Civil War Firsts

Civil War Firsts

The Legacies of America's Bloodiest Conflict

GERALD S. HENIG

and

ERIC NIDEROST

STACKPOLE
BOOKS

Published by
STACKPOLE BOOKS
5067 Ritter Road
Mechanicsburg, PA 17055

Printed in the United States of America

ISBN 0-8117-0354-1

FOR

Lori,
Jennifer, Rebecca, and Adam
and
in memory of my parents,
Sarah and Joseph Henig

GSH

❖ ❖ ❖

To my students,
past, present, and future

EN

Contents

Acknowledgments

No book of this scope could reach fruition without the help and support of many people. We are especially grateful to Kristina Werk Gatkin, a student in Professor Henig's U.S. history survey class. It was Kristina's rather innocent-sounding question—"Was Mary Surratt the first woman ever executed by the federal government?"—that ignited the idea for this project.

We would like to express our gratitude as well to the California State University, Hayward, library and its staff, particularly Librarian Carol Castagnozzi, and library assistants Paula D. Kapteyn, Carolyn Chun, and Melisa H. Broussin. Lynn LaFleur, in charge of interlibrary loans, deserves special mention. Always with good cheer, but with the fierce determination of a bounty hunter, Lynn tracked down and supplied us with *every* microfilm, article, or book we requested.

Other members of the Cal State Hayward community also went beyond the call of duty. Peter Chamberlain, an academic computing consultant at the university, scanned, refined, and formatted the manuscript for submission to the publisher, performing much of the work on his own time. We are additionally indebted to Rose Carrillo and Jason Coleman, former history department secretaries, and to Wanda Washington, who currently serves in that capacity, for the myriad of tasks they each carried out in our behalf. Gerald Henig would like to acknowledge as well the continuous encouragement and suggestions he received from his colleagues in the history department, in particular Professor Emeritus David B. Chan, and Professors Tom G. Hall, Henry F. Reichman, Richard J. Orsi, Pablo-Raúl Arreola, Jr., Dee E. Andrews, Sophia Lee, and adjuncts Dr. Richard B. Speed and Dr. Terry P. Wilson. Henig is further grateful to the university's administration and to the members of the Professional Leave Committee (1996–1997) for the award of a sabbatical leave, allowing him to devote his energies full time to research and writing.

There were others who helped in other ways. Our thanks to Janice A. Wilson for her clerical assistance; to Carolyn Harrell Kilgore, who provided some key leads; to research assistants Michael S. Chisholm and James Kostecka, who volunteered countless hours checking the accuracy of our assertions and surfing the Internet for fresh ideas; and to Chabot College instructional support staffers Arlene Adamson and Winnie Wong for their computer expertise, conveyed always with unfailing good humor.

Gerald Henig would also like to offer a very special thanks to Distinguished Professor Emeritus Hans L. Trefousse of Brooklyn College and of the Graduate Center of the City University of New York. Teacher, Civil War scholar, and mentor, Hans has remained over the decades a good friend and constant source of professional inspiration.

Linking up with Stackpole Books was yet another stroke of good fortune. We were truly blessed with a superb publishing house staff. Above all, we are most grateful to our editor, William C. Davis, a leading Civil War historian in his own right, who first saw merit in our manuscript, and to our associate editor, Leigh Ann Berry, who has been an indispensable source of help from the manuscript's acceptance through publication. Our deep appreciation, moreover, to copyeditor Joyce Bertsch, typist Eileen Connors, and page designer Robert Kowkabany at Doric Lay Publishers.

With much affection I would like to thank the following members of my family: To my sister and brother-in-law, Lynn and Norman Binger, and to my nephews, Joseph Binger and Scott C. Binger, I am truly indebted for their hospitality, encouragement, and willingness to check out material on the East Coast, which otherwise was inaccessible to me. Finally, to my wife, Lori, and to our children, Jennifer, Rebecca, and Adam, I am most grateful for their support, devotion, and unwavering love—all of which sustained me throughout this work and, as always, continues to do so.

—G.S.H.

Preface

America's Civil War, the popularly acclaimed historian Bruce Catton once wrote, "was the first of the world's really modern wars. This is what gives it its terrible significance. . . . If it says nothing else it says this to all men involved in it, at the moment of its beginning: Nothing is ever going to be the same again."

In fact, not long after the outbreak of hostilities between North and South, many Americans believed that nothing would ever be the same again. Men and women, young and old, black and white, elite and ordinary people, Unionist and Confederate—all seemed to share an uneasiness over the profound transformations resulting from the conflict.

As Northern armies invaded the Confederacy, inflicting upon it what Union general William Tecumseh Sherman called "the hard hand of war," more and more Southerners realized the portentous times in which they lived. Emma Mordecai, for example, fifty-two years of age, unmarried, and residing with her widowed sister-in-law just outside of Richmond, was deeply distressed by "this strange, new state of things." Recalling in far more graphic terms his sense of alienation, a young Confederate lieutenant described in his memoirs the "blood and flame" and how, as he put it, "the temples of our lives were tumbling about our heads." In 1864 a correspondent wrote to the *Montgomery Daily Advertiser*: "We are passing through a great revolution, one of those grand convulsions. . . . The surface of society, like a great ocean, is upheaved, and all the relations of life are disturbed and out of joint." A year later, upon returning home after serving as an officer in the Confederate army, a Louisiana planter observed that "society has been completely changed by the war. The [French] revolution of '89 did not produce a greater change in the 'Ancien Regime' than has this in our social life." Whites in the South, according to a black army chaplain, appeared to be unsure "as to whether they are actually in another world, or whether this one is turned wrong side out." One thing was certain, however. As nineteen-year-old Lucy Buck, the daughter of a wealthy planter in Virginia's Shenandoah Valley, noted sadly in her wartime diary, "We shall never *any* of us be the same as we *have* been."

African-Americans, on the other hand, were jubilant over the revolutionary nature of the war, well aware that they stood at the close of one era and the beginning of another—and that there would be no turning back. Thomas Long, a corporal in the first black regiment officially mustered into U.S. military service, the 1st South Carolina Volunteers, told his comrades in arms:

> If we hadn't become sojers, all might have gone back as it was before; our freedom might have slipped through de two houses of Congress & President Linkum's four years might have passed by & notin been done for we. But now tings can never go back because we have showed our energy & our courage & our naturally manhood.

One of the founders of the American Anti-Slavery Society, Robert Purvis, "a distinguished, urbane, wealthy Negro who lived in a fine house in a Philadelphia suburb," in May 1863 proclaimed at a society meeting: "For the first time since your government was a government, it is an honor to be a citizen of the United States! Old things are passing away, all things are becoming new."

Northern whites could not have agreed more. Antislavery crusader Wendell Phillips was convinced that Americans were "never again to see the republic" as it was. The war, editorialized the *New York Times,* "touches everything, and leaves nothing as it found it." Writing in 1869, George Ticknor, a retired Harvard professor, concluded that the Civil War had created a "great gulf between what happened before it in our century and what has happened since, or what is likely to happen hereafter. It does not seem to me as if I were living in the country in which I was born."

Even foreigners sensed the transformational power of the conflict. Karl Marx characterized the Civil War as "a world upheaval." The British statesman and author, and soon to be prime minister, Benjamin Disraeli "looked upon the struggle in America. . . [as] a great revolution." And Charles Dickens, who had visited the United States before the war, on a return trip in 1868 told an audience how "astounded" he had been by "the amazing changes" he had encountered throughout the country.

Modern scholars do not deny the changes engendered by the Civil

War, but some take issue with their overall significance, questioning whether collectively they represented *the* great watershed in the history of the American nation. In other words, how much had that world changed over four years? Was the country that came out of that struggle very different than the one that went into it?

In his study of late-nineteenth-century America, Morton Keller has argued that "by most indices" the war did not fundamentally alter American life. Although he conceded that "Americans of the Civil War generation had a profound sense of living through events that changed their world," he believed that they were overreacting. Not so, according to other students of the period. Frank E. Vandiver, for one, has maintained that the war, by "building its own momentum . . . had become a great rolling change agent . . . that left America forever different." And James M. McPherson, in his Pulitzer Prize-winning *Battle Cry of Freedom* and various other works, has viewed the conflict as no less than America's second revolution, a vast and profound transitional event without parallel in American history.

This debate has raged for decades, largely because no one has attempted a comprehensive investigation of the actual changes produced by the war, both on the battlefield and on the home front. Given the magnitude of the literature (more than 50,000 books or pamphlets on the war have been published since the guns fell silent), it is all the more incredible that no single volume has yet been published documenting in detail the many firsts experienced by the American people as a consequence of the conflict. We are hoping that our book will fill that void.

It is our contention that the Civil War produced unprecedented change; that Americans were never the same once Lee surrendered to Grant at Appomattox on April 9, 1865. We realize, of course, that many of the new developments spawned by the war would have taken place in spite of it. But it was the war, as Professor William Hesseltine said years ago, that served as "the fiery crucible in which the old nation was melted down, and out of which modern America was poured."

Our book is organized along topical lines, allowing the reader to open it at random and read any chapter or section without the need for additional information. To avoid cluttering the text with footnotes, the sources are located in the back of the volume, identified by page numbers and section titles.

This book has been designed for a wide audience, especially for the general reader and the Civil War buff. But we hope the scholarly community will approve of it and perhaps discover in some of the material we have unearthed areas of study worthy of further investigation.

CHAPTER 1

On the Eve of Civil War

Americans have always been an optimistic people, but as 1859 drew to a close, the new year was looked upon with anxiety and dread. The sectional rift between the free North and the slaveholding South had deepened to the point where compromise and conciliation seemed impossible. The threads of unity that bound the country together—ties of history, common language, culture, and political institutions—were strained to bursting and barely able to contain the raging forces of partisan politics and sectionalism.

The John Brown raid at Harpers Ferry, Virginia, in October 1859 underscored divisions even as it heightened tensions. When Brown's attempt to foment a slave rebellion failed, he was captured, tried, and hanged that December. In parts of the North, especially New England, the old man became a martyr, but throughout the slave states, he was viewed as an archfiend bent on destroying the very foundations of Southern society.

For those Americans struggling to prevent the disruption of the Union, the timing of the raid was a disaster. The 1860 presidential election was not far off, and if the Republican party took power, Southern extremists vowed secession. They viewed their opponents as "black Republicans," allies of Northern abolitionists, the very people who had supported John Brown.

New York City lawyer George Templeton Strong captured the temperament of the time when he recorded in his diary, "It's a sick nation, and I fear it must be worse before it's better." Strong's voice was only one in the growing chorus of concern. Writing to her son from St. Augustine, Florida, Frances Smith informed him that "the whole country is in a state of fearful agitation—disunion! disunion! is the cry of our Southern friends."

Yet for all the impassioned rhetoric, in January 1860 no one knew how far the South would go, or if there would still be a genuinely *United* States a year hence.

WILLIAM PENNINGTON

William Pennington became speaker of the U.S. House of Representatives on February 1, 1860, after two months of partisan politics and acrimonious debate. A man of mediocre talents, Pennington nevertheless was the first freshman congressman to be chosen speaker in half a century.

The new speaker, a veteran politician who had served as governor of New Jersey, was sixty-three years old at the time of his sudden rise to national prominence. Originally a Whig, Pennington had been elected to Congress as a candidate of the "People's Party," a coalition of anti-Democratic groups in his state that were unwilling to join the Republicans, whom they considered too radical, but detested their rivals, the Democrats.

Pennington owed his election as speaker to the tumultuous times, not to any ability. The process began on December 5, 1860, when the Thirty-sixth Congress met in its first regular session. No one party held a majority in the House; the Republicans had 109 members, the Democrats 101, and the antiforeign and anti-Catholic American party, also known as the "Know Nothings" (so-called because their members, bound by secretive oaths, usually responded to questions by saying that they knew nothing), had twenty-seven representatives in the lower chamber. In order to win the speakership, a candidate needed to obtain 117 votes. The first ballot was inconclusive, with leading Republican congressman John Sherman of Ohio falling far short of the required number. Then, before the session could proceed any further, Missouri representative J. B. Clark introduced a long-winded resolution saying that any congressman who endorsed a book called *The Impending Crisis in the South* was not fit to be speaker.

Written in 1857 by Hinton Rowan Helper, a white Southerner, *The Impending Crisis* was highly critical of the slave system, arguing that it hurt the South both economically and socially. The author made some good points, but by including dull lists of statistics, he weakened the impact of his thesis for the average reader. In any case, whether Helper's criticisms of slavery were well presented or not, they were blown out of proportion by an overly touchy and apprehensive South.

In saner times, Sherman probably would have won the speakership with little controversy and less comment. But it was revealed that Sherman had been one of sixty-eight Republican congressmen who had signed a circular advertising the book. Sherman admitted that he hadn't even read *The Impending Crisis,* yet those few penstrokes had effectively ended his chances for the speaker's job.

The result of all this controversy was a bitter deadlock that lasted two months. In ballot after ballot, Sherman would gain a plurality but fall short of a majority—sometimes by only three or four votes. The House was unable to pass laws or transact any business until a speaker was chosen. New Year's Day 1860 came and went, and still the House was deadlocked. Southern congressmen refused to support anyone who endorsed the "infamous" book. As the weeks dragged on, tempers flared; at one point, John Logan of Illinois pulled a pistol out of his pocket, though he did not fire the weapon. Frustrated and exhausted, members of the House finally agreed upon a settlement. Sherman withdrew his name, and Pennington was put forward as a compromise candidate.

As a "People's Party" representative, Pennington was technically not affiliated with either major political organization; best of all, he had not signed the book endorsement, which pleased the Southern Democrats. On the other hand, Sherman and the Republicans favored him because, once in office, he would follow their lead on committee appointments. As speaker, Pennington would demonstrate "a pitiful inability to control the chamber," but at least with his election the immediate crisis was resolved.

RABBI MORRIS J. RAPHALL

On February 1, 1860, Rabbi Morris J. Raphall opened the day's proceedings in the U.S. House of Representatives with a prayer, the first clergyman of his faith ever to do so. The significance of the invocation, delivered in both Hebrew and English, was somewhat lost amid all the relief later that same day when Congressman William Pennington was elected speaker, breaking a two-month long deadlock.

But for Rabbi Raphall, his opening-day prayer was a high point in a religious career that included both acclaim and controversy. Born in Sweden, Raphall was educated in Denmark and Germany and spent twenty-five years in England. In 1849 the rabbi's peripatetic odyssey ended when he came to New York on a life contract with Congregation B'nai Jeshurun.

Later the rabbi caused quite a stir in the North when he delivered a long sermon defending slavery. Arguing that the Bible condones, even sanctions, human bondage, he reminded members of his congregation "that Abraham, Isaac, Jacob, [and] Job—the men with whom the Almighty conversed, with whose names he emphatically connects his own most holy name . . .—that all these men were slaveholders." Raphall's comments were widely circulated, receiving a warm reception in the South and refuted by abolitionist elements in the North.

In spite of his proslavery sermon, Raphall and his family remained loyal to the Union when the war came. His son Alfred, a Union officer, lost an arm at Gettysburg.

"BUCHANEERS"

Corruption and scandal, in one form or another, have plagued most administrations in American political life. But the first to be held to task publicly for its malfeasance—and deservedly so—was the administration of Democratic president James Buchanan. During the four years Buchanan was in office (1857–61), his regime, in the words of one historian, "was undoubtedly the most corrupt before the Civil War and one of the most corrupt in American history."

How much President Buchanan was involved is an open question. He was courtly and dignified, his appearance marred only by wryneck, a condition that caused him to cock his head to one side. The wryneck sprang from the fact that he had one farsighted eye and one nearsighted eye; if looking in the distance, he'd close his nearsighted orb. When it came to the corruption of his appointees, however, he seemed to turn a blind eye.

Benjamin B. French, a Democrat and Washington lobbyist, was deeply disappointed with the president. "I had considerable hope of Mr. Buchanan," French admitted in a letter to his brother. "I really thought he was a statesman, but I have now come to the settled conclusion that he is just the d—ndest old fool that has ever occupied the Presidential chair."

Buchanan would occasionally preach about virtue in politics, but these pronouncements were taken with a liberal grain of salt. At the very least, the president was unwise in his choice of appointees— described aptly by some "as a gang of 'Buchaneers.'" Secretary of War John B. Floyd headed the list of plunderers. Caring more about profit than public trust, Floyd sold Fort Snelling, Minnesota, a strategically important military reservation of about 8,000 acres, to speculators at a price far below its market value. Conversely, the secretary had the Federal government purchase properties from cronies and influential Democrats at inflated prices. In California, the U.S. government paid $200,000 at Lime Point for fortifications, even though the estimated value of the property was only $5,000.

Government contracts were awarded not to the lowest bidder, but to those who had contributed most to the Democratic party war chest. Secretary of the Navy Isaac Toucey, for instance, granted a lumber contract to an individual because he had contributed $16,000 to Buchanan's presidential campaign. On another occasion, the secretary used his influence to award a ship-building contract to a machine shop, with the expectation that the owners of the business would persuade the new employees hired to do the work to vote Democratic. And this was only the tip of the iceberg. Blatant fraud—kickbacks, favoritism, outright graft—was uncovered in almost every government agency, the worst occurring in the War, Navy, Interior, and Post Office Departments. The corruption had become so widespread that the House of Representatives began investigations. A committee headed by Republican representative "Honest John" Covode of Pennsylvania, not entirely unbiased, still found enough concrete evidence of malfeasance to convince the most loyal Democrat.

Buchanan didn't emerge from these revelations entirely unscathed. The president was shown to be a weak-willed and at times willing tool of the dishonest men who surrounded him, endorsing their shady dealings when required. A climax of sorts came on June 13, 1860, when Congress passed a series of resolutions condemning the Buchanan administration's sordid record of corrupt contracts, bribery, and outright thievery. The president himself was censured for his role in these dubious affairs.

The Republicans made sure the House revelations were publicized; they planned to make Democratic corruption a major theme in the 1860 presidential election.

DEMOCRATIC NATIONAL CONVENTION

When the delegates to the Democratic National Convention began arriving in Charleston, South Carolina, to choose their presidential standard-bearer for the 1860 race, little did they realize that they were about to attend the first national nominating convention ever to meet for a total of fifteen days. No party selecting a presidential nominee exceeded that record until the Democratic Convention of 1924.

The Democratic delegates who assembled in 1860 were not oblivi-

ous to the potentially divisive problems within their political organization. They were well aware that the party had managed to retain the
White House for eight years because they had remained united and
appealed to voters in both North and South. But the question of whether
slavery should be allowed in the territories had poisoned relations
between the country's two disparate halves. As the only remaining
political party in the United States with a national constituency, the
Democrats would have to confront this explosive issue—and
Charleston would serve as the site of that confrontation.

Then, as now, the city exuded an old-world grace melded with a
languid Southern charm. Colonial mansions lined the streets, and the
sweet perfume of azaleas scented the air. Yet for all its crowded
charms, the decision to select Charleston as the host city of the Democratic National Convention was not just a miscalculation; it was an
unmitigated disaster.

To begin with, the weather, even in April, was stiflingly hot, and
since Charleston was a small city of some 50,000, there were not
enough accommodations for all the delegates. To make matters worse,
the city was a citadel of sectionalism, a place where Southern rights and
slavery were regarded as sacred principles. Many a Charlestonian
remembered that one of South Carolina's greatest citizens, John C. Calhoun, had challenged the Federal government almost thirty years earlier
with his doctrine of nullification, declaring that a state had the right to
disobey federal law. In all respects, then, Charleston wasn't neutral
ground; it was passionately, even rabidly, pro-Southern. And if slavery
wasn't upheld, and even encouraged to grow, there was serious talk of
secession from the Union.

The Democratic National Convention began its opening session on
April 23, 1860, in the hall of the South Carolina Institute. The atmosphere inside became oppressive in more ways than one, with the
unbearable heat and the "hot air" of long-winded and fiercely partisan
debate. The spectator galleries added to the misery by raucously cheering pro-Southern speeches and greeting Northern speakers with hoots
and catcalls.

The fabric of unity began to unravel at once. Sen. Stephen A. Douglas of Illinois was a leading contender for the party's presidential nod,
but most Southerners did not support him. His "Freeport Doctrine"
position, which had attracted much attention during the debates with
Lincoln in 1858, seemed to suggest that the Supreme Court's Dred
Scott decision, denying Congress the authority to prohibit slavery in the
territories, could be evaded. Douglas had also rejected the pro-Southern

Lecompton constitution for Kansas, a stand that had won him few friends south of the Mason-Dixon line.

A yawning chasm opened between Northern and Southern delegates, and no bridge of compromise seemed able to span the gap. William L. Yancey of Alabama set the tone. An intractable advocate of Southern rights, Yancey declared that Northerners were in error when they accepted the view that slavery was evil. Fully supported by most of the Southern delegates, Yancey demanded a plank in the party platform that would create a slave code—that is, federal protection of slavery in the territories.

The Northern delegates predictably balked at this proposal. Sen. George E. Pugh of Ohio responded to Yancey's barbs without equivocation. "Gentlemen of the South," Pugh said, "You mistake us—You mistake us. We will not do it." When a more moderate, Douglas-oriented platform was adopted, fire-eating Southerners took another vote—with their feet. Led by Yancey and the Alabamians, the delegations of Mississippi, Louisiana, South Carolina, Texas, and Florida left the hall, accompanied by scattered groups from other Southern states.

Since a candidate needed a two-thirds majority of *all* delegates to win, not just two-thirds of the rump that remained, the business of the convention ground to a halt. On May 3 it was decided that a six-week recess might cool tempers and promote unity. Altogether, the convention met in Charleston for a total of nine days. (Sunday, April 29, was set aside as a day of rest.)

When the Democrats reconvened in Baltimore on June 18, some Southern delegates had returned to the fold—only to bolt again later. Stephen A. Douglas eventually won the presidential nomination on the sixth day of the convention, but the party he led was composed mainly of Northern Democrats. The largely Southern wing of the party met separately in Baltimore and nominated John C. Breckinridge of Kentucky, then vice president of the United States, as their presidential standard-bearer. Thus, the last remaining bond that had held North and South together—the Democratic party—was irreparably shattered.

CHICAGO

Chicago has hosted more presidential nominating conventions than any other city in America. To date, a total of twenty-five national political conventions have been held in the Windy City, fourteen Republican and eleven Democratic.

The first time Chicago was chosen as a convention site was in

1860. In retrospect, the midwestern metropolis seemed a perfect setting for such an event. A burgeoning town of some 110,000 people, the city owed much of its greatness to its location, since it sat squarely on a natural artery of commerce. Even before the coming of the railroad, the Illinois and Michigan canal, opened in 1848, provided the first navigable link to the commerce-laden Mississippi River. By 1860 fifteen railroads served Chicago, and the city had surpassed New York as a major cattle and hog market.

Geography, commerce, and a more-than-adequate transportation network all contributed to Chicago's edging out its competitors as a convention site, but the primary reason for its success was the adroit political maneuvering of one man, Norman Judd. Judd was chairman of the Illinois Republican State Central Committee and also had a seat on the party's National Committee. On December 21, 1859, the Republican National Committee met in New York to decide the location of the next year's presidential nominating convention. Judd suggested Chicago, pointing out that it was neutral ground, as no major Republican candidate hailed from Illinois. A majority of the committee went along with Judd's proposal, and Chicago won out over St. Louis by one vote.

Judd was being disingenuous. Apart from boosting his home state, he had his own political ax to grind. Judd was but one of a number of Illinois Republicans who were backing the then not widely known Abraham Lincoln as a presidential candidate. As Illinois's "native son," Lincoln's chances for receiving the nomination might well receive a boost if the convention was held in Chicago.

THE "WIGWAM"

Big, bustling, and rambunctious, Chicago is a place that does things on a grand scale. When the city received word that it had been selected as the site of the 1860 Republican National Convention, it built the first auditorium in the United States with a capacity to seat 10,000 people.

A sum of $5,000 or $7,000 (sources vary) had been raised for the purpose, and an empty lot at Lake and Market Streets chosen for the grand design. Carpenters swarmed over the site, and before long the huge two-story auditorium, dubbed the "Wigwam," began to rise.

The building was indeed large for its time, measuring 180 by 100 feet. Inside, a broad wooden platform faced a spacious floor and galleries on three sides. The interior was huge, decorated with portraits and busts of American statesmen on the speakers' platform, while the upright beams were adorned with bunting, rosettes, and evergreens. The decorative items, however, did little to enhance what was basically a "raw and ugly" cavernous hall. But what the Wigwam lacked in beauty it made up in utility. Acoustics were perfect—vital for speechmaking— and gas lights provided illumination for night sessions.

Architecturally, then, the Wigwam was well designed for its purpose, though no one seemed overly concerned about issues of safety. With its bunting, tinder-dry evergreen boughs, and flaring gas jets, the building, according to a modern scholar, "must have been one of the most dangerous fire traps ever built in America."

REPUBLICAN NATIONAL CONVENTION

On May 16, 1860, when Republicans gathered at their national nominating convention, they were in an ebullient mood. Earlier that month, the Democrats had recessed in Charleston without choosing a presidential candidate. With the Democrats in disarray, prospects of a Republican victory in November brightened considerably.

To ensure that victory, Republican leaders were willing to open their deliberations to the public at large. After all, there were only some 500 delegates, yet the convention hall was capable of holding a total of 10,000. Whether or not Republican politicos had a say in the actual construction of the Wigwam (it was probably the grand design of Chicago's city fathers, who wanted the biggest and best), the fact remains that the facility afforded party leaders the opportunity for a sort of mass nominating process—and apparently they liked the idea. The 1860 Republican National Convention in Chicago was the first in American political history where more than 10,000 spectators—a greater number than there were seats or space for—were admitted.

The people, "crammed almost to suffocation," packed the galleries and aisles, and from the moment the proceedings began, it was clear that they were not going to be passive observers. They shouted, cheered, and applauded, transmitting their desires to the delegates in no uncertain—and at times earsplitting—terms. Bands would play, parades would march, and braggadocio would mix with ballots. Those in the galleries intended to participate fully in candidate selection by creating an atmosphere of momentum—real or imaginary—for the man they favored.

Sen. William H. Seward of New York was the front runner, but some had begun to doubt his chances to win the nomination. Prior to the convention, he had made two anti-Southern speeches, costing him the support of many conservative delegates. The first nominating ballot catapulted Abraham Lincoln of Illinois—the man most spectators favored—from a dark horse to a major Seward rival for the presidential nod. When the ballot was counted, it was 173½ for Seward, 102 for Lincoln, and a scattering of votes for others. Thus, the senator fell short of the 233 he needed to win the nomination.

To make matters worse for Seward, he found himself with few supporters in the galleries. His partisans marched around Chicago to the foot-tapping sounds of a band—only to discover later they had missed the boat. They might have been drumming up support for their candidate on the outside, but when they arrived at the Wigwam, the building was already full of Lincoln backers.

"Old Abe's" supporters had arrived early, jamming each nook and cranny of the cavernous building. It was said that counterfeit admission tickets were used to enable Lincoln men to pack the galleries. True to their western origins, the Lincoln-dominated galleries had some of the "strongest-lunged hog callers" around. The roars for the man from Illinois drowned out any cries for other candidates.

The second ballot showed Lincoln gaining strength, the delegates seemingly egged on by the tremendous shouting in his behalf. A reporter tried to convey to his readers the high-decibel tumult. "Imagine," he wrote, "all the hogs ever slaughtered in Cincinnati giving their death squeals together, [and simultaneously] a score of big steam whistles going."

The third ballot proved the charm for Lincoln, when it was announced that he now had 231½ votes. The chairman of the Ohio delegation jumped up and declared four more votes for the "rail-splitter," putting him over the top. Lincoln was the Republican nominee, which triggered a bellowing storm of jubilation, "thousands cheering with the energy of insanity."

JAPANESE DIPLOMATIC MISSION

In the spring of 1860, while Americans selected nominees for their forthcoming presidential contest, a foreign embassy appeared in Washington that provided a momentary diversion. It was the first Japanese diplomatic mission to the United States, dispatched in compliance with an American-Japanese Commercial Treaty that had been signed in 1858.

In 1860 Japan was feudal, ruled by an all-powerful warlord called the shogun. In theory, the shogun was an agent of the Japanese emperor, but in reality, the monarch, though much revered, was a political figurehead. The real authority was wielded by the shogun, backed by powerful feudal lords, who were part of an aristocratic warrior class called *samurai.*

Insular in thought as well as geography, the Japanese wanted no contact with the outside world. Centuries of relative isolation had produced a kind of ethnic and cultural arrogance that viewed all outsiders, whether Western or Asian, with disdain. Two American expeditions under Commodore Matthew Perry in 1853 and 1854 had finally opened Japan to limited diplomatic contact and trade with the United States. Now it was the Japanese's turn to visit America.

On February 13, 1860, the seventy-seven-member delegation, composed mostly of samurai, left Japan aboard the USS *Powhatan,* Commodore Perry's old flagship. Encountering storms almost at the outset, they took a brief stopover in Hawaii before arriving in San Francisco. After a few days in the Bay City, they proceeded to the Isthmus of Panama, crossed that narrow strip of land, then boarded the U.S. frigate *Roanoke* for the last leg of the trip.

The Japanese embassy reached Washington on May 14, their arrival witnessed by nearly 5,000 people, with another 20,000 lining the streets as the procession made its way to the hotel. Three days later the mission met with President James Buchanan. After diplomatic documents were exchanged, a state dinner was held for them at the White House. "They are really a curiosity," wrote Harriet Lane, the president's niece.

To Americans the Japanese were exotic, from the fabled East of Marco Polo, and their very appearance and demeanor made them seem like beings from another planet. They wore colorful flowing silk and brocade kimonos. As samurai, they each carried two swords, encased in beautifully jeweled scabbards, but it was clear that the weapons were anything but ceremonial. Their heads were partly shaved, the bald pates surmounted by curious boxlike hats. "They looked for all the world," one observer commented, "like little old ladies dressed up to kill."

The younger, more junior members of the delegation seemed the most curious about American ways. Tateishi Onojiro, nicknamed "Tommy" by the American press, surprised his companions and delighted his hosts by kissing a young American lady's fingertips. Yet despite Tommy's antics and the generally warm reception given to the Japanese, the two cultures were almost incomprehensible to one another. "So strange is everything," wrote Muragaki Norimasa in a poem, "their language, their appearance/That I feel as if living in a dream-land."

The Japanese were astounded at the deference American men paid to American women. Why, females were even guests at official receptions! Sometimes American men even served their wives, unthinkable in Japanese society. As for American food, the visitors found most of it too greasy and indigestible, except for ice cream and champagne, which made a big hit with them.

If ordinary American life gave the Japanese a "sensory overload" of strange sights, smells, tastes, and sounds, American political life was totally beyond the pale. With the presidential campaign of 1860 getting under way, and Lincoln having been nominated during their visit, the Japanese seemed not to have noticed. The issues of slavery and sectionalism also seem to have been beyond their comprehension. The Japanese delegation made a few racist statements in their writings, like "blacks are inferior as human beings and extremely stupid," but these were probably secondhand sayings picked up from their American hosts.

The American system of government was also incomprehensible. Coming from a feudal society, the Japanese had equated the president with the emperor, or at least the shogun. Yet they were astonished to find that President Buchanan was an "unassuming" man, who wore plain clothes, had no bodyguards, and lived in a house (not a castle), which he occupied only while he was in office. And when taken to a session of Congress, the Japanese were shocked by its freewheeling nature, one of the ministers referring to it as a "crazy talking-place," where its members shouted and gestured at each other like "a cage full of monkeys."

But some of the younger Japanese visitors—perhaps because of their youth—were less judgmental and more receptive to American ways. Fukushima Yoshikoto, a nineteen-year-old attendant to one of the senior deputies, wrote: "We are treated kindly by the foreigners [Americans]. . . . High-ranking people do not look down on the lower class or oppress them, so most people are happy. . . . I believe that the lower classes in Japan would be eager for the American way of life if they ever tasted its freedom."

After Washington, the Japanese envoys went to Baltimore, Philadelphia, and New York. The grand finale was in New York, where the city shelled out the princely sum of $90,000 (equivalent to millions in today's dollars) for a gargantuan reception attended by an estimated 10,000 people. The group departed for Japan on June 30, 1860.

THE PRINCE OF WALES

Americans have always been fascinated by royalty, a paradox in a country dedicated to republican principles. Yet royalty, with its heady mix of history, tradition, pedigree, and power, seems to have an innate appeal that can win over the most patriotic American.

This was certainly the case in the fall of 1860, when His Royal Highness Albert Edward, Prince of Wales, arrived in the United States. It was the first time an heir to the British throne ever visited America's shores.

In his later years Prince Albert Edward (future King Edward VII) became celebrated in Britain as a kind of genial libertine, an antidote to the straitlaced Victorianism his mother personified as well as gave her name to. He grew a beard and became enormously fat, his expanding waistline testifying to his love of good food. A notorious womanizer, he was once named in a messy divorce case and as king had an acknowledged mistress. Following in the tradition of his mother, his name was also used to describe an era, the Edwardian age, a time of sophisticated decadence.

But in 1860 Americans saw quite another incarnation. The prince was young, only eighteen, and cut a dashing figure in his finely tailored coat and stovepipe hat. As befitting the heir to the throne, Prince Albert Edward was accompanied by a large entourage, including his chief chaperone, the duke of Newcastle.

President James Buchanan was the catalyst for the royal visit. Learning that Albert Edward was scheduled to visit Canada, Buchanan suggested to Queen Victoria that his itinerary might also include the United States. The offer was accepted, and the prince set foot on American soil from Canada on September 18, 1860. Almost as if in deference to America's democratic sensibilities (but actually for security purposes), the prince traveled "incognito" as Baron Renfrew, one of his real but lesser titles.

This transparent incognito fooled no one, and the prince immediately became a celebrity. Following a tour of several Midwestern cities, the royal guest arrived in Washington, D.C., in October. Albert Edward was much taken with Buchanan's niece Harriet Lane, and the pair slipped out to a gymnasium, where the prince swung on rings, climbed a rope ladder, and lost a game of ninepins to the young lady.

After his stay in the capital, the royal heir visited George Washington's Mount Vernon, where he paid homage to the man who had rebelled against his great-grandfather George III. In Boston he even shook hands with Ralph Farnham, the last survivor of the Revolution's battle of Bunker Hill.

But it was in New York City that he encountered his most memorable reception. Some 300,000 people crowded the streets to acclaim him as he was taken by carriage to the Fifth Avenue Hotel. All went well until the prince attended a grand ball given in his honor at the Academy of Music at East 14th Street. It was here, one might say, that his Gotham visit fell through—quite literally. About 3,000 were invited to the reception, but an additional 2,000 gate-crashed and jammed into the ballroom. As the guests lined up to greet His Royal Highness, suddenly there was a loud cracking sound, and part of the floor gave way. Several people dropped with the flooring, but apparently no one was seriously hurt. Carpenters were summoned, who hastily—too hastily, it turned out—made repairs. When the new floor was in place, Albert Edward and the guests returned—only to hear a frantic hammering coming from below the boards. A carpenter had been overlooked and sealed below the new floor!

Sailing for England on October 20, the prince of Wales had helped to revive positive feelings between Americans and his own countrymen, the likes of which had not been known since pre-Revolutionary days. True, within a year the United States and Britain were on the brink of war, but the goodwill generated by the royal visit was not entirely forgotten. As for the prince, he gained a new confidence. In fact, rumor had it that he had experienced his first sexual encounter in a New York brothel. For their part, Americans remembered the month-long visit with affection. In obvious reference to the royal guest, Lincoln's oldest son Robert was briefly dubbed the "Prince of Rails."

CAMPAIGN BIOGRAPHIES OF LINCOLN

In the nineteenth century the principle means of mass communication was the printed word. Newspapers were the primary source of information, but during political contests, they were supplemented by hastily published pamphlets and other literature. The 1860 presidential campaign was no exception, saturated as it was with much political pulp, perhaps more than ever before. In this deluge of printed matter, however, one publication stood out among the rest. John L. Scripps's *Life of Abraham Lincoln* was the first campaign biography of a presidential candidate to become a bestseller.

Lincoln's capture of the Republican presidential nomination had taken most publishers, and not a few politicians, by surprise. Although not entirely obscure, Lincoln was largely unknown outside of Illinois. True, the publication of his 1858 debates with Douglas had given him an audience, and a celebrated speech in February 1860 at New York's Cooper Institute was widely reported. Yet if the electorate had some vague notions of his political stands, they had absolutely no idea of his personal life or background. Republican newspaper editor Horace Greeley expressed the concern of many party regulars when he said that there should be "at least one million copies of some cheap life of Lincoln" made available to the public.

Ever eager to make a quick buck, publishers rushed to fill the need. A flood of campaign biographies were produced in the months after the convention, patchwork quilts of information stitched together by hacks. Not all were spurious, but the public's curiosity about Lincoln was such that the bad was equally snapped up with the good. Some cheap pamphlets went through several editions; a Reuben Voss advertised an "irrepressible" edition of his life of Lincoln, an unfortunate label, because it apparently *was* "repressed" and never saw print!

The first campaign biography of the "rail-splitter" to appear was the so-called "Wigwam edition," published by Rudd and Carlton of New York on June 2, 1860, scarcely two weeks after Lincoln became the Republican standard-bearer. But what the Wigwam edition gained in speed, it lost in accuracy, because the anonymous author spelled Lincoln's first name "Abram."

Undoubtedly the best account in this flood of printer's ink was the biography by Chicago *Press and Tribune* senior editor John L. Scripps. The newspaper's owner, prominent Republican Joseph Medill, had heeded Greeley's pleas and assigned Scripps to the task.

John Scripps was the right man for the job, a thoroughgoing professional who chose to do much of his own primary research. A lawyer by training, in 1847, at twenty-nine years of age, Scripps moved to Chicago but found that there were so many attorneys in the city he would have to scramble for clients. Rather than risk starvation, he went into journalism, where he prospered.

Scripps went down to Springfield to interview Lincoln, finding the candidate besieged with party politicos, reporters, and office seekers, yet still cordial. Lincoln even granted Scripps a private interview, but proved evasive when it came to the details of his boyhood and youth. "Why, Scripps," Lincoln protested, "it is a great piece of folly to attempt to make anything out of my early life. It can all be condensed into a single sentence, and that sentence you will find in Gray's Elegy: 'The short and simple annals of the poor.'"

Actually Lincoln was indulging in some equivocation. The truth is that he rarely if ever spoke of his origins to friends, much less wanted it publicized to the whole country. As a self-made man, he thought it best not to dwell on his crude frontier past, preferring to forget, or at least minimize, his log cabin birth, his illiterate or nearly illiterate parents, and his rough country upbringing.

Nevertheless, Scripps managed to persuade Lincoln to write a short autobiography for reference purposes. Using this sketch as a source, Scripps then wrote a thirty-two-page campaign biography. It became a bestseller, though precise numbers of copies sold are open to question. During the 1860 campaign itself, some hundreds of thousands of Scripps's *Life of Abraham Lincoln* were sold, and perhaps as many as a million, if postcampaign retail figures are added to the overall total.

Scripps's work had more than literary merit; it was also affordable. The cost of the pamphlet was a nickel for a single copy, but if purchased in bulk it was 2 cents each. These prices stand in sharp contrast to some of the competition; David Bartlett's life of Lincoln retailed at 25 cents a copy, bound in paper, and a cloth edition was a pricey $1.

Lincoln must have been pleased with the Scripps biography, because as president, he appointed the author U.S. postmaster at Chicago.

"LITTLE GIANT"

Small in stature, large in reputation, Sen. Stephen A. Douglas of Illinois was one of the most famous men of his day. Only five feet, four inches tall, he was known as the "Little Giant" in tribute to his dynamic nature and many accomplishments. Yet when Douglas received the presidential nomination of a fragmented Democratic party, he knew the task before him was almost insurmountable.

Although in failing health and plagued by troublesome sore throats, Douglas decided on an unprecedented move: He would personally take his message to the people. As he knew, this violated a long-standing tradition dating back to George Washington, a tradition that dictated that it was not proper for a candidate seeking the highest office in the land to stump the nation. Convinced that the perilous times offered no other choice, Douglas became the first major presidential nominee in American political history to campaign actively in his own behalf. The notion was so novel that many people found it hard to accept. He "demeans himself," sneered the *North Iowan,* "as no other candidate ever yet has, who goes about begging, imploring, and beseeching the people to grant him his wish." Comparing Douglas to an organ grinder's monkey, the same paper went on to suggest that the candidate should "be attended by some Italian, with his hand organ to grind out an accompaniment."

Simian similes notwithstanding, Douglas, whose other nickname was "Steam Engine in Britches" because of his indefatigable energy, took the stump with a will. Not altogether unmindful of criticism, Douglas began his campaign with a "cover story" intended to mask his true intentions. He kicked off his presidential bid with a trip east, explaining that he was going to New York to see his aging mother.

But filial devotion took second place, as Douglas's "journey to mother" lasted over a month and included many speech-making stops. The Republicans made a laughingstock out of the transparent ploy. "A Boy Lost" crowed one Republican pamphlet, then continued tongue-in-cheek: "He has not yet reached his mother, who is very anxious about him. He has been seen in Philadelphia, New York, Hartford, Conn. [and] at a clambake in Rhode Island. He has been heard from at Boston, Portland, Augusta, and Bangor, Me."

While campaigning in Iowa, Douglas received news that the Republicans had swept the October state elections in Pennsylvania, Ohio, and Indiana. A realist, he saw clearly that these victories presaged an overall Republican win in November. "Mr. Lincoln is the next president," Douglas told his secretary. "We must try to save the Union. I will go South."

Above all, he wanted to impress upon those in the slave states that the legal election of any president, even a Republican one, was no excuse for secession. Anyone who contemplated such a move was, in his view, a traitor. As Douglas toured the states below the Mason-Dixon line, at great personal risk and at the cost of his health, he cautioned Southerners against secession. "I believe there is a conspiracy on foot to break up this Union," Douglas declared on November 2 as he stood on the steps of the state capitol in Montgomery, Alabama. Little did he know that the conspiracy of which he spoke would take shape four months later in the very building behind him.

Railing against the disunionists, Douglas risked being shot; pelted by tomatoes and eggs, it could have easily been hot lead. The "Little Giant" survived the campaign, but he died on June 3, 1861, at the age of forty-eight, his demise no doubt hastened by his herculean efforts to save the Union he loved.

THE CAMPAIGN OF 1860

The 1860 presidential election was one of the most momentous in U.S. history, and Americans knew it. The issues of freedom and slavery, Union or secession, had been tearing at the body politic for years, and a crossroads had been finally, painfully, reached. The great mass of the electorate had watched with growing concern as political leaders grappled with national issues. Now, as the November election approached, it was their turn to express their views at the ballot box.

And express them they did, in unprecedented numbers. The 1860 contest for the White House was the first to attract a voter turnout of 81.8 percent, more than in any previous presidential election.

This unparalleled interest registered at the ballot box was reflected in the campaign itself, with its emphasis on pageantry, parade, and all forms of hoopla. Although not uncommon in national political life (it all began two decades earlier in the "Tippecanoe and Tyler Too" 1840 campaign), there was something decidedly novel about the 1860 canvass. Hundreds of thousands of Americans became involved in what were called marching clubs. Composed largely of young men, they were best known for their colorful outfits and banners as they sang and marched in cadence at political rallies throughout the country. The Northern Democrats had the "Little Giants," a reference to their candidate Stephen A. Douglas, and the Constitutional Unionists, a third party composed of former Whigs and Know Nothings, had the "Bell Ringers," a reference to their man John Bell. But perhaps the most famed of the marching clubs were the Republican party's "Wide Awakes."

The Wide Awake clubs, which first appeared during the 1856 presidential contest, could trace their origins in the 1860 campaign to Hartford, Connecticut. In late February, when Cassius M. Clay, a Kentucky Republican, arrived in town to deliver a political speech, a group of young men decided to escort him from the railroad depot to his quarters in town. They put on glazed capes to protect themselves from the dripping oil of their torches and created quite a stir with their marching. Later, they organized along paramilitary lines, met on a regular basis to practice drill formations, and called themselves the Wide Awakes.

The idea caught on, and within a few months Wide Awake clubs sprouted all over the Republican North and had some 400,000 members. One of the greatest Wide Awake parades took place in New York City in early October. The marchers, about 90,000 strong, tramped down Broadway, the colorful cavalcade illuminated by salvos of rockets and other fireworks blazing high into the sky. Bands played, and when thousands of voices joined to sing the party song "Ain't You Glad You Joined the Republicans?" the effect was mesmerizing.

The discipline, color, and sheer spectacle the Wide Awakes had to offer created a sense of paranoia in the slave states. After all, if Northerners were willing to turn out en masse to march at political rallies, would they not go to the polls in record numbers on election day? And even more frightening, if Lincoln won, might not the Wide Awakes serve as the vanguard of a Northern invasion to force abolition in the South?

To counter this "black Republican" threat, Southern Democrats, supporting John C. Breckinridge, organized their own marching clubs under the banner "Minute Men." Whatever the purpose of these clubs, either to rally voters or to protect against an invasion, or perhaps both, one thing was abundantly clear: The fact that they were called Minute Men was no coincidence. If the original Minute Men (ironically, Northerners) resisted British tyranny, then Southern Minute Men were a guard against that of the Republicans.

ABRAHAM LINCOLN

On November 6, 1860, Abraham Lincoln was elected president of the United States, the first Republican candidate ever to win the White House. His was a clear-cut victory, at least in the electoral college, but not in terms of the popular vote. Lincoln was a minority president, having won less than 40 percent of the ballots cast by the electorate. Altogether, he polled 1,866,452 votes, while his closest rival, Northern Democrat Stephen Douglas, tallied 1,376,957 (29.4 percent), Southern Democrat John Breckinridge, 849,781 (18 percent), and Constitutional Unionist John Bell, 588,879 (12.6 percent).

How can one account for Lincoln's triumph? No doubt the breakup of the Democrats into two opposing North-South factions strengthened Lincoln's position, but it was hardly decisive. In addition, the introduction of a third party, the Constitutional Unionists, probably hurt the Democrats more than the Republicans.

Of far greater importance in determining the outcome of the contest was Lincoln himself. Regarded as neither a radical nor a conservative, the Republican nominee was viewed as a moderate, firmly opposed to the extension of slavery, but having no ties to the abolitionist movement. His position was misinterpreted in the slave states, however, especially among those in the lower South, where his image as an abolitionist ogre was so deeply entrenched that they refused to believe anything else.

Instead of trying to persuade them otherwise, Lincoln upheld the tradition of the times by maintaining a political silence during the campaign. An enigma to begin with—indeed, as historian Robert W. Johannsen has reminded us, "no presidential candidate of a major party had been so little known at the time of his nomination"—this turned out to be a source of political strength for Lincoln, at least in the North. Since he was an unknown commodity in most respects (except when it came to the nonextension of slavery, where his position coincided with the vast majority of those in his party), he offended few people in the free states and consequently provided little if any verbal ammunition for his rivals to use against him.

On the other hand, his silence was a two-edged sword. It might have helped in the North, but it hurt him in the South, because it did nothing to assuage that region's fears of a "black Republican" presidency. Lincoln said his positions on slavery were a matter of public record, so he would say no more. But lack of reassurance made Southern paranoia on Lincoln run wild. The Republican standard-bearer wasn't even on the ballot in many of the slaveholding states.

Thus, Lincoln was a distinctly Northern president who had garnered only 26,000 Southern votes out of an overall total of 1,866,452. When the votes were all counted, Lincoln had carried 17 1/2 free states; Breckinridge, 11 slave states; Bell, 3 upper South states; and Douglas, Missouri and half of New Jersey's electoral votes. In the 1860 presidential election, therefore, most voters chose their candidate along strictly regional lines—and herein lies the main reason for the Republican triumph.

Lincoln was victorious because he was strong in the populous Northern states that had large numbers of electoral votes. It didn't matter if his popular vote lead was comparatively slim; once a state was won, he won the lion's share of the electoral votes. As for the division in Democratic ranks and the challenge posed by the Constitutional Unionists, these developments had little if any impact on Lincoln's ultimate victory. Even if all three of his opponents' votes had gone to a single candidate in the North, Lincoln would have lost only Oregon, California, and New Jersey, and that outcome would have reduced his electoral vote from 180 to 169—still comfortably above the 152 needed to win.

HENRY VILLARD

The White House press corps is an integral part of the American presidency, but that was not always the case. It all began with Henry Villard, who in December 1860 became the first reporter in the history of American journalism to cover a president-elect on a full-time basis.

Villard was born Ferdinand Heinrich Gustav Hilgard on April 10, 1835, in Speyer, Rhenish Bavaria. Scarcely more than a boy when the Revolution of 1848 swept Germany, he sympathized with the democratic movement, participating in it to the best of his ability. His revolutionary sympathies caused a rift with his father, and eventually Hilgard emigrated to the United States when barely eighteen years of age. Arriving in New York in 1853 with $20 in his pocket, Hilgard couldn't speak a word of English.

After learning the language of his adopted country, he then tried a variety of jobs—law, real estate, peddling books—before taking up newspaper reporting in 1857. Because he did not want his father to know his whereabouts, he assumed the name of Henri, later Henry Villard. Proving successful at his new profession, in 1858 he was given the assignment to cover the Lincoln-Douglas debates for the German language newspaper *Staats Zeitung* of New York. It was during this period that Villard and Lincoln became friends. Despite the age difference and the obvious difference in background and culture, the two had much in common. Both were self-made men who became successful in worlds far removed from the ones they grew up in.

With his personal ties to Lincoln, Villard was the ideal candidate to cover the president-elect in Springfield and during his long journey from Illinois to Washington. Although it was the New York *Herald* who actually posted him with Lincoln, Villard's dispatches were given a wider circulation to other papers via the Associated Press.

Villard must have struck a responsive chord in Lincoln, because the young reporter seems to have captured the essence of the inner man beneath the public facade. While traveling by rail with the Lincoln entourage to the nation's capital, Villard sent the following piece to his editors in New York (it appeared in print on February 20, 1861):

> It was plain to see that the Lincolns are common sense, homelike folks unused to the glitter and flutter of society. Towering above all, with his face and forehead furrowed by a thousand wrinkles, his hair unkempt, his new whiskers looking as if not yet naturalized, his clothes illy arranged, Mr. Lincoln sat toward the rear of the car. . . .

No one can see Mr. Lincoln without recognizing in him a man of immense power and force of character and natural talent. He seems so sincere, so conscientious, so earnest, so simple-hearted that one cannot help liking him. . . .

[W]ith the intimate knowledge of politics and politicians, and with the uncommon homespun common sense which his friends claim for him, Lincoln seems a man to act and decide for himself.

From December 1860 to February 1861, many in the North were reading reports such as the above—in the clear, concise English of a German immigrant. It was a magnificent achievement, considering he had mastered the written English sentence only a few years before. In later years Villard became a successful businessman, eventually controlling the Northern Pacific Railroad. He died in 1879.

GRACE BEDELL'S LETTER

Abraham Lincoln was the first president ever to wear a beard. Of all his predecessors, Martin Van Buren perhaps came the closest to a beard by sporting large sideburns. But his chin was bare, which disqualifies him from consideration.

In the 1840s and 1850s facial hair was coming into vogue, and it was only a matter of time before a bearded president would have been elected. In fact, had the full-bearded John C. Frémont been elected president in 1856, it would have been he, not Lincoln, who claimed to be the first bewhiskered chief executive.

The story of Lincoln's beard has been enshrined in American folklore. Apparently Grace Bedell, an eleven-year-old girl, wrote Lincoln during the campaign of 1860, suggesting that he should "let [his] whiskers grow." The pert little miss added: "You would look a great deal better for your face is so thin. All the ladies like whiskers and they would tease their husbands to vote for you and then you would be President."

Lincoln replied to Grace's letter in his usual self-deprecating way. "As to the whiskers," he wrote, "having never worn any, do you not think people would call it a piece of silly affec[ta]tion if I were to begin it now?"

Whatever his concern over public reaction, Lincoln began to grow a beard soon after he won the November election—a decision that seems to have pleased others besides Grace. A number of "very earnest" Republicans in New York expressed a desire for a bearded president, thinking that Lincoln's "dignity might be enhanced."

But it was little Grace Bedell who was recognized as having inspired the idea. When Lincoln's Washington-bound train on February 16, 1861, stopped at her hometown of Westfield, New York, she was in the crowd that greeted him. He called for her, and an old man brought her up to the rear platform of the car where Lincoln was standing. "You see I have let these whiskers grow for you, Grace," he told her. The president-elect then kissed the little girl, and pointed her out to the crowd as the one who had advised him to grow a beard.

KATE WARNE

In 1860 career opportunities for women were few. Denied the vote and equal judicial rights, females were still considered inferior to males. Conventional wisdom of the time said women were creatures of emotion, not intellect. Their role was primarily in the home, as wives and mothers, where their natural instincts as nurturers of children and help-mates of their husbands could best be utilized.

A few courageous women fought hard against these restricting stereotypes. One such was Kate Warne, the first professional woman detective in U.S. history, who achieved a high point in her career when she also became the first woman to guard a president-elect. Given male attitudes of women as the weaker sex, being a trusted—and armed—presidential bodyguard was an incredible achievement, all the more incredible as women were not part of American police departments until 1891, and then only as prison matrons. It would not be for another dozen years, in 1903, before they first served as police investigators—almost half a century after Warne began her groundbreaking career.

Warne was no token, but a good private detective who worked for the Pinkerton National Detective Agency. Her career began in 1856, when she introduced herself to agency chief Allan Pinkerton. She was then a widow of about twenty-three. At a time when such women were expected to seek another husband at the earliest opportunity, Warne took the bold course of wanting a career as a private detective. Impressed by her determination and intelligence, Pinkerton hired her, and she soon became one of his most successful operatives.

Eventually Warne was assigned to guard Lincoln because of the so-called "Baltimore plot"—an alleged conspiracy to assassinate the president-elect before he could be sworn in. It first came to the surface in early 1861, when Samuel Felton, president of the Philadelphia, Wilmington, and Baltimore Railroad, heard disturbing rumors in Baltimore that a plan to kill Lincoln was in the works. He hired Pinkerton to investigate the matter.

Because Lincoln's train journey from his home in Springfield, Illinois, to Washington, D.C., would be a long and roundabout one (it would take eleven days, since the president-elect had so many speaking engagements and events to attend), there was ample time and opportunity to strike at him. Yet nowhere would Lincoln be more vulnerable than in that storm center of secessionist intrigue, the city of Baltimore. There was no direct rail route to Washington; Lincoln would arrive at Baltimore's Calvert Street Station, then have his railroad car drawn by horses over the streetcar tracks across town to be attached to another train at the Camden Street Station for the last leg of the journey to Washington.

Pinkerton and his operatives went undercover, hoping to sniff out any clandestine plots. Mrs. Warne, code named "M. B." for the alias of Mrs. M. Barley, also went to Baltimore. Although a Northerner, she must have been adept at accents, because she passed herself off as a resident of Montgomery, Alabama. She had been on a case there and was thoroughly familiar with that Southern city. Her main duty was to "cultivate" the wives and daughters of any assassination conspirators.

Another Pinkerton man, one Harry Davies, befriended an O. K. Hillard, who happened to be part of the Baltimore plot. After a few drinks at the Fountain Hotel, Hillard's tongue was loosened enough that he confided he would kill Lincoln if called upon to do so. Hillard was a member of a small, fanatical band of assassins headed by an Italian named Cypriano Ferrandini (sometimes called Fernandina). A barber by trade, Ferrandini was a fiery secessionist who was known as "Captain" to his followers. He had a bristling black mustache, was given to pompous, posturing speeches, and was armed with a stiletto. But if his appearance and style seemed comic opera, his intentions were deadly.

A narrow corridor of the Calvert Street Station was selected as the assassination site. Some of the plotters would create a diversion, and when the police rushed elsewhere, Lincoln would be unguarded and quickly dispatched.

The Ferrandini plotters had no inkling that they had been infiltrated. While Davies befriended Hillard, Pinkerton gained the confidence of Ferrandini himself. Pompous as ever, the "Captain" called his men together to draw lots to determine who would kill Lincoln; the person who drew a red ballot would be the assassin. The room in which they met was darkened, and "everyone was pledged to secrecy as to the color of the ballot he drew." Actually, Ferrandini and one or two other leaders of the plot, "doubting the courage of some of their number," had decided to place eight red ballots in the box, increasing the likelihood that at least one of the band would carry out the deed.

Pinkerton now had to convince Lincoln and his entourage of the imminent danger. On the evening of February 21, 1861, the detective visited the president-elect in the latter's Philadelphia hotel. Once Lincoln was persuaded that the plot was real, Pinkerton then huddled with members of the president-elect's entourage, railroad officials, and army officers and came up with a suitable plan to neutralize the threat. Lincoln would leave for Washington about a day in advance of his scheduled departure. By boarding a night train in Philadelphia, moreover, the president-elect could pass through dangerous Baltimore in the wee hours of the morning. As an added precaution, he would travel incognito as Kate Warne's "invalid brother."

In keeping with this subterfuge, Mrs. Warne arranged to have tickets purchased for her "brother" and his companions and made sure she secured the rear sections of the sleeping car. She charmed the conductor into allowing an unusual concession: The back door of the sleeper would be left open to allow her "sick sibling" to enter his berth with privacy. A curtain divided Lincoln's part of the car from the rest of the passengers.

When Lincoln arrived at the Philadelphia station, Mrs. Warne kept up the ruse by greeting her "brother" warmly. The president-elect was in disguise, wearing an overcoat and eschewing his signature stovepipe hat for a fedoralike brown "Kossuth hat." Lincoln's entourage included Allan Pinkerton and Lincoln's close friend and bodyguard, Ward Hill Lamon. Lamon was burly, tough, and armed to the teeth, carrying two revolvers, two derringers, and two Bowie knives.

Detectives Kate Warne and George Bangs were also part of the president-elect's security force. Armed with a seven-shooting revolver, Warne was posted near the door to Lincoln's compartment during the all-night vigil. At about 3:15 A.M. Lincoln's train rolled into Baltimore, the station deserted. The sleeping car was then hitched to a team of horses and taken across town via streetcar tracks to the Camden Street depot.

There was some anxiety when the Washington train was two hours late, temporarily stranding the party in Baltimore. Lincoln eased the tension by telling funny stories, but the group remained on alert, keeping a wary eye on those milling about the station. Despite the early hour, there were a number of passengers on the platform just outside waiting for the train. Lincoln and his party could even hear people singing the Southern song "Dixie," one drunk roaring the lyrics at the top of his voice.

At last the Washington train chugged in, its clatter of pistons and squeal of wheels shattering the tension of the night. Lincoln arrived in Washington about 6:00 A.M., and as he stepped off the sleeping car, he was accompanied by Pinkerton and Lamon (Detectives Warne and Bangs had remained in Baltimore). The president-elect passed unnoticed through the capital station, when suddenly a loud voice said, "Abe you can't play that on me." Pinkerton gave the speaker a sharp elbow in the ribs, and Lamon raised a fist. Lincoln interceded, explaining that the stranger was a friend, Congressman Elihu Washburne.

The nerve-wracking journey was over, successfully concluded. Kate Warne continued to work as a detective for Allan Pinkerton—and as he recalled, "Mrs. Warne never let me down." She died prematurely at age thirty-five in 1868.

THE CONFEDERATE STATES OF AMERICA

By February 1, 1861, secession was a reality. All seven states of the lower South had broken their bonds with the Union and were determined to create a government of their own. Meeting in Montgomery, Alabama, on February 4—a full month before Lincoln even took the oath of office—the delegates from six of the seceded states (Texas would send representatives later) were called to order. With a deep sense of reverence, the president of the convention, Howell Cobb of Georgia, reminded his colleagues of the "great work" committed to their care.

One of the first orders of business was to draft a new constitution for the fledgling nation. To the surprise of many observers and the satisfaction of most delegates, the task was completed within just five weeks. On March 11 the convention unanimously adopted a governing document that formally established the Confederate States of America.

In several respects, the new government was progressive and innovative, with its single-term presidency, line-item veto, self-sufficient post office, and civil service reform. On the other hand, this neophyte Southern nation could not have been more backward. Put succinctly, the Confederacy was the first government in modern history to commit itself firmly to a policy of racism.

Indeed, the Montgomery gathering was composed of men who passionately believed in the racist tenets of the day. Few Southern leaders had the moral qualms about slavery that, say, Virginian Robert E. Lee had. Human bondage was justified purely in terms of skin color. Persons of African descent were not slaves because of debt or the misfortunes of war, as had been the case in other lands and times. They were slaves because they were, in the opinion of most white Southerners, physically and mentally inferior to whites.

The Montgomery convention (unlike the Philadelphia convention of 1787) specifically used the term "slavery" in its constitution; no more watered-down phrases or vague euphemisms in the name of compromise. No law could be passed denying or impairing the right to own slaves, and slavery was protected in the territories.

Thus the Confederate Constitution reaffirmed the plantation way of life as the nucleus of the Southern system, a system that seemed to need slavery for its continued existence. By 1860 only one Southern family in four owned slaves, but even nonslaveholding whites (the yeomen) liked the idea of being superior to another group by the sheer fact of being Caucasian. Besides, there was always that hope, however remote, that fortune might smile and they, too, would become slaveholders.

Confederate vice president Alexander H. Stephens was a product of the yeoman class, a former Georgia congressman who had opposed secession but ultimately succumbed to the wishes of his state. Sickly, never weighing more than ninety pounds, Stephens had a wizened face that was the image of an unwrapped mummy. Yet for all that, he could be a powerful speaker, and in March 1861 he gave an address in Savannah that came to the heart of the matter. Stephens was a racist, proud of it, and to him racism was the chief pillar of the Confederacy. He had little tolerance for those people—Northerners were implied—who professed to believe in the equality of all men, proclaiming:

> Our new government is founded upon exactly the opposite idea; its foundations are laid, its corner stone rests upon the great truth that the negro is not equal to the white man. That slavery—the subordination to the superior race, is his natural and normal condition. This, our new Government, is the first in the history of the world, based upon this great physical and moral truth.

AN ARMED CAMP

When Abraham Lincoln arrived in Washington, D.C., on February 23, 1861, his personal safety was far from secure. Washington was still a Southern city that harbored Confederate sympathizers. True, most of the capital's 61,000 citizens were loyal, and surrounding Virginia and Maryland thus far had made no attempt to break their bonds with the Union. But the District of Columbia was a Federal island in a Southern sea, where an assassination attempt or pro-Confederate coup was not out of the question. With that possibility hovering over Washington, Lincoln's inauguration became the first in American history to have tight security precautions. The next time such protective measures were taken was when Franklin D. Roosevelt was given the oath of office in March 1933, another period of national crisis.

Gen. Winfield Scott was general in chief of the U.S. Army, and though a Virginian, he was utterly loyal to the Union. On March 3, 1861, Scott held an unprecedented conference at his headquarters to discuss inauguration security. There were some 600 regular army troops on hand to guard the new president, backed up by around 2,000 volunteer militiamen. Unlike all previous inaugural ceremonies, this time the soldiers were there for protection, not pageantry.

It was planned that outgoing president James Buchanan escort Lincoln from Willard's Hotel down Pennsylvania Avenue to the Capitol in an open carriage. A double file of District of Columbia (volunteer) cavalry would flank the presidential carriage, while a company of West Point Sappers (engineers) and Miners (explosive experts) would precede it. Infantry units would bring up the rear, completing the cordon around Lincoln.

Scott was thorough. Sharpshooting riflemen were posted on the rooftops along the parade route, with orders to watch the opposite side of the street and to fire upon any building "should any weapon appear in any of the windows." Regular cavalry was also posted along the side streets that crossed Pennsylvania Avenue, thus sealing off the grand thoroughfare.

At the Capitol itself, additional sharpshooters eyed the crowds for trouble, and artillery was on hand for more than just presidential salutes. The night before the ceremony, information was received of a plot to blow up the inaugural platform as Lincoln took the oath of office. As a precaution, a whole battalion of District of Columbia militia guarded the structure, and plainclothes detectives mixed with the spectators.

The presidential procession went off without a hitch. The carriage, however, was so closely guarded that one could scarcely see Lincoln and Buchanan in the smear of blue uniforms. Inspector General Charles P. Stone, moreover, took his own precautionary measures. Riding near the carriage, he purposely spurred his mount in such a way as to keep the escort's horses nervous and agitated. Stone reasoned it would be harder to get a clear shot past a screen of edgy, skittish, constantly moving horses.

For many, it was a sad commentary on the times. Here was a spectacle, a Philadelphia newspaper pointed out, to "terrify the heart of every patriot." When Lincoln gave his inaugural address, he was "surrounded and guarded not by the honest hearts of a happy people, but safely esconced [*sic*] out of the people's reach, within a military cordon bristling with bayonets."

BORN IN KENTUCKY

Abraham Lincoln, the sixteenth president, was the first born outside the original thirteen states. He was born February 12, 1809, in an area known as the Sinking Spring, near Nolin Creek about three miles south of Hodgenville, in central Kentucky. The Lincoln family stayed at the Sinking Spring farm for two years, living the typical "hardscrabble" pioneer life of the period. In 1811 Lincoln's father, Thomas, a restless sort, always seeking greener pastures, pulled up stakes and moved his family to Knob Creek farm, some ten miles east of Lincoln's birthplace. It was near the main road from Louisville and Nashville, so young Abraham was treated to a perambulating pageant that included peddlers, pioneers with their wagons, and even slaves and overseers. Abraham's earliest memory was of Knob Creek, helping his father plant pumpkin seeds.

But Thomas Lincoln's title to Knob Creek was clouded, so in 1816 the family moved again, this time to Indiana. Government surveys in Indiana meant there was less chance of litigation or disputed titles. Besides, Kentucky was a slave state, and Thomas Lincoln hated slavery. In later years his son Abraham commented that Thomas left Kentucky "partly on account of slavery; but chiefly on account of the difficulty in land titles in Ky."

And so Abraham Lincoln became a Northerner, thanks to his father. Another baby boy born in Kentucky, on June 3, 1808, almost eight months before Abraham, would experience a different fate. This was Jefferson Davis, destined to become Lincoln's nemesis as president of the Confederate States of America. While Davis was still an infant, his family moved to Mississippi, where he grew up to be a slaveholding plantation owner. It is interesting to speculate how history would have been changed if Thomas Lincoln had not been hostile toward slavery. What if the Lincolns had settled deeper South like the Davis clan?

Thomas Lincoln erected a one-room log cabin near Gentryville, Indiana. The Hoosier State was still a wilderness—in the words of

Abraham Lincoln, "a wild region, with many bears and other wild animals still in the woods." The Lincolns lived in Indiana until 1830, when they picked up stakes and moved farther west to Illinois.

Prior to Lincoln, the only other president who was considered a "Westerner" was Andrew Jackson, having spent most of his adult life in Tennessee. In truth, "Old Hickory" was born in South Carolina. Lincoln, by contrast, was a true son of the West, a region that was coming of age by 1860.

LINCOLN'S WORKING-CLASS ROOTS

As a self-made man, Abraham Lincoln downplayed his working-class origins. He had come far and did not want to be reminded constantly of his humble roots. But Lincoln's background remained a constant source of wonder, since he was the first president of the United States from the working class, a man who had known years of physical toil in his youth and early adult years.

Stripped of its romantic aura, frontier life was dirty, backbreaking, and sometimes heartbreaking. Chopping wood, clearing the land, plowing, planting, and tending the livestock were pursuits not for the weak and sickly. The future president was physically well suited for life on a farm, though his lankiness might have suggested otherwise—at twenty-one, he was six feet, four inches tall and weighed 160 pounds. With his massive hands and long, powerful arms, his relatives and acquaintances remembered him as one of the strongest men they had ever known. He could "strike with a mall a heavier blow than any man," recalled a neighbor. "If you heard him felling trees," his cousin Dennis Hanks later told an interviewer, "you would think there were three men in the woods cutting."

Ambitious enough as a youth to know farming wasn't for him, Lincoln tried several different occupations, sometimes just to make a little extra cash, sometimes as a serious career move. He did some carpentry, was hired to help guide a riverboat up the Sangamon River, ferried a flatboat of goods down the Mississippi to New Orleans, and at one point considered blacksmithing.

Convinced that he could make a better living as a businessman, Lincoln opened a general store in New Salem, Illinois, with a partner by the name of William Berry, but he discovered that he had no knack for retailing. Nor was his partner of any assistance. Berry drank himself to death, leaving Lincoln holding the bag with a debt of over $1,000—

a huge sum for the time, which Lincoln called "the National Debt." It took him years to pay it off.

At various times from 1833 to 1836 Lincoln worked as a farmhand, helped at the mill, and served as New Salem's postmaster. He even did a stint as deputy county surveyor, a job that demonstrated his ambition and nerve, since he knew nothing about surveying when he started the work. Basically picking up what he needed to know from books, Lincoln went on to successfully survey several town sites.

Eventually, Lincoln became a lawyer, and a very good one. Although he didn't dwell on his origins, he was proud of the fact that there was social mobility in the country. "There is no permanent class of hired laborers amongst us," Lincoln explained in 1859 to an audience in Cincinnati. "Twenty-five years ago, I was a hired laborer. The hired laborer of yesterday, labors on his own account today; and will hire others to labor for him tomorrow."

As an occupant of the White House, Lincoln's early years as a manual laborer did not go unnoticed. In 1864 a Lansing, Michigan, newspaper editor pointed out to his readers that "Mr. Lincoln is the only President we have ever had who may be said to be from the working class of people. . . . No other President has ever worked with his hands for a livelihood after arriving at the full maturity of manhood."

FIVE FORMER PRESIDENTS

Abraham Lincoln's inauguration on March 4, 1861, was the first to take place while five former presidents were still alive. It was an occasion that did not happen again until President Bill Clinton was sworn in on January 20, 1993.

The five ex-chief executives still alive in March 1861 were Martin Van Buren, John Tyler, Millard Fillmore, Franklin Pierce, and James Buchanan. The oldest of the surviving presidents was Van Buren, who had served from 1837 to 1841.

During the 1860 campaign, the five former presidents had their own personal preferences, reflecting the divisions in the country as a whole. Van Buren supported Stephen A. Douglas, in part because of the "Little Giant's" popular sovereignty theory, which called for the settlers in a territory to determine whether to include slavery. John Tyler and Franklin Pierce threw their support to John C. Breckinridge of the Southern Democratic party. Outgoing president James Buchanan also backed Breckinridge.

Millard Fillmore's choice for standard-bearer is far more difficult to pin down. Something of a political chameleon, he was at various times an Anti-Mason, a Whig, and in 1856 the presidential nominee of the American or Know-Nothing party. It is not known who Fillmore supported in 1860, but it probably wasn't Abraham Lincoln.

In mid-April 1861 Franklin Pierce wrote to Martin Van Buren proposing that all five ex-presidents meet in Philadelphia, "the cradle of the Union." From there they would issue a call for a peace convention as a last-ditch effort to avoid civil war. Pierce felt Van Buren should summon the other former chief executives by reason of his seniority. Owing partly to his advanced age, Van Buren declined, thinking that it would do no good in any case.

MAJ. ROBERT ANDERSON

When South Carolina seceded from the Union in December 1860, the leaders of the state naturally assumed that all Federal property within their borders would fall under their jurisdiction. The U.S. forts guarding Charleston harbor soon became a bone of contention. After South Carolina declared its independence, the "sovereign nation" sent commissioners north to negotiate for these military installations.

The controversy centered on two major fortifications, Moultrie and Sumter. Most of the soldiers still loyal to the United States occupied Fort Moultrie, an out-of-date fortress that was vulnerable to attack from the rear. Fort Sumter, at least on paper, was the more formidable of the two. Perched on a man-made granite island just within the entrance to Charleston harbor, it was designed to mount 146 guns and be garrisoned by 650 troops. Its walls were forty to sixty feet high and eight to twelve feet thick, a masonry mountain that rose in tier after tier of brick. The problem was that Sumter was still under construction, most of its cannons were not yet mounted, and it was unmanned.

Charleston represented the heart of the secessionist cause, full of fire-eaters willing to expel the "Yankees" by force, if necessary. With around eighty U.S. soldiers at Moultrie, the thousands of South Carolina militiamen surrounding the Union stronghold were confident of an easy victory—if only they could attack. But the South Carolinians were under strict orders not to open fire—that is, until a Confederate government was in place and gave its approval.

It was a volatile situation, and the job of the U.S. garrison commander was one that required tact as well as courage. Maj. Robert Anderson was given the assignment shortly after Lincoln's election in

November 1860. Anderson, fifty-six, was a career soldier who hailed from Kentucky. A former slaveholder, he sympathized with Southern aspirations, but thirty-five years in the army had bred an unshakable loyalty to the Union.

Anderson was haunted by the specter of civil war, and he wanted to avoid conflict if at all possible. Charleston was a powder keg, the garrison a lighted fuse. It was only a matter of time before an explosion. To dampen the fuse, Anderson decided to strengthen his position, hoping that this might discourage the South Carolinians from taking action. On the evening of December 26, 1860, the major spiked the guns of Fort Moultrie and executed a brilliant withdrawal to Fort Sumter under the very noses of the secessionist troops.

Beginning with this single act, and continuing with the defense of his tiny island outpost, Major Anderson found himself "the first American to become a folk hero literally overnight." Anderson had withdrawn to maintain the peace and prevent capitulation to South Carolina, but the North saw it as a magnificent act of defiance.

The major became not only a hero, but a living symbol of the Northern effort to maintain the Union. Newspapers across the free states sang his praises, and gun salutes were fired to honor him. Since South Carolinian authorities (at least for the time being) allowed postal delivery to the island, Anderson also received a flood of mail from admirers. "You are today the most popular man in the nation," wrote one. Another said, "While you hold Fort Sumter, I shall not despair of our noble, our glorious Union."

Before matters got out of hand, photographer George S. Cook of Charleston was allowed to take a boat out to Fort Sumter and photograph Major Anderson. The negatives found their way North, where Anderson's picture was sold at twenty-five cents a copy. The commander of Sumter was so popular, in fact, that during the remainder of the crisis a photographer made upward of 1,000 prints a day of his likeness.

But Anderson could not hold out indefinitely. Supplies were dwindling. With a lame duck administration in Washington, there seemed little hope that any attempt would be made to resolve the crisis. Outgoing president James Buchanan surprised everyone, however, when in early January 1861 he sent the merchant vessel *Star of the West* with reinforcements (200 soldiers) and supplies to Charleston harbor. It was a courageous decision by a president who had previously demonstrated little backbone, but it proved to no avail. When the *Star of the West* appeared at the harbor entrance, Confederate shore batteries opened fire, forcing the ship to turn back.

"My dear sir," Buchanan remarked to Lincoln on March 4, the day of his inauguration, "if you are as happy in entering the White House as I shall feel on returning to Wheatland [Pennsylvania], you are a happy man indeed." Once Lincoln received a detailed briefing of Anderson's plight, he probably understood better his predecessor's sense of relief. Informed that Fort Sumter had barely a month's rations left and was surrounded by South Carolinians itching for a fight, the newly installed president found himself in a no-win situation. If he failed to aid the Union garrison, this would be viewed as a sign of weakness, and there was no telling what the recently created Confederate government might do in light of that inaction. But if he launched an aggressive relief force, he might have to bear the onus of starting a war. Recognizing that neither policy would yield satisfactory results, Lincoln shrewdly adopted a middle course, authorizing an expedition that would contain neither ammunition nor reinforcements, only provisions. And he made certain to notify Southern authorities of his decision.

In the meantime, the Confederates demanded that Anderson surrender. He refused but made it clear that he would have to abandon the fort if not resupplied soon. Unwilling to wait and starve him out, at 4:30 A.M. on April 12, 1861, and before Lincoln's relief vessels had arrived, the Confederates opened fire on Sumter. The huge cannons hurtled solid shot against the smooth outer walls of the fort. The barrage, once begun, seemed endless, causing interior fires and sending shattered pieces of brick and masonry all about.

Although outgunned, Anderson's men were not entirely defenseless. The Sumter garrison consisted of the major, nine officers, and about seventy men of the 1st United States Artillery. Some workmen who had been building the fort were also part of the defense complement. One of the officers, Capt. Abner Doubleday, who some believe invented and named the game of baseball, scored in another way by firing the first shot in defense of the beleaguered fort. In all, Sumter's defenders managed to get off 1,000 rounds, knocking out several Confederate cannons and demolishing the barracks at Fort Moultrie.

After suffering thirty-three hours of continuous bombardment, Major Anderson felt his men had done enough to uphold the honor of the Stars and Stripes. He surrendered on April 14, 1861. Confederate batteries had fired 3,341 shot and shell, leaving Sumter's walls pitted with 600 direct hits. Yet while the fort was badly damaged, with its facade pock-marked and scarred, not a single man had been lost.

Exactly four years to the day, April 14, 1865, a victorious North staged a ceremony at the battered Fort Sumter. Anderson, now a brevet major general, raised the same American flag that he had been forced to haul down four years before. Events had come full circle, only now the Union was restored, not sundered.

NEW YORK *HERALD*

When Confederate batteries opened fire on Fort Sumter in the early morning hours of April 12, 1861, it was clear that a civil war between the Northern and Southern states, long anticipated with a mixture of jubilation and dread, was at last begun.

Probably at no point in the history of the Republic—and perhaps not again until Pearl Harbor—were Americans so consumed by an outbreak of hostilities as they were by what had transpired at Charleston harbor. In response to this unprecedented public interest, the New York *Herald* on April 14, 1861, published more than 135,000 copies of a single issue—the first time ever that a newspaper had printed so many copies. Few, if any, Americans realized, however, that the events reported in the *Herald* and in thousands of newspapers across the divided nation marked the beginning of what would be the bloodiest conflict in U.S. history.

CHAPTER 2

Raising and Administering an Army

Until the post–World War II era, the United States never maintained a large military establishment in time of peace. A powerful but idle army, it was felt, might breed a military dictatorship and extinguish hard-won liberties. One only had to look across the Atlantic, where European armies were often used as instruments of despotism and absolute monarchy.

Mid-nineteenth-century Americans were especially vigilant, almost to a point of risking the very safety of the Republic. At the outset of the Mexican-American War, for instance, Mexico had 32,000 men in arms, more than four times as many as the United States. But as they had done in the past, Americans rallied to the cause, and by the time they had defeated their neighbor to the south, they had 50,000 men in uniform. True to their traditions, however, once the two-year war came to an end in 1848, America's conquering army was demobilized and returned almost to its prewar skeletal size. For the next dozen or so years, nothing changed. On the eve of the Civil War, therefore, the U.S. army consisted of a lilliputian force of 1,105 officers and 15,259 enlisted men—most of whom were on outpost duty in the West, guarding against possible Indian uprisings.

Soon after the bombardment of Fort Sumter in April 1861, both sides began raising mass armies, something completely alien to an America that had barely recognized the need for professional armed forces at all. The Confederacy would have to create an army from scratch, while the Union, with only 1,000 soldiers in organized units east of the Mississippi, and with nearly a third of its officers resigning and entering Rebel ranks, was not much better off. Yet despite a lack of precedent and a complete reliance on volunteerism, at least in the beginning, North and South mobilized men on a scope and scale actually exceeding America's efforts in either of the World Wars in the twentieth century. By the time Lincoln addressed a special session of Congress on July 4, 1861, the Union had 235,000 men in military service, more than a fifteenfold increase since the outbreak of hostilities. The president himself was astonished by the sheer numbers of volunteers recruited. "So large an army as the government has now on foot, was never before known," Lincoln told members of the House and Senate, emphasizing that every soldier in that force was there "of his own free choice." When Congress convened in regular session in early December 1861, the Union army had increased to more than 640,000 men.

The Confederacy's recruitment efforts were even more remarkable. Although its white population was only one-third that of the Union, it established an initial fighting force two-thirds as large.

Putting men into uniform, however, was only one part of the task. An army also needs proper training and discipline, without which it is not an army, but an armed mob. It needs seasoned noncommissioned officers—like the ubiquitous drill sergeant, who was scarce in the North and practically nonexistent in the South—to mold a disparate collection of civilians into full-fledged soldiers. An army also needs good officers to provide leadership, though at the very beginning of the war, there were only two officers in the entire country—Union generals Winfield Scott and John E. Wool, both well into their seventies—who had commanded armies of more than 10,000 men, and that was during the conflict with Mexico. In the Civil War, the major armies in the field numbered anywhere between five and twelve times that amount.

As the war progressed, both sides developed systems of command and discipline, which helped bring some sense of order and professionalism to Civil War armies. Yet throughout the conflict, the vast majority of recruits received no basic training to speak of. Nor was it unusual if they found themselves on the front lines a month or so after signing up. As one Northern soldier remembered his unit's baptism under fire: "Within three weeks from the day this regiment was mustered into service, and before it had ever had what could properly be called a battalion drill, it was in the battle of Antietam." Most officers, who were appointed from civilian ranks, experienced a similar situation. Indeed, for almost all of the 2 million men who had served in the Union army, and for the nearly 1 million in the Confederate armed forces, combat itself would serve as their first and only training ground.

CONSCRIPTION

During the first year of the Civil War, neither side had any difficulty raising troops. Fired by patriotic zeal and dreams of romantic glory and adventure, hundreds of thousands of young men rushed to defend their colors. The states handled the recruitment process. Raising—and in many cases, outfitting and arming—the volunteer regiments, the states then sent them off to be mustered into the service of the central government for periods ranging from three months to three years. Whatever the agreed-upon length of service (eventually three years became the standard), each regiment—made up of ten companies with a combined total of about 850 to 1,000 men—retained its original identity and was designated by number and state name, such as the 20th Maine infantry regiment, the 45th Virginia, the 69th New York, or the 14th Tennessee. As for the officers, those on the company level, captains and lieutenants, were elected by the men themselves; on the regimental level, colonels, lieutenant colonels, and majors were commissioned by the state governors, who generally followed the recommendations of the company officers. Since the units were composed of men from the same locality, it was not surprising that the most influential leaders of the community were usually the ones elected or recommended for command positions.

At first, the volunteer system seemed all that either side needed to fill up its armies. After all, had it not worked in past struggles? In the Revolution, the War of 1812, and the Mexican conflict, the Regular army, supplemented by the existing state militia and volunteers, proved more than sufficient to meet each of the crises. But the Civil War was like no other in U.S. history. As the conflict dragged on with no end in sight, as the casualties mounted well beyond anyone's expectations, and as the desertions increased (more than 100,000 for the Union and nearly the same for the Confederacy by the end of 1862), the initial burst of enthusiasm disappeared and so did the volunteers. Before long it became evident that something would have to be done to replace the depleted ranks of the combatants. Both sides ultimately resorted to conscription. With its smaller manpower pool, the Confederacy was the first to feel the pinch, and on April 16, 1862, passed a general draft law. The Union followed suit nearly a year later, on March 3, 1863. For the first time on a national level Americans were subjected to compulsory military service.

Neither Southerners nor Northerners were pleased with conscription. As the vast majority of Confederates viewed it, a draft controlled and administered by the central government in Richmond violated the very foundation upon which the new nation was based, namely, the sovereignty of the individual states. At least, this was the opinion of such powerful governors as Zebulon B. Vance of North Carolina and Joseph E. Brown of Georgia—an opinion also shared by Confederate vice president Alexander H. Stephens. Not one to mince words, even if it antagonized Jefferson Davis and others in the administration, Stephens argued that the conscription system was "radically wrong in principle and in policy." Although most of his fellow citizens agreed with him, they were probably less interested in the theoretical implications of the draft and far more concerned with how it was going to affect them.

To begin with, all able-bodied white males between the ages of eighteen and thirty-five (soon raised to forty-five) were to serve for three years. The age limits (even when the range was modified from seventeen to fifty in early 1864) did not appear to be a major source of contention among Southerners, many of whom accepted them as necessary if the war was to be waged successfully. But when it came to the provisions regarding exemptions, that was another story. Small-scale farmers and unskilled laborers in particular felt that they were unjustly targeted for conscription, while those who were in skilled occupations were able to avoid military service. Practically every position requiring some special expertise was considered exempt, including "schoolteachers of twenty pupils, ministers, college professors, druggists, mail carriers, postmasters, civil officers of state governments and of the Confederacy, employees of railroads, ferrymen, telegraph operators, employees in cotton and woolen mills, mines, furnaces, and foundries, shoemakers, blacksmiths, tanners, millers, saltmakers, printers, and one editor for each paper."

As might be expected, a number of these exempt occupations became popular "careers." Many potential draftees decided that they had an inclination for teaching, and new "schools" began to appear throughout the Confederacy. Others became druggists by opening apothecaries that were little better than "variety stores or produce depots." Because civil servants were exempt, the most obscure government post now became valuable; some men paid as much as $500 to became a bailiff or postmaster in some backwoods community.

One could buy an exemption in other ways as well. A person eligible for the draft could pay a substitute to take his place. But this proved to be a costly alternative. Since there were few individuals available to serve as a proxy, the asking price was so high that only the very wealthy were able to exercise the option. Inevitably, more and more Southerners were beginning to view the struggle against the North as "a rich man's war but a poor man's fight." Instead of attempting to defuse this simmering resentment, the Confederate Congress added fuel to it by approving the so-called "twenty Negro law." Passed in October 1862, it excused from service one overseer or owner of a plantation of twenty or more slaves. Public reaction to the measure was swift and for the most part hostile. The legislation was enacted, a North Carolina private told his wife, "to get the big men out." "How can we go in to battle and fight. . . ," another soldier asked, while "the rich men who beca[u]se he owns twenty negros is permitted to stay at home with his family?"

Legislators in Richmond were well aware of the negative fallout. "Never did a law meet with more universal odium than the exemption of slave owners," wrote a Mississippi senator to President Davis. Eventually the lawmakers responded to the outcry, but their response was far from satisfactory. Although they eliminated the substitution loophole in December 1863, two months later, when they reviewed the "twenty Negro law," the best the congressmen were willing to do was reduce it to fifteen, hoping to placate the smaller plantation owners.

But for the common folk of the South, no significant relief was provided. The draft remained a major source of dissatisfaction and unrest throughout the war. In fact, conscription was second only to inflation as the reason why Southerners turned against the Confederacy. Yet in terms of its original purpose, to raise men for the Confederate army, the draft was far from a failure. Most authorities agree that conscription in the South was probably responsible for adding nearly 300,000 men to the army (100,000 draftees and another 200,000 who volunteered to avoid the stigma of being conscripted), in total about one-third of all Confederate combatants.

In early March 1863 the Union Congress passed its own conscription law. Officially termed the "Enrollment Act," the statute provided that all men between the ages of twenty and forty-five were liable for three years of military service. The youngest of the group, twenty- to thirty-five-year-olds, as well as unmarried men from thirty-six to forty-five, would be the first to be called up; once their numbers were exhausted, then married men between thirty-six and forty-five would be mustered into service.

For administrative purposes, the 185 congressional districts in the Northern states were designated as enrollment districts, each with a provost marshal whose task was to register all eligible inductees. When a call-up was made, each district was assigned its required quota and given an opportunity to fill it with volunteers. But if the community failed to do so, then a public drawing of the names of potential conscripts was conducted.

Unlike the Southern system, the Northern had very few occupational exemptions, though one could escape the Union draft for other reasons, especially in cases of personal hardship. The only son of parents who could not support themselves, a widower with children under twelve, an older brother of orphaned young children, or a member of a family with two or more men already serving in the military were the kinds of situations Congress considered as legitimate grounds for an exemption.

For men who could offer no humanitarian reason or physical condition (there were fifty-one "diseases and infirmities" allowing for an exemption), one could always buy his way out. A drafted man could hire a substitute. Or in the event he could not find someone to serve in his place, he could pay a flat $300 commutation fee, but this option could only get him off the hook for the particular draft in which his name was selected. He was still eligible for possible future call-ups.

On the surface, it appeared that the commutation clause favored the rich over the poor. But in truth, most wage earners could avoid the draft almost as easily as the wealthy. If their names were drawn, working men had the benefit of various support groups capable of providing the money to pay the $300 commutation fee or to hire a substitute. Some laborers were assisted by their employers, who had set up draft insurance funds. Others secured financial assistance from political machines, local community organizations, or private clubs. Whatever the source of funding, most workers could buy their way out of military service. The 1863 draft call bears this point out. Of the 88,171 men held to service, 52,288 paid the $300 fee and another 26,002 hired substitutes, leaving only 9,881 men to serve as conscripts. And if further evidence is necessary, one only has to look at the poorest districts of New York City, where 98 percent of the men called up paid the $300 exemption fee or hired someone to take their place.

Since this was not commonly known in the North, many contemporaries were convinced that the burden of the draft fell most heavily on the lower classes. The conscription law, in the words of one congressional leader, "was a rich man's bill." The measure was also viewed in racial terms. White men were now compelled to lay down their lives to carry out Lincoln's "abolitionist crusade" (keeping in mind that the Emancipation Proclamation had been issued only two months before passage of the draft law). Winning freedom for slaves, most white urban workers feared, would result in a black exodus out of the South into Northern cities, serving only to depress wages and ruin neighborhoods. It was this uneasiness and anger—fueled by a combustible mixture of antidraft sentiment, class resentment, and racial hatred—that exploded into full-scale rioting in some of the major metropolitan areas of the North soon after the draft was put into effect.

The worst occurred in New York City in mid-July 1863, when mobs of mostly Irish working men and women thronged the streets, burning, pillaging, and killing. During the four-day uprising, no one was safe. The rioters burned the provost marshal's headquarters, destroyed public buildings, plundered fine homes and stores, savagely beat the city's police superintendent, killed two disabled veterans who tried to restore order, and stoned to death an unarmed military officer home on leave. Most of the rioters' venom, however, was focused on African-Americans, who "were hunted like wolves"; dozens of the city's black residents were tortured, lynched, and mutilated. With the help of 4,000 troops dispatched from the battlefield of Gettysburg, the outbreak was finally suppressed, but not until at least 105—possibly 119—people died. It was the bloodiest urban riot in U.S. history.

Anxious to placate popular opinion, and convinced that the commutation fee was the most objectionable feature of the draft, in early July 1864 Congress abolished it, except in cases of conscientious objectors. But instead of calming class divisions, it aggravated them. The original purpose of commutation had been to hold down the cost of substitutes, and it did, keeping it below the $300 figure. Now that it was no longer in operation, the price of substitutes soared, in many instances well out of the reach of the average wage earner.

To be sure, someone like George Templeton Strong, a prominent New York attorney and member of the social elite, had no problem finding a substitute, "a big 'Dutch' [German] boy of twenty or thereabouts, for the moderate consideration of $1,100." Moderate perhaps for Strong, but most Northerners could not come up with that kind of money. One way to eliminate or limit this kind of problem was for enrollment districts to fill their quotas with volunteers, thereby avoiding the draft—and consequently the need for substitutes—altogether. This gave rise to what became known as the "bounty system," whereby local communities, states, and the federal government paid bonuses to those who volunteered for service.

Actually, cash incentives for recruits were not something new, having been used prior to the draft, but the amounts involved had been small compared with the payments beginning in mid-1863. In some districts, an enlistee signing up for a three-year stint could earn a total of $1,000 from government bounties. In the end, hundreds of millions of dollars (the wartime total has been estimated at $700 million) were spent by all levels of government to encourage men to fill the depleted ranks.

With so much money at stake, it's not surprising that the system attracted the unsavory. A large number of "bounty brokers" sprang up to supply districts with potential volunteers and substitutes in return for a percentage of their bounties and fees. Primarily interested in obtaining their commissions, most brokers couldn't care less about the physical or mental condition of their recruits; all "they asked was that a man be able to walk." And even that requirement was compromised. In March 1864 the cavalry corps of the Army of the Potomac reported that "32 percent of its recruits were on the sick list when they reached camp and that 8 percent of the lot were permanently crippled." Even more revealing were the comments of a brigade commander who had received 300 newly arrived substitutes just as he was about to launch an assault against Lee's line at Petersburg in early April 1865. In later years he maintained that all "300 should have been shot or hung," as they vanished before the attack took place and were never seen again.

Deserters were nothing new to the Union army, but the bounty system spawned a unique type of deserter called a "bounty jumper." These were men who enlisted, collected the bounty, then deserted at the first opportunity, only to repeat the process in another district. There's no telling how many got away with it, though a number were caught (one of whom admitted to a record thirty-two desertions). Most were jailed, and several were executed.

It's easy to overemphasize the chicanery of bounty brokers, the cowardice of some substitutes, and the outright fraudulent behavior of the bounty jumpers. But recent studies have made it clear that "of the hundreds of thousands of troops raised, the great majority of them did not desert. And just as certainly this great majority, while impelled by the lure of the bounty, intended to serve patriotically and did so serve."

Although the Northern draft produced only 46,000 conscripts and 118,000 substitutes (a mere 8 percent of the Union's total fighting force), these numbers can be misleading. As designed by its congressional architects, Union conscription was never intended to compel men to enter the ranks, but rather to goad them into volunteering. True, the system contributed to serious internal dissension, and commutation should have remained linked with substitution, or both should have been abolished, not just commutation. Yet the legislation achieved much of what its authors had in mind. From 1863 to 1865, nearly 1 million men volunteered for the Union army, determined to avoid the stigma of being drafted and eager to receive enlistment bounties and choice units. How many would have joined *without* the threat of a draft?

AFRICAN-AMERICAN SOLDIERS

Until the Civil War, African-Americans had served as soldiers infrequently and without any official standing. Only when the crisis was severe—as it was during the Revolution, with its shortage of manpower, and in the War of 1812, when Andrew Jackson needed help to defend against the British attack on New Orleans—were blacks called upon to fight. But once the crisis was over, the men of color were immediately disarmed and excluded from any further participation in the military. This was indeed confirmed by a Federal law passed in 1792, which prohibited African-Americans from enrolling in state militias and barred their entry into the regular U.S. Army.

As far as most white Americans were concerned, blacks were a racially inferior people best suited for field work and other kinds of menial labor. They were thought to have neither the discipline nor the courage to engage in combat. Moreover, it was believed that white soldiers would be demoralized by the prospect of serving side by side with blacks. And could they be trusted? As far back as the Colonial period, white Americans had always kept a wary eye out for possible insurrection. Would African-Americans, if armed, be more inclined to rise up in an attempt to win their freedom and that of their loved ones?

All of these concerns and questions in one form or another resurfaced when Northerners debated the use of black troops during the Civil War. As the conflict entered its second year and there seemed to be no end in sight, the issue of recruiting men of color inevitably came to the forefront. Given past views, the initial reaction among those in the Union was predictable. This was "a white man's war," many in the loyal states angrily insisted. Any attempt to enlist the aid of "these semi-barbaric hordes," declared a congressman from the borderland, would prove "derogatory to the manhood of 20 millions of freemen." The antiadministration and racist New York *World* was just as forthright in its views when it asserted that "it is unjust in every way to the white soldier to put him on a level with the black." And the men in blue could not have agreed more. "We don't want to fight side by side with the nigger," wrote Sgt. Felix Brannigan of the 74th New York regiment. "We think we are a too superior race for that." Another Union soldier, blinded by racial bigotry, took the argument to a point where he was defending the honor of the enemy. The Southern people, he noted, "are rebels to the government but they are White and God never intended a nigger to put white people Down."

Racial prejudice aside, Northerners were also convinced that blacks simply could not do the job. Even some abolitionists harbored reservations about the black man's fighting ability. Young William Channing Gannett, a recent graduate of the Harvard Divinity School and a volunteer teacher of former slaves at Port Royal, South Carolina, was of the opinion that "Negroes—plantation negroes, at least—will never make soldiers in one generation. Five white men could put a regiment [of blacks] to flight." Charles Francis Adams, Jr., serving as an officer in the 5th Massachusetts cavalry, shared a similar view. A member of the most prestigious political family of the nineteenth century, and one that had firm antislavery roots, Adams believed that recruiting blacks as soldiers would do "more harm than good." As he explained to his brother in the summer of 1862: "Under our system . . . we might make a soldiery equal to the native Hindoo regiments in about five years. It won't pay and the idea of arming the blacks as *soldiers* must be abandoned." Several months later, meeting with a delegation from Chicago, President Lincoln expressed his own reservations regarding this matter: "I am not so sure we could do much with the blacks. If we were to arm them . . . in a few weeks the arms would be in the hands of the rebels."

Presidential doubts notwithstanding, a small but determined group continued to put pressure on the administration, demanding the enrollment of African-Americans into the military. Frederick Douglass, a former slave (he had escaped in 1838) and now prominent abolitionist leader, was perhaps the most eloquent and persistent on behalf of the cause. As early as September 1861, in the editorial columns of his antislavery monthly, Douglass had upbraided the government for its refusal to utilize blacks militarily. "Why does the Government reject the negro? Is he not a man? Can he not wield a sword, fire a gun, march and countermarch, and obey orders like any other?" Douglass asked. "This is no time to fight with one hand . . . when they might fight with two, and a man drowning would not refuse to be saved even by a colored hand."

The wisdom of Douglass's argument could be denied only so long. With the war dragging on, the numbers of dead and wounded escalating, and the rate of new enlistments decreasing dramatically, whites were compelled to reassess their views regarding black recruitment. Nowhere was this change of sentiment more prevalent than among those in the ranks, many of whom previously had been opposed to serving with men of color. But more and more soldiers were beginning to feel that whatever it would take to stop the enemy was acceptable. "If a bob-tail dog can stick a bayonet on his tail, and back up against a rebel and kill him, I will take the dog and sleep with him—and if a nigger will do the same," a Union officer said, "I'll do the same by him. I'll sleep with any thing that will kill a rebel." Enlisted men, in growing numbers, felt the same way. "If they [blacks] can kill rebels," a sergeant in the 34th Illinois declared, "I say arm them and set them to shooting. I would use mules for the same purpose if possible." A private in the 9th Illinois was even more direct when he confessed: "[I] wouldant lift my finger to free them if I had my say, but if we cant whip the rebils without taking the nigers I say take them and make them fite for us any way to bring this war to a close."

Enlisting blacks to kill Rebels, however, was only one reason why Northern whites wanted them in uniform. Self-preservation was another. In other words, African-Americans could stop bullets just as well as whites. "I am willing that they risk their lives as I mine. It is but fair," Pvt. Edwin Wentworth of Maine argued. Fair, perhaps, but few would deny the existence of an underlying assumption that black lives were not as valuable as white ones. Iowa governor Samuel J. Kirkwood, for one, did not disguise the fact that he "would prefer to sacrifice the lives of niggers; rather than those of the best and bravest of our white youths." An officer in a Massachusetts regiment concurred emphatically. "You can't replace these [white] men," he declared, "but if a nigger dies, all you have to do is to send out and get another one."

Although Northern whites were slowly coming around in support of lifting the military's color barrier, it was hardly for the benefit of the black man. Yet no matter how repugnant their motives, according to Frederick Douglass, it was the end result that would prove critical. "Once let the black man get upon his person the brass letters, U. S.; let him get an eagle on his button, and a musket on his shoulder and bullets in his pocket," Douglass maintained, "and there is no power on earth . . . which can deny that he has earned the right to citizenship in the United States."

But before citizenship could be considered, men of color would have to be given the opportunity to prove themselves on the battlefield. Douglass and others, therefore, refused to ease up on their demands for the military recruitment of blacks, keeping pressure on the administration to reverse its position. Their efforts finally paid off. In August 1862 Secretary of War Edwin M. Stanton authorized Brig. Gen. Rufus

Saxton, military governor of the South Carolina sea islands, to raise five regiments of black soldiers. On November 7, the first of the five regiments, the 1st South Carolina Volunteers, was mustered into federal service—the first time ever that African-American soldiers were officially recognized as part of the United States armed forces.

Over the next two and a half years, approximately 180,000 African-Americans—nearly 10 percent of all Union land forces—served in Civil War regiments. They took part in 449 separate engagements, of which 39 were major battles. Combat, however, was less of a threat to the black enlistee than was illness. Where one in twelve white Union soldiers died of disease during the war, one in five blacks did. All told, more than 37,000 men of color made the ultimate sacrifice for their country, close to 3,000 suffering battle-related deaths, while most of the rest fell victim to disease.

Black soldiers proved their worth almost immediately. On November 13, 1862, only six days after they were sworn in, 240 of the 1st South Carolina Volunteers saw combat for the first time. Assigned to a foraging expedition to gather lumber near Darien, Georgia, the men ran into some Confederate troops. A skirmish broke out in which the blacks bested the whites. Although small in scale, the victory loomed large in political and even psychological significance. For one thing, most of the African-American soldiers had never handled a gun before, and for another, these particular blacks were ex-slaves, in bondage since birth. Depicted as childlike and subservient, the volunteers proved the stereotype false, as they stood their ground, fought, and defeated their former masters.

But their true test under fire came some six months later, in the late spring and early summer of 1863, in a series of battles that would leave no doubt of their determination and valor. The first of these occurred on May 27, when two Louisiana black regiments participated in an assault on Port Hudson, Louisiana, a major Confederate stronghold on the lower Mississippi River. Throughout the attack, though it was repulsed, the African-Americans demonstrated a raw toughness and courage that did not go unnoticed. In a letter to his father, a Wisconsin soldier wrote that the "negroes fought like devils, they made five charges on a battery that there was not the slightest chance of their taking, just (as their officers said) to show our boys that they could and would fight." Another eyewitness, a soldier in the 156th New York, had no doubt that what he had seen that day "settles the question about niggers not fighting well. They, on the contrary, make splendid soldiers and are as good fighting men as any we have."

Barely ten days later, African-American troops rose to the occasion once again. On June 7 two black regiments at Milliken's Bend, Louisiana, successfully defended against an attack by a Confederate force estimated to be as large as 3,000. The casualties sustained by the black soldiers were staggering. One of their two units, the 9th Louisiana Regiment, had nearly 45 percent of its men killed or mortally wounded; no Union regiment in the entire war suffered such a high proportion of losses. Assistant Secretary of War Charles Dana, who was traveling with the army, reported to his boss Stanton that the "sentiment [in] . . . regard to the employment of negro troops has been revolutionized by the bravery of the blacks in the recent battle of Milliken's Bend. Prominent officers, who used in private to sneer at the idea, are now heartily in favor of it." For that matter, even the Confederate officer who had commanded the attacking forces acknowledged that the "charge was resisted by the negro's portion of the enemy's force with considerable obstinacy, while the white or true Yankee portion ran like whipped curs almost as soon as the charge was ordered."

The following month, on July 18, probably the most famous of all black regiments, the 54th Massachusetts, led the frontal assault on Fort Wagner, situated on Morris Island at the entrance to Charleston harbor. The attackers, including two of Frederick Douglass's sons, encountered massive resistance, though they were able to get their regimental colors up to the parapets—but no farther. Forced to pull back, over 40 percent of the men in the 54th were killed, wounded, or missing. In the wake of the carnage on Morris Island, Judge Advocate General Joseph Holt reassured the War Department that "the tenacious and brilliant valor displayed by troops of this race at Port Hudson, Milliken's Bend, and Fort Wagner has sufficiently demonstrated . . . the character of service of which they are capable."

For the remainder of the conflict, black soldiers could be found on almost every front, taking part in some of the worst fighting of the war. During the nearly year-long siege of Petersburg, for example, one out of eight Union combatants was black. But despite their record on the battlefield and the glowing testimonies received from a cross section of comrades in arms, many white commanders, unable to shake their prejudice, harbored an uneasiness about men of color in uniform. As a result, black soldiers continued to be assigned to a disproportionate amount of garrison and fatigue duty—guarding prisoners, bridges, supply dumps, railroad tracks, vital passes, and the like. This explains why black combat fatalities were only 1.5 percent compared to 6 percent for whites, and why their rate of death from disease was almost twice as high as among their white counterparts. Stationed in one place for an extended period of time, African-American soldiers had a greater likelihood of exposure to foul water and other fatal accumulations of bacteria than if they had been on the move. To make matters worse, with only eight commissioned black physicians (and only a few volunteer white doctors), medical treatment for African-American soldiers was woefully inadequate.

Insufficient medical care was only one of many points of contention among black troops. Segregated in all-black regiments, they were led for the most part by white officers. Of the some 7,000 men commanding United States Colored Troops, as they officially became known, less than 100 officers were black, and the vast majority of them (except for the chaplains and surgeons) were eventually forced to resign because of racial bigotry. This policy caused considerable resentment among African-Americans, most of whom would have preferred leadership from their own ranks. "If we heave [sic] to fight for our rights," one black soldier declared, "let us fight under Colored officers."

More distressing to black enlistees was their day-to-day treatment. Although they faced the same trials and tribulations as their white counterparts, many of them believed—and justifiably so—that they were being treated as second-class soldiers. To begin with, they were more likely to be abused by their officers. When going into combat, moreover, many black soldiers were often armed with substandard weapons and equipment. Even in the most basic matters, such as rations, men of color were shortchanged. Writing directly to the president in August 1864, a member of the 20th U.S. Colored Troops complained of conditions in his unit. Despite his misspellings, grammatical inaccuracies, and lack of punctuation, the message contained in his letter was crystal clear. "We are treated," he wrote, "in a Different maner to what others Rigiments is Both Northern men or southern Raised Rigiment. . . . We All Listed for so much Bounty Clothing and Ration And 13 Dollars A Month. And the most has fallen short in all thes Things. . . . And Another thing we are Cut short of our Ration in A most Shocking maner. . . . Hardly have Anough bread . . . to Do A Soldier 24 Hours on Gaurd or eney other Labor."

All things considered, nothing proved as frustrating to African-Americans in uniform than the difference in pay between black and white soldiers. Regardless of rank, all black soldiers received $10 per month, out of which $3 was deducted for clothing; a white private at the time received $13 per month plus a $3.50 clothing allowance. Outraged by this injustice, some regiments, such as the 54th and 55th Massachusetts, refused all compensation until the issue was resolved. Other men of color suffered more severely. About two dozen members of the black 14th Rhode Island Heavy Artillery were sentenced to imprisonment at hard labor for their unwillingness to accept the lower wages, and a sergeant in the 3rd South Carolina Volunteers was executed by a firing squad after being convicted of inciting mutiny by persuading his men not to fight until they were properly compensated. Prodded by Lincoln, Congress finally took action to rectify the iniquity. In mid-June 1864 a law was passed establishing equal pay for all Union soldiers.

As African-American combatants struggled with injustice at the hands of those in authority at home, they also had to confront a far more perilous situation—the possibility of falling into the hands of the enemy. Right from the beginning, the Confederate government refused to recognize blacks as legitimate soldiers, threatening their enslavement if captured. Lincoln responded with his own admonition, proclaiming that for every man of color in uniform enslaved by the enemy, "a rebel soldier shall be placed at hard labor" until the black soldier "shall be released and receive the treatment due to a prisoner of war." The president never carried out his threat, even though there were reports of captured freedmen returned as slaves to their former masters, and of black soldiers executed on charges of inciting servile insurrection. But since it was difficult, if not impossible, to confirm official Confederate involvement in these instances, the Union administration decided not to retaliate.

On the other hand, atrocities committed against black soldiers on the battlefield itself were more blatant, involved larger numbers of victims, and could not be ignored. The most notorious incident occurred on April 12, 1864, after Confederate general Nathan Bedford Forrest's cavalry captured Fort Pillow, Tennessee, a Union outpost on the Mississippi River, about forty miles north of Memphis. Surrendering and wounded African-American soldiers (estimates range from 150 to 300) were denied POW status and were cut down in cold blood. "Damn you, you are fighting against your master," one Southerner exclaimed as he unloaded his gun into an unarmed black soldier. Realizing their fate, other men of color fell upon their knees and begged for mercy, but were "shot down like dogs." Six days later there were more atrocities, this time at Poison Springs, Arkansas, when several black prisoners were executed outright and others who were wounded had wagons driven over their bodies. These were not isolated instances. They were repeated at Petersburg, Virginia, on July 30, 1864; at the battle of Saltville, Virginia, the following October; and in numerous minor engagements during the remaining months of the war.

After the massacre at Fort Pillow, Confederate general Forrest had hoped that the Northern people would come to their senses and realize "that negro soldiers cannot cope with Southerners." Instead, just the opposite occurred. Outraged by the atrocities, Northerners rallied behind their black troops. And as for the men themselves, they were determined to get even. "'Remember Ft Pillow' is getting to be the *feeling* if not the word," an officer of the U.S. Colored Troops wrote to his wife. "It looks hard," he added, "but we cannot blame these men much." In an attack on Fort Blakely, Alabama, in early April 1865, a Union lieutenant observed that when the black units charged, "the rebs were panic-struck. . . . [They] threw down their arms and [ran] for their lives over to the white troops on our left, to give themselves up, to save being butchered by our niggers[.] [T]he niggers did not take a prisoner, they killed all they took to a man."

Whether engaged in retaliatory action or not, for the black man, service in the Union army offered him an opportunity to shatter the racial stereotypes that white Americans had held for centuries. Given the history of postwar relations between the races, those stereotypes were far from shattered, but a few holes had been poked in them—enough that even the Confederacy, during its eleventh hour, began recruiting and training black soldiers, though Lee surrendered before any of them fought for the South.

For those African-Americans who bore arms for the United States, however, no one could deny the sense of pride they experienced. "This was the biggest thing that ever happened in my life," recalled a former slave. "I felt like a man with a uniform on and a gun in my hand." W. E. B. DuBois, the early-twentieth-century black political activist and historian, could not help but see a cruel irony in this turn of events. Only when the African-American "rose and fought and killed" white men, DuBois pointed out, then "the whole nation with one voice proclaimed him a man and brother"—at least for a brief moment.

FREE MILITARY SCHOOL FOR APPLICANTS FOR COMMANDS OF COLORED TROOPS

Once black men were enlisted in the Union army, it was understood that whites—and whites only—would lead them. Even when some officer positions were staffed by blacks, as in the case of three Louisiana regiments raised by Gen. Benjamin F. Butler, it was only a matter of time until most of these men of color, one way or another, were eased out of their commands.

Reflecting the racism of the era, most whites were of the opinion that blacks had no business in leadership positions. "You should have a look here at these negro Captains, appointed by Gen. Butler," a Northern officer wrote to a friend after arriving in New Orleans. In his view they looked "like dogs in full dress, ready to dance in the menagerie. Would *you* like to obey such a fool?" he asked. Another Union officer, Col. Charles G. Paine, left no question where he stood on the matter when he said, "They ought never to put a shoulder strap on a darkey."

To most Northern whites, civilian or military, African-Americans were incapable of leading, only following. Considered inferior, blacks were viewed as infantile, lazy, and ignorant, and therefore in need of well-trained and authoritarian officers. As William M. Findley, a civilian quartermaster clerk, assured his mother in May 1863, after seeing for the first time black regiments at Hilton Head, South Carolina, "They are of course under the charge of white officers, who doubtless keep them under the strictest discipline." Even an antislavery advocate like Sgt. Nathan Webb of Maine believed in the necessity of white commanders. As long as that arrangement continued, he thought, black soldiers "will, with proper discipline and good Officers, make just as good soldiers as white men."

If the key to the success of black troops was good officers, as Sergeant Webb and many others maintained, then a process would have to be established to single out the best men for the job. In May 1863 the War Department created the Bureau of Colored Troops, which had as its purpose the recruitment of black units and the selection of officers to lead them. Those soldiers and civilians interested in obtaining a commission applied in writing to the bureau, enclosing letters of recommendation. If coming from the civilian sector, the supporting documentation usually included statements testifying that the candidate was an upstanding member of the community; if applying as a soldier, a reference letter was written by his commanding officer, who then circulated it throughout the unit for other officers to endorse or to add their own comments.

Once the candidate's application and references passed initial muster, he was then directed to appear before one of the boards of examiners, which were located in various cities, including Washington, New Orleans, St. Louis, Nashville, and Cincinnati. Composed of four members each, the boards administered an oral examination covering such topics as tactics, army regulations, and general military knowledge, in addition to arithmetic, history, and geography. The subject matter was so diverse that many who were otherwise worthy candidates had difficulty mastering all of the required material. Those who were in uniform generally did better on the military part of the test, while those coming from the civilian sector had the edge when it came to basic knowledge. In any case, the end results did not reflect well on either group, though civilians on the whole tested better than soldiers. Of the first 1,000 or so applicants, nearly 50 percent failed the examination.

Seeking a way to reverse this trend, Maj. Gen. Silas Casey, head of the Washington examining board, met with a group of Philadelphians responsible for recruiting black regiments. The general suggested to them that if the officer candidates were given a few weeks of concentrated study, the failure rate would decrease significantly. As chairman of Philadelphia's black recruiting committee, Thomas Webster was well aware of the difficulty of finding qualified whites to serve in command positions. Seizing upon Casey's suggestion, Webster went to work immediately, securing a building for instructional purposes, gathering a faculty, formulating a thirty-day course of study, and publishing a descriptive brochure. On December 26, 1863, the Free Military School for Applicants for Commands of Colored Troops opened its doors at 1210 Chestnut Street in Philadelphia—and thus became the first officer candidate school in American history.

Operating privately and without official standing, the school nevertheless had the War Department's full cooperation. When potential officer candidates needed thirty-day furloughs to attend classes, the department issued General Orders no. 125, strongly advising army commanders to release "non-commissioned officers and privates . . . who may desire to enter the free military school at Philadelphia." In most cases, the applicant's request was granted.

Once accepted to the school, the candidate was exposed to a rigorous course of study—six days a week, each day including three hours of classroom work, three hours of drill, morning and afternoon dress parades, and nighttime study. The curriculum also provided actual field experience, with students allowed to "exercise the functions of officers, in assisting to drill and train" black troops at Camp William Penn near Philadelphia. As the student neared completion of the month-long program, the school tested him to ensure his readiness for the examining board. After passing the school tests, the confident graduate then applied for an appearance before the Washington board. Of the first ninety-four graduates to be examined, all but four were recommended for officer-level appointments.

With that kind of track record, the Free Military School attracted large numbers of applicants—nearly 170 requests for admission per week, after only four months in existence. Its popularity was so widespread that the school could boast of a student body that represented seventeen states and the District of Columbia, as well as a dozen foreign countries.

In view of the application process, the appearance before the examining board, and the sheer risk involved in the command of black troops, one wonders why so many men wanted to serve in that capacity in the first place. After all, no one knew at the time that Jefferson Davis's threat to "put to death" those who trained or led African-American soldiers would turn out to be nothing more than bluster. But whether or not the danger was real, it was obviously outweighed by the advantages of being an officer, which carried with it social prestige, better food and quarters, and a significant increase in pay—from, say, $13 a month as a private to $120 once the shoulder straps were attached.

The possibility of rapid advancement was also attractive. Having recently graduated from West Point, Lt. John R. Winterbotham of Chicago saw an opportunity he could not resist. The "darkeys make splendid troops," he told his family, "and I shall be devilish well satisfied if I can get a Lieutenant Colonelcy, which I am going to aim for and try my best under the circumstances to obtain." Considered too young for such a high rank (he was only twenty), Winterbotham was turned down for the appointment.

Others sought a commission for reasons that had little to do with material rewards. There were those who had been active in the antislavery crusade and saw their role as officers of black soldiers as a natural outgrowth of their prewar activities. One abolitionist regarded his appointment as the fulfillment of his dreams—as a youth, he had visualized himself "marching at the head of an army of blacks, proclaiming liberty, and rallying the slaves to my standard." Still others became involved as a means to help the African-American through his transition from slavery to freedom. Here was an opportunity—"a field for christian and philanthropic labor"—as a New York soldier put it, "to elevate and enlighten" the man of color so that "he may be prepared for the future."

Whatever their motives, they all had to meet the rigorous demands of the examining boards. And the Free Military School played an unprecedented role in that regard, successfully preparing 484 of its graduates for service as officers in black regiments. Despite the school's premature demise in mid-September 1864 due to a lack of funding, it proved that a well-run program in a relatively brief period of time could train civilians and enlisted men to serve, in the words of Secretary of War Edwin M. Stanton, as "a class of instructed and efficient officers."

"THE SERGEANT TURNS OUT TO BE A WOMAN"

War has always been a man's occupation, while women remained at home, lonely, anxious, and sometimes even envious of their brothers and husbands as they marched off to the glories of battle. This was certainly true during America's Civil War, when many women on both sides expressed a desire to do more than simply maintain the home front in the absence of their men. A young Northern girl, for instance, wrote to the New York *Herald* in search of a physician who would be willing to certify her as a man so that she could enlist. And when the Confederate army was having a hard time attracting recruits, a Southern woman asked: "Why does not the President call out the women if there are [not] enough men? We would go and *fight,* too—we would better all die together." Sharing this same sentiment, the young and spirited Julia LeGrand of New Orleans confided in her journal the dreams she had of serving on "the red fields where great principles are contended for. . . . I am like a pent-up volcano. I wish I had a field for my energies. I hate common life, a life of visiting, dressing and tattling, which seems to devolve on women, and now that there is better work to do, real tragedy, real romance and history weaving every day, I suffer, suffer, leading the life I do."

Like many of her contemporaries, what LeGrand did not know was that a significant number of women—Union and Confederate—refused to suffer these frustrations. Disguising themselves as men, they took to the battlefield. Indeed, the Civil War was the first conflict in which hundreds of American women served as combat soldiers.

Since women passed as men when they enlisted, and some of them kept the secret to the grave, it's impossible to determine precisely how many served. In her recent study of the subject, Elizabeth Leonard has taken the position, similar to other modern scholars, that anywhere between 500 and 1,000 women saw combat during the war.

Why did they choose to fight? Some women wished to be near their husbands or sweethearts. Others, like their male counterparts, were either patriotic and wanted to make a contribution to the cause or wanted the cause to make a contribution to them, in the form of cash bounties given to new recruits. Still others signed up for the chance of adventure, to escape the passive role of Victorian domesticity, and to do new things and see new lands. After having her true identity revealed, one female soldier admitted, "I thought I'd like camp-life, and I did."

Most woman combatants fit in so well, in fact, that they were rarely detected. Nor was their deception threatened by existing military procedures. For one thing, army induction physicals were cursory, almost laughable, by today's standards. Physicians were mainly interested in such things as a working trigger finger, enough teeth to bite a paper cartridge, and adequate hearing to follow orders. Unless you were afflicted with tuberculosis or had a glaring physical malady, you qualified. Few, if any, recruits were required to remove coats or shirts, so women were safe in that regard. Once in uniform, a loose tunic would hide the most obvious feminine physical characteristics, but if necessary some women bound their breasts.

Modern readers might question why women would not be discovered while bathing or answering nature's call. It was here that Victorian social mores came to a woman's rescue. It was not unusual for men to exhibit modesty in front of their fellow soldiers, even to bathe in their underwear. No less a personage as Ulysses S. Grant was excessively modest, almost prudish. Whenever he had to bathe, he did so in a closed tent. No one, not even close aides, were allowed to glimpse him naked.

In the eastern theater of the war, armies often marched, camped, and fought in thickly wooded regions. If a female soldier had any personal business to attend to, it would be simple enough to slip into the trees or bushes. Even in camp this would be a common practice, since many refused to use the odorous and open-trenched latrine systems.

But in the final analysis, it was Victorian male assumptions, not ingenious disguise, that allowed many women to escape detection. Males were taught from childhood that females were the "weaker vessels," unable to engage in "manly" pursuits. Then, too, modes of dress were gender-based. To most men, it was unthinkable for a woman to dress like a man, so they never assumed that their comrades in arms could possibly be of the opposite sex. Besides, there were so many preadolescent boys in uniform that their presence in the ranks provided the perfect cover for the beardless and high-voiced women soldiers.

Not that they all escaped detection. Usually women soldiers were discovered if they were killed or wounded in battle. At Gettysburg, a female combatant was found dead alongside the body of her husband, both casualties of Confederate general George Pickett's ill-fated charge. Another Southern soldier of the opposite sex was unmasked when she lost a leg on that same battlefield. Women in the ranks of the Union army shared the same kinds of experiences. After serving eighteen months before being wounded, Fanny Wilson of New Jersey had her true identity revealed, as did Mary Wise, a two-year veteran of an Indiana regiment who was hit by enemy fire. Both women were discharged.

If a woman soldier was captured by the enemy, there was also a good likelihood that she would be discovered. Living in close quarters, with no opportunity for privacy, and more prone to illness as a POW, it was only a matter of time until she would be found out. Once detected, both sides frequently went out of their way to offer the woman better treatment and acted with dispatch (usually out of a sense of gentlemanly honor) to send her back under a flag of truce.

But nothing was more shocking to the men in blue or gray than when they heard that a comrade in arms had given birth to a baby. "The sergeant turns out to be a woman," wrote Michigan soldier James Greenalch to his wife, as he tried to explain how the orderly sergeant in the neighboring 74th Ohio regiment had produced a child. And this was not the only case. There is evidence of at least five other instances where female soldiers delivered children, including a Confederate officer imprisoned at Johnson's Island camp on Lake Erie, where "he" gave birth to a "bouncing baby boy."

Although most female combatants were discovered as a consequence of pregnancy, capture, serious wounds, or death in battle, several women warriors chose to go public on their own. Sarah Emma Edmonds, a.k.a. "Franklin Thompson," published her memoirs soon after the war came to an end, and in time she became one of the most celebrated women soldiers of the war. Unlike the majority of her sisters in uniform, who came from poor and rural backgrounds, Edmonds was Canadian-born, urban oriented, and well educated. Leaving home to escape an abusive father, she earned a living selling Bibles until her enlistment at the age of twenty in the 2nd Michigan regiment.

Her military career was fraught with irony. She served first as a "male nurse," one of the few war-related occupations allowed women. But when a young soldier, who might have been her lover, died, she volunteered for more hazardous duty as a spy. While posing as a black male slave, she sketched the fortifications of Confederate Yorktown; on another occasion, she donned a Confederate uniform to infiltrate Rebel lines. In a situation reminiscent of the modern musical *Victor/Victoria*, she was also asked to disguise herself as a woman. So a woman was playing a man playing a woman!

During the war Edmonds contracted malaria, which seriously impaired her health. After hostilities came to an end, she married, had a family, and eventually was awarded a veteran's pension of $12 a month.

The Confederacy also had its share of female soldiers, in spite of the fact that a Southern woman's lifestyle seemed even more prescribed than that of her Northern sister. Mary and Molly Bell enlisted in the

Confederate army as "Tom Parker" and "Bob Martin," serving two years before being discovered. Gen. Jubal A. Early, scandalized to the very bottom of his boots, declared that they had been "common camp followers"—by implication, prostitutes. But there is no evidence to support that charge. It's more than likely that the Bell sisters had served in the ranks as soldiers, and that Early's accusation was an expression of his own prejudices as well as an attempt to cover up his failure to discover the deception sooner.

Whatever the reasons for the general's charges, the case against Mary and Molly Bell is a prime example of the twofold dilemma that confronted women soldiers in the Civil War. Facing the enemy on the battlefield, they also had to deal with the sexual bigotry of their own comrades in arms—a situation that continues to linger in one form or another in the U.S. armed forces today. True, the role of women in combat has changed dramatically since Operation Desert Storm in the early 1990s, but the debate still rages over precisely what that role should be. In this regard, as one modern student of the subject has so well stated, "the women combatants of 1861 to 1865 were not just ahead of their time; they were ahead of our time."

"HOLY JOES"

The American tradition of a military chaplaincy dates as far back as the seventeenth century, when spiritual leaders accompanied Colonial militia units in the early Indian wars and later in the intermittent conflict with France. Providing guidance and comfort to those in the ranks (even seemingly invincible young men start to think about God when death is near), the clergy became an integral part of the American military experience. During the Revolution, more than 100 chaplains served in the Continental army and another 100 ministered to the needs of those in the state militias.

Less than a decade after the Revolutionary War, on March 4, 1791, the chaplaincy was given permanent and official standing when John Hurt, an Episcopal clergyman, was commissioned as the first chaplain in the U.S. Army. Although the position carried no rank, the $600 annual pay was slightly above that of a captain. As for duties, since none were specified, it was understood that conducting services, teaching, giving solace to the sick, and burying the dead were all part of the job.

Over the next half century or so, hundreds of clergy served their country as military chaplains. But all men of the cloth were not eligible to serve in that capacity. With America's antebellum population overwhelmingly Protestant and steeped in racism, an applicant had to be Protestant and white to secure a chaplaincy. Catholic, Jewish, and free African-American spiritual leaders were denied access to the position, despite the fact that members of their communities had fought and shed blood in America's wars.

As more and more minorities donned the uniform of the U.S. Army, restrictive barriers against their clergy began to crumble. Catholics were the first to reap the benefits brought by an increase in numbers, a result of a massive influx of Irish immigrants to America in the 1840s. When war broke out with Mexico in 1846, one-fourth of the invading army headed by Gen. Zachary Taylor was Catholic. Determined to maintain harmony in the ranks, and eager to dispel charges that this was a Protestant crusade to destroy Catholicism in Mexico, President James K. Polk appointed two priests to provide religious services for Catholic troops in the field. Since these clergy served in a civilian capacity, the Protestant monopoly on the chaplaincy seemed in no danger of being broken, at least until the Civil War, when, for the first time in American history, Catholics, Jews, and blacks received official commissions as U.S. Army chaplains.

At the time Rebel batteries opened fire on Fort Sumter, one out of every ten Americans was Catholic. Totaling three million in number, many of Irish ancestry, and a majority living in the loyal states, they were instrumental in creating several all-Catholic regiments. But for the most part, the Sons of Erin, along with fellow Catholics from other nationalities, served in nondenominational units. A demand for official recognition of military clergy of their own faith from the Catholic community, which represented nearly one-sixth of the Union army's total manpower, could no longer be put on hold. Over the course of the struggle, forty priests in the North and nearly thirty in the South were fully commissioned as military chaplains in American armies.

Similar to Catholics, Jews experienced an unprecedented rise in population during the antebellum decades. In 1840 there were only 15,000 Jews in the U.S.; that number rose to 150,000, a tenfold increase over the next twenty years. Caught up in the liberal revolutions of 1848, German Jews fled to America, escaping political persecution and seeking greater economic opportunities. Soon after arriving, most of the Jewish newcomers were drawn to the antislavery movement and became active in the Republican party. Once the war broke out, they did not need much encouragement to defend the colors of their adopted country.

Some 7,000 Jews wore the Union blue; another 3,000 served the Confederacy. They represented more than 7 percent of American Jews, a figure far out of proportion to their $1/2$ percent of the general population. With this kind of overrepresentation, Jewish leaders in the North called upon the government to provide military clergy for men of their faith serving in the armed forces. (No apparent effort was made in the South.)

Members of the administration, including Lincoln and Secretary of War Simon Cameron, were sympathetic to the commissioning of Jewish chaplains, but existing legislation tied their hands. In the summer of 1861 Congress had passed a law requiring that a chaplain "be a regular ordained minister of some Christian denomination." When Jewish spokesmen protested the action, insisting that it was a violation of the constitutional rights of non-Christians, conservative editors of the Protestant press reacted accordingly. "Our government has already gone a great length in this respect in appointing Roman Catholic and Universalist chaplains to the army. . .," argued the Cincinnati *Presbyter.* "These denominations at least call themselves Christians, and profess to honor the Lord Jesus, however much they may really dishonor Him. But Jews regard Jesus of Nazareth as an impostor, a deceiver, and one worthy of every term of reproach."

As usual in most matters of this sort, Lincoln took the high ground, believing that "the exclusion of Jewish chaplains to have been altogether unintentional on the part of Congress," and promised a change in the legislation "in behalf of the Israelites." The president kept his word. Although it took a year of executive pressure and congressional wrangling, in July 1862 lawmakers amended the original act to read that "no person shall be appointed a chaplain in the United States army who is not a regularly ordained minister of some religious denomination."

Within two months after passage of the law, Jacob Frankel, the spiritual leader of Philadelphia's Rodeph Shalom Congregation, became the first rabbi to be commissioned a U.S. military chaplain. Assigned to army hospitals in Philadelphia and surrounding areas, Frankel's primary assignment was to minister to the needs of sick and wounded Jewish servicemen. As the war progressed, two other rabbis also received appointments. One served as a medical chaplain in the heavily populated German-Jewish regions of Kentucky and Missouri, and the other as a field chaplain with the 54th New York infantry regiment (a unit composed mainly of non-Jewish Germans who apparently favored an educated clergyman conversant in their language even if not of their faith). During the entire conflict, only these three rabbis were commissioned, but the fact that they were commissioned at all was something most Americans would never have thought possible prior to the Civil War.

The same held true for black military chaplains. Their numbers were also unimpressive—only 14 of the 133 chaplains assigned to African-American regiments were black—but here again, the fact that there were any at all was remarkable. Since almost all officers of the Civil War's 180,000 black troops were white, it was no easy matter commissioning African-Americans as chaplains. Gov. John A. Andrew of Massachusetts found this out early in the conflict. As the first chief executive of a state to recruit black regiments, Andrew, a longtime antislavery activist, asked the War Department in January 1863 for its approval "to commission Colored chaplains, assistant surgeons, and a few second lieutenants." The administration turned him down, arguing that it was much too soon to consider blacks as officers, when blacks as enlisted men were not yet tried and tested. Not one to accept rejection, Andrew continued to lobby for black officers, using his influence with fellow abolitionist and Secretary of the Treasury Salmon P. Chase. By the summer of 1863, his persistence paid off. Although the War Department refused to reconsider its position regarding blacks as combat officers, it relented in the matter of clergymen and approved the commission of William Jackson, a Baptist minister attached to the 55th Massachusetts regiment, as the first African-American chaplain in the U.S. Army.

Other appointments followed, but they were few and far between. Only those black spiritual leaders with extraordinary credentials and outstanding references seemed to have had any chance of landing a chaplaincy. To cite a few examples: Henry M. Turner received his commission by presenting endorsements of nearly a dozen Washington, D.C., ministers; Samuel Harrison was recommended by the president of Williams College; and Garland H. White, a fugitive slave who had studied theology in Canada, was strongly supported by Secretary of State William H. Seward, who had first met the applicant before the war when he had been a slave to Georgia senator Robert Toombs.

Since minority chaplains—Catholics, Jews, and African-Americans—were more closely screened and scrutinized than their Protestant counterparts, they were probably better qualified for the job. But even if true, such a comparison is unfair if one bears in mind that the total number of minority clergymen in both armies combined was less than 100, while in the Union army alone, over 2,500 Protestant ministers served as wartime chaplains.

Qualified or not, why were so many clergymen attracted to the position in the first place? No doubt many were interested in the $100-a-month paycheck, comparable to a captain's pay. And then there was the matter of status. Even though chaplains held "rank without command," whereby they had neither established grades nor promotional opportunities, they were still recognized as officers, since their names were entered below those of surgeons on field and staff rolls.

Of course, good pay and officer status hardly guaranteed an exemplary job performance. Men of the cloth are no more or less human than their congregations, and Civil War army chaplains were no exceptions. Whether performing their official responsibilities (conducting worship services, ministering to the sick and wounded, burying the dead, and reporting monthly to the adjutant general on the moral state of the regiment) or carrying out their unofficial duties (teaching, counseling, and setting a proper example for their men), chaplains varied in quality. Some were lazy, incompetent, or too old to stand the rigors of campaigning or camp life. Most of these men, but by no means all, were weeded out or reassigned. And yet there were those clergy who rose to the occasion. A young Union soldier who was addicted to gambling attended a "Regular Methodist Style" meeting in camp. Later he joyfully noted, "The best meeting I ever attended in the Army [was] at Holy Jo's tent." Eventually he gave up cards and even signed a temperance pledge.

Maybe that soldier's resolve lasted, maybe not. But in time of death and upheaval, and of seeming ethical decay and uncertainty, there were many Civil War chaplains, whatever their faith or color, who remained anchors of morality and spiritual comfort.

MONTGOMERY C. MEIGS, QUARTERMASTER GENERAL, U.S.A.

For all its horrors, war can exert a powerful, almost hypnotic attraction. There is high drama in the decisions of generals and the clash of armies. But behind the great events, there is another kind of war, perhaps less dramatic yet just as pivotal—the war of supply. Before soldiers can fight, they must be equipped, clothed, fed, sheltered, and provided a means of transportation. Supplies and equipment also have to be delivered, oftentimes to far-flung encampments, forts, and battlefields.

During the Civil War, supplying the Union armies—except for food and weaponry—was the concern of the Quartermaster General's Office in the War Department. In early 1861 that bureau employed thirteen clerks and spent some $4 to $5 million annually. Since the U.S. Army at the time was composed of about 16,000 men, neither the quartermaster general's clerical staff nor its budget was unreasonable. But once hostilities broke out, the department was inundated with an overwhelming number of requests.

Like the army it served, the quartermaster's bureau grew from a "minnow" to a "whale" during the course of the struggle. By the end of the war, the office in Washington had nearly fifty times the number of civilian employees that it had at the beginning of the conflict, and it had spent seventy-five times more than a peacetime bureau would have spent over a comparable period. Fortunately for the Union, presiding over this unparalleled growth was Quartermaster General Montgomery C. Meigs—the first government official in U.S. history in charge of spending more than $1 billion.

A Southerner by birth, Meigs was born in 1816 in Augusta, Georgia. After graduating from West Point in 1836, he was commissioned a lieutenant of engineers. Over the next two and a half decades, Meigs was involved in a variety of projects, including the extension of the Capitol, the General Post Office, and the aqueduct system in Washington, D.C. Meigs was well over six feet in height and his impressive bearing matched his personality. Devoted to duty and loyal to country, Meigs was able, incorruptible, and hardworking, leaving little doubt that he was the right man for the job when he was appointed quartermaster general of the U.S. Army in mid-June 1861.

As qualified as he was, Meigs was caught off guard by the size of the task before him. "Troops, thousands, wait for clothes to take the field," he complained to a fellow officer only a month after his appointment. "Regiments have been ordered here [Washington] without clothes. Men go on guard in drawers for want of pantaloons. The necessity is far greater than I imagined. . . . I had no idea of this destitution, this want of preparation by this department when I took charge of it."

The supply challenge Meigs faced was truly a formidable one. First and foremost, as he himself noted, men had to be clothed before they could fight. Northern soldiers wore out a uniform every four months. Using the last year of the war as a case in point, with 1 million Union men in arms, Meigs's department needed to furnish at least 3 million uniforms. And apparently it did, with some to spare. According to the quartermaster general's annual report for the fiscal year ending on June 30, 1865, the department purchased 3,463,858 uniform trousers, 3,708,393 drawers, and 3,268,166 flannel shirts.

Shoes were an even greater problem. A soldier required a new pair every two months, which meant that millions of pairs of footwear had to be furnished by the quartermaster's office in any given year. In addition, the bureau was responsible for supplying massive quantities of overcoats, tents, blankets, hammocks, knapsacks, canteens, and mess kits to those in camp and on the front.

Although purchasing and distributing clothing, shoes, and miscellaneous wartime gear was the primary task of the department, it had other responsibilities as well. Meigs's office also had to provide animals to the Union forces. In one year alone, the quartermaster's department authorized the procurement of nearly 200,000 cavalry horses, more than 20,000 artillery horses, and almost 60,000 mules (used mainly for hauling wagons). Supplying feed for these animals was yet another job for the bureau. Each horse, for instance, consumed about twenty-six pounds of food a day, which explains why more than half of the daily provisions shipped to an army in the field consisted of forage.

In fact, transporting supplies, whether for humans or animals, posed an almost insurmountable logistical challenge to the Union's quartermaster bureau. Unlike its Southern counterpart, which, with few key exceptions, spent most of the war distributing provisions to troops on the defense never far from their supply bases, Meigs's department had to meet the needs of Northern armies penetrating deep into enemy territory. An invasion force of 100,000 men required delivery of 600 tons of supplies per day, a task of enormous proportions given the condition of Southern roads, not to mention the possibility of inclement weather or the threat of enemy attack. Yet the bureau rose to the challenge, and it did so superlatively. By coordinating its efforts with private and government-run railroads, and by operating its own huge fleet of water transports—hundreds of ocean, river, and bay vessels—along with thousands upon thousands of wagons, the Quartermaster General's Office created a delivery system that was unprecedented in terms of speed and efficiency. As Meigs's biographer, Russell F. Weigley, has pointed out: "For the most part the Union soldier who fought the Civil War probably could count himself better provided for than any soldier ever before in history."

Montgomery C. Meigs continued to serve his country after the war, remaining in his position as quartermaster general until his retirement in 1882. He died ten years later.

TAPS

The bugle call taps—first used by the U.S. Army during the Civil War—has had more of an impact on the consciousness of Americans than any other military music. Everyone is familiar with those long, mournful notes, spine chilling in poignancy and profound in meaning.

Much of the music's sad, wistful aura comes from its association with military funerals, even though that was not its original purpose. Gen. Daniel Butterfield, the composer of taps, penned the tune to be a lights-out signal in camp, never intending it to be a kind of funeral dirge.

Butterfield was born in Utica, New York, in 1831, and by background was neither a full-time professional soldier nor a composer. At the time the war broke out, he was working as a superintendent of the American Express Company and was also serving as an officer in the New York State militia. Mustered into the Federal army, Butterfield rose rapidly in rank. Within a few months of Fort Sumter he was already a brigadier general, and by 1863 he was chief of staff of the Army of the Potomac.

Fond of music, Butterfield especially liked to dabble in bugle calls. On a summer day in July 1862, when the army was in camp at Harrison's Landing on the James River in Virginia, the general summoned bugler Oliver W. Norton of the 83rd Pennsylvania to his tent. Butterfield whistled a tune he had invented, and asked Norton to repeat it on the bugle. It took some trial and error, but after a time the bugler sounded the new call to the general's satisfaction.

Butterfield then ordered the tune to be used in his brigade in lieu of the existing call for lights-out. It became an instant hit and soon spread throughout the Union army, first in the East, then in the West. Most soldiers so enjoyed the melody that they sang impromptu lyrics when it was sounded. "Put out the lights," they would chorus, "go to sleep, go to sleep, go to sleep . . ."

As the years passed and old soldiers "faded away," taps was often sounded at their funerals, as it was at General Butterfield's burial service in 1901. A distinguished officer, Daniel Butterfield served in numerous Civil War campaigns and was the recipient of the Medal of Honor, but he would be best remembered for composing taps, one of the more beautiful things to come out of America's costliest war.

CHAPTER 3

The Land War

The Civil War was the first large-scale conflict to employ the industrial technology and scientific discoveries of the nineteenth century. More than ever before, soldiers were better prepared to fight, to destroy, and to kill, while their commanders now had the means to transmit orders almost instantaneously, to coordinate combat movements more efficiently, and to shift forces more swiftly from one theater to another. From 1861 on, the fate of armies would be determined as much, if not more, in the factory and laboratory as it would be on the battlefield.

Rifled muskets, breech-loading and repeating rifles, machine guns, explosive bullets, land mines, rifled artillery—all were introduced or widely used for the first time in the Civil War. Placed in the hands of millions of combatants, this new weaponry produced a volume of firepower greater than in any previous conflict. During the three days of fighting at Gettysburg in early July 1863, for instance, "an estimated 566 tons of ammunition were expended, amounting to about 24 pounds for every casualty on both sides." Or take, as another example, the Wilderness and Spotsylvania campaigns nearly a year later, when Confederate ordnance officers retrieved from those battlefields over 120,000 pounds of lead, prompting one authority to estimate that as many as 19 million bullets were fired in a single week of combat.

The Civil War had transformed the battlefield, formerly a place of limited engagement, into an all-out killing zone. The battle of Shiloh in April 1862, the deadliest encounter of the war up to that time, marked a point of departure from which there was no return. As novelist and historian Shelby Foote has pointed out:

The bloodiness of Shiloh was astounding to everyone. Out of 100,000 men, over 20,000 were killed, wounded, captured, or missing. Shiloh had the same number of casualties as Waterloo [the massive battle that ended the Napoleonic Wars]. And yet when Shiloh was fought, there were another twenty Waterloos to follow.

Those additional "Waterloos," fought over the next three years, cut across vast geographical areas and involved hundreds of thousands of men. Here, again, the industrial and scientific advances of the period, especially the electric telegraph (used initially in the Crimean War, but employed extensively for the first time in the Civil War) and a newly introduced visual signal system allowed field officers to command and control armies not in eyesight. And when they had to move their troops over long distances, Civil War armies were transported and supplied by railroads on a scope and scale unparalleled in world history.

The strategy of warfare and its tactical implementation were inevitably influenced by all of these developments. As the Civil War approached its final year, the frontal assault, long considered the avenue toward victory, was now deemed too costly. Although generals on occasion still ordered offensive attacks, more and more the emphasis was on defense. Soldiers in all branches—infantry, cavalry, artillery—were forced to take cover outside the extended range of the enemy's more accurate and concentrated fire, a tactical realization that foreshadowed World War I a half century later.

THE MINIÉ BALL

For centuries the infantry's standard firearm was the smoothbore musket. Smoothbores, so called because the inside of the gun barrel was perfectly smooth, were reliable enough and relatively easy to load, but notoriously inaccurate. The weapon's effective range was only about eighty yards. Beyond that, as Ulysses S. Grant observed, a man armed with a smoothbore "might fire at you all day without you finding it out."

Not that there wasn't an alternative. The rifled musket had been around for a long time. Like the smoothbore, it was loaded by dumping gunpowder followed by a small lead ball down its muzzle, but unlike the smoothbore, the rifled musket had spiral grooves cut into the inner surface of its barrel to make the projectile spin through the air, thereby increasing its range and accuracy. Effective at 400 yards, in the hands of an above-average marksman the rifled musket could be deadly at 1,000 yards. If this was the case, why didn't the gun become the weapon of choice for the infantryman? Put simply, it was difficult to load. The ball, inserted into the muzzle, had to be a tight fit in order to grip the barrel's inner grooves. Using a ramrod, it took enormous force to push the projectile down the barrel; sometimes riflemen pounded the ramrod with a mallet. Slow and cumbersome to load, the rifled musket was simply not feasible under combat conditions.

The problem was resolved in the 1840s, when several inventors, principal among them a French Army captain by the name of Claude Étienne Minié, developed a cylindrical projectile. Rounded off at the front, the projectile was hollowed at the base and fitted with an iron or wooden plug. Called a minié ball (actually, it looked like a bullet rather than a ball), it was slightly smaller in diameter than the rifle bore, making it much easier to push it down the barrel. When fired, the plug at the base would enter the hollow of the projectile, forcing it to expand. This would allow it to tightly grip the rifled grooves and thereby achieve the desired spin. The minié ball was further perfected by an American, James H. Burton, of the Harpers Ferry armory. Eliminating the plugs, which had a tendency to malfunction, Burton developed a bullet capable of expanding solely from the gas produced by the powder's explosion. Less expensive and more reliable, it quickly replaced Minié's projectile, though it was still referred to as the minié ball.

The rifled musket as an infantry weapon made its debut in the Crimean War in the mid-1850s, when English and French troops used it against the Russians, still armed with the smoothbore. Later in the decade, in 1859, during the brief Franco-Austrian War, most of the soldiers involved in the fighting were equipped with the gun. But it was not until the American Civil War that the rifled musket for the first time was the primary weapon of both sides in an extended and large-scale conflict.

The Union and Confederacy used a variety of muskets in the war, but the two basic ones, both rifled and muzzle-loading, were the .58 caliber Springfield (named after the Massachusetts armory where it was produced) and the .577 caliber British Enfield. Considered the jewel of the Union armaments industry, the Springfield was fifty-six inches long and weighed approximately nine pounds. Over the course of the war, the Union manufactured more than 1.6 million of them, at a cost of $14.93 each. As for the Confederacy, at first it was unable to match the industrial productivity of the North, and either imported its arms from abroad or scavenged them directly off the battlefield, which accounted for several hundred thousand Union rifles falling into Southern hands. By 1863, however, the South depended less on imports and retrievals, and more on its newly created armaments industry. "Johnny Reb" might not have been well fed, well clothed, or well shod, but in most cases he was well armed. Midway through the war, therefore, the vast majority of infantrymen on both sides carried rifled muskets.

What impact did this have on battlefield tactics? Above all, it gave the advantage to those on the defense. Charging columns now had far less of a chance to reach the entrenched enemy, dislodge him, and claim victory. Even though the rate of fire remained roughly the same as the smoothbore (no more than three times a minute), the rifle's range and accuracy were far more lethal. Attacking foot soldiers could be brought under fire much earlier, at a half mile's distance, and take heavier and more serious casualties. With at least a fivefold increase in range, defending riflemen could decimate charging cavalry as well, cutting down both riders and mounts. The same would be true for advancing artillery. The cannoneers, along with their horses dragging the field pieces, could be picked off before the artillery was placed in a position to do any damage. "One rifle in the trench was worth five in front of it," wrote Union general Jacob D. Cox.

Cox might have exaggerated a bit (current scholarship has suggested that the rifle "made defense three times as strong as offense"), but his point is still well taken. The traditional close-order assault had indeed become futile at best and suicidal at worst, as Lee learned at Gettysburg, when half of the 15,000 men in Pickett's charge failed to return, and as Grant experienced at Cold Harbor, when 7,000 of his advancing troops were killed or wounded in a matter of hours. In the closing months of the war, although some generals persisted in taking the offense, most wanted to avoid a repeat of the bloodbaths at Gettysburg and Cold Harbor. Opposing armies drew their battle lines farther and farther apart, seeking cover behind the fortifications of a town or city, or in an elaborate network of trenches. The soldiers rarely saw their enemy anymore, except for mounds of earth "from which came clouds of powder smoke and a storm of bullets." With battlefield formations spread over vast areas, the engagements inevitably became longer, less aggressive, and more nerve-wracking. It may not have been entirely clear to the participants at the time, but Captain Minié's invention had forever changed the tactical face of warfare.

BREECHLOADERS AND REPEATING RIFLES

The Civil War infantryman, armed with a rifled musket, was capable of killing his enemy with more accuracy and at longer distances than ever before in the history of mass warfare. Here was a soldier, especially if he was a good shot, who could cut down a man 1,000 yards away. Compared to the smoothbore, with its limited range, the rifle was unquestionably the superior weapon, but it was not without problems.

The rifle's chief flaw was in its loading. True, the minié ball had eased the process, allowing for the projectile to be inserted into the barrel without difficulty; still, the overall procedure was long, tedious, and downright dangerous. To begin with, the soldier had to stand the rifle up, while he took out a cartridge wrapped in paper, consisting of gunpowder and a bullet. He then bit open the paper and put the powder down the muzzle, followed by the bullet. Next he took a ramrod, inserted it into the barrel, and pushed the contents as far down as they would go, all the while standing there and exposing himself to enemy fire. And the process was yet to be completed. The soldier now had to half cock the hammer, place a firing cap on the small nipple beneath the hammer, then fully cock the hammer, aim, and pull the trigger. This caused the hammer to strike the cap, producing a small explosion, which ignited the powder in the chamber, propelling the bullet out of the barrel. Once the weapon was fired, the rifleman would have to start the entire procedure all over again from scratch.

If one or more of the steps were forgotten, the rifle would not fire. In the noise, smoke, and fear of battle, soldiers might load and reload like automatons without actually firing their weapons once. After the fighting at Gettysburg, of the 27,500 loaded muskets found on the field, more than 12,000 had two loads each, 6,000 had from three to ten rounds of ammunition, and one had twenty-three bullets in the barrel. If any of those rifles had been discharged, it would have been deadly to the soldier who pulled the trigger, just as deadly as if he stopped an enemy bullet.

There was a solution: breechloaders. These weapons—fed ammunition at the breech, located at the base of the barrel just above the trigger—had been in use for hundreds of years. The gun could be traced as far back as the reign of Henry VIII in the first half of the sixteenth century. During the Revolutionary War, a British officer, Patrick Ferguson, used one at the battle of the Brandywine in 1777; an American named John Hall patented a breechloader in 1811.

The breechloader certainly eliminated all of the loading problems inherent in a muzzleloader. The soldier, no matter how much he tried, could put in no more than one load at a time; he had no need for a ramrod; and he could be in a prone position while loading, instead of having to stand. Accuracy and range also improved, since tighter-fitting bullets could be used. And finally, the rifleman employing a breechloader could fire as many as nine (on the average six) rounds per minute, compared with the muzzleloader's maximum of three.

But a major stumbling block prevented adoption of the breechloader. Thus far manufacturers were unable to stop the escape of gas from the weapon's breech. When the gun was considered for adoption by the army's Ordnance Department in the early 1840s, the gas leak problem convinced the military that it was not worth including in its arsenal.

That decision prevented the weapon's use in the war with Mexico later in the decade. Soon after the conflict, however, Christian Sharps, a former employee of John Hall, who had patented a breechloader nearly forty years before, introduced a firearm with a breech mechanism that allowed less gas to escape than previously. Encouraged by the Sharps rifle, in 1854 Congress appropriated $90,000 for testing and purchasing the breechloader, which caused a rash of new patents and proposals. Secretary of War Jefferson Davis (the future Confederate president) and his successor John B. Floyd (a future Confederate general) were both vigorous advocates of the weapon. The breechloaders, reported Floyd in 1860, "surely will . . . drive out of use those that load at the muzzle." An accurate prophecy, but one that had no immediate effect on the military establishment.

Like that of most entrenched bureaucracies, the U.S. Army's leadership was innately conservative. In early 1861 the entire officer corps numbered little over 1,000 men, a tight-knit body of career professionals. At the top were senior officers, many of whom had served for close to half a century, including seven of the eight heads of the army bureaus. The heavy hand of time-honored routine and hallowed tradition caused these men to resist change. Even worse, the junior officers knew that if they had any hope of promotion, they had better not rock the boat.

At the beginning of the war, weapons approval rested with the chief of ordnance, Brig. Gen, James W. Ripley. Close to seventy years of age, Ripley was a career soldier, a veteran of the War of 1812—in short, the very personification of hidebound military conservatism.

When the matter of breechloaders came before the Ordnance Department, Ripley and his cohorts, as expected, offered a host of reasons why they should not be adopted. The weapons were prone to breakage, they argued, and with the lack of standardized parts, there would be great delay in repairing them. Besides, the soldiers would misuse the breechloaders by relying on total firepower instead of taking accurate, deliberate aim. This wastage of ammunition would cause a supply problem of nightmare proportions, in view of the many kinds of cartridges the various models of breechloaders used. Members of the Ordnance Department also emphasized that it would take at least a year to convert government and most private armories to the mass production of breechloaders, impacting negatively on the supply of desperately needed arms in the field.

The arguments advanced by the army's old guard had little substance in fact. The breechloaders were no more likely to break down than the muzzleloaders. Given the technology available, in time replacement parts and ammunition could have been standardized and made available for the breechloaders. As for the assertion that soldiers fired a great deal more with breechloaders than if armed with muzzleloaders, this was true, but it was also true that the increased rate of firepower did far greater damage to the enemy. And finally, it would have been possible to contract the weapon out to foreign manufacturers and thereby not interfere with the production of muzzleloaders at home.

Refusing to acknowledge the validity of some of these counterarguments, Ripley and his supporters in the Ordnance Department held firm in their commitment exclusively to the muzzleloader, determined to resist any hint of innovation. If a nonmuzzleloading weapon could not be rejected outright, then it was referred to a board of inquiry, which could be counted upon to drown the proposed firearm in a sea of red tape.

However clever and discreet Ripley's obstructionist tactics were, a faster-loading rifle capable of producing greater firepower could not be resisted for long. Governors, congressmen, and the soldiers themselves were demanding access to the weapon. Even Lincoln became an advocate. Always interested in new weaponry, the president sometimes tested experimental guns, firing them at a rifle range in the Treasury Park not far from the White House.

In September 1861 Lincoln visited the camp of Col. Hiram Berdan's 1st Regiment of United States "Sharpshooters," a term that was first used in the early 1800s and, despite the coincidence, did not owe its origins to breechloader manufacturer Christian Sharps. Colonel Berdan, one of the best shots in the country, had raised a special force of marksmen but was having difficulty obtaining from the Ordnance Department the Sharps breechloaders he had promised his men. Lincoln interceded, and though it took nearly a year of pressure from the White House, Berdan's unit was finally armed with the weapon.

The marksmen, angered and demoralized by the delay, somehow put all that aside and fully justified the president's confidence in them.

On the second day of the battle of Gettysburg, July 2, 1863, to cite just one of many instances when they overwhelmed the enemy, 100 of Berdan's sharpshooters, fighting alongside 200 Maine troops armed with muzzleloaders, held off a superior force of Confederates. In the twenty-minute action, the marksmen unleashed a hail of fire with their breechloaders, so heavily concentrated and deadly that many of the Southerners were under the impression they had confronted "two Federal regiments." A Union sharpshooter, who was captured by the enemy and taken through their lines, could not believe the "slaughter" that he and his comrades had "made in their ranks." The Rebels were "piled in heaps and across each other," he later recalled. Another eyewitness, a Confederate doctor, was convinced that his unit must have encountered a force even greater than two regiments, perhaps a corps, since he "never saw lead so thick in his life as it was in those woods."

In terms of sheer firepower, then, the breechloader was in a class by itself. Yet one should bear in mind that the breechloader, like the muzzleloader, was still a single-shot weapon. For years, Union arms manufacturers had been well aware of this limitation, and by the summer of 1863, they were prepared to produce in large quantities a firearm that did not have to be loaded after each shot. The "repeating rifle," as it was called, was used for the first time in combat during the Civil War.

There were several kinds of repeating firearms to choose from in 1863, but the most popular one was the Spencer rifle (which also came in a carbine model—a rifle with a shorter barrel designed for cavalrymen). Patented in 1860, the Spencer weapon was the brainchild of Christopher Minor Spencer. A twenty-seven-year-old Connecticut Yankee, Spencer had had a passion for firearms since his boyhood and worked for a time in the Colt Armory in Hartford. His weapon was a seven-shot repeater that had a magazine in the stock into which a metal tube with seven bullets could be inserted. After each time the Spencer was fired, the empty shell case was ejected by a downward thrust of the leverlike trigger guard, and when returned to its normal position, another cartridge was in place ready to fire. By preloading a number of tubes, the soldier was capable of firing at least fifteen rounds per minute, with a maximum range of over a mile (approximately 2,000 yards).

Predictably, when Spencer attempted to sell his weapon to the Ordnance Department, Ripley showed little enthusiasm, offering the same reasons he had used to reject the breechloader. However, in late December 1861, Secretary of War Simon Cameron (soon to be replaced by Edwin M. Stanton) had received from several officers independent test results on a number of repeating rifles, including the Spencer. All of the reports were positive, and the Spencer itself was considered the most durable and effective. In need of no further convincing, Cameron told Ripley to purchase the Spencer, which he did on December 26, ordering 10,000 of them. But when delivery was delayed because of production problems, the order was cut to 7,500.

Until the summer of 1863, that was the total number of Spencer repeaters in the hands of Union soldiers. Unable to persuade Ripley to place additional orders now that his factory was in full operation, Christopher Spencer went West to visit with Union commanders in the field and provide some practical demonstrations of just what his weapon could do. Well received—he even dined with General Grant outside of Vicksburg—Spencer decided next to go right to the top, securing an interview with Lincoln in late August. After personally testing the weapon by firing it several times, the president was duly impressed and endorsed it warmly—so warmly, in fact, that the Spencer repeater henceforth was dubbed "Mr. Lincoln's Gun."

Thanks to the president's interest and influence, the government soon began purchasing the weapon in large quantities. Around the same time, in mid-September 1863, Brig. Gen. James Ripley was formally retired from active duty. At first he was replaced by two generals sharing authority, but when that "dubious division of power" proved unworkable, Brig. Gen. Alexander B. Dyer was named chief of the Ordnance Department. Unlike Ripley, Dyer "brought a more advanced outlook" to the purchasing of weaponry.

During the latter part of the war, some 5,000 repeating rifles and more than 94,000 repeating carbines were bought from Spencer, along with thousands of other repeaters from smaller manufacturers. By 1864 most Union cavalrymen were armed with a repeating carbine. On the other hand, the vast majority of foot soldiers continued to rely on the muzzle-loading rifled musket. Only select infantry units were outfitted with repeating rifles, the most famous of which was a brigade in the Army of the Cumberland, commanded by Col. John T. Wilder. Known as the "Lightning Brigade," it was the first military force ever to be armed with repeaters. On June 24, 1863, at Hoover's Gap, near Chattanooga, Tennessee, Wilder's men were ordered to clear the area of rebel troops. Confronting an enemy force of superior numbers, the Union brigade laid down such a heavy fire with their repeaters that the Confederate officer in charge ordered a retreat, actually believing that he was outnumbered five to one.

The following September, at the battle of Chicamauga in northern Georgia, the Lightning Brigade unleashed a barrage of lead on an approaching Confederate column, so devastating in effect that Colonel Wilder himself admitted that it "seemed a pity" to kill men in such a fashion. Subjected to "a continuous blast of fire," the "head of the [Confederate] column, as it was pushed on by those behind, appeared to melt away or sink into the earth, for, though continually moving, it got no nearer." After the fighting stopped, Wilder observed, "one could have walked for two hundred yards . . . on dead rebels without touching the ground."

In the last year of the war, as Spencer repeaters found their way into more and more Union hands, the Confederates understandably were "getting rattled" by the firepower they had to face. "They are afraid of our repeating rifles," wrote a soldier in Sherman's army. "They say we are not fair, that we have guns that we load up on Sunday and shoot all the rest of the week."

One can only wonder what would have happened if those repeater guns had been produced in much larger quantities and placed in Union hands much earlier in the war. Of course, repeater weapons were relatively new at the time the conflict broke out, and speculation regarding those arms might seem too far-fetched. But single-shot breechloaders had been available for some time before the war. What if the Union infantry had been armed from the first with those weapons? In *Lincoln and the Tools of War,* Robert V. Bruce pondered that question, offering the following:

> If a large part of the Union Army had been given breechloaders by late 1862, Gettysburg [July 1863] would certainly have ended the war. More likely, Chancellorsville [May 1863] or even Fredericksburg [December 1862] would have done it, and history would record no Gettysburg Address, no President Grant, perhaps no carpetbag reconstruction or Solid South. Instead, it might have had the memoirs of ex-President Lincoln, perhaps written in retirement during the administration of President Burnside or Hooker.
>
> But it did not happen that way.

MACHINE GUNS

Similar to rifled muskets, machine guns also predated the Civil War by centuries. As far back as the middle of the 1300s, a weapon existed that could discharge a volley of projectiles. Known as the organ gun, it featured a series of musket barrels—as many as twenty—lined up side by side on a cart, looking like organ pipes and thus the weapon's name. A lighted linstock, the same instrument used to fire a cannon, was applied to the barrel touchholes, igniting the powder and emitting lead balls in rapid succession. The concept was crude yet sound, but the limited technology at the time rendered the gun slow to reload, difficult to aim and maneuver, and likely to malfunction because of the clogging effect of the heavy black powder. A machine gun in the more modern sense of the term would have to wait until the nineteenth century, when significant advances in science and industry took place.

Once a self-contained cartridge, consisting of powder and projectile wrapped in paper, was developed, there was no further need for scoops of powder and separate lead balls, and the appearance of the percussion, or firing, cap made the flint (successor to the linstock) obsolete. Around the early 1860s munitions manufacturers took the technology a step further, first by inserting the paper-wrapped cartridge into a reusable steel container, and then replacing it altogether with a metallic cartridge. By the outbreak of the Civil War, the machine gun was ready to be used in combat.

Of the various models of the weapon on the market, one of the most popular was the "Union gun," claimed to have been designed by businessman Wilson Ager, though others filed patents as well. Capable of firing 120 rounds per minute, the weapon was mounted on a two-wheel light artillery carriage. It consisted of a single rifle barrel, with an opening at the rear of the barrel, topped by a funnel or hopper. The ammunition was placed into the hopper, and turning a crank on the side of the gun automatically fed the cartridges into a revolving cylinder, which in turn deposited each of them into the chamber for firing. Further rotation struck the firing cap, causing the bullet to be ejected, while its empty container dropped into a receptacle, and another round fed immediately into the barrel. Witnessing a demonstration in June 1861, President Lincoln thought it looked like a device for grinding coffee beans and dubbed the weapon the "coffee mill gun," a name that stuck to it throughout its brief history.

During the first year of the war, the coffee mill gun was at the height of its popularity, but it was soon eclipsed in fame by another rapid-firing weapon, the Gatling gun, named after its inventor, Dr. Richard J. Gatling. Born and raised in North Carolina, Gatling was a mechanical genius who in 1839 at the age of twenty-one patented his first invention—a seed-sowing machine called a rice planter. After moving North, Gatling converted the machine to plant wheat and experienced considerable success in its manufacture and sale.

By the winter of 1845-46, Gatling was on his way to fame and fortune, when his career and life almost came to an abrupt end. Stricken with smallpox, he languished three months, several times on the verge of death, but somehow recovered. This near-fatal experience convinced Gatling that only by obtaining a medical education could he be better prepared to deal with serious illness if in the future he or a member of his family were afflicted. Entering medical school in 1847, he took his training at the Ohio Medical College in Cincinnati. Whether or not he graduated is open to dispute but of little significance; though he assumed the title of doctor, he never practiced medicine. Instead, he continued to invent agricultural machinery and other mechanical devices, earning for himself a vast fortune and a position of prominence in Indianapolis, where he had married and settled.

Not one to rest on his laurels, Gatling remained as active as ever in the field of labor-saving machinery for the farmer. In 1860 alone, he was granted five inventions. His most famous one, however, was yet to come.

Perhaps Gatling himself explains best the events leading up to the invention of his famous gun. "I witnessed almost daily the departure of troops to the front and the return of the wounded, sick and dead," Gatling remembered years later. "It occurred to me if I could invent a machine—a gun—which could by its rapidity of fire enable one man to do as much battle as a hundred," then the number of men exposed to disease and death, he reasoned, would "be greatly diminished." Here then, as Gatling saw it, was another of his labor-saving inventions, but this one had a far more important purpose than simply conserving human energy—it would also save lives, at least those not on its receiving end.

Gatling patented his gun in early November 1862. Like the coffee mill gun, it used a crank-operated action and funnel-type feeding system. But unlike its competitor, the Gatling featured six barrels designed to rotate about a central axis. While it was being fired, the barrels not in use had time to cool, allowing the Gatling to discharge more rounds (about 150 to 200 per minute) and for a greater length of time than the single-barrel coffee mill gun.

It was an improvement, to be sure, but the army's Ordnance Department, right from the beginning of the war, wanted nothing to do with machine guns, be they the coffee mill or the Gatling variety. Intractable as ever, most members of the department were of the opinion that a war for national survival was not a time for experimentation with new military inventions. The weapon was doomed from the start, and its tactical purpose was also misunderstood. Ordnance officers were under the erroneous impression that the machine gun was an artillery piece, and as such, it appeared inferior to the more powerful field pieces available.

Whatever the basis for their opposition, they did not figure on J. D. Mills, a salesman representing the manufacturer of the coffee mill gun. An indefatigable pitchman, with a seemingly innate ability to showcase his product, Mills went straight to Lincoln. Referring to the weapon as "an Army in six feet square," in early June 1861 he demonstrated it to the president and a number of other government officials, military and civilian. After a second demonstration in October, the president, without consulting the Ordnance Department, authorized the purchase of ten coffee mill guns at $1,300 a piece. Two months later, J. D. Mills arranged an even bigger sale, persuading Gen. George B. McClellan, commander of the Army of the Potomac, to buy fifty of the weapons at cost plus 20 percent, which came to $735 each.

Precisely when the coffee mill gun was put into action is a matter of debate. Some scholars have suggested that it was first used by men of the 28th Pennsylvania regiment in a skirmish at Middleburg, Virginia, on March 29, 1862, but the evidence remains sketchy. Based on the most recent study, it's more likely that the weapon's baptism of fire—indeed, the first time ever that a machine gun was used in warfare—occurred on April 21, 1862, when men of the 56th New York opened fire with a coffee mill gun during the siege of Yorktown. The action was witnessed by a correspondent of the New York *Evening Post,* who reported that "a novel kind of weapon was brought into service . . . which loads and fires by turning a crank. . . . In fact," he added, "it is one continuous discharge. The balls flew thick and fast, and the Yankee invention must have astonished the other side."

Astonishing as the impact might have been, it was also short-lived. The coffee mill guns proved unsafe to operate and prone to breakdowns. By the end of 1862, while some of these weapons remained in service to be used by the infantry in defense of bridges or by the navy on the Mississippi, most had been sent back to Washington and placed in storage.

Enter Dr. Gatling. Having had his machine gun predictably spurned by the Ordnance Department, Gatling appealed directly to Lincoln in early 1864. "I assure you," he wrote to the president, "my invention is no 'Coffee Mill Gun'—but is entirely a different arm, and is entirely free from the accidents and objections raised against that arm." Lincoln did not reply, probably having had his fill by now of inventors and inventions. But Maj. Gen. Benjamin F. Butler, eager as always to try new military hardware, saw merit in the weapon and purchased a dozen Gatling guns out of his own pocket. The unorthodox general had found an unorthodox gun, and it was only a matter of time before he would put it to the test. In the trenches outside Petersburg in May 1864, Butler himself opened fire with a Gatling gun on "some unarmed & unsuspecting rebels who were strolling up & down the top of their earthworks." Beyond that incident, however, the use of Gatlings by Union forces are based more on rumor than fact.

Turned down by the Ordnance Department and used only sporadically in the field, the machine gun, despite its enormous potential, had no impact on the Union war effort. But its possibilities as a combat weapon, even if misunderstood, were not overlooked for long. A year after Appomattox the army adopted the Gatling gun as part of its arsenal. Yet for decades, it continued to be thought of as an adjunct to artillery or as a defensive weapon useful in guarding fixed positions. As an arm of the infantry, capable of providing massive firepower for the foot soldier—this was not demonstrated until the Spanish-American War in 1898 and not fully understood until World War I.

MUSKET SHELLS

When the *Louisville Journal,* a pro-Union Kentucky paper, reported on March 19, 1862, that "a lot of poisoned bullets" had been found in Nashville, Tennessee, "left behind by the rebels in their flight from the city," it was probably the first time that most of its readers had ever heard of such ammunition. Poisoned bullets, or musket shells, as they were more commonly called, were rifle cartridges designed to explode once they made contact with the target. Resembling sort of miniature artillery shells, these projectiles were not new to warfare, but the first conflict in which they were used extensively—by both sides—was during America's Civil War.

Explosive bullets had their origins with the British in India around the middle of the nineteenth century. Never intended for antipersonnel use, their original purpose was to explode artillery caissons or cartridge boxes from afar. In fact, the British used these projectiles to blow up ammunition wagons during the Indian Mutiny of 1857. Fired from long-range rifles, the bullets, .52-caliber rounds filled with powder charges, detonated on impact.

A similar kind of musket shell, but of larger caliber, was used by the Confederates half a decade later. The Union version, however, employed a different principle. Instead of explosion on contact, the

Yankee musket shell, containing a time fuse, could be set to detonate from one to three seconds after firing. Its inventor, a New Yorker by the name of Samuel Gardiner, Jr., believed that this would allow the bullet, with its delayed reaction, to penetrate deep into an ammunition box before bursting.

In theory, the bullet's target was supposed to be nonhuman, but it did not always turn out that way. The Confederates were the first to use musket shells, and if they were unable to find an enemy ammunition storage chest to blow up, they turned their attention to Northern soldiers. At least, that's what Confederate captain William Farley did. In late June 1862, at the battle of Gaines' Mill on the Peninsula, Farley, equipped with explosive bullets and a long-range "double-barrel English rifle," was "looking out for a caisson to blow up." Unable to get a shot at one, he decided to use his musket shells as ordinary bullets. "I had eighty rounds in my haversack," he confessed, "and I used them all up that day before I got through."

According to Farley, no less than six Union officers had been hit by his musket shells, suffering what were probably agonizing deaths. The normal, nonexplosive minié ball was bad enough; its soft lead tended to smash and splinter bone, or cut through internal organs without exiting. But the explosive bullet caused even more horrible wounds; when it exploded, it ripped flesh apart, mangling and tearing its victim into a bloody pulp. "To my dying day," wrote a New York *Tribune* correspondent, "I shall have in my ears the wailing shrieks of a private of the 1st Long Island, shot dead beside my horse with a percussion musket-ball, whose explosion within its wound I distinctly heard."

Although not standard issue, musket shells were used by soldiers on one side or the other (sometimes on both) in some of the major battles of the war. In the eastern theater, there's evidence that they were used on the Peninsula, at Antietam, Chancellorsville, Gettysburg, the Wilderness, and Cold Harbor; and in the West, at Vicksburg and Missionary Ridge. One regiment in particular—the 2nd New Hampshire— had a unique experience with explosive bullets. In the late spring of 1862, during the Peninsula campaign near Glendale, Virginia, the New Englanders came under heavy Confederate fire. As the Southerners opened up on them, the air was peppered by loud popping explosions, puzzling to the men of the 2nd New Hampshire, until one of their officers, a Captain Sayles, had his chest ripped open as if with an invisible cleaver. The gaping, jagged wound left no question that the Confederates were using musket shells. A little more than a year later, the 2nd New Hampshire got a measure of revenge at Gettysburg when the regiment went into battle with Sharps rifles loaded with explosive bullets. As one Yankee itching to get even put it, "Woe to the Johnny that stops one." And many a Confederate probably did, since the 2nd New Hampshire expended 14,000 rounds of musket shells in the fighting.

Unfortunately, the explosive bullets could be almost as lethal to the user as to his intended target. Each man's cartridge box, usually carried on his belt, was in effect a small powder keg, a potentially fatal accident waiting to happen. One New Hampshire soldier had the bad luck to be at the wrong place at the wrong time; a piece of hot shrapnel landed on his cartridge box with horrifying results. For thirty seconds, which must have seemed like thirty minutes, the victim's body quivered and jerked in spasmodic agony as each bullet went off in almost firecracker fashion, rending the soldier into a bloody mass.

During and after the war, leaders of both sides, apparently unaware that some of their own men were issued musket shells, condemned use of them. At Vicksburg, for example, General Grant denounced their use by the Rebels, insisting that the bullets were "barbarous, because they produced increased suffering without any corresponding advantage to those using them." And years after the conflict, former Confederate president Jefferson Davis denied any Southern involvement with explosive bullets, considering them "abhorrent to Civilization."

Outlawed by most European nations in the post–Civil War era, musket shells were also excluded from America's arsenal. In 1868 Gen. Alexander B. Dyer, chief of ordnance, officially condemned explosive bullets as "inexcusable among any people above the grade of ignorant savages."

GAS WARFARE

From a tactical standpoint, nothing was more challenging to the Union army than when it had to dislodge an entrenched enemy force. Whether the Rebels were behind the barricades of a town or taking cover in a system of earthworks, it was always at the expense of a great number of Union lives before the Southerners surrendered their defensive positions. If the Yankees experienced limited success in this regard, it was not for a lack of ideas, many of which were sent directly to the War Department for consideration.

Some of these proposals were legitimate and farseeing, deserving of further study, while others, well-meaning no doubt, were sheerly ludicrous in concept and implementation. Joseph Lott of Hartford, Connecticut, for instance, suggested that fire engines be dispatched to the Confederate strongholds at Yorktown, Virginia, and Corinth, Mississippi. Once the engines arrived on the outskirts of these towns, Lott proposed that they spray large quantities of chloroform on the Rebel defenders, thereby anesthetizing them and allowing Union forces to capture both garrisons without resistance.

No one could fault the War Department for ignoring Lott's proposal, and probably having a good laugh to boot, but the department, overburdened and subjected to many such preposterous schemes, sometimes allowed a viable idea to slip through the cracks. On April 5, 1862, a New York City schoolteacher, John W. Doughty, wrote a letter to the recently appointed secretary of war, Edwin M. Stanton, enclosing a plan for the use of gas warfare—the first time in U.S. military history that such a proposal was made.

The gas Doughty wanted to employ was liquid chlorine, which he pointed out "is so irritating in its effects upon the respiratory organs, that a small quantity diffused in the atmosphere, produces incessant & uncontrollably violent coughing." By loading the liquid chlorine into artillery shells and exploding them over "an *entrenched* enemy," Doughty maintained, it would only be a matter of minutes before the gas, which was heavier than air, would sink into trenches, bombproofs, and all other kinds of earthworks, rendering the men defenseless "as though both their legs were broken."

To his credit, Doughty recognized that the use of such a weapon raised moral questions. But as he noted in his letter to Stanton (using the same rationale that pro-atomic bomb advocates embraced nearly a century later), if the gas shells could end the war sooner, despite their terrible effects, then why prolong the agony and death by more conventional means. Sound reasoning, perhaps, but no one seemed interested in his weapon or his justification for it. After Stanton failed to reply, Doughty sent a similar letter to Lincoln, who, it appears, never had an opportunity to read it, since one of his secretaries referred it directly to the War Department. Somehow the letter ended up in the graveyard of innovation, the Ordnance Department. Not surprisingly, Doughty was informed that the department was too busy to test the concept. Poison gas was never used in the Civil War.

During World War I, in an attempt to break the stalemate of trench warfare, the Germans used chlorine gas shells for the first time on April 22, 1915. Greenish yellow clouds emerged from the shell bursts and soon enveloped Allied soldiers. According to a British observer, the men abandoned their positions, "reeling and retching, eyes bloodshot and weeping, some with blistered flesh." Civil War soldiers had to endure much, but at least they were spared this particular horror.

LAND MINES

On May 4, 1862, as Union troops entered Yorktown, Virginia, abandoned by the Rebels the evening before, the men in blue received a rude and nerve-shattering shock. Without warning, the earth along the deserted streets and beneath trees and telegraph poles erupted into gouts of flames, smoke, and flying pieces of metal. The unsuspecting Yankee soldiers hit by these explosions were torn to shreds; four or five were killed outright, and about a dozen were severely wounded. Even those unscathed were left traumatized and filled with terror. The explosions were caused by Confederate land mines, more commonly referred to by contemporaries as torpedoes or subterra shells.

Understandably, Northern commanders were outraged by the use of these weapons, which they considered immoral and uncivilized. As head of operations on the Peninsula, Gen. George B. McClellan declared that the Rebels were "guilty of the most murderous & barbarous conduct in placing torpedoes *within* the abandoned works." Instead of defending what had been done, most Southern officers, at least in the early years of the war, agreed with McClellan. Confederate general James Longstreet was of the opinion that subterra shells were not "a proper or effective method of warfare," while Gen. Joseph E. Johnston, at the time in charge of the Army of Northern Virginia, flatly decreed that all further use of them should cease immediately.

Although outranked by both Johnston and Longstreet, Confederate brigadier general Gabriel J. Rains, the former commander of Yorktown and the man responsible for ordering the mines planted before retreating from the town, gave no apology for his actions. Nor did he have any intention of shelving the weapon. "Deception is the art of war," Rains told his critics, and he would employ whatever it took to deceive and cripple the enemy. And employ it he did. The first large-scale use of land mines in the history of combat took place during the Civil War.

Gabriel Rains's involvement with land mines could be traced to his pre–Civil War military career. A graduate of West Point, he was commissioned a second lieutenant in 1827 and spent the next thirty-four years serving his country at a variety of posts and in two wars, one against the Seminoles in Florida in 1840, and then against Mexico in the latter part of the decade. It was during the hostilities with the Seminoles that Rains first used land mines as a means of alerting his garrison to possible penetration by the Indians.

More than twenty years passed before Rains's name was again linked to these explosive devices. In the summer of 1861, fifty-eight-year-old Rains, a native of North Carolina, surrendered his commission in the U.S. military and accepted a brigadier generalship in the Confederate army. Once hostilities began in earnest, it did not take long for Rains to realize the important role that land mines could play in this conflict.

Similar to the mines he had employed against the Seminoles, Rains's subterra shells were essentially artillery shells filled with powder. Concealed under the surface, they were rigged to explode either by direct contact with a pressure-sensitive friction primer or by moving an article (serving as a decoy) attached to the primer by a hidden string or wire.

Contrary to the objections raised by his superiors, Rains had no reservations, ethical or otherwise, regarding the use of land mines. As far as he was concerned, these underground weapons offered several tactical advantages: They could help repel an attack by their unexpected and deadly impact; they could slow down the advance of the enemy and allow retreating Confederate forces to regroup and prepare to renew the battle; and they could discourage night assaults, since they were almost impossible to detect in the dark. Whatever their purpose, Rains believed, land mines were perfectly legitimate weapons, as acceptable to warfare as, say, an ambush, or hidden artillery guns, or tunnels dug under enemy fortifications, filled with explosives and ignited without warning. Confederate secretary of war George Randolph, for the most part, sided with Rains. If subterra shells were planted "to repel an assault or in a road to check pursuit," this was "admissible in civilized warfare," the secretary ruled; but under no circumstances, he emphasized, were they to be used "to take life with no other object than the destruction of life."

Randolph's decision cleared the way for the continued use of mines. Not that Rains would have needed it anyway. As Confederate reverses mounted, Southern authorities, even those who had previously taken an antimine stance, grew less squeamish about their use. Soon after the fall of Vicksburg in early July 1863, Rains was ordered by none other than his former nemesis, Gen. Joseph E. Johnston, to mine a riverbank and two roads in order to cover his withdrawal from the area. The subterra shells, it was reported, "stopped and stampeded Grant's army," inflicting hundreds of Union casualties and allowing Johnston to conduct a successful retreat.

For the remainder of the war, Confederate generals, suffering a steady erosion of manpower, found themselves relying more and more on land mines to halt advancing Union forces. For example, at Fort Wagner, located on Morris Island at the entrance to Charleston Harbor, subterra shells were put into place to protect against an enemy assault. When that attack was finally launched in early July 1863, and continued intermittently until the Confederates abandoned the fort on September 6, the land mines inflicted their share of damage on unsuspecting Union soldiers. Planted in the sand and either camouflaged with a board over them or attached to a booby trap such as a pocketknife, those who ran afoul of these devices either suffered the sudden loss of a limb or two or were blown to bits. And even though the casualties sustained from these hidden explosives were few in number, the sheer terror they produced spread through the ranks like a prairie fire. In retaliation, once Fort Wagner was secured, Confederate prisoners were forced to find the unexploded mines and disarm them.

Gen. William Tecumseh Sherman instituted the same policy more than a year later. After taking Atlanta in early September 1864 and advancing toward Savannah, Sherman's men encountered land mines and all kinds of booby traps. The general himself witnessed firsthand a young officer who had all the flesh blown off one of his legs by an exploding subterra shell. "This was not war, but murder," Sherman exclaimed. As a result, he ordered Confederate POWs, whom he equipped with picks and shovels, to march ahead of his own columns in order to detect and dig up the hidden explosives.

Compelling Rebel prisoners to clear minefields, however, did not deter use of the weapon. In fact just the opposite occurred. As Union armies advanced deeper into the South, the Confederate command increased its requests for land mines. Gabriel Rains interpreted this as complete vindication. "These shells are now appreciated," he wrote in late October 1864. "I now have more calls for their use than I can possibly fulfill."

Channeling most of his energies and resources into the defense of Richmond, Rains supervised the planting of mines in and around the fortifications protecting the Southern capital. By the time the Confederates surrendered the city on April 3, 1865, a total of 2,363 subterra shells had been placed in position.

Americans should be grateful that Gabriel Rains's professional vindication came late in the war. One can only speculate what might have been if the Confederacy had had the commitment and wherewithal early in the conflict to support a massive effort to mine the battlefields, cities, and towns of the South. That there would have been a greater number of dead and wounded, and of soldiers suffering from posttraumatic stress disorder, is undeniable. But the outcome of the war would have been the same. What would have been different, however, was that generations of postwar Americans in the South—similar to Southeast Asians today—would have lived lives filled with terror as each dormant mine eventually exploded and left its deadly mark.

BRASS POUNDERS

The first practical suggestion for the construction of an electric telegraph was made in 1753 by British surgeon Charles Morrison, though credit for its invention—or at least for its perfection—is given to the American painter and inventor Samuel F. B. Morse. In November 1837 he developed an instrument capable of conveying a signal for a distance of ten miles; seven years later the first public message was sent from Baltimore to Washington by Morse telegraph.

The sending device, called a key, transmitted electrical current of short or long duration, all at the pressure of a finger. These impulses were received by an instrument equipped with an electromagnetically controlled pencil that made marks on a paper tape moving over a clockwork-operated cylinder. The markings—dots and dashes—would be interpreted via a code developed by Morse that corresponded to the alphabet and could form words. The entire process, relatively simple in design, was revolutionary in application.

Before long, telegraph wires were strung throughout much of the country. Within four years of the historic Baltimore-Washington transmission, every state east of the Mississippi except Florida had some connection with a telegraph network. By the 1850s, the miles of telegraph line jumped more than tenfold, from under 5,000 to 56,000. A culmination of sorts was reached in October 1861, when President Abraham Lincoln received the first transcontinental telegraph message from Sacramento, California.

At the very time the chief executive had received that message, Union armies were training in the East and massing in the West, preparing to do battle with the enemy. With its forces in separate theaters, scattered over hundreds of miles, the strategic control of military operations and tactical direction of troops in battle would have been near impossible if not for the telegraph. Actually, its military potential had already been demonstrated by the British and French in the Crimean War in the mid-1850s, but the Americans were the first combatants to use the telegraph on a scope and scale unprecedented in the history of warfare.

Soon after the Rebel bombardment of Fort Sumter in April 1861, the United States Military Telegraph (USMT) was organized. Attached to the Quartermaster's Department and headed by Anson Stager, the prewar superintendent of Western Union, the USMT was charged initially with securing the telegraph lines around the capital. Within a year Congress expanded its jurisdiction, enabling the USMT to assume authority over all private telegraph companies throughout the United States. As a former director and attorney for the Atlantic and Ohio Telegraph Company, Secretary of War Edwin M. Stanton realized the enormous potential of such a vast communications network. Almost immediately, he assumed full authority over the organization, though he retained Anson Stager as its administrative head. Henceforth, few dared to interfere with the secretary's "autocratic" hold on the military telegraph. Fearful that its coded messages and overall operations could be compromised, Stanton made certain that no officer, whatever his rank, including Grant himself, was ever allowed to exercise authority over the USMT.

To ensure maximum control, Stanton made certain that the United States Military Telegraph, which in later years he called his "right arm," remained a nonmilitary operation. The USMT, therefore, was made up of civilians, approximately 1,200 to 1,500 of them, who served either as operators or as part of the support staff—foremen, teamsters, battery keepers, and linemen. Only Stager, who was appointed colonel, and his dozen or so top associates were given military commissions, and the sole reason for this was to enable them to requisition money and supplies from the Quartermaster General's Office. In all other respects, the military telegraph was a civilian bureau, which meant that its personnel were directly answerable to Stanton, Stager, or their administrative assistants, not to officers in the field. Understandably, military commanders resented the situation, since they needed the services of the operators but had no authority over them.

Though disconcerting for the officers involved, this anomalous situation was worse for the telegraphers. Those who pounded the key— often called "brass pounders"—were operating on fields of battle at great personal risk, without the benefits of being in uniform. Having no military status, if wounded or killed, they or their loved ones were not entitled to a pension; and if captured, technically they could be charged with espionage if they were found tapping the enemy's wire. Such was the fate of a young Southern telegrapher by the name of David O. Dodd, who was taken into custody by Federal troops, accused of picking up some information off Union wires, and hung before a crowd in Little Rock, Arkansas. There's no evidence that the Confederacy ever executed a Union operator as a spy, but members of the USMT still experienced their share of suffering, with at least 100 (some estimate as many as 300) telegraphers and their helpers killed, wounded, or captured.

Despite the risks involved, the brass pounders, many of whom were boys in their teens—not to mention Louisa Volker of Missouri, the first woman ever to be employed as a military telegrapher—performed heroically under the pressures of wartime, including actual combat. Every operator in a battle zone carried a portable telegraph with a wire that he could hook up to an existing line, allowing him to send information until the very moment of an advance or a retreat. If capture was inevitable, then it was his duty to destroy the sending instrument so that the enemy could not force him to use it against his own side.

Union operators were even more guarded when it came to the secret code that they employed to transmit messages. Devised by Anson Stager in the early months of the conflict, it was the first military telegraph cryptographic system ever used in warfare. The Union telegraphers, who sent more than 90 percent of their messages by this cipher (which employed code words and plain-language equivalents), were sworn to secrecy and not permitted to share it with anyone. Fear of the wrath of Secretary of War Stanton apparently was all that was needed to ensure a cloak of secrecy over Stager's cryptographic system. Improved and revised numerous times during the course of the war, the Union's telegraph code was never broken by the Confederacy.

The USMT could also take pride in the miles of telegraph wire it had strung and the sheer volume of messages it had sent. During the four years of war, 15,000 miles of line (compared to the Confederacy's 500) were erected by the USMT. Over those wires, moreover, an unprecedented number of messages were sent and received. For the fiscal year ending June 30, 1863, some 1.2 million telegrams were transmitted, ranging in length from ten to a thousand words. The volume of messages increased further in the last years of the conflict, for a wartime total of 6.5 million transmissions, which came to a daily average of around 4,500.

For President Lincoln, the telegraph proved indispensable, affording him the opportunity, as one of his modern biographers has noted, "to be the first commander-in-chief in almost constant communication with his generals in distant fields." A frequent visitor to the War Department, where Stanton's USMT communication center was located, Lincoln not only followed the course of the war, but also made informed decisions based on up-to-date information.

Of course, the chief beneficiaries were the commanders on the battlefields. Thanks to the telegraph, Civil War generals now had communications that Napoleon would have envied a scant half century before. Throughout the Peninsula campaign, the USMT had twenty-three operators manning stations at all major points, providing day and night service for Gen. George B. McClellan and his officers in the field. At Gettysburg George Meade, commanding general of the Army of the Potomac, was probably the first military leader in history to have instant contact with the staff officers of a nearly 90,000-man force actively engaged in a battle. But nothing came close to the coordination and direction exercised by Ulysses S. Grant in his capacity as general in chief. In the last year of the war, he had direct communication with General Meade in Virginia, Gen. William Tecumseh Sherman in Georgia, Gen. Franz Sigel in West Virginia, and Gen. Benjamin F. Butler on the James River. Altogether, Grant's telegraphic system enabled him to monitor and control the movement of more than half a million men, operating over an area of some 800,000 square miles.

As a civilian agency with no official standing in the army, the United States Military Telegraph was dissolved soon after the war ended, and its duties were assumed by the signal corps. In the wake of its demise, it left a rather ironic legacy. The USMT had strung thousands of miles of line to assist Union generals in their operations to destroy the Rebel cause; now those same lines would be used to rebuild the South by reconnecting it to the Union. Within two months after Lee's surrender, New York City had a direct wire to New Orleans, Charleston, and other leading cities of the former Confederacy.

COL. ALBERT J. MYER, U.S. ARMY SIGNAL CORPS

Regarded as the "father" of the U.S. Army signal corps, Albert J. Myer, a physician by profession, had always been interested in the art of communication. Born and raised in upstate New York, Myer attended Buffalo Medical College. For his graduation thesis, he developed a sign language for the deaf, which he intended to implement once established as a physician. But after only three years of practicing medicine, Myer, described as "tall and robust," grew tired of the day-to-day life of a rural doctor and, in search of adventure, decided to join the army.

Commissioned in 1854 as an assistant surgeon, Myer was sent to Fort Davis, Texas, a typical military post of the period, having as its main purpose the protection of settlers against hostile Indians. Not one to sit idly by and wait to treat patients at the fort's dispensary, the young doctor volunteered to accompany the troops on their patrols. During these missions, Myer first observed through his field telescope Indian scouts signaling by use of cloths or flags of different designs. Recognizing the potential of such a system, he set to work almost immediately to create a signal code of his own. Determined to keep it simple so that even a lowly (but literate) private could master it, after two years of experimentation, Myer came up with a workable visual signal alphabet. To transmit it in daylight, square-shaped white flags with a red center square or red or black flags, both with a white center square, would be used. These color combinations were considered the most visible at great distances. At night, however, either torches or lanterns would serve as the means to convey the signals.

The alphabetical system that Myer devised was far less complicated than the Morse code, yet in its way it was every bit as effective. A signaler would begin by holding a flag upright. The number "one" was indicated by moving the flag in a semicircle to the signaler's left, then immediately returning it to the upright position. "Two" was formed by a similar motion to the right, and "three" by dipping the flag to the front. These were the basic movements, the building blocks of Myer's alphabet. Letters for messages would be formed by repeating these motions in particular patterns. The letter *A,* for example, was formed by the sequence 1-1, *B* by 1-2-2-1, *C* by 2-1-2, and so on. Letters were separated by a brief pause, and words or sentences were delineated by several dip motions to the front. Once mastered, a signalman could send (by what would become known as the "wigwag" system) a fifteen- or twenty-word message in five minutes or so.

The next step was to gain army approval, no easy task given the geophysical pace at which the military bureaucracy moved when it came to new ideas. In 1856 Myer inquired if the War Department was interested in his signaling system. He heard nothing until 1859, when a military board headed by Lt. Col. Robert E. Lee approved the idea, pending further field tests. Eventually, Myer's system passed muster, and on July 2, 1860, the thirty-three-year-old doctor from Newburgh, New York, became the world's first signal officer.

Soon after his appointment, Myer, now a major, was ordered to the Southwest, where he used his invention in an expedition against the Navajo. But once the Civil War began, his Indian-fighting days were over. Summoned back East, he arrived in June 1861.

Myer was the Union's only signal officer, yet he had no men under his authority. This situation would drag on for nearly two long, frustrating years as the War Department debated whether the signal corps should be a separate unit or attached to the infantry, artillery, engineers, or Quartermaster Department. Meanwhile, Myer had to conduct his work with men detailed to him on a temporary basis, never certain how long they would stay or whether it was worthwhile training them before they were transferred to other duties.

With the Union War Department bogged down by indecision, it was the Confederacy in April 1862 that achieved the distinction of formally creating the first Signal Corps ever within a military organization. Actually, in the early years of the conflict, the South seemed more aware than the North of the tactical advantages of signaling. Soon after hostilities broke out, E. P. Alexander, one of Myer's protégés, now a captain in gray, began training a handful of recruits to serve as signalmen. At the battle of Bull Run in July 1861, Alexander and his trainees proved their worth. In the midst of the fighting, Alexander spotted an advancing Union column that otherwise went undetected and sent a wigwag message allowing the Confederates enough time to react successfully. Civilian leaders in Richmond and Southern generals in the field were quick to praise the work of Alexander and his men, some observers going so far as to suggest that they had saved the day. From then on, the Confederate signalers had strong support in high places and took part in may of the key struggles of the conflict—Island No. 10, Shiloh, Vicksburg, Atlanta, Nashville, and Petersburg-Richmond, just to name a few. But in the end, the South's Signal Corps never really lived up to its early promise.

Hardly a glamorous job, signaling failed to attract an adequate number of officers, most of whom were neither interested nor inclined toward the technological demands of the service. With so little talent available (Alexander himself left to serve as an artillery officer), the Confederacy used the same set of signals for most of the war, allowing the Union Signal Corps to intercept and read their messages on a regular basis. Concerned about the security of their transmissions, by the closing months of the conflict Southern field officers depended less on signaling and more on the traditional courier system.

The Union army's Signal Corps had a far different history. On March 3, 1863, with the War Department's approval, Congress finally passed a law establishing the position of chief signal officer with the rank of colonel, assisted by one lieutenant colonel and two majors. Each army corps or military department would be provided a signal service, headed by a captain, with no more than eight lieutenants, and with a sergeant and six soldiers for each of the officers in the unit.

Unlike the Confederacy, the Union had no trouble attracting officers and men to serve in the Signal Corps, despite the fact that all of the volunteers, whatever their rank, even Albert Myer, would have to be examined and approved by a military board. As expected, Myer received a unanimous recommendation to fill the position of colonel and chief signal officer, a process that was probably pro forma. But that was not the case for other officers interested in securing an appointment. In order to pass the examination, a candidate had to be well prepared. In addition to basic language and mathematics skills, he also had to be well groomed in science and related areas, since he might be called upon to operate a field telegraph system. "I found out what studies would be necessary," a young Connecticut lieutenant noted in his diary, "and sent North for an elementary chemistry, Prescott's Electricity, a grammar & arithmetic & crammed." While some studied privately, many officers and enlisted men prepared for the examination at a Signal Corps training camp (the first of its kind) established by Myer on Red Hill in Georgetown, just outside of Washington. In all, more than 300 officers and some 2,500 enlisted personnel were members of the signal corps at one time or another during the course of the war.

As these men found out soon enough, skill alone would not ensure their success as signalers. There were other pivotal prerequisites: height, for one. To achieve maximum efficiency, a signalman would need to secure a high observation post. Church steeples, rooftops, courthouse cupolas, even the mastheads of ships, if the action was near navigable waters, made great vantage points. Yet man-made objects were not always available. Occasionally the Signal Corps turned to nature. "Crow's nest" platforms were built on the tops of tall trees, the signalers reaching their precarious perches by means of ladders. And in the absence of trees, or other natural heights such as hills or mountains, platforms were constructed from scratch. On the Petersburg-Richmond front in 1864, towers as high as 150 feet were erected, providing a sweeping panorama of the battlefield.

Height was only one part of the equation. Good atmospheric conditions and favorable terrain were also necessities. Rain, fog, thickly wooded areas, sometimes battlefield smoke, could bring an entire signaling operation to a halt. But if all conditions were favorable, signalers, armed with flags and telescopes, could send and receive messages over an average distance of ten miles, and in some instances up to twenty-five miles.

Technically a noncombatant corps, the signalers took far more than their share of casualties. By its very nature, signaling was conspicuous work, yet vital to Union operations, something the Confederates were well aware of. Members of the corps, therefore, drew heavy enemy fire, and their death rate was alarmingly high, even by Civil War standards.

After all, if hit by a bullet or shrapnel high up in those observation posts, the difficulties of being transported and obtaining medical aid were much greater than on the ground. As Colonel Myer reported, his signalmen had a 50 percent chance of dying from wounds if shot in battle, as opposed to a rate of only 20 percent if they had served in the infantry.

Nevertheless, the risks involved did not discourage men from joining the corps. As a branch of the Union army, it was well officered and well manned, and it served in almost every important campaign. Prior to its official recognition, Myer and his volunteers could be found with McClellan on the Peninsula, and later in the midst of the carnage at Antietam and at Fredericksburg. Once organized on a more permanent basis, its towers and flags were visible at Chancellorsville, and especially at Gettysburg, where, for the first time ever, signal officers were invited by a commanding general to participate in the planning of a battle. And through the remainder of the war, whether providing intelligence to the navy—Farragut at Mobile Bay—or accompanying Sherman on his march to the sea or with Grant's armies before Petersburg and Richmond, the Signal Corps had etched a place of prominence for itself in military history.

Such a record should have secured for it a permanent position within the army; instead, its existence remained tenuous at best. In part this was due to a dispute involving the Signal Corps' founder, Colonel Myer, and Anson Stager, head of the United States Military Telegraph (USMT). Early in the war Myer, aware of the drawbacks of visual signaling, had sought to supplement his use of flags and torches with a field telegraph system. Developed by George Beardslee of New York, it was entirely portable, operating on a pile of magnets instead of batteries. At first Myer had his men employ the telegraph only for front-line communications, when the terrain or weather did not permit the wigwag system. But when he attempted to expand its use by recruiting additional operators, he ran afoul of Stager, who feared that his military telegraph organization might be depleted of trained personnel. As a close friend of Secretary of War Stanton, Stager had no difficulty winning his support. On November 10, 1863, Myer was dismissed as head of the signal corps, and all field telegraph equipment was turned over to the USMT.

While the Signal Corps continued its wartime activities, its standing was clearly diminished by the dismissal of Myer, who remained in the corps as a subordinate officer. The signalers were also hampered by no longer having access to the field telegraph, which severely limited their ability to send and receive messages in the immediate combat area. Once the war came to an end, the Signal Corps itself was disbanded on the premise that a peacetime army would have no need of its services. Within a year, however, members of Congress reconsidered, deciding that the signal unit should become a permanent part of the army, and in a reversal of previous policy, it also authorized the corps to take over the duties of the military telegraph. In the process, Albert J. Myer received vindication as well. On July 28, 1866, Congress reinstated him as chief signal officer, a position he held until his death at age fifty-two in 1880.

THE RAILROADS

Although invented by the British, railroads were made to order for Americans. By the first quarter of the nineteenth century, the United States was a sprawling nation in need of a fast and efficient transportation network. The Baltimore and Ohio was the first U.S. rail line, beginning operations in 1830. Its opening ceremonies featured Charles Carroll of Carrollton Manor, Maryland, the last surviving signer of the Declaration of Independence. Just as Carroll and his contemporaries fostered a revolution against political tyranny, this new technology wrought a transportation revolution that conquered the tyranny of distance.

Progress was slow but soon quickly accelerated. The nation was stitched together by ribbons of steel. From 1850 to 1860, some 21,000 miles of track were laid, reducing travel times significantly. At speeds averaging 30 miles per hour, trains were the fastest transportation in America. The trip from New York to Chicago, for instance, was cut from three weeks to two days.

By 1860 there were over 30,000 miles of track crisscrossing the nation, more rail mileage than in all other countries of the world combined. Yet these figures are somewhat misleading, since America's railroad lines were not equally distributed throughout the nation. The North predominated, with more than 21,000 miles; the South, an area of comparable size, had less than half that amount, some 9,000 miles. Northern railroads were also in better shape than Southern ones, with larger quantities of replacement parts available and access to more advanced technology. As early as 1859, Northern locomotives were already beginning to convert from wood to coal as their source of fuel, a process that would be completed by 1865. In addition, the free states, compared to those below the Mason-Dixon line, had far greater uniformity in track gauges (the width between the rails) from one state to another. This meant that Northern railroads could travel over long distances, crossing state borders without interruption of the flow of passengers and freight.

On the eve of the Civil War, few, if any, Northerners realized the military advantage they possessed because of their superior rail system. Even if they were aware of the fact that the British had constructed a short military railway during the Crimean War of 1854–56, and the French had moved several army corps by rail to ports of embarkation in the Franco-Austrian War of 1859, these events were hardly evidence of the railroad's potential as a critical instrument of warfare. Most Americans viewed railroads in terms of commerce and convenience, not as a conveyance for military purposes. All this would change overnight. America's Civil War would be the first conflict in the history of the world in which large numbers of troops and vast amounts of supplies were moved frequently by rail.

From the very outset, railroads proved their value. Within days after the fighting began, in mid-April 1861, Washington, D.C., found itself isolated and vulnerable to attack. Having failed to prepare adequately for the crisis, the Lincoln administration found itself in dire straits. The capital's situation looked hopeless, surrounded and threatened by pro-Confederate Virginia, soon to break its bonds with the Union, and the loyal but wavering slaveholding state of Maryland. Some 15,000 Rebel troops were reported near Alexandria, just outside of Washington, and another 8,000 at Harpers Ferry, Virginia, all making preparations to seize the city. The *Richmond Examiner* urged them on: "Our people can take it, and [General Winfield] Scott the arch traitor, and Lincoln the Beast, combined cannot prevent it." The president feared the worst, waiting anxiously for Union troops to enter the capital. Pacing in his office, Lincoln was overheard muttering, "Why don't they come? Why don't they come?" Finally, on April 25, the 7th New York Regiment arrived by train, followed by more trains, carrying troops from Massachusetts, Pennsylvania, and Rhode Island. Within two days 10,000 soldiers, transported most of the way by rail, converged on the capital. Washington was secure—and American armies had found a new means of transportation.

To ensure that the military would have ready access to the Union's rail system, in January 1862 Congress authorized the president to take possession of any railroad line if the public safety required it. The next month Lincoln appointed Daniel C. McCallum, former superintendent of the Erie Railroad, to serve as head of a new War Department agency called the United States Military Railroads (USMRR). Its chief purpose was to run and maintain lines seized by the government. At first this might have sounded ominous to the privately owned companies in the loyal North, but early on Lincoln made it clear that if a railroad supported the war effort, it had nothing to fear. As a matter of fact, the military would assist cooperative lines, helping to reconstruct and repair them, and even provide track protection if necessary. Basically the intent of the legislation (which also called for the court-martial of anyone interfering with its execution) was to frighten potentially recalcitrant owners and managers who otherwise might refuse to perform what the administration believed was their patriotic duty. The law, though of dubious constitutionality, produced the desired effect. Almost all privately owned lines in the Union extended full consideration to the military; only a few of them, either close to the battlefield or involved in a labor dispute, were ever taken over by the government.

The situation was entirely different in the war zone. As Union forces struck deep into Dixie, the United States Military Railroads took over captured lines, repaired them, ran them, and sometimes extended them. When Daniel McCallum was first appointed director of the USMRR, its personnel were few in number, and it was in possession of only a seven-mile line from Washington to Alexandria. By war's end McCallum's bureau employed 25,000 men and operated fifty different Southern lines, extending over 2,100 miles. With a combined rolling stock of 419 locomotives and 6,330 cars, the USMRR was by far the largest railroad system in the world at the time.

The Confederacy had no such organization. Lacking critical resources, unable to centralize the system because of states' rights purists, and vulnerable to seizure from invading Union forces, the Southern railroads operated under severe limitations. Ironically, however, it was the Confederacy, not the Union, that initiated the tactical use of railroads in combat. At the first battle of Bull Run on July 21, 1861, Confederate general Pierre G. T. Beauregard's outnumbered defenders of Manassas, a rail junction about 30 miles southwest of Washington, probably would have gone down in defeat if not for the arrival by train of reinforcements. By the time Union forces launched their attack, three Confederate brigades (more than 9,000 men) under the command of Gen. Joseph E. Johnston arrived on the Manassas Gap Railroad from the Shenandoah Valley. These were the troops, fresh from the trains, along with a fourth brigade, arriving 4:00 P.M. on the day of the battle, that emboldened the Confederate command to order a counterattack all along the front, forcing the Northerners into a disorderly and humiliating retreat.

Unfortunately for the South, as the war progressed its railroads grew less reliable. Without available parts, maintenance was impossible. And to make matters worse, by the end of 1863 a good part of the system had fallen into Union hands. Yet the Confederate army remained resourceful, continuing to use whatever lines were available and operational to meet their transport needs. Perhaps the most daring of all wartime tactical feats involving Southern railroads occurred in September 1863, when Confederate lieutenant general James Longstreet's 12,000-man corps was taken by train from Virginia to northern Georgia. The trip lasted nine days, required the use of sixteen different lines, and covered some 900 miles of track. Most of Longstreet's men arrived in time—either just before or during the first day of fighting—to reinforce Gen. Braxton Bragg's Army of Tennessee and contribute to the victory over Union general William E. Rosecrans's forces at Chicamauga Creek on September 19–20. It was the bloodiest two-day battle of the war, with combined casualties totaling over 34,000. Forced to retreat across the Georgia border into Chattanooga, Tennessee, Rosecrans's Army of the Cumberland soon realized that it was trapped in the city, cut off from necessary supplies and in danger of being starved out.

Like its adversary just two weeks before, the Union now had to reinforce one of its major armies in a distant theater. Within a matter of days, Lincoln issued orders that the Army of the Potomac's XIth and XIIth corps be sent by rail to break the siege of Chattanooga. Placed under the command of Gen. Joseph Hooker, the first troops boarded the train in northern Virginia on September 25 for the 1,233-mile trip to southern Tennessee. Over the next eleven and a half days, thanks to a joint effort by the United States Military Railroads and private companies, more than 23,000 men, ten batteries of artillery with their horses, and 100 cars of baggage all safely reached their destination. It was truly an unprecedented logistical feat—the first time in military history that so many troops were transported so quickly over such a long distance. And as for the outcome of the mission, it accomplished just what it set out to do. With the arrival of Hooker's relief force, the stage was set for operations leading to the eventual rescue of the beleaguered Union garrison at Chattanooga.

Less dramatic but no less important were the day-to-day Union troop transfers conducted by rail. Since only a few Northern railroads maintained separate accounts of military and nonmilitary passenger traffic, it's impossible to come up with accurate wartime totals. Yet a cursory look at one or two of those Northern rail systems that kept separate records can shed some light on the sheer numbers of soldiers involved. The Pennsylvania Railroad is a prime example. From the relief of Washington in April 1861 to the immediate postwar demobilization era, the Pennsylvania transported nearly a million bluecoats. Another line, the Illinois Central, began serving as a troop carrier in 1862 and, by the end of the conflict, had moved a half million soldiers to their destinations.

The statistics for nonhuman cargo were also unprecedented. Transporting almost every conceivable item for troops in the field—ammunition, artillery, horses, mules, cattle, pigs, wagons, tents, blankets, medical supplies, water, food, clothing, boots, and above all else, mail—railroads proved the speediest and most reliable carriers. In one year alone (1864–65), the USMRR delivered over 5 million tons of supplies to the men on the front.

Probably no troops were more dependent on this service than Gen. William Tecumseh Sherman's "boys" on their famous march to Atlanta from the first day of May to early September 1864. These men are often portrayed as rampaging "locusts" devouring and living off the land, thereby making their general's concept of total war a grim reality. They did cut a swath of destruction from Atlanta to the sea, but the truth of the matter is that Sherman's forces during most of the campaign were not cut off from their bases as is commonly believed. A single railroad served as their lifeline, supplying most of their needs in such a way that foraging never could.

Eventually that single line stretched 473 miles, all the way back to Tennessee and Kentucky, and took almost as many soldiers to guard it as were being supplied in the campaign. With a steady stream of puffing USMRR locomotives operating in convoys of four ten-car trains, the system provided about 1,600 tons of supplies each day for the advancing 100,000-man army and its 35,000 animals. "The Atlanta campaign would simply have been impossible," Sherman later wrote, "without the use of the railroads."

Modern students of the war not only are in agreement with the general, but are inclined to expand his point, arguing that the railroads played a decisive role in the outcome of the conflict itself. In "this first great railroad war of world history"—as Allan Nevins described it in his authoritative eight-volume *Ordeal of the Union*—the railroads were the main arteries through which flowed the men, the guns, and the supplies that were needed to produce a Union victory. Just as the railroads had served to bind Northerners together during the antebellum era, the rail lines sustained them in their struggle to keep the nation united in the 1860s.

GEN. ULYSSES S. GRANT

In March 1864, when President Lincoln elevated Ulysses S. Grant to a lieutenant generalship with full command of all Union armies, it was the first time since George Washington that a U.S. military officer was promoted to three-star rank. Considering the fact that only three years before, Grant was working in his father's leather goods business in Galena, Illinois, having been unable to make it on his own, the career of this extraordinary yet modest man was truly remarkable.

Born in Ohio in 1822, Grant was the son of a prosperous business-man, whose "greatest desire . . . was for the education of his children." Since there were no free public schools, Grant attended the "subscrip-tion" schools of the village. These were essentially one-room school houses, with a single, privately funded teacher offering instruction to thirty or forty students from early elementary to upper high school level. Having learned the basic fundamentals, described by Grant as "the three R's, 'Reading, Riting, Rithmetic,'" at age seventeen he received an appointment to West Point. It was his father who made the arrangements, much to the young man's chagrin. "A military life had no charms for me," he later noted in his memoirs, "and I had not the faintest idea of staying in the army even if I should be graduated, which I did not expect."

Self-doubts aside, Grant graduated from the Academy in 1843, ranking twenty-first in a class of thirty-nine. After assignments at sev-eral military posts in the South, Second Lieutenant Grant saw service in the Mexican War. Participating in no less than eight battles, he com-piled a distinguished record for himself and was promoted to first lieu-tenant—a promotion that might not have been made if his superiors had been aware of his true feelings about the war. Privately believing that the United States was the aggressor, Grant regarded the conflict with Mexico "as one of the most unjust ever waged by a stronger against a weaker nation."

Such views were rare among the soldiers who fought in Mexico. But then, Grant hardly fit the popular image of a warrior. Mild-man-nered and soft-spoken, at five feet, eight inches tall and a mere 135 pounds, the future general's personality and appearance never seemed to square with his demeanor on the battlefield. Here was a man, more-over, who hated all forms of bloodshed—even hunting. Squeamish at the sight of animal blood—an aversion that can probably be explained by the many hours he had worked in his father's tannery curing blood-soaked hides—he always wanted his meat burnt to a crisp. And he refused to touch chicken or any fowl; as he put it, "I could never eat anything that went on two legs."

By the early 1850s Grant had become a family man, devoted to his wife and children, though separated from them for extended periods of time because of military service. Assigned to outpost duty, first in Washington territory and later in Humboldt, California, Grant suffered from bouts of loneliness and depression. Despondent, he took to whiskey, something he would struggle with throughout his life. While not a chronic alcoholic, he was, in the words of a recent biographer, "a binge-drinking type of alcoholic," who might not indulge for a long time, even years, but once he started drinking again, it would be in excess.

Loneliness and alcohol were only two of his problems; he was also unhappy with his commanding officer at Humboldt, a mean-spirited man who took his frustrations out on junior officers. Having had his fill, Grant quit the army in 1854, rejoined his family, and took up farming in Missouri. He failed as a farmer. Nor did he succeed as a rent collector in St. Louis. Discouraged and suffering from migraine headaches and rheumatism, thirty-eight-year-old Grant returned home to Illinois in the summer of 1860 and worked as a clerk in his father's store.

The outbreak of war proved his salvation. Soon after taking command of an Illinois regiment, Grant's hometown congressman and self-chosen mentor, Elihu B. Washburne, saw to it that the former West Pointer and Mexican War veteran was appointed a brigadier general. Grant lived up to Washburne's expectations. In February 1862 he surrounded Fort Donelson on the Cumberland River in Tennessee, demanded "immediate and unconditional surrender," and delivered to the North its first major land victory of the war. Promoted to major general, Grant's career was on the rise—but suddenly, in early April, it almost came to an inglorious end. Confederate forces caught his army by surprise, launching a massive counterattack in southeastern Tennessee near a backwoods church called Shiloh. During the first day of the battle, Union troops were pushed back to the edge of the Tennessee River, dug in, and expected to be overrun. Grant, who had been downriver in a gunboat at the beginning of the fighting, returned in time to rally his men. On the second day, with the help of reinforcements, he took the offensive, driving the Rebels from the battlefield. It was a costly victory, with more than 13,000 bluecoats killed, wounded, or missing, compared to the Confederacy's 10,500; nevertheless, Lincoln was pleased with Grant's performance, despite rumors that the general might have been drunk at the time of the surprise attack. To a Republican politician who demanded Grant's removal, Lincoln responded: "I can't spare this man. He fights."

Whether Grant was drinking or not—and there is no evidence to indicate that he had consumed any alcohol before or during the battle of Shiloh—his reputation suffered only temporary damage. In early July 1863 his prestige in Washington and popularity throughout the North soared to new heights with his seizure of Vicksburg, the Confederacy's last remaining stronghold on the Mississippi. Less than five months later, his triumph over Chattanooga convinced practically everyone, particularly Lincoln, that Grant's place was in the East at the head of all Union armies. In early March 1864 the man from Galena, Illinois, who had never really wanted a military career, traveled to Washington to meet with the president, accept a third star, and assume command as general in chief.

With Grant's promotion came a new strategy. During the first three years of the Civil War, armies in the field fought each other along traditional lines. A campaign would begin, there would be extensive maneuvering, then all would be capped by a big and sanguinary battle. And no matter who was the victor, the pattern remained the same. After a bloody engagement of a few hours or days, the battered armies would withdraw to rest, regroup, and prepare for another contest a month, two months, or six months down the road.

But this pattern of sporadic combat became a thing of the past once Grant took charge. For the first time in American military history, soldiers were going to experience "continuous campaigning," fighting that entailed constant contact with the enemy—until it capitulated. Capitalizing on the Union's superior resources and greater manpower, Grant hoped that massive and unrelenting military pressure on the South would ultimately tip the scales in favor of the North.

With Lincoln's concurrence, the general in chief positioned the Union armies in such a way as to strike the Confederacy on several fronts at once, not easing up until all Rebel resistance was smashed. In the eastern theater, Gen. George Meade's Army of the Potomac would pursue Robert E. Lee's Army of Northern Virginia, allowing it no rest, no time to rebuild, no time to secure supplies. "Lee's army will be your objective point. Wherever Lee goes, there you will go also" were the simple and direct orders Grant gave Meade.

Meanwhile, other Union armies were to apply pressure on their respective fronts. Gen. Nathaniel Banks was instructed to move on Mobile; Gen. Benjamin F. Butler to begin operations against Richmond; Gen. Franz Sigel to secure the Shenandoah Valley; and Gen.

William Tecumseh Sherman to wreak havoc on the Deep South by taking Atlanta and Savannah. Although Banks, Butler, and Sigel failed to carry out their missions, Sherman understood perfectly the concept of continuous campaigning, as he pressed the enemy and moved forward, destroying all in his way.

Accompanying the Army of the Potomac in northern Virginia, Grant saw to it that George Meade followed his orders explicitly. "Whatever happens, there will be no turning back," the general in chief assured Lincoln. No longer would the outcome of a single battle matter; win, lose, draw—the objective was to pursue the enemy to the death. After two days of fighting in early May 1864, in a heavily wooded area known as the Wilderness, fifty miles north of Richmond, the Army of the Potomac sustained close to 18,000 casualties. Repulsed and demoralized, the men in blue were preparing to retreat as they had done so many times before. But Grant had just begun to get his hands on the enemy's throat, and heavy losses weren't going to persuade him to let go. Orders went out to advance, not retreat, a move that elicited cheers from his men, most of them not realizing, as one combat veteran later put it, that for the next month or so they were about to live "night and day within the 'valley of the shadow of death.'"

What followed were a series of indecisive yet incredibly gory battles in northern Virginia—Spotsylvania Court House, North Anna, Totopotomoy Creek, and finally Cold Harbor. In the month and a half of continuous campaigning, from early May to mid-June 1864—where, according to a Rhode Island soldier, "no one was safe, even for an instant"—the Union suffered 65,000 casualties, the Confederacy 35,000. Proportionately, however, the losses were far more damaging to the South than they were to the North. By the time Lee's Army of Northern Virginia took refuge in the trenches surrounding Petersburg, just south of Richmond, the Confederacy's main fighting force was at its lowest point. Grant's overall strategy had worked. As he explained afterward:

> Lee had to fight as much as I did. . . . Every blow I struck weakened him, and when at last he was forced into Richmond it was a far different army from that which menaced Washington and invaded Maryland and Pennsylvania. It was no longer an invading army. The Wilderness campaign was necessary to the destruction of the Southern Confederacy.

No one understood this better than Robert E. Lee. Once his crippled army retreated to the earthworks and fortifications of the Petersburg-Richmond area, Lee realized, it was "a mere question of time."

As for the architect of the Confederacy's defeat, he went on to scale new heights. A little more than a year after Appomattox, Ulysses S. Grant became the first four-star general in American history; served two terms as president of the United States; traveled around the world; and wrote a two-volume memoir, considered today a timeless classic. Yet as Grant contemplated his life shortly before his death, in his usual unassuming manner he seemed more mystified than impressed by his achievements. On July 25, 1885, he died of cancer at the age of sixty-three.

CHAPTER 4

The Naval War

The major land battles of the Civil War were so epic in scale and sanguinary in execution that they tend to overshadow the naval aspects of the conflict. Certainly the naval war, though not without dramatic incidents, has nothing to compare with such titanic struggles as Antietam or Gettysburg. Yet naval power—whether on ocean or river—was to have a profound effect on the course of the war.

When hostilities began in April 1861, vessels of canvas and wood were about to be displaced by a new kind of warship—steam-powered, propeller-driven, and iron-plated. The North, controlling 90 percent of the nation's industry, had the potential to develop into a leading naval power. The South, on the other hand, had to start virtually from scratch. As it was essentially an agrarian society, it was anyone's guess whether the Confederacy, lacking a skilled labor force and without adequate physical plants—shipyards, workshops, steam mills, and foundries—could mount a serious challenge to Union seapower.

In the early months of 1861, however, Union seapower posed little threat to the Confederacy. All told, the U.S. Navy maintained an official roster of ninety ships, but many were obsolete and out of commission. On March 4, the day of Lincoln's inauguration, only forty-two vessels were ready for action, and even this figure is misleading, since many were on foreign stations and unavailable for immediate home service. In short, Northern naval superiority was more apparent than real when Confederate batteries first opened fire.

SECRETARY OF THE NAVY GIDEON WELLES

It did not take long for the United States Navy to realize how truly ill prepared it was for operations against the South. To be sure, it had a proud fighting tradition that dated back to the Revolution and John Paul Jones, but modern techniques of war were developing that demanded more than simple courage and determination. Ship design was in transition all over the world. France and Great Britain, the first powers to build ironclad warships, were in the forefront of this naval revolution. The United States lagged far behind. Its most recently constructed vessels—wooden and propeller-driven—were essentially hybrids, amalgams of old and new that employed both sail and steam.

For the moment, the Union navy's immediate concern was sheer numbers. The exigencies of war demanded a rapid expansion of its fleet. Was the Navy Department equal to the challenge? Not only did it measure up to the task at hand, but the department succeeded beyond all expectations. The United States became the first country in the history of the world to increase its naval strength from 42 combat-ready vessels to 427 such vessels—more than tenfold—in less than two years. Nor did the growth end there; by December 1864, the navy totaled 671 ships, including 71 ironclads.

The man most responsible for this miracle was Lincoln's secretary of the navy, Gideon Welles. Welles was a fifty-eight-year-old Connecticut native whose stern visage and long white beard gave him the appearance of an Old Testament prophet. A former Democratic newspaper editor who joined the Republicans in 1855, he was efficient, incorruptible, and perceptive. Although his appointment was purely a political one, designed to placate New Englanders, Welles actually had some experience in naval affairs. During and immediately after the Mexican War, he served in James K. Polk's administration as chief of the navy's Bureau of Provisions and Clothing, where he proved himself competent and honest, never once using his office to further his own ends. In fact, there was not one false note about the man—except the ill-fitting henna-gray wig he wore to hide his bald head.

To Washington insiders, Welles was old "Father Neptune," and the secretary knew where to poke his trident to get the desired results. One of his first orders was to recall vessels on foreign stations, several of them taking as long as two years to come back. More importantly, the secretary coordinated the effort to charter or purchase ships from civilian sources and to order new ones from both private and government shipyards. Personnel kept up with the expansion; in 1861, the 42 ships were crewed by 7,600 men, and by 1864, the 671 vessels were manned by 51,500 sailors. Shipbuilding facilities also expanded to meet the unprecedented demand. When the war began, the shipyards employed 3,844 men; four years later, 17,000.

It was with justifiable pride that Secretary of the Navy Gideon Welles declared, "The annals of the world do not show so great an increase in so brief a period to the naval power of any country."

THE BLOCKADE

The Confederacy had an agricultural economy, largely dependent on outsiders for manufactured goods. For decades, cotton—some called it "white gold"—fueled that economic system, and as long as the South continued to export it, the credit needed to wage war would be available. But if the Rebel coastline were blockaded, denied the vital sea trade from Europe and elsewhere, economic strangulation might ensue. With its economy in ruins, the South would have to submit.

At least that was the strategic theory embraced by the Lincoln administration early in the war. Whether or not it would work depended upon the U.S. Navy, which—for the first time in its history—imposed a major blockade. Such tactics were not unprecedented; the British had blockaded Napoleonic Europe some fifty years before. Continental in scope and scale, the British effort, however, was dwarfed by the Union navy's Civil War blockade.

At first, the job seemed impossible; the South's 3,500 miles of coastline included ten major ports and 180 inlets, bays, and navigable river mouths. On the very day Lincoln announced the blockade, April 19, 1861, Secretary Welles had exactly three ships available for the task.

Southern blockade runners wasted no time exploiting the situation. Making a name for themselves as well as a good deal of money, the runners shipped out of port loaded with cotton and came back with a wide variety of goods. But in some ways their successes, if measured strictly in terms of the war effort, were not as impressive as they appeared to be. Too much cargo space was allotted to luxury goods (which yielded the highest profits), not to precious war-related materiel. Rifles, saddles, and saltpeter were mixed with brandy, bonnets, fine wines, and soap. Not until 1864 did the Confederate government try to stop the wasteful importation of luxuries, but by then it was too late.

As scores of Union ships—eventually hundreds—were drafted for patrol duty off the Southern coastline, the blockade grew more effective. In 1861 the chance of a blockade runner being captured was only one in ten; by 1864 it was one in three; and as the war drew to a close in early 1865, it was one in two.

This was an impressive accomplishment for the Union navy, but apparently it gave little satisfaction to the men who helped bring it about. For them, despite an occasional exciting chase or capture of a rich prize, blockade duty was monotonous in the extreme. Ships were crowded, discipline was harsh, the diet plain. Boredom, not projectiles from enemy cannons, was the chief risk Union sailors took while on station. A seaman serving off the coast of Wilmington, North Carolina, wrote to his mother, suggesting that she could get some insight into what blockade duty was like if she were to "go to the roof on a hot summer day, talk to a half dozen degenerates, descend to the basement, drink tepid water full of iron rust, climb to the roof again, and repeat the process at intervals until . . . fagged out, then go to bed with everything shut tight."

Was the blockade successful? Some historians believe that it virtually won the war for the North by destroying the Southern economy. But others maintain that the blockade was ineffective, pointing out the half a million rifles, the thousand tons of gunpowder, and the several hundred cannons that were imported. Still others adopt a more balanced view, stressing that the blockade alone did not defeat the South, but there's no question that it weakened and isolated it, softening it up for the final, land-based blows.

Whatever the impact, no one can deny the grandeur of the effort. Secretary Welles did not exaggerate when he noted that the blockade was "greater in extent than the whole coast of Europe from Cape Trafalgar to Cape North . . . an undertaking without precedent in history."

THE CSS *VIRGINIA*

A new epoch in naval warfare dawned when on March 8, 1862, the Confederate ironclad *Virginia* sank the USS *Cumberland* and the USS *Congress* off Hampton Roads in Virginia. These two sail-driven, wooden warships were simply no match for the Rebel ironclad. A disaster of unprecedented proportions for the U.S. Navy, it was the first time ever that an enemy ship had sunk two of its vessels in a matter of hours.

How did the Confederacy, if only for a brief moment, achieve this upper hand in the naval war with the Union? Perhaps it could be understood best by bearing in mind that the South had no navy to begin with, so it was open to innovation and experimentation. Literally, something was better than nothing. As a fledgling service, the Confederate navy had no entrenched bureaucracy or narrow-minded officer corps to deal with. It was also blessed with a secretary who had both vision and experience—a potent combination for a wartime leader.

The secretary of the Confederate navy was Stephen Russell Mallory. Born in 1813 in Trinidad, West Indies, he moved with his family to Key West, Florida, in 1820. After securing a position as a customs inspector there in 1833, Mallory studied to become a lawyer. An amiable fellow, "he had much calm common sense [and] great patience"— which probably contributed to his political success. In 1851 Mallory was elected to the U.S. Senate from Florida, and over much of the next decade, he served as chairman of the Naval Affairs Committee. But all this came to an abrupt end when he resigned his seat and followed his state out of the Union in 1861.

As head of the Confederate navy, Mallory was free to test his ideas with little interference from President Jefferson Davis. Open-minded and innovative, Mallory immediately recognized the enormous potential of ironclads. These iron-plated vessels might disrupt the blockade and might even bring the war to the North by bombarding New York or other coastal cities. The latter idea proved overambitious, however, since ironclads were poorly designed as seafaring craft. But they were fully capable of wreaking havoc upon the Union blockade, along with providing protection to Southern coastal rivers.

The most famous of all Southern ironclads was the CSS *Virginia,* built from the salvaged hull of a Union vessel called the *Merrimack.* Much of the credit for transforming the *Merrimack* into a new iron-sheathed creation belonged to Confederate navy commander John Mercer Brooke. A professional sailor who had served in the U.S. Navy before the war, Brooke resigned his commission after his state Virginia seceded and became a lieutenant in the infant Confederate navy. In late June 1861 Brooke, supported by naval builder J. L. Porter and chief engineer William P. Williamson, presented his plans for the *Merrimack* to Secretary Mallory, who accepted the proposal without hesitation.

After many delays, the *Merrimack*—rechristened the *Virginia*— was finally rebuilt. The hull, almost entirely submerged, was approximately 270 feet long (no precise measurements have survived) and served as a platform for a large central portion, housing the artillery, that rose like a metal mountain about 180 feet in length and some 24 feet above the waterline. The four-inch armor-plated superstructure was angled at 36 degrees to allow enemy shot to bounce off instead of penetrating. This strange craft was neither fish nor fowl, and contemporaries were hard pressed to describe such a monstrosity. "A barn floating with its roof above water" was one try, but another observer with even more imagination saw the *Virginia* as "a huge, half-submerged crocodile."

The CSS *Virginia* was armed with ten guns, and crewed by about 320 men. One drawback, which might be considered the vessel's Achilles' heel, was its slow, sluggish engines. Steerage was also so poor it took thirty to forty minutes to turn 180 degrees. And for all its "futuristic" design, one feature was wedded to the distant past. The ship had a submerged cast-iron ram that was designed to penetrate and sink wooden hulls. Ramming is almost as old as naval warfare itself; it was successfully employed by the Greeks against the Persians at Salamis in 480 B.C.

There was no time for sea trials; instead, the *Virginia* was to have a trial by fire. It was hoped the ironclad would break the back of the Union blockade at Hampton Roads. The Roads is a body of water where the James, Elizabeth, and Nansemond Rivers flow into the broad Chesapeake. The U.S. ships on duty there included the *Minnesota, Roanoke, St. Lawrence, Cumberland,* and *Congress.* The last three were sailing ships, considered antiquated by many, and today's action would give them a final push into oblivion.

On March 8, 1862, the *Virginia* ventured forth on its first combat mission, accompanied by two Confederate vessels named *Raleigh* and *Beaufort.* It took time for the lumbering leviathan to reach its targets, so the element of surprise was lost. It was hardly a tactical setback, since the commander of the *Virginia,* Commodore Franklin Buchanan, a long-time navy man who knew his business, had already zeroed in on his first target. His intended victim was the *Cumberland*, which he hoped to ram and send to the bottom.

As the *Virginia* approached the *Cumberland*, the *Congress* exchanged fire with the ironclad. But the *Congress*'s shots caused little serious damage, simply bouncing off the *Virginia*'s thick iron hide. By contrast, the *Virginia*'s broadsides were lethal, its mushrooming shell bursts tearing great holes in the Union vessel. Direct hits not only killed those unfortunate enough to be in their path, but also sent up wooden splinters from the shattered hull. Showers of splinters lacerated and impaled; men were disemboweled, decapitated, or had their limbs blown off. Blood was everywhere—but the *Congress* still remained afloat, at least for the time being.

Yet nothing could stop the ironclad's inexorable advance. The *Cumberland* was rammed, its hull sustaining a wound that proved mortal. As the ship sank, it nearly took the *Virginia* with it, because the ram was stuck fast in the very hole it created. Luckily the ram broke off, enabling the ironclad to escape disaster. The *Cumberland* went down with its flag still flying, taking with it 121 officers and men.

Now it was the *Congress*'s turn. The ship had been deliberately grounded in shallow waters, so the *Virginia* simply kept its distance and pounded the Union vessel into submission. After an hour of punishment, the *Congress* hauled down its ensign and surrendered. Shortly after, the *Congress* was aflame, with great, black coils of smoke rising into the sky signaling its demise. The flagship *Minnesota* was the next intended victim, having also run aground in an effort to succor its sister ship. With the coming of night, however, the *Minnesota* was given a reprieve. The *Virginia* broke off the attack, planning to return the next day.

It had been a frustrating and demoralizing day for the U.S. Navy. Massive Union broadsides had little effect on the Confederate ironclad. Casualties aboard the *Virginia* were light, standing at two dead and several wounded. Two guns had been knocked out and a few iron plates loosened, but for the most part, Union fire had "no more effect than peas from a pop-gun."

When the sun set that Saturday, March 8, 1862, it also set on the great days of sails and wooden ships.

THE USS *MONITOR*

Official Washington was thrown into a frenzy when it first received reports that the CSS *Virginia* sank the Union ships *Cumberland* and *Congress* at Hampton Roads. Lincoln himself was shaken by the news, as were most members of his cabinet when they met in an emergency session the day after the battle on March 9, 1862. Secretary of War Edwin M. Stanton, in particular, seemed on the verge of panic, pacing up and down and gesticulating wildly. Conjuring up horrific images of the *Virginia* on a destructive rampage, the secretary pictured New York and Boston destroyed, and Washington itself reduced to rubble.

Stanton's pessimism was not shared by everyone. Secretary of the Navy Gideon Welles was a rock of calm in a sea of emotion; the tough, old New Englander wasn't about to lose his head. He knew that, if all went well, the Union would have an answer to the Confederate ironclad. Expressing these views to the president and members of the cabinet, Welles went on to inform them that as he spoke, a Union ironclad was on its way to Hampton Roads. Christened the USS *Monitor,* it was more than a match for the *Virginia*, the secretary assured them.

Welles's confidence was not misplaced. The *Monitor,* an armored ship, was truly a unique and formidable vessel, the first in U.S. naval history to be armed with a revolving gun turret. As a matter of fact, that turret can claim to be the "ancestor" of today's gun turrets, and the

Monitor itself an early prototype of the "all-big-guns-on-the-center-line" kind of vessel—in other words, the modern battleship.

The Union's decision to support construction of the *Monitor* was in direct response to the Confederacy's involvement with ironclads. When the *Virginia* was being built from the salvaged remains of the USS *Merrimack,* Union spies kept Washington apprised of the situation. Secretary Welles wasn't an ironclad promoter, but the news of Confederate activities pushed him in that direction. Since the entrenched navy bureaucracy was notoriously conservative and unwilling to move forward on the matter, Welles got Congress to take it up. Capitol Hill solons passed a bill that called for the creation of a navy board to review plans for the "construction or completing of iron or steel clad steamships or steam batteries."

The navy board thus formed approved two conventional designs that became the ironclads *Galena* and *New Ironsides* respectively. But the third proposal, submitted by maritime engineer John Ericsson, was radical in concept and innovative in design. Ericsson's drawings would soon take concrete shape in the form of the celebrated *Monitor.*

A highly talented if erratic engineer, Ericsson was born in Sweden on July 31, 1803. Blessed with an unusual aptitude for things mechanical, he soon made a name for himself as a nautical engineer. It was Ericsson, for example, who was instrumental in having the screw propeller adopted in place of inefficient paddle wheels, a major contribution to naval technology. On a personal level, however, the Swede was cranky and thin-skinned, ready to take offense at real or imagined slights. Proud and difficult to work with, Ericsson seemed unable to acknowledge mistakes or share credit in triumphs. But he was a brilliant man.

Although Ericsson did not design the *Monitor* to challenge the *Virginia* (it had already been on the drawing board before word of the *Virginia* surfaced), the inventor was still under a construction deadline set by Washington. Thriving under the pressure, and despite his irascibility, Ericsson lived up to the agreement. When the *Monitor* was launched from Greenpoint, Brooklyn, on January 30, 1862, it was two weeks ahead of the *Virginia*'s own launch.

The *Monitor* featured a flat deck 172 feet long, covered with iron plating $4\frac{1}{2}$ inches thick. The ironclad had only 2 feet of freeboard; in other words, its raftlike deck barely rose above the bobbing waterline. That meant that the *Monitor*'s engines, boilers, magazines, staterooms, and crew berths were below the waterline. Sailors who wished to relieve themselves could not go to an open-air "head," so another means of waste disposal had to be devised. Ericsson came up with an air pump device that was attached to a privy—in essence a flush toilet, the first time a warship ever had one.

The *Monitor*'s revolving gun turret, however, was its most significant innovation, and its crowning glory. Sitting squarely in the middle of the ship, the turret measured nine feet high, with an inside diameter of twenty feet, and was heavily armored and rounded to have enemy shot ricochet off. The turret was turned by a small steam engine, and that enabled it to revolve a full 360 degrees. Since the turret could move, the ship did not have to maneuver as much to fight. Armament was provided by two smoothbore guns with eleven-inch-diameter bores, each capable of firing 180-pound round shot.

Recent scholarship has suggested that Ericsson borrowed the concept of a revolving gun turret from another inventor, one Theodore Timby. In the early 1840s Timby began peddling his turret idea to such disparate personalities as John C. Calhoun and the emperor of China. Interest was expressed in Washington, but in the end it was "sound and fury," signifying nothing. Timby could not get anyone to use his idea. Refusing to capitulate, he developed a working model, which he displayed in New York City, and his efforts were detailed in a number of newspapers. It is more than possible that Ericsson saw the model or read the accounts.

In any event, no one can deny that Ericsson was a genius who took various elements—perhaps borrowed, perhaps products of his own brain—and combined them to produce a unique vessel. The USS *Monitor,* variously described as a "cheese box on a raft" or a "tin can on a shingle," would have a profound influence on naval design.

ENCOUNTER AT HAMPTON ROADS

It was Sunday morning, March 9, 1862, but for the sailors of the CSS *Patrick Henry* it was anything but a day of rest. In the distance, the USS *Minnesota* lay helplessly aground at Hampton Roads, Virginia. The day before, the Confederate ironclad *Virginia* had gone through the Union blockading fleet like a wolf in a sheepfold, sinking two federal ships with near impunity. Aboard the *Patrick Henry,* a small vessel accompanying the *Virginia* on its second sortie, Lt. James Rochelle fixed his gaze on the USS *Minnesota* in the distance. But the *Minnesota* had a companion, a protector, who guarded the larger ship with bulldog tenacity.

Rochelle was almost mesmerized by the newcomer. It was, as he put it, "a craft such as the eyes of a seaman never looked upon before, an immense shingle floating on the water, with a gigantic cheesebox rising from its center; no sails, no wheels, no smokestack, no guns. What could it be?"

The coming battle of Hampton Roads would soon answer Rochelle's question. The strange apparition was the USS *Monitor.* For the first time in the history of naval combat, two ironclads would meet in open battle. The *Monitor* was commanded by Lt. John L. Worden and had a complement of fifty-eight men. The vessel had been named *Monitor* because a monitor is one who admonishes and corrects wrongdoers. The ship's two smoothbore cannons were fully prepared to give the Southerners a taste of "correction" with the first salvo.

The Union ironclad had only just arrived in the nick of time. The *Monitor* had to protect the *Minnesota* from being finished off by the rapacious *Virginia.* The ironclads approached each other. They then circled and maneuvered in a deadly, lumbering *pas de deux,* a "ballet" accompanied by the thundering reports of their own salvos. According to an observer on board the *Minnesota,* "Gun after gun was fired by the *Monitor,* which was returned with whole broadsides by the Rebels with no more effect, apparently, than so many pebblestones thrown by a child."

The *Monitor* and the *Virginia* kept fighting for four grueling hours, armored leviathans that couldn't seem to get the better of one another. Cannons roared and flamed, spouting huge puffs of smoke, but the monsters' "barks" seemed worse than their "bites." Neither ship suffered a single man killed nor serious damage, even though they were less than a hundred yards apart for most of the battle.

The *Virginia*'s commander, Lt. Catesby ap R. Jones, who had succeeded Capt. Franklin Buchanan when the latter had been wounded in the previous day's action, tried to ram the *Monitor,* with scant success. But a direct hit on the *Monitor*'s pilothouse threw up bits of iron, powder, and cement into Lieutenant Worden's eyes, temporarily blinding him. Command of the Union ironclad was turned over to Lt. Samuel Dana Greene, though by then the battle was winding down. Both ships broke off the fighting as if by mutual consent.

Who won the battle? Most authorities say it was a draw, which it was in the strict technical sense. But perhaps the North won in the long run, because the Confederate ironclad threat to its vulnerable wooden fleet was neutralized.

Two months after the battle, the Confederates had to fall back from Hampton Roads, forcing them to blow up the *Virginia* to prevent its capture. The *Monitor* met a watery end on December 31, 1862, while being towed south for blockade duty. A heavy storm struck and sunk the iron-clad off Cape Hatteras, North Carolina, with a loss of sixteen hands.

In 1973 the wreck of the *Monitor* was discovered lying upside down in 230 feet of water. Although divers have continued to explore the sunken vessel in efforts to salvage what they can, recent surveys show that the ironclad's condition is deteriorating, a victim of ocean corrosion.

BY SEA TO THE PENINSULA

"On to Richmond!" was the cry that rallied the North during the early months of the war. The Confederate capital became the ultimate goal in the minds of many Northerners, as if its capture would make the Rebels magically collapse like a house of cards. Richmond's fall would have been a grievous blow, but since when was a capital a country? Recognizing the futility of the Union's strategy, *The Times* of London noted, "It is one thing to drive the 'rebels' from the south bank of the Potomac, or even to occupy Richmond, but another to reduce and hold in permanent subjection a tract of country nearly as large as Russia in Europe."

Nevertheless, Richmond remained a major goal. But how to take it? Union general George B. McClellan, commander of the Army of the Potomac, devised a plan that was conceptually bold as well as strategically sound. He would take his army down to the Virginia Peninsula flanked by the James and York Rivers. That way, McClellan would be only seventy miles from Richmond and would have to cross only two rivers to get to the city. The more direct landward approach from Washington, D.C., would mean a distance of one hundred miles and a half dozen rivers to cross. And since the approach was from a peninsula, the Union navy could guard his flanks and resupply him by sea in the bargain.

McClellan's plan called for 100,000 men to be transported by sea to the Peninsula, a gigantic undertaking that fell upon the shoulders of Quartermaster General Montgomery C. Meigs and Assistant Secretary of War John Tucker. Using the resources at their disposal almost to the point of exhaustion, they were able to gather all sorts of seagoing craft, including 71 side-wheel steamers; 57 propeller-driven steamers; 187 schooners, brigs, and barks; and 90 barges. Altogether there were 405 vessels, an aggregate of 86,278 tons.

Right from the very beginning, McClellan had assumed that his transported army would be secure, thanks to Union naval power, but he had not reckoned with Confederate ingenuity. On March 8, 1862, well before the first Union soldiers set foot aboard the assembled flotilla, the Confederate ironclad *Virginia* sank the Union warships *Cumberland* and *Congress* at Hampton Roads. The fate of McClellan's plans hung in the balance; a rampaging *Virginia* might conceivably attack Union troop ships as they arrived. Fortunately for the general and his men, the *Virginia*'s threat was neutralized the next day by the Union ironclad *Monitor,* so the seaborne invasion could proceed safely.

Embarkation began on March 17. Not only did the assembled ships carry over 100,000 troops, they also transported 300 pieces of artillery, 3,600 supply wagons, 700 ambulances, 25,000 horses and mules, 2,500 head of cattle, and 600,000 rations. The entire operation went off without a hitch, and by early April all men and cargo had been deposited at the Peninsula's tip at Fort Monroe.

Despite the spectacular success the War Department had in transporting the army, it had no such success in getting it to fight. The Peninsula campaign, as it became known, was ultimately a failure, and much of the blame rests with McClellan. Having made the Army of the Potomac a truly magnificent fighting force, the general seemed to lack the will to use it effectively. As a field commander, he was slow, over-cautious, and readily believed exaggerated reports of enemy numbers. On the Peninsula, McClellan wasted a precious month laying siege to Yorktown, rather than taking the city quickly, then following it up with a rapid advance. There were other reasons for the debacle as well. The weather didn't cooperate; April rains turned dusty roads into muddy quagmires. And then there were the brilliant maneuvers of Confederate generals Robert E. Lee and Thomas "Stonewall" Jackson. But probably it was McClellan's own poor generalship that doomed the campaign.

Yet nothing could take away the magnificent achievement of Quartermaster General Meigs and his associates. Not only did they transport a huge army by sea—the first large-scale seaborne movement of troops in American history—but they also managed to keep the 100,000-man force supplied in the ensuing months, feats not often appreciated by most scholars.

TORPEDOES

The Civil War was the first conflict ever in which water mines, or torpedoes, as they were then called, were used extensively. The concept was not new to naval warfare. David Bushnell had attempted to sink a British warship with a small barrel filled with gunpowder during the American Revolution, and Robert Fulton, best known as the inventor of the first commercially successful steamboat, did some experimenting with explosive devices early in the nineteenth century. Later the Russians tried to use torpedoes during the Crimean War.

At a time when war was still regarded as a sort of gentlemanly endeavor, torpedoes, whether used in land or sea combat, were considered to be unsporting at best and diabolical at worst—truly "infernal machines," as contemporaries called them. They were sinister because they gave no warning when they exploded. The idea of a night mine blowing up a shipload of sleeping sailors, for example, was viewed with horror.

Partly because it was well suited to their overall defensive strategy, but primarily because they had no choice, Southerners embraced the torpedo concept. The Confederacy had some 3,500 miles of vulnerable coastline to guard. With lethal necklaces of torpedoes protecting such vital ports as Wilmington (North Carolina), Charleston, and Mobile, the Union navy might be less inclined to launch an attack.

The Confederacy's wholesale adoption of torpedoes owed much to one man, Matthew Fontaine Maury. When the war broke out, Maury was a fifty-five-year-old career naval officer of international renown. Called the "Pathfinder of the Seas," Maury was an oceanographer whose careful studies made major contributions in the fields of meteorology and hydrography. His books, such as *The Physical Geography of the Sea,* offered detailed information for mariners around the world.

After Virginia seceded from the Union, Maury, like Robert E. Lee, could not find it in his heart to draw his sword against his native state. Resigning his commission in the U.S. Navy, he was subsequently appointed a commander in the Confederate sea services. Crippled some years before in a carriage accident, he was not an agile man, which put his life in considerable jeopardy once he began experimenting with torpedoes.

Torpedoes came in all shapes and sizes. Probably the most common water mine in the Southern arsenal was the keg torpedo, a five- or ten-gallon, cigar-shaped wooden container filled with powder. Then there were torpedoes made by using iron cylinders, which in turn were loaded with powder and suspended beneath floating casks or barrels. Sometimes torpedoes would be launched in a hit-or-miss fashion by releasing them to float free in the current. Detonation methods varied as well. Some ignited on contact via percussion or chemical fuses, others went off via a trigger that was pulled by a lanyard, and still others were detonated electrically by a galvanic battery.

It did not take long for Maury to come to the conclusion that torpedoes were an absolute, if grim, necessity of war. In his view, these explosive water devices were a way the resource-starved South could counter Federal sea power. As for any moral qualms about using such "instruments of terror," if Maury harbored any, they were dispelled once the North declared that medicines and medical instruments were contraband of war to be denied the Confederacy.

Once he convinced himself that torpedoes were the answer, Maury went to work with a will. In mid-June 1861 a demonstration was arranged for the Confederate secretary of the navy Stephen Mallory and several other dignitaries. The place chosen for the test was on the James River, off what was appropriately called Rockett's Wharf. With the help of his young son Richard, Maury set off a torpedo that sent a white plume of water spurting skyward some 20 feet into the air. It was a highly impressive display, and the government officials who witnessed it were more than willing to use their influence to advance Maury's ideas. Eventually, the Confederate Congress appropriated $50,000 for the further development of the weapon, raised Maury to the rank of captain, and placed him in charge of the "Sea-Coast, Harbor, and River Defenses of the South."

Torpedoes served the Confederacy well, inflicting both material and psychological damage on the Federals. During the course of the war, no less than forty-three Union vessels were sunk or damaged by mines. Years later a Union sailor wrote, "We dreaded torpedoes more than anything else."

MINESWEEPERS

In early December 1862 Union naval captain Henry Walke was ordered to take his squadron and ascend the Yazoo River in northwestern Mississippi. His mission was to clear the river of all Confederate vessels and to prevent the enemy from establishing any position of strength along the tributary. The operation was part of an overall plan to neutralize the surrounding area so that the Union army would have less resistance when they attempted to capture the Confederate fortress of Vicksburg on the Mississippi River.

Captain Walke proceeded up the Yazoo with a powerful squadron, which included the *Marmora* and *Signal* (popularly known as "tinclads" because they were lightly armored), the ironclads *Cairo* and *Pittsburgh,* and the ironclad ram *Queen of the West.* Upon arriving at the mouth of the Yazoo, Walke ordered a reconnoitering probe upriver. On December 11 the tinclads *Marmora* and *Signal* cautiously steamed up the Yazoo, where they encountered scows and "stationary" floats bobbing innocently in the water. Suddenly, there was an explosion near the *Signal*. Although no damage was done to the vessel, the Union commanders decided to leave the area. As they withdrew, riflemen on board the *Marmora* fired shots at the floats, and another explosion occurred, producing a towering geyser of water not fifty feet away from the tinclad. It was thought that the musket fire had hit a mine and exploded it, when, in fact, both explosions, the first near the *Signal* and the other as they were leaving, were "command-detonated," which meant that Confederate torpedo corps members onshore, who had rigged these mines to explode by pulling on a lanyard, were actually responsible for the detonations.

When the captains of the vessels reported their findings, Walke decided to dispatch a reconnaissance in force. The tinclads went back upriver the next morning, this time accompanied by the *Cairo, Pittsburgh,* and *Queen of the West*. Their specific orders were to clear the river of enemy torpedoes. The *Signal* and *Marmora* led the flotilla, with small boats preceding them searching for any suspicious objects. Just behind the tinclads were the ram and the ironclads. The sailors in the lead boats located the mines; when possible, lifted them from the water and deactivated them; and if that proved too dangerous, fired upon the objects in an attempt to cause them to explode. It was the first minesweeping mission in American naval history.

USS *CAIRO*

The USS *Cairo* was an ironclad built in St. Louis by James B. Eads, the engineer later famed for constructing the first steel bridge over the Mississippi River. The ship was 175 feet long, and to allow enemy shot to bounce off, it was sheathed in armor 35 degrees at the bow and 45 degrees at the stern. The *Cairo,* a powerful vessel, earned a place in history not by its design, but because it was the first warship ever to be sunk by a mine during combat.

The vessel was part of a five-boat flotilla that, on December 12, 1862, ascended Mississippi's Yazoo River. The squadron moved with great caution since a previous reconnaissance trip had discovered Confederate mines about twenty miles from the river's mouth. The tinclads *Signal* and *Marmora* led the stately procession, with small boats out front to clear mines. The ironclad *Cairo* was just behind the *Marmora,* but when the tinclad rounded a bend of the river it was momentarily lost from sight.

The captain of the *Cairo* was Lt. Comdr. Thomas Selfridge, who came from a seafaring family. A good officer, Selfridge realized later that he had acted impulsively. When he heard firing from the direction of the still unseen *Marmora*, he ordered full steam, but his "rescue attempt" proved a false alarm. The tinclad was not under enemy fire, just shooting at Confederate torpedoes. Moments later, however, the *Cairo* was rocked by two explosions under the port quarter and port bow—the ship had struck mines.

The stricken vessel sank within a matter of twelve minutes, but luckily, though half a dozen men were hurt, there were no fatalities. The *Cairo* had fallen victim to a pair of five-gallon powder-filled demi-johns attached to wooden floats and connected by some fifty feet of wire suspended below the surface. The wire had been caught and tripped by the unfortunate ship, resulting in the ignition of the torpe-does' friction fuses.

Selfridge came under a lot of sarcastic criticism from those who were abundantly blessed with twenty-twenty hindsight. One officer humorously noted, "On December 12 Lieutenant Commander Selfridge of the *Cairo* found two torpedoes and removed them by placing his ves-sel over them." Such mockery tended to obscure the positive effect the *Cairo*'s loss had in that it spurred the Federals to greater caution and ingenuity. Col. Charles R. Ellet invented a huge 65-foot torpedo rake made of logs festooned by grappling hooks designed to gather up the mines and pull them to the surface. Crude but effective, the torpedo rake was not foolproof but at least neutralized the mines in the Yazoo River.

CSS *DAVID*

The CSS *David* was yet another Confederate attempt to drive the all-powerful Union navy from Southern shores. A group of men headed by Theodore Stoney and Dr. St. Julien Ravenal pooled their resources and created the Southern Torpedo Company of Charleston, South Carolina. Its first venture was the creation of the *David,* a peculiar little vessel that was a cross between a surface craft and a submarine. Yet this strange incarnation was destined to leave its mark on naval history—as the first torpedo boat ever to inflict damage on a warship.

The fifty-foot-long, sardine-shaped little craft kept a low profile in the water—so low, in fact, that its deck was awash. What little of the superstructure remained above the surface was semicamouflaged by bluish gray paint. Powered by a steam engine, its main armament was a spar torpedo, a sixty-pound explosive charge that was attached to the tip of a fourteen-foot shaft and projected from the vessel's nose like the "sword" of a swordfish. Ideally, the torpedo boat would poke its spar nose into the hull of an enemy ship, the pressure detonating the torpedo.

The *David* was named probably because its intended targets were the Goliaths of the Union navy, powerful ironclad warships. Only six feet wide, the torpedo boat was so small that the rest of its armament included double-barrel shotguns and handguns, not cannons. Once completed, the vessel was turned over to the Confederate navy for use at Charleston. Blockading Union ships ringed the outside harbor, tempting targets for the lilliputian ship's maiden mission.

After some consultation, the monstrous Union ironclad *New Ironsides* was selected as the *David*'s first target. The *New Ironsides* was a Goliath indeed, a lumbering metal beast that was a thorn in the Confederacy's side and a virtual symbol of Union predominance at sea.

Lt. William T. Glassel was placed in command of the *David*. Also among the six-man crew were Pilot J. Walker Cannon and Engineer James H. Tomb. The night of October 5, 1863, was chosen as the time of the attack on the *New Ironsides*. The *David* was finally going into combat, its steam engines throbbing a rhythmic tattoo. Darkness, coupled with the ship's low profile, enabled the torpedo boat to escape detection until the last moment.

The *David* managed to get so close to the *New Ironsides* that the iron behemoth's guns could not bear—that is, elevate low enough to put the torpedo boat in harm's way. Although Union sailors aboard the ironclad peppered the *David* with small-arms fire, and the torpedo boat crew replied with shotgun blasts, this was just the curtain raiser to the main event. The *David*'s torpedo rammed into the *New Ironsides*' massive hull, resulting in a huge explosion that sent a "tidal wave" of water welling upward. The geyserlike spout rained down on the torpedo boat, pouring into its smokestack and extinguishing its boiler.

The *New Ironsides* did not sink, but it was badly damaged. Those aboard the *David* were too concerned with survival to be in a jubilant mood; with no power, the little torpedo boat bobbed about the Union fleet like a toy in a bathtub. Glassel gave the order to abandon ship, but he and another member of the crew, James Sullivan, were spotted by Union sailors, plucked from the water, and made prisoners.

The attack had a curious epilogue. Engineer Tomb noticed that the *David* was still intact, so he swam back. With the help of the ship's pilot, J. Walker Cannon, Tomb got the *David* under way. The little boat managed to reach base safely.

Eight more *David*-like torpedo boats were made, but none were used. It's open to speculation as to why they were never employed. Perhaps it was because the spar torpedo arrangement was almost as dangerous to the attacker as it was to the target.

THE UNIVERSITY OF VIRGINIA

Today universities and colleges play a leading role in the research and development of new technologies, but back in 1861 the idea was novel. Confederate naval captain Matthew Fontaine Maury, who was in the midst of developing electrical water mines and other such devices for the defense of Confederate harbors and rivers, decided to enlist the aid of the University of Virginia. At his urging, the Board of Visitors of the university was requested to set up a research lab to be manned by faculty under the overall auspices of the Virginia Ordnance Department.

The University of Virginia was an obvious choice for such a venture. The defense of the Old Dominion was a primary concern, so it was natural for its premier institution of higher learning to become involved. A research lab was set up on campus in the summer of 1861, focusing on the production of gunpowder and chemicals for use in electrical devices, especially galvanic batteries.

Soon the university lab was in full swing. Maury worked closely with faculty Professors Socrates Maupin and James Lawrence Cabell. But in the end, plagued by shortages of chemicals—"our minds are at a loss with regard to sulphur," Maury conceded—their efforts contributed little to the Confederate cause. The University of Virginia, however, had broken new ground as the first American institution of higher learning involved in the research and development of military technology.

A TORPEDO GONE AWRY

The image, reinforced by scores of World War II movies, is an indelible one. A submerged submarine stalks a surface ship, then launches a torpedo to sink it. Yet few are aware that the first time a self-propelled torpedo ever sunk a ship occurred not in World War II, or even World War I, but in the Civil War.

It began as the brainchild of Washington, D.C., inventor Pascal Plant. In those days, the president of the United States was more accessible to the general public, so Plant, armed with nothing but enthusiasm and a small model, was able to have an interview with Abraham Lincoln. The inventor was basically trying to sell his idea of a rocket-propelled gunboat. Lincoln must have thought the idea had merit, because he sent Plant on to the Navy Ordnance Bureau. But as far as the bureau was concerned, Plant's vessel was "altogether speculative" and not even worthy of a trial.

Undaunted, Plant returned again with plans for a rocket-driven torpedo, His persistence paid off. On December 9, 1862, a demonstration of Plant's rocket torpedoes was arranged, with Secretary of the Navy Gideon Welles and Assistant Secretary Gustavus Vasa Fox in attendance. Two rocket torpedoes were launched from a large, flat-bottomed boat about forty feet offshore from the Washington navy yard. The first torpedo had the good grace to plow into a mud bank and explode.

The second rocket torpedo was more typically unpredictable and suddenly veered off and struck the *Diana,* a nearby schooner. The little vessel, which had never been intended as a target, sunk within a few minutes. The Washington *Evening Star* dryly commented, "The destructive properties of the rocket were certainly proven." As it was, the rampaging rocket might have blown up a large nearby steamer, the ironically named *State of Georgia,* which was in range nearby.

Another test a month later literally fizzled out when the rocket drowned itself in the Anacostia River. Plant's idea sunk with it, but at least he etched a place for himself in naval history, having launched the first self-propelled torpedo to sink a ship, even though he didn't intend to do it.

ADM. DAVID GLASGOW FARRAGUT

David Glasgow Farragut was one of the outstanding naval figures to emerge in the Civil War. His capture of New Orleans in 1862, together with his brilliant attack at Mobile Bay in 1864, are regarded as two of the most notable exploits in the annals of the sea. Farragut's fame and honors are commensurate with his deeds. In fact, he was the first officer to hold the ranks of rear admiral, vice admiral, and admiral in the U.S. Navy.

There was little in Farragut's pre-Civil War record to indicate future greatness. He was one of those quietly competent officers who rose to great heights when given the opportunity, but if not given the opportunity, languished in obscurity. In this sense, Farragut was much like Ulysses S. Grant, whose military record before the Civil War was satisfactory but unremarkable. And Farragut had to deal with one other issue that Grant did not—he was a Southerner, which made his loyalty to the Union at least initially suspect.

Farragut was born July 5, 1801, near Knoxville, Tennessee. After the death of his mother, seven-year-old Farragut and his sisters were sent off to the homes of various friends. Famed naval officer David Porter, who was grateful to the Farraguts for the kindness and care they had given his dying father, agreed to take the young lad under his wing and later adopted him. As was the custom during that period, Farragut became a midshipman at the tender age of nine. When Porter took his epic cruise as commander of the frigate *Essex* during the War of 1812, Farragut was aboard. And he was soon in the thick of things; the youngster took one of the ships that the *Essex* had captured and sailed it to Valparaiso, Chile—no mean feat for a twelve-year-old.

Farragut stayed in the navy, and by the secession winter of 1860–61, he had served fifty years. But neither his tenure in the navy nor his announced loyalty to the Union won him a position of command once the war broke out. A Southerner married to a Southern woman, Farragut was viewed with distrust by some of the bureaucrats in the Navy Department. Finally, after months of inactivity and brief service on a naval retirement board, Farragut's chance came when a New Orleans expedition was being planned. New Orleans was queen of the Mississippi River, a great port and the Confederacy's largest city. Taking it would be part of the Union's overall strategy to seize control of the Mississippi and split the Rebel South in two.

Who would command the Union's seaborne assault on the Crescent City? Although several candidates were mentioned, in the end Secretary of the Navy Gideon Welles chose Farragut. It was a bold move to pluck a man from obscurity, but the times demanded boldness.

On the surface, Farragut did not cut a heroic figure. He was only 5 feet, 6½ inches in height and weighed about 150 pounds. Graying hair clustered about his ears, and he combed it in a way to compensate for a balding crown. Because of his nearsightedness, and his refusal to wear eyeglasses, his eyes "gave a quizzical, half-smiling appearance to his face." At sixty, he was generally fit, though his health was perpetually under siege by bouts of cholera and other ills.

Farragut may have been nearsighted, but his strategic sense was anything but myopic. He had moral courage and imagination, attributes of good commanders. On January 9, 1862, he was formally appointed to the command of the West Gulf Blockading Squadron. The task force included eight steam sloops, one sailing sloop, and fourteen gunboats. There were also nineteen mortar schooners and transports loaded with some 15,000 Union troops under Gen. Benjamin F. Butler. The troops would occupy New Orleans after it was taken.

New Orleans was guarded by two forts that sat beside the Mississippi's mouth, Forts St. Philip and Jackson. Situated seventy-five miles below the city, the forts had been strengthened and bristled with 126 cannons. The Confederates also had two unfinished gunboats, and even though they were unable to move they could still bring their guns into

action. In addition, there was a swarm of small gunboats guarding the
river channel.

Capt. David Dixon Porter (son of the man who had adopted Farragut) tried to reduce the forts by means of mortar bombardment, but
six days of heavy shelling did not produce the desired results. Farragut
decided to run the gauntlet—take seventeen of his ships and push his
way past the forts to the city beyond. At 2:00 in the morning, April 24,
1862, Farragut ordered his ships up the Mississippi. It was a major
gamble, and the old salt himself later remembered it as "the most anxious night" of his life.

The seventeen Union vessels moved forward, Farragut's flagship,
the *Hartford*, among them. The forts opened fire, and the ships replied.
Hot tongues of flame spouted from cannon mouths, simultaneously
punching through gray-white masses of powder smoke. Mortar shells
arched through the night sky in fiery parabolas, and Confederate rafts
filled with burning pine and pitch floated downriver. It was a pyrotechnic display to end all pyrotechnic displays, a hellish "Fourth of July" in
April that was as dazzling to the eye as it was deafening to the ear.

Against all expectations, Farragut made it through with only four
ships lost. New Orleans capitulated, and the downriver forts also surrendered. For his magnificent achievement, Lincoln made Farragut a
rear admiral in July 1862. One New York newspaper christened Farragut an "American Viking," a man who had the courage and seaman-
ship of the Norseman of old.

Early in 1864 Farragut planned his next major mission: to seal off
the port of Mobile, Alabama, by seizing control of Mobile Bay. The
three-mile-long bay mouth was guarded by two forts and a double string
of floating mines. The entrance was also protected by the Confederate
ironclad *Tennessee*, whose powerful guns and formidable ram, coupled
with its six-inch-thick armor, made it a worthy opponent. The *Tennessee*
was the flagship of Adm. Franklin Buchanan, who had catapulted to
fame as the commander of the ironclad *Virginia* some two years earlier.

Admiral Farragut chose August 5, 1864, as the day of his attack.
The Union flotilla included fourteen wooden ships and four powerful
ironclad monitors. By 7:00 A.M. the engagement began in earnest.
Between the broadsides of the opposing fleets and the barrage from
the defending forts, the battle smoke was so thick that Union gunners
were afraid of hitting their own ships. With his own vision obscured,
Farragut climbed the port-side rigging of his flagship, the USS *Hartford*. Although he was lashed to the rigging to prevent him from

falling, it was still a very dangerous and exposed position for a senior commander.

One of the Union ironclads, the *Tecumseh*, struck a mine and sank, taking ninety-three men to the bottom. The *Hartford* plunged into the fray, despite the torpedoes floating all about. "Damn the torpedoes!" Farragut cried, "Full speed ahead!" After three and a half hours of intense fighting, the Rebel flotilla, including its leader, the *Tennessee,* capitulated. For this victory at Mobile Bay—in many ways the capstone of his career—Farragut was promoted to vice admiral in December 1864.

After the war, on July 25, 1866, he was named full admiral. Weighed down with age and honors, America's first admiral died in 1869.

ADM. DAVID DIXON PORTER

In the fall of 1862 the Union was well on its way toward controlling the Mississippi and splitting the Confederacy in two. But there was still one hard nut that remained to be cracked—the fortress city of Vicksburg, Mississippi. Along with Port Hudson, Vicksburg guarded the middle section of the Mississippi not far from its confluence with the Red River. The Red River was a vital conduit of grain and cattle from Texas and elsewhere, a lifeline to the famished Confederate armies in the east.

Secretary of the Navy Gideon Welles had a disparate collection of ships on the great river, a flotilla appropriately named the Mississippi Squadron. But Welles knew he needed a good commander for the mid-Mississippi—bold, but not rash, and able to instill confidence and fighting spirit in his men. In late September 1862 the navy secretary decided on David Dixon Porter for the assignment. Porter was given the temporary and local rank of rear admiral, with control over the naval forces of the middle and upper part of the river. By assuming that assignment, Porter became the first officer in American naval history to have nearly ninety vessels under his direct command.

Porter came from a seafaring tradition. His father, Commodore David Porter, was a celebrated figure in the War of 1812. At the age of ten, David Dixon Porter took his first sea voyage, accompanying his father on a naval cruise in the West Indies. Six years later he was appointed a midshipman in the U.S. Navy. His career followed the usual course—tours of sea duty as well as assignments onshore—until the Mexican War, when his commander singled him out as a "brave and zealous officer." Yet promotion remained glacially slow, and Porter was still a lieutenant at age forty-seven.

With the coming of the Civil War, however, opportunities opened for career military men. Porter was given the command of the mortar flotilla during the campaign to capture New Orleans in April 1862. Overly confident, Porter predicted that his guns alone would batter into submission the Crescent City's twin sentinels, Forts St. Philip and Jackson. But the forts did not surrender, even after six brutal days of continuous bombardment.

In spite of his embarrassment in New Orleans, Porter's "great energy . . . and daring" were recognized by Secretary Welles, who gave him the nod as commander of the Mississippi Squadron. Porter soon found himself cooperating with the Union army in the siege of Vicksburg.

Gen. Ulysses S. Grant was in charge of the land operations, commanding an army of some 45,000 men. To support him, Porter had eleven ironclads, thirty-eight wooden and tinclad boats, and forty or so auxiliary craft. Altogether, naval operations could muster 5,500 men and some 300 guns—an impressive array of firepower by any index.

The bloody land fighting around Vicksburg, particularly Grant's sanguinary yet fruitless assaults, have tended to obscure the navy's role in the reduction of the city. Actually, the navy was indispensable in the campaign—transporting reinforcements and supplies, suppressing Confederate guerrilla activity along the river, and shelling the fortress city on a regular basis.

Siege warfare is a tedious, dirty business, and the tactics used are far from subtle. The inhabitants of Vicksburg found this out the hard way, as their city was bludgeoned into submission. On May 22, 1863, Porter began shelling night and day, with devastating results. Hundreds of mortar shells, solid shot, and shrapnel rained down on the city, forcing Vicksburg's soldiers and citizens alike to find shelter in makeshift caves or trenches.

Not content with operations around Vicksburg proper, Porter—the "Terror of the Mississippi," as he was now called by the Confederates—sent a naval force up the Yazoo River. The admiral considered the Yazoo region Vicksburg's granary and was determined to cut off this source of sustenance. The gunboat *Dekalb* and several other union vessels steamed up the Yazoo River to Yazoo City, where they began a land bombardment that destroyed a Confederate navy yard, mills, carpentry shops, and two ironclads, the whole estimated at $2,000,000.

On July 3, 1863, the last Confederate gun at Vicksburg roared a final defiance. The Confederate commander, Gen. John C. Pemberton, had requested an armistice to arrange for a surrender. At 5:00 A.M. on July 4, Porter received a telegram from Grant announcing that the enemy had agreed to his terms of surrender. And with Vicksburg finally in Union hands, a great deal of the credit belongs to David Dixon Porter and his Mississippi Squadron.

SUBMARINE SCHOOL

The concept of a vessel designed to operate underwater and attack ships floating on the surface had long held a fascination for those who fought on the high seas. The first known submarine to be used as an instrument of war was David Bushnell's one-man *Turtle,* which came close to sinking a British warship during the American Revolution. Famous steamboat engineer Robert Fulton (who, like Bushnell, had experimented with water mines) built an underwater vessel around 1800. Nothing ever came of Fulton's invention; when he tried to sell it to Napoleon's government in France, it was rejected.

The idea of a submarine, seemingly defunct with Fulton's failed attempt, was revived by the Civil War. Desperate for a means to break the Union naval blockade, the Confederacy tried a number of inventions, including ironclads, torpedo boats, and floating mines, all with varying success. The submarine, on the other hand, seemed to offer the most promise, since it could inflict damage on the enemy and, at least in theory, go entirely undetected. But could Southerners transpose theory into action? No one could fault them for not trying. During the course of the war, Confederate inventors and investors together built not one, but three submarines: the *Pioneer,* the *American Diver,* and the more famous CSS *H. L. Hunley.*

The South's first underwater vessel was developed by James R. McClintock and Baxter Watson of New Orleans. Although anxious to assist the cause, they were not averse to turning a dollar. In early 1861, Southern president Jefferson Davis solicited applications for letters of marque; in essence, he was giving the green light for privateers to raid Union shipping. To sweeten the appeal, the Confederate government promised to pay handsomely for any Union ships destroyed. If McClintock and Watson could get their idea operational, they might reap profits as well as praise.

The submarine project began in late 1861. Several others joined the effort, in particular Horace L. Hunley, who, in addition to his enthusiasm, supplied the much-needed capital for constructing the underwater craft. Dubbed the *Pioneer,* it measured some twenty feet long, four feet deep, and six feet wide. The egg-shaped vessel consisted of iron plates bolted to an iron frame. Small and cramped, the *Pioneer* was barely able to accommodate a crew of four (some scholars say two).

The *Pioneer* seemed to function well during the initial testing, but it was never tried in combat conditions. Before the sub could become operational, the Union navy's David Farragut captured its New Orleans home base. Sunk by accident or design, the *Pioneer* was discovered in 1957 and subsequently put on display.

The simultaneous loss of both their workshop and their submarine did not cool the builders' enthusiasm for the concept. Relocating to Mobile, Alabama, McClintock, Watson, and Hunley began anew. In the summer of 1862, the men set up their operation in Parks and Lyon's Foundry and enlisted the aid of two young engineers from the 21st Alabama infantry, Lt. George E. Dixon and Lt. William A. Alexander.

A second submarine, the *American Diver,* soon took shape. High hopes were pinned on this craft, but the swells of Mobile Bay proved a greater adversary than any Union ship. The *American Diver* was true to its name—it sank to the bottom. Some accounts say there was a loss of life; others maintain there were no casualties.

The gallant little band of builders tried again. This time, they used a ready-made cylinder—a twenty-five-foot ship's boiler. The boiler was cut in two, tapered fore and aft, then had bow and stern castings attached. Ballast tanks were located in the castings, whereby water could be allowed in or out in order to lower or raise the vessel. When completed, the sub measured 40 feet long by 3 1/2 feet wide by 4 feet deep.

But how to propel the craft? The submarine was cramped, and coal-burning steam engines were obviously out of the question. Even if such an engine could be installed, there would not be enough air, and the ship would of necessity lack a smokestack to vent off burning emissions. Adequate storage batteries had not yet been invented, and attempts to concoct an electromagnetic battery came to naught. There was no other alternative but to use human muscle power. The propeller shaft ran the length of the vessel, with eight cranks spaced at intervals for crew use. Of course, cranking the shaft would be work—and the men would further eat up the limited oxygen supply. The captain was supplied with a lighted candle, which provided illumination in the dark and was also a flickering "early-warning system" if oxygen ran low.

Confederate general P. G. T. Beauregard was so impressed with this third submarine that he had it transferred from Mobile to Charleston,

South Carolina, where he thought it might break the tightening grip of the Union blockade. But misfortune dogged the vessel from the start. In mid-October 1863 the submarine was unable to surface during test trials, suffocating its entire nine-man crew. Among the victims was Horace L. Hunley, the builder and commander of the craft, who had put his money and his life on the line and ultimately lost both.

Despite the loss of their comrades, Lieutenants Dixon and Alexander still had faith in the submarine concept. Nine days after the accident, the vessel was raised, cleaned and repaired, and made ready for use. It was christened the CSS *H. L. Hunley*.

Determined to avoid future tragedies, Dixon, who had been placed in command of the sub, and Alexander, appointed as his executive officer, felt the crew should receive specialized training. Beginning in November 1863, at Mount Pleasant on the north side of Charleston's harbor, the program was implemented. In the morning the submariners attended classes and exercised, and in the afternoons they took the *Hunley* out for short cruises and practice dives. Civilians onshore probably had no idea that the men they were observing were actually students of the world's first submarine school.

REMAINING UNDERWATER

One problem plagued the Confederate submarine *H. L. Hunley* more than any other: How long could it remain underwater? The vessel's ability to attack by stealth and surprise would be severely compromised if it was compelled to surface before the arranged time.

The *Hunley*'s crude design featured an air box that was supposed to draw in fresh oxygen to the crew while the sub prowled just below the surface. Unfortunately, the air box didn't do its job very well, so the *Hunley* had to surface just enough for crew members to open an aft hatch cover. But when they did this, they usually heard voices over the harbor—voices coming from Union sailors aboard blockading ships. If the Confederate submariners could hear the enemy, the enemy might just be able to *see* them.

The officers in charge of the *Hunley* decided on a little test: They would see just how long the sub could remain completely underwater—or, to put it another way, how long the nine-man crew could hold out without fresh air. The Back Bay area off Battery Marshall near the entrance to Charleston Harbor was chosen as the site of the experiment.

Before they took the plunge, the ground rules were laid out. The *Hunley* was going to submerge and rest on the bottom. The crew agreed to stay down as long as humanly possible, but when the limit was reached, anyone's cry of "Up!" would bring the sub to the surface immediately. When everything was ready, the *Hunley* submerged and settled to the bottom. Dixon lighted a single candle, in part for illumination, but more importantly to gauge the oxygen supply in the container.

The men sat still, each no doubt absorbed in his own thoughts. The only movement came from the candle's flickering flame, a tiny pinprick of light almost swallowed up in the *Hunley*'s claustrophobic darkness. After twenty-five minutes the candle gave up the struggle and went out. Repeated attempts to relight it proved fruitless. There simply wasn't enough oxygen available to support the flame—but if there wasn't enough oxygen for a tiny candle, was there enough for a full-grown man or, for that matter, nine grown men?

Crewmen coughed and gasped as the air grew fouler, yet no one wanted to show signs of weakness by crying "Up!" Sitting in the pitch dark, listening to their companion's labored breathing and no doubt thinking about the tragic fates of the previous crews, the nine were reaching the limits of their endurance. Finally, almost all shouted "Up!" together, as if it was a single voice. The vessel rose with difficulty, but when it broke to the surface, the men flung open the hatch cover and inhaled the cool, fresh air. It was not long before they checked their watches. For the first time in history, a submarine crew had remained submerged for two hours and thirty-five minutes—a record not only of time, but of human endurance.

CSS *H. L. HUNLEY*

After months of preparation, the submarine CSS *H. L. Hunley* was at last ready to set out on its first combat mission. Its target was the USS *Housatonic,* one of a number of Union ships blockading Charleston, South Carolina.

The egg-shaped, forty-foot-long *Hunley* had a crew of nine, including its commander, Lt. George Dixon. The men provided the propulsion by cranking a long propeller shaft. Originally the boat was designed to tow a cylinder torpedo. The idea was for the *Hunley* to dive under the target, then come up on the other side. As it completed this maneuver, the torpedo would make contact with the target vessel's hull and explode. But because this scenario did not work well in shallow water, the armament was switched to a spar torpedo. In this configuration, a torpedo was attached to a long pole affixed to the front of the sub, much like a swordfish's snout.

The evening of February 17, 1864, was chosen for the attack. There was a full moon, its baleful eye silvering a sea that was as smooth as a millpond. The submarine's intended victim, the USS *Housatonic,* was a 1,240-ton screw steam sloop. At about 8:45 P.M. the *Housatonic*'s officer of the deck, Master J. K. Crosby, noticed that something was disturbing the water, the ripples casting off little sparkles of moonlight.

The crew was bedding down for sleep, but thoughts of repose were banished when a drummer beat to quarters at Crosby's warning shout. The object causing the ripples was about 100 yards away, moving toward the *Housatonic*'s starboard quarter. The *Housatonic*'s guns could not be brought to bear, but Union sailors peppered the unidentified object with rifle fire.

It was too little, too late. The *Hunley* had managed to bring its torpedo in direct contact with the *Housatonic.* A deafening roar sent tons of water skyward, the explosion tearing apart the Union vessel's stern, sending it to the bottom almost immediately. Thus the *Hunley* became the first submarine in history to sink a warship. Unfortunately, the *Hunley*'s triumph was also its last. The sub went down with its target, and all hands were lost (while, ironically, almost all of the *Housatonic*'s crew survived).

There are several schools of thought as to why the sub sank. One argues that the *Hunley*'s forward hatch was on the surface and open, and the submarine was swamped by water from the explosion. Others maintain that the sub was sucked into the hole torn into the *Housatonic*'s hull and, unable to back out, went under with its target.

In 1995 a wreck was found that some thought might be the *Hunley.* In May 1996 a team from the Submerged Cultural Resources Unit of the National Park Service dived to examine the ruins. They concluded that it was indeed the *Hunley,* a discovery of immense archaeological significance on par with the finding of the USS *Monitor* in the 1970s. The researchers were surprised to find that the *Hunley* was much less cruder in design than was previously supposed. As one member of the unit commented, "The thing's no basement tinkertoy; it's surprisingly well made."

A hole in one of the hatches suggests that the *Hunley* may have been sunk by small-arms fire, one of several theories that scientists and archaeologists are now in a position to investigate thoroughly. On August 8, 2000, the *Hunley* was lifted from the Atlantic.

CHAPTER 5

Fighting the War from the Air

The dream of flight is a very old one. Around 1290 a Franciscan monk named Roger Bacon wrote that air, like water, has certain properties and wondered if men could build a machine that air could support, much like water supports a ship. About 1500 the great Renaissance artist Leonardo da Vinci sketched something he called ornthopters, birdlike contraptions that a man could strap on and theoretically fly.

The age of human flight truly began in 1783, when two French brothers, Jacques Étienne and Joseph Michel Montgolfier, experimented with a hot-air balloon. Tethered firmly to the ground, the craft would rise as the air inside of its envelope was heated from dry straw burned on an iron grate just beneath the open neck of the balloon. The siblings successfully launched several balloons, one of which carried a duck, a rooster, and a sheep as passengers. The three animals survived unscathed, paving the way for humans to try their hand.

Not long after the animal flight, King Louis XVI's historian Jean François Pilâtre de Rozier decided to make some history, not just record it, by coming forward and volunteering as the first human in flight. Pilâtre de Rozier made his groundbreaking ascent in Paris on October 15, 1783. Staying in the air about four and a half minutes, the intrepid aeronaut reached an altitude of about eighty feet. This only served to whet his appetite for a far more adventurous undertaking, an untethered flight through the air. On November 21, 1783, the ubiquitous Pilâtre de Rozier and the Marquis d'Arlandes made the world's first free ascent, reaching altitudes of about 300 feet. The use of hot air as fuel, however, proved unsatisfactory; once the warm air trapped in the balloon envelope cooled, it lost its lift. As a result, hydrogen gas was substituted, volatile and sometimes dangerous, but overall more effective.

Free ballooning had its drawbacks, chief of which was its dependency on the whims of the wind to carry the craft along. The great man of letters Dr. Samuel Johnson considered this a major liability. "These vehicles," Johnson remarked in 1784, "can serve no use till we can guide them. I had rather now find a medicine that can ease an asthma." But Benjamin Franklin, more prescient, saw possibilities in flight. Franklin, then in Paris as America's diplomatic representative, witnessed one of the early balloon ascents. When a spectator turned to him and asked, "What good is it?" Franklin quickly responded, "What good is a newborn baby?" As always, the sage of Philadelphia was right on the mark; flight was in its infancy.

Not long after ballooning was introduced, the French military recognized its potential and in April 1794 formed a balloon corps, calling it the *Aérostiers*. During the French Revolutionary wars, notably at the battle of Fleurus, the *Aérostiers* performed a valuable service. For nearly ten hours while the battle raged, two balloonists stayed aloft, transmitting vital information that helped the French win the fight against the Austrians.

The French balloon corps was disbanded in 1799, but the idea of military ballooning would gain new life in years to come. In the meantime, ballooning became a craze in France, a contagion that soon spread to other countries. The first American ascent was made by French showman Pierre Blanchard in Philadelphia, then the nation's capital, on January 9, 1793. A gala event, the flight was witnessed by thousands, including such distinguished observers as President George Washington, Thomas Jefferson, John Adams, and James Monroe. Washington, a dignified man not given to speculative statements, was inspired enough to predict that there would be transcontinental flights to Europe.

Washington may have been the first, but certainly not the last, American to suggest Europe by air. Beginning in the early nineteenth century the idea was given serious consideration—and much attention in the press—though in the end, no one ventured forth. Nor did ballooning in America have any success as a weapon of war. In 1840, for example, Secretary of War Joel Poinsett—the same man who introduced the Christmas flower poinsettia—suggested using balloons against the Seminole Indians in Florida, but the proposal never came to fruition, a victim of red tape. During the Mexican-American War, John

Wise, dean of American balloonists in the mid-nineteenth century, proposed an aerial bombardment of the fortress of San Juan de Ulúa at Vera Cruz but couldn't get the green light from the War Department.

A decade and a half later, on the eve of the Civil War, the War Department reversed itself on the use of balloons in combat. Confronting an enemy far more formidable than the one it had fought south of the border, the U.S. Army was now willing to give the aeronauts an opportunity to prove their military worth. Soon, thanks to these pioneer aviators, America would have its first air force.

JOHN WISE

On June 26, 1861, Maj. Hartman Bache, acting chief of the topographical corps in Washington, D.C., telegraphed aeronaut John Wise, asking for a cost estimate of a balloon made of the "best India raw silk, capacity twenty thousand cubic feet, cordage of linen, everything complete." Since time was of the essence, Bache also wanted to know just how long such an envelope would take to build. Wise replied that the vehicle would cost about $800 and take two weeks to construct. The deal was made, and Wise began work on the first aircraft to be built for the U.S. military.

John Wise was in many ways the perfect choice for the job. At the time the Civil War broke out, Wise, a Pennsylvanian, had some twenty-six years of practical experience as an aeronaut. Slender, almost gaunt, with a long face and Lincolnesque beard, Wise was a man with reserves of stamina and an unshakable conviction in the future of flight.

Wise completed construction of the balloon on July 16, well within the promised time limits. And, as events unfolded, not a moment too soon. Union forces under Gen. Irvin McDowell were advancing into Virginia, and a major action was expected within a matter of days. Wise was ordered to Washington, where he would inflate his balloon and report to McDowell's headquarters in the field.

The aeronaut was proud of his creation, convinced that it would hold up under combat. Not only did he follow government specifications to the letter, but he also included a unique contribution of his own. Fearing that the balloon's wooden car or basket, which held the passengers, might not be able to withstand enemy fire, the aeronaut saw to it that the bottom of the basket was armored with thick sheet iron. With this addition, Wise was responsible for yet another first: the first aircraft ever to be armor-plated (even if only partially).

Upon arriving in the capital, Wise and his balloon were placed under the command of Maj. Albert J. Myer, who would later distinguish himself as head of the army's Signal Corps. Myer's unit, some twenty soldiers from the 26th Pennsylvania infantry, were to tow the inflated balloon via mooring ropes, much in the manner of the balloons of the modern Macy's Thanksgiving Day Parade. Having enlisted to fight Rebels, one wonders what these infantrymen thought of their unique and possibly, to them, bizarre assignment.

In any case, the soldiers had their hands full; it was tricky work to shepherd the massive balloon through such obstacles as telegraph poles and wires. Worried that they would not get to McDowell in time, Major Myer ordered the balloon tied to an accompanying wagon and horse team, much like a child might tie a toy balloon to the back of his bicycle. Once the balloon was attached, the horses were whipped up to a trot. The onrushing horses made good progress at first, the balloon bobbing and swaying in protest. But then the wagon went down a tree-lined road, and the balloon stuck fast between the upper branches. Efforts to free the balloon from the trees' leafy embrace proved initially unsuccessful, so a meddling Major Myer (who proved far more successful as a signal officer) intervened again. The horse team was urged to go forward at a trot, the idea being that the sudden lurch would free the captive balloon. It did, but at the cost of severe damage to the silk envelope. The tree branches tore great rents in the balloon, causing a large volume of gas to escape. Inevitably, the balloon collapsed, along with Wise's great expectations.

Having missed the first battle of Bull Run, the disappointed aeronaut hoped to redeem himself, but his next field expedition also proved abortive. While being towed to Ball's Cross Roads in northeastern Virginia, the balloon escaped from its handlers, abetted by a stiff wind. A series of musket volleys fired by Wise's men punctured the envelope enough to partly deflate the fugitive craft, and it came back to earth.

This second mishap spelled the end of Wise's military career. Capt. A. W. Whipple, who was in charge of overseeing the operation and served as a liaison with headquarters, was disgusted by the two failures and was soon ready to wash his hands of the aeronaut. Writing to his superior in August 1861, Whipple declared that he "would have nothing more to do with balloons."

John Wise had received no pay, rations, or even quarters for himself. On top of that, the aeronaut had paid for the repairs of the balloon out of his own pocket. Thus shabbily treated, Wise left Washington in early August 1861.

Yet nothing can expunge Wise's achievements as an American

aeronautics pioneer. In addition to his precedent-setting work on behalf of the government, he also held the record (briefly) for the longest balloon flight—804 miles. In 1879, while trying to set another long-distance record, John Wise and a companion crashed and drowned in Lake Michigan.

THADDEUS S. C. LOWE

In the summer of 1861, after the War Department severed its relationship with balloonist John Wise, his chief rival, Thaddeus Sobieski Constantin Lowe, emerged as the Union's premier aeronaut. A man of extraordinary vision and talent, Lowe was born in Jefferson Mills, New Hampshire, on August 20, 1832. As early as he could remember, he had been interested in aeronautics, on one occasion even sending the family cat aloft. Like Thomas Edison, Lowe had no formal scientific training but had a natural talent for gadgets and invention. In his late teens, the future aeronaut became a traveling magician, delighting rural audiences with his simple chemical experiments.

In 1854, at the age of twenty-two, Lowe took up aeronautics full-time, supporting himself by continuing to perform "scientific" demonstrations. Although he couldn't afford a formal university education, Lowe studied the various elements of aerodynamics on his own, and in 1858 his hard work bore fruit; he built his first balloon.

It was around this time that Lowe caught "transatlantic fever," the dream of going to Europe by air. Prevailing east winds, he believed, might well propel a balloon and its passengers from the New World to the Old. Brimming with enthusiasm, Lowe constructed a huge airship which he called the *City of New York,* despite the fact that it was built in Hoboken, New Jersey. Bad weather and other delays postponed his Atlantic attempt until 1860.

In the interim, Lowe went to Philadelphia, where he enjoyed both professional and financial support from a number of scientific and wealthy backers. In the summer of 1860, the *City of New York*, now rechristened (at the suggestion of Horace Greeley's *Tribune*) the *Great Western,* prepared for a transoceanic flight. But the balloon's change of name did not prove a good omen. On a trial voyage, its envelope was damaged, and so the *Great Western* got no farther than a New Jersey sand flat.

Discouraged but not down, Lowe met with Professor Joseph Henry, secretary of the Smithsonian Institution in Washington. Henry suggested that a trial voyage over land should be undertaken first, to become familiar with the problems and challenges of long-distance flight. Risks were always present, of course, but there was a better chance of surviving a forced descent over land than being lost at sea.

Taking Henry's advice, Lowe went to Cincinnati, which would serve as the point of departure for his test flight—a flight he hoped would take him to the southeastern part of the United States. He arrived in the city in early April 1861 and was warmly welcomed by both the business community and the public at large. Lowe began his ascent about 3:30 A.M. on April 20. His balloon, the *Enterprise,* was smaller than the *Great Western* but was also less unwieldy. The brave aeronaut rose to a height of 12,000 feet, only a thin layer of wicker between him and a fatal plunge to earth. Wanting proof of both his time and point of departure, Lowe took with him an early morning edition of the *Cincinnati Commercial.*

Some nine hours later, around 1:00 in the afternoon, Lowe gently descended at a point 9 miles west of Unionville, South Carolina. It was a moment of undeniable triumph; the aeronaut had accomplished a flight of 900 miles. The previous long-distance record of 804 miles for a similar time span had been set by John Wise in 1859. Lowe's courage was great, but his timing was poor. Fort Sumter had been fired upon, and the country was now in the grip of a civil war.

Lowe's initial reception in South Carolina had little to do with politics, however; superstitious locals, both black and white, took Lowe for some kind of demon, even though he came from the heavens. At first he was threatened, but saner heads came to his rescue, and he was taken to Unionville.

Holding on to his deflated balloon and instruments, Lowe boarded a train at Unionville for Columbia, South Carolina, intending to go from there back home to the North. But as soon as he set foot in Columbia, Lowe was arrested, charged with being a Yankee spy. As the sheriff conducted his prisoner to jail, mobs of fire-eating secessionists howled for the aeronaut's blood, demanding a "necktie" party that would soon have Lowe at the end of a rope. Some of the less bloodthirsty in the mob "merely" advised their friends to "tar and feather the damn Yankee."

It looked bad, because copies of the *Cincinnati Commercial,* a leading abolitionist journal, were discovered in his gondola. Luckily, several South Carolinians stepped forward to vouch for him, including faculty members of South Carolina College. Apparently the publicity attending his transatlantic attempt had preceded him. In any event, It must have been a terrifying experience for Lowe, though he dismissed it by humorously declaring that he was "the first prisoner of the Civil War."

After making it safely back to the North, Lowe traveled to Washington in early June 1861 in order to offer his services to the Union. Anxious to impress officialdom, the aeronaut made sure he took the *Enterprise* with him, the same balloon that had taken him on his long-distance southern odyssey.

After arriving in the capital, Lowe visited with his friend Professor Henry of the Smithsonian, who he knew had influence in the corridors of power. Henry proved a faithful ally and an influential advocate, selling the idea of military balloon flights to the highest authorities. After a round of discussions with officers in the topographical engineer corps, Secretary of War Simon Cameron, and President Abraham Lincoln, Henry secured a test trial for Lowe, with the War Department footing the bill. And if that weren't enough, Henry obtained for the young aeronaut an invitation to the White House. As expected, Lincoln seemed genuinely interested, promising Lowe that his balloon would be given serious attention.

Not long after the presidential interview, the War Department appropriated money for the trials, "not to exceed $200 or $250." The grounds of the Columbian Armory were chosen as the test site, and all preparations proceeded apace. By June 18 all was ready for the great experiment. But what did Lowe plan to do? After all, everyone knew balloons made good observation platforms; there was nothing to test about that. Some newspapers seemed to think that it was all an elaborate subterfuge for secret observations on Confederate forces. Actually, Lowe was going to try something no one had ever done before—to send a telegraphic message from the air.

The balloon *Enterprise* was colorfully decorated for the occasion, its 20,000-cubic-foot envelope festooned with two large American flags and—inexplicably—a British Union Jack. The balloon basket, or car, would have a small Morse telegraph apparatus that would be attached by a wire to a ground station below, which in turn would be connected to the War Department, the Alexandria office of the telegraph company, and the White House.

At the appointed hour on June 18, Lowe entered the basket, together with telegrapher Herbert C. Robinson and Superintendent George McDowell Burns of the American Telegraph Company. Gradually the mooring rope unwound, allowing the lighter-than-air leviathan to rise more than 500 feet over Washington. Once at maximum height, the nation's capital at their feet, Lowe dictated to Lincoln the following telegraphic message, the first ever sent from an aircraft:

Balloon *Enterprise*
June [18, 1861]

To the President of the United States

Sir:

This point of observation commands an area nearly fifty miles in diameter. The city, with its girdle of encampments, presents a superb scene. I take great pleasure in sending you this first dispatch ever telegraphed from an aerial station, and in acknowledging my indebtedness to your encouragement for the opportunity of demonstrating the availability of the science of aeronautics in the military service of the country.

T. S. C. Lowe

AERIAL RECONNAISSANCE

Thaddeus S. C. Lowe's balloon demonstrations in Washington on June 18, 1861, gained wide publicity, most of it favorable. Brig. Gen. Irvin McDowell, Union commander of the newly created Department of Northeastern Virginia, was particularly interested in Lowe's aeronautical talents. Rumors were circulating that there were reports of "20,000 Confederate troops in the vicinity of Manassas and Fairfax Court House." The general believed that Lowe, from his high perch, could confirm or deny the presence of the enemy.

Lowe responded to McDowell's summons with enthusiasm, even though he was still a private citizen with no official status. Provided with $150 for gas and a fifteen-man detail from the 8th New York infantry, the aeronaut and his balloon *Enterprise* left Washington and arrived at McDowell's headquarters at Arlington, Virginia, on the afternoon of June 22. On that very day Lowe made his first ascension, but according to the press, his observations were "of no particular interest."

The next day Lowe and his balloon detail went forward, arriving at Baily's Cross Roads only to hear that a large Confederate patrol had recently been seen in the area. Undaunted, the aeronaut and his party proceeded to Camp Tyler, near Falls Church. After resting briefly, Lowe went aloft around noon, but the *Enterprise* was rudely buffeted by winds, so the mission was aborted. By 6:00 P.M. the turbulence died down, allowing Lowe to make a smooth ascent. Yet once again his view was obscured, this time by the thick green cluster of trees. The attempt was not a total failure, however; Lowe reported large clouds of dust in the direction of Fairfax Court House, telltale signs—or so the balloonist reported—of Confederate cavalry. In the evening Lowe conducted a final ascent, and after detecting no trace of flickering campfires, he concluded that there was no enemy presence in the area.

Overall, Lowe's inaugural military flights had produced mixed results. Certainly, it was shown that a region's tree cover or inclement weather could prevent detection of an enemy and largely neutralize the benefits of air observation. On the other hand, Lowe's efforts in late June 1861 should not be minimized; they represented the first transmission of aerial reconnaissance data in the history of American warfare.

MAPMAKING IN THE AIR

When Thaddeus S. C. Lowe tried to sell his idea of military ballooning to an initially skeptical Washington bureaucracy, the emphasis was on aerial reconnaissance of enemy movements and positions. But early on it was recognized that a balloon's unique bird's-eye view of surrounding terrain might produce other worthwhile advantages as well, including the opportunity to draw more accurate maps.

In late June 1861 Union army commanders discovered to their dismay that their maps of Fairfax County, Virginia (in the northeastern part of the state), were terribly out of date and not detailed enough for the requirements of their mission. Apprised of the situation, on June 24 Brig. Gen. Daniel Tyler sent Maj. Leyard Colburn of the 2nd Connecticut infantry up with Lowe to make a map of the surrounding region. Colburn's keen eye and meticulous attention to detail, coupled by the high view afforded by the balloon, produced dramatic results. His map—the first in the world sketched for military purposes from an aircraft—was so accurate that local Virginians vouched for its many unerring details, such as roads, streams, and even individual houses.

At first a balloon skeptic, General Tyler became a true believer once he saw Colburn's map. As he explained in a telegram to his commander, Gen. Irvin McDowell, "I have not been much of a convert to ballooning in military operations, but the last ascent made by Major Colburn of the 2nd Connecticut Volunteers . . . convince[s] me that a balloon may at times greatly assist military movements."

The original aerial map has been lost, so there is no way to verify Tyler's lavish praise. But the balloon had proven itself, and the United States was one step closer to the creation of its first true air force.

FLYING OVER ENEMY TERRITORY

Military ballooning, like all ballooning at the time, was an inexact science at best, which explains why most of the hydrogen-filled envelopes were tethered to the ground. After all, there was no way to steer the bulbous craft, putting the aeronauts at the mercy of wind currents. In time of war, they also risked being at the mercy of the enemy if they had the misfortune of going down in hostile territory. For balloonist Thaddeus S. C. Lowe, however, these risks seemed minor compared with what was at stake in the summer of 1861.

On July 21 at Bull Run, a creek near Manassas Junction, Virginia, around thirty miles southwest of Washington, Union forces under Brig. Gen. Irvin McDowell clashed with Confederate troops led by Pierre Gustave Toutant (P. G. T.) Beauregard. McDowell might have won, but most of his men were green three-month-enlistment volunteers who marched at a snail's pace. The Confederates weren't much better; in fact, Bull Run was a contest between two untested, ill-trained mobs.

But the Confederates gained the upper hand, forcing McDowell to order a retreat. The withdrawal soon turned into a rout, a mad scramble of panic-stricken men seeking the safety of Washington's defenses. Only the handful of Regular army units remained calm and covered the precipitous retreat. The demoralized troops who streamed into the capital presented a terrible spectacle to anyone who loved the Union cause. In the words of one eyewitness, a "cruel, crazy, mad, hopeless panic possessed them. . . . [T]he men were . . . a mass of ghastly wretches."

The panic seemed infectious, a contagion that soon spread to Washington's civilian population. The Confederate enemy was, or seemed to be, at the gates. In truth, the Southerners had won a tactical victory, but they were just as exhausted as the Union soldiers, and just as inexperienced, making it unlikely that they would think of pursuit. Of course, the North had no way of knowing this at the time.

Thaddeus Lowe and his balloon detail were at Falls Church, Virginia, some dozen miles west of Washington, when the first mobs of Union refugees began streaming back to the capital. Fearful of falling into Confederate hands, the aeronaut and his men left Falls Church and proceeded east about eight miles to Fort Corcoran. Three days later, on July 24, Lowe boldly decided on a free, untethered, ascent. He did not seem to have fully spelled out his reasons for doing so, but it's likely that he felt he could obtain more information about the enemy's location if he had movement and higher elevation. Such knowledge, moreover, might prove critical, given the reports of panic in Washington. If his reconnaissance could prove the existence of a major Confederate thrust toward the capital, the authorities could be alerted; if such an advance proved false, public fears could be put to rest and confidence restored.

The flight began about 5:30 A.M. on July 24. Supremely confident, Lowe climbed into the basket and rose to make his observations. Freed of all restricting bonds, the balloon went higher and higher, eventually reaching an elevation of three and a half miles—around 18,000 feet. Lowe's altitude, though no record, was certainly one of the highest recorded to that date, and at those heights the atmosphere is cold, the oxygen starting to thin. Risking altitude sickness, the balloonist could have succumbed to unconsciousness and death.

Apparently unaffected by these high elevations, Lowe performed his mission, perhaps without realizing that he had just become the first pilot in history to fly over enemy territory for reconnaissance purposes. While Virginia lay at his feet like a living, three-dimensional map, he carefully observed the terrain and detected no massing of Confederate troops, yet he could see Rebel encampments. Obviously, fears that Washington was going to be immediately attacked were groundless.

But before he could get the information to the authorities, he had to deal with more pressing matters. Subject, as balloons were, to the vagaries of the wind, Lowe's craft started to drift toward Alexandria, Virginia. Union troops in the area, unaware that the balloonist was one of their own, fired off some warning shots. "Show your colors," they shouted, but the aeronaut had no American flag in the basket with him. The soldiers peppered the balloon with lead, but as the bullets whizzed by, Lowe had the presence of mind to release ballast and gain some altitude, putting himself and the balloon outside the range of the riflemen. As Lowe was dodging those bullets, he probably had no idea that he was directly involved in establishing yet another military precedent— as the first U.S. pilot subjected to "friendly fire." Fortunately, the men in blue who shot at him did not find their mark, and Lowe managed to land in an area known as Mason's plantation, five and a half miles from Alexandria and some two and a half miles from the nearest Union picket. Having escaped death at the hands of his own troops, Lowe now found himself behind enemy lines, with his balloon, which was anything but inconspicuous.

There is a story, redolent of romantic fiction, that Mrs. Lowe disguised herself as a farm woman and took a horse and wagon team to retrieve her husband. Eventually, Lowe and his balloon reached safety, but he made no mention of his wife's alleged rescue. It may have happened, but in his official report, the aeronaut only acknowledged the help of the 31st New York infantry.

Upon arriving at military headquarters, Lowe presented his findings to the army brass. Apparently his observations helped restore calm in beleaguered Washington.

AN AMERICAN AIR CORPS

When Thaddeus S. C. Lowe came to Washington in early June 1861, he had a single purpose in mind: the creation of a U.S. Army balloon corps. But despite the positive attention the twenty-eight-year-old New Englander initially attracted as a civilian aeronaut assisting the military, his original mission remained unfulfilled.

Not that he didn't have support for his project. Both President Lincoln and Secretary of War Simon Cameron endorsed it. What he lacked, however, was the backing of the third member of Washington's military triumvirate, General in Chief Winfield Scott.

In late June, with a letter of introduction from Lincoln in hand, Lowe met with the aging general, who had recently turned seventy-five. Finding Scott "very infirm, pompous, and with many of the affectations that sometimes go with extreme age," Lowe got nowhere with the man. The general's mind, according to the aeronaut, "was centered on the make-up of an army as he had always known it, and he did not care for innovations." In short, Scott "had no interest in a balloon corps."

About a month later Lowe's hopes were renewed. After meeting with the president and explaining to him what had transpired, Lincoln took pen in hand and wrote the balloonist yet another letter of introduction to Scott. Lowe made a beeline to Scott's office, only to cool his heels in an anteroom. At first Lowe was informed that the general was too busy to see him; then he was told that Scott was eating his lunch and could not be disturbed. The last straw came when Lowe received word that the elderly commander was taking a nap! Furious, Lowe stormed back to the White House, where the president of the United States apparently was more accessible than the general in chief. Informed of Scott's stonewalling, Lincoln laughed and simply said to Lowe, "Come on." Lincoln and Lowe walked across Seventeenth Street, heading for the Winder Building, where General Scott's office was located. The two men must have been studies in contrast: Lincoln, with his tall and lanky frame, his weather-beaten face and whiskers, wearing his "fuzzy, old stovepipe hat" and his ill-fitting suit; Lowe, six feet, one inch in height, "well-proportioned, with broad, massive shoulders," an unusually handsome man with coal black hair, curling mustache, piercing blue eyes, and as always, stylishly dressed.

With the president by his side, doors opened for Lowe as if by magic. Formerly unavailable, General Scott now was all ears, listening intently and agreeing to support the aeronaut's proposal. Lincoln's intervention had saved the day; the United States would have a balloon corps.

One of Lowe's initial tasks was to begin the actual construction of the balloons, making certain to follow the War Department's specifications. In August 1861 he busied himself with the first of these balloons, which he proudly named the *Eagle.* Gradually the balloon corps expanded, and by November Lowe had built five new military balloons. Besides the *Eagle,* there were the *Constitution, Washington, Intrepid,* and *Union.* Each of these inflated envelopes were capable of lifting three men more than 1,000 feet. At its peak in 1862, the U.S. balloon corps—in actuality America's first air force—had seven balloons in operation.

In terms of appearance, the balloons themselves were gaudy expressions of Victorian verve and wartime patriotism. Made of fawn-colored Indian silk, sewn in double thickness, the envelopes were painted with designs and symbols that evoked the Union cause. The balloon *Union,* for example, boasted the Stars and Stripes, as well as an American Eagle with talons open and wings outspread; the *Constitution* had a huge portrait of George Washington painted on its curved silken surface. The wicker baskets were similarly decorated, a kaleidoscope of variously colored designs such as sky blue punctuated by white stars.

While the balloons were under construction, Lowe searched for crewmen. The "chief aeronaut," as Lowe liked to refer to himself, sought balloonists of proven experience, but the pickings were slim. Eventually the corps had a complement of nine members, including men such as John H. Steiner, a German immigrant, a colorful man who before the war had "enjoyed a wide reputation" as a balloonist. Once a rival of Lowe's, Steiner grew to be a major supporter.

In March 1862 Lowe invited James Allen to join his group. An "outstanding" aeronaut, Allen would take part in at least three major campaigns in the eastern theater. Another member of the corps was Ebenezer Mason, Jr., a "competent balloon maker as well as an aeronaut," but his talents were never fully employed. Disgruntled over delays in receiving his pay, a problem shared by the other members of the corps as well, Mason, whose family "was practically destitute," refused to perform his duties until his wages were forthcoming. Having no choice, the chief aeronaut had to discharge the striking balloonist.

In Mason's case, Lowe probably felt misgivings, but he had no such regrets when it came to firing another subordinate, one Jacob C. Freno. Freno, "a mixture of lawyer and balloonist," proved to be a man of dubious morals, prone to backbiting and insubordination. When he was dismissed from the balloon corps, Freno took malicious revenge by ripping the envelope of the balloon *Constitution.*

As head of the U.S. Army balloon corps, however, Lowe's problems were far more serious than the insubordination of a couple of assistants. The corps itself was an anomaly. Although operating with official government sanction, in reality it did not fit into the normal grooves of the military. None of the aeronauts, from Lowe on down, were soldiers. Similar to other civilian employees of the War Department serving on the front, they did not have the protection of the uniform. If caught behind enemy lines, they might be branded as spies and shot. There were combat risks as well. Confederates soon grew to hate snooping Union balloons and did all in their power to shoot them down. When sniper fire proved ineffective, on August 29, 1861, the Confederates trained a rifled cannon on Lowe and his balloon, the *Union*, while in the air near Fort Corcoran in northeastern Virginia. The shot missed, but it was yet another precedent—the first use of antiaircraft artillery fire in American combat.

Lowe's U.S. balloon corps served on far-flung fronts, including the Mississippi River, Union-occupied Port Royal, South Carolina, and during the Peninsula campaign in Virginia. In fact, it was during the Peninsula's battle of Fair Oaks on May 31 and June 1, 1862, that military ballooning really came into its own. Lowe's observations during that battle probably saved the Union army from disastrous defeat. The chief aeronaut observed a massing of Confederate troops for an all-out attack, a movement Union commanders initially took as a feint. Lowe telegraphed warnings that enabled reinforcements to be dispatched to the area in the nick of time. Otherwise, as several scholars have pointed out, the Army of the Potomac would have suffered "a major defeat."

In the aftermath of the Peninsula, the balloon corps served in two other major campaigns: Fredericksburg in December 1862 and Chancellorsville in May 1863.

JOHN LA MOUNTAIN AND THE USS *FANNY*

Aircraft carriers are generally considered to have been developed in the First World War. Actually these vessels have a long pedigree, and their roots can be traced to the USS *Fanny*, an armed transport that operated in Virginia in 1861. A purist may dispute the claim, but the fact remains that the *Fanny* carried a balloon into position, then the aircraft was launched from its deck. Since balloons were the aircraft of their time, the *Fanny* was indeed the first aircraft carrier in U.S. history.

John La Mountain was the man behind the *Fanny*'s landmark status. It's known that La Mountain was born about 1830, but his early life is obscure and lacking in concrete detail. Apparently he was a seaman who traded riding on currents of water for currents of air. La Mountain first gained real attention in 1859, when he, along with two fellow aeronauts and a newspaper reporter, flew 1,100 miles from St. Louis, Missouri, to Henderson, New York, in less than twenty hours, establishing an American distance record for that time span.

Gen. Benjamin F. Butler, commander of *Union* troops around Fortress Monroe, asked La Mountain to be an aerial observer in his Department of Virginia. La Mountain accepted, and a novel idea emerged from this assignment. Instead of the normal land-based balloon operations, La Mountain's aircraft would operate from the armed transport *Fanny*. That way Confederate coastal emplacements and forts could be readily observed and the data passed on to Union forces. If successful, such balloon operations could also be expanded to take place on the open sea, to observe Southern naval activities.

One of La Mountain's balloons was inflated and secured to the *Fanny*'s stern by mooring ropes. On August 3, 1861, the boat steamed out into the channel opposite Sewall's Point, Virginia, and once in position, La Mountain lifted off—the first pilot ever to be in an aircraft that ascended from the deck of a vessel. At an altitude of 2,000 feet, the aeronaut could easily see the Confederate positions. The Rebels were busy constructing additional gun pits and embrasures, fortifications that were not detectable from the ground.

La Mountain sketched the enemy positions, and his keen observations resulted in some finely detailed reports. A typical dispatch read: "On the left bank of the James River, about eight or nine miles from Newport News, is a large encampment of the enemy, from 150 to 200 tents." It was a promising start, but La Mountain's hydrogen gas supply ran out after two weeks of operations. La Mountain received permission to go back to Troy, New York, to get a bigger balloon and gas generator, but when he returned to Fortress Monroe, much to his chagrin, there was a new commander who didn't care for balloons.

That was discouraging enough, but then the *Fanny* was captured by Confederate gunboats off Loggerhead Inlet, North Carolina, in late August. Its nascent career as the world's first aircraft carrier, ground-breaking though it was, came to an end.

La Mountain's days as a military balloonist were also numbered. He refused to serve under the Union's chief aeronaut, Thaddeus S. C. Lowe, whom he disliked intensely. As far as Lowe was concerned, the feelings were mutual. The two aeronauts started to bicker, a situation made worse by La Mountain's unwillingness to surrender his status as an independent military balloonist and join the corps. Unfortunately for the stubborn balloonist, his rival, Lowe, was at the peak of his influence and had powerful friends. John La Mountain was dismissed from his position in February 1862. He continued as a professional aeronaut until his death eight years later at the age of forty-one—a death that might have been related to injuries sustained in a previous air accident.

AERIAL SPOTTING OF ARTILLERY FIRE

The first aerial spotting of artillery fire in military history took place in northeastern Virginia on September 24, 1861, when Thaddeus S. C. Lowe directed guns from a balloon high in the air. This was truly unique in warfare in that the artillerymen could fire at targets that were not visible to them.

The action itself was more of a trial run to test the concept, but the ammunition nevertheless was real and the enemy was on the receiving end. Union general William F. Smith ordered his gunners at Chain Bridge to fire on Confederate-held Falls Church, while Lowe, from the vantage point of his balloon, gauged their shots for range and deflection. Using a telegraphic hookup, the aeronaut would convey his observations to the mortar batteries some two miles away. The experiment worked splendidly, with the artillerists pinpointing their targets based upon Lowe's input.

Pleased with the results, General Smith then tried a system of flag signals, anticipating the possibility that use of the telegraph might not be feasible under certain combat conditions. When shots fell to the right, a white flag was raised vertically in the basket; when a shot fell too far left, that movement was indicated by lowering the flag. An overshot was shown by holding the flag stationary in a horizontal position; too short a shot was communicated by waving the flag in a horizontal arc. Secondary observers trained their field glasses on the balloon basket to read the signals, which proved to be just as effective as the telegraph.

The experiments conducted by General Smith and aeronaut Lowe on that September 24, 1861, did not lead to a major breakthrough in military science, nor was the mortaring that day of any strategic significance. Yet it presaged a time when artillery spotting from the air would be of major import, and in that sense, then, their efforts were pioneering.

BOMBARDMENT OF ISLAND NO. 10

Early in February 1862, George B. McClellan, then commanding general of all Union armies, decided to send an observation balloon to the Mississippi River theater of the war. At this time, Gen. John Pope's newly formed federal Army of the Mississippi was marching on New Madrid, a strategic point on the Mississippi River above a bend at the Kentucky–Tennessee border. The bend was defended by a Confederate fortress located on what was known as Island No. 10. Unless this stronghold was reduced, Union forces could make no further progress along the great "Father of Waters."

Upon receipt of McClellan's order, Chief Aeronaut Thaddeus S. C. Lowe dispatched John H. Steiner, one of his ablest balloonists. A German immigrant who may not have mastered all the intricacies of his adopted country's tongue, Steiner still had wide experience as an aeronaut. Even before the war he had enjoyed a degree of fame, having performed the first balloon ascension in Toronto, Canada. Prior to his western assignment, he had served in the balloon corps with Union forces on the upper Potomac.

Arriving in Cairo, Illinois, in late February, with balloon and support equipment in tow, Steiner was ready and eager to begin his ascents. But local army commanders did not share McClellan's enthusiasm for aeronautics, and the German had to wait in idle frustration. When Steiner tried to convince officers of the usefulness of his mission, he was simply made a laughingstock. Heaped ridicule upon and stonewalled by the army, the aeronaut finally received recognition from an unexpected quarter—the U.S. Navy.

On March 13 New Madrid was taken, but further progress was impeded by the Island No. 10 fortress some ten miles below the captured town. General Pope made the island the next major objective of the campaign, and Commodore Andrew H. Foote's gun and mortar boats were charged with softening it up. Steiner approached Foote, and to the aeronaut's great relief, the commodore gladly accepted his offer of assistance.

By the time Steiner had won his assignment, Island No. 10 had already been subjected to bombardment by the Union navy's mortar boats, but with little apparent effect. The Yankee shells were just too inaccurate to cause significant damage. It was hoped Steiner's observations would help the mortars zero in on their targets.

A large flatboat was placed at Steiner's disposal, and on March 25, 1862, the aeronaut went aloft, but poor visibility—brought on by smoke from the continuous bombardment and haze from the river—prevented him from accurately gauging Union mortar fire. The next day Steiner went up again, but this time he was not alone in the balloon car; Col. N. B. Buford and Capt. H. E. Maynadier, both artillery officers, were there to direct the fire themselves. Shells were seen to be overshooting the target, and corrections were made. Soon the mortars had found the range, and their 13-inch shells were ripping through the Confederate emplacements.

Within ten days Union troops crossed the Mississippi below the island and severed its communications. Battered and now isolated, Island No. 10 surrendered April 7. The first aerially directed naval artillery fire in history had clearly played a role in the reduction of the fortress.

The siege of Island No. 10 was the last military milestone established by the U.S. balloon corps. There was too much red tape, too much bureaucratic inertia, and too many hidebound army officers for the corps to fight. There were occasional high spots, but all too often the balloonists were either ridiculed or simply ignored. Take, for example, John Steiner's situation. Although his accented English and phonetic spelling probably added to his difficulties, Steiner reported that he could "not git eny ascistence" from the Union officers. "They even laugh ad me. . . . Give me a paper from Headvauters," he asked Lowe, "to show theas blockheads hoo I am." John Starkweather, a balloonist sent to South Carolina, met with an even chillier reception. Ignored, he pleaded, "All I want is the chance."

The fact that Lowe and his fellow aeronauts were civilians without military status helps explain at least in part their shabby treatment by many army officers. Of course, the dead hand of bureaucracy—administrative snarls, lack of adequate supplies, infrequent paychecks—exacerbated the already low morale of the balloonists.

But the final straw was the appointment of Capt. Cyrus Comstock of the corps of engineers as Lowe's immediate superior. Comstock reduced the chief aeronaut's pay from $10 a day to $6 and added insult to injury by insisting that Lowe's father be dismissed from the balloon ground crew. Most galling of all, however, was Comstock's firm insistence on "going through channels" when doing business. Refusing to be strait-jacketed in that way, fed up with the petty slights, and privately feeling unappreciated, Lowe resigned in May 1863. A month later the balloon corps was officially disbanded. Lowe himself blamed its demise on three critical factors: "first, the very limited means allowed; secondly, want of authority to properly organize a corps; and thirdly, the very few persons experienced with glasses to take observations from the Balloons."

Whatever the reasons, the Confederates were thankful. Gen. James Longstreet, for instance, was unable to conceal his envy of the U.S. balloon corps when he wrote after the war, "We were longing for the balloons that poverty denied us." And another Southern officer noted that the Union aeronauts, at the very least, "forced upon us constant troublesome precautions in efforts to conceal our marches."

THE "SILK DRESS BALLOON"

The Union balloon corps, which operated from 1861 to 1863, was obviously a thorn in the Confederate side, providing vital data on Southern numbers and troop movements. Rebel authorities were well aware of the advantages of these hydrogen envelopes but were unable to muster the means to respond in kind. For one thing, the South lacked the materials to build a balloon fleet, and besides, the Union blockade prevented, or at least impeded, getting such supplies from abroad.

In spite of these difficulties, the Confederates tried to construct a balloon at least a handful of times. At the beginning of the Peninsula campaign, to cite one of the first attempts, Confederate general John Bankhead Magruder threw together a crude cotton bag, filled it with hot air, and sent it forth with a somewhat unwilling aeronaut named John Bryan. Hot air as a propellant hadn't been used since the Montgolfier brothers in the eighteenth century, so this effort was a step backward in more ways than one.

The Magruder balloon performed with predictable results. It soon deflated, also deflating Confederate hopes of competing with the Union in the air. But the South was not yet willing to concede the skies to the Yankees. In the spring of 1862 Langdon Cheves, Jr., tried his hand at building a balloon. A South Carolina rice planter and businessman, forty-eight-year-old Cheves served the South as a captain of engineers. In June 1862 he was responsible for the Confederacy's only major venture in aeronautics.

The Southern cause is often enmeshed in a nostalgic romanticism, and in such a favorable soil myths and legends take root and grow. Cheves's aircraft soon became known as the "silk dress balloon." According to the story, patriotic Southern belles contributed to the cause their silk dresses as material to make the balloon envelope. Such is the enduring strength of myth that even modern sources repeat the tale, though it is completely false.

In reality, the balloon was made of new imported silk, which must have been costly because of the Union blockade (Cheves paid for the material out of his own pocket). Its volume was a not inconsiderable 7,500 cubic feet. There was one drawback: hydrogen was not available, so Richmond city gas was used to inflate the envelope.

The "silk dress balloon"'s service was brief, but not inglorious. From June 27 to July 4, it made several ascents and relayed information on Northern forces during the battle of Gaines' Mill. The Union's chief aeronaut, Thaddeus S. C. Lowe, was also aloft at this time, telegraphing data to the ground below. The battle of Gaines' Mill stands unique in the annals of military aviation, because for those few days in mid-1862, two opposing armies—for the first time ever—were employing aircraft.

During this brief moment, the Confederacy had a fully operational balloon, an "air force" to rival the Union in observations if not in numbers. The Rebels even attached their balloon to the small armed tug *Teaser,* making the vessel a kind of Confederate "aircraft carrier." But the "silk dress balloon"'s operational service days were numbered. In fact, its waterborne service ultimately proved its undoing. On July 4 the *Teaser* ran aground on the James River below Malvern Hill and was captured, balloon and all, by the Union gunboat *Maritanza.* It was another unprecedented moment in the history of American warfare, since this was the first enemy aircraft—and enemy aircraft carrier— ever captured by U.S. military forces.

The "silk dress balloon" was the last serious attempt by the Confederacy to match, or at least counter, the Union balloon corps. Lack of materials, coupled by a scarcity of trained personnel, brought the matter to a close.

PROPAGANDA LEAFLETS FROM THE AIR

Union general Benjamin F. Butler was one of the most controversial military figures of his day. A politician before the war, Butler achieved a certain notoriety as military governor of occupied New Orleans.

Southerners grew to loathe him, branding him "Beast Butler" for his threat to treat the overly zealous Confederate ladies of the city as common prostitutes. If not his actions, Butler's very appearance made him a figure of contempt, even ridicule; his bald head, squinting eyes lost in crevasses of flesh, and walrus mustache made him seem to one critic like a "cross-eyed cuttlefish."

But there was more to Butler than being a strict disciplinarian or having an ungainly exterior. Beneath the portly facade, he had an innovative mind and was ever ready to try new things. Indeed, he was the first American military officer to authorize the dropping of propaganda leaflets behind enemy lines.

Butler was hoping to capitalize on the leniency of President Lincoln's reconstruction plan, which he had announced in December 1863. As part of the program, Lincoln offered a full pardon to most Southerners, if they would pledge their allegiance to the Constitution of the United States. Only high-ranking Confederate military officers and civilian officials would be exempt from this decree.

As shortages of food, clothing, shoes, and medicine took their toll on the ordinary Confederate soldier, Butler thought that the presidential offer of amnesty might have military applications. Perhaps the amnesty proclamation would provide just the right inducement for Confederate troops to bolt a lost cause and surrender.

In the spring of 1864 General Butler was in command of the Army of the James, more than 30,000 men and eighty-two guns. Frustrated by the fact that the Union's drive to Richmond was stalled, Butler decided to try a little psychological warfare. A kite was devised that held a bundle of leaflets detailing Lincoln's amnesty offer. When the kite flew over Confederate positions between Petersburg and Richmond, a string released the captive circulars to rain down on Southern heads.

The paper "cloudburst" seems to have had little effect on Confederate troops. There was no mass exodus to Union lines to surrender, and Southern soldiers fought on as bravely as before. But it was still a novel idea and worth a try.

CHAPTER 6

Intelligence Gathering and Security Measures

M ilitary espionage dates back to biblical times. Around 1200 B.C., as recorded in the Book of Joshua, the Israelite leader "secretly sent out two spies from Shittim, saying 'Go, reconnoiter the land and Jericho.'" Throughout the ages, military strategists have long recognized the pivotal role played by those courageous men and women who have risked imprisonment, torture, and death to glean vital information from the enemy. "Too much attention cannot be given to spies," declared the eighteenth-century French military commander Marshal Saxe. "They are as necessary to a general as the eyes are to the head."

The first notable American experience in intelligence gathering was during the American Revolution. George Washington, celebrated as the "father of his country," is also the father of American espionage. Saddled with a small, amateur army, scanty resources, and a fractious Congress, Washington faced an uphill battle against a well-financed, professional British military force. In order to level the battlefield, the general became his own intelligence chief, using the information he gained from a network of agents to anticipate and, if possible, counter British moves.

Yet Washington's spy ring was his own creation, unofficial, and with no professional standing within the new government. By the time the second war with Great Britain broke out in 1812, the U.S. lacked an intelligence service, leaving its armies pretty much in the dark as to British strategy. Without accurate information, the Americans allowed themselves to be duped—not once, but twice—into believing that they were outnumbered by the British, resulting in the loss of Detroit and Washington.

During the Mexican War, the U.S. at least made an effort to gather intelligence. Aside from the army engineers who provided reports on terrain and the enemy's defenses, Gen. Winfield Scott set up the "Mexican Spy Company," consisting of some 200 Mexican bandits who succeeded in giving the Americans some valuable information—that is, for a price (the total cost was over $16,000). But the employment of turncoats, outcasts, and traitors set no precedent for a permanent intelligence organization.

The sheer scale of the Civil War, coupled by the fact that momentous issues were being decided, finally placed espionage, counterespionage, and security in the forefront of national concerns. While the conflict raged on, those in the Union witnessed the birth of several organized intelligence operations, two created by prominent detectives and a third, more modern agency formed by a U.S. Army general. Internal security was also a concern, and counterintelligence as well as the suppression of disloyal activities proceeded apace during the war. And for the first time, a measure of control was placed over the movements of Americans when they attempted to leave or reenter the country.

Establishing security through a military or police presence inevitably poses a threat to the very liberties of citizens living in a democracy. Striking a balance between the right of a government to maintain itself and the right of an individual in a free society has always been a difficult task. It is indeed a credit to the basic soundness of American political institutions, as well as a credit to the political leaders who had to deal with such issues during the Civil War, that the liberties of the people remained intact after the greatest upheaval in U.S. history.

ALLAN PINKERTON

Today the Pinkerton agency is one of the most recognizable in the private security industry. Created a century and a half ago, its founder, Allan Pinkerton, was a bold and innovative man, who not only made a name for himself as the foremost private investigator of his day, but also played a pivotal role gathering intelligence for the Union during the Civil War.

Pinkerton was a Scotsman, born in Glasgow in 1819, the son of a policeman. After his father was injured on duty, Allan was apprenticed to a barrelmaker, and at nineteen he became an independent craftsman. Young and idealistic, Pinkerton soon got involved with the Chartists, considered a radical group, since it was seeking social reform and political democracy for the working class. Having taken part in several demonstrations, Pinkerton feared arrest and fled the country, immigrating to the U.S. He and his wife, whom he had married the day before sailing to America, settled in Dundee, Illinois, and there the young Scotsman opened a cooperage. Not long afterward, however, an incident occurred that would alter his life forever. While cutting hoops for barrels on an unfrequented island not far from his home, he stumbled upon a group of counterfeiters. After seeking help, he captured the entire gang. This launched his police career, and in 1850 the Pinkertons moved to Chicago, where Allan joined the city's newly organized police force and at the same time established a private detective agency.

The Pinkerton agency almost immediately gained a reputation for both professionalism and results. Its main mission, during these early years, was to deal with the rising number of railroad robberies that were seemingly increasing with each new mile of track. Having cracked several cases, Pinkerton became so successful that he left the Chicago police force and devoted himself full-time to his company, whose logo—a wide-open human eye with the words "We Never Sleep" printed under it—earned Pinkerton the nickname "The Eye" for his well-known vigilance, and also led to the coining of the expression "private eye."

After the clash at Fort Sumter in April 1861, it was only a matter of time before Pinkerton, the nation's most famous detective, would be sought after. A firm antislavery man who at one time had befriended and supported the martyred John Brown, Pinkerton was ready and willing to do his part for the Union. Within weeks he received a request for his services from none other than Gen. George B. McClellan, a former railroad executive who had known Pinkerton on both a personal and a professional level. In May 1861 the general, in command of the Department of the Ohio (which encompassed western Virginia, Kentucky, and Tennessee), was interested in obtaining information on Rebel activity within his jurisdiction. Pinkerton accepted the assignment and at once sent agents into the field, while he himself in disguise traveled through Kentucky, Tennessee, and some say as far south as Mississippi. Upon his return, after providing McClellan with accurate reports of Confederate forces in the immediate and outlying areas, Pinkerton set up his bureau—the first organized intelligence agency in U.S. history.

When McClellan was appointed commander of the Army of the Potomac in July 1861, Pinkerton moved his operation to Washington. But his mission remained essentially the same: to gather information through intelligence and to ferret out spies, civilian and military alike, through counterintelligence. In several respects, Pinkerton's bureau performed its duties well, particularly when it came to the interrogation of prisoners, deserters, or runaway slaves. But it had its shortcomings, a direct result of the quirky personality of its creator.

Basically, Pinkerton's operation was a civilian business contracted by the army and paid by the War Department, and therefore had no official standing. Nevertheless, the modern term "government spooks" could apply to Pinkerton and his agents, given the fact that there was something insubstantial and spectral about the organization. Secrecy is normal for espionage and other such clandestine operations, but with the bushy-bearded Scot it became a passion, almost a mania. Pinkerton went under the cover name of "E. J. Allen" and later in the war as "Major Allen." His operatives also had code names, their real names known only to the chief himself, and unknown even to the highest Union officials who used their information. Monthly pay vouchers either listed initials or went through the alphabet as "Operative D," "Operative E," all the way down the line, including even an "Operative X."

This cloak-and-dagger subterfuge got to be too much for Secretary of War Edwin M. Stanton, who tried to force Pinkerton to reveal the names. The intelligence chief refused. Stanton was a formidable individual, not easily thwarted, but in this case he met his match. The War Department ended up paying blind for operatives they knew nothing about, remaining as much in the dark about Pinkerton's men as everyone else.

Yet for all his eccentricities, Pinkerton cannot be dismissed as a mere crank. He exposed enemy agents and was successful in gleaning information on the Confederate army. Then why was Pinkerton's work for the military short-lived and subjected to severe criticism? In order to answer these questions, one would have to be aware of the limitations of Gen. George B. McClellan, the man who hired Pinkerton for the job.

McClellan has been held to task, and justifiably so, as a mediocre battlefield commander, overly cautious and dilatory in movement. Insisting that he was outnumbered or lacking necessary reserves, he refused to march against Richmond while on the Peninsula in the spring of 1862, and less than six months later, he failed to pursue the retreating Lee after defeating him on the battlefield at Antietam. He was, as Lincoln said in his folksy way, infected with the "slows."

Still McClellan's apologists have often blamed Pinkerton for misleading the general by producing reports that inflated enemy numbers. Modern studies have shown that, in the main, such charges against

Pinkerton are not accurate. "Far from being a victim of the overestimates," most scholars tend to believe that "McClellan was party to them." To be sure, Pinkerton idolized McClellan to the point of sycophancy and might have tailored figures to what the general wanted to hear. But "Little Mac"—as his admirers affectionately referred to him—compounded the problem by his own indelible mental image of a vastly superior enemy. Perhaps the final verdict, unless new evidence comes to light, has been rendered by intelligence expert and historian Edwin C. Fishel. "Among Civil War generals McClellan had many companions in believing himself outnumbered," Fishel wrote. "With no other army commander, however, did this belief so condemn his campaigns to failure, as on the Peninsula, or deny him a decisive victory, as on the Antietam."

On November 7, 1862, the very day McClellan was relieved of command, Pinkerton submitted his resignation as head of intelligence for the Army of the Potomac. Despite Stanton and Lincoln urging him to stay on, Pinkerton returned to Chicago. For the duration of the conflict, he accepted nonespionage investigatory assignments from the War Department, checking out claims against the government and unearthing frauds, which sent many a crooked businessman to jail. After Appomattox Pinkerton returned to the private detective trade, where his company continued to be foremost in its field. During the last quarter of the nineteenth century, a period of increasingly violent labor unrest, the Pinkerton agency was often called upon to provide armed guards to protect companies being picketed. As far as the workers were concerned, the "Pinkertons" were nothing more than strike breakers. Ironically, the founder of the company, who had always championed the underdog, was now viewed by labor as the despised head of corporate America's private police force. Pinkerton died in 1884.

BUREAU OF MILITARY INFORMATION

The Bureau of Military Information was the first intelligence agency in U.S. history to collect, evaluate, and synthesize *all* sources of information. Prior to the appearance of the bureau, the Union war effort was served by much smaller intelligence operations performing limited functions. The very first, of course, was Allan Pinkerton's group serving the Army of the Potomac. But there had also been another spy corps of sorts, the National Detective Bureau, organized by Lafayette C. Baker, a former San Franciscan who had helped bring law and order to that city as a member of its famous (or infamous) Second Vigilance

Committee. Upon arriving in Washington, Baker secured employment first as an intelligence agent for Gen. Winfield Scott, then for Secretary of State Seward, and ultimately ended up reporting to Secretary of War Stanton. Characterized by a modern researcher as "an overzealous gumshoe and self-important rascal," Baker was chiefly involved in counterespionage in and around Washington, D.C.

Whatever the scope of their duties, neither Pinkerton nor Baker provided their superiors with what is now called "all-source intelligence." Pinkerton is a good case in point. The reports he submitted to Gen. George McClellan were at best fragmentary, based solely on his efforts at espionage and interrogation, and thereby ignoring a wide array of data. To weaken the operation's effectiveness even further, McClellan chose to do his own analysis of Pinkerton's findings in addition to all other raw intelligence items sent to him, a near impossible task for a busy commander of an army totaling some 100,000 men.

The Bureau of Military Information did much to set things right. Gen. Joseph "'Fightin' Joe" Hooker is often remembered as the man who suffered a catastrophic defeat at the hands of Robert E. Lee at the battle of Chancellorsville in May 1863. Yet the much maligned Hooker deserves recognition for his positive contributions to the war effort as well. Several months before his ill-fated encounter with Lee, Hooker established the Bureau of Military Information—America's first all-source intelligence operation.

The chief of the bureau was Col. George H. Sharpe. A graduate of Yale Law School, well traveled, and having served at the U.S. legations in Vienna and Rome, the thirty-five-year-old Sharpe had the necessary background and skills to get the job done. When it came to the enemy, he left no source untapped. Information was culled from prisoners, deserters, refugees, newspapers, scouts working for individual generals, the cavalry, the signal corps, aerial observations from the balloon corps, and dispatches from Washington and various field commands. In addition, Sharpe employed a corps of 200 spies and scouts (he called them "guides" for payroll purposes) who provided even more information. Sometimes Sharpe's "guides" wore Confederate uniforms for infiltration purposes, but for the most part, forged identity papers, passes, and the like seem to have been little used.

The Bureau of Military Information proved its effectiveness before the battles of Chancellorsville and Gettysburg. In the case of the former, Sharpe had produced detailed information on Gen. Robert E. Lee's Army of Northern Virginia, accurately reporting to Hooker that the enemy had only 60,000 effectives to the Union's 130,000. But military intelligence in and of itself cannot produce victory. Having suffered a devastating defeat at Chancellorsville, Hooker, disgraced and resentful, didn't want to hear that he had been defeated by an enemy with inferior numbers. In a sense, he took his frustration out on the bureau, casting aspersions upon his own creation. The provost marshal general of the Union army, Marsena Rudolph Patrick, noted that the bureau had furnished Hooker with "the most astonishingly correct information" yet was treated "with indifference at first, and now with insult."

After Hooker was relieved of command, Gen. George Meade was placed at the head of the Army of the Potomac. Once again, Sharpe and the bureau supplied accurate reports of Confederate strengths and troop movements, which helped contribute significantly to the Union victory at Gettysburg. By contrast General Lee invaded Pennsylvania virtually "blind," deprived of his cavalry reconnaissance "eyes" because of Gen. J. E. B. Stuart's grandstanding ride around Union forces.

The bureau continued operating throughout the remainder of the war. In March 1864 Sharpe was appointed as head of intelligence for Ulysses S. Grant, then general in chief of the Union armies.

The Bureau of Military Information chalked up an altogether impressive record. Its emphasis on all-source gathering and analysis of information made it decades ahead of its time. The bureau was disbanded after the Civil War and nothing like it existed until World War II. With passage of the National Security Act of 1947, the bureau's spiritual descendant—the Central Intelligence Agency—achieved permanent status within the U.S. government.

WOMEN SPIES

The Civil War was the first American conflict in which hundreds of women served as spies for the military. Because their activities were of necessity cloaked in secrecy, the precise number involved in espionage will never be fully known. Rumor and innuendo have often been substituted for concrete facts. If you broaden the definition of spy to include informants, however, then according to Mary Elizabeth Massey in her pioneer work, *Bonnet Brigades,* "countless women . . . aided one or the other army, for there were thousands who by a single deed rendered valuable service."

When it came to espionage women had many advantages over men. First, there was the matter of feminine attire. Bell-shaped hoop skirts, petticoats, and corsets made ideal hiding places for secret messages and other data. Women also wore their hair long, often reaching to midback, allowing them to conceal notes and other tokens of the spy trade.

By today's standards, women were second-class citizens in the 1860s, worshiped as icons of feminine beauty and charm but denied substantive rights in what was essentially a male world. Yet paradoxically, their inequality had its advantages in espionage. Because women were "on a pedestal," they were in a sense above reproach and better able to get away with things than a man. They were also, as ladies, less likely to be searched carefully by men.

Even when caught, their gender protected them, at least to some extent. No woman was ever executed for espionage, though in one instance a Union female spy came very close. On the other hand, hapless male spies, Yankee or Rebel, faced hanging. Two Union agents, Timothy Webster and Spencer Brown, went to the gallows, as did two Confederate operatives, Sam Davis and David O. Dodd.

This is not to say that women did not confront death, but such a possibility was more likely while they were engaged in the actual commission of espionage rather than at the hands of an executioner. Some received prison sentences when convicted, but here again their gender sometimes softened the blow. In 1864 Sarah Hutchings was convicted of supplying arms to Confederate guerrilla Harry Gilmore and sentenced to a term of two to five years in the Fitchburg (Massachusetts) House of Corrections. Given the public outcry over the ruling, Lincoln pardoned her after a few weeks when she promised to "conduct herself in a loyal manner."

Perhaps the most famous member of Dixie's espionage sorority was Rose Greenhow, celebrated as "Rebel Rosie," the person who provided information to Gen. P. G. T. Beauregard and thus helped the Confederacy win the first battle of Bull Run. In 1861 Greenhow, a forty-two-year-old widow, well placed and well connected, was active in Washington society. When she gained secret information that the Union army was definitely going to move on Manassas, she sent this vital intelligence to General Beauregard's headquarters. And when she learned of the timetable of the advance, she sent the Confederate general a second dispatch as well. Although some question the importance of these warnings—Manassas Junction was an obvious target, Union troop movements were common knowledge, and Beauregard was certainly no fool—no one could deny the courage it took to pass this information on.

In any event, "Rebel Rosie's" operation was soon shut down. She had long been suspected as a Confederate informant, and her residence was under surveillance by Union counterespionage agent Allan Pinkerton, who, on August 23, 1861, ordered her arrest. Having bungled badly by leaving around copies of the reports she had forwarded to Beauregard, Greenhow tried to destroy all the incriminating evidence before being taken into custody, but was not entirely successful. Greenhow had influential friends who secured her release, however, and they helped her relocate to the Confederacy. In August 1863 President Jefferson Davis sent her on a diplomatic mission to Europe, where she had some success, securing an audience with Napoleon III and Queen Victoria. But on the return voyage, her blockade runner was chased by a Union gunboat. Demanding to be put ashore before the Yankees seized the ship, even though the captain warned her that the seas were rough, Greenhow had her way. While being rowed ashore, she fell overboard and drowned. Fearless to the end, "Rebel Rosie" was buried with full military honors.

Belle Boyd was another Southern spy who gained fame, probably with more justification than most of her fellow operatives. Only seventeen when the war broke out in 1861, the Virginia-born Boyd wasted no time making a name for herself. While a Yankee sergeant attempted to raise a flag over her house in the Shenandoah Valley, an altercation ensued in which the soldier cursed Boyd's mother. Considering his action an unpardonable offense, the impulsive teenager shot and killed the soldier on the spot. Luckily for Boyd, her sex, age, and a strict code of conduct for Union troops in the area all worked to her advantage; a group of officers investigating the incident concluded that it was justifiable homicide. Rather than feeling a sense of gratitude for the verdict, Boyd was emboldened by it, soon taking on the role of a full-fledged Confederate spy. During the course of the war, her greatest exploit was delivering critical information to Gen. Thomas "Stonewall" Jackson in May 1862, enabling his forces to capture Front Royal, Virginia, and move forward to Winchester. Not usually one to hand out praise, Jackson thanked young Belle "for the immense service you have rendered your country."

In July 1862 her luck ran out, or at least so it seemed. She was seized by Union authorities and incarcerated at Washington's Old Capitol Prison. Masterful at manipulating men, in her two months of captivity she became engaged to a fellow prisoner and simultaneously so charmed the warden of the prison that after her release he sent her a trousseau. Once in the South, Boyd broke off her engagement, apparently believing that "all's fair in love and war."

In the spring of 1864, with smuggled dispatches in her possession, Boyd tried to sail to England aboard the blockade runner *Greyhound,* but the vessel was captured by the U.S. Navy. The ship was taken back to Boston as a prize, and en route, a young Union navy officer named Samuel Hardinge became smitten with Boyd. Blinded by his love for her, Hardinge let the Confederate captain of the *Greyhound* escape. For this he was court-martialed and imprisoned, but he somehow fled to England, where he met up with Boyd, who had made her way across the Atlantic and was waiting for him. The pair married and produced a daughter, but soon afterward Hardinge died—the causes are disputed— and Boyd found herself a twenty-one-year-old mother and widow. A survivor above all else, Boyd, who became known as the "Cleopatra of the Secession," after the war cashed in on her fame with speaking engagements on her life as a spy.

The Union, too, had its women operatives. Although Harriet Tubman is best known for conducting an antebellum underground railroad, which rescued anywhere between 60 to 300 slaves, she also proved to be one of the most effective spies for the Union. A fugitive slave herself, Tubman was living in Canada when the war came. In view of her reputation, she easily procured passes to enter Union lines and ended up serving as a spy and scout for Maj. Gen. David Hunter in Beaufort, South Carolina, where Union forces had retaken several of the Sea Islands. Sometimes she worked alone, and sometimes she led troops deep into Confederate territory, "usually returning with valuable information and slaves she had spirited away from their masters." While the military made good use of the intelligence Tubman secured, it also benefited from her activities as an emancipator. Of the more than 750 slaves she ferried to freedom, "nearly or quite all the able-bodied men" went on to join the Union army. She was an extraordinary woman who had served her country in an extraordinary way, yet her efforts went unrecognized. Denied a pension by the government, Harriet Tubman died penniless and in obscurity.

Elizabeth Van Lew was a woman of far different background than Tubman, but they had more in common than what appeared on the surface. Both were shrewd and courageous, and they shared a deep commitment to the Union cause. Van Lew was a Virginian, a scion of a wealthy aristocratic family, which allowed her to mask her true anti-slavery and Unionist sentiments. Eventually Van Lew became an agent of the Bureau of Military Information, using her own considerable fortune to create a spy network within Richmond.

She managed to play the role of a slightly addled "spinster" to perfection, even to twitching her head and rambling nonsense in the streets. As "Crazy Bet," a harmless eccentric, she managed to throw off suspicion until nearly the end of the war. Perhaps her greatest coup was planting a supposedly illiterate African-American maid named Mary Bowser in the home of President Jefferson Davis. Van Lew had freed Bowser and all the other slaves on her plantation but made certain that they had been taught to read and write. Because she was black and a former slave, everyone assumed that Bowser was uneducated and nothing more than a simple-minded domestic. In fact, she was a highly intelligent woman capable of recalling in detail conversations she overheard between Davis and members of his cabinet and army command. She also read and memorized classified documents left lying about on the Confederate president's desk. As such, Bowser turned out to be the source of much of the intelligence Van Lew transmitted to the Bureau of Military Information.

Van Lew never considered herself a traitor to the South but a Southern abolitionist loyal to the concept of the Union. In the last days of the war, with Richmond finally about to fall to Union forces, rumors of Van Lew's "treason" circulated, and an angry mob collected in front of her house. Facing her accusers squarely, she let it be known that if her house was touched, General Grant would burn their houses to the ground. The crowd relented.

After the war Mary Bowser moved North, and we know nothing of her later life. As for Van Lew, she was ostracized by the people of Richmond and neglected by the very government she had served so well. Having spent most of her fortune on Unionist espionage activities, she filed a claim for $15,000 in reimbursement. General Grant himself approved the request, writing, "From her I received the most valuable intelligence that ever came from Richmond throughout the entire conflict." Yet in spite of this ringing endorsement, the claim was turned down. Refusing to allow Washington's bureaucracy to have the last word, Grant took matters into his own hands when he became president and appointed Van Lew postmistress of Richmond with a salary of $4,000 a year.

LINCOLN'S SUSPENSION OF HABEAS CORPUS

During the Civil War Abraham Lincoln had to maintain a precarious balance. On one hand, he was compelled to take the necessary steps to ensure the Union's continued survival, but on the other, he was bound to protect the liberties of individual citizens as guaranteed by the Constitution. Hardly an easy task in view of the "enemy in the rear"—an enemy, as the president phrased it, consisting of "a most efficient corps of spies, informers, suppliers, and aiders and abettors" of the rebellion who used as their cover "Liberty of speech, Liberty of the press and *Habeas corpus.*" Determined to maintain a *United* States whatever the cost, Lincoln took decisive action, even if it meant suppression of some of those very liberties he had taken a solemn oath to uphold. As a result, for the first time in American history, thousands of civilians were imprisoned without charges or trial in civil courts.

By suspending the privilege of the writ of habeas corpus, which requires that a citizen be told the charges against him and the court then determines whether there is sufficient cause to hold him, Lincoln was treading on dubious constitutional ground. At the time, many argued, including Chief Justice of the Supreme Court Roger B. Taney, that only Congress could legally suspend the writ—but in truth, the Constitution did not specify precisely who held that power, so the president did not think he had violated the law of the land.

In any event, Lincoln first suspended habeas corpus in parts of Maryland where Rebel guerrilla activity had occurred or where there had been mob violence directed at Union forces. A slave state of divided loyalties, with an active secessionist minority, Maryland had to be held for the Union. It bordered Washington, D.C., on three sides; Rebel Virginia was on the fourth. If Maryland joined the Confederacy, the North's capital would be completely surrounded and untenable, a situation that many in the administration considered too chilling to even contemplate.

In mid-September 1861 Union troops arrested a number of pro-Southern Marylanders, including the mayor and chief of police of Baltimore and thirty-one secessionist members of the state legislature. These legislators were incarcerated for about two months, until a new legislature sympathetic to the North was elected in November. Once Maryland was firmly in the Unionist camp, the Federal government relaxed its grip. Many were released upon taking an oath of allegiance to the United States; a few hard-core "Secesh" were kept in jail until all Maryland political prisoners were freed in December 1862.

But the writ of habeas corpus remained suspended in Maryland, and eventually the policy was extended to the entire country in order to prevent, as Lincoln explained, "disloyal persons [who] are not adequately restrained by the ordinary processes of law from . . . giving aid and comfort in various ways to the insurrection." Under this blanket suspension (and factoring in those incarcerated prior to it), probably more than 14,000 people were arrested and imprisoned during the course of the war.

Much controversy concerns the offenses of the detainees. Although there was a hue and cry against Lincoln as a suppresser of civil liberties, it seems that most prisoners deserved confinement and were in jail not for dissent or political opposition, but for serious crimes. Pulitzer Prize-winning historian Mark E. Neely, Jr., has mustered an enormous amount of evidence to prove that most of those taken into custody and held without benefit of habeas corpus were either citizens of the Confederacy or borderland residents who were suspected spies, smugglers, blockade runners, bushwhackers, and the like. What is most significant, according to Neely, is that "a majority of the arrests would have occurred whether the writ was suspended or not. They were caused by the mere incidents or friction of war. . . . [Those arrested] may have been civilians, but their political views were irrelevant."

Lincoln ably defended his seemingly "dictatorial" measures, insisting that suppression, or partial suppression, of civil liberties was only a temporary policy, a bitter medicine, that would help break the fever of rebellion that had infected the body politic. Using a medical metaphor, as he often did to drive home his point, the president maintained that he could no more believe that the infringements on civil liberties in wartime would set a peacetime precedent than he was "able to believe that a man could contract so strong an appetite for emetics during a temporary illness, as to persist in feeding upon them through the remainder of his healthful life."

The record speaks for itself. In fact, there are those who have argued that "Americans' personal liberties fared better during the Civil War than during either World Wars I or II."

PASSPORTS

Passports have not always been a requirement for U.S. citizens leaving or entering the country. The first time Congress mandated such a document was in 1815, while America was at war with England. At that time, a passport was required only under "certain circumstances"— namely, if a traveler from the United States planned to enter territory occupied by the enemy. Otherwise, Americans were free to depart and return to the country without documentation, a situation that remained in effect until 1861.

The Civil War raised a whole new set of problems concerning travel into and from the United States. In the first place, there were those persons residing in the Union whose loyalty was open to question. Should they be allowed unrestricted mobility, perhaps enabling them to make direct contact with the enemy? And second, there were those on the outside who might wish to enter the United States for purposes of sabotage and the like. Should their movements go unmonitored? Early in the war Secretary of State William H. Seward took a firm stand on these matters. In August 1861 he issued a directive, requiring for the first time in U.S. history that those leaving or entering the country must have passports.

By 1863, with implementation of a national conscription act, the passport was also used as a means to ensure that potential draftees would not evade military service. Men between the ages of eighteen and forty-five were denied passports unless they furnished a "surgeon's certificate" confirming that they were physically unable to perform military duty, provided evidence that they had a substitute ready to take their place, or posted a financial bond promising to fulfill their obligation if called upon.

The passport system lasted only through the Civil War years. It was not implemented again until World War I and then was discontinued in 1919 until World War II. Finally, in 1952, the passport was made a requirement of "all U.S. citizens for departure and reentry into the United States, except for travel within certain countries of North, South, and Central America."

FEDERAL TROOPS AS STRIKEBREAKERS

War often brings prosperity. The Second World War's insatiable demand for military goods ultimately ended the Great Depression in the United States. The Civil War had a similar effect. After years of economic hard times following the Panic of 1857, and once the shock of war itself had worn off, the Union's economy not only recovered, but entered a period of unprecedented well-being. It was America's first experience with what later would be called "war-induced prosperity." And it seemed to impact all sectors of the economic community. "Everybody admits that, in the main, the industry of the North is very flourishing," commented the *New York Times* on July 2, 1863. "The farms teem, the workshops and the factories whir, and the bustle of trade fills the streets. Labor was never in greater demand, or more largely paid."

All true, and yet in some respects, this prosperity was not shared by all. Wartime inflation, for example, had a devastating impact on certain segments of the Northern working class, causing their purchasing power to decline by one-third. Then there were the higher taxes, which eroded the wage earners' capacity to keep up with the cost-of-living even more. Given these circumstances, Northern workingmen felt they had no choice; if their demands went unanswered, their only recourse was to go out on strike—a dangerous move in wartime, especially if one is employed in an industry vital to the war effort.

And that was the wage earners' essential dilemma. Work stoppages gave aid and comfort to the enemy, even if that was not the intention. But what could workingmen do? Certainly strikes were "unfortunate," a labor spokesman said, but "if the issue is forced upon us we must accept it. If capitalists will persist in their efforts to drive us to the wall, and reduce us to beggary and want, and deprive us of the rights due every citizen, and their persistence leads to open war, upon them rests the responsibility."

Realizing the potential for a public backlash, workers moved with caution, sometimes putting ads in newspapers in an effort to explain their position. They pointed out that while employers reaped enormous profits due to government contracts, they were reduced to poverty. As "loyal citizens, sound uncompromising Union friends of the Government [and] as respectable mechanics," they merely wanted their wages to keep abreast of the cost of living.

When employers turned a deaf ear, strikes broke out—at the coal mines in Pennsylvania, at the Parrott Armaments Works in Cold Springs, New York, at factories producing machinery, clothing, and assorted industrial goods in St. Louis, and elsewhere. Some of these labor disputes touched the war effort directly; others did not. But the government was deeply concerned and reacted accordingly. For the first time in U.S. labor history federal troops were used as strikebreakers.

In March 1864, after workers at the Parrott gun factory went on strike, the army dispatched two companies of troops to the town. Declaring martial law, the soldiers seized four of the labor leaders, imprisoning them for seven weeks without trial, and eventually broke the back of the strike. Similar tactics by the military, but on a larger scale, were employed to put down the work stoppage staged by miners in the anthracite coal fields of Pennsylvania. And in St. Louis, after members of the machinists', blacksmiths', and tailors' unions walked out, the army took an even bolder stand by issuing orders "prohibiting refusal to work, meetings, and picketing."

But perhaps the most significant instance of military intervention occurred in July 1864, when the workers of the Philadelphia & Reading Railroad walked off the job because of a wage dispute. Since the Philadelphia & Reading was the main carrier of coal to Philadelphia for use by military railroads and Union naval vessels, the War Department acted swiftly, seizing and operating the railroad—the first time ever that the Federal government took full control of a privately owned company and kept it functioning in the midst of a labor dispute. Charles E. Smith, president of the Philadelphia & Reading, could not have been more pleased. As he explained in a letter to Maj. Gen. George Cadwalader, who was in charge of the takeover, "Your action brought the strike at once to a crisis, and hastened a result favorable to us."

Outraged by the army's antilabor stance, the editor of *Fincher's Trades' Review*, a leading workingman's journal, asked, "Has it come to this, that the Government we all love . . . must array its armed citizens against their fellow-citizens because of a difference among civilians?"

WHITE HOUSE SECURITY

When the Civil War broke out, there was no White House security worthy of the name. Edward Moran, "a short, thin, humorous Irishman" who had served as an usher for years, covered the front door, while another veteran employee named Louis Bargdorf was stationed in the upstairs corridor. With only these two men on duty, sightseers, office seekers, politicians, and a few cranks and idlers roamed the White House with near impunity. The lax security for the president's residence, however, was just part of the story. In truth, until the twentieth century, the president of the United States was probably the least guarded head of state in the western world.

Not that there hadn't been disturbing incidents in the past that should have raised concerns. President Andrew Jackson, for example, had more than his share of violent encounters. Charismatic and controversial, "Old Hickory's" larger-than-life personality was bound to produce enemies as well as friends. On May 6, 1833, Jackson was on a steamboat when a stranger entered his cabin. It was easy to do; the president was as accessible at the time as a private citizen. As the stranger approached, Jackson thought the man was an admirer who wanted to shake hands. Instead, the man "dashed his hand" into Jackson's face. Fortunately, the captain of the steamboat happened to be close by and subdued the president's assailant.

But worse was to follow. On January 30, 1835, Jackson was the victim of the first presidential assassination attempt. As the president left the Capitol building, Richard Lawrence, a deranged house painter, pulled a pistol and fired at him. Seconds later, the would-be assassin produced another loaded pistol and pulled the trigger. By some miracle—it can be described in no other way—the caps exploded in both pistols but failed to ignite the main charges. In short, the bullets were not fired, and Jackson was left unharmed. Lawrence was declared insane, institutionalized, and died in 1861. As for the malfunctioning guns, they were found to be in perfect working order. The odds of two pistols simultaneously misfiring was reckoned at 125,000 to 1.

Yet forewarned did not seem to be forearmed, at least when it came to presidential security. Jackson's near misses seem to have been forgotten almost as soon as they occurred.

During the Lincoln years, however, not everyone was so lax. Ward Hill Lamon, one of the president's old friends from Illinois, urged greater protection for Lincoln and occasionally acted as a bodyguard himself. On November 8, 1864, the evening of Lincoln's reelection, Lamon was so concerned for the president's safety that he "curled up on a blanket in the corridor outside his door, where he slept till daybreak."

Lincoln's own attitude didn't help matters. Since he was a popularly elected leader, he believed that it was inappropriate for a president to appear in public with armed guards like some pompous monarch. It was crucial, as he put it, "that the people know I come among them without fear." And then there was Lincoln's personal fatalistic streak to contend with. He was convinced that if someone was *really* determined to murder him, no amount of safeguards could prevent it. "I long ago made up my mind," Lincoln confided to California newspaperman Noah Brooks, "that if anybody wants to kill me, he will do it. If I wore a shirt of mail, and kept myself surrounded by a body-guard, it would be all the same. There are a thousand ways of getting at a man if it is desired that he should be killed."

But with the crank letters increasing and the threats growing louder in the wake of his successful bid for reelection, in November 1864 Lincoln finally gave in and approved the formation of an armed guard—the first time in the history of the presidency that a police detail was assigned to the White House. It was composed of four District of Columbia policemen in plain clothes. Two of them were placed on daytime duty from eight till four, and the other two divided the night shift. They were responsible for guarding Lincoln at all times, remaining outside of his office and other official rooms while he performed his presidential duties and patrolling the corridors when he occupied the family quarters. In addition, they were to accompany the president on his walks, escort him to and from the War Department, and protect him when he went to the theater.

Although he consented to the guard, Lincoln was never comfortable with it. As far as he was concerned, the detail was forced upon him by overcautious friends. Ward Hill Lamon, Lincoln privately told a cabinet officer, "is a monomaniac on the subject of my safety." And besides, the president asked, "What does anyone want to assassinate me for?"

UNITED STATES SECRET SERVICE

Today the Secret Service is associated in the public mind with the protection of the president of the United States. But this was not its original purpose; initially, it was organized to combat the alarming rise in counterfeiting that had taken place during the Civil War.

The amount of forged paper money circulating in 1862, a year after the war began, was staggering. Based on a *New York Times* report, 80 percent of all bank notes (the primary source of currency in the Union) were counterfeit. Most of those responsible for this criminal activity were operating out of America's urban centers, especially its two largest cities—New York and Philadelphia—which "controlled a combined 70 percent of the engraving, lithographic, and printing firms in the United States." With nearly 10,000 workers involved in the industry, there were always a few willing to sell their talents to the highest bidder, legal or not.

Considered a problem for local law enforcement, the Federal government offered little if any assistance to suppress the counterfeiters—that is, until 1862. In that year Congress passed the Legal Tender Act, providing for the issuance of $150 million in non-interest-bearing treasury notes, more commonly known as "greenbacks." Ultimately more than $430 million of the currency was put into circulation during the war. Since the public had grown suspect of paper money—and with good cause, given the enormous amount of fake bills floating around—the government was concerned that the integrity of its notes might be open to question. A Federal crackdown on counterfeiters would go a long way toward restoring the people's confidence in paper money. But who would conduct it? Customs officers and postal inspectors were neither trained nor equipped to deal with this kind of criminal activity. And even U.S. marshals, who qualified more than any other group of lawmen as a national police force, were essentially court officers with no experience in matters concerning the urban underworld. Recognizing the need to go outside of existing channels, in 1863 Congress allocated funds and authorized both the Interior and Treasury Departments to take whatever measures necessary—use of army provost marshals, employment of private detectives, rewards, and the like—to stamp out counterfeiting. Despite the very generous allocation ($100,000) and the grant of broad administrative powers, neither department measured up to the task. Over the next year or so, the problem grew even worse.

In early 1865 another plan was proposed, this time by Hugh McCulloch, the newly appointed secretary of the treasury. "In my opinion," McCulloch told Lincoln and members of the cabinet at a meeting on April 14, "everything possible has been done that could be done under the plans pursued, but as you see, it is not enough." The president asked if there was a better way. "I think so," the treasury secretary responded. "I believe there should be a continuous organized effort, aggressive rather than merely defensive, and that the work should be undertaken by a permanent force managed by a directing head." Other cabinet members at once expressed their approval, but the final decision rested with the president. Lincoln was favorable, saying, "Work it out your own way, Hugh. I believe you have the right idea." The chief executive had given the verbal green light, but nothing had been formally drawn up, nor would it be for another two months. The cabinet meeting of April 14 was Lincoln's last; that very evening he was assassinated by John Wilkes Booth at Ford's Theatre.

Once the grief and turmoil surrounding the president's death subsided, plans for creating a Federal anticounterfeiting agency was put into operation. The organization—the first permanent intelligence agency in American history—was formally created on July 5, 1865, when William P. Wood was sworn in as the chief of the Secret Service of the Treasury Department, later known as the United States Secret Service.

At first glance, William P. Wood might have seemed a bit too shady a character to be installed as first head of the Secret Service. Described as "a man without fear, without a complete stock of morals, and sometimes without good judgment," Wood nevertheless always seemed to land on his feet. A veteran of the Mexican War, Wood was superintendent of Washington's Old Capitol Prison at the time of his appointment. As head of the prison, he had interviewed inmates who were incarcerated for counterfeiting and had developed some expertise in the matter. This, in turn, had attracted the attention of government officials, who had been impressed enough to appoint him as a treasury agent in December 1864. Not surprisingly, Wood had managed to hold on to both positions until he took over the Secret Service.

No matter how much of a wheeler and dealer he had been in the past, Wood proved highly effective in his new role. Heading a force of thirty agents, he soon began arresting big-time counterfeiters, criminals who had operated for years without fear of the authorities. There was, for example, one Lewis M. Roberts, also known as "Mysterious Bob." Actually, there was nothing mysterious about his counterfeiting operation, a large-scale affair that ranged through three states. Each month he sold about $50,000 in counterfeit bills and thus was responsible for annually injecting into the currency some $600,000 in fake money—a sizable sum for that period. An acknowledged master of the trade, "Mysterious Bob" was engaged in this activity for half a decade until Wood and his agents finally shut him down. He was sentenced to twenty years in prison. By 1866, after only a year in existence, the Secret Service had compiled an impressive record, having captured more than 200 counterfeiters.

When the Secret Service uncovered a plot against the life of Grover Cleveland in 1894, the agency started to protect the president—but only on an intermittent basis if threats were known. In 1902, less than a year after the assassination of President William McKinley, the U.S. Secret Service was assigned to guard the nation's chief executive on a permanent twenty-four-hour basis, a mission that continues to this day.

CHAPTER 7

Health and Medical Care

On August 11, 1880, Gen. William Tecumseh Sherman gave a brief, impromptu speech at Columbus, Ohio. He was addressing some 5,000 Union veterans—"good old boys," as he called them—many of whom no doubt worshiped him as a romantic warrior and still thought of war as a grand adventure. Sherman caught the mood of his audience, and proceeded to throw cold water on such notions. "There is many a boy here today," the general declared, "who looks on war as all glory, but boys, it is all hell."

Although war can have brief moments of glory, even elation, and undoubtedly exudes a powerful fascination, few would dispute Sherman's assertion—especially as it relates to the Civil War. By the time Rebel guns fell silent, approximately 620,000 men lay dead (360,000 Union, 260,000 Confederate), nearly equal to the 680,000 combined losses for all other American wars.

Civil War casualties on the battlefield were often horrific, but from a statistical vantage point, the average soldier faced greater dangers from disease. Thousands of men found themselves crowded together in unsanitary conditions—a recipe for disaster. The problem was exacerbated by the fact that many recruits came from rural areas—isolated farms and small communities—and therefore had developed no natural immunity to communicable diseases such as measles, chicken pox, mumps, and whooping cough, in many cases proving fatal to its victims. And then there were the more serious killers—typhoid fever, malaria, chronic diarrhea, dysentery, pneumonia—which could scythe through regiments like a biblical plague.

The problem was made even worse by the state of medical knowledge at the time. Perhaps Union surgeon general William A. Hammond summed it up best when he wrote years afterward that "the Civil War was fought at the end of the medical Middle Ages." Unfortunately for the diseased or wounded Union or Confederate soldier, the most critical medical discoveries were just a little too late to help him. In 1864, for example, the French chemist Louis Pasteur introduced the "germ theory"—the idea that diseases were caused by infectious organisms—yet the concept was so novel that it took time to disseminate. Not long after Pasteur's finding, British surgeon Joseph Lister cured his first patient by using antiseptic techniques. It was undeniably a major medical breakthrough, but it occurred in the summer of 1865; by then, the Civil War had been over for several months.

Compounding the inadequate state of medical knowledge was the inadequate condition of the U.S. Army medical department. At the beginning of the conflict, the entire medical staff numbered only thirty surgeons and eighty-three assistant surgeons (physicians in the military were commonly called surgeons at the time). That number was further reduced by Southern defections, so when the war broke out, there were only ninety-eight medical officers left.

By 1863, however, the Union medical department had undergone a thorough reorganization. With the help of private relief organizations, such as the U.S. Sanitary Commission, doctors and nurses were recruited in unprecedented numbers, scores of hospitals were built, and new systems were devised for the treatment of the wounded and the diseased.

Yet the likelihood of death, either from suffering a gunshot wound on the battlefield or succumbing to illness in camp, was ever present, even more so for the Southern soldier. Not that the Confederate medical department failed to perform heroically; it did. But the South lacked skilled manpower and resources—a situation that grew worse over time.

Just the opposite was the case for the men in blue. As the war progressed, their chance of survival grew better, although disease continued to ravage their ranks. On the average, two Union soldiers died of disease for every one who succumbed to battlefield wounds. Yet these grim statistics should be put into perspective. When judged by nineteenth-century standards, not twentieth-century ones, the survival rate of sick and injured soldiers was truly unprecedented. The surgeon general made certain to point this out at the end of the war, when he reported that the U.S. Army's mortality rate from both disease and wounds was "lower than had been observed in the experience of any army since the world began."

STANDARDS FOR PHYSICIANS

The single most important task for the Union army's medical department at the outset of the Civil War was to recruit competent physicians. This was hardly a simple undertaking. Up to this point, there were no real standards in place to determine the expertise of an American medical practitioner. And to complicate matters further, medical training itself was in a state of major transition. Most of the older generation of doctors learned their trade in a hands-on manner by serving an apprenticeship with a practicing physician. This was not the case for a majority of the younger doctors, who received their education from medical schools. But whether a medical diploma in antebellum America made one a more competent practitioner of the healing arts is an open question. The standard medical course was two years of nine months each, with the second year a time-wasting rehash of the first year's lectures. No time was given to laboratory or clinical instruction, though such omissions were truly academic in some states, where dissection was legally prohibited.

Given the diverse quality of medical education and practice in the civilian sector, it became clear early in the war that some sort of standard level of competency must be established for army physicians. Qualifying examinations might separate the wheat from the chaff by exposing and weeding out incompetents, quacks, and charlatans. Sen. Henry Wilson of Massachusetts authored a medical department reorganization bill that embodied these goals. Passed in April 1862, Wilson's act set up a series of competency exams for prospective Union army doctors—the first time in American medical history that standards were established for a large number of physicians.

The tests probed general knowledge as well as medical competency. A typical examination given by the army medical board in the fall of 1862 started with a one- or two-hour oral test, a grilling that covered such diverse subjects as history, geography, literature, science, and languages. No doubt still reeling from this "third degree," the candidate next faced a three-hour-long written exam, in which seven or eight questions had to be answered from a lengthy list of topics, including surgery, anatomy, pathology, physiology, chemistry, and toxicology, just to name a few. Oddly enough, obstetrics was included as a topic for test questions, probably to confirm that the physician was competent to treat female civilians, either in camp or in the field.

Eventually some 12,000 physicians went through the exam system. No one doubted that the incompetent had to be culled out, but at first so many doctors failed the tests that it seemed truly a case of the cure being worse than the disease. Secretary of War Edwin M. Stanton wanted more positive results, and examining board members were informed that a greater number of candidates should be passed or the boards themselves would face extinction. Seeing the handwriting on the wall, the examiners complied with the secretary's wishes. Passing scores were lowered, but to the board members' relief, the "Stanton physicians" proved just as competent in the field as their higher-scoring colleagues.

The Confederates, too, had an examination system for prospective army doctors. Of the some 3,000 Southern physicians who served, however, it is impossible to determine how many were actually tested. Neither the exams nor the records of those who took them have survived. According to historian Bell I. Wiley, a number of Confederate doctors purposely avoided taking the examinations to hide their deficiencies, and in some instances the examiners themselves were incompetent.

Yet most doctors, North and South, were skilled and dedicated men, devoted to the arts of healing. It was the medical ignorance of the time that gave physicians such bad reputations among the troops, not the doctors themselves. "All but a few," the poet Walt Whitman observed, "are excellent men." And Whitman's extensive nursing experience put him in a position to know.

In 1918, looking back at his Civil War service after half a century, surgeon William W. Keen wrote:

> It can be understood why we surgeons in 1861–1865 . . . in our ignorance committed grievous mistakes which nearly always imperiled life and often actually caused death. . . . We operated in our blood-stained and often pus-stained coats. . . . We operated with clean hands in a social sense, but they were undisinfected hands. . . . If a sponge or an instrument fell on the floor, it was washed and squeezed in a basin of tap water and used as if it were clean.

Despite the ignorance, the Civil War medical record was a good one, thanks in part to the standards of professionalism that the military examinations upheld.

THE "LETTERMAN SYSTEM"

Prompt treatment of wounds can often mean the difference between an agonizing death or eventual recovery. During the first year or so of the Civil War, the methods of collecting and evacuating wounded were "traditional" ones, scarcely changed from the Napoleonic wars of a half century earlier. Noncombatants—usually musicians (many in their teens), cooks, and teamsters—were assigned as stretcher bearers. Young or old, such battlefield caregivers lacked adequate training, and many of them had little, if any, commitment to the task at hand. If the fighting got too intense, it was not unusual for the stretcher bearers to take to their heels.

The wounded were also carried by ambulance, but early in the war, many U.S. Army ambulance wagons were found to be poorly designed for the rigors of active service. In particular, the two-wheeled vehicles, known among the soldiers as the "avalanche," had structural weaknesses; if they didn't break down on the battlefield, they tormented their wounded passengers by bouncing and jolting them unmercifully. There were times, in fact, when "blood trickled from the ambulances like water from an ice cart." Adding to the problem were the drivers themselves, mostly civilians whose primary concern was to flee from the danger rather than help the wounded, often driving at high speeds, whether they had passengers or not. In a report filed in 1862, Union army physician George Henry Gay maintained that the ambulance drivers were "the most vulgar, ignorant, and profane men [he] ever came in contact with."

Poor equipment, little organization, and unfit personnel made the evacuation of the wounded chaotic at best. Even after the last shot of the battle was fired, the ambulance system as it existed early in the conflict was so inadequate that it would usually be overwhelmed by the sheer logistics of transporting thousands of sufferers. Some wounded soldiers had to wait days before being collected; many of them died before they could be reached. Sometimes a soldier's only hope of succor was if a relative was able to get to the battlefield and search for him.

Determined to end this scandalous situation, Surgeon General William A. Hammond, in the summer of 1862, appointed Dr. Jonathan Letterman as medical director of the Army of the Potomac. Letterman proved to be an ideal choice.

Born in 1824, Letterman was the son of a Pennsylvania physician. Following in his father's footsteps, he obtained his medical degree in 1849. But unlike his father, young Letterman opted for an army career— an act of considerable courage. The U.S. Army of the 1850s was small, neglected, and largely scattered throughout the western frontier to guard against Indian depredations. An army surgeon's life was anything but glamorous, and duty on some isolated frontier post was hardly the path to fame and fortune. Yet the twelve years Letterman spent in the West tending casualties of Indian warfare would stand him in good stead when the Civil War finally came. The frontier taught him to use his ingenuity, to be less conventional, and to care about what actually worked rather than what the rulebooks said was supposed to work.

Soon after assuming the medical directorship of the Army of the Potomac, Letterman introduced a system, the first ever in American military history, designed to care for and evacuate battlefield wounded. His so-called "Letterman system," which became standard for the U.S. Army and was eventually copied by many foreign nations, was subdivided into three categories: ambulances, medical supplies, and field hospitals.

In the late summer of 1862 Letterman put the first part of his plan into operation: an ambulance field service for the Army of the Potomac. "The system I devised," Letterman explained in later years, "was based upon the idea that they [the ambulances] should not be under the immediate control of Medical officers, whose duties, especially on the day of battle, would prevent any proper supervision." Instead Letterman appointed a nonmedical officer holding the rank of captain to head the ambulance service for each army corps; to assist him, a first lieutenant was placed in charge of ambulances for each division within the corps, a second lieutenant for each brigade, and a sergeant for each regiment. Those in charge of their respective units would be responsible, under the captain's direction, for "inspecting the ambulances weekly, drilling the crews, and instructing them on casualty handling." The crews—ambulance drivers and stretcher bearers—were to be recruited directly from the ranks, and after interviews and examinations, the medical staff would decide which candidates were most suitable. Those who passed muster were provided special insignias—a green band on the cap, plus inverted chevrons of the same color on each arm above the elbow for sergeants or half chevrons for privates. The insignias, designed to allow easy recognition of medical personnel on the battlefield, had the added effect of instilling a sense of pride among its members.

That *esprit de corps* was soon put to the test. On September 17, 1862, the Army of the Potomac engaged Lee's forces at Antietam—the bloodiest single-day battle of the war. The casualties were heavy on both sides, yet the 9,500 Union wounded were treated and evacuated within twenty-four hours. A few months later, at the battle of Fredericksburg (December 13), the ambulance corps proved even more effective, collecting all 9,000 wounded Northern soldiers within twelve hours. But it was at Gettysburg (July 1–3, 1863) that the system "approached perfection." With 1,000 ambulances (largely four-wheeled vehicles, most of the two-wheeled ones having been scrapped) and 3,000 drivers and stretcher bearers under his command, Letterman oversaw the removal of some 14,000 Union wounded during the course of the battle, the entire operation completed by the morning after the three days of fighting. Word of Letterman's success spread fast, and soon his ambulance system was embraced by other commands and armies, with Congress ultimately mandating it by law in 1864.

Letterman's other procedural innovations were also well received. In 1862 he required all physicians in the Army of the Potomac to carry a standardized medical kit and every brigade to maintain a fully equipped medical wagon. Designed by Letterman himself, this mobile field medical transport carried seventy-six different medicines, various types of dressings, all kinds of medical instruments, medical books, and a host of hospital stores, including bedding, basins, bedpans, vials, pillboxes, and food staples (six two-pound cans of beef stock and ten pounds of hard bread), as well as kettles, tin plates, tumblers, and tablespoons. To ensure that these wagons would never suffer shortages, medical supplies were stockpiled in many locations and often overstocked. To those who accused the medical director of extravagance, Letterman responded, "Lost supplies can be replaced, but lives lost are gone forever."

Once Letterman put into motion his plans to evacuate the wounded and guarantee that there would be adequate medical supplies at the ready, he then introduced his final reform. He recalled in his memoirs, "As far as I knew, no system of field hospitals existed in any of our armies, and, convinced of the necessity of devising some measure by which the wounded would receive the best surgical aid which the Army afforded, with the least delay, my thoughts naturally turned to this most important subject." On October 30, 1862, Letterman introduced a field medical system, which included one assistant surgeon of each regiment conducting a dressing station at the front and the remainder of the army's medical staff organized as teams in divisional field hospitals set up a mile or two from the battle. There, only the most skilled physicians (about one out of every fifteen) were permitted to engage in surgical procedures, while the others were assigned as wound dressers, record keepers, or supervisors of food, clothing, bedding, and the like. Some physicians regarded the division hospital system "a slur upon their capacities," but most experienced medical personnel agreed that it was "a brilliant achievement in hospital management."

Indeed, Letterman's system to evacuate and treat the wounded was so successful that it would be the model "for most armies of the world down to World War I."

THE U.S. SANITARY COMMISSION

The United States Sanitary Commission was the first civilian relief organization in American history to enlist a large segment of the public in helping to meet the medical and health needs of U.S. soldiers. Its origins can be traced to the Crimean War of 1854–56, which left an indelible impression on American minds, in large part because of the appalling casualties the British Army sustained due to disease. Of the 28,000 British troops who landed in the Crimea in 1854, no less than 10,000 were dead of disease a mere six months later.

These were sobering statistics, and there were many in the United States who resolved not to let such things happen to their soldiers. A number of local aid societies arose soon after Fort Sumter was fired upon, societies, mostly organized by women, whose main mission was to supplement the government in providing supplies to men in the ranks. The largest of these early wartime groups was the Women's Central Association for Relief, founded in New York City in late April 1861.

Although inspired by women, men, not surprisingly in that day, assumed the leadership roles of these various organizations. The men drew up the constitutions, nominated the committees, chaired the meetings, and helped coordinate activities between the relief agencies and the government. In mid-May 1861, during a trip to Washington, a New York delegation, which included Unitarian minister Dr. Henry W. Bellows and the prominent physician Dr. Elisha Harris, came up with the idea of the U.S. Sanitary Commission, an organization that would serve as the coordinator for all of the local relief chapters.

Upon arriving in the capital, however, the delegation met with predictable reluctance on the part of Federal officialdom. Innately suspicious of change to begin with, government bureaucracy did not look kindly upon the proposal to create a Sanitary Commission, fearing that it might be more disruptive than helpful. After all, members of the commission wanted authority to investigate the soldier's diet, clothing, housing, and campgrounds; determine how medical supplies were procured; and check the adequacy of the ambulance system. Perhaps most radical of all, the "Sanitary," as it became known, wanted to explore the use of women as nurses, following the lead of Florence Nightingale, who had made female nursing respectable during the Crimean War, but which was still a novel idea in the U.S.

The administration remained skeptical. Even President Lincoln, usually open-minded to innovation, seemed to have believed that the Sanitary would turn out to be a meddlesome civilian organization—in his words, a "fifth wheel to the coach." But after struggling three weeks with what Bellows called "the apathy, preoccupation, [and] suspicions of the government," Secretary of War Simon Cameron issued an order officially establishing the commission, followed by presidential approval on June 13, 1861.

The commission's intent was to prevent or retard disease, but it was the inspectors themselves who were treated like the plague in the early years of the war. The army brass didn't like the idea of civilian "watchdogs" snooping around and, even worse, telling them what to do. Army of the Potomac medical director Dr. Charles Tripler characterized the commissioners as being made up of "sensation preachers, village doctors, and strong minded women."

Resented at first, the inspectors—many of them physicians recruited by the commission—were eventually well received. They traveled from camp to camp, carefully noting the quality of water and rations, methods of cooking, condition of privies, drainage of each site, and disposal of garbage. When deficiencies were uncovered, inspectors contacted the officers in charge and gave advice on how to remedy the situation.

The original mission was the prevention of disease, but the commission soon expanded its activities to other areas. It sent out badly needed bandages, medicines, clothing, and food to hospitals and camps. Lodging was established for soldiers on leave, as well as "homes" and "refreshment saloons" for sick and destitute soldiers, veterans, and paroled prisoners of war.

Organizations often mirror society, and the U.S. Sanitary Commission was no exception. The national officers and most of the paid agents were men, but the rank-and-file volunteers were women. Though unequal by today's perspective, the commission was actually a step forward for most women. At a time when society offered women few options other than homebound positions as wives and mothers, the Sanitary allowed them to showcase their talents as administrators and fundraisers. Actually, if not for the hundreds of thousands of dedicated volunteers, largely women, who gave of their time and talents, the commission's debts would have been much higher. As it was, by 1864 the Sanitary's paid employees numbered about 450, and its monthly payroll amounted to $28,000—a sum that would be equal to hundreds of thousands of dollars in today's money. Salaries, however, constituted a small part of the organization's budget; its greatest expense was purchasing supplies. To cite but one example, at the battle of Gettysburg, the commission distributed $73,838.52 worth of goods, including 11,000 pounds of poultry and mutton, 12,500 gallons of milk, 6,430 pounds of butter, and—no doubt more to a soldier's taste—1,168 bottles of whiskey and 1,148 bottles of wine.

In 1863 and 1864 the commission relied on "Sanitary Fairs" as a major means of raising funds. Usually held in large exhibit halls or temporary structures built specifically for the occasion, these fairs proved to be veritable cash cows. A vast array of donated items were sold, such as "knitted scarves and mittens, appliances, jewelry, agricultural and dairy products, evergreens, flowers, food supplies, war relics and trophies, works of art, and manufactured goods . . . pumps, reapers, and cultivators," in addition to "'cologne by the barrel,' wine, pianos, organs, washing machines, nails, and lumber." Tickets were also sold that enabled the public to try its luck in lotteries, with prizes that appealed to all tastes, everything from a racehorse to a collection of presidential autographs. Perhaps the most unusual item was offered by the New York Sanitary Fair—a cardboard eagle "feathered" with head and beard hairs from Lincoln and his cabinet. New York City raised $1 million, surpassed only by Philadelphia's $1.2 million—the first time ever that American private philanthropic ventures produced such enormous sums of money.

As time went on, the Sanitary did more than just succor the physical needs of the soldiers. Claim offices were established for enlisted men who had lost their papers and records and were thus in danger of losing the bounties and pensions they were entitled to. Even back-pay agencies were set up, though it's hard to determine how effective these were in securing overdue wages.

To help families keep track of their loved ones, the commission published a hospital directory that contained the names of over 600,000 patients. Friends and relatives could then determine the location of wounded or sick soldiers in any of the more than 200 military hospitals. The Sanitary also distributed the latest medical literature to army surgeons, keeping them abreast of the most current findings in their field.

By contrast, the Confederacy never developed an agency equivalent to the U.S. Sanitary Commission. Part of the problem stemmed from the fact that the South, essentially a rural society, was simply not equipped to coordinate a massive civilian relief effort. To be sure, Southern women were as active as their Northern sisters, and Confederate fairs and bazaars did wonders in raising much-needed funds. The fictional Charleston bazaar so colorfully detailed in the classic film *Gone with the Wind* had its real-life counterparts. Yet the South did not have the resources to match the Northern effort. "We had no Sanitary

Commission," a Southerner recalled, then went on to explain, "We were too poor; we had no line of rich and populous cities closely connected by rail."

As for the U.S. Sanitary Commission, its greatest contribution was saving lives. Cornelia Hancock, a young Quaker nurse, in her own way put it well: "Uncle Sam is very rich, but very slow, and if it was not for the Sanitary, much suffering would ensue." The commission suspended operations in 1878, but it left an enduring legacy, serving as the forerunner of the American Red Cross and the United Service Organizations (USO) of World War II.

AMERICA'S "FLORENCE NIGHTINGALES"

One of the traditional roles for women has been that of caregiver, but nursing the sick was largely confined to home and family. Nursing outside the home, particularly in military hospitals or on the battlefield, was unthinkable within the straitjacket of Victorian conventions. Men ruled society, and there was a great wall of male prejudice that barred women from military nursing.

Objections were legion. Some claimed that women would faint at the sight of blood or disturb the wounded with hysterics. There was also the very real specter of impropriety. It was just not fitting for a "good" woman to see men in various stages of undress, much less see all the blood and torn flesh. And single, attractive women might experience unwelcome advances from recovering soldiers. For that matter, some women might even welcome them, having been lured to hospital work in hopes of finding a husband.

These ingrained chauvinist attitudes were hard to change, but American women—and some American men—took inspiration from the pioneer work in nursing performed by Florence Nightingale during the Crimean War. Nightingale's perseverance, diligence, and sheer courage in the face of seemingly insurmountable odds not only made nursing a respectable job for women, but made it into a profession. Before Nightingale's arrival on the scene, the death rate among British wounded was scandalous. She and her dedicated band of female nurses improved conditions, cut the death rate, and even won grudging approval from at least some members of the British military.

There had been "unofficial" women nurses before, but usually from the "lower orders"—camp followers like washerwomen, prostitutes, and maybe a few common soldiers' wives. But Nightingale was firmly middle class, eminently respectable, and very much part of the establishment. Her work made her a legend in her own time. "The lady with the lamp," she was called, a Victorian icon who was often thought of as an "angel of mercy."

Yet there was a core of iron beneath the "angelic" facade. Courageously, she stood up to the medical men of her time and was a tireless worker. In the Crimea during the winter of 1854, Nightingale worked twenty hours a day, often on her feet the entire time. Her spreading fame produced reform; in 1860 she opened the Nightingale School and Home for Nurses at Saint Thomas' Hospital in London. Though she was a role model in the United States, Nightingale's example alone, as American women would soon find out, would not suffice to break the long-standing traditions of the male-dominated medical establishment.

In the early months of the Civil War, all nurses were men. And these men were decidedly a mixed bag. Some were recovering invalids themselves, some were misfits judged unsuitable for other duty, and others were petty criminals who accepted the job to avoid imprisonment. Probably a few were sincerely committed to their assigned task, but virtually all lacked training for the job.

Not long after the war broke out, Dorothea Dix traveled to Washington to offer her services "in the hospital branch" of the military. Dix's fame had preceded her; she was known—and rightly revered—as a humanitarian reformer who had been a leading advocate for the mentally ill.

Born in Maine in 1802, Dix experienced loneliness as a child, which did not improve as she grew into adulthood. A broken engagement completed the isolation. But she soon found her calling. After visiting a prison where both criminals and the mentally ill were kept, she was appalled at the medieval treatment accorded the latter. In the 1840s and 1850s she dedicated her life to the reform of prisons, almshouses, and insane asylums, meeting with considerable success. By 1861 she was a woman of experience, able to deal with bureaucrats and politicians with equal aplomb.

Dix's offer of her services were accepted, in part because of who she was, but also because of the anticipated need for a corps of trained nurses—even if they were women. In June 1861 Dix became superintendent of female nurses, and in August Congress passed an act providing that women could serve in hospitals "when it seems desirable to the Surgeon General or the surgeon-in-charge." With a salary of 40 cents a day (about the pay of a private) and one ration, thousands of American women, for the first time ever, were to be employed as nurses.

The new superintendent of female nurses was determined to put her imprint on the fledgling nursing corps. It was Dix who set the standards and saw to it that applicants were screened according to the rules. Prospective nurses had to be over thirty, plain looking, dressed in brown or black, and were to have "no bows, no curls, no jewelry, and no hoop shirts." Dix herself conducted many of the interviews, and scores were turned away as being "too young," "too attractive," or "over anxious." The superintendent also insisted that the nursing candidates who were selected must agree to be "in their own rooms at taps, or nine o'clock, unless obliged to be with the sick; [and] must not go to any place of amusement in the evening."

The U.S. Army nursing corps thus became a reflection of Dix's own personal and social values. But the rules were too rigid, and many a good potential nurse was rejected because she had a pretty face. One spurned applicant complained, "Dragon Dix . . . won't accept the services of any *pretty* nurses." Some of the women who were considered too young or too pretty went on to successful nursing careers elsewhere. Cornelia Hancock, a twenty-three-year-old Quaker, soon proved her worth at Gettysburg; Helen Gilson of Massachusetts was a beauty who wore a short-skirted costume and entertained convalescing soldiers with her songs. Nevertheless, Dix remained inflexible, even rejecting Dr. Esther Hill Hawks—one of America's handful of women physicians!

Generally speaking, the women both in and out of Dix's nursing corps were white and solidly middle class. Virtually all were untrained, but most learned quickly. In spite of Dix's draconian rules against fraternization, a few nurses did romance patients and leave the service to marry them. But fears of rampant "immorality," of "women's virtue" being sorely tested, proved groundless.

Most nurses served in general military hospitals behind the lines, sometimes working sixteen-hour days. Wearing "calico dresses, bonnets, and shawls," they performed all sorts of hospital chores—administering food and medicine, changing bedding, keeping track of medical supplies, washing and dressing wounds, writing letters for their patients, and so on. A few women, however, saw duty in the more horrific field hospitals near the fighting. One nurse walked through a battlefield so bloody, she remembered, "the edge of my dress was red, my feet were wet with it." If experienced enough, or if there was a need, women nurses also assisted in surgical operations such as amputation. But exposure to such procedures were never easy to take. On one occasion the nurses had become physically ill at the sight of amputated limbs "thrown out of one of the windows [of an operating room] until they made a pile *five feet high just as they fell.*"

Of all the nurses who did not serve under Dix, probably the most famous one was Clara Barton. A former clerk in the U.S. Patent Office (in 1854 Barton was "the first woman who was regularly appointed as a civil servant"), once the war broke out she left her position and took it upon herself to minister to the needs of the sick and wounded, eventually serving—without pay or allowances—as head nurse of the Army of the James.

As many as 2,000 African-American women, many of them escaped slaves, also served in Union hospitals. Although a few worked as unpaid volunteer nurses (the most celebrated was Susie King Taylor, who cared for the casualties in her husband's regiment), most black women fulfilled roles as laundresses, cooks, and hospital aides.

Besides former slaves, there was yet another group of women who traditionally kept a low profile in American society but lent their talents to the war effort as well. For the first time in American history, a significant number of Catholic nuns served as military nurses. During the course of the war, more than 600 sisters from twelve separate orders nursed both Union and Confederate soldiers. Having trained and worked in Catholic hospitals, of which there were some twenty-eight in the U.S. before the war, these "Sisters of Charity," as they were commonly called, had far more experience and discipline than their Protestant counterparts. Understandably, doctors showed a preference for the sisters. This fueled an anti-Catholic sentiment within the official nursing corps, instigated by Dix herself. Yet Protestant nurses had to concede that the soldier patients (once they grew accustomed to the nun's strange garb, especially their head gear which was described as "a cross between a white sunbonnet and a broken-down umbrella") deeply appreciated the care they received from the sisters.

Recent studies show that there were more women, both black and white, engaged in all aspects of hospital work than has been previously supposed. The currently accepted total is somewhere around 20,000, including 5,600 mostly white nurses. Despite these new estimates, women were still a minority among hospital staffs, and made up no more than one-third of the nursing corps. Although their small numbers hardly made them a threat to male doctors' authority, the medical community refused to accept these women on any basis of equality. Most Civil War nurses, a modern scholar has pointed out, had "at least one confrontation with an ill-tempered, arrogant physician who resented sharing his territory." Congress, moreover, contributed to the problem by authorizing the payment of $12.00 a month to women nurses, while their male counterparts received $20.50 for much the same work.

Women of the Confederacy had perhaps even more of a challenge than their Northern sisters, since the "woman on a pedestal" tradition was deeply embedded in the Old South. But Southern chivalry soon crumbled in the face of grim reality. By 1862, with the war heating up and casualties mounting, the Confederate Congress enacted a law permitting women to serve as nurses in general army hospitals.

The most famous Confederate nurse was Sally Tompkins of Virginia. Soon after the first battle of Bull Run in July 1861, Tompkins, twenty-eight, unmarried and a member of a wealthy slave-holding family, converted a private Richmond home into a hospital. There, working side by side with her slaves, she compiled an unparalleled record of healing for a medical facility—North or South—with only seventy-three deaths out of 1,333 patients admitted for care during the four years of war. President Jefferson Davis himself was impressed. When Confederate medical regulations required the closing of all private hospitals, Davis appointed Tompkins to a captaincy in the Confederate army so her infirmary would qualify as a military hospital. As a result, Sally Tompkins became the first American woman ever to hold an officer's commission and the first to be a commissioned army nurse.

The sheer hell of many hospitals affected some women's physical and mental health, and at least one in ten suffered a physical breakdown. But the vast majority put to rest the stereotyped notion of women as the "weaker sex." On the whole, women—black and white, North and South—established an outstanding record of both service and self-sacrifice. The male-dominated press acknowledged their contributions by declaring that "all our women are Florence Nightingales," which was a high accolade indeed. Nothing had done more than the Civil War to help establish nursing as both a profession and a serious career for women. By 1873 the first nursing school was established, laying the foundations of modern nursing as we know it today.

PAVILION HOSPITALS

The Civil War stimulated the first large-scale hospital construction program in American history. Prior to 1860, there were few medical facilities of any kind in the United States. Excluding Catholic health-care institutions, in all of New England there were only three hospitals; in the entire South, only four or five. This was in part because the United

States was still a rural society, but also because self-reliance and individualism were deeply rooted national traits. Most people preferred to be treated at home.

Before Rebel guns opened fire, there were no general military hospitals, only a scattering of small post infirmaries west of the Mississippi. The largest of these was at Fort Leavenworth, in Kansas, containing forty beds. Since the prewar army was small and primarily engaged in Indian fighting out west, it made sense to locate most post hospitals in that region.

But the Civil War changed all that. The sheer scope and scale of the conflict and the unprecedented numbers of casualties it produced prompted the army medical department to reconsider the location of its health-care facilities. At first the situation bordered on the chaotic. In the early part of the war the Union wounded were deposited in such places as hotels, schools, warehouses, barns, churches, and jails. In Philadelphia, a railroad station became a makeshift hospital; in Washington, the halls of Congress were converted into an infirmary; and in Arlington, Virginia, Robert E. Lee's mansion, which fell into federal hands, was used to house the wounded.

In spite of the obvious need, the Quartermaster Corps—then in charge of new construction—hesitated to sanction the building of additional medical facilities. The cost would be high; besides, soldiers needed guns, not beds. By 1862, however, with casualties increasing and the end nowhere in sight, even the most obtuse saw the necessity to construct new military hospitals.

In terms of their architectural design, U.S. hospitals were strongly influenced by Europe. Since the germ theory of disease was not yet established, medical care facilities across the Atlantic were constructed on the theory that mysterious "poisons" or "effluvia" collected in the air and spread from patient to patient. It was an old concept—malaria, for example, came from the Italian word for bad air. With such views in vogue, the pavilion concept of hospital construction became popular in the Old World. The idea was to have a series of well-ventilated buildings or pavilions, each radiating from a circular corridor like spokes from a wheel. Overcrowding in the pavilions was to be avoided at all costs, with adequate space between beds so that infection—it was hoped—could be contained. London's Blackburn Hospital was a pavilion type, as was Lariboiserie Hospital in Paris.

These developments had been studiously followed by William A. Hammond, who, as U.S. surgeon general early in the war, deserves much of the credit for initiating hospital construction. Having received his degree in medicine in 1848 when he was only twenty, Hammond joined the army a year later as an assistant surgeon. Like most newly appointed military doctors, he ended up on the frontier, isolated from much of civilization. Nonetheless, Hammond made the best of it. During the decade he spent out west, he conducted research on certain foodstuffs to prevent scurvy, earning him an award in 1857 from the American Medical Association.

After the war broke out, Gen. George B. McClellan chose Hammond for surgeon general, plucking his name from the bottom, not the top, of the seniority list. At the time of his appointment in April 1862, therefore, Hammond was not well known in Washington's corridors of power. But at six feet, two inches in height, and weighing 240 pounds, he had a commanding presence and was also blessed with a dynamic personality enabling him to cut through red tape. In all respects, then, he was the right man for the job, especially when it came to building medical facilities. Considered an expert in such matters, he had written a book, *Military Hygiene,* which included over 100 pages detailing the construction of pavilion hospitals, with an emphasis on one-story buildings (so that the "exhalations and secretions of the ill would be rapidly dissipated and not rise to affect patients on a second story"), adequate cross ventilation for each ward, and the placement of toilet facilities at a distance from the beds.

Beginning in early 1862, the Union launched a massive hospital construction program. The first facility completed was at Parkersburg, Virginia (now West Virginia). Construction soon accelerated. By 1863 the North had 151 hospitals with 58,715 beds; by the end of the war, 204 hospitals with 136,894 beds. The largest of these was the 4,000-bed Mower General Hospital in Philadelphia.

The South did the best it could with its sick and wounded, handicapped as it was by scanty resources and war-torn conditions. But hard work and dedication paid off. The 8,000-bed Chimborazo Hospital in Richmond was probably the largest in the world at the time. A sprawling complex, Chimborazo boasted 150 buildings, a bakery that could turn out 10,000 loaves of bread a day, a 400-keg brewery, five icehouses, a soap factory, Russian bathhouses, cultivated fields, herds of livestock, and a small fleet of vessels.

Confederate surgeon general Samuel Preston Moore was also very aware of the benefits of the pavilion-style construction and saw to it that such hospitals were built throughout the South. But lack of means, material and financial, particularly in the last years of the war, limited the effectiveness of these facilities. Even Richmond's Chimborazo

Hospital by late 1862 left much to be desired. Overcrowding, dwindling supplies, and poorly trained personnel produced, in the words of a visiting Texas chaplain, a "charnel house of living sufferers." In the end, the death rate at Chimborazo was more than 20 percent.

On the other hand, the North had the resources to spend, and the results were unprecedented. Of the more than 1 million sick and wounded Union soldiers treated in Union hospitals, the mortality rate was 8 percent—the lowest of any war up to that time.

ANNIE WITTENMYER

Annie Wittenmyer is not a familiar Civil War–era name, but she deserves recognition for her contributions to the field of hospital dietetics. In fact, as a result of Wittenmyer's tireless efforts, special diet kitchens were established for the first time in American hospitals.

Wittenmyer had Southern roots. Her family originally hailed from Kentucky, but since she was born and raised in Ohio, her loyalties were firmly for the Union. The outbreak of war in 1861 found her living in Keokuk, Iowa, a wealthy thirty-four-year-old merchant's widow. Given the narrow range of opportunities afforded women at the time, Wittenmyer seems to have been quite an activist. Aside from philanthropic church-related work, she was instrumental in establishing a free school for the underprivileged children of her town, ultimately enrolling some 200 students. Such organizational talents would serve her well in her new role as a wartime volunteer.

Wittenmyer soon became the guiding force of the local volunteer aid society. Like thousands of other women throughout the North, the ladies of Keokuk gathered bedding, clothing, food, bandages, medicine, and other supplies for Iowa's soldiers. Wittenmyer, however, was not content to merely gather supplies. She wanted to determine firsthand how her community's relief society could best serve the troops. In the summer of 1861, leaving her only child, a son, in the care of her parents and married sister, Wittenmyer made the first of many trips into the South in order to ascertain the needs of Iowa's men in blue. Her visits would usually last several weeks, then she would return home with the necessary information, collect the supplies, and leave once again for the field. By the spring of 1862, she even managed to obtain a Federal government pass, presented by Secretary of War Stanton and signed by President Lincoln, allowing her and her cargo full access to the various theaters of war.

For Wittenmyer, the war truly came close to home when, in the winter of 1862, she visited her brother—only sixteen years of age—languishing in a Sedalia, Missouri, military hospital. Flushed with patriotism, the young man had rushed to the colors, only to fall ill. Seeing her brother so sick was depressing enough, but Wittenmyer was really appalled at the hospital food that was given to the patients. Arriving at the breakfast hour, she described the meal: "On a dingy-looking wooden tray was a tin cup full of black, strong coffee; beside it was a leadenlooking tin platter, on which was a piece of fried fat bacon, swimming in its own grease, and a slice of bread." Wittenmyer could scarcely believe her eyes. "Could anything," she later wrote, "be more disgusting and injurious to fever-stricken and wounded patients?"

Soon discovering that her brother's diet was hardly atypical (some hospitals were far worse, serving moldy bread and worm-infested hardtack), Wittenmyer decided to develop a system of special diet kitchens. In need of backing, she successfully lobbied the United States Christian Commission—a national relief agency sponsored by the YMCA—to underwrite her efforts and to appoint her supervisory agent for the project. By 1864 her program was in full swing, with over 100 special diet kitchens in U.S. military hospitals, run by over 200 women managers.

The system worked well. A bill of fare would be provided for each patient, with food items sanctioned by the attending physician. Thus, a patient could choose what he wanted to eat within prescribed guidelines. The meals themselves, prepared under the close supervision of dietary managers, reflected the freshest and healthiest foodstuff available. Instead of greasy bacon or moldy hardtack, patients were offered soup, chicken, eggs, milk, fruits, and vegetables. By 1865 millions of special diet meals had been served, no doubt saving the lives of thousands of soldiers—and establishing a precedent for the system used in modern hospitals today.

In the post-war era Wittenmyer remained active in social causes. She served as national president of the Woman's Christian Temperance Union but devoted most of her energy and time doing missionary work for the Methodist Episcopal Church. She died in 1900 at the age of seventy-three.

HOSPITAL SHIPS

Even in the best of times, nineteenth-century American travel could be a bone-jarring, bruising adventure. Roads were often poor—dust-choked tracks in the summer and viscous bogs in the winter—if they were passable at all. Wagons and stagecoaches bumped and rattled along, throttling passengers with sudden jolts or nauseating them with motion sickness.

These conditions were bad enough on a healthy traveler; to a sick or wounded Civil War soldier, they were excruciating torture. Even the railroad, the marvel of the age, as swift and efficient as it was, had its drawbacks. Cars were often unheated, sometimes lacked water, and rattled and jerked almost as unmercifully as wagons. But there existed yet another alternative—water transportation. Steamboats in particular were a comfortable, almost luxurious, way to travel before the war. Not surprisingly, then, within a year after Rebel guns fired on Fort Sumter—and for the first time ever in an American war—ships of all kinds were used extensively to treat and transport wounded soldiers.

For most wounded men, treatment in field hospitals served only as a holding action. Whether they would recover fully or suffer debilitation (or death) often depended upon how swiftly they could be evacuated to general military hospitals, the vast majority of which were located far from the battlefields. Since land conveyances were overwhelmed by the sheer numbers of casualties, water transportation was pressed into service. The first vessel in the western theater to be used for the large-scale evacuation of wounded was the steamboat *City of Memphis,* ordered by Gen. Ulysses S. Grant to pick up Union casualties at Fort Henry on the Tennessee River. On February 18, 1862, after taking 475 wounded aboard, the *City of Memphis* left the fort for Paducah, Kentucky. It was the first of many such trips it would conduct in the region; within the next five months the steamboat carried some 7,000 casualties to hospitals in Memphis, St. Louis, Cincinnati, and other points.

The *City of Memphis* was typical of the vessels used in the western theater to transport the sick and injured. The Mississippi Valley region was richly veined with rivers of varying sizes but generally broad and slow-moving, making it the domain of the steamboat, both sidewheeler and sternwheeler. These generally had low drafts and luxurious appointments, the kind of vessel celebrated in the writing of Mark Twain. On the eastern seaboard, however, the rougher waters of the Atlantic compelled the use of oceangoing ships, mostly converted merchant vessels known for their versatility.

By late 1862 the hospital transport service was functioning but lacked centralized supervision. Some vessels, for instance, were rented by the U.S. government, though outfitted and operated by the U.S. Sanitary Commission, the largest and most powerful of the wartime civilian relief agencies. Under this agreement, the commission would furnish surgeons and attendants and retain the day-to-day operation and control of the craft, while the government would provide food, clothing, and other general supplies. There were also state hospital ships, vessels equipped and run usually by the western states. They performed their missions effectively, but some state boats earned bad reputations by refusing to take patients that were not "native sons."

A measure of order and stability was introduced in 1863, when the U.S. Army medical department took control of all hospital ships from the Sanitary Commission and discouraged further use of state hospital boats. The *D. A. January,* a 450-bed hospital steamboat, was the first vessel specifically purchased, not chartered, by the U.S. government for its missions of mercy. Having first seen service during the bloody battle of Shiloh in April 1862, for the next three years the *D. A. January*—equipped with a "full corps of nurses and surgeons, and a fine operating room"—traveled the Missouri, Ohio, Illinois, and Iowa rivers, transporting 23,738 patients to military hospitals mostly in St. Louis or Memphis. The vessel was noted for its low mortality rate of 2.3 percent, better than most (if not all) land-based hospitals of the period.

The *J. K. Barnes* was another U.S. Army hospital ship of note, a craft that had the distinction of being the first built specifically for the transportation of the sick and wounded. The guiding force behind the vessel was Dr. Alexander Henry Hoff, who in 1864 supervised its construction. A coastal steamer, the *J. K. Barnes* was the largest seagoing hospital ship in the Civil War. Active only for a brief period, from January to November 1865, it still chalked up an impressive record. Out of the 3,655 patients it transported, only 29 died.

But pride of place certainly goes to the *Red Rover,* the first hospital ship launched by the U.S. Navy, and justly celebrated as a "floating palace." Originally a Confederate ship, it had been used as a barracks to house Southern soldiers stationed on Island No. 10 on the Mississippi River. Damaged by a Union shell, the vessel was captured and taken to St. Louis, where it was converted to a hospital ship. The craft, a side-wheeler steamer, emerged as the finest medical facility on the Mississippi. A true hospital ship, the *Red Rover* was designed for long-term patient care, not merely transportation. It had well-equipped operating rooms, elevators between decks, "two separate kitchens for sick and well," a cold-storage locker capable of holding 300 tons of ice, bathrooms, a laundry, and even gauze blinds for the windows to keep the cinders and smoke from annoying the patients. At the time, it was considered the "most complete thing of her kind that ever floated" and was "in every way a decided success."

The *Red Rover* had one other distinction: It carried the first women nurses to serve on a U.S. Navy hospital ship. According to the log of the vessel, the nursing corps on board included four African-American females and a like number of sisters of the Order of the Holy Cross.

The U.S. hospital ships operated from 1862 to 1865. During those three years, the fifteen steamboats and seventeen oceangoing vessels transported about 150,000 wounded and sick soldiers and sailors to hospitals in the rear.

HOSPITAL TRAINS

Since the United States led the world in rail mileage, it was inevitable that railroads would be used for military purposes once the war broke out. Moving men and supplies was of prime importance, but it wasn't long before trains were conveying troops for medical reasons as well. America's Civil War was actually the first conflict in history in which large numbers of wounded and sick soldiers (mostly Northerners) were transported to hospitals by rail.

In August 1861, only months after the start of the conflict, the first hospital train was put into operation when it transported Union wounded from the battle of Wilson's Creek in southwestern Missouri to the city of St. Louis. Hastily pressed into service, the train had facilities that were primitive even by contemporary standards. The wounded, laid out in rows on the floor of each car without as much as a wisp of straw to cushion their agonies, had to endure the 110-mile journey to St. Louis on new, unsettled track. The bouncing and rattling the men experienced must have been excruciating beyond belief.

Throughout the war, various kinds of rigging and suspension devices were introduced, in part to provide more space for the wounded, in part to give the men a more comfortable ride. Sometimes tiers of wooden bunks would be built on the inside walls of the cars, one over the other, but the ride could be just as jarring as lying on the floor. Dr. Elisha Harris, a prominent New York physician and one of the founders of the U.S. Sanitary Commission, came up with a system by which incoming litters were suspended on rubber rings. Unfortunately, the rings proved too elastic, and the patients were still bounced around. Nevertheless, the "Harris car," as it became known, was still considered an improvement over previous rail transportation because of its other innovative features, such as heavier springs to cushion shocks, a kitchen equipped with a water tank, a washbasin, cupboards, and copper boilers.

Although railroad tracks and the trains that rode them were legitimate targets of war, both sides agreed to exempt hospital trains from harm. To avoid any mistakes, the smokestacks, cabs, and tenders were painted scarlet, and each car had "HOSPITAL TRAIN" painted in bold letters across its sides. Union and Confederate forces honored the code, but there was one incident, conspicuous because it was so rare, in which Confederate cavalry raiders burned a hospital train in April 1863, yet made certain that all of the wounded were removed beforehand.

By the middle of the war, the Union hospital train system had become highly efficient, playing a vital role in transporting casualties. After the battle of Chancellorsville in May 1863, some 9,000 wounded Northern soldiers were evacuated by rail; two months later, at Gettysburg, over 15,400 of the 20,300 Federal wounded were transferred by train to medical facilities in Washington, Baltimore, and other cities. Trains were also able to keep pace with Gen. William Tecumseh Sherman's celebrated march to Atlanta in 1864, even though by the time he reached his destination, the rail link was 472 miles from the front to the nearest base hospitals. Despite such distances, over 20,000 ill and wounded soldiers in Sherman's Georgia invasion force were transported by rail, with the loss of only one man en route.

As might be expected, Confederate wounded saw far less train travel. Besides the relative lack of resources, a ubiquitous theme, the South had fewer miles of track than the North. Also, too, the South was the major battle zone, exposing its rail traffic to inevitable disruption and destruction.

The railroads not only saved lives; they increased overall battlefield efficiency. For one thing, armies in the field were relieved of the burden of sick and wounded, and for another, the quick evacuation to general hospitals gave men a better chance to recover and return to duty. Altogether, some 225,000 Union soldiers were evacuated by train, the figure a testament to the crucial part hospital trains played in America's fratricidal conflict.

DISABLED VETERANS

"The trade-mark of Civil War surgery was amputation," a modern scholar has written. "More arms and legs were chopped off in this war than in any other conflict in which the country has ever been engaged."

Why was the Civil War soldier who took a bullet in one or more of his limbs placed in such an unenviable position? Certainly the limited medical knowledge of the time contributed to this suffering, but perhaps it can be best understood by focusing on the unique nature of the wounds themselves. The rifled muskets of the period fired soft lead bullets of a high caliber. This fact, coupled with the generally low muzzle velocity of such weapons, meant that bullets stayed in human flesh instead of passing through. Moreover, if these lead bullets hit bone, they generally shattered it. Gangrene or septicemia or osteomyelitis could develop, and Civil War medicine did not have in its arsenal the drugs necessary to combat such maladies. The only recourse, drastic as it may seem today, was amputation.

Of course, surgically severing a limb posed a severe risk itself, especially if performed in a germ-laden field hospital. Soldiers by the thousands died of infection, yet statistics show most of them survived the scalpel and bone saw. In the Union army, there were 29,980 documented cases of amputations of arms and legs, and of that figure, 75 percent of the wounded made it through the ordeal.

But what was to become of them? Disabled, most of these men could not resume their old occupations. Young and for the most part determined to make something of themselves, they wanted neither charity nor the enforced idleness of institutionalized care in an old soldiers' home. Essentially, they wanted as normal a life as possible.

The public was highly sympathetic, as it usually is toward its limbless veterans. Returning soldiers harbor many scars, some psychological, some physical, and often not apparent to the naked eye. But seeing a man in uniform without an arm or leg evokes a special blend of emotions—compassion, sorrow, gratitude. *Harper's Weekly* caught the poignant mood many felt when it published *The Cripple at the Gate,* an artist's depiction of a returning veteran in a travel-stained uniform reduced to begging because he had lost his leg.

All sorts of plans were advanced for employment of the disabled veterans. They could become clerks, messengers, or telegraph operators if they had a mind to. But before this could become reality, the amputees had to have their mobility restored, at least as much as humanly possible. Since they had performed so faithfully and courageously in behalf of the nation, it seemed to many that artificial limbs should be supplied at public expense.

On July 16, 1862, Congress responded positively, passing a law requiring the government to pay for soldiers' prostheses. An allowance of $50 was granted for the purchase of an arm or foot, $75 for a leg. Those who wished for more expensive models had to pay the difference out of their own pockets—but still, by allocating money for artificial limbs, for the first time ever the Federal government was committing itself to a program designed to physically rehabilitate veterans.

Compared to today's prostheses, the metal or rubber limbs of the Civil War era were crude, and in most cases, they must have been very uncomfortable to wear. Although they were an improvement over the eighteenth-century stump hook and peg leg of pirate fame, the artificial limbs were so poorly made that they sometimes caused more pain than they were worth. On top of that, vendors on occasion tried to cheat their clients. A New York veteran complained to a newspaper that one fitter attempted to charge him $100 for a $25 leg.

Because of all the potential problems involving a prosthesis, few veteran amputees availed themselves of the government's offer, preferring a cash commutation instead. Disabled ex-soldiers also enjoyed a monthly pension, which was low—$8 a month for the loss of a limb (later to be increased)—but for the moment, better than nothing at all.

Confederate amputees faced a double handicap: They had to cope with their disability, and they had the misfortune of being on the losing side. There were roughly 25,000 amputations performed in the Confederate army, and those who survived had to rely on funds from depleted state treasuries or private charities. In the spring of 1866, for instance, a benevolent society was organized by women in Nashville, with dues of $1 a month, to purchase artificial limbs for the boys in gray. In some areas of the former Confederacy, a "shoe exchange" was established, by which one-legged men "equipped with the cheap old-fashioned peg-leg could swap the unwanted half of a pair of shoes." Southern veterans themselves tried to help their less fortunate comrades by forming Confederate Soldiers' Associations. These efforts, though worthy, lacked the scope and financial resources of the Federal response, and therefore it was not unusual, as a British visitor observed, that human mutilations left by the war were "everywhere in town and farm communities through the South."

FOOT PROBLEMS

The three most essential parts of a soldier's equipment, the duke of Wellington once said, were "a pair of shoes, a second pair of shoes, and a pair of half soles." Like most commanders, Wellington was well aware of the fact that an army's effectiveness depended much on the mobility of its infantry—a mobility that would be seriously compromised without proper footgear. This was certainly the case during the

Civil War, a war fought predominantly by infantry. Union and Confederate generals often relied on lengthy but fast-moving marches to fulfill their tactical and strategic objectives.

To maintain the pace, a Civil War soldier had much to contend with. After all, he was already limited by what he had to carry, including haversack, cartridge box, canteen, blanket, rifle, and bayonet, a load that could come close to fifty pounds. And besides transporting that extra weight, he had to deal with mud, rough ground, and varying elevations of terrain. Under the circumstances, well-made, good-fitting shoes were essential, yet such shoes were often unobtainable for the average man in the ranks—at least during the first year or so of the war.

Ill-fitting footwear would rub and chafe mercilessly, until every step was agony. As a case in point, take the New Jersey sergeant whose feet became "swollen, blistered, and infected" during the course of grueling marches in the Fredericksburg campaign. Poor-fitting shoes chafed his feet raw; when the regiment halted and the sergeant removed his footwear, he found "blood and pus acting as a glue between sock and skin." Once the march continued "fresh scabs 'cut into the raw flesh like a knife.'"

Such cases, however, grew rare as the war progressed. By mid-1862 Northern industry was producing a better-fitting shoe, though hardly perfect, and as a result of technological advances in the mass production of footwear, manufacturers were able to keep pace with the demand.

For the men in gray, the situation got worse rather than better. As one modern student of "Johnny Reb" has pointed out, "The most pervasive and most keenly felt of all deficiencies [by Confederate soldiers] was that of shoes." Almost from the start, there was a critical shortage of shoe leather. Not long after the first battle of Bull Run in July 1861, Confederate quartermaster general A. C. Myers expressed apprehension that he would be unable to meet the footwear needs of the army. This became apparent when Lee prepared for his invasion of the North in September 1862, and it was estimated that the Army of Northern Virginia needed 40,000 pairs of shoes. While the Confederate government scrambled as best it could to meet the needs of its main army, the men in the ranks made do with what they had. Some infantrymen crafted so-called "utility" shoes, ankle-high leather nailed to a wooden sole, but the sole usually split and left the wearer no better off than before. Still others tried to make crude moccasins from rawhide, but after two or three days the hide shrank, became ill fitting, and emitted a terrible "slaughterhouse" stench that attracted flies. Many Southern soldiers were forced to go barefoot, a terrible hardship, especially in winter. At times, even some Northern soldiers went without footwear, victims not so much of shortages as of poor distribution systems.

Dr. Charles Harley Cleveland was a Union physician who became interested in foot-related problems. In 1862 the forty-two-year-old doctor wrote *Causes and Cures of Diseases of the Feet,* the first medical book published in the United States to deal strictly with podiatry, or chiropody, as it was then called. Some 100 pages in length, Cleveland's paperbound volume was designed as an instructional manual for surgeons as well as for the infantryman himself, who "suffered so much from various diseases of the feet" and needed "to be instructed in their causes and cure." The doctor did not see the results of his book, since he died in 1863 while serving with Union forces in Memphis. Still, his was a seminal work, helping establish the foundations for podiatry as a legitimate medical field.

DENTAL CARE

Blessed with greater wealth and seemingly unlimited resources, the Union was often able to pioneer innovations during the Civil War. But dentistry was one field where the Confederacy, not the Union, was the trailblazer. Even before the war, Southerners led the way in dental care. In 1842 Virginia dentists organized a state dental society, the first such organization in the world. And Confederate president Jefferson Davis, as secretary of war in the 1850s, proposed an army and navy dental corps, but the proposal fell on deaf ears and was not adopted.

As the Civil War dragged on, it was obvious that the men fighting for the South could use quality dental care. For most soldiers in the field, tooth care was the last thing on their minds unless a problem set in, which was more than likely, since most Civil War soldiers prior to entering the service probably had never visited a dentist. And if they were in need of one during the war, the vast majority, especially those in the Confederate army, couldn't have afforded a dentist's services anyway. Dental care in the wartime South, given the continuing devaluation of the currency, was prohibitively expensive. Even during the early stages of inflation, the charge was $20 for an extraction, $120 for a gold filling, and anywhere between $1,800 and $4,000 for an upper set of teeth.

In March 1863 a plan was introduced for the Confederate government to contract the military's dental work out to private dentists. But once that failed to be implemented, dentists were then drafted into the military with the rank of hospital steward. The Confederate army, therefore, had access to its own corps of dental practitioners, making it the first military organization in American history to provide professional and organized dental care to its soldiers.

Once the program was put into operation, Confederate dentists were not at a loss for patients. "A day's work," Dr. W. Leigh Burton of Richmond wrote, "consisted of from twenty to thirty fillings, the preparation of the cavities included, the extraction of fifteen or twenty teeth, and the removal of the tartar ad libitum!"

In addition to "plugging, cleaning, and extracting teeth," Southern military dentists also made contributions in the treatment of wounds affecting the face and jaw. Dr. James Baxter Bean, an Atlanta dentist, experimented with an interdental splint in treating fractures of the maxillary bones. Impressed by the success of Bean's procedure, Confederate medical inspector Edward N. Covey moved all facial wound cases to one hospital in Atlanta, making it "the first [medical facility] in military or dental history to be used for maxilla-facial surgery."

At a time when many people considered dentists little better than tooth pullers, the Confederacy's efforts to secure dental care for its fighting men no doubt gave an added lift to the status of the profession. Regrettably, the dental treatment that the Confederates enjoyed was not shared by their counterparts in blue. The idea of dental care for Union soldiers was rejected by Northern authorities, though the rationale behind that decision remains unclear.

MEDICAL STOREKEEPERS

Before the Civil War, medical supplies for the U.S. Army came from the Medical Purveying Depot, a central depository located in New York City. From there, supplies were sent to subdepots in the South and West—chiefly New Orleans, San Antonio, Camp Floyd in Utah, and Albuquerque—for distribution to various army posts. The vast majority of subdepots were in the West, where most of the 16,000 men of America's peacetime force were stationed.

With the outbreak of war, and as thousands flocked to the colors and armies grew, the distribution of medicines, surgical instruments, hospital beds, and scores of related items had to keep pace. In addition to New York City, Philadelphia became a major purveying depot. Other, smaller supply hubs sprung up as well, until by the end of the war there were no less than thirty such centers.

An increase in medical distribution centers meant that there had to be an increase in personnel—preferably personnel who could manage to sort, store, and forward vital medical supplies to field hospitals. In January 1862 the editor of the *American Journal of Pharmacy* suggested that pharmacists were ideal candidates for the positions and should be given "a distinct standing and the rank of Pharmaceutist as in the French army."

Innately conservative, the army medical department did not favor such recognition to persons whom they considered mere "handmaidens" within the medical community. But the need for trained distribution agents was so great that Congress overruled the department's entrenched bureaucracy and, on May 20, 1862, created the post of "medical storekeeper"—authorizing the U.S. Army, for the first time in its history, to recruit qualified pharmacists. The act empowered the secretary of war to appoint six medical storekeepers, "who shall be skilled Apothecaries or Druggists," between the ages of twenty-five and forty, with business experience and "a good English education." They also would be required to pass an examination administered by a board of not less than three medical officers and give a bond in the sum of $40,000.

Medical storekeepers were charged with the receiving, storing, safekeeping, and issuing of medical and hospital supplies, in addition to maintaining a detailed record of all transactions. For these responsibilities, they were paid $124.16 a month and provided quarters equal to those of a first lieutenant. But like other professionals employed by the army and given the pay and living allowance of an officer, medical storekeepers remained civilians with no military standing. Out of courtesy, they could be addressed as "Captain," an honorary title and only to be used on base; elsewhere they would be merely "Mr."

Of the six original recruits, four were appointed acting medical purveyors, positions in which they were accountable for millions of dollars worth of transactions. But that did not relieve them of their more traditional pharmaceutical tasks. At Mower General Hospital in Philadelphia, for instance, an army pharmacist reported that 500 to 800 new prescriptions were filled each month, and the procedures he described were similar to those of a modern hospital pharmacy.

Although medical storekeepers received little recognition and no official status within the U.S. Army, their services were not without significance. In several respects, they served as a vanguard for their profession, helping establish the practice of pharmacy as a separate but respectable part of the health-care community.

VETERINARY SURGEONS

Modern readers tend to forget the integral role played by four-legged animals in the Civil War. Horses served the cavalry, and mules were used as draught animals pulling supply wagons and other vehicles. During America's four-year struggle, the U.S. Army alone purchased over 1 million such animals.

To keep these horses and mules in peak condition, they would need care. In the first two years of the war (and ever since formation of the first U.S. cavalry regiment in 1833), farriers were responsible for the well-being of military animals. As self-taught laymen, farriers knew the basics of horse care; they could shoe a horse and administer the standard medicine but had no real substantive veterinary knowledge. Actually, there were just a few, possibly only fifty, professionally trained veterinarians in the entire country—and most of them were foreign-born and educated. With only one veterinary school in the United States—the New York College of Veterinary Surgeons—Americans were far behind Europeans in this field of medicine.

Ill-prepared or not, with the creation of 200 Union cavalry regiments (there had only been 5 before the war), Congress soon recognized the need to attract college-educated veterinarians. On March 3, 1863, legislation was passed authorizing one veterinary surgeon for each cavalry regiment—the first time in U.S. military history that professionally trained veterinarians were to be employed by the army. Paid $75 a month, they would serve in a civilian capacity but were given the honorary rank of sergeant major and allowed to wear a uniform with horseshoe-shaped brassards on their sleeves.

Since there was neither screening nor testing of the applicants, it's impossible to identify the professionally educated veterinary surgeons as opposed to the lay people—farriers or blacksmiths—who also held the title. To compound the problem, because veterinary surgeons were civilians, their names do not appear on official military rosters, and therefore there is no way of knowing precisely how many served in that capacity.

Whatever their qualifications or numbers, those who practiced veterinary medicine in the military had helped pave the way for its acceptance as a genuine field within the medical community. Official recognition, however, was more than a half century away, not to take place until 1916, when veterinarians finally received commissions as officers in the U.S. Army.

DR. MARY WALKER

Dr. Mary Walker was a feminist and proud of it. Refusing to accept the constraints imposed upon women during her lifetime, she rose—nay, soared—above them. Not only was she the first woman to be employed by the U.S. Army as a physician, she was the first—and to date only—woman to win the Medal of Honor.

That she managed to become a doctor at all was something of a miracle, given the status of women at the time. Largely confined to the home as wives and mothers, women might work on the farm, in a family store, or tend the sick (often becoming skilled midwives), but most professions were closed to them. It was not until 1849 that Elizabeth Blackwell beat the odds and became the first female physician in the United States, paving the way for others to follow suit.

Mary Edwards Walker was born on November 26, 1832, in Oswego, New York. Her father was liberal, open-minded, and something of a radical when it came to his beliefs in the inherent equality of women, convinced that they should be educated on an equal basis and even have professional careers. Such views imbued Mary with a sense of her own self-worth. At eighteen, she attended Falley Seminary in Fulton, New York, where she studied algebra, natural philosophy, grammar, Latin, and, somewhat unusual for a young lady at the time, physiology and hygiene. Soon after leaving the academy, Mary took a teaching position not far from her home, but by 1853, at age twenty-one, she decided to become a doctor. Walker was accepted by Syracuse Medical College and went through the standard two-year course of study. When she was awarded her medical diploma in June 1855, she was the only woman in her class.

Getting a diploma was one thing; finding acceptance was another. Walker set up practice in Columbus, Ohio, but could find few patients. The idea of a woman doctor was so novel, so "unnatural," few people could stomach the idea. Walker's manner of dress didn't help her cause, either. In part as an expression of her feminism, and in part because of sheer comfort and good health (in her view, tight-fitting corsets and long, heavy skirts ran counter to a woman's physical and mental well-being), Walker adopted aspects of male dress. She wore slacks buttoned to the waist or held up by suspenders, and "an upper garment resembling a knee-length dress, cinched in at the waist and with long sleeves, a high neck, and a full skirt." To see a woman's legs—however covered—was shocking to Victorian sensibilities. But beyond that, trousers were the very symbol of male power and dominance, and it was unthinkable that a woman would attempt to usurp their garb.

Walker managed to eke out a living for a few years, but the coming of war seemed to signal new opportunities. The Civil War created a demand for physicians, so Walker applied for a commission from the U.S. surgeon general. She was rejected; despite the need for doctors, it was not great enough to break male prejudices.

This was to prove the first of many rebuffs Walker was to receive during the war, but she was indefatigable in her desire to serve her country. In the fall of 1861, Walker volunteered her services at a Washington, D.C., military hospital. The physician in charge, a Dr. J. N. Green, was desperately short-handed and agreed to take her on as his assistant. Tending to some 100 patients, she diagnosed their illnesses, treated them, and even assisted in their operations, leading Dr. Green to conclude that Walker was a highly competent physician.

About a year later, still determined to serve in the field as an army doctor, Walker took it upon herself to head for Warrenton, Virginia, where a typhoid epidemic raged through the Army of the Potomac. Given the state of emergency, her offer to help was accepted. And so impressive was her work with the stricken soldiers that after the battle of Fredericksburg in December 1862, attending surgeons welcomed her back to assist them in caring for the wounded. Once again she performed her duties well—so well that one of the Army of the Potomac physicians, Dr. Preston King, wrote to Secretary of War Edwin M. Stanton urging him to compensate Walker for her work and grant her a position in the army. But the request elicited no response.

Although Walker's efforts to secure a commission were repeatedly frustrated, her fame as a military doctor was spreading. One newspaper paid tribute by calling her a "daughter of Esculapius," a reference to the ancient Greek physician of great skill and renown. Yet the army remained unmoved, prompting Walker to take matters into her own hands. In November 1863 Walker proposed to raise her own regiment, to be called "Walker's U.S. Patriots," with herself as its medical officer. The idea of a woman doctor was horrible enough to Washington officialdom, but the possibility that she would raise a regiment was so unthinkable that the government rejected it out of hand.

Discouraged but unwilling to acknowledge defeat, Walker took her case to the president himself. To no avail; Lincoln, too, refused her request for a commission. The Medical Department, he informed her, was "an organized system in the hands of men supposed to be learned in that profession," and he did not want "to thrust among them anyone, male or female, against their consent."

Only an act of God, it seemed, would be necessary to break down this wall of male prejudice—and that's just what happened. An assistant surgeon in the 52nd Ohio Regiment of the Army of the Cumberland died, leaving a vacancy. The commanding general, George H. Thomas, who knew of Walker's work, assigned her to the 52nd Ohio to be a civilian contract surgeon. To have been hand-picked by Thomas was certainly a stroke of good luck, but Walker was far from out of the woods yet. Like most of the civilian physicians appointed as noncommissioned army contract surgeons, Walker would have to undergo an examination of her medical skills by a board of military doctors. The medical staff of the Army of the Cumberland was aghast at the appointment; why should they be saddled with such a "medical monstrosity," particularly one "dressed in that hybrid costume," as one member of the examining board put it. The results of the test were a foregone conclusion; the board ruled that she failed her oral exam. Fortunately for Walker, General Thomas stood by her, and her appointment as an assistant surgeon was upheld.

Beginning her service with the Army of the Cumberland in early 1864, she must have cut quite a figure in her blue uniform. Slender and barely five feet tall, she wore a knee-length coat, with brass buttons and shoulder straps, over a pair of male trousers. No doubt some of the troops resented her, but most simply did not know what to make of her. She was an anomaly, something completely out of their experience. In any event, Walker found little to do at first, the soldiers being healthy, so she treated local civilians, sometimes beyond the camp and perilously close to Rebel lines. On April 10, 1864, only two months after her appointment, she strayed a bit too far and was captured by the Confederates.

If Northerners didn't know what to make of her, Southerners were positively dumbfounded. One Confederate captain wrote that they were "all amused and disgusted too at the sight of a *thing* that nothing but the debased and depraved Yankee nation could produce—a 'female doctor.'" The officer, tongue firmly in cheek, recommended that she be dressed in a frock and bonnet and be sent back to the Union lines, or put in an insane asylum.

Imprisoned for four months at Richmond's Castle Thunder, a place infamous for its filth and vermin, eventually Walker was exchanged for a Confederate officer with the rank of major. The conditions of her release—man for man—were almost as much a source of satisfaction as freedom itself.

After a period of recuperation, Walker was appointed superintendent of the Female Military Prison at Louisville, Kentucky, leaving that position at war's end. On November 11, 1865, in "recognition of her services and sufferings," President Andrew Johnson awarded her the Medal of Honor.

Walker wore the medal with enormous pride, but in 1917, a commission reviewed all awards and set up stringent rules for the honor. More than 900 medals, including Walker's, were revoked. In Walker's case, it was pointed out that she was not a regular member of the Ohio infantry regiment, and besides, her service did "not appear to be distinguished in action or otherwise." When asked to return her medal, Walker, feisty as ever at eighty-five, reportedly replied, "Over my dead body." She continued to wear it until her death two years later in 1919. In 1977 the U.S. Army posthumously restored her Medal of Honor, a result of the lobbying efforts of several feminist groups.

ALEXANDER T. AUGUSTA, M.D.

Dr. Alexander T. Augusta was the first black man commissioned as a surgeon with the rank of major in the U.S. Army. His was an outstanding achievement, given the mistrust, prejudice, and violence he had to endure.

The Virginia-born Augusta had received his medical training in Canada, having been compelled, as he explained in a letter to President Lincoln, "to leave my native country and come to this on account of prejudice against colour." After earning his medical degree from Trinity College in Toronto, Augusta set up a practice there, serving mostly white patients. While the Civil War raged in the United States, Augusta (who became a British citizen) could have stayed in Canada and continued to prosper, but he wanted to serve his former country and "be of use to [his] race."

At first the army medical board in Washington flatly rejected his request to serve as a physician, insisting that Augusta was unsuitable because he was "a person of African descent" and also "an alien & a British subject," the latter of which would make his acceptance "an evident violation of her Britannic Majesty's Proclamation of Neutrality." Unwilling to back down, Augusta responded by pointing out that he had traveled "near a thousand miles at a great expense and sacrifice," and that his chief purpose was to minister to the medical needs of his own people. With few white doctors willing to serve in black units, Augusta's statement apparently struck a responsive chord among members of the board, since they reversed themselves and invited the thirty-eight-year-old black physician to take the qualifying examination. Passing the test, Augusta was duly commissioned as a surgeon in the U.S. Army on April 14, 1863.

But an officer's shoulder bars did not shield him from the racism of the era. Only a month after receiving his commission, upon boarding a train at Baltimore and taking his seat, he was roughed up by a railroad guard and "8 or 10 toughs" and in the attack had one of his oak leaf insignias torn off his uniform. Refusing to be intimidated, Augusta returned to the depot, but this time with a military squad and several detectives. Even with this protection, he was hit in the face and had to be escorted aboard the train with revolvers drawn.

Unfortunately for the newly commissioned major, his problems had only begun. Once Augusta reported for duty at Camp Stanton, Maryland, assistant white surgeons expressed dismay that the new senior surgeon was black. Complaining to President Lincoln himself, they requested that a termination be put to "this unexpected, unusual, and most unpleasant relationship in which we have been placed." It is not recorded what Lincoln's response was, but Augusta was soon put on detached duty, in effect relieved of command and assigned temporarily to another post.

As if to add insult to injury, Dr. Augusta found himself caught up in the dispute over pay for black soldiers. At the time of his appointment, all men of color, no matter their rank, were paid $7 a month, the standard wage for a black private. As an army surgeon holding the rank of major, Augusta deserved $169 a month. A complaint was lodged with Secretary of War Stanton, but nothing was done for more than a year, until Congress finally equalized the pay situation in June 1864.

Technically, Augusta was part of the 7th Regiment of U.S. Colored Troops, but his position and rank continued to spark so much controversy that throughout most of the war he was stationed at a rendezvous camp for black soldiers. In the postwar era he taught anatomy in the department of medicine at Howard University, the first black doctor to serve on the faculty of any American medical school. At the same time, Dr. Augusta earned a reputation as one of the leading physicians of Washington, D.C.

BATTLING VENEREAL DISEASE

Prostitution flourished during the Civil War. Whether in camp, on furlough, or passing through an urban area en route to the front, the soldiers were more than eager to partake in what was popularly termed "horizontal refreshments."

The cities in particular were major centers of the trade. In the North, New York City reportedly had 20,000 "ladies of the evening," and even staid Boston, citadel of the Puritan spirit, in the words of one visitor, "absolutely swarms with strumpets." Before the war Washington, D.C., harbored around 500 prostitutes. By 1863 the nation's capital had become "a mecca for whores," with 450 known brothels and no less than 7,000 women plying the world's oldest profession. Many bordellos had colorful names, like "Headquarters U.S.A.," "Fort Sumter," "The Ironclad," or "Unconditional Surrender." According to a newspaper correspondent residing in the city, Washington was probably "the most pestiferous hole since the days of Sodom and Gomorrah. The majority of the women on the streets were openly disreputable."

The Confederacy also saw a marked increase of prostitution. George Avery, a Southern soldier, was so shocked that he retreated into forgivable hyperbole. "I do not believe," Avery told his wife, "there is more than one woman in a thousand in the whole southern Confederacy who is virtuous, & the men are universal libertines." Avery obviously exaggerated, but certainly places like Richmond were hotbeds of prostitution, with brothels lining many streets and Southern courtesans using the very grounds of the Confederate capitol building for soliciting.

Casual, unprotected sexual activity has its risks, and many soldiers contracted venereal disease. Among Union army troops, gonorrhea and syphilis were the most common sexually transmitted forms of the ailment, with an annual average of eighty-two cases per 1,000—a low incidence, if compared with that among European armies. Victoria's British redcoats, for example, had a 200 per 1,000 rate. Yet the American rate of venereal disease was probably much higher, since many cases were not reported, leading several historians to conclude that if all unreported cases were added, the numbers would double or possibly triple.

At the time, there was no cure for venereal disease. But that didn't seem to deter some physicians, who gamely prescribed pokeroots, elderberries, sassafras, potassium iodide in sarsaparilla, mercury, zinc sulfate, quinine, or even cauterization. Sometimes the "cures" were worse than the disease. The use of mercury produced side effects ranging from abdominal pain and kidney failure to hallucinations and insanity.

Unable to defeat the disease medically, U.S. military authorities attempted to stop it by suppressing the prostitutes. The Union command ordered raids and deportations in various jurisdictions, North and South, but nowhere were these efforts more ambitious than in Nashville and Memphis.

Important as supply and logistical centers, both of these Tennessee cities were captured by Union forces early in the war. Nashville fell in late February 1862 and Memphis in June of that year. Thousands of Northern troops poured into both areas, and as was usually the case, prostitutes in search of Yankee dollars were not far behind. Memphis was soon called the "Gomorrah of the West." "Virtue," declared a Union soldier, "is scarcely known within the limits of the city." Nashville had an even more infamous reputation, with its red-light district called "Smokey Row." Pvt. Benton E. Dubbs of Ohio recalled, while stationed in Nashville, that "there was an old saying that no man could be a soldier unless he had gone through Smokey Row. . . . The street was about three fourths of a mile long and every house or shanty on both sides was a home of ill fame. Women had no thought of dress or decency. They said Smokey Row killed more soldiers than the war."

In the winter of 1863–64, the Union command in Nashville came down hard on the city's prostitutes. Some 1,500 "women of the town" were rounded up and shipped off by train to Louisville, Kentucky, but within a short time most came right back. Refusing to acknowledge the futility of their approach, the city's provost marshal, Lt. Col. George Spalding, staged another mass raid six months later, gathering up the women and deporting them this time by river via a chartered steamboat. Spalding must have thought he solved the problem, but he found that the vacuum he had created in Nashville was soon filled by African-American women of ill repute. And if that weren't enough, the white prostitutes soon returned from their temporary exile. Deportation was no solution.

Faced with a deteriorating public health situation, in August 1863 Spalding established a system of licensing Nashville's prostitutes—thereby initiating for the first time in American history legalized prostitution. The colonel's plan called for each prostitute to obtain a license at the cost of $5 and to provide the authorities with an employment address. She would then be examined for venereal disease by a physician once every seven to ten days; those passing would get a certificate of soundness, while those not passing would be sent to a special hospital set up for the purpose. The prostitutes themselves would be taxed 50 cents a week for the upkeep of the hospital. And finally, those unwilling to obtain a license and a certificate could be "at once arrested and incarcerated in the workhouse for a period not less than 30 days."

As of April 30, 1864, 353 prostitutes were so licensed, and by June 30 of that year, close to 1,000 infected women had been admitted to the female hospital for treatment. On the whole, the experiment worked. The surgeon general commented that "under these regulations, a marked improvement was speedily noted in the manner and appearance of the women." As a matter of fact, the program proved so successful, the surgeon general further reported, that "many of the better class of prostitutes had been drawn to Nashville from Northern cities by the comparative protection from venereal disease which its license system afforded."

As for the disease itself, though not completely eradicated, it was brought under control. Dr. H. R. Fletcher, in charge of Nashville's female venereal hospital, came right to the heart of the matter when he stated:

> It is not to be supposed that a system hastily devised, established for the first time on this continent . . . should be other than imperfect. . . . This much is to be claimed, that after the . . . forcible expulsion of the prostitutes had utterly failed, the more philosophic plan of recognizing and controlling an ineradicable evil has met with undoubted success.

In September 1864, about a year after legalized prostitution had been put into effect in Nashville, Memphis embraced a similar plan and experienced similar results. But once the war came to an end, so did the programs. Civilian authorities in both cities, as well as in other American municipalities considering adoption of the program, were uneasy with a system that seemed to encourage loose morals. As far as they were concerned, legalized prostitution had been a war measure essentially designed to preserve the health of soldiers rather than to improve the medical well-being of the community at large.

POST-TRAUMATIC STRESS DISORDER

All wars eventually end, and once peace is concluded, soldiers are discharged and return home to take up the threads of their former lives. Time often heals, and with the passage of years the terrifying reality of combat usually fades, or at least is transformed into a memory that evokes pride in having done one's duty in the face of trying conditions. Yet for some soldiers, the horrors remain as fresh as the day they were first experienced.

In the aftermath of the Vietnam War, for example, veterans seemed beset with a host of problems, including anxiety disorders, severe depression, alcoholism, drug abuse, unemployment, rootless wandering, homelessness, and suicide. For the most part these problems are said to be related to post-traumatic stress disorder (PTSD). Some veterans' advocates maintain that the condition was made worse because the Southeast Asian conflict was so unpopular with the American people. Lack of support from the public at large, and indeed, out-and-out rejection of returning vets by at least some segments of society, it has been argued, produced a fertile soil of alienation that allowed PTSD to take root.

But were Vietnam veterans unique in their manifestation of PTSD? What about those who served in other American wars? Did they escape this mental disorder because they were well received upon returning home? A recent groundbreaking study by Eric T. Dean, Jr., has suggested that Vietnam was not the first conflict to produce cases of PTSD, that home front reception had little to do with triggering the disease, and that postwar adjustment problems could best be explained by the traumatic experiences of combat. In short, the more grisly the battlefield encounters, the greater the likelihood that veterans would suffer from PTSD.

This being the case, it's not surprising that the Civil War, given its sheer scale of slaughter, was actually the first American conflict in which a significant number of soldiers and veterans experienced acute and delayed stress problems. Letters, diaries, and memoirs often spoke of "dead bodies everywhere." After the bloodbath at Shiloh, for instance, Grant himself remembered: "I saw an open field . . . so covered with dead that it would have been possible to walk across the clearing, in any direction, stepping on dead bodies, without a foot touching the ground." Still worse were those who witnessed death firsthand. "I never shall forget how awfully I felt on seeing, for the first time, a man killed in battle," wrote Leander Stillwell of the 61st Illinois. "I stared at his body, perfectly horrified! Only a few seconds ago that man was alive and well, and now he was lying on the ground, done for, forever!" A Massachusetts soldier described an even more graphic scene involving hand-to-hand combat at Gettysburg: "Foot to foot, body to body, and man to man they struggled, pushed, and strived and killed. Each had rather die than yield. The mass of wounded and heaps of dead entangled the feet of the contestants, and, underneath the trampling mass, wounded men who could no longer stand, struggled, fought, shouted and killed."

In the midst of such carnage, men's reactions varied. There were those like the Pennsylvania infantryman who, after witnessing two of his tent mates wounded by Confederate fire, lost all sense of proportion. "The feeling that was uppermost in my mind was a desire to kill as many rebels as I could." Other soldiers reacted to the trauma of combat with numbness, while some broke down completely. Entrenched near Bermuda Hundred, not far from Richmond, Union soldier Albert Frank offered a drink to a man sitting next to him, when suddenly a shell blew the man's head off, "splattering blood and brain fragments" on Frank. That evening Frank acted strangely, began screaming, and then ran toward the enemy. He was later found "huddled in fear," making incoherent sounds, and after an examination by a doctor was sent to a government hospital for the insane in Washington, D.C.

Frank is but one of hundreds of documented cases of acute or delayed service-related stress problems. There were probably thousands, perhaps tens of thousands, of additional cases that went unrecorded primarily because the illness was poorly understood in the nineteenth century. Some Civil War physicians identified the problem physiologically, without fully grasping the meaning behind the symptoms they were describing. A few spoke of an "irritable heart" or "trotting heart," failing to recognize that this was a calling card of stress. Others noted headaches, paralysis, and even a kind of "sunstroke" among those afflicted with what they diagnosed as "melancholia." And still others advanced a theory of "nostalgia" or "homesickness" that was said to hit soldiers as a short-term reaction to combat.

After the war many veterans could not adjust to civilian life. Surviving pension records and surgeons' certificates testify to the difficulties they encountered, ranging from restlessness, inability to sleep, apathy, and partial loss of memory to far more serious disorders, such as incoherence, severe depression, and other behavior patters, which today would be diagnosed as various forms of schizophrenia. Like their Vietnam counterparts a century later, many ex–Civil War soldiers found themselves unable to hold jobs, to maintain harmonious marital and family relationships, and to simply put the war behind them; indeed, many succumbed to alcohol or drugs, and, prone to violence, a number had confrontations with the law.

We will probably never know the extent of the PTSD problem created by the Civil War, but it did exist. Records are imprecise, psychological care as we know it today was not available, and the patina of romanticism that soon grew about the conflict in its aftermath covered and obscured this dark side of the war.

RACISM CONFIRMED

Anthropometry—the collecting and classification of body measurements to better understand the dynamics of human behavior—is a thoroughly discredited discipline. It was closely allied to phrenology, studying character and mental capacity by the physical formation of the skull. Casts were sometimes made, as in the case of the notorious nineteenth-century Scots murderers Burke and Hare, to study the "criminal type."

The first major anthropometric studies in the United States were conducted during the Civil War. After the Union's disastrous rout at Bull Run in July 1861, the administration asked the U.S. Sanitary Commission, the best staffed and equipped of the civilian relief agencies, to undertake anthropometric measurements of the troops to determine if there had been a physiological cause for the defeat. Since studies cost money even then, the major life insurance companies agreed to underwrite the commission's work. All things considered, they had much to gain from this kind of an investigation, which could help their industry acquire useful statistical averages on the physical condition of the male population.

Meanwhile, the government also requested that the Provost Marshal General's Bureau conduct a similar study, independent of the commission. Both agencies set to work almost immediately, but were soon diverted from their original task when the War Department in August 1862 authorized the recruitment of African-Americans. Here was an opportunity to study racial differences on a scope and scale never before available. Investigators for the bureau and the commission soon abandoned their original objective and focused their interest and energies on the racial diversity within the ranks.

A variety of measurements were taken and statistically recorded, among them height, weight, length of head, neck, forearms, torso, legs, feet, and width of shoulders and chest—as well as facial angle, height to knee, distance from tip of middle finger to kneecap, between nipples, from perineum to most prominent part of pubes, circumference around hips, and so on. By the end of the war, 10,876 white soldiers, 1,146 white sailors, 68 white marines, 2,020 so-called "full-blooded" blacks, 863 mulattos, and 519 Native Americans (mostly Iroquois, who had fought for the Confederacy and were POWs held near Rock Island, Illinois) were examined and measured. In addition, 405 autopsies were performed (381 on African-Americans and 24 on whites) to determine the average size and weight of the brain for both races.

Four years after the hostilities ceased, the U.S. Sanitary Commission published its findings under the title *Investigations in the Military and Anthropological Statistics of the American Soldier.* Still later, in 1875, the *Statistics, Medical and Anthropological of the Provost-Marshal-General's Bureau* was added to the literature. Both studies came up with similar findings, validating preconceived notions of Caucasian superiority. White soldiers attained the highest level of "physical perfection"; they were better proportioned, stronger, and had greater stamina than people of color. Native Americans were a distant second in the rating, with so-called "pure-blood" blacks third, and mulattos last. In terms of mental capacity, the autopsies further confirmed black inferiority, with white Americans having brains on the average 10 percent larger and five ounces heavier than those of full-blooded African-Americans. Mulattos, however, had a brain weight of only three ounces less than whites, making them intellectually superior to pure-blood blacks but still physically inferior, and thereby reinforcing the antimiscegenationist views of the time that the mixing of the races would serve no positive purpose.

Upon arriving at these conclusions, the investigators gave little thought to their own prejudices, nor did they factor in environmental conditions, such as health, diet, education, even state of mind. At any rate, it is a sad irony that the very war ending slavery in the United States was also responsible for producing studies that fostered, even helped institutionalize, racism. In that sense, the Civil War freed African-Americans only to enslave them in less overt ways.

ARMY MEDICAL MUSEUM

The Army Medical Museum, founded in 1862, was the first institution in the United States to specialize in pathology. It was the brain child of Surgeon General William A. Hammond. Soon after taking office, Hammond ran across files containing medical information dating back to the early days of the Republic. In one particular box, he discovered a human arm, amputated during the Mexican War and properly labeled and preserved. Refusing to discard these items, he decided instead to establish a museum where they could be displayed and also be made available to physicians for purposes of enhancing medical and surgical knowledge.

On May 21, 1862, Hammond issued the following order:

> As it is proposed to establish in Washington, an *Army Medical Museum,* Medical officers are directed diligently to collect, and to forward

to the office of the Surgeon General all specimens of morbid anatomy, surgical or medical, which may be regarded as valuable; together with projectiles and foreign bodies, and such other matters as may prove of interest in the study of military medicine or surgery. These objects should be accompanied by short explanatory notes.

At first there was little response from physicians in the field, most of whom were overwhelmed by their own work and had neither the time nor the inclination to prepare specimens with accompanying case histories. Dr. John H. Brinton, the museum's newly appointed curator, realizing that perhaps he should set an example, went to the front himself to collect artifacts. At various battle sites, Brinton and his associates were seen digging up the trenches in which amputated arms and legs had been buried. Soon "the idea got around" that the medical department "was really in earnest, that a great work was in progress," and that it would be to the best interests of military surgeons to cooperate. It was not long before kegs and barrels filled with specimens from field and general hospitals arrived at the museum. Within its first year of operation, more than 1,300 human limbs, organs, and the like were sent, requiring the museum to move to new quarters on Pennsylvania Avenue, and within a half year to still a larger facility on "H" Street. By December 1866 it would relocate once again, this time to the building housing Ford's Theatre (which had been taken over by the government after the assassination), and would remain there for the next twenty years.

Although the museum received most of its pathological specimens directly from battlefield physicians, sometimes medical artifacts were donated privately. Probably the most famous of such "gifts" was Gen. Daniel E. Sickles's amputated leg, enclosed in a small, coffinlike box and accompanied by a calling card that cordially expressed the general's compliments. Such slightly bizarre behavior was typical of the man. In 1859, while serving as a member of Congress from New York, Sickles had learned that his wife, Teresa, was having an affair with Philip Barton Key, son of Francis Scott Key of national anthem fame. The enraged husband promptly shot Key down in the street, shouting, "You Scoundrel, you have dishonored my bed—you must die!" It was Victorian melodrama par excellence, but Sickles was soon arrested for murder and placed on trial. Defended by Edwin M. Stanton, the future secretary of war, Sickles was acquitted on the grounds of temporary insanity, the first time such an argument was successfully used in American legal history.

By the middle of the Civil War, Sickles was a major general commanding the Army of the Potomac's III Corps at Gettysburg. There, on the second day of the battle, he received the wound that ultimately cost him his leg. On recovering somewhat, the general decided to donate the limb to the Army Medical Museum. Sickles, who survived the war and died in 1914 at the age of ninety-six, would often go to the museum to visit his leg, which had been placed on exhibit in a special display case.

Actually, the general's limb was one of the main attractions of the museum during its early years. But the institution, as its first curator, Dr. John H. Brinton, had predicted, would "in time be productive of real use." As a research facility, its reputation soon reached overseas. In 1870 a leading French physician paid homage to the museum by declaring that the United States had made as much progress in the field of pathology "as had been done in Europe in a century."

By 1887 the museum moved out of Ford's Theatre into a "new red brick" four-story structure on "B" Street, which would also house temporarily the soon-to-be-established Army Medical School. There the museum remained for nearly seventy years, serving as a major center for pathological study both at home and abroad.

After World War II the Army Medical Museum became known as the Army Institute of Pathology, and five years later it assumed its current name, the Armed Forces Institute of Pathology (AFIP). Not long afterward, in 1955, it moved to its present quarters at the Walter Reed Army Medical Center in Washington, D.C. An internationally acclaimed medical institution, currently the AFIP maintains twenty-two subspecialty departments, employs more than 120 pathologists, and reviews an annual average of 50,000 surgical pathology and autopsy requests from around the world.

And yes, General Sickles's leg can still be seen at the institute's Museum of Health and Medicine.

CHAPTER 8

Reporting the War

In the nineteenth century the printed word reigned supreme as the main medium of news and information. Much of the United States was still rural, with the bulk of the population in small towns or farms. Isolated from the greater world that lay just outside their community, people looked to newspapers to provide them with the information they needed. The press kept them apprised of national and international affairs and shaped public opinion even as it informed and entertained.

On the eve of the Civil War there were more than 3,000 newspapers nationwide, including about 400 dailies. Americans seemed to hunger for news; New York State alone had more dailies than all of Great Britain. And as for New York City, it was considered the hub of newspaper publishing in the United States, home to such industry giants as the New York *Herald* and the New York *Tribune*, the latter published in a daily and weekly format. In 1860 the *Herald* boasted a daily circulation of 77,000, the weekly edition of the *Tribune* a circulation of 200,000. Altogether, seventeen daily newspapers were based in New York City.

Newspaper growth was helped by the relatively high literacy in the United States. By the time the war began, most citizens in the North and a good majority of whites in the South had received at least the rudiments of the "3R's," leaving only about 9 percent of white adult Americans unable to read.

The country was awash in newsprint, thanks not only to increasing demand, but also to advances in technology. Presses improved, as did paper-making machines, which made newspapers cheaper to produce, allowing the savings to be passed on to the consumer in the form of lower prices.

Postal rates were also reduced, important for people who received their news through the mail. With a well-organized format that usually had four pages per issue (eight for metropolitan papers), each page having six columns, newspapers seemed easier to read and handle compared with tabloids of the previous era. The only drawback, seen from the modern perspective, was the almost "microscopic" typeface of antebellum newspapers.

But nothing could quench the public's thirst for news. "The American," one foreign journalist concluded, "might be defined as a newspaper-reading animal." This craving for news was heightened by the war. Millions of lives were affected; there was hardly a family in America who didn't have a son, brother, father, or other male relative fighting on some distant battlefield.

People wanted news, and they wanted it as fast as humanly possible. The newspapers responded to this voracious demand, and circulation rose as never before. The New York *Herald* witnessed a dramatic increase from 77,000 to over 100,000 daily copies in the very first year of the war. During that same period, the *New York Times* saw its numbers catapult from 45,000 to 75,000. Other newspapers experienced similar growth as well.

The rise in circulation figures, however, reveal only a small part of the Civil War's impact on the press. Actually, the field of journalism itself was irrevocably transformed by this bloodiest of all American conflicts.

THE "SPECIALS"

The Civil War was an unprecedented event, and the nation's newspapers responded in an unprecedented way. "Never before," in the words of one student of American journalism, "had a war of any magnitude been covered so comprehensively, so accurately, and with such dispatch." During the course of the struggle, more than 200 special war correspondents, or "specials," for short, were dispatched to Union battlegrounds—and that figure does not take into consideration hundreds of part-time reporters, nor does it include those covering the Southern side. The Civil War was truly the first conflict in history to have hundreds of journalists who were close to the action and provided firsthand accounts for those at home.

Reporters seemed to be everywhere. In the early months of the conflict, Franc B. Wilkie, a *New York Times* correspondent stationed in Washington, observed: "You meet a newspaper man at every step; they block up the approaches to Headquarters; one of them is attached to the button of every officer; they are constantly demanding passes, horses, saddles, blankets, news, copies of official papers, [and] a look into private correspondence."

Newspaper mogul James Gordon Bennett, publisher of the New York *Herald,* was responsible for having the largest contingent of correspondents (over forty at one time) accompanying Union armies in the field. Bennett was no stranger to the concept of war reporting; he had helped pioneer the technique, having been the only New York newspaperman to send a reporter to the Mexican War. Convinced that Americans wanted fast news from the front presented in a lively, entertaining manner, Bennett spent lavishly (well over half a million dollars during the war) to hire and equip the best reporters. And apparently it paid off; the *Herald* was considered by many to be the most widely read newspaper in Civil War-era America.

Of course, the *Herald*'s popularity with the reading public, like that of any newspaper, depended much upon the quality of its correspondents. Fortunately for the wartime news industry, it had access to a large pool of mostly talented and dedicated reporters anxious to make a mark in their field. They were also blessed with youth, their average age somewhere in the late twenties, though there were several who were in their teens as well as in middle age. As a group, moreover, Civil War journalists were well educated, many of them holding degrees from Harvard, Yale, Columbia, or other institutions of higher learning. In the prewar years they had held down jobs such as "school teachers, lawyers, government clerks, telegraphers, bookkeepers, poets, preachers, and even soldiers," but four out of five had been involved—one way or another—in some kind of journalistic endeavor. Picturesque in appearance, they were not difficult to spot once in the field. A typical reporter was described as a man "in mud-spattered mufti or Federal blue, astride the inevitable sway-backed nag—saddlebags bulging with mackintosh, notebooks, Faber No. 2's, field glasses, pipe, sometimes potables—riding among the troops."

These specials were certainly not in it for the pay. Salaries averaged around $25 a week, not too bad (about as much as a second lieutenant in the Union army received), but not a sure path to wealth. Always on the prowl sniffing out stories, these news hounds feared being scooped by rivals more than they feared bullets. No source of information would go untapped, from the highest general to the lowliest supply clerk. If persuasion didn't work, a good bottle of whiskey might loosen tongues. As Charles Page of the New York *Tribune* confessed: "If I have the watermelons and whiskey ready when the officers come [back] from the fight, I get the news without asking questions."

The specials had to be everywhere at once, but being so ubiquitous often put them in harm's way. Reporting in the field wasn't merely fatiguing or uncomfortable; it was also dangerous. The New York *Herald*'s perambulating reporters suffered a number of casualties, including one killed and three dead from illness or exposure in the line of duty. And then there was the Chicago journalist who was killed by a cannonball while riding next to General Grant, and another special who literally had a close shave when a shell fragment sheared off most of his long beard.

Southern journalists faced similar peril and suffered their share of hardships, but unlike their Northern brethren, they also had to contend with dislocations at home. As the Confederacy declined, its newspapers suffered the inevitable shortages and chaotic conditions associated with defeat.

Correspondents North and South gave readers the information they craved. But on the whole, was it accurate? It's probably safe to say that most Civil War reporting was good, solid journalism. Some reporters were guilty of intentional inaccuracy or downright fraud, though they seem to have been a very small minority. For the most part, Civil War news accounts contained sound information, written in a clear, sometimes dynamic style, making it fine descriptive literature.

Putting their literary talents aside, however, the Civil War specials made a far greater contribution, one that wrought a newspaper "revolution." Prior to the war, the chief purpose of the press was to shape public opinion rather than provide the news. But once the correspondents started reporting the conflict "voluminously and incessantly," the American people began to expect their news immediately and grew far less interested in the editorial column. "For the first time in American history," wrote Elmer Davis in his study of the *New York Times,* "a situation had arisen in which the public wanted to know what had happened yesterday rather than some man's opinion on what had happened last week." The intrepid journalists who had covered the great fratricidal conflict had redefined the role of the American newspaper.

AERIAL NEWS COVERAGE

In the fall of 1861 John La Mountain, serving as a balloonist for the U.S. military, conducted a series of aerial reconnaissance missions that reported Confederate troop movements around Centreville and Manassas in northeastern Virginia. On November 16 a reporter from the *Boston Daily Journal* accompanied him on one of his free-flying forays. It was the first time ever that a newspaper correspondent flew over enemy lines.

The name of the reporter is lost to history, because in those days it was common editorial practice for journalists not to identify themselves in newsprint. But sometimes a correspondent would use a pen name or sign his initials. The anonymous newsman who flew with La Mountain called himself "Frank"; it's possible that Frank was his real name, but it is not known for certain.

What *is* important is that Frank gave a rich, detailed account of his aerial experience. His dispatch, which was printed in the *Boston Daily Journal* on November 22, 1861, forms a vivid contrast to the somewhat dry official reports that the aeronauts usually penned. After Frank stepped into the balloon's basket with La Mountain, they "cut loose, and in a moment," as the reporter informed his readers, they viewed the entire Army of the Potomac from the sky, "a sight well worth a soul to see—brown earth fortifications, white tented encampments, and black lines and squares of solid soldiery in every direction."

The balloon then drifted over Fairfax Court House, well within enemy territory. "Soon Centerville and Manassas came in full sight, and there," wrote Frank, "in their bough huts lay the great army of the South. All along they stretched out toward the Potomac, on whose banks their batteries were distinctly visible. So plain were they below, their numbers could be noted so carefully that not a regiment could escape the count."

Since the balloon was behind enemy lines, Frank realized with some apprehension that to come down now "was death, or at least the horrors of a Richmond tobacco prison." But the journalist relaxed once he saw that La Mountain was calm and confident and in full control of the craft. An upper current of air toward the east gently pushed them back to their own lines, and they descended "gradually and smoothly" into the Union encampments.

Enormously impressed by the flight, Frank concluded his dispatch by pointing out that aerial reconnaissance had great potential as a tool of war, since it could provide "a daily map of the enemy's position, even the guns of his batteries, at the same time the number of his forces." With these advantages, the correspondent assured his readers, Union armies would achieve a "success that is formidable, that is resistless."

JOURNALISTIC ARTISTS

As the fighting continued and the casualties mounted, it became apparent to most Americans that their ordeal would be long and bloody—and that few, if any, would escape unscathed. Fearful for their loved ones at the front and determined to stay abreast of developments, the American public craved information, whether it be in the form of news stories or pictures. Visual images of any kind were especially in demand. Three Northern illustrated weeklies published in New York City—*Leslie's Illustrated Newspaper, Harper's Weekly,* and the *New York Illustrated News*—led the way in graphically documenting the Civil War. Other papers across the country followed as well as their resources allowed. Most of the pictures appearing in the press were supplied by journalistic artists rather than photographers. This had little to do with editorial preference; in truth, photographs had greater clarity and detail than artistic sketches. But the technology had not yet been developed to allow reproduction of photographs in published form, and that included drawings as well. The only way this could be achieved was for an engraver to redraw the picture on a block of wood, then cut away a portion of the top of the block, leaving the desired image as a printing surface for use on the presses. Since drawings were far easier than photographs to transfer to wood, the journalistic artist emerged as the chief supplier of pictures for the daily and weekly papers.

There were some 150 artists in the field, almost all of whom were Northerners. Numbers are disputed, but about twenty were "special" artists, full-time employees of one of the illustrated weeklies. The rest were freelancers, a mixed group of professional artists, officers, and soldiers of varying talent.

Like their print counterparts, the special artists shared some common characteristics. All had artistic training in one form or another, a few having attended prestigious art schools. Most were young, in their early to mid-twenties. Field conditions were tough, and youth was the best defense against hardship. Thomas Nast, later famous for helping expose New York's infamous Tweed Ring and for such symbols as the Republican elephant and the Democratic donkey, was only twenty in 1861.

Usually confronted with a lack of time and poor visibility, most field artists resorted to sketching rather than drawing pictures. For battle scenes, pencil was used; for camp life, crayon and charcoal were generally preferred. When sketching a battle, artists employed a kind of visual shorthand—men, guns, horses, and cannons were all limned in with a few short, deft strokes. Sketches thus drawn were done in a couple of minutes and would be submitted with notes so that the engraver could fill in the blanks as he made a woodcut for the printer. The engraver could be the field artist's best friend—or his worst enemy. Sometimes much was lost in translation from paper to wood.

Most journalistic artists had their own "beat" from which they rarely if ever strayed. Alfred Waud, who studied at the highly respected Royal Academy in London, covered the war in Virginia, while his colleague Alex Simplot went west. Generally speaking, artists tried to stay out of the fighting, though sometimes they got too close to their subject for comfort, as in the case of James R. O'Neil of *Leslie's Illustrated News,* who was killed in battle. A few were seriously wounded. Still others, particularly the "older men" in their thirties, suffered terribly while in the field. Exhaustion, chronic diarrhea, sunstroke, and disease took its toll.

Special artist Arthur Lumley, a talented member of the guild, was lucky enough to escape most of these ordeals. Lumley's sketches of the war helped launch his career as an artist and in the process earned for him a special place in the history of pictorial journalism.

Born in Dublin, Lumley came to the United States in 1858 and studied at New York's National Academy of Design. To pay his tuition and expenses he worked as an illustrator for several weeklies, until he landed a full-time position at *Leslie's.* Once the war began, the twenty-four-year-old artist was assigned to cover the Union's Army of the Potomac. In early 1862, after leaving *Leslie's* and joining the staff of the *New York Illustrated News,* Lumley found himself recording the events of the protracted Peninsula campaign. When chief balloonist Thaddeus S. C. Lowe arrived on the scene, the artist scented an opportunity in the making. The two men became friends, and it wasn't long before Lowe allowed the young Irishman to accompany him aloft in tethered flights. In April 1862, during the siege of Yorktown, Lumley became the first journalistic artist ever to sketch a picture from an aircraft, when, as a passenger in Lowe's balloon, he made a drawing of Union and Confederate entrenchments.

A few months later, again ascending the skies with Lowe, Lumley sketched Richmond from a vantage point of 1,000 feet above the ground. The tethered balloon was only four miles from the prize, with Richmond's church towers spiking the sky and making the Confederate capital seem so tantalizingly close. Lumley's illustration was the best view Northerners would get of Richmond until the closing days of the war in 1865.

After the war Lumley continued to work as an artist for journals both at home and abroad. In later years he also won recognition as a landscape and portrait painter. He died in 1912 at age seventy-five.

THOMAS MORRIS CHESTER

Thomas Morris Chester was the first African-American to serve as a war correspondent for a major daily newspaper. As a reporter for the *Philadelphia Press*, he covered the Union campaigns against Richmond during the last nine months of the war. It was a grueling and dangerous assignment, but it all seemed worthwhile when, in early April 1865, Chester accompanied the black troops of the XXV Corps under Maj. Gen. Godfrey Weitzel as they marched victoriously into the Confederate capital. For the Philadelphia journalist, it was a sweet moment of triumph in a bittersweet career that had known both accomplishment and disappointment.

Thomas Morris Chester was born in Harrisburg, Pennsylvania, on May 11, 1834. His parents owned and operated a restaurant that became a center of abolitionist activities; one could buy a copy of William Lloyd Garrison's *Liberator* as well as a meal. As successful restaurateurs, the Chesters, unlike most free blacks, had the means to educate their children, enabling sixteen-year-old Thomas to enter the Allegheny Institute, not far from Pittsburgh. Originally a preparatory school, it later became a "college for the education of colored Americans." The two years Chester spent at this "fountain of learning," as he referred to it, left a lasting impression upon him, morally and intellectually.

Defiant, self-confident, and imbued with the passions of youth, Chester was not about to accept the second-class status accorded Northern blacks in antebellum America. Rather than "submit to the insolent indignities" that most African-Americans had to endure, in 1853, at the age of nineteen, he announced his intention to migrate to Liberia, the West African nation founded by the American Colonization Society in the early 1820s and settled by former slaves.

Within a year, however, Chester returned to the United States to continue his formal education. Not that he abandoned Liberia; he kept in touch with frequent visits, crossing the Atlantic more than a dozen times between 1853 and 1870—a period during which he was involved intermittently in various colonization and educational projects, as well as serving as the publisher and editor of a newspaper in Monrovia, the capital of Liberia.

But Chester's brief stint as a newspaperman in Africa was hardly the reason why the *Philadelphia Press* in August 1864 crossed the color line and hired him as a war reporter. The *Press* had no ties with the black community, and both owner John W. Forney and editor John Russell Young had shown no previous interest in racial equality. Since the paper did not intend to make a political statement, it is possible that Chester might have been given the job on the strength of his more recent journalistic endeavor, having produced earlier in the year what was considered by many an "excellent report" on the proceedings of the African Methodist Episcopal General Conference.

Chester was assigned to cover the Army of the James and spent most of his time on the Petersburg-Richmond front. His dispatches focused largely on the actions of black troops. To those who still doubted the freedmen's ability to fight, Chester missed no opportunity to point out that black soldiers in battle were just as brave and dedicated to the Union cause as were their white counterparts. Yet African-Americans in uniform continued to suffer prejudice, particularly at the hands of their superiors. Outraged, Chester insisted that there was no excuse for this and took it upon himself to let the public know when white Union commanders refused to treat "a negro patriot as a man."

The capstone of Chester's wartime journalistic career came when he entered the fallen city of Richmond on April 3, 1865. The reporter made his way to the Confederate House of Representatives, now somewhat forlorn and empty in the wake of Southern defeat. He walked down an aisle, then sat at the speaker's desk to start writing his dispatch. He must have relished the moment; here was a black man seated at one of the citadels of the Confederacy, a nation that had defended slavery and racial inequality to the last.

His fevered scribbling was interrupted by the sudden appearance of a paroled Confederate officer. The Rebel was livid at the "presumption" of the black man and shouted, "Come out of there, you black cuss." Chester refused to acknowledge him and kept on writing, prompting the Southerner to yell once again, "Get out of there, or I'll knock your brains out." Still ignored, the Confederate rushed up to Chester, intending to grab him from the chair. The reporter rose and punched the officer so hard it sent him sprawling on the floor.

Just then a Union captain appeared, and the Southerner recovered enough to ask him for his sword "to cut the damned nigger's heart out!" The Union officer declined but offered to make a ring for a fair fight. "You'll get damnably thrashed," the amused Yankee advised the still-seething Rebel. The Confederate stormed off, leaving Chester to comment that he had simply exercised his "rights as a belligerent."

After the war Chester served for two years in Europe as a diplomatic representative of Liberia. When the country's president, whom he supported, failed to win reelection, however, Chester vacated the post. Returning to the United States, he got involved in Reconstruction politics in Louisiana, until white conservative Democrats resumed control of the state. In the late 1870s and early 1880s he was appointed to two minor Federal positions but held them only briefly. He ended his career as head of a black-owned railroad construction company, which, lacking adequate capital and suffering severe competition, went out of business within a year. On September 30, 1892, Thomas Morris Chester died—in the words of his biographer—"a disillusioned man."

CAPTURED JOURNALISTS

War correspondents are noncombatants. They wield a pen instead of a sword and generally are more interested in observing and reporting than participating in combat. Despite this, journalists who fall into enemy hands might well expect imprisonment for their pains. During the Civil War, for the first time in U.S. history, American reporters, both Northern and Southern, were captured and held as prisoners. Although precise numbers are impossible to come by, it appears that only four or five Rebel newspapermen (relatively few were in the field to begin with) ended up in Yankee prisons and usually for brief stays. But more than thirty members of the Northern press corps, including a few journalistic artists, fell into Confederate hands and suffered varying degrees of incarceration.

Some Union correspondents were treated with kindness and consideration, others with indifference or active brutality. It seems that journalists from the New York *Tribune* were singled out as supposed representatives of an "abolitionist" paper. Since the Confederates couldn't get their hands on editor Horace Greeley, who was particularly hated as a radical Republican and archfiend, they took vengeance on his reporters instead. One *Tribune* journalist, who regularly signed himself with the initials "J. B. H.," was captured in Virginia by John Singleton Mosby's Confederate guerrillas. The hapless newsman was readied for hanging on the spot as an "abolitionist liar for Horace Greeley." Only the timely arrival of a Union patrol prevented the lynching.

But nothing could surpass the experiences of *Tribune* reporters Albert D. Richardson and Junius H. Browne. Captured near Vicksburg in May 1863, the pair were prisoners some twenty months before they successfully escaped. Theirs is a tale of human courage and endurance in the face of unspeakable conditions.

Their ordeal began as a routine assignment to cover Gen. Ulysses S. Grant's campaign for Vicksburg, the last remaining Confederate strong point on the Mississippi. Anxious to join Grant's army, then some fifty miles below Vicksburg, they had to come up with the fastest route. From their location at Milliken's Bend, Louisiana, an overland journey would take too long, at least three days; but there was a better, if riskier, alternative. They could take a hay barge down the Mississippi and get to Grant in only eight hours. The problem with the water route, however, was that Union vessels had to run past Vicksburg and its formidable array of Confederate shore batteries that stretched for miles. So far, ten of fifteen Union vessels had successfully run the gauntlet and evaded sinking or capture. The odds seemed pretty good.

And so, on the evening of May 3, 1863, Richardson and Browne, accompanied by New York *World* reporter Richard Colburn, went aboard one of two hay barges pulled by the same steam tug. At first they made good progress down the river. Then, around 1:00 the next morning, a rocket went up, signaling the beginning of the gauntlet. Confederate artillery opened fire with a roar, a storm of shot and shell that seemed to bracket and envelop the two barges. Then a shot crashed into the tug, ripping its boiler into flaming shards of metal and sending it to the bottom. The barges were soon aflame, the hay alight, and there was nothing the reporters could do but plunge into the Mississippi.

Richardson, Browne, and Colburn were captured by the Confederates and taken by train to Libby Prison in Richmond. It was the start of a long and harrowing odyssey for two of the three prisoners. At first the men were treated with respect, even kindness, by their captors. But attitudes soon hardened, and a transfer to Atlanta signaled a change for the worse. One seeming catalyst for this shift in opinion was a scathing editorial published by the fire-eating *Confederate,* considered the "most fanatical" newspaper in the state of Georgia. The *Confederate* viewed the journalists as villains who had glorified the "vile deeds" of the Yankee invaders. "We would greatly prefer," the *Confederate* thundered, "to assist in hanging these enemies to humanity, than to show them any civilities or courtesies."

Since Colburn was a reporter for an anti-Lincoln newspaper, the New York *World,* he was eventually released, but Richardson and Browne remained in captivity. As time wore on, it was increasingly clear that the pair was being targeted for their affiliation with the pro-abolitionist New York *Tribune*. As soon as Colburn was free, he did what he could to lobby for their release. His appeals did not fall on deaf ears; the list of persons who at one time or another tried to secure their freedom reads like a who's who of Northern officialdom. Generals Ulysses S. Grant and Benjamin F. Butler, Secretary of War Edwin M. Stanton, and Ohio governor John Brough all contacted Confederate authorities, but to no avail.

President Lincoln himself entered the fray, telegraphing the U.S. exchange commissioner, Col. W. H. Ludlow, to "get them off if you can." Yet even Lincoln's intervention failed to set the men free. The Confederate commissioner of exchange, Robert Ould, refused to countenance their release. Officially they were being held as hostages for Southern civilians incarcerated in the North. But the real reason slipped out when Commissioner Ould made intemperate remarks regarding Horace Greeley's newspaper. "The *Tribune*," Ould told his Union counterpart, "did more than any other agency to bring on the war." And on yet another occasion, the Confederate commissioner informed the head of the U.S. Exchange Commission that "such men as the *Tribune* correspondents . . . have had more share than even your soldiery in bringing rapine, pillage, and desolation to our homes. . . . They are the worst and most obnoxious of all non-combatants."

While protracted negotiations continued, Richardson and Browne endured sickness, filth, and at times semistarvation. The pair were sent to no less than seven different Confederate prisons during the course of their captivity; each change of venue varied from the tolerable to the hellish. The last stop on the road of misery was the military prison at Salisbury, North Carolina. At first conditions were spartan though bearable, but then the Union prison population swelled from 600 to 10,000.

The overflowing made a bad situation intolerable. There was scant food and little shelter for the newcomers. Sickness and exposure to winter cold undermined the health of the prisoners, and many—between twenty and fifty—were dying daily. Richardson and Browne concluded that their only chance for survival was to flee the garrison. In December 1864 the two reporters, assigned to a hospital detail, were able to deceive the guards and made their escape. After twenty-seven days on the run, much of it in the dead of winter across the mountainous Tennessee country, they managed to reach Northern lines. Foot sore, ragged, half starved, crawling with vermin, they had beaten the odds.

The news of their escape made them heroes in the North, and they found themselves in the unaccustomed position of making news, not just reporting it. Richardson telegraphed the *Tribune* as soon as he was able, neatly and succinctly encapsulating twenty months of captivity: "Out of the jaws of death, out of the gates of Hell."

A LEAK IN THE WHITE HOUSE

Government secrets—especially in a democracy—are the hardest to keep. Yet until the Civil War, the U.S. government seems to have had no major break in confidentiality, at least in terms of classified or otherwise inappropriate material disclosed to the press. Indeed, the very first leak of a major government document to the news media occurred during the Lincoln presidency. And the person accused, rightly or wrongly, of complicity in the leak was the first lady, Mary Todd Lincoln.

The scandal broke when the New York *Herald* published portions of President Lincoln's annual message before it was delivered to Congress in December 1861. Angered by this breach of protocol, Congress began an immediate investigation. A frequent visitor to the White House, one Henry Wikoff, was subpoenaed to appear before the House Judiciary Committee on February 10, 1862. Wikoff, a *Herald* correspondent, admitted that he was responsible for publication of parts of the document but refused to divulge his source. Declared in contempt, Wikoff was placed in custody.

As the affair became public, rumors began to circulate that Mary Todd Lincoln was the source; after all, it was well known she favored Wikoff and the *Herald,* if for any reason, because the reporter and his paper often flattered her. Wikoff was a charming rogue, a man whose duplicity was obscured by a colorful and cosmopolitan facade. Mrs. Lincoln, who had been mocked by Washington society as a vulgar westerner, was easily taken in by Wikoff's "compliments on her looks and attire."

But did the first lady give Wikoff portions of her husband's annual message or let him see a copy? Before the incident was investigated any further, a White House gardener named John Watt came forward and confessed to being Wikoff's source. Supposedly Watt was in the library fixing some flowers when he happened to see Lincoln's speech lying on a table. Recognizing its importance, the gardener memorized the sheets and passed the information on to Wikoff, presumably for money. The tale seemed implausible, and there was a suspicion that Watt "took the fall" to spare Mrs. Lincoln any further embarrassment. In spite of the dubious nature of Watt's confession, the House accepted it, and the case was deemed closed.

Technically cleared, Mary Todd Lincoln was still condemned in the court of public opinion. At the very least, she was shown to be susceptible to flattery and carelessness in her choice of friends and associates.

NEWS TRANSMISSION BY TELEGRAPH

During the Civil War—for the first time in the history of journalism—the telegraph was used extensively to transmit news. Never before had such a voluminous amount of information been conveyed over the wires for the purposes of informing the public.

Using the telegraph to send a news story was not new. It started in New York City as early as 1848, when seven Gotham newspapers, anxious to reduce the high costs of obtaining such information, banded together to form the Associated Press. The AP—the forerunner of today's celebrated news agency—maintained reporters with access to a wire in certain major cities so that they could transmit news as soon as possible to all seven New York papers. Before long, editors outside of the city wanted these telegraphed stories, which the New York publishers were more than happy to supply—for a fee.

In the prewar period, these telegraphic news items were confined to two or, at the very most, three columns of a newspaper. There seemed to be no real need for instantaneous news; the public wasn't accustomed to it and so didn't demand it. But after Fort Sumter fell, there was a dramatic increase in the public's appetite for news that was steady, reliable, and most of all, fresh. With reader demand high and competition fierce, newspapers had no choice but to turn to the telegraph as a fairly dependable source of up-to-the-minute information. By the winter of 1861–62, some journals were printing two or three pages of telegraphic news.

Articles sent by wire bore the legend "By Telegraph," which became a kind of reassuring talisman that told readers they were getting the very latest information. Access to the lines, therefore, was of primary importance. Even reporters for New York's leading papers vigorously sought use of the wire, since membership in the Associated Press did not always guarantee the most current news, a fact that many independent telegraph companies were quick to exploit for profit. The New York *Herald,* for example, spent a total of $1,000 for transmitted reports of the capture of New Orleans and paid $250 a column for its telegraphic account of the battle of Chickamauga. Nor was the *Herald* an exception. During the first two years of the conflict, the major New York papers each shelled out an estimated $60,000 to $100,000 annually to fill its columns with dispatches "By Telegraph."

But money alone did not guarantee access to a telegraph line. Since only one story at a time could be sent over the wire, the competition for its use was severe. At first the telegraph companies insisted on a first-come, first-served policy, which often led to journalists hogging the line. If they didn't have their copy ready, for example, some reporters would instruct operators to tap out whole passages of the Bible, anything to prevent competitors from using the wire. Denied access, frustrated correspondents were not above cutting the telegraph line in reprisal. In an attempt to bring order to the industry, the telegraph companies instituted a "fifteen minute system," whereby no one reporter was allowed to hold the line for more than a quarter-hour span.

The telegraphic transmission of the news had come a long way since 1848. On February 12, 1865, reporters sent a total of 59,600 words over the wire from Washington to New York—more in a single day than had been transmitted in a week before the war began. As consumers of this virtually instantaneous information, Americans were in the vanguard of a communications revolution. "For the first time in history," in the words of journalism historian Louis Starr, "an entire nation knew what it was about, knew its leaders, knew what had happened yesterday and what might be happening today."

OFFICIAL NEWS BULLETINS

During a war the dissemination of information by a government is particularly vital to those on the home front. By the same token, withholding facts, or preventing their wide circulation, can also be just as important to the prosecution of a war. The Union had to grapple with these issues as it struggled for its very destiny in the midst of a civil conflict. Ultimately the Lincoln administration recognized the need to keep the public informed, prompting for the first time the issuance by the Federal government of official news bulletins to the press.

The system was fairly haphazard in the early part of the war, largely because the government had little experience releasing sensitive information for public consumption. Newspapers did print official announcements when they could, and occasionally the sources were unusual. When Confederate president Jefferson Davis wired his wife giving her the details of the Southern victory at the first battle of Bull Run, the telegram fell into the hands of the U.S. War Department, which in turn passed it on to the press. Sometimes commanding Union generals formally congratulated their troops by proclamation, reviewing the fighting that had taken place in the process. These proclamations were later published by the newspapers.

The first official news statements directly issued by the administration were in essence military communiqués sent by commanders in the field to the War Department. These reports simply announced a battle won, an enemy town captured, or other such news in skeletal form. From time to time Washington released these bulletins to select newspapers, which in turn would print them, and then a few days later the paper's special correspondent would put flesh to the bones by providing a lengthy and detailed description of whatever the communiqué had announced.

But this arrangement was not satisfactory to members of the press corps, who demanded more substantive information delivered at specific intervals. In early May 1864 the U.S. government acquiesced and began issuing official bulletins on a regular basis. As a major news organization, the Associated Press became one of the first recipients of this information. The reports were drafted by Secretary of War Edwin M. Stanton or one of his assistants, then telegraphed to Maj. Gen. John A. Dix, commander of the New York military district, who in turn relayed the news to the AP.

This was a commendable and noteworthy gesture on the part of the secretary of war, but Stanton's "New York only" pipeline of information proved too roundabout and clumsy for the rest of the country's papers. Washington, D.C., editors found the process particularly irritating, and they appealed to President Lincoln. After all, it seemed ridiculous to receive Washington news from New York when they themselves were based in the nation's capital. On September 9, 1864, Lincoln wrote to Stanton about the matter, and thereafter the official dispatches coming from the War Department were available to all newspapers directly from the source.

But what prompted Stanton in the first place to begin issuing the official bulletins the press had been clamoring for? Perhaps Lincoln had a hand in the matter, influenced by a phase in the Wilderness campaign in early May 1864, when Grant and some 125,000 Union troops seemingly disappeared, with no outside contact. The nation's capital, as well as New York, "was close to a standstill," waiting desperately to hear word of Grant's army. The president himself was under enormous strain.

A young reporter, Henry E. Wing, was with Grant, and he telegraphed Washington proposing to tell all if he was allowed first to use the military lines to wire his paper the New York *Tribune*. Lincoln telegraphed back accepting the terms but also proposed that the reporter's statement to the paper "be so full as to disclose to the public the general situation." Soon after, Wing met with the president, assuring him that Grant's army was determined to pursue the enemy and "that there would be no turning back."

The evidence is circumstantial, but it's more than possible that it was Lincoln who was behind Stanton's bulletin policy, having come to the realization—in the wake of Grant's temporary disappearance—that the people should be kept informed under all circumstances.

GOVERNMENT CENSORSHIP

Before 1861 the United States had no real experience in government censorship of military news. This contrasted with Europe, where restrictions imposed upon newspapers, especially as it related to information from the battlefield, were commonplace. Old World governments were not above prohibiting the publication of war-related information, withholding it, or even falsifying it for political ends. In the early nineteenth century Napoleon Bonaparte was notorious for distortions of the truth in his public bulletins; "to lie like a bulletin" became a proverb among French troops.

The United States had been fairly free of such practices—until the 1860s. During the Civil War, Americans experienced for the first time a major effort by their government to censor military information.

The first target was the telegraph. In the early weeks of the conflict, with telegraph lines remaining open between North and South, Confederate intelligence was obtaining vital military information from private messages transmitted over the wire. Most of the senders were merely foolish or indiscreet; others were Rebel sympathizers or out-and-out secessionists. On May 20, 1861, Federal agents in New York, Washington, and other large Northern cities seized records of these telegrams, identifying the names of the traitors. James E. Harvey, a friend of Lincoln's and a recent appointee as minister to Portugal, was one of the people so exposed.

A far more comprehensive effort to control the flow of military information was undertaken on August 2, 1861, when Gen. George B. McClellan, in the aftermath of the Union's disastrous defeat at Bull Run, summoned a press conference of Washington journalists. He presented a plan to them that was in effect voluntary censorship, a kind of "gentlemen's agreement" that all parties could adhere to. Each of the press representatives signed a statement pledging to transmit no information that would be useful to the enemy. For his part, McClellan assured those present that he would use all his influence to facilitate the gathering of nonsensitive news.

To allow reporters to monitor themselves seemed reasonable and promising, but it broke down within three months. Bureaucratic wrangles and interdepartmental jealousies were largely responsible for the plan's eventual demise. On October 22 Secretary of State William H. Seward ordered H. E. Thayer, at first the "official censor" of the War Department but now under State Department jurisdiction, to prohibit telegraphic messages from Washington concerning military *and* civil operations of the government. Since Seward's order included nonmilitary matters, this was a clear violation of the "gentlemen's agreement," so the press considered the pact void.

Things improved for the better when the censor post was taken from the State Department and returned to the War Department, where it remained for the duration of the conflict. In late February 1862 Secretary of War Edwin M. Stanton announced new censorship rules, requiring that newspaper correspondents submit their copy to provost marshals for approval before telegraphic transmission. This was an improvement of sorts, since now it was understood that censorship would apply only to military matters.

In terms of actual implementation, the Stanton directive continued to allow journalists considerable latitude. After all, reporters could still deliver their dispatches in person or send them through the mail. Control over the wires meant simply that the speed of communication would be affected, and even in this regard the War Department's order created more problems than it solved. The policy gave far too much weight to the interpretation of the individual provost marshal. For that matter, since the local provost marshal was responsible to his commanding officer, the latter might attempt to manipulate the news to his favor, and this did occur. But it was not a common practice; most army brass didn't like the idea of snooping journalists reporting their every move and did what they could to get rid of them.

Gen. George Meade, for instance, took offense at a story filed by Edward Crapsey of the Philadelphia *Inquirer* and expelled the unfortunate journalist from the army's lines. Crapsey was placed backward on an old nag, a placard bearing the legend "Libeler of the Press" put on his chest, and he was paraded through the ranks while a regimental band played the "Rouge's March." Meade later expressed regret over his actions, but it was too late. He became a nonperson to the press, with Crapsey's colleagues deciding that the general would never be mentioned in dispatches again. Such was the power of the fourth estate.

The pen may be mightier than the sword, but it had little effect on William Tecumseh Sherman, another general who despised reporters with a passion. It took some time for the fiery officer to come to a boil, but when he did, someone was going to get scalded. In truth, Sherman had taken a lot of press abuse in silence. Newspapers railed against him; some even flatly said he was insane. Sherman grew tired of the endless stream of lies and calumnies; freedom of the press was one thing, defamation of character was quite another.

Matters came to a head when Sherman read an account by Thomas Knox of the New York *Herald* criticizing the general's actions. When Sherman confronted him, Knox replied blandly, "I had no feeling against you personally, but you are regarded [as] the enemy of our set [the press] and we must in self-defense write you down." It was the last straw for the lava-tempered Sherman, who decided to make an example of one of these "dirty newspaper scribblers," as he put it. On February 4, 1863, the general issued an order for the reporter's arrest, charging him with giving information to the enemy, spying, and disobeying the orders of the commander in the military district. Knox was to be tried in a military court.

The first accusation was based on the fact that Knox had published a story in the *Herald* estimating the size of the Union army engaged in operations against Vicksburg, a direct violation of military regulations. It could mean the death penalty. Not that Sherman wanted the journalist shot, but he was determined "to establish the principle that such people cannot attend our armies, in violation of orders, and defy us, publishing their garbled statement and defaming officers who are doing their best.

After a fifteen-day trial, Knox was convicted of the third charge, disobeying Sherman's orders. The verdict, which had "no criminality attached to it," sentenced Knox to be banished from the lines of the Army of the Tennessee, "not to return under penalty of imprisonment."

Sherman was disappointed; to him, this was just a slap on the wrist. Journalists were also unhappy with the verdict, though obviously for different reasons, and an appeal was made to the president. Lincoln attempted to intervene and have the reporter reinstated, but Sherman said, "Never," and Grant concurred—and there the matter ended.

BYLINES

Newspaper articles usually give the names of reporters who wrote them, but this was not always the case. Until the 1860s, hardworking journalists labored in obscurity; their articles either were left unsigned or went by some pen name. The Civil War changed all this. By the time the fighting ceased, it was common practice for reporters to sign their handiwork, making the byline, for the first time, a standard part of American journalism.

Its origins could be traced to an order issued by Gen. Joseph Hooker on April 30, 1863, just before the beginning of the Chancellorsville campaign. As commander of the Army of the Potomac, Hooker required all reporters in his military jurisdiction to sign their dispatches. Like other generals in the field, "'Fightin' Joe" was concerned about the press leaking the location of army units, their strength, or other vital information. Author-identified dispatches, the general hoped, might discourage such action. At any rate, if members of the press cooperated, Hooker pledged an open-door policy, "including the license to abuse or criticize . . . [him] to their heart's content."

One would think that Hooker's decree would be welcomed by the newspapermen—especially by the front-line reporters who labored under the most trying conditions, yet remained unidentified. But the reaction to the order seemed more negative than positive. To begin with, most editors didn't like the idea of signed articles; the tradition of journalistic anonymity was just too deeply ingrained. Surprisingly, some correspondents didn't like the idea either. Lazy or dishonest journalists sometimes manufactured stories whole, describing imaginary clashes from the safety of a hotel room. Still others fashioned pieces from wild rumor or unfounded supposition. Not that there were very many unscrupulous reporters, but the signing of articles not only identified the writer, but also firmly fixed the responsibility for shoddy news coverage when it occurred.

American journalism ultimately profited by General Hooker's order. Compelled to have their names printed with their dispatches, some reporters took pains to improve the quality of their news stories. And even after Hooker was removed from command, many correspondents, enjoying for the first time public recognition, continued to identify themselves with their work, establishing the byline as a permanent fixture of their profession.

FRONT-LINE NEWSBOYS

Civil War soldiers were voracious readers. With the exception of letters from home, which they complained were always too few and infrequent, newspapers were the most popular reading material in camp. Staying abreast of the news let the men in the ranks know how the war was progressing, kept them informed of national affairs, and in some cases provided a welcome link with the home front. It was also a means of staying in touch with the latest developments, since major city papers were available to soldiers usually two days after publication. Of course, such convenience had a price. At a time when a copy of a newspaper might be three or four cents at most, newspapers at the front sold for as much as ten cents a copy.

A lieutenant in the 50th Ohio wrote: "I receive the 'Chronicle' regularly. The boys all want to read it. . . . The officers subscribed $4.75 each for papers for the benefit of the boys." Responding to this demand, the news media soon had newsboys hawking their papers at the front. In the midst of some of the worst battles, a Union officer recalled, "one could hear the squeaking voice of the 'newsboy' over the sound of the fusillade, crying 'New York Tribune, New York Herald.'"

Although little is known of these boys who worked on the front lines selling their papers, a few did leave memoirs, including a young Vermont lad by the name of Cullen "Doc" Aubrey. In 1861 Aubrey accompanied his four brothers when they joined the 2nd Vermont Regiment. Before long, Doc was hired as a kind of orderly and jack-of-all-trades about the camp. But the youngster always had an eye out for profit, so he began selling newspapers to soldiers. Soon he had a horse and a "paper route" that covered several regiments.

But Doc's greatest coup was selling newspaper accounts of Gettysburg to the combatants while the fighting was still going on—the first time ever that soldiers were able to read about a battle in a newspaper as they fought it. Aubrey met a Baltimore train at Westminster, Maryland, and loaded his horse with as many Philadelphia *Inquirer*s as the animal could carry. This particular edition included an account of the first day's fighting at Gettysburg on July 1, 1863. The struggle still raged when Aubrey reached the battlefield on July 3, his papers selling "like ginger-bread at a state fair."

NEW ORLEANS *TRIBUNE*

In 1860 New Orleans was a cosmopolitan city, a curious mix of Spanish, French, African, and American cultural influences. Serving as the port of deposit for the mighty Mississippi River, it was one of the South's largest cities, with a strong loyalty to the section and yet so unlike any other part of Dixie. The city's 168,000 residents were a unique community, especially in terms of its free black population, considered "the most prosperous and sophisticated" not only in the South, but in the entire United States.

Louisiana was a slave state, but New Orleans's free population of color could trace its roots as far back as the early 1720s. By the eve of the Civil War, the free black community stood at 10,939. Having grown wealthy, with investments in real estate and small businesses, many free African-Americans of the Crescent City were well educated, bilingual (speaking both French and English), and active in community affairs.

Far more fortunate than most blacks in the antebellum era, New Orleans's free people of color still had to deal with severe handicaps. Although they could sue in court, they were "usually denied" the vote and could not always be sure of equal treatment in the judicial system. And then there were the humiliating social restrictions; for instance, free blacks were "required to be respectful in the company of whites," could not own an establishment where liquor was sold, and before leaving the city had to obtain the permission of the mayor. In the late 1850s, the increasing debate over slavery hardened white Louisianians' views toward blacks. More and more controls were imposed on free African-Americans, and in 1857, manumission—the private or individual act of freeing slaves—was expressly forbidden by the legislature.

Once the war came, however, conditions in Louisiana, particularly in the southern part of the state, changed dramatically. In late April 1862, New Orleans fell to the U.S. Navy; the city itself and much of the surrounding region was occupied by Union troops. The African-American community had good reason to welcome the "bluecoats," believing that a "great revolution" was now under way, with planters to be toppled from power, slaves freed, and blacks armed.

The presence of Federal soldiers in New Orleans "so emboldened the free men of color" that they soon launched a campaign for equal rights. To spread the word, several of the city's black business leaders in September 1862 founded *L'Union,* a biweekly newspaper first published in French only, but later in an English edition as well. Proclaiming the Declaration of Independence as the paper's platform, its inaugural issue trumpeted a call for action: "Let all Friends of Progress unite! The hour has come for the struggle of the great humanitarian principles. . . . 'You were born for liberty and happiness! Do not deceive yourselves in this and do not deceive your brother!'"

Editorials of this nature served more to anger white extremists than to rally black supporters. Almost on a daily basis, there were threats to kill the editor and to torch the paper. Several of the financial backers of *L'Union* grew frightened, especially when it became apparent that the occupation forces were indifferent to their plight. After a difficult two years, *L'Union* folded, its editor putting most of the blame on the black community's unwillingness to support the paper's so-called "radical" agenda.

Refusing to accept defeat, one of the financiers of the defunct *L'Union,* Louis Charles Roudanez, immediately set down plans to publish a new paper. Described as "a man far above the crowd," Roudanez had impressive credentials. Born in 1823, he was the son of a French merchant and a free black woman. His formative years were spent in New Orleans, but he received his college education in France, earning three degrees, including one in medicine in 1853; four years later he received a second medical degree from Dartmouth College in New Hampshire.

As one of the leading black physicians and businessmen of the Crescent City, Roudanez certainly had the means to support an African-American newspaper. Almost immediately after the collapse of *L'Union,* Roudanez threw his financial support behind a newspaper he called *La Tribune de la Nouvelle Orleans,* or the *Tribune* for short. The *Tribune* began publishing on July 21, 1864, only two days after *L'Union* had gone out of business. At first it appeared three times a week, but after a new press arrived from New York in October, the *Tribune* started publishing every day—thus becoming the first African-American daily newspaper in U.S. history.

The other driving force behind the *Tribune* was its newly appointed forty-four-year-old editor, Jean-Charles Houzeau. A white Belgian, his complexion was swarthy enough to pass for black, and once in the States, he made no attempt to correct the impression; in fact, he seemed to enjoy the subterfuge. Regarding himself as a "liberal," Houzeau felt strongly about human freedom and racial equality. But he was not anti-American, despite the "shameful evil" of slavery, which he believed would soon be abolished. More than simply an admirer of the United States, the Belgian confessed that he loved the country "for the moral and material well-being that it is able to pour forth upon all its children."

The *Tribune* had two editions: a French version and an English one. In New Orleans itself, the French edition was more important, since most of the paper's subscribers were French-speaking African-Americans. But Houzeau felt the English-language edition was important too, as a forum to promote African-American civil rights. The *Tribune* campaigned unceasingly for black suffrage, equal justice under the law, greater economic opportunities, integrated schools, and even desegregated restaurants and theaters.

The paper's proposals anticipated the 1960s civil-rights agenda of Dr. Martin Luther King, Jr., and his supporters by a century. Houzeau made sure members of Congress and other prominent people received copies of the *Tribune* on a regular basis. Well thought of in many circles, the paper seemed destined for a long run. Not so. It folded in 1868 after only four years of publication, a victim of the internecine political quarrels that wracked Louisiana during Reconstruction. Financial backer Roudanez supported a white ex-slaveholder for Louisiana governor on an independent ticket, while Houzeau supported a Republican slate headed by a former Union officer. After Houzeau's candidate won the election, Roudanez shut down the paper.

"We record with regret," the New Orleans *Daily Picayune* reported in April 1868, "the fact that the New Orleans *Tribune,* the only newspaper both owned and edited by colored people in the South, and the only daily thus conducted in the whole Union, has been compelled to suspend publication."

CHAPTER 9

Photographing the War

The photograph first made its debut in 1839, when a Frenchman named Louis Jacques Mandé Daguerre announced that he had developed a process that virtually duplicated reality. Called the daguerreotype, after its inventor, it was a silver-coated copper plate that, when exposed to sunlight, could create true-to-life images. Even in this primitive form, photography created a sensation, opening up new artistic and commercial vistas.

But it soon became apparent that the daguerreotype had its limitations; for one, because of its mirrorlike surface, the image could be seen only when held in a certain position, and for another, it could not be duplicated. Around the same time, an Englishman, William H. F. Talbot, did much to solve the latter problem when he introduced a photographic procedure that used a light-sensitive paper. The paper was coated with salt and silver nitrate, and it produced a negative from which positive prints could be made. This was a step forward, but Talbot's innovation, which he dubbed the calotype (from the root of a Greek word meaning beautiful), suffered in comparison to the daguerreotype. Talbot's early images were not as clear and crisp, his process was longer than Daguerre's, and the calotype had a tendency to fade.

Despite these shortcomings, word of this new art form continued to spread rapidly, especially across the Atlantic. One of the first Americans to promote photography was the painter-inventor Samuel F. B. Morse. Having gone abroad in the summer of 1838 to secure patents in England and France for his electronic magnetic telegraph, Morse happened to be in Paris when Daguerre's process was formally revealed. The American was fascinated; unlike some who thought photography would be a rival to such visual arts as painting, he was convinced the new medium could be of great assistance to the artist. Primarily a portrait painter, Morse felt that if he had photos of his subjects at hand, the need for lengthy and tedious posing sessions would be eliminated. Calling photography "Rembrandt perfected," he became one of its most enthusiastic supporters.

Morse contacted Daguerre, and the two men met in early March 1839. Soon afterward Morse described the daguerreotype in a letter published in the New York *Observer* and reprinted in newspapers throughout the country. This wasn't the first time photography was discussed at length in America's press; a description had already been published some months before. Nevertheless, Morse's unqualified endorsement did its part in popularizing this new visual art form in the United States.

Frederick Scott Archer, an English engraver and sculptor, was responsible for the next technological advance in photography by inventing the wet plate process in 1851. He coated a glass plate with a wet, sticky substance called collodion, then dipped the exposed plate in light-sensitive salts. The one major advantage of the process was that a finely detailed negative could be made, from which many positives could be produced. But there was a serious drawback: The glass plate had to remain wet throughout the procedure. The plate had to be freshly prepared and sensitized while moist, exposed in the camera still wet, and developed immediately before it dried. That meant a darkroom had to be nearby, a major problem in the field, especially if that field was a battleground.

Military photographers certainly had their work cut out for them. Cameras, lenses, chemicals, and the all-important glass plates would have to be transported over roads that were often muddy, pitted, or downright impassable. Even if this fragile equipment survived undamaged, where in the combat zone could one find a room dark enough to develop the photographs? Nor were these the only obstacles. Because of the slowness of exposure, the camera could produce only static scenes; action photos were still some years into the future. And finally, the publishing technology of the time did not permit the reproduction of photos in newspapers or magazines, except when an artist redrew the photograph and then an engraver made a woodcut of the drawing—an expensive and laborious process.

Given all of these limitations, the photographic coverage of America's Civil War—its scope, its grandeur, its horror—was truly an extraordinary achievement. Never before had there been such an extensive visual representation of a great upheaval, captured not only for the generation that lived through it, but for all generations to come.

WARTIME PHOTOGRAPHY

War photography is almost as old as the medium of photography itself. During the Mexican-American War, an unknown photographer made several daguerreotypes, including one that some authorities believe might have been the battlefield of Buena Vista. Evidence suggests that he was a street-corner photographer in Saltillo, Mexico. In 1846–47, he photographed American soldiers, in one instance surrounded by Mexican street urchins. There's even a picture of Gen. John Wool on horseback, accompanied by his staff. But these photos, though historic, come nowhere near being true combat or battlefield pictures.

The first identified photographer to record wartime scenes was Roger Fenton, an Englishman who documented aspects of the Crimean War in 1855. Usually the photojournalist's mission is to complement the correspondent's story, but Fenton was sent to the Crimea for the very opposite reason, to counteract published reports of mismanagement and horror at the front. *The Times* of London correspondent William Russell had written scathing dispatches revealing the full extent of how the British soldier was suffering, with meager rations, poor clothing, and inadequate hospital care. In his attempt to calm public fears, Fenton took pictures mostly depicting camp scenes of officers in conference or soldiers enjoying a few drinks while off duty. The photographs suggested an army engaged in peacetime maneuvers, rather than one on the front lines. But to his credit, Fenton was also determined to secure pictures "likely to be historically interesting" and occasionally photographed a deserted battlefield, hoping to evoke images of the nature of war.

Photographers like Fenton set a precedent that Americans were quick to follow. Around 1860, some 3,000 photographers plied their trade in the United States, with the greatest number residing in the North. Once the war broke out, hundreds of these cameramen followed the armies to the battlefields, making portraits for the soldiers to send home and at the same time visually recording the conflict itself for a civilian population eager to see what was happening.

With the exception of combat photos, unobtainable because of long exposure times, all other aspects of the struggle were dutifully recorded. Not only were battlefields, camps, and supply depots documented, but the camera caught every level of military society, from top-ranking generals to the humblest hospital orderly. With an estimated one million pictures taken, the Civil War was the first conflict ever to be photographed in such volume and detail.

Risking life and limb, enduring heat and cold and bone-rattling roads, the hundreds of photographers responsible for creating this visual record were goaded on by two powerful forces: profit and patriotism, with the former exerting the greater influence. War photography was a potential gold mine, a chance to recoup after some lean years that followed the economic slump of 1857.

The real money was in portraiture. Hundreds of thousands of fledgling soldiers had their pictures taken to commemorate their participation in such an epochal event. As a British reporter observed in 1862:

> America swarms with the members of the mighty tribe of cameristas, and the civil war has developed their business in the same way that it has given an impetus to the manufacturers of metallic air-tight coffins and embalmers of the dead. The Young Volunteer rushes off at once to the studio when he puts on his uniform, and the soldier of a year's campaign sends home his likeness that the absent ones may see what changes have been produced in him.

The so-called *carte de visite* was a popular format for such soldier portraits. They were small and handy, and called *carte de visite* because they were about the size of a visiting card (2¼ by 3¾ inches). Their very popularity caused an overburdened post office endless headaches. At one point, early in the war, so many soldier portraits were in the mail that the postal service ground to a halt for a time.

Although the vast majority of photographers were in the North (actually there were more professional cameramen in New York City alone than in almost the entire Confederacy), there was still a great demand for images in the South. Johnny Reb was just as eager for a chance at immortality as his Yankee counterpart. But the South's limited resources of paper, chemicals, and other necessary supplies ultimately took its toll on the profession, forcing many photographers out of business. Also, as Southern reverses grew worse, photographers were compelled to trade their cameras for rifles and join the Confederacy's ragged and dwindling ranks.

As long as the fighting continued, however, demand for *carte de visite* photos and war scenes remained high. But once the fighting came to an end, so did interest in the photographs that had captured it. In the postwar era many thousands of glass plate photographs were sold to gardeners to be used as panes in greenhouses, their precious images gradually scoured away by the burning rays of the sun. The war had been too traumatic, and for many Americans of that generation, poring over war photos threatened to open old wounds and renew old sorrows. As the sun beat down on greenhouse panes, it was as if the fading images also helped fade, or at least mute, the anguish many still felt. Fortunately a good number of the photographic plates survived and with the passage of time would be appreciated as a treasured mirror of a crucial period in American history.

MATHEW B. BRADY

Mathew B. Brady is the most famous photographer of the Civil War, a man whose very name conjures up images of duster-coated artists laboring behind bulky black cameras. Hundreds of photographers were active during the war, yet most are anonymous. Civil War historians are familiar with a few, but only Brady's name has stood the test of time, at least in the popular mind.

At the height of his fame in the early 1860s, Brady was the lionized dean of American photographers. But Brady the man, as opposed to his carefully cultivated public image, is much harder to pinpoint. In many ways, he is an enigma, his work far better known than the details of his life. Even his middle name is disputed. Some sources say it stood for Benjamin; others insist that it was simply an initial that stood for nothing, a way of endowing its bearer with some superficial importance. It is likewise uncertain when he was born (probably in 1823) and where (either Cork, Ireland, or Fort Warren, New York). But in truth, these details of his personal life are far less important than his extraordinary career.

It began when he met Samuel F. B. Morse. From that moment, as Brady put it, he was "inextricably enmeshed with the infant art of photography." Some time in 1840 or 1841, he enrolled in Morse's photography school, the first of its kind in the United States. Blessed with a natural talent for operating a camera, Brady also had a strong sense of its limitless commercial possibilities.

The fledgling photographer set up his own daguerreotype gallery in 1844 on the corner of Broadway and Fulton Street in New York City. It was a prime location; Broadway was the heart of the city, a bustling hive lined with shops and restaurants, and its streets congested with horse-drawn conveyances of every description. Brady's establishment was right across the way from P. T. Barnum's popular museum, which drew such crowds the young daguerreotypist was bound to benefit.

Brady hit upon the idea of taking photos of notable men and women of his era, especially all living former presidents. Offering a free sitting to those willing to have their portraits displayed in his

"Gallery of Illustrious Americans," Brady was successful in attracting the great and the near great, including Daniel Webster, John C. Calhoun, Henry Clay, John Quincy Adams, James K. Polk, and Zachary Taylor. But it was the photograph of an aging Andrew Jackson shortly before the old hero's death that was the main feature—if the most disputed part—of the collection. Some say the historic picture, taken on April 15, 1845, was by Dan Adams of Tennessee, while others give Brady credit. In any case, Brady did emerge with a Jackson photograph and exhibited it with forgivable pride.

In February 1860 a rising western politician by the name of Abraham Lincoln stepped into Brady's studio-gallery for a picture. Lincoln was going to make a speech at the Cooper Institute in Manhattan, an address that he hoped would broaden his base of support in his quest for the Republican presidential nomination. The speech proved a success, and Brady's photo of Lincoln was in great public demand. By May it appeared in the widely circulated *Harper's Weekly,* and during the campaign itself, the photo was used on all sorts of cards, banners, and buttons.

In 1861 Brady was at the peak of his fame and prosperity. "Photographed by Brady" became a kind of trademark, a badge of status as well as of quality. As if to underscore his standing as America's premier photographer, Brady opened a new and magnificent studio on the west corner of Broadway and Tenth Street and grandly dubbed it the National Portrait Gallery. Duly impressed by the establishment, the *New York Times* referred to its creator as "the prince of photographers on our side of the water."

When the Civil War broke out, Brady thought about becoming a pictorial war correspondent—roughly what we would call a photojournalist today. But whether he was the first one to suggest photographing the war is not entirely certain. In June 1861 a committee of the American Photographic Society tried to get the War Department to sanction just such a project, but to no avail. Brady's associate and future rival Alexander Gardner was another who claimed to have come up with the idea, though how much Gardner's assertions are based on professional jealousy or a latent resentment of his treatment at Brady's hands is unclear.

At any rate, Brady used all his powers of persuasion, and not a little string-pulling, to be allowed to travel with the Union army. His wife and friends "had looked unfavorably upon this departure from commercial business to pictorial war correspondence," the photographer later recalled, but a "spirit in my feet said 'Go' and I went." Equipped with a special darkroom vehicle (soon to be called the "What-is-it wagon" in reference to soldiers' constant queries), Brady accompanied the army in late July 1861, when the first battle of Bull Run was fought, a Union defeat that soon became a humiliating rout. Newspapers did a post-mortem of the disaster, and Brady was the butt of some malicious humor. One story claimed in jest that the photographer was partly responsible for the debacle. It was Brady's big camera, a "mysterious and formidable instrument that produced the panic." The retreating troops mistook it for a "great steam gun . . . and took to their heels when they got within focus."

Lampoons notwithstanding, Brady's experiences at Bull Run con-vinced him that the nation was undergoing an ordeal worth recording for posterity. To this end, Brady organized a corps of field cameramen to cover the conflict—the first time ever in the brief history of pictorial journalism that there was an organized and extensive effort to photo-graph a war. Although Brady himself didn't entirely abandon the camera or darkroom, he now became more of an impresario, orchestrating, with the approval of the government but at his own expense, a twenty-man photography corps, making sure they were organized, equipped, and well supplied with chemicals and other tools of the trade.

The corps ranged far and wide, and could be found in most the-aters of the war. Many in the group were men of real talent, such as Alexander Gardner, Timothy O'Sullivan, and George Barnard. Over time, some members of Brady's organization grew to resent the impre-sario's domination. They worked in relative obscurity, and the prod-ucts of their labor were invariably labeled "Photo by Brady," though the master might have been miles away at the time. More galling to the men in the field, however, was that even if Brady had been on loca-tion, he couldn't have taken most of the photographs anyway, since he was badly nearsighted from childhood. The extent of his visual impair-ment and its impact on his professional duties remain subjects of con-troversy. That he took at least some of the war photos attributed to him there is no question; yet the vast majority bearing his imprint were taken by others.

Brady's hogging the credit was irritating enough, but there was also the matter of his tight purse strings. Corps members put their lives at risk and endured terrible hardships for $35 a week—a decent salary at the time, but not comparable to what they could earn on their own. When they couldn't stand it anymore, they left; Gardner, the number-two man in the organization, departed in 1863. Others soon followed his lead.

The Civil War proved a mixed blessing for Mathew Brady. On the one hand, it catapulted him to new heights of fame; on the other, it helped bring about his downfall. He spent $100,000 of his own money to finance the photographers' corps, a sum equal to millions in today's money. It finally came to the point where his expenses exceeded his income; the man who was once at the pinnacle of success and freely hobnobbed with the rich and famous eventually had to declare bankruptcy.

Brady began to drink heavily, but the balm of alcohol only provided momentary relief from financial woes. His wife died in 1887, and he ended his days as a nearly blind pauper. When he died in 1896, he was already a half-forgotten relic of an earlier age. Yet the passage of time restored, even augmented, his reputation. Altogether, Brady and his men took over 7,000 photos, a rich visual record that stands as his monument and most enduring legacy.

THE CAMERA AS A TOOL OF WAR

Photography at its best records objects as they are, not as we wish them to be. It was this quality of an exact and accurate rendering that made the photograph a major tool during the Civil War. The wet plate or collodion process then used also had the advantage of producing negatives that could be replicated. Before long, military documents, maps, and plans were being photographed, copies of which would be distributed to high-ranking officers in the field or functionaries within the War Department.

Since the army had no experience in this new medium, civilian cameramen were hired—the first time ever that photographers were employed by the military for war-related purposes. None of these photographers had any official status; they might be called captain or some other military title, but these were purely courtesy ranks and had no authority attached to them.

Alexander Gardner was one of the many photographers who offered his services to the North. He was born in Paisley, Scotland, on October 17, 1821. Shortly after his birth, the family moved to Glasgow, where at fourteen, he was apprenticed to a jeweler. After learning the craft, the young Scot turned to various financial ventures but soon found that he was less the businessman and more the idealist. Subscribing to the utopian dreams of Robert Owen and others, in 1849 Gardner traveled to the United States and helped to establish a Scottish socialist-type community in Clayton County, Iowa. After several months he returned home to Scotland, where he continued to aid the cause by lecturing and recruiting new members for the colony.

By the mid-1850s, now working as a newspaper editor in Glasgow, Gardner became involved in photography, probably influenced by what he saw of Roger Fenton's work in the Crimean War. Fascinated by these visual images, he studied the wet plate or collodion method, developing expertise in the process. There is even evidence of his attempt to launch a career as a photographer, but this was cut short when he decided to migrate with his family to America, hoping to join the Iowa community.

Upon arriving in Newfoundland, however, Gardner and his fellow travelers received the tragic news of a tuberculosis outbreak that ravaged the colony. With Iowa now out of the question, Gardner settled his family in New York City and sought work with Mathew Brady. His experience as a businessman and photographer paid off; by 1858 he was managing Brady's Washington, D.C., gallery.

Gardner's war service began in early 1862. While remaining in Brady's employ as a field cameraman, he accepted a civilian appointment to serve as "Photographer to the Army of the Potomac." Officially attached to the topographical engineers and given the courtesy rank of captain, his initial responsibilities were to photograph maps and other diagrams. Prior to the Civil War, copies of maps were painstakingly drawn by hand, a time-consuming and tedious process. Photography allowed an unlimited numbers of copies to be distributed to field commanders almost immediately.

But there was also a covert, or semicovert, aspect to "Captain" Gardner's many tasks. In addition to his routine duties, the photographer was also a member of the army's intelligence service. Gardner struck up a friendship with its head Allan Pinkerton; no surprise, since the two had common Scottish roots. As a free-roving army photographer, Gardner had a perfect cover for counterespionage activities. At Pinkerton's direction, Gardner and his men would set up their camera in a camp where it was suspected a Confederate spy had infiltrated the ranks. Various groups of soldiers were photographed, and the pictures were then studied to ferret out the intruder.

Besides Gardner, the Union army and navy employed a number of other civilian photographers. Several, such as George N. Barnard, Sam F. Cooley, and John Wood, specialized in taking pictures of roads, railroads, bridges, and fortifications for the army engineers. Others served in camera units that scouted ahead of the armies, photographing potential battle sites, hospital or barracks sites, or even locations for temporary military headquarters. And then there were those who worked for the Union navy, taking photos, for example, of captured coastal fortresses, perhaps to study the damage inflicted by naval artillery.

Even the South, despite shortages of talent and materials, might have used the camera for war-related purposes. There is some documentation suggesting that an A. D. Lytle of Baton Rouge, Louisiana, secretly photographed occupying Union forces, including artillery and cavalry units, and sent the pictures to Confederate authorities. A modern scholar disputes whether Lytle engaged in such activity, since "there is nothing in his surviving images that would have any military value." It is possible, though, that the photos Lytle had passed on to Confederate intelligence were purposely destroyed or simply lost. If that was the case, Lytle was very brave and Union forces not very observant.

Whether or not the South took advantage of this new art form, the fact remains that the U.S. military had clearly established photography as a nearly indispensable tool of war.

CAPT. ANDREW J. RUSSELL, U.S. ARMY

The hundreds of photographers who covered the Northern side of the Civil War were either self-employed or worked for one of the major galleries. Several of these cameramen were also hired by the military but maintained their civilian status. During the four long years of bloodshed, only one member of the armed forces, Andrew J. Russell, served as an official military photographer, the first man ever to perform those duties in behalf of the U.S. Army.

Like many photographers of the period, Russell's roots were in art. A native New Yorker, he was a painter of landscapes and panoramas, and it's more than likely that it was his sense of the pictorial that caused him to dabble in photography. In any event, the Civil War soon interrupted Russell's artistic pursuits—or at least diverted them to another direction. In August 1862, at the age of thirty-two, he enlisted and was made a captain in the 141st New York Volunteers. But the time he spent as a conventional soldier was brief. By a special order, Russell was placed on detached service and sent to Alexandria, Virginia.

Classified as a "Government Artist," which in those days meant photographer, the young captain found himself assigned to the construction corps, a unit responsible for maintaining the U.S. military railroads. As might be expected, Russell's primary duty was to take photos of railroads, bridges, and transportation routes in general. His work apparently reached the highest echelons of government; after his photographs were developed, they were usually sent to Washington for Secretary of War Edwin M. Stanton's perusal.

Russell also played a major role in the production of the first U.S. Army instructional manual ever to include photographs. Designed by Gen. Herman Haupt, head of the construction corps, the manual's primary purpose was to provide information, with photographic examples, to engineers about "the most practical and expeditious" methods to build roads and bridges. In addition, the book showcased new ways to ease the movement of troops, using pictures of pontoon bridges and barges. And lastly, it included a section on the disruption of enemy lines of communication, with illustrative photos and detailed guidelines describing how the Confederacy's railroads, tracks, and bridges could be "most rapidly and effectually destroyed."

The final product was entitled in part *Photographs Illustrative of Operations in Construction and Transportation, as Used to Facilitate the Movements of the Armies of the Rappahannock, of Virginia, and of the Potomac. . . .* Distributed to officers in command of "Departments, Posts, and Expeditions," the manual featured a total of eighty-two photographs by Andrew J. Russell. Since the technology of the period did not permit the actual publication of these visual images, the photos were "tipped in," which meant that the easily duplicated paper photographs were pasted into the pages of the book.

After the war Russell continued his professional career and became well known as a railroad photographer and "western chronicler." He died in 1902.

"THE DEAD OF ANTIETAM"

In late September 1862 Mathew Brady hung a placard outside of his gallery on Broadway in New York City. It bore the simple legend "The Dead of Antietam" and was announcing an exhibition of photographs taken on the battlefield. Antietam had been the bloodiest single day of the war, and for the first time ever, the American public was about to view graphic images of its own combat dead.

The photos showed war or, more specifically, the aftermath of war with a brutal realism that created an immediate sensation. Up to this point, armed combat had usually been romanticized by artists. The French painter Jacques Louis David, for example, showed Napoleon crossing the Alps on a huge charger with flowing mane; in reality, he rode a common mule. Most battlefield scenes were even more theatrical, especially as they depicted the carnage and death, with carefully composed corpses and dramatically gesturing wounded.

The photograph pulled away the veil of myth and romanticism, substituting grim reality for dreamy-eyed artistic convention. Here at the Brady gallery, one could see torn flesh, bloated dead bodies, and faces contorted in agony. All the glorious trappings of war—the bright banners, heroic postures, dashing uniforms—are conspicuously absent. The crowds that thronged the exhibition were exposed to a view of combat usually experienced by the participants themselves. As the *New York Times* commented: "Mr. Brady has done something to bring home to us the terrible reality and earnestness of war. If he has not brought bodies and laid them in our dooryards and along the streets, he has done something very like it."

For those with loved ones at the front, the photographs had an even greater poignancy. Physician and author Oliver Wendell Holmes acquired a set of these Antietam photos but found the images "almost unbearable to look at." Holmes's son Oliver, Jr., the future associate justice of the Supreme Court, had been shot in the neck at Antietam. The older man had actually been at the battlefield looking for his son, so he knew more than most civilians how painfully accurate the photos really were. Speaking of these pictures, he explained: "It was so nearly like visiting the battlefield to look over these views, that all the emotions excited by the actual sight of the stained and sordid scene . . . came back to us, and we buried [the photos] in the recesses of our cabinet as we would have buried the mutilated remains of the dead they too vividly represented."

Mathew Brady should receive full credit for displaying such images, even though he didn't take them. It was his employee Alexander Gardner who, trudging through the blood-soaked fields of Antietam, was responsible for those photos. Brady's habit of imprinting his name on pictures that he didn't shoot was a major factor in the eventual rift between these two men.

But such unpleasantness did little to cramp Brady's style. Soon after his Antietam exhibit, he put much of his energy and money behind the publication of war photos, using such formats as album cards and stereographs. Album cards were designed to be viewed from a specially prepared book, much like today's photo album, but instead of several pictures mounted on a page, there would only be one. *Brady's Album Gallery,* the first of several to be offered for sale, was a set of war prints together with an album to mount them. Buyers could arrange the set as they pleased or follow a numbered system that came with the album.

Stereography allowed a person to view photographs with an illusion of depth—in other words, appearing three-dimensionally in space. This image would be created by placing two almost identical scenes next to each other on an apparatus attached to a binocular device. Dr. Oliver Wendell Holmes, a man of many talents, was the inventor of a hand-held stereoscope in 1859. It became the most popular and widespread of all such devices on the market. Originally used for education and entertainment, during the war years many Americans used their stereoscopes to view battlefield scenes, particularly the ones at the Brady exhibit.

For Civil War Americans who did not serve in the armies of the North or South, there was no way they could visualize the horror of combat. The work of Gardner and his fellow photographers in the field, combined with the exhibits and publications prepared by Brady, revealed the true face of war to their contemporaries—and to those who would come after.

CHAPTER 10

The Wartime Presidency

Once he received word of the Rebel bombardment of Fort Sumter on April 12, 1861, Abraham Lincoln, who had served as president for only five weeks, did not hesitate to take whatever measures were necessary to meet the crisis. Congress, on the other hand, was unable to act with a similar sense of dispatch and decisiveness. Out of session when the war broke out, it was dependent upon the president to call it into special session. Even if Congress had been seated, no one expected it to take immediate steps against the Confederates. Legislative bodies are deliberative by nature, with as many opinions as there are members. Before action can be taken, some sort of consensus must be reached, and more often than not consensus takes time. In the early months of 1861, events crowded upon events in such a manner that time was the one thing the government did not have.

Sensing this at the outset, Lincoln supplied the strong hand needed to guide the Union war effort—and he never relinquished it. But while he considered prosecution of the war largely his domain, the president neither assumed the role of a despot nor treated Congress as a mere "rubber stamp." Throughout the conflict, Lincoln demonstrated that he was willing to work with the legislative branch and support its initiatives—so much so that he became the first president to sign more than 1,000 bills in a four-year term, hardly a sign of congressional indifference.

A masterful politician and a strong and capable leader, Lincoln was also a man of great humanity and compassion. As the war progressed, a large and diverse group of people, many of whom never had cause to view an occupant of the White House with favor, grew to trust the sixteenth president of the United States and to admire his commitment to basic American principles. Blacks in the States and in foreign lands, labor unionists both male and female, and common soldiers all fell under his spell. Largely self-educated, Lincoln was able to express himself in a way that most average Americans could understand. His speeches and his correspondence—public and private—are models of simplicity, eloquence, and grace. He was blessed with an ability to synthesize concepts such as democracy and freedom with a few deft strokes, and ordinary people as well as the elite found hope and inspiration in his words—words that he translated into deeds. As commander in chief, Lincoln upheld the preservation of the Union, a victory for democracy; as a foe of slavery, he issued the Emancipation Proclamation, a declaration of freedom; and as president, he made the office he held somehow more compassionate, a statement of his decency and his devotion to national ideals.

AN "UNLIMITED DESPOT"

By early February 1861, with the breakup of the Union a reality, Abraham Lincoln was well aware of the enormity of the challenge confronting him. "I go to assume a task more difficult than that which devolved upon General Washington," the president-elect told his friends and neighbors as he departed Springfield for the nation's capital.

After taking the oath of office on March 4, Lincoln made it abundantly clear that his primary goal was to preserve the Union. He would allow nothing, he emphasized, to interfere with that commitment. Five weeks later the president's pledge was put to the test. With Congress out of session and Fort Sumter taken by the Rebels, he alone was responsible for the Federal government's reaction, a situation that could work to his advantage but could also backfire. For the moment he was free to act as he saw fit, without interference from those on Capitol Hill who might attempt to block him with hair-splitting constitutional constraints. Yet the absence of any opposition could turn out to be a disaster, laying him open to charges of arbitrary rule or outright despotism.

Trusting that Congress, which was to meet in special session on July 4, would ratify his actions, Lincoln moved swiftly. On April 19 he proclaimed a blockade of Southern ports, which, according to those familiar with international law at the time, was beyond the president's authority, since it was an act tantamount to a declaration of war—a power granted exclusively to Congress. Less than two weeks later, again without the approval of lawmakers, Lincoln enlarged the size of the Regular army and navy. He also usurped congressional authority in fiscal matters, advancing some $2 million of public money to several citizens in New York "for military and naval measures necessary for the defense and support of the government." Perhaps more troubling was Lincoln's curtailment of civil liberties, suspending the writ of habeas corpus at first from Washington, D.C., to Philadelphia and then on July 2 extending the suspension as far north as New York City. Hundreds—eventually thousands—of people suspected of "disloyal" activities were rounded up and thrown in jail, without benefit of charges or trial in civil court.

To modern Americans, having grown accustomed to the "Imperial Presidency" of the post–World War II era, Lincoln's actions might not appear all that alarming. But viewed in the context of the nineteenth century, the president's initiatives seemed to threaten the very soul of the Republic. No previous chief executive had ever pushed the governing document to such limits. Whether justifiable or not, Lincoln was the first president in American history to undertake sweeping actions of questionable constitutionality.

Not surprisingly, his contemporaries criticized him severely. The abolitionist Wendell Phillips called Lincoln an "unlimited despot," and Associate Justice Benjamin R. Curtis was of the opinion that the president had established "a military despotism." Adding to the chorus of protest, former Democratic president Franklin Pierce considered it highly dangerous for a chief executive to believe as Lincoln did that "in time of war the arbitrary will of the President takes the place of the Constitution." In full agreement, George Ticknor Curtis of Massachusetts, one of the leading constitutional scholars of the period, warned that if the public continued to acquiesce in these "serious infractions" carried out by the chief executive, it "will be an end of this experiment of self-government."

Aware of those who held opposing views, Lincoln sought to answer them. In defense of his actions, the president referred to what he called the "war-power." As he saw it, this granted him emergency powers, at least implicitly, in his role as commander in chief. The exigencies of war demanded one brain and one will to exercise power efficiently. Given the situation, Lincoln argued, he had "no choice" but to implement the "war-power."

When Congress met in special session in early July 1861, Lincoln presented his case. Although he expressed the "deepest regret" for having taken actions authorized by the "war-power," the president was unrepentant. "These measures," he explained to the reassembled Congress, "whether strictly legal or not, were ventured upon, under what appeared to be a popular demand, and a public necessity; trusting then, as now, that Congress would readily ratify them."

Not all the legislators were convinced. Massachusetts senator Charles Sumner asked why "these vast War powers" were not applicable to Congress. As far as he was concerned, it made more sense that the legislative branch should have war power authority over the executive, since the president "is only the instrument of Congress, under the Constitution." While Sumner's remarks were worthy of further discussion, the immediacy of the crisis prevented that from happening; Congress approved retroactively all of Lincoln's actions.

Modern scholars are divided as to whether Lincoln's actions were constitutional or not. Some, echoing the critics of Lincoln's own day, have maintained that he knew exactly what he was doing—that he knew he was acting in an arbitrary manner but proceeded to disregard constitutional precepts anyway. Not so, in the opinion of Herman Belz, one of the foremost constitutional authorities on the Civil War era. In a recent study, Belz has argued convincingly "that Lincoln was neither a revolutionary nor a dictator, but a constitutionalist who used the executive power to preserve and extend the liberty of the American Founding."

Perhaps Lincoln should have the last word. As always, he illustrated truths by means of commonsense metaphors. "By general law," he noted, "life *and* limb must be protected; yet often a limb must be amputated to save a life; but a life is never wisely given to save a limb." If Lincoln had saved the "limb" by adhering strictly to constitutional procedures, the "life"—the nation itself—might well have perished.

PRESIDENTIAL ACCESSIBILITY TO THE PRESS

Abraham Lincoln was the first president of the United States to make himself accessible to the press. At a time when newspapermen were the major transmitters of mass public information, Lincoln the politician knew how important they were to the overall success of his administration. During the war, according to one scholar, "almost every Northern journalist of prominence" was a visitor to the White House at least once. As sounding boards for public policy, these editors and correspondents were greeted warmly by the president, who sought their advice, listened patiently to their criticism, and sometimes acted on their suggestions.

Unlike today, Lincoln's contact with the newsmen remained informal; there were neither press conferences nor scheduled interviews. Essentially, the relationship between the chief executive and the press was based on a one-on-one personal level. Reporters would call on the White House frequently, even after hours, but the president usually accommodated them. Associated Press correspondent L. A. Gobright showed up one night only to find Lincoln fretting over the Vicksburg campaign. In typical fashion the president invited the newspaperman to accompany him as he walked over to the War Department. Sometimes journalists were pushy, sending their cards to the president when he was in conference. Occasionally Lincoln would get up in the middle of such a meeting to go out and tell the reporters what they wanted to know, or write the information on their calling cards and send them back by messenger.

Not everyone was happy about this unprecedented access. Secretary of the Navy Gideon Welles complained that the president "permits the little newsmongers to come around him and be intimate." Lincoln, Welles went on, "likes to hear all the political gossip. . . . But the President is honest, sincere, and confiding—traits which are not so prominent in some by whom he is surrounded." Others characterized the newsmen collectively as "shameless liars" and "unauthorized hangers-on," though Lincoln did not agree with these assessments. Members of the press had "tremendous power for both good and evil," he informed a New York *Herald* reporter, but on the whole they were "trustworthy."

Yet they were not without fault, as Lincoln himself acknowledged. Journalists, the president once noted, were "sure to be 'ahead of the hounds,' outrunning events, and exciting expectations to be later dashed into disappointment." This was clearly the case early in the war, when newspaper editors had whipped up public opinion with their "On to Richmond!" exhortations, only to have Union hopes extinguished with the defeat at Bull Run.

Unlike other chief executives, however, Lincoln never held the press responsible for his errors in judgment. One would assume that such a position would endear him to the news corps. Apparently not. For all his rapport with journalists, few presidents have been attacked so savagely by the press as Lincoln was during his years in the White House. No doubt this vilification, aside from the usual political motives, can be explained by the pressures of war. Everyone had a pet project, a war strategy, or an opinion on emancipation, and when the president did not comply, dissatisfaction was expressed in the columns of the newspaper. An engulfing wave of newsprint attacked Lincoln's leadership, his loyalty, his honesty, his morality, his masculinity, his sobriety, even his personal appearance, with one New York newspaper ridiculing him as a "hideous baboon" whom showman P. T. Barnum should exhibit "as a zoological curiosity."

By nature, the president was a forgiving man, but these written assaults were not easy to bear. Although holding firm in his view that the press was essentially "trustworthy," it must have been difficult for Lincoln to live with the knowledge that more editorial abuse had been heaped upon him than on any of his predecessors.

"PUBLIC OPINION BATHS"

The presidency of the United States, Andrew Jackson once remarked, was a form of "dignified slavery." His successor, Martin Van Buren, called the office "toilsome and anxious probation," and James K. Polk later said that it was "no bed of roses." Enormously demanding of time and energy, the office has its own way of inevitably isolating its occupant from the very people he is pledged to represent. This was particularly so in the nineteenth century, when residents of the White House did not have access to sophisticated public opinion polls afforded presidents in recent decades.

After his inauguration, it did not take long for Abraham Lincoln to recognize how easily he could lose touch with the average citizen. A man of humble origins, a man who, despite melancholy moods, loved human contact, he was not about to let the terrible responsibilities of office cut him off from the rest of humanity. Almost instinctively, the prairie politician from Illinois understood the need to be informed, to keep his fingers on the pulse of the nation, and that did not simply mean consultation with generals, politicians, and the social elite. As president, that came with the territory. But he was most anxious to hear directly from the people, to get some idea of their concerns, their needs, and in general what they thought.

In the early days of Lincoln's administration, there was no organized system for such public contact. At all hours droves of people came to see the president, leaving him scarcely enough time for pressing government business. His two young private secretaries, John Nicolay and John Hay, did their best to screen visitors, but it was all getting to be too much. To bring order out of chaos, Lincoln worked out a schedule with his assistants. It was decided that he would meet with the citizenry on Monday, Wednesday, and Friday from 10:00 till 2:00, and on Tuesday and Thursday from 10:00 till 12:00 noon—the first time ever that a president of the United States made himself available to the public on a regularly scheduled basis.

Lincoln referred to these sessions as "public opinion baths," but most of the time those with whom he met were more interested in securing a favor than expressing an opinion. Noah Brooks, the Washington correspondent for the *Sacramento Daily Union* and a White

House insider, described in detail how the process worked. After breakfast, Brooks explained,

> The President sits at his table and kindly greets whoever comes. To the stranger he addresses his expectant "Well?" and to the familiar acquaintance he says, "And how are you to-day, Mr. ———?" though it must be confessed that he likes to call those whom he likes by their first names. . . . With admirable patience and kindness, Lincoln hears his applicant's requests, and at once says what he will do, though he usually asks several questions . . . trying to completely understand each case, however unimportant, which comes before him.

The cases, according to Brooks, might involve

> a poor widow who wants a writership in one of the departments . . . or it may be a Brigadier wanting promotion, an inventor after a contract, a curiosity hunter with an autograph book, a Major General seeking a command, a lady with a petition for a pass to Richmond, a Cabinet Minister after a commission for a favorite, a deputation asking an impossibility, or a Committee demanding an impertinence; it may be all or any of these who come next, and the even-tempered statesman . . . patiently sits there, interlarding the dull details of business with a good-natured joke or anecdote. . . . Of course, during all of these interviews he is liable to interruption from his Cabinet Ministers, who have free access to him at all business hours; Senators and Governors of States come next in precedence, and Representatives come last before "citizens generally."

As was his nature, Lincoln was courteous to all who called upon him and genuinely sympathetic to those in need, but he was no pushover. He could be as harsh as a Puritan elder to anyone he felt was trying to manipulate him for a selfish or dishonest purpose. When a visitor apparently wanted to use Lincoln's name to promote a business, he got an angry response from the chief executive. "No!" Lincoln said firmly. "Do you take the President of the United States to be a commission broker? You have come to the wrong place, and for you and every one who comes for such purposes, there is the door!"

Most encounters, however, remained pleasant. But the constant parade of people trooping through his office took its toll on the president, who often appeared physically and emotionally exhausted. Sen. Henry Wilson of Massachusetts remembered calling upon him one day on pressing business. The anteroom "was crowded with men and women seeking admission." Lincoln "seemed oppressed [and] care-worn." The senator said to him, "'Mr. President, you are too exhausted to see this throng waiting to see you; you will wear yourself out, and you ought not to see these people to-day.'" With "one of those smiles in which sadness seemed to mingle," Lincoln replied, "'They dont want much and they dont get but little, and I must see them.'"

Stories of the accessibility and kindness of the president spread quickly throughout the Union. "For the first time in American history," Lincoln biographer David Herbert Donald has pointed out, "citizens began to feel that the occupant of the White House was *their* representative."

LINCOLN AMONG THE TROOPS

Throughout history, military commanders who rose to become heads of state were usually idolized by the men they had led. Having shared similar dangers, common hardships, and the glories of victory, a special bond existed between them. Napoleon Bonaparte was one such example in the early nineteenth century.

The United States also had its share of military heroes who served as chief executive. George Washington, a reserved man, not one to excite affection, nonetheless was greatly admired by the men he had led and as president retained that respect. Gen. Andrew Jackson is another case in point. Catapulted to national fame after his victory at the battle of New Orleans, "Old Hickory" was highly regarded by the troops under his command, a feeling that did not diminish when he entered the White House in 1829.

Abraham Lincoln was yet another chief executive beloved by the men in the ranks, but what made his relationship so special was the fact that he was the first president of the United States from civilian life to enjoy this popularity. Although a nonmilitary man (his brief stint in the Black Hawk War hardly qualified him as a member of the fraternity), Lincoln developed a solid, almost mystical, rapport with the boys in blue. A frequent visitor to the battlefield, to discuss strategy or to size up his generals, the president always made it his business to be with the troops. In the summer of 1861, during one of his very first trips to the field, an immediate bond seemed to form between the commander in chief and his men. Felix Brannigan, a sergeant in the 74th New York regiment, related this feeling of camaraderie to the folks back home: "Old Abe was here a few days ago. . . . He, we are all convinced, is the soldier's friend. We feel he takes an interest in us. . . . Talk of McClellan's popularity among the soldiers. It will never measure a hundredth part of Honest Abe's. Such cheers as greeted him never tickled the ears of Napoleon in his palmiest days." Later in the year another New Yorker, Pvt. A. Davenport of the 5th regiment, recorded similar impressions: "President Lincoln reviewed the whole Army in a flying visit. The men were all glad to see him & like him & have full confidence in him to a man."

As the war progressed, more and more soldiers caught a glimpse of Lincoln during his travels to the front. One of his most memorable visits occurred midway through the war in early April 1863. The Army of the Potomac, quartered in Falmouth, Virginia, had just undergone some internal organizational changes, all orchestrated by its commanding officer, Gen. Joseph Hooker. A separate cavalry corps had been created, about 11,000 troopers strong, and it was the first to be reviewed by Lincoln on April 6. Two days later the Army of the Potomac went all out for the president, staging a grand parade, probably the greatest public spectacle of American military might up to that time. Four corps participated, a total of some 75,000 men. It was a magnificent sight, rank after rank of blue-clad troops in tight formation, flags flying, bayonets glistening, drums beating, marching legs rising and falling as one. Lincoln was on horseback, his plain black suit set off against his generals' gaudy epaulettes and rows of gleaming brass buttons. Few, if any, soldiers marching in the parade could miss seeing their president. "We passed close to him," Sgt. Ira Dodd of the VI Corps recalled, "so that he could look into our faces and we into his. None of us to our dying day can forget that countenance!" Terribly sad and haggard looking, Lincoln appeared as if he alone were "bearing the burdens of the nation." The sergeant's impressions were confirmed by many others, including a Pennsylvania chaplain, who was so taken by the chief executive's "care worn" demeanor that he prayed for him that very evening.

In between reviews, Lincoln, on horseback, rode through the sea of tents that marked the various army corps. Some housed the wounded from the battle of Fredericksburg, and the president went out of his way to stop by, chat with the men, and offer a sympathetic word. Here, again, Lincoln had difficulty hiding his feelings, one observer noting that "over [his] whole face was spread a melancholy tinge."

As he continued to make his way through the encampment, soldiers came up to the president to shake his hand or cheer his presence among them. "Thousands of them crowded around his horse," an officer later remembered, "hoping to touch his hand or hear his voice or look into his eyes—those deep, fathomless eyes, half closed, as if to hide their sadness."

By the last day of military reviews, the president's emotions finally got the better of him. "As Mr. Lincoln rode by," a Maine private observed, "I noticed that he was weeping. Why he wept I know not—whether he was thinking how many had fallen, or how many will soon fall. . . . But this I do know: under that homely exterior is as tender a heart as ever throbbed, one that is easily moved toward the poor and downtrodden."

The bond between Lincoln and his soldiers never dissolved. It seemed to strengthen with time, as evidenced by his return visit to the Army of the Potomac in late June 1864. For the Union, that summer was one of the darkest periods of the war, a nightmare of blood and horror where final victory seemed more remote than ever. Yet when Lincoln met with the troops encamped at City Point, Virginia, he was greeted with "cheers and enthusiastic shouts." African-American soldiers, in particular, demonstrated their support, as they "cheered, laughed, cried, sang hymns of praise, and shouted . . . 'God bless Master Lincoln!'"

For those in the ranks, the president symbolized and defined better than anyone else the purpose of the war and the reasons why it had to be fought until its triumphant end. Sgt. Ira Dodd of the VI Corps articulated these very thoughts when he described how he and his fellow soldiers felt after seeing Lincoln in person: "Concentrated in that one great, strong yet tender face, the agony of the life [and] death struggle of the hour was revealed as we had never seen it before. With new understanding we knew why we were soldiers."

HAITI AND LIBERIA

Haiti and Liberia, though separated by geography and differing in national origins, share one common experience: They were the first black countries formally recognized by the leading powers of Europe. A diplomatic victory of enormous import, it was neither quickly nor easily achieved.

Haiti, occupying the western third of the Caribbean island of Hispaniola, became free of French colonial rule in 1804. The bulk of the population was former black slaves, and their successful fight for freedom under the brilliant generalship of François Dominique Toussaint L'Ouverture challenged prevailing racist assumptions in the white world. But challenging them was one thing; overturning them was another. For more than two decades the international community snubbed the black Caribbean government; diplomatic recognition implied equality, something the European world was not ready for.

Finally, in 1825, the French came around and recognized Haiti; the British followed suit eight years later.

Around the same time Haiti achieved international legitimacy, Liberia, the second oldest black republic, was founded. In 1821 members of the American Colonization Society purchased land on the west-central coast of Africa, hoping to establish a refuge for freed African-American slaves. The colony, named Liberia, encountered extreme hostility on the part of the indigenous population yet somehow survived. But the experiment failed. Antebellum American blacks, most of whom were born in the United States, had no interest in migrating if freed from bondage; America, not Africa, was their homeland. The handful of African-Americans who had relocated, however, made a go of it, and in 1848 they proclaimed Liberia an independent republic. Great Britain extended diplomatic relations that very year, France, four years later.

Despite the fact that most of the major countries of Europe recognized Haiti and Liberia, the United States refused, primarily because of Southern opposition. As early as 1826, when several Northern newspapers raised the issue of an exchange of ministers with Haiti, slaveholders refused to consider the idea even worthy of discussion. South Carolinian John C. Calhoun, at the time vice president of the United States, noted: "It is a delicate subject, and would in the present tone of feelings to the South lead to great mischief. It is not so much recognition simply, as what must follow it. We must send and receive ministers; and what would be our social relations to a Black minister in Washington? Must he be received or excluded from our dinners, our dances and our parties, and must his daughters and sons participate in the society of our daughters and sons? Small as these considerations appear to be, they involve the peace and perhaps the union of this nation."

But after the "peace" and "union" were broken in 1861, there was no longer any need to placate the South. With most of the slaveholding states out of the Union, the North was now in a position to take a long overdue step toward progress and freedom.

As always, much depended on the president. In early December 1861, in his annual message to Congress, Abraham Lincoln left no doubt where he stood. "If any good reason exists why we should persevere longer in withholding our recognition of the independence and sovereignty of Hayti and Liberia," the chief executive said, "I am unable to discern it." A half year later, on June 5, 1862, having secured the approval of lawmakers, Lincoln became the first president of the United States to extend diplomatic recognition to black nations.

The president's support for recognition, however, was not entirely motivated by the fact that it was long overdue. He was spurred on by another reason as well: the colonization of African-Americans. A long-time admirer of Henry Clay, one of the founders of the American Colonization Society, Lincoln had grown to believe that whites and blacks could not live harmoniously in an integrated society. Now that Haiti and Liberia had official ties with the United States, colonization might move along more smoothly.

In mid-August 1862 the president met with a delegation of African-Americans and delivered what was in essence a policy statement to "test the waters." He began:

> You and we are different races. We have between us a broader difference than exists between any other two races. Whether it is right or wrong I need not discuss, but this physical difference is a great disadvantage to us both, as I think your race suffer very greatly, many of them by living among us, while ours suffer from your presence. . . . If this is admitted, it affords a reason at least why we should be separated.

Lincoln went on to offer financial assistance and to ask for volunteers—"a number of able-bodied men, with their wives and children, who are willing to go"—not necessarily to Liberia, which might be too far away, but perhaps to Central America or to Haiti, where they "are more generous than we are here. To your colored race they have no objection."

Reaction to the president's proposal was swift and unmistakable. Throughout the Union, African-Americans declared that they were opposed to colonization, had no desire to migrate, and that the United States was their country too. Antislavery leaders—black and white—were furious with the president. Black abolitionist Frederick Douglass, who later came to genuinely like Lincoln, on this occasion held nothing back when he angrily denounced the president's proposal—a proposal which showed "all his inconsistencies, his pride of race and blood, his contempt for negroes and his canting hypocrisy." White antislavery crusaders were just as outraged. William Lloyd Garrison characterized Lincoln's remarks as "humiliating . . . impertinent . . . untimely," and insisted that they reflected his "education(!) with and among 'the white trash' of Kentucky."

Ever the pragmatist, Lincoln knew when it was time to back down. If anything, he was not set in his ways, and his flexibility was genuine, not the product of desperation or sheer political expediency. Those to whom he had directed his proposal had spoken, rejecting it in no uncertain terms.

Thus, by mid-1863, Lincoln abandoned colonization as unfeasible. How could it be otherwise when tens of thousands of African-Americans were joining the Union army and proving themselves on the field of battle? Why fight and die for your country, only to leave it when the guns cease fire?

Although wartime colonization proved abortive, in one respect it was productive of good. Indirectly, it was responsible for the United States breaking the international color barrier and extending diplomatic status to two black republics. And with Lincoln at the helm, there would be no turning back. When the State Department attempted to sabotage the effort by refusing to accept a black diplomat from Haiti, the president stepped in and let it be known that the representative from that country was welcome.

LINCOLN'S BID FOR REELECTION

In late August 1864, Columbia College professor Francis Lieber, a loyal and active Republican, was deeply concerned about the fate of his party and, more importantly, about the future of the Union itself. Lincoln's bid for reelection, to be decided in a little more than two months, was far from a certainty. "If we come triumphantly out of this war, with a presidential election in the midst of it," wrote Lieber, "I shall call it the greatest miracle in all the historic course of events."

An overstatement, to be sure, but Lieber was not far from the mark. The presidential contest of 1864 was one of a kind. By running for a second term, Abraham Lincoln was the first popularly elected leader in history to seek reelection in the midst of a long and costly war. Only once before had a chief executive sought reelection in time of war— James Madison in 1812—but that was during a conflict that had just gotten under way.

In Lincoln's case, the Civil War was approaching its fourth year when, in early 1864, his candidacy for reelection was made public. It was hardly a propitious time for such an announcement. The euphoria of the previous summer, inspired by Union victories at Gettysburg and Vicksburg, had been replaced with a growing war weariness. The months had gone by, the casualties had mounted, and there were still no signs that the ordeal was coming to an end. Even Ulysses S. Grant, appointed general in chief of Union armies in March 1864, proved a disappointment, making little headway against an entrenched and determined Confederate enemy. The miracle worker of the West, the man who had captured Fort Donelson, turned disaster into victory at Shiloh, and conquered Vicksburg, seemed unable to repeat his magic in the East.

With the war going badly, most of the president's supporters, including many of his closest friends, were of the opinion that his bid for reelection would most likely be turned down by the voters. Leonard Swett, one of Lincoln's most vigorous campaigners, who had known him since 1849, when they both had practiced law in Illinois, believed that there was little if any chance for success. "Unless material changes can be wrought," Swett confided to his wife, "Lincoln's election is beyond any possible hope." The president himself saw the handwriting on the wall. "You think I don't know I am going to be beaten," he told an army officer, "*but I do,* and unless some great change takes place, *badly* beaten."

In view of the pessimism within the Lincoln camp, it is truly remarkable that no thought seems to have been given to postponing or suspending the presidential contest until the present crisis was resolved. Facing almost certain defeat, the president nevertheless refused to allow consideration of such a notion. As far as he was concerned, the election was a "necessity." "We can not have free government without elections," he told a crowd of serenaders on the White House lawn. "And if the rebellion could force us to forego, or postpone a national election, it might fairly claim to have already conquered and ruined us."

With the election sure to take place, the Democrats were elated. A victory was more than likely, if they could find the right candidate, one capable of attracting a wide constituency and at the same time exploiting the Northern malaise. Eventually they chose the former commander of the Army of the Potomac, George B. McClellan, who had name recognition, symbolized anti-Lincolnism, and was a man still revered— or so it seemed—by many soldiers in the field. And even if his record as a combat general was decidedly mixed, there was no question regarding his organizational talents. "Little Mac," as his men affectionately had called him, had been responsible for shaping the Union's eastern army into a unified and well-structured fighting force. Could McClellan use those same strengths to unite Democrats behind him in his forthcoming battle with Republicans?

It would be a more challenging task than when he had taken command of the Army of the Potomac. His party was divided between "War Democrats" and "Peace Democrats." McClellan himself was a "War Democrat," and his position ran counter to the party's platform, which, as a result of some shrewd political machinations, was drafted by the "Peace Democrats." McClellan favored a restoration of the Union first and then a discussion of terms, while those who authored the so-called "peace platform" wanted an armistice above all else; in other words, peace before Union. The platform, moreover, called the war a failure, proving an embarrassment to General McClellan, who believed that this negated the efforts of those whom he had led and dishonored those who had died on the battlefield. In his acceptance speech, McClellan virtually repudiated the document, which served only to exacerbate divisions within the organization and caused further confusion as to where he and the party stood.

Like all previous presidential candidates, except Stephen A. Douglas, neither Lincoln nor McClellan played a public role in the contest. They did not deliver formal speeches, attend rallies, or engage in debate, and they were very careful to avoid saying anything negative about each other. But privately, both presidential standard-bearers did what they could to advance their cause, though McClellan was no match for Lincoln when it came to maneuvering behind the scenes. A consummate politician with thirty years of experience, Lincoln left nothing to chance. The president wrote numerous letters to party leaders, helped decide who would speak and where, distributed patronage to his political advantage, made it clear that Federal employees should kick in 10 percent of their paycheck for the party (a common practice strictly enforced during this campaign), and didn't hesitate to ask for donations from war contractors and even from members of his own cabinet. Lincoln was kind and tender hearted, but when it came to his political life, he was all business, leaving no room for sentimentality.

Thanks to Republican donors, and government clerks who helped as processors and distributors, the Union was flooded with pro-Lincoln literature. In fact, no previous campaign came close to the sheer volume of material published in behalf of the president, later estimated at more than three pieces of printed items for every Lincoln voter. Whether they were pamphlets or one-page flyers, the message was always the same: a vote for McClellan was a vote for treason and disunion.

The Democrats fought back. Pulling no punches, they accused Lincoln of inept military leadership and political tyranny. Using the "race card," they also hit below the belt. Two reporters from the New York *World,* a staunch Democratic paper, anonymously drafted a seventy-two-page pamphlet extolling the virtues of the social and sexual mixing of the races, and in the process they coined a new word, *miscegenation,* from the Latin *miscere* ("to mix") and *genus* ("race"). The booklet was sent to Lincoln and other Republican luminaries, hoping that they would acknowledge receipt and endorse the content. A few abolitionists took the bait and responded in the affirmative, but Lincoln and most others in the party offered no comment, suspecting the pamphlet for what it was, a Democratic attempt to inflame racist passions. Failing to entrap the president, the Democrats still didn't ease up on the matter, dubbing Lincoln "Abraham Africanus the First" and insisting that his reelection would be a victory for interracial marriage.

The Democrats might have overplayed their hand on the race issue. At least Lincoln thought so, privately joking that miscegenation was a Democratic "mode of producing good Union men, and I don't propose to infringe on the patent." How many Northern voters, disgusted with Democratic race-baiting, actually joined the Republicans? Of course, it's impossible to determine, but there's no question that miscegenation as a campaign tactic fell short of achieving its goal. To most voters, according to a recent study of the election, miscegenation as a word "was not only too long, but the issue was too remote. Though emotionally loaded, it didn't rank with treason."

Treason, disunion, winning the war—these were the issues that seemed to carry the most weight. This was especially so among those in uniform away from home, who for the first time in American history were allowed to cast absentee ballots in a presidential contest. During the previous year or so, nineteen states had either amended their constitutions or legislatively made provision for soldiers in the field to take part in the electoral process. In those states where no action was taken on soldier suffrage, the War Department, confident that the men in blue were partial to Lincoln, furloughed large numbers of servicemen home to cast their ballots.

The confidence of the War Department was not misplaced. Most soldiers genuinely liked the president and saw him as one of their own. "He has proved a good and faithfull soldier," wrote Pvt. John Lee to his father. Not that McClellan was so disliked, but most of the men had doubts as to whether he would stay the course once elected. As for "Old Abe," they knew that he would accept no truce until the objectives of the war were fulfilled. "We all want peace," one of them said, "but none *any* but an *honorable* one." The soldiers, a Lincoln supporter observed, were "quite as dangerous to Rebels in the rear as in front."

But it was their actions on the front that guaranteed Lincoln's victory in the rear. On September 2, 1864, after months of stalemate, Gen. William Tecumseh Sherman took Atlanta, one of the last major strongholds of Confederate resistance in the Deep South, and then in late

October, the diminutive but dashing Union general Philip Sheridan whipped Gen. Jubal A. Early's forces in the Shenandoah Valley. Both victories electrified the North, refreshing a public thirst for good news after an extended drought of bad tidings. No longer could the administration be convincingly accused of military ineptness.

When the votes were tallied, Lincoln won reelection handily. In terms of the popular vote, the president received 55 percent of the overall count, while in the electoral college, his victory was far more impressive, gaining a majority of 212 over his opponent's 21. McClellan carried only three states, New Jersey, Delaware, and Kentucky.

The general fared even worse among his former comrades. Nearly 80 percent of the soldiers threw their support behind the president, and though their vote was not decisive (with or without it, Lincoln would have carried most states because of his large popular majority), the military ballot was still unprecedented. Never before in history had men in combat, representing all ranks, been asked to pass judgment on their commander in chief.

Considering what might have been, like many Northerners, New York lawyer George Templeton Strong was relieved. "The crisis has been past," he noted in his diary, "and the most momentous popular election ever held since ballots were invented has decided against treason and disunion." Lincoln, too, took great pleasure in the victory, never losing sight, however, of the process by which it came about. The election proved that democracy was not as fragile an experiment as many had believed. "It has demonstrated," the president declared, "that a people's government can sustain a national election, in the midst of a great civil war. Until now it has not been known to the world that this was a possibility."

"THE BLACK MAN'S PRESIDENT"

Enshrined in popular folklore as the "Great Emancipator," the traditional, if paternalistic, view of Lincoln is that he was the true champion of African-Americans. Upon closer examination, Lincoln the man, as opposed to Lincoln the myth, had decidedly ambivalent attitudes toward racial equality. In his early years in public life, he left no question that he detested the institution of slavery, but social justice for blacks was another matter. During his debates with Stephen A. Douglas in 1858, he made a number of statements that would be considered racist today. In Charleston, Illinois, he admitted that he was not nor ever had been "in favor of bringing about in any way the social and political equality of the white and black races." To have said anything less, especially in the bottom half of the state populated by people with roots in the slaveholding South, would have probably catapulted Lincoln to political oblivion. But motivation aside, Lincoln's remarks could still be construed as representative of his true feelings—at the time.

Midway through his presidency, however, it was obvious that Lincoln was no longer the prairie politician of the 1850s. As the war evolved, so did he. Blessed with an enormous capacity for growth, and having always harbored an innate compassion for the underdog, the president's views of the black man changed, his racism muted, if not entirely erased. Nothing illustrates this better than the change of protocol at the White House. Until the Civil War, people of color worked at the presidential mansion but were not welcome in any other capacity. Lincoln changed all this, becoming the first chief executive of the United States to receive African-Americans at the White House, both as visitors and as guests at social gatherings.

They came in groups and sometimes alone. In early March 1864 two Louisiana blacks met with the president to discuss suffrage for their people; two months later a delegation of five "colored citizens of North Carolina" brought up the same issue. In September a group of African-Americans from Baltimore visited with Lincoln, presenting him with a pulpit-size edition of the Bible, bound in royal purple velvet, with two heavy gold clamps. The front cover bore an engraving on a gold plate depicting Lincoln in the act of striking the shackles from the wrists of a slave. The gift, according to presidential artist Francis B. Carpenter, gave the president "more genuine pleasure" than any other public tribute ever bestowed upon him.

In late October 1864 Lincoln received a visit from one of the most dynamic black women of the era, Sojourner Truth. A slave for the first forty years of her life, Truth was over six feet tall, rawboned, and outspoken. After escaping bondage, she repeatedly risked her own life and freedom by bringing out other fugitives on the Underground Railroad. Close to seventy years of age, she remained a shrewd judge of character. When she met Lincoln, she liked him immediately. Afterward, Truth commented that she was never treated "by any one with more kindness and cordiality" and was thankful that she had "always advocated his cause."

But not all black leaders had always advocated Lincoln's cause. During the first eighteen months of the war, for example, ex-slave and abolitionist Frederick Douglass had serious misgivings about Lincoln, a man whom he believed would have accepted the status quo—a Union with slavery still intact—if he had been given the opportunity. After the issuance of the Emancipation Proclamation, and after meeting the president face-to-face at the White House, however, Douglass's feelings changed dramatically. Lincoln, the black abolitionist reported, was "entirely free from popular prejudice against the colored people. He was the first great man that I talked with in the United States freely," Douglass emphasized, "who in no single instance, reminded me of the difference between himself and myself of the differences of color."

Informal meetings with blacks in a private setting were one thing, gala events were another. The more popular the act, the more noteworthy. Would Lincoln be willing to mingle socially in public with people of color? At the White House New Year's Day reception in 1864, he left no doubt how he felt about the matter. Among the guests who were greeted by the president and his wife were "four colored men of genteel exterior, and with the manners of gentlemen." Today that might be dismissed as "tokenism," but in 1864 it was a bold step forward, the first time that African-Americans were allowed to attend such a function at the Executive Mansion. Nor was it the only time. The following New Year's "a throng of colored folk" attended the festivities.

Perhaps no event underscored the changes wrought by Lincoln's open-door social policy than what occurred at the White House inaugural reception on the evening of March 4, 1865. Frederick Douglass had attempted to enter the mansion but was barred by two policemen. Managing to get a message to Lincoln, he was finally permitted to pass. Once in the East Room, the president spotted the black leader and exclaimed in a voice that carried through the room, "Here comes my friend Douglass." As Douglass approached, Lincoln gave his guest a cordial handshake and said: "Douglass, I saw you in the crowd to-day listening to my inaugural address. There is no man's opinion that I value more than yours: what do you think of it?"

Several of the guests who were present might have thought that Lincoln's question was disingenuous—a president of the United States in public asking an ex-slave what he thought of a national speech. But there is no reason to suspect that Lincoln was insincere. He truly wanted Douglass's feedback and was pleased to hear that the abolitionist liked his inaugural address, calling it "a sacred effort."

The president had come a long way since his days on the stump in Illinois. It was clear that the impact of the war or, in Douglass's words, "the educating tendency of the conflict" was decisive in revising Lincoln's views on racial matters. This "most remarkable man," Douglass believed, could now be regarded as "the black man's president."

LINCOLN AND ORGANIZED LABOR

Wars are mixed blessings for labor. Those not taken for military service usually find jobs plentiful, but the hours can be very long and conditions poor, with few options to redress grievances. For the sake of national security, strikes, especially in key war industries, are discouraged, if not actively suppressed.

During the Civil War, employers resorted to all sorts of techniques to keep workers in line, including blacklists, lockouts, and "yellow dog" contracts, whereby employees agreed not to join a union while on the job. Exploiting the war effort, management also secured the cooperation of Federal officials, who sometimes authorized Union generals to use their troops to disperse or imprison strikers.

In the midst of this labor unrest, Abraham Lincoln's position could best be described as incongruous. At the very time that his military forces were serving as strikebreakers, he became the first president of the United States to be openly sympathetic to organized labor. A clever politician or a genuine supporter of the wage earner? Labor leaders of the time were convinced that it was the latter, arguing that "upstart officials" were responsible for their troubles and that Lincoln, who had always been a friend of the workingman, was kept in the dark.

It is not difficult to see why the leadership, and the rank and file, arrived at this conclusion. Lincoln had been a manual laborer in his youth and early manhood, and on occasion made a point of it. In late 1859, to a crowd in Indianapolis, Indiana, he proclaimed with pride that he "himself had been a hired man twenty-eight years ago." In his very first annual message to Congress on December 3, 1861, he included a brief but revealing comment on the relationship between labor and capital. "Labor is prior to, and independent of, capital," he informed the legislators. "Capital is only the fruit of labor, and could never have existed if labor had not first existed. Labor is the superior of capital, and deserves much the higher consideration."

None of his predecessors ever expressed these ideas. Nor were they confined only to formal state papers. Lincoln spoke in similar terms when he met with disgruntled laborers. In the fall of 1863, some 7,000 members of the New York Machinists and Blacksmiths Union went on strike for higher wages to keep up with the wartime cost-of-living increases. Since many of their employers had contracts with the war and navy departments, it was feared that the Federal government would favor management. To protect their interests, a delegation of workers went to Washington to see the president. In his official capacity, Lincoln explained, he had to remain neutral. But off the record, his sympathies were with the workers. As far as he was concerned, the employers were actually "the first strikers as they refused to accept the terms offered by the men, and compelled the latter to cease work." Lincoln arranged for the group to have an immediate interview with Secretary of the Navy Gideon Welles, who assured the workers that his department would show no favoritism to either side.

Several months later another delegation of striking laborers visited the White House and received a similar reception. Once again, Lincoln pointed out that he could not officially take sides, but there was no question as to where he stood. "I know the trials and woes of working men," the president said, "and I have always felt for them. I know that in almost every case of strikes, the men have just cause for complaint."

On at least one occasion, the president went further than words of sympathy. In 1864, when Union troops were sent to St. Louis to break a strike by printers, Lincoln took the position that "servants of the Federal Government should not interfere with legitimate demands of labor" and ordered the soldiers withdrawn.

Lincoln's sympathy for the wage earner was not restricted to men only. In January 1865 he was the first president to meet with a group of women labor leaders in the White House. The delegation, representing more than 10,000 seamstresses in Philadelphia, visited with the president for two hours, informing him of the substandard compensation they received from war contractors. Convinced that they were underpaid, Lincoln ordered the quartermaster general to make certain that the women obtain fair wages for their work.

While Lincoln's support of organized labor was isolated and sporadic, reflecting personal views rather than official policy, his overall position was unprecedented. Never before, and not again until Theodore Roosevelt in the early 1900s, would a president of the United States demonstrate any degree of sympathy for organized labor.

CHAPTER 11

The Wartime Congresses

There have been only a half dozen or so times in American history that Congress, stimulated by momentous events, has risen to the occasion with far-reaching legislation. In the midst of the Great Depression, a special session of Congress, inspired by the leadership of Franklin Delano Roosevelt, passed a flurry of bills during the celebrated "one hundred days" in 1933. In similar fashion, the 89th Congress reshaped America by approving Lyndon Johnson's "Great Society" programs in the mid-1960s.

The Civil War Congresses, though not as famous in the public mind as later sessions, were every bit as dynamic. The stimulus here wasn't an economic collapse, or a landslide victory at the polls, but a sectional division that had shaken the Republic to its foundations. Compelled to deal with a wide range of political, economic, and social issues—not to mention military ones—Civil War lawmakers did not shrink from the challenge. On the contrary, they capitalized on it, enacting legislation of such sweep and significance that they were responsible for creating, in the words of one historian, "a future different enough from the past to merit the label of revolution."

How was this possible? How could the 37th Congress (1861–63) and the 38th Congress (1863–65), in session during the bloodiest conflict in America's history, with the very destiny of the nation at stake, pass such a large number and diverse array of legislative measures "to merit the label of revolution"? Of course, the war itself served as the primary catalyst. In order to finance it, for example, members of Congress would have to revise the nation's tax, monetary, and banking systems. But the crisis also produced an environment for change that went far beyond immediate necessity. The departure of Southern senators and representatives, nearly all Democrats, cost that party close to half of its voting strength in both houses of the legislature. With virtually no opposition from the states' rights, laissez-faire Southerners, Republicans of the North, committed to an activist Federal government and convinced of the need to "promote development in all sectors of the economy," would now have their way.

WARTIME TAXATION

In 1860 the United States depended on two major sources of income: a tariff—that is, a tax on imports—and sales of Federal lands. These government revenues were more than enough to meet the needs of America's antebellum budgets, but once Rebel guns opened fire, the fiscal situation changed dramatically. "War is not a question of valor, but a question of money. . .," New York congressman Roscoe Conkling declared only days after the Union rout at Bull Run. "Who can afford the most iron or lead?" To make certain that the North could, legislators in Washington set to work almost immediately and, before their session ended in 1863, produced the first broad-based set of internal tax measures ever passed by an American Congress—changing forever national revenue policy. In August 1861 Congress enacted the first Federal income tax. Primarily designed to tap into the increasing nonagricultural wealth of the nation, its secondary purpose was to reassure buyers of national bonds that the government would have the necessary funds to pay them for their investments. By imposing a 3 percent tax on all annual incomes over $800, the Republican majority was careful not to burden the average wage earner, who earned less than $400 per year. Over the course of the war, Congress readjusted the rate on three separate occasions, each time seeking to prevent the burden from falling on lower-income Americans, but at the same time not wanting to discriminate against the rich. In July 1864, for instance, yearly incomes of $600 to $5,000 were subjected to a 5 percent tax; $5,001 to $10,000, 7.5 percent; and above $10,000, 10 percent.

Although the income tax had the potential to cause discontent among the general population, its impact was far less onerous than might be expected. The most vehement protests came from the business community in the Northeastern states, but in terms of sheer numbers, barely 1 percent of wartime Northerners were actually affected by the income tax. And by the time it was repealed in 1872 (on the grounds that it was unnecessary, given an existing fiscal surplus), only 0.2 percent of Americans had incomes high enough to warrant payment of the levy.

Since the income tax touched few Americans and generated no more than $55 million in total wartime revenue, a paltry sum in light of the $1.75 million average cost per day of the conflict, members of Congress sought other sources of fiscal support. In late June 1862 they passed a massive tax measure, known as the Internal Revenue Act. Signed into law by Lincoln on July 1, the act was described by James G. Blaine, at the time an aspiring Maine politician, as "one of the most searching, thorough, comprehensive systems of taxation ever devised by any Government." Comprehensive, indeed. Filling more than seventeen triple-column pages of fine print, the law tried to tax almost everything and everybody. "Spirituous and malt liquors and tobacco. . . . Manufactures of cotton, wool, flax, hemp, iron, steel, wood, stone. . . . Banks, insurance and railroad companies, telegraph companies, and all other corporations. . . . Every profession and every calling, except the ministry of religion, was included. . . . Bankers and pawnbrokers, lawyers and horse-dealers, physicians and confectioners, proprietors of theaters and jugglers on the street."

Nor did the legislation stop there. The measure also included the first inheritance tax in American history. On any legacy of more than $1,000, taxes ranging from 0.75 to 5 percent were imposed, depending on the relationship of the heir to the deceased. The closer the family tie, the lower the tax. For example, a brother or sister of the deceased paid only 0.75 percent; a distant relative or friend, 5 percent; and a husband or wife was exempt from the tax altogether.

The Internal Revenue Act of 1862 had still another novel feature. For the first time ever, some Americans would have their taxes withheld. All Federal employees, civil and military, with incomes over $600 per year, "including senators and representatives and [territorial] delegates in Congress," were to have 3 percent of their wages withheld by government paymasters. In the private sector, only dividends from stocks and bonds would be subjected to withholding.

Like most comprehensive tax measures, this act also provided the means by which the revenues were to be collected. Congress established as part of the Treasury Department an "Internal Revenue Bureau," to be overseen by a "Commissioner of Internal Revenue." George S. Boutwell, a prominent Massachusetts attorney, was appointed as the first head of the bureau, a bureau that would extend itself through a network of 185 district offices into almost every Union village, town, and city. Although Boutwell vacated the post in March 1863 to take a seat in the House of Representatives, beginning a distinguished national political career, the Internal Revenue Bureau under new leadership continued to grow in import and numbers. By the close of the war, it was the Treasury Department's largest agency, with 4,031 civilian employees.

Suffering the same fate as the income tax, most of the internal levies on goods and services, and on inheritances, were allowed to expire in the immediate postwar years. But the infrastructure created to collect the taxes—the office of the commissioner and the bureau—remained intact, clear acknowledgment that wartime revenue policies had set important precedents for the future.

"FINANCIER OF THE WAR"

During the course of America's fratricidal conflict, Northerners and Southerners alike could count themselves among the most heavily taxed peoples of the world. Yet those taxes were not as productive as their architects had anticipated. In the case of the Union, for instance, the total amount raised by internal revenues covered only 20 percent of the war's cost. Since lawmakers in Washington, fearful of the political backlash, had no desire to impose additional levies on their constituents, they came up with another approach to finance the struggle.

Rather than tax the people, why not borrow from them? Prior to the war, the government had raised modest amounts of money through the sale of bonds to bankers and investment houses both at home and abroad. Now it considered enlarging that sales base, by selling hundreds of millions of dollars of securities directly to the general public, even though the public consisted largely of small-scale farmers and businessmen without previous investment experience. It was purely experimental, with an undeniable potential for disaster, but there were some compelling reasons to give it a try.

To begin with, in the late summer of 1861, when Secretary of the Treasury Salmon P. Chase tried to sell long-term U.S. bonds to foreign investors, he met with little success. Most financial brokers abroad were far from convinced that the Union was going to come out ahead in this contest. Domestic bankers, especially in New York, shared a similar reluctance. While eventually America's financiers came around and advanced the funds for the first $50 million of war bonds, they were still plagued with reservations, anxious over the drain it would put on their gold reserves.

In view of this response within the financial communities, abroad and at home, Chase decided to appeal directly to the people. On September 1, 1861, the secretary issued a public statement calling upon private citizens to purchase three-year government bonds at 7.3 percent interest. To stimulate and facilitate sales of these bonds—or "seven-thirties," as they were called—the Treasury Department hired general subscription agents throughout the Union. Ultimately more than $30 million of this first offering was sold, but most revealing was the distribution of these sales. One hundred forty-seven agents were responsible for selling close to $25 million worth; however, one agent alone, Jay Cooke of Philadelphia, sold the remaining $5 million worth of securities.

Cooke was truly in a class by himself. The son of a prosperous Ohio attorney, he moved to Philadelphia in 1839 at age eighteen and over the next two decades established himself as one of the city's most prominent bankers. Once the war broke out, Cooke offered his personal services to Secretary Chase, of course expecting a "fair commission," but since he was a committed Unionist, "pay or no pay," as he confided to his brother, "I will do all I can to aid him."

At the very outset, Cooke recognized the advantages of selling bonds to average Americans. Small investors, he believed, would be more susceptible than institutional investors "to appeals to patriotism"; they "would not be so likely to resell their bonds at once and thus throw them on the market where they would interfere with new issues"; and by virtue of their numbers, small investors would offer the added advantage of "democratizing" the loan, which in turn would bind "the loyalty of many people to the cause of the North."

With these views to guide and inspire him, Cooke emerged as the Treasury Department's leading bond agent. After having sold $5 million worth of the "seven-thirties," the Philadelphia banker launched a far more ambitious campaign to sell "five-twenties," 6 percent bonds redeemable in not less than five nor more than twenty years. Between late 1862 and early 1864, Cooke and his agents sold more than $400 million of the "five-twenties." And then in early 1865, Cooke returned to selling the "seven-thirties," eventually wracking up a whopping $800 million in sales.

Critics, keeping a vigilant eye out for profiteering, complained that Cooke was making undue profits from these transactions. In the end, his firm made $4 million in commissions, which amounted to $1/3$ of 1 percent of his total sales, hardly an exorbitant figure, then or now.

In any case, Cooke was a master of public relations, a man who knew instinctively what would appeal to the common man. He plastered the Union with "hundreds of thousands of miscellaneous posters and handbills," and it was said that he made the bonds "stare in the face of the people in every household from Maine to California." Using newspapers as well, he wrote articles and advertisements explaining in clear terms the provisions of the bonds, always including a patriotic appeal to the cause. Nor did he ignore the competitive spirit of the American people, making certain that the total amount of bonds sold each day were reported in the newspapers, along with sales by regions, states, and municipalities, with occasional praise for those locales that purchased more than the ordinary.

A marketing genius, Cooke ordered his employees to establish nighttime agencies, advertised as "workingmen's savings banks," where coffee and doughnuts were served, and where "the mechanic, the peddler, the clerk, the sailor, and saloonkeeper" congregated to discuss and hopefully purchase the "seven-thirties." Even the boys in blue were targeted. Agents were sent to demobilization points to sell bonds to the soldiers as they received their mustering-out pay.

Cooke's efforts trumpeted a revolution in the public investment sector. It was the first time that more than a million Americans purchased government bonds to finance a war—predating the war-bond drives of the twentieth-century world wars.

All in all, it was a towering achievement. Cooke had appealed directly to the people, and they had responded in the affirmative. True, the majority of investors were still the wealthy, but there was no denying the broad-based nature of the constituency. "The history of the world," Secretary of the Treasury Chase reported proudly to Congress, "may be searched in vain for a parallel case of popular financial support to a national government." In four years the Union's citizenry had absorbed a Federal debt of over $2.5 billion—nearly half of which had been raised under Cooke's leadership. After the war was over, the *Philadelphia Press* reminded its readers of this fact when it said: "The nation owes a debt of gratitude to Jay Cooke that it cannot discharge. . . . Now that we have come out of the struggle successfully no one . . . will hesitate to place the financier of the war along side its great generals."

"GREENBACKS"

Before the Civil War the U.S. government did not issue paper money. The nation's money supply consisted of state bank notes—currency issued by privately owned, state-incorporated banks—and Federal specie, gold and silver coins in denominations ranging from half dollars, quarters, and dimes to smaller fractional amounts. Since all Federal transactions were required to be in "hard money," this meant that the government's ability to pay its debts was dependent upon how much gold and silver it had on hand. This was fiscally primitive, no doubt, yet not unworkable as long as the government's operations were on a small scale, as they were prior to the conflict. Take the fiscal year ending on June 30, 1861; annual Federal expenditures were only $67 million. But the following year, as the war got into full swing, the government spent $475 million, an increase of more than 700 percent.

Inevitably a crisis was in the making, and it erupted in late winter 1861. With the Union army having suffered a humiliating defeat the past summer at Bull Run, the prospects for an early victory looked increasingly remote. Then, in November, a clash with England over the seizure of two Confederate envoys from the British vessel the *Trent* threw financial markets at home and in Europe into chaos. Anxious investors stopped buying government securities, gold and silver were hoarded or sent out of the country, and specie reserves in state banks and in the U.S. treasury became seriously depleted. The State Department's defusing of the *Trent* dispute did little to allay the anxiety, and on December 30, 1861, all banks and the treasury suspended specie payments.

Suspension meant simply that the Federal government had no means to pay its debts; it had suffered a financial breakdown. As the bills began to mount and as the payroll—for soldiers and contractors— could not be met, it seemed as if the Confederacy might very well achieve a relatively bloodless triumph.

Congress was not about to allow that to happen. Early in January 1862, Elbridge G. Spaulding of New York, chairman of the House subcommittee to frame a national currency bill, introduced a measure calling for the issuance of paper money *not* redeemable in specie, but simply based on the faith of the U.S. government. Considered revolutionary, not only by hard-money advocates of the Democratic party but also by many Republicans, the proposal was debated intensely for more than a month.

Opponents declared that paper money was unconstitutional, arguing that the founding fathers empowered Congress to *coin* money, not print it. Others painted a dark picture, saying "prices will be inflated . . . incomes will depreciate; the savings of the poor will vanish." One banker with a more religious bent proclaimed that "gold and silver are the only true measure of value. These metals were prepared by the Almighty for this very purpose."

Rather than invoke the divine, however, most opponents simply pointed to the chaotic fiscal impact that "printing press" money was having on the enemy's economy. The South's paper currency was already beginning to spiral out of control, inflating prices and the cost of services, and was proving to be a major source of discontent on the Confederate home front. Was Congress willing to risk creating a similar situation for the Union?

Since the government was on the verge of bankruptcy, the Republican majority in Congress really had no choice. Congressman Spaulding warned his colleagues that without "at least $100,000,000 during the next three months," all government operations—military and civil—would cease. Secretary of the Treasury Chase, himself a staunch opponent of paper money, also pleaded on the grounds of necessity. *"Immediate action,"* he reported to Congress in early February, *"is of great importance. The Treasury is nearly empty."* Another hard-money man, William Pitt Fessenden of Maine, the chairman of the Senate finance committee, reluctantly joined the ranks of those who saw no way out. Even if paper money "encourages bad morality, both public and private," Fessenden argued, "to leave the government without resources in such a crisis is not to be thought of." Necessity, and necessity alone, therefore, drove most Republican members of Congress to vote in favor of the so-called Legal Tender Act. Approved by Lincoln on February 25, 1862, the measure created America's first national system of paper money not backed by specie.

The law authorized the secretary of the treasury to issue $150 million of the new currency. Popularly known as "greenbacks," because they were printed with a patented green ink, the notes were legal tender for all debts public and private, except in two cases: They could not be used to pay customs duties, nor could the government use them to pay interest to those investors who purchased government securities with specie. In all other financial matters, the greenbacks—printed in denominations of $5, $10, $20, $50, $100, $500, and $1,000—were an acceptable medium of exchange.

Within a matter of months, the paper money, put into circulation largely as payments to army contractors and soldiers, ran out. In July 1862 Congress authorized issuance of an additional $150 million and also lowered the minimum denomination from $5 to $1. A third and final increase was approved in 1863, so that by the close of the war, $431 million of the notes were in circulation.

The Union's paper money policy was never as disastrous as its opponents had predicted. To be sure, the greenbacks were partly to blame for wartime inflation, losing at one point as much as 65 percent of their value. But overall, the North's inflation rate of 80 percent was minuscule compared to the South's 9,000 percent and was actually less than America's 84 percent rate during World War I, and not that much higher than the 70 percent in World War II.

In any case, it would be unfair to blame greenbacks alone for the inflation. Since most of the war costs were raised by borrowing, interest rates had to remain attractive; inflation was inevitable. Perhaps most significant in the long run was that Congress, by authorizing the issuance of money based solely on the faith of the government, had taken a major step toward the modernization of currency policy in the United States.

A NATIONAL BANK SYSTEM

When war came in 1861, the United States did not have an efficient central banking system to handle such an unprecedented emergency. Instead of a unified system, there was a hodgepodge of some 1,600 privately owned banks scattered across the country. These state-chartered banks issued their own notes, which served as the nation's currency and were redeemable in specie from the issuing institution. But the value of these notes and whether or not they could be redeemed depended on the solvency—and honesty—of the institution of origin. Banks that were corrupt or poorly managed, many of which were located in the western states, would issue banknotes that might be—unknown to the customer—literally not worth the paper they were printed on. Reputable and more solvent banks, found mostly in the New England and Middle Atlantic states, issued paper money that was for the most part reliable and stable, yet even these notes were suspect in view of the chronic counterfeiting problem existing at the time. In Massachusetts alone, with 185 banks in operation, authorities found counterfeits on the notes of 174 of them.

The system cried out for reform, but there were too many people committed to its ideological underpinnings for change to come quickly or easily. Some three decades earlier, President Andrew Jackson had helped establish that ideological base. Backed by his Democratic supporters, Jackson had succeeded in divesting the Federal government from the banking system, arguing that a national bank such as had been in existence prior to 1836 was an aristocratic monopoly at odds with the egalitarian principles that founded the country.

Jackson's legacy probably would have prevented any movement toward a centralized banking system until late in the century, if not for the Civil War. The escalating cost of the conflict, the North's nonuniform and unreliable currency situation, and its chaotic banking structure propelled Secretary of the Treasury Chase to recommend an overhaul of the country's fiscal institutions. On February 25, 1863, in spite of the negative votes of 91 percent of the Democrats in Congress (a testament to the lingering influence of "Old Hickory"), Republicans were able to muster enough support to pass the National Banking Act—creating the first network of nationally chartered banks in the United States.

Amended in June 1864, the legislation required state banks wishing to obtain national charters to purchase U.S. bonds with at least a third of their capital and deposit those securities with the treasury. They would then have the authority to issue gold-backed national bank notes in an amount equal to 90 percent of the value of their bonds held by the government.

The beauty of this system was that it stimulated the sale of U.S. bonds at the same time that it stabilized the nation's currency. Since the national banknotes were secured by the bonds, no longer would there be fluctuations in their value. The notes, moreover, were printed by the government itself, so that instead of thousands of styles of engraving, there was now a single set of designs, easily recognizable and difficult to counterfeit.

State banks were encouraged to join the system; if they didn't, they were subjected to a 2 percent tax on their notes. But this carrot-and-stick approach won few converts. Preferring to remain independent, most bankers refused to participate. By October 1864, only 508, less than a third of the state-chartered banks in the Union, had become part of the system.

Faced with such resistance, passive though it was, Congress took action. In March 1865 the lawmakers increased the tax on state banknotes to 10 percent, which took out all the profit. Recognizing the inevitable, most of the hold-out banks applied for national charters, so that by the end of the year there were 1,294 national banks, with only 349 state banks still in existence.

Under tremendous pressure to conform, it seemed as if the state banks would not survive, but to the surprise of many fiscal insiders, they staged a comeback in the postwar era. Discouraged by the requirement to use a third of their capital to purchase U.S. bonds, more and more state-chartered banks, particularly in the West and South, chose to remain outside of the system. In 1873 there were 1,330 state banks, compared to 1,968 national banks, and less than twenty years later, state financial institutions actually outnumbered Federal ones. Thus by the early 1890s, America's Civil War banking structure was proving

unattractive and inadequate as the country was approaching the twentieth century. With a concentration of investment capital and national
bank notes in the hands of New England and New York bankers, and
with a majority of banks under no Federal regulatory control to speak
of, the National Bank System—in effect for half a century and having
served its purpose—was superseded by the Federal Reserve in 1913.

"IN GOD WE TRUST"

"In God We Trust" is a familiar inscription on U.S. coins and currency,
yet few are aware that its origin can be traced to the Civil War. Early in
the conflict, a number of Northerners, perhaps wanting to enlist the
Almighty on behalf of their cause, wrote to Secretary of the Treasury
Chase suggesting that a reference to God be inscribed on U.S. coinage.
A man of strong religious convictions, Chase liked the idea and sent a
letter to the director of the U.S. mint, James Pollock, asking him to
come up with a briefly worded motto expressing the belief that "no
nation can be strong except in the strength of God." At first Pollock proposed "God Our Trust," then "God and Our Country"; both were turned
down by the secretary. It took some time, almost two years, but finally
Pollock produced the slogan "In God We Trust." Officially adopted by
an act of Congress on April 22, 1864, the first U.S. coin ever to bear
that inscription was a two-cent bronze piece issued that same year.

   As drafted, the law did not make the motto mandatory for every
coin minted. Nearly a century passed before Congress, on July 11, 1955,
required that all coins and currency be engraved with the inscription "In
God We Trust."

DEPARTMENT OF AGRICULTURE

Until the late nineteenth century, agriculture was the backbone of the
Republic. The independent, self-sufficient farmer was held up as an
icon, a man to be exalted and praised. Yet paradoxically, official Washington had long neglected America's yeomen. Even President Thomas
Jefferson, who once said that farmers were the chosen people of God,
made no attempt to establish a national agricultural agency of any kind.
In Jefferson's case, political ideology—he was a firm advocate of limited central government—probably triumphed over personal sentiment.

   In any event, the first steps toward Federal involvement in agriculture were taken in 1836, when Congress established the U.S. Patent
Office. At first glance, it would seem that the granting of patents had

little to do with growing food, but by happy coincidence, the man chosen to head the office was Connecticut farmer Henry L. Ellsworth. An independent-minded New Englander, Ellsworth began distributing free seeds and plants under the postal franks of congressmen and also began publishing agricultural information and statistics. Not long afterward, Congress officially endorsed Ellsworth's initiatives, appropriating $1,000 for the Patent Office to continue its agricultural outreach programs. Over the next few years, as western farmers increased in numbers and became more active politically, their demands for Federal recognition could not be ignored. Responding to the pressure, in 1849 President Zachary Taylor recommended creation of an agricultural bureau, but it failed to attract the necessary support in Congress.

A decade later, in September 1859, an Illinois lawyer-politician named Abraham Lincoln, speaking before members of the Wisconsin State Agricultural Society, contributed to the farm bureau movement by presenting a strong case for the application of "book-learning" to agriculture. "No other human occupation," Lincoln maintained, "opens so wide a field for the profitable and agreeable combination of labor with cultivated thought, as agriculture." And with a succinct eloquence for which he would become well known during the war, the future president added, "Every blade of grass is a study; and to produce two, where there was but one, is both a profit and a pleasure." Lincoln knew what he was talking about, having grown up in a succession of hardscrabble farms in Kentucky and Indiana.

As chief executive, Lincoln was now in a position to implement his ideas. When Secretary of the Interior Caleb B. Smith recommended the establishment of a "Bureau of Agriculture and Statistics," the president endorsed the proposal vigorously. In his very first annual message to Congress on December 3, 1861, Lincoln noted that "agriculture, confessedly the largest interest of the nation, has not a department, nor a bureau." If the legislators saw fit to institute such an agency, the president explained, it would present annual reports on "the condition of our agriculture, commerce, and manufactures . . . a fund of information of great practical value to the country."

Congress responded in the affirmative. A majority of its members reasoned that if Northern farmers could be helped with scientific and statistical information, more grain could be exported to Europe in return for gold. And domestically the Union would also profit, since the population—and its armies—would be better fed. Spearheaded by the "Farmer Congressman" in the House, Owen Lovejoy of Illinois, and in the Senate by James F. Simmons of Rhode Island, a bill creating a Department of Agriculture was passed on May 10, 1862, and endorsed by Lincoln's signature five days later. The *Bureau County Republican,* a hometown newspaper from Lovejoy's district, recognized immediately the historical significance of the legislation, pointing out that Congress had established the first Federal agency devoted exclusively "to the interests of the man who cultivates the soil."

Although the department was not granted cabinet status, it was now independent of the Patent Office and headed by a commissioner of agriculture, paid an annual salary of $3,000. The post went to a man with the improbable name of Isaac Newton. A former Pennsylvania dairy farmer who had delivered milk to the White House and other prominent Washington residences (which he was not above using to his political advantage), Newton had been in charge of the agricultural bureau while it was part of the Patent Office. Soon after assuming the position of commissioner of agriculture, he was subjected to a barrage of criticism, with opponents arguing that his appointment was purely a political one since he lacked scientific credentials. The attacks were based on more than a kernel of truth, but Newton ignored them, compensating for his academic deficiencies by demonstrating strengths in more pragmatic areas. As chief administrator of the department, Newton was both innovative and daring, becoming the first head of a Federal civilian agency to hire scientific and technical personnel—a botanist, an entomologist, chemists, and statisticians.

The newly established department continued its previous practice of distributing seeds, but also expanded its activities, which now included tending a six-acre propagating garden, maintaining a museum, translating foreign publications, and performing a small amount of taxidermy and chemical work. Its most valuable function, however, was the issuance of monthly reports containing statistics on rainfall and temperature, the number of acres of crops under cultivation, average yields, market conditions, and export and import figures.

Despite what appeared to be an ambitious start, Newton failed to win over the nation's agricultural press or the leaders of the various farming societies. Considered ineffectual and "uneducated," the commissioner continued to suffer severe criticism but managed to remain in office until his death in 1867.

Modern historians have been more generous to Newton than his contemporaries. In his seminal study of agriculture and the Civil War, Paul Gates was of the opinion that Newton had left a positive mark on the department, emphasizing that "the new lines of statistical enquiry, experimentation, and scientific activity which he had fostered were continued and developed by his successors."

His successors would also enjoy greater prestige within the councils of government. In 1889 the department was elevated to cabinet status.

THE HOMESTEAD ACT

In the antebellum decades of the 1840s and 1850s, aside from slavery extension, no issue generated as much controversy in or out of Congress as did homestead legislation—the allocation of free land to western settlers. Opponents, largely Democrats, were firmly against handing over the public domain free of charge. Arguing along various lines, they insisted that it was unconstitutional; that free homesteads would drain off laborers from the eastern states; and that the government had no business surrendering a source of its revenue (at the time, land sales made up about 8 percent of the national income, the remainder provided by tariff duties). The strongest opposition, however, came from Southern Democrats, who visualized hordes of free-state yeomen settling in the West, isolating slavery more than ever until it could no longer survive.

Republicans were well aware that a homestead bill would advance their political agenda, but they were goaded on by other reasons as well, especially the desire to prevent further land speculation in the West. In the past the Federal government had sold large parcels of public domain to individual and corporate investors, who held the land off the market until there was widespread migration into the area, then sold the property for enormous profits. Free land in the West, Republicans believed, would go far to alleviating this problem, and besides, contrary to what their opponents argued, rather than siphon off eastern workers, a homestead law would strengthen the economies of the industrializing states by giving the unemployed urban poor a fresh start in the West. It was the "duty of Congress," advocates of free land declared, "to help the cities to disgorge their cellars and their garrets of a starving, haggard, and useless population."

On three separate occasions in the prewar era, the House had passed a homestead act, only to have it rejected each time by the Southern-dominated Senate. In 1860 the bill had finally won approval in both chambers but encountered the veto of Democratic president James Buchanan, who maintained that it was unconstitutional. Almost as if in response to Democratic policy, the Republicans included a homestead plank in their 1860 platform. The party's standard-bearer, Abraham

Lincoln, was a staunch advocate of the proposal, reaffirming after his victory that he favored "cutting up the wild lands into parcels, so that every poor man may have a home."

Congress would carry out the new president's wishes. With the secessionist Southern Democrats gone, leaving the Republicans in charge of both the House and Senate, it was not long before the details were ironed out and a homestead bill was sent to the president. Lincoln signed the measure on May 20, 1862—offering Americans, for the first time, the opportunity to obtain free lands in the West.

The Homestead Act granted ownership of 160 acres of public land to the head of a household who could claim five years' residency on the property. For those without adequate means, but with enough money to get them out West and settled, the legislation seemed too good to be true. New York *Daily Tribune* editor Horace Greeley, for one, exulted in the act, urging all to take advantage of it: "Young men! Poor men! Widows! resolve to have a home of your own."

Greeley's thundering advice was well intended, but his message was somewhat misleading. In the first place, the homestead land itself "was distinctly limited" in amount and locale. The 160 acres offered were simply not enough in many areas for successful farming, and much of the land available was in the drought-ridden central prairies. Furthermore, the measure contained enough loopholes to allow for massive speculation, in many cases leading to outright corruption.

Yet in spite of these shortcomings, the Homestead Act fulfilled much of its framers' expectations. Even before the war came to an end, some 25,000 families settled on more than 3 million acres. Ultimately 500,000 heads of farm households would lay claim to 80 million acres of homestead land in the West. As for the law itself, it remains in effect and is still being used.

HIGHER EDUCATION

Most Americans have long held an ambivalent attitude toward formal education. On the one hand, they have always been anti-intellectual, wary and suspicious of those with higher learning, yet on the other hand they have consistently supported programs to advance education. As early as 1785, the Articles of Confederation Congress passed a land ordinance that reserved one section of each township in the Northwest territory for public schools. In 1850, at the time of California's admission, two sections were set aside, and by the early twentieth century, the allocation was increased to four. The peoples' representatives were also generous when it came to higher education. In 1803, beginning with Ohio's entry into the Union, two entire townships—some 46,000 acres of Federal land—were granted to each new state for establishing a university.

For those states that had entered the Union prior to 1803, however, there was no Federal assistance for institutions of higher learning. Of course, most of those states, particularly the original thirteen, had prestigious private schools. But beginning in the mid-nineteenth century, America's colleges were being asked to include in their curriculum agricultural course work as well as mechanical training for the "industrial classes." Without Federal support for these areas of study, the pre-1803 states were clearly at a disadvantage compared with the newer ones.

In the decade before the Civil War, Representative Justin S. Morrill of Vermont emerged as the acknowledged spokesman for a uniform system of Federal aid to higher education. A self-made man who had not gone to college but keenly appreciated its advantages, Morrill pressured his colleagues to support tuition-free agricultural and mechanical colleges where the average citizen—the farmer and the laborer—could become better educated and by extension become better citizens.

Similar to previous educational enactments, Morrill's proposed bill called for the use of proceeds from the sale of Federal lands in the West to finance the construction of these colleges. It was innocuous perhaps on the surface, but the measure had more opposition than support, and Congress voted it down when it was first introduced in 1856. Demanding a second vote in 1858, the Vermont congressman was now backed by the influential United States Agricultural Society. His two major adversaries—states' rights Southerners as well as Westerners who believed that the public lands in their states should benefit only them—continued to mount a vigorous opposition, and they almost succeeded a second time. By the narrowest of margins, the bill squeaked by both houses of Congress. All to no avail; in 1859 pro-Southern president James Buchanan vetoed the measure (for the same reason that he would veto the Homestead Act a year later), claiming that lawmakers had gone beyond their constitutional powers.

Reintroducing his bill in December 1861, this time Morrill anticipated a different outcome, given the absence of Southern obstructionists in Congress and a more receptive president in the White House. But he still had to contend with Westerners who felt it unfair to use the lands within their states to finance eastern colleges, and he also had to confront a bias against agricultural education, derisively referred to as "book-farming"—a classic case of American anti-intellectualism.

Critics of "book-farming," for example, argued that farmers had no need of formal training; what they needed was hands-on experience. Countering with a forceful dissent, Morrill maintained that education would improve the quality of life on the farm, result in more efficiency, and inevitably create more wealth for the community and the nation. How could it be otherwise? "Science, working unobtrusively," he emphasized, "produces larger annual returns and constantly increases fixed capital, while ignorant routine produces exactly the reverse."

With the war raging, Morrill made his bill even more attractive by including military training as part of the curriculum of these schools. Congress passed the measure in late June 1862, and Lincoln signed it into law on July 1.

The Land Grant College Act—also known, and deservedly so, as the Morrill Act—was America's first program of Federal aid to higher education for every state in the Union (including future states and those temporarily out of the Union). It provided to each state 30,000 acres of public land for each senator and representative it had in Congress. The proceeds from the sale of this land would support colleges "to teach such branches of learning as are related to agricultural and the mechanical arts" as well as "military tactics," but not at the exclusion of scientific and classical studies.

The New York *Daily Tribune*'s nationally prominent editor Horace Greeley, with his usual foresight, was quick to see the overwhelming significance of this measure. Although most of the press took little notice of the legislation, Greeley saw in it a "wide and lasting good."

Its impact would indeed be profound. The Land Grant College Act, as one modern scholar has written, marked "a major shift in the structure of American education." No longer would it be "largely classical in curriculum, church-related, and privately supported." Justin Morrill's measure signaled the beginning of a new system that would educate farmers and members of the "industrial classes," while providing "equality of access to higher learning, and acceptance of public responsibility for maintaining the colleges."

In terms of implementation, the act gave the states considerable latitude. They could use their newfound wealth either to enrich existing institutions of higher learning (as long as they incorporated the new curriculum) or to build new colleges. For the most part, the eastern states gave their bounty to schools already in operation. Massachusetts divided its money between MIT and Amherst Agricultural College (now the University of Massachusetts); Rhode Island gave its funds to Brown; Connecticut to Yale; New York to Cornell; New Jersey to Rutgers. In the West, where there were fewer established universities, new ones were created—the Universities of Illinois, Wisconsin, Minnesota, Nevada, and California, to name but a few. And after the Southern states returned, A&M colleges sprang up throughout most of the former Confederacy. All told, sixty-nine institutions of higher learning, in one way or another, benefited from an act sponsored by a Vermont blacksmith's son who had never attended college.

THE TRANSCONTINENTAL RAILROAD

As early as the 1840s, Americans considered the possibility of constructing a transcontinental railroad. But it was not until 1850, when California joined the Union, that the idea gained fresh impetus, even a sense of urgency. California was rich in gold and other resources, and its Pacific ports held great promise as gateways to the wealth of Asia. As a transcontinental power, moreover, there was also a need for the United States to reevaluate logistically its military position. In case of foreign war, a rail line would prove the most expeditious way to move men and supplies to protect America's interests on the Pacific coast. The alternatives, if one could call them that, were highly impractical.

The 17,000-mile sea journey around South America was long and hazardous, taking about 5 months, depending on the type of vessel and the weather conditions. The famed clipper ship *Flying Cloud* managed a record-breaking passage of eighty-nine days, twenty-one hours in 1851, but most ships were far slower. If anything, the overland journey by horse or wagon was even more hazardous. There were deserts and mountains to cross, and the fear of Indian attacks was ever present, though in the 1850s quite rare. Death was more likely from thirst, fatigue, and most especially from disease, with maladies like cholera decimating whole wagon trains. Going west by land was often hot, dusty, and dirty in the summer, bitterly cold in late autumn. If the immigrants did not cross the Sierra Mountains before the coming of winter, they might become trapped in snowdrifts and perish from hunger.

Safer and faster than all other modes of transportation, the railroad, most Americans believed, could best conquer the nearly 2,000 miles of inhospitable wilderness separating California from its sister states. This explains why, at least in theory, the concept of a transcontinental railroad enjoyed bipartisan and biregional support, but its implementation was another story. With sectional differences between North and South becoming more pronounced in the 1850s, it was getting to the point where even the most benign of measures became entangled in increasingly bitter debate.

Would the railroad be constructed along a Northern or Southern route? Which city—New Orleans, St. Louis, Memphis, or Chicago— would be selected as its eastern terminus? And would government or private funds, or both sources of capital, be used to finance the project? Most Democrats were convinced that the Federal government had no constitutional authority to involve itself fiscally in this matter; Republicans held an opposite view, declaring that public appropriations for internal improvements of this kind were "authorized by the constitution, and justified by the obligation of the Government to protect the lives and property of its citizens."

The debate came to an abrupt (and for the Republicans, a favorable) conclusion in the wake of the secession crisis of 1860–61. After eleven Southern states bolted the Union, there was no longer any significant opposition in Congress to a Federally subsidized Northern-based rail route to the Pacific. In mid-June 1862 the lawmakers passed the Pacific Railroad Act, and it was approved by the president on July 1. Given the immenseness of the task, not one but two private companies were authorized to build the railroad. The Central Pacific (later called the Southern Pacific) would start from San Francisco Bay and proceed eastward; the Union Pacific would begin construction westward from Omaha. Both companies were awarded rights of way, the right to take timber and stone from public domain, plus grants of ten alternate sections of public lands per mile of track laid—that is, sections alternating to the left and right of the tracks in "checkerboard" fashion—altogether totaling 6,400 acres for each mile of road built. The act also permitted loans to the Central Pacific and Union Pacific in the form of bonds, $16,000 per mile of track across the low level plains, $32,000 in in-between areas, and $48,000 across the mountains, where construction would be the most difficult. And finally, the railroads were allowed to sell 100,000 shares of stock to raise additional capital for construction.

A railroad to the Pacific had enormous potential, but because of the risks involved in its financing and construction, private investors were slow to buy in to the venture. Many were of the opinion that despite the generosity of the government, the project was still not adequately funded; that the road itself, running through hundreds of miles of barren areas inhabited by Indians, would take decades before generating a profit; and since the government held the first mortgage, if the companies failed, private investors would have to wait until Federal claims were settled.

Determined to see the project through, in July 1864 Congress passed an amended Pacific Railroad Act. The land grants were doubled, the stock offerings were increased to 1 million shares, and government security was reduced to second mortgage status. Encouraged by the new provisions, investors poured money into both companies. The overall success of the transcontinental railroad was all but virtually assured, though there were still some difficult times ahead. The crossing of the Sierra Nevada was a major engineering challenge for the Central Pacific, and Sioux and Cheyenne attacks harassed the Union Pacific. Nevertheless, in May 1869, the project was finally completed. The Union Pacific had laid more than 1,000 miles of track, the Central Pacific around 700, before they linked up in Promontory, Utah, establishing the first transcontinental railroad in the United States.

The railroad's impact was both dramatic and far-reaching. A solid link was made to California and its wealth, and a potential link was made to a developing Asian market via the port of San Francisco. If you put aside American Indian land claims, the Great Plains region was also a major beneficiary, with its towns and farming communities cropping up along the tracks, nurtured and sustained by the railroads that gave them birth.

Whatever its positive impact, the Pacific railroad was hardly free of criticism. The financial machinations of investors in later years, and the monopolistic practices of the railroad companies involved, would cast a dark shadow over the industry. But there was no denying that the Civil War Congressmen who shaped the transcontinental railroad legislation had fulfilled their original mission, as expressed in the measure itself: to "strengthen the bonds of union between the Atlantic and Pacific coasts."

ENCOURAGING IMMIGRATION

As hundreds of thousands of men and boys from farms, towns, and cities enlisted or were drafted for military service, the Union, unlike the Confederacy with its large slave population, experienced severe labor shortages on the home front. Rallying to the cause, Northern women filled some of the shortfall, particularly in the fields; yet existing social conventions would not allow them to work in the mines or do heavy industrial labor. In normal times some, if not all, of the slack would have been taken up by immigrants, but ever since the bombardment of Fort Sumter, immigration was down. Fearful of being conscripted into military service once on American shores, foreigners were reluctant to come. Who, then, was going to grow the crops to feed the swelling armies, work the mines to supply industry with the necessary resources, and make the guns to arm the troops?

Many urged the government to do something to stimulate immigration. One of the country's most eminent economists, Henry Charles Carey, lobbied strenuously for more newcomers. "Every man imported is a machine that represents capital of at least $1,000," he wrote to Secretary of the Treasury Chase. "Half a million men are worth more than $500,000,000—*more than the total cost of a year of war.*"

Although Lincoln was not comfortable placing a dollar figure on the value of men, declaring instead that men are "better than gold," he was essentially in agreement with Carey. In his annual address to Congress on December 8, 1863, the president called for "establishing a system for the encouragement of immigration." Here, at home, he pointed out, there "is still a great deficiency of laborers in every field of industry, especially in agriculture and in our mines." Yet at the same time, "tens of thousands of persons . . . are thronging our foreign consulates, and offering to emigrate to the United States if essential, but very cheap, assistance can be afforded them."

Congress got the message. In early July 1864 it passed a law entitled "An Act to Encourage Immigration." In exchange for payment by an employer of the immigrant's travel expenses to the United States, the measure stipulated that the newcomer would be obliged to work for that employer and surrender no more than a year's future wages to pay off the incurred debt. To oversee all labor contracts, the office of commissioner of immigration was created, and to guarantee that the new arrivals would have transportation to their job sites, the position of superintendent of immigration was also established. And lastly, immigrants were assured by the legislation that as long as they did not declare their intention to become citizens, they would be draft exempt.

The Contract Labor Law, as it was more commonly known, was the first attempt by the U.S. government to manage immigration. A well-intended gesture, perhaps, but it simply did not go far enough to ensure success. Without providing for Federally assisted travel fees, the act proved unworkable, since most employers found it too expensive. Repealed in 1868, the government returned to its nonactivist position, refusing to involve itself in immigration on any major level until the 1920s.

POSTAL SERVICE REFORM

The Civil War was the first conflict in history to be fought between two literate mass armies. More than 90 percent of white Union soldiers and more than 80 percent of Confederate soldiers could read and write.

Away from their loved ones in most cases for the first time, it was only natural that these fighting men (a total of about 2 million serving the North and nearly 1 million in arms for the South) would take every opportunity to write letters home. Given their numbers and the high rate of literacy, the sheer volume of their correspondence was mind-boggling. A representative of the U.S. Christian Commission, a soldiers' aid organization, reported that in some of the 1,000-man Union regiments he visited, an average of 600 letters were posted daily. With the war in full swing, it was estimated that a total of 45,000 pieces of correspondence were sent each day through Washington from the Union soldiers in the eastern theater, and *double* that number were mailed through Louisville, Kentucky, from Federal troops in the West.

Based on Northern postal records, it seems that equal numbers of letters were also received. For men on the front, except for survival itself, nothing was more important than hearing from family and friends. "Often a cheer would go up when the postman, with mail bags slung across his horse, came in sight," a sergeant in the Army of the Potomac recalled. Nor did it matter if the correspondents just scribbled a few words or so. According to an Indiana corporal, "A little token from home no difference how small" was all that was necessary to bring joy to those in the ranks. Writing from Memphis in December 1862, another Union soldier observed that after returning from a month of reconnaissance missions, mail call had a very calming effect on the men. "All the men will have letters and papers from mothers, wives, sisters, and friends; and there is a change immediately. A great quiet-ness falls on the men; they become subdued and gentle in manner; there is a cessation of vulgarity and profanity, and an indescribable softening and tenderness is *felt*."

In order for the U.S. post office to process the more than 8 million pieces of military-related mail sent each month, in addition to its non-military correspondence, Congress instituted an unprecedented series of postal reforms. Here, again, Southern secession served as a catalyst for the modernization of yet another aspect of Northern society. Prior to the war, the post office had suffered from soaring deficits ($7 million by 1859). Once the Confederacy was created, the Post Office Department suspended hundreds of nonproductive mail routes throughout the South, so that by 1863 the deficit was wiped out, leaving available capital for postal innovations. It could not have come at a better time, in view of the wartime demands made on the department.

On July 1, 1863, the day the battle of Gettysburg began, the U.S. post office instituted for the first time ever free delivery of mail. Before this policy change, patrons had the option of either paying to have their mail delivered or going to a central office in their community to pick it up. Now mail would be delivered free, beginning first in the forty-nine largest cities in the Union, and if successful, it would be introduced to other parts of the country. The backbone of the program were the letter carriers themselves, who walked approximately twenty-two miles on their routes each day, seven days a week, fifty-two weeks a year, and were paid an annual average wage of $670. Within three years the free city delivery idea proved workable and profitable, producing ten times more in revenue than it cost and leading ultimately to its implementation throughout the nation.

In the same year that Congress provided for free delivery of mail in America's urban centers, it also took action to eliminate distance as a determinant of postage fees. The cost of mailing a letter was 3 cents in most parts of the country, except when sending correspondence to the far West, say to California, which required a postage of 10 cents. In 1863 lawmakers in Washington established for the first time a standard postage rate (3 cents) for sending a letter anywhere in the country.

The enormous volume of mail generated by the war resulted in yet another major innovation in postal service. On March 25, 1864, Congress authorized a railway mail service, whereby clerks would sort the mail aboard specially fitted trains en route between cities, thus preparing it for delivery the moment it arrived. Previously, the railroad, like its predecessor the stagecoach, simply delivered the mail "raw," but under this new arrangement, as much as twenty-four hours was cut from the delivery time.

The postal money order was also spawned by the Civil War. For years businessmen had clamored for a safer way to transmit money through the mails, and now the demand took on a new urgency as more and more money was sent from and to soldiers in the field. On May 17, 1864, Congress enacted legislation instituting a postal money order system. For a small fee patrons could forward a draft or money order (up to $30, soon raised to $50) safely and conveniently through the mail, without actually putting cash in the envelope. The procedure, which was already in use by banks and express companies, was an almost instantaneous success. In its very first year of existence, 419 post offices issued a total of $1,360,122 in money orders, a hefty sum for that period.

In 1910 Emerson D. Fite, one of the pioneer historians of the period, wrote, "It is doubtful if so many valuable reforms in the postal service have ever been achieved in any other administration in the whole history of the nation." At the time Fite arrived at his conclusion, it was an entirely valid one. No one could fault him for not anticipating the major impact that airmail would have on postal delivery, or the great success experienced by the highly innovative and competitive U.S. Postal Service of today—both of which, incidentally, are lineal descendants of what Fite called the "valuable reforms" of the Civil War era.

ANTIOBSCENITY LEGISLATION

Americans have always had access to pornographic books and pictures, but until the mid-1840s, this material was largely imported from Europe rather than homegrown. All of this would change with the immigration to the United States of an Irish surgeon, one William Haynes, regarded by some as the founding father of American pornography. Arriving in New York City in 1846, Haynes published a reprint of the eighteenth-century novel *Fanny Hill,* the bawdy and graphic "memoirs" of a prostitute. He then reinvested the money he had made in that venture, producing a number of "cheap erotic novels." During the 1850s the industry took off, with sexually explicit and not-so-explicit (perhaps best described as "titillating") literature readily available at railroad stations, steamboat docks, and hotels and inns. By the end of the decade, pornographic photographs began to make their appearance as well—adding further to the general public's concern over this "Satanic Literature."

Once the Civil War broke out, a new and even larger market for pornography appeared almost overnight. Apart from their families and communities, living in an all-male environment, and facing unknown danger, hundreds of thousands of soldiers were an easy mark for the purveyors of "licentious" prints and literature. Whatever taboos might have repelled most of these teenage boys and men from viewing or reading this material in the past seemed no longer relevant under their current circumstances. One Union infantry officer admitted that "obscene prints and photographs" were "quite commonly kept and exhibited by soldiers and even officers." The same was true in the case of reading material, with William Haynes's books in particular considered "barracks favorites."

The relatively low cost and ease in obtaining such materials contributed to their widespread appeal. For only 12 cents apiece the men could purchase through the mails twelve-by-fifteen-inch prints, depicting, for instance, groups of young women, naked or seminaked, in "interesting frolic" and conveying the impression that they cared not whether they were being observed. And if the men in blue wished to pay a bit more, for $3 a dozen they could receive postage-paid, calling-card-size photos of "London and Paris voluptuaries," revealing "the mysteries and delights of naked female beauty, male and female together and separate." Pornographic books were also reasonably priced and available by mail order. A catalog published by G. S. Hoskins and Company of New York City listed twenty-three books, nine of which cost only 50 cents, including titles such as *Venus in Cloister, The Marriage Bed, Secret Passions,* and *Physiology of Love.*

Horrified by how widespread pornography was among the men in the ranks, those in authority, military and civilian, took matters into their own hands. In June 1863 Marsena Patrick, the provost marshal general of the Army of the Potomac, burnt "a large quantity of obscene books, taken from the mails." Another officer, Capt. M. G. Tousley, wrote directly to President Lincoln, informing him of the problem and sending along as evidence a brochure from the mails advertising "New Pictures for Bachelors." Civilian officials also took action. The War Department's chief detective, Lafayette Baker, confiscated large amounts of pornographic material. But the one government official who brought matters to a head was Postmaster General Montgomery Blair. Reporting to Congress that "great numbers" of "obscene books and pictures" were being sent to the men in uniform, Blair called for legislation to prohibit the transmission of this material through the mails.

In early 1865 Congress dealt with the postmaster general's request, but from the outset, it was apparent that the lawmakers had little if any understanding of the complexity of antiobscenity legislation. The debate in the Senate was brief and involved few of its members, and in the House there was no debate at all. Although some concern was expressed in the Senate about giving too much power to postmasters, there was absolutely no indication that anyone thought it was necessary to define "obscenity" or to explain the difference between licit and illicit sexual expression.

As for the power of the postmasters, it was agreed that they would be allowed to ban the "offensive" material, as long as they did not tamper with the envelope or break the seal. Since "many of these publications" were "sent all over the country from the City of New York with the names of the parties sending them on the backs [of the envelopes]," it was felt that postal officials would not encounter much difficulty carrying out their duties.

On March 3, 1865, for the first time in U.S. history, Congress approved a law prohibiting the mailing of obscene material. Specifically, the measure stated "that no obscene book, pamphlet, picture, print, or other publication of a vulgar and indecent character shall be admitted into the mails of the United States." It went on to say that any person or persons who intentionally mailed such materials could be guilty of a misdemeanor and, if convicted, would receive a $500 fine or a year in prison, or both.

If the intent of the law, enacted in March 1865, was to target the U.S. military, it was of questionable value, as the war would be over in a month or so. But its long-range impact was another matter. Supplanted by a new piece of antiobscenity legislation in 1873, the coverage was broadened to include the prohibition of mailing sexual devices (contraceptives and abortion aids, among other things) "designed" for "immoral use." Additional revisions followed, but the intent of the original law passed by Congress during the Civil War remained in effect in one form or another until the 1950s, when the courts began to question the constitutionality of such legislation.

YOSEMITE

Through the spring and summer of 1864, Union armies engaged in some of the bloodiest and longest fighting of the war. The Wilderness, Spotsylvania Court House, and Cold Harbor were fought one after the other in Virginia, while in the Deep South, Sherman launched his Atlanta campaign, followed by his destructive "March to the Sea." At the very same time that the American landscape was being disfigured beyond recognition and drenched in blood, a piece of legislation of supreme irony was winding its way through the halls of Congress. Introduced by Sen. John Conness of California, the bill called for the Federal government to grant to California some 20,000 acres of land known as the Yosemite Valley and the nearby Mariposa Big Tree Grove. Located in the Sierra Nevada range in the east-central portion of the state, the land would be handed over to California "upon the express condition that the premises shall be held for public use, resort, and recreation, and shall be inalienable for all time." It's doubtful whether the lawmakers who passed the legislation or President Lincoln, who signed it in late June 1864, understood its profound environmental implications for the future. But whether they realized it or not, their actions were truly unprecedented; for the first time in history, a government set aside a large scenic and natural area for the recreational purposes of its citizenry.

A number of dedicated individuals were responsible for the establishment of Yosemite Park, but if any one person can claim credit as the driving force, that would have to be Frederick Law Olmsted. A writer, editor, and landscape architect, Olmsted was the principal designer of New York's Central Park during the late 1850s. After the war broke out, unable to serve in the military because of a badly crippled leg, Olmsted became general secretary of the U.S. Sanitary Commission, the largest of the privately administered soldiers' aid organizations. Dedicating a good deal of his time and energy, he served the commission until the spring of 1863, when he became involved in an internal administrative dispute, causing him to leave and accept a position in California as superintendent of Gen. John C. Frémont's estates in Mariposa County. Not far from Yosemite, Olmsted first visited the valley in November 1863 and was not all that impressed. As an Easterner, he was not used to the dryness of California's summer and early fall, with its sparse vegetation and overly rugged-looking terrain. But after a year's residence, Olmsted was captivated by the valley's genuine beauty, referring to it as "the greatest glory of nature."

Determined to convert the Yosemite Valley into a state park, Olmsted was fortunate to have articulate and influential allies. Thomas Starr King, a Unitarian minister from New England transferred by his church to California, wrote popular articles on the park idea for an Eastern newspaper; Jessica Benton Frémont, wife of the general and a vigorous advocate for Western expansion, used her connections and capable talents in behalf of the movement; Josiah Dwight Whitney, chemist and geologist (Mount Whitney was later named after him), lobbied for the project; and finally, businessmen of every stripe, including those in railroads, steamships, and road-building, served as boosters for the park, hoping that it would encourage settlement and tourism.

Whatever their motives, their combined efforts persuaded Congress to create the nation's first natural preserve and entrust its management to California. If for any reason the Golden State did not measure up to the task, a proviso was included in the legislation allowing the Federal government to take over at any time.

During its first decade as a state park, Yosemite's well-advertised snow-capped mountains, spectacular waterfalls, giant sequoia redwoods, and abundant wildlife attracted visitors from all over the country. New England author and philosopher Ralph Waldo Emerson himself, though in his sixty-seventh year, took a trip across the continent to see Yosemite. Others—naturalists, writers, artists, photographers, geologists, botanists, even a few political leaders—traveled thousands of miles to witness what Emerson called the "grandeur of these mountains perhaps unmatched on the globe; for here they strip themselves like athletes for exhibition and stand perpendicular . . . showing their entire height and wearing a liberty cap of snow on the head."

For the first ten years or so of its stewardship, California demonstrated through various state-funded studies and commissions that it was determined to succeed in the management of the park. But by the late 1870s, with lumbering interests poaching on the land, ranchers allowing their livestock to roam freely in the region, and farmers setting up homesteads in violation of the preserve, the state was failing to fulfill its mission. The pioneer naturalist John Muir organized a campaign to save Yosemite. Though it would take decades, Muir rallied the support of conservationists in both the East and West, and in 1906 managed to get Congress to reclaim Yosemite and make it part of the National Park System—a system, modern historians maintain, that owed its "point of departure" to the Yosemite Act of 1864.

THE FREEDMEN'S BUREAU

When the war began, the preservation of the Union, not the abolition of slavery, was the chief objective of the Lincoln administration. On a personal level, the president was firmly opposed to slavery, but from a public standpoint, he recognized the need to proceed cautiously on the matter, otherwise the loyal slaveholding border states such as Kentucky and Missouri might join the Confederacy. In late August 1861, when Gen. John C. Frémont issued an order freeing slaves of all citizens in Missouri who actively supported the Rebels, Lincoln asked him to rescind the decree, explaining that his emancipatory action would "alarm our Southern Union friends, and turn them against us."

Officially, then, the Lincoln administration went on record against any outright attempts to eradicate slavery. But that did not exclude indirect assaults on the institution. As early as May 1861, Gen. Benjamin F. Butler, commanding Fortress Monroe in Virginia, declared that runaway slaves entering his lines would be considered "contraband" of war and would not be returned to their masters. By law, the fugitives were property, and therefore the general believed that he had the authority to confiscate all possessions belonging to the enemy that might be used against the United States. Lincoln discussed the matter with his cabinet, and while he was uneasy over Butler's action, in the end he allowed it to stand. Henceforth, all slaves who sought Federal protection, or lived in areas taken over by the Union army, were to be recognized as spoils of war.

Soon after the policy became known, African-Americans, first in small groups, then by the hundreds, and eventually by the thousands, deserted the plantations and made their way to Union lines. Masters had long claimed that their slaves were happy in bondage, but most, when given the opportunity, had demonstrated by "voting with their feet" that such an assertion was a self-serving lie. By war's end, it is estimated that half of the Confederacy's nearly 4 million slaves in one way or another, as a consequence of Northern military operations, had become "contrabands."

Once in Union-held territory, many ex-slaves—men and women—served the U.S. Army in a variety of capacities, such as guides, scouts, cooks, laundresses, teamsters, stevedores, carpenters, blacksmiths, nurses, hospital orderlies, grave diggers, and the like. After the Emancipation Proclamation was issued on January 1, 1863, tens of thousands were also recruited as soldiers. But the army was neither willing nor able to absorb all of the refugees, many of whom were women and children, the aged and infirm. With nowhere to go, many former slaves found themselves in makeshift communities called "contraband camps," supported in large part by Northern freedmen's aid societies. Operating out of Boston, New York, Philadelphia, and Cincinnati, these philanthropic groups sent money, clothing, and books, along with teachers and missionaries. The effort was noble and generous, but it fell far short, lacking effective coordination and adequate resources. Under pressure to help these groups, in 1863 the War Department created the American Freedmen's Inquiry Commission, a three-man team that would investigate conditions in the Union-occupied South and suggest how to deal with the burgeoning emancipated black population. Shocked by what they had encountered, the commission reported that neglect and disease were responsible for the death of one-fourth of the African-Americans herded into the contraband camps. Unless the Federal government intervened, the investigators warned, half of the freedmen were "doomed to die in the process of freeing the rest."

Despite these dire predictions, it would take more than a year before the government finally agreed upon a plan. In March 1865, with the collapse of the Confederacy in sight, Congress approved a bill establishing in the War Department a Bureau of Refugees, Freedmen, and Abandoned Lands—the first Federal welfare agency in American history. More commonly known as the Freedmen's Bureau, its job was to provide food, clothing, fuel, and medical care to the former slaves (and destitute whites) in the war-torn South. It also was responsible for reuniting black families separated in slavery, seeking employment and overseeing labor contracts for the freedmen, and most importantly, providing for their education.

In view of its unprecedented mission, almost immediately the bureau came under severe attack. Ex-Confederates, quite naturally, led the charge, calling the agency an "engine of mischief" and regarding it as "virtually a foreign government forced upon them and supported by an army of occupation." Unexpectedly, Northerners joined in the criticism. Some argued that the bureau had the potential to foster idleness and promote pauperism, and by coddling blacks it might create a permanent dependent class in America. Even those who championed the cause of the African-American, particularly radical Republicans, had reservations, fearful that the bureau would steer a conservative course. Rather than provide the black man with confiscated Rebel land, they believed, it would uphold the South's plantation system and its labor organization, thereby preventing any real economic or social advancement for the former slave.

Were any of these criticisms justified? Did the South, for example, have cause for alarm? On the contrary, the bureau actually helped the states of the former Confederacy recover from the war's devastation, by promoting a stable labor situation in which ex-slaves were encouraged to return to the fields, convinced by agency officials that they had negotiated fair contracts. As for the accusation that African-Americans would become wards of the state, several observers pointed out that in many communities of the South former slaves showed a greater willingness than whites to care for their own, and that more whites than blacks were in need of assistance. And in response to the criticism that the bureau was not committed to the transformation of Southern economic institutions (namely, land reform on behalf of African-Americans), it is essential to note that there was little, if any, public sympathy in behalf of such change. Aside from the radicals, the vast majority of Republicans, and almost all Democrats, did not support the confiscation of land and its redistribution to the freedmen, which, many whites believed, was far too extreme, unconstitutional, and might, by rapidly elevating blacks, encourage their exodus northward.

What, then, did the Freedmen's Bureau accomplish? If one bears in mind that it was established only as a temporary agency, to exist during the remainder of the war and one year thereafter, that it was grossly underfunded, and that it never was adequately staffed (at its height, it had no more than 900 agents to serve millions of people), it is remarkable that the bureau achieved as much as it did. Under the able leadership of Gen. Oliver Otis Howard, during the seven years it existed (Congress had granted it several extensions), the bureau provided some 20 million rations, each ration consisting of a week's supply of corn-meal, flour, and sugar; established more than fifty hospitals; granted medical care to a million people; and negotiated several hundred thou-sand labor contracts. Its greatest impact, however, was in the area of education. The bureau spent a total of $5.3 million on more than 4,300 schools. In 1870 alone there were close to a quarter of a million South-ern black students in day and night educational institutions. Equally as impressive were the start-up costs and administrative help that the agency extended to Fisk, Atlanta, and Howard Universities. By the time the Freedmen's Bureau closed its doors in 1872, opportunities for African-American children in the South to receive at least a rudimen-tary education, and some even to attend a university, unthinkable less than a decade before, were now reality.

CHAPTER 12

The First Family

A braham Lincoln and Mary Todd were an unlikely pair, he a rough-hewn, self-educated frontier lawyer, she a well-bred Southern belle from a prominent Kentucky family. The exact nature of their relationship is difficult to pin down. Relatives, friends, political associates, and historians all have offered opinions, many differing widely, though on one point there seems to be a consensus. No two people were more dissimilar, at least on the surface, than the sixteenth president of the United States and his wife.

There's no question that the Lincolns were a study of opposites, not only in background, but in temperament as well. Mary Lincoln was, or could be, charming and vivacious, the perfect hostess in an era when such things were a large part of what society expected of a woman. On the other hand, she was emotionally unpredictable, given to outbursts of shrewish temper. By contrast, Lincoln was easygoing and informal, but he also had a dark side, suffering from bouts of depression, sometimes severe, which he called "the hypo."

In addition to social class and personality, the Lincolns were worlds apart in terms of sheer physical appearance. He was thin; she was plump, if not fat. Given the president's unusual height of six feet, four inches, and Mrs. Lincoln being just five feet, two inches, the difference in appearance between them was further exaggerated. It was typical of Lincoln that he often spoke in jest of their physical disparity, saying he was the long and she was the short of it.

When Lincoln met Mary Todd in 1839, he was a young lawyer and member of the Illinois state legislature. Mary was in Springfield visiting with her sister and brother-in-law, Elizabeth and Ninian Edwards. Lincoln and the twenty-one-year-old Kentucky socialite began courting, though it is said that the Edwardses disapproved of the potential match. After all, Mary's father was a wealthy banker, socially well connected, and a friend and close political ally of the great Henry Clay. Lincoln was only a few years removed from the backwoods. True, he was an intelligent fellow obviously on the rise, but it was also apparent that he sprang from the "lower orders." Why, even his speech was heavily flavored with a rural Indiana frontier accent—that is, when the socially taciturn Lincoln spoke at all.

Regardless of the family's reservations, the couple were engaged, then suddenly the engagement was broken off for reasons that are still not entirely clear. But eventually there was a reconciliation, and Lincoln and Mary became husband and wife on November 4, 1842. They moved into a small room at the Globe Tavern in Springfield, and it was there, ten months after their marriage, that their first child, Robert Todd, was born. Another son, Edward Baker, arrived in 1846, only to die four years later. A third child, William Wallace, born on December 17, 1850, turned out to be a precocious little boy who, like his father, had a love for books. The family was rounded out two years later with the arrival of Thomas, born with a cleft palate, which would cause him to speak with a lisp, an affliction prompting his parents to fuss over him all the more.

Until recently, the Lincoln marriage has been characterized as literally a hell on earth for the president. Lincoln is depicted as long-suffering, his wife a "hellion—a she devil," in the words of one Springfield resident. The stories of their tumultuous union are legion. Mary's temper, if aroused, could boil to the surface like a volcanic eruption. Lincoln was once seen escaping through the back door of their Springfield home, dodging a barrage of potatoes thrown by his irate wife.

Yet many of these stories, though probably true, show only one side. No doubt Mary was high-strung and erratic, but she also had much to contend with. Permanently scarred by the death of her mother when she was six, she developed a fear of abandonment, a morbid concern that loved ones would be snatched away by death, leaving her alone and inconsolable. These anxieties, always lurking just below the surface, were in part responsible for her emotional instability. And the condition grew worse as her fears inevitably, and in some instances prematurely, were transformed into reality. In 1849 and 1850, first her father died, then her beloved grandmother, and then the cruelest blow of all, the death from tuberculosis of her second son, Eddie.

A compassionate and loving husband, Lincoln was a source of comfort to Mary during these tragedies. But under normal circumstances—that is, on a day-to-day basis—Lincoln was not an easy man to live with. He could be moody and withdrawn, wrestling with one of his periodic bouts of depression. Then there were the times that he got so caught up in what he was doing that he became oblivious to those around him. Once, Mary asked him to poke up a dying fire, but he was too self-absorbed in his reading to hear her. After three polite—and unheeded—requests, Mary lost her temper and hit him on the nose with a piece of firewood.

In time, Mary learned to cope with Lincoln's taciturn moods, even using them as opportunities to display her own brand of tart wit. On one occasion, her half-sister Emilie Helm recalled, Lincoln and one of his boys were playing checkers when someone asked him a question. Absorbed in the game, Lincoln did not answer. After a long pause, Mary said, "Your silence is remarkably soothing, Mr. Lincoln, but we are not ready for sleep just yet." Everyone, Lincoln included, enjoyed a good laugh.

All things considered, the Lincolns were a classic case of opposites not only attracting, but also complementing one another. Mary's older sister, Frances Wallace, saw this firsthand. "They knew each other perfectly," Wallace wrote. "They did not lead an unhappy life at all." Whatever friction existed in their relationship was overcome by a genuine love and admiration they had for each other. Immensely proud of her husband, Mary was convinced that no one in the political arena was his equal. And that included Stephen A. Douglas, the "Little Giant," so nicknamed because of his small stature but inexhaustible energy and political acumen. "Mr. Douglas is a very little, little giant by the side of my tall Kentuckian," Mary told Emilie Helm, "and intellectually my husband towers above Douglas just as he does physically."

Actually, Lincoln and Mary had much in common. They were both ambitious—socially, economically, and most of all, politically. In the 1840s and 1850s they were equally strong partisans of the Whig party. The future president admired the Whig leader Henry Clay, and so did the future first lady, who had known the Kentucky statesman in her youth.

As a girl growing up in Lexington, Mary had dreamed of being a president's wife. For all her quirks, she seems to have sensed a greatness, or at least a potential, in Lincoln earlier than most. A young woman of less foresight would have tried to marry a more obvious choice, a man of more impressive breeding, of greater wealth. No matter, in the end Mary made the right decision.

The children also brought them close. Although Mary's almost paranoid fear that more of her children might die—a fear tragically well founded—must have made her possessive at times, nevertheless she was a good mother by all accounts. Lincoln, too, adored his children, regaling friends and colleagues about their accomplishments.

In the winter of 1860–61, the Lincoln family looked forward to taking up residence in the White House. For the boys, particularly the younger ones, it was anticipated with great excitement, and for Mary, her dream had come true.

"HAPPY AND UNRESTRAINED BY PARENTAL TYRANNY"

In March 1861, when the Lincolns moved into their residence at 1600 Pennsylvania Avenue, they were the first family to live in the White House with more than one child. All previous occupants save one had been either childless or parents of adult children. The exception was President John Tyler, whose ten-year-old son was the first and only child to live in the mansion before the arrival of the Lincoln boys.

At seventeen, Robert Lincoln, or Bob, as he was known, was a student at Harvard when the family moved to Washington and therefore was an infrequent visitor to the White House. But his younger brothers, William (Willie), ten, and Thomas (called Tad because as a baby he had a big head and wriggled like a tadpole), nearly eight, lost no time in converting their new home into a vast playground, with few restraints imposed by their mother and father.

As if to make up for their own sometimes unhappy childhoods, the Lincolns were doting and permissive parents. At a time when mothers and fathers rarely "spared the rod," and parental authority was as absolute as it was severe, the Lincolns were the exception, not the rule. "We never controlled our children much," Lincoln told a Springfield physician, a statement his friends and neighbors would have agreed with. "He was the most indulgent parent I ever knew," recalled John Gillespie, an Illinois lawyer and a close friend of Lincoln for thirty years. "His children litterally ran over him and he was powerless to withstand their importunities." So it seemed. In actuality, conviction rather than weakness dictated Lincoln's child-rearing views. According to Mary Lincoln, her husband, with whom she fully agreed on the matter, had said: "'It is my pleasure that my children are free—happy and unrestrained by parental tyranny. Love is the chain whereby to lock a child to its parent.'"

Well ahead of his times, Lincoln's philosophy on raising children often caused resentment among his contemporaries. When the boys visited their father's law office in Springfield, for instance, they drove his partner, William Herndon, to distraction. The children, Herndon later wrote, "would take down the books—empty ash buckets—coal ashes—inkstands—papers—gold pens—letters, etc. etc. in a pile and then dance on the pile." Meanwhile, Herndon remembered, "Lincoln would say nothing, so abstracted was he, and so blinded to his children's faults. Had they s—t in Lincoln's hat and rubbed it on his boots, he would have laughed and thought it smart." Many a time Herndon wanted to reprimand the youngsters and "wring their little necks," but out of respect for Lincoln, he said and did nothing.

Others learned to do likewise, as Willie and Tad got into all sorts of mischief at the White House. They ran through the corridors, played hide-and-seek everywhere, interrogated visitors to determine why they came to see "Paw," and then collected from them nickel "entrance" fees, which they donated to the philanthropic U.S. Sanitary Commission. Having virtually free run of the place, the boys soon turned the White House into a zoo, with kittens, rabbits, a turkey, ponies, and a pet goat that slept in Tad's bed.

With limitless opportunities for deviltry, Lincoln's sons reacted predictably. Once Tad—usually the instigator in such matters—found the bell rope system that summoned the servants to rooms. The temptation was too great; the youngster made all the bells go off, sending servants scurrying in all directions. On another occasion, the president was reviewing troops from the White House portico as they were marching by on Pennsylvania Avenue. Standing with great dignity holding a Union flag in his hands, Lincoln noticed that the spectators were reacting strangely. It seems that a mischievous Tad was behind his father waving a Confederate flag. Quickly scooping up his son and the flag, the president handed both to an aide, who hustled the boy inside.

Lincoln found such antics welcome diversions from the pressures and grim responsibilities he had to bear as commander in chief. When his schedule permitted, Lincoln joined the boys and their friends in play, even wrestling "roughhouse" style on the floor. At other times, he would gather them all around him and read or tell stories.

The boys themselves had their quiet—and more constructive—moments. Tad had developed a genuine compassion for those less fortunate, often inviting street urchins to the White House to be fed. And he was seen regularly collecting flowers, fruit, and books for the "good soldiers," as he called them, who were stationed in Washington. Willie was far different from his younger brother. More studious and pensive, he had a serious side and, unlike Tad, needed no prodding to accompany his mother to church.

As the Lincolns approached their first-year anniversary in the White House, things seemed to be falling into place, at least on a personal level. Robert was doing well at Harvard, the boys were happy, and Mary's redecorating of the mansion, though not without problems, was soon to be completed. Then, suddenly, without warning, tragedy struck. In early February 1862, Willie became seriously ill.

"THE HOPE AND STAY OF HER OLD AGE"

William Wallace Lincoln was considered to be the brightest of the Lincoln children. Although he was fond of his younger brother, Tad, joining him in fun and games, Willie, who turned eleven in December 1861, could be just as happy curled up in a chair reading poetry. An introspective youngster, he also wrote his own verses, several of which have survived, indicating even at his tender age a definite flair for the language.

But we will never know if Willie Lincoln would have enjoyed success as a writer, or perhaps as a businessman or a politician. A boy of great potential, his life was tragically cut short when he died on February 20, 1862. No strangers to tragedy, the Lincolns now had the unenviable distinction of being the first presidential family to suffer the death of a young child while residing in the White House.

Before this time presidents had lost offspring, but not minors and not in the White House itself. President John Adams had lost his son Charles to alcoholism when the young man was thirty; Thomas Jefferson lost his twenty-six-year-old daughter Maria from complications of childbirth in 1804. Shortly before Franklin Pierce's inauguration in 1853, his son Benjamin was killed in a train accident. Only eleven years of age, his tragic death cast a pall on the Pierce presidency.

Willie Lincoln was a bright, healthy, and lively boy, and his sudden death was a shocking blow to the family. In early February he and his brother Tad had both come down with a high fever. At first the doctors had assured the president and his wife that the boys would recover, but Willie showed little improvement. Diagnosed as having "bilious fever" (a malarial infection), actually Willie had contracted typhoid, probably from the fecal-contaminated White House water supply. Of course, it's easy to blame Washington's relatively primitive city services for the problem, but the truth is that typhoid was a worldwide disease. Even royalty was not exempt. Queen Victoria's beloved consort, Prince Albert, died of typhoid in December 1861, a victim of Windsor Castle's polluted pipes.

Throughout the two-week course of Willie's illness, the Lincolns ran the emotional gamut, from rising hope to prayerful despair. But nothing could have prepared them for the boy's death. Overwhelmed by grief, the president wandered into the office of John Nicolay, one of his private secretaries. "Well, Nicolay, my boy is gone—he is actually gone," Lincoln said, before breaking down in tears. For some time after the funeral, every Thursday (the day on which his son died) the president would lock himself in Willie's room and there sit alone and weep. "I never saw a man so bowed down with grief," wrote Elizabeth Keckley, an ex-slave who served as Mrs. Lincoln's seamstress.

In time, Lincoln came to grips with the loss of his son. The press of events and the need to attend to the nation's business compelled him to cope with his sadness. And then there was Tad, who needed him and in turn was a tremendous source of consolation for him. Never known to have disciplined the boy, now Lincoln spoiled his youngest son more than ever before, constantly making excuses for his misdeeds and showering him with gifts. Like most children raised under these circumstances, Tad took advantage of the situation, earning a reputation as the "tyrant of the White House." But Lincoln refused to take a hard line with the youngster, who remained his greatest source of personal joy during these grief-stricken years.

Mary Lincoln's reaction to the loss of Willie was even more severe than her husband's. She was emotionally unstable to begin with, and her son's passing seemingly pushed her to the very brink of insanity. As much as she loved all of her children, she favored the affectionate Willie, believing that he would "be the hope and stay of her old age." Devastated by his death, Mary refused to eat, suffered convulsions, and took to her bed for weeks, sobbing uncontrollably. The mere mention of Willie's name would trigger cries of anguish and outbursts of tears. Never again did she enter the room where Willie died. When she finally emerged from her initial spate of grief, she was dressed in black, covering her face in veils. In the meantime, finding little solace in her church, Mary became convinced that she could contact her departed son with the help of spiritualists. A séance was held in the presidential cottage on the grounds of the Soldiers' Home just outside of Washington, and possibly as many as eight others in the White House itself—all without success.

After a year of mourning, of searching for her son in the "beyond," Mary recovered sufficiently to resume her normal schedule of duties. But no matter how hard she tried to pick up where she had left off, it was patently clear that Willie's death had changed her forever. Those close to Mrs. Lincoln observed that she was more irritable, more likely to fly off the handle at the slightest provocation, and less interested in entertaining than she had been before.

Less than two years after the Lincoln household had buried their son, in a rather tragic twist of fate, the other first family also suffered the crippling loss of a child. Confederate president Jefferson Davis and his wife, Varina Howell Davis, had five children when he took office in 1861. In common with the Lincolns, they had already lost one son, Samuel, in 1854 just before his second birthday. And they were destined to lose another during their residence at the Confederate White House in Richmond. In April 1864 young Joe Davis, an active five-year-old, fell from a veranda to the brick pavement below. Never regaining consciousness, he died minutes after a servant reached him.

Like Willie Lincoln, Joe was the "most beautiful and brightest" of his siblings and the favorite of his parents. Heartbroken, Varina Davis, who was pregnant at the time, grieved for weeks. Her husband was also crushed, but similar to his counterpart in the North, Jefferson Davis had a country to run—a country that was already spiraling down to defeat. Yet no matter how weighty the distractions, one never entirely gets over the loss of a child. In one respect, however, the Davis family was more fortunate than the Lincolns. They soon had another baby to renew their spirits. On June 27, 1864, Varina Anne Davis was born. Nicknamed Winnie, the baby girl survived and was known as the "Daughter of the Confederacy."

"STABS GIVEN MARY"

From the moment she set foot in Washington on February 23, 1861, Mary Todd Lincoln became almost as controversial a figure as her husband. Whether she brought it upon herself, whether it was the volatility of the times, or whether it was a combination thereof, Mrs. Lincoln's years as first lady were turbulent and tumultuous ones. None of her predecessors had ever excited so much attention—and much of it negative. Indeed, Mary Lincoln was the first president's wife to suffer severe and unrelenting public criticism.

Things went wrong from the very start. When Mary and the family arrived to join Lincoln, they were quartered in Washington's Willard Hotel until the inauguration. Few of the capital's society ladies called upon her, an obvious snub that was a portent for the future. Arrogant, entrenched, and pro-Southern in outlook, Washington's matrons of good taste had only contempt for these upstart Westerners, whom they considered barely civilized. To further demonstrate their disapproval of the Lincolns in general, and Mary in particular, they boycotted the inaugural ball and the first few White House receptions.

To be rejected as a "country hussy" who was better suited for the barnyard than the White House must have been particularly irritating to Mary. Hailing from a socially recognized Kentucky family, she did not deserve to be called a parvenu. Nor was she uneducated. By the standards of the day, she was academically better prepared than most women and could even speak French. Compared with her social adversaries in the capital, Mary was every inch a well-bred lady.

But the fact that she was originally from the South served only to ignite further criticism. No matter how hard Mary tried to be accepted, one group or another found fault with her. If it wasn't Washington's pro-Southern Tidewater gentry dismissing her as a vulgar Westerner, then it was the capital's Eastern establishment suspecting that she was a Confederate sympathizer, some going as far as to say that she was a spy. Her accusers pointed to the fact that her family owned slaves, that three of her half-brothers fought (and ultimately died) for the Confederacy, and that a full brother served the Southern cause as a surgeon. All of this was true, but what her detractors either lost sight of or refused to acknowledge was that Kentucky, a border Southern state, had divided loyalties, with many of its families split between the Union and the Confederacy. As for Mary, she could not understand why anyone would consider her disloyal. "Why should I sympathize with the rebels," she once asked, "are they not against me? They would hang my husband tomorrow if it was in their power, and perhaps gibbet me with him. How then can I sympathize with a people at war with me and mine?"

Despite her sincerity, not to mention the soundness of her reasoning, her critics refused to ease up. Having declared open season on the first lady, they considered nothing off bounds. Even her very physical appearance was a target. When the president sought a second term, not only was he subjected to a barrage of personal abuse, but so was his wife, whom the Democratic Illinois *State Register* described as "a sallow, fleshy, uninteresting woman."

Mary's taste in clothing was also a topic of private and public mockery. Determined to reflect the latest fashions, no matter the immodesty of the style, the first lady raised numerous eyebrows. Partial to large hoop gowns and long trains, with bare shoulders and arms, and low necklines, Mary's taste was considered more vulgar than elegant. Newspapers reported that she wore "absurd costumes" and was "a coarse, vain, unamiable woman" who had "no conception of dignity." The president himself was sometimes embarrassed by her display of so much flesh. Before meeting their guests at a lavish ball held on February 5, 1862, he noticed that the plunging neckline of Mary's long, flowing gown was inappropriate and said to her, "Mother, it is my opinion, if some of that tail was nearer the head, it would be in better style." Attending the reception, Sen. James Nesmith of Oregon came to the same conclusion, noting disdainfully in a letter to his wife, "The weak minded Mrs. Lincoln had her bosom on exhibition." Before coming to Washington, the senator added, "she used to cook Old Abes dinner, and milk the cows with her own hands." Now "her only ambition seems to be to exhibit her own milking apparatus to the public gaze."

Not only were Mary Lincoln's fashions considered tasteless, but so were her parties, particularly the one she gave on February 5, 1862. Breaking with tradition, the affair was by invitation only. In the past, all receptions at the White House either had been official—for diplomats, cabinet members, and the like—or had been open to the public. Predictably, this new arrangement alienated many. Presidential secretary John Nicolay reported that half the city was overjoyed at being invited, while the other half was furious at being "left out in the cold." Then there were those who thought the event was inappropriate altogether. "Are the President and Mrs. Lincoln aware that there is a civil war?" Republican senator Benjamin F. Wade asked in response to his invitation. "If they are not," the Ohio senator declared, "Mr. and Mrs. Wade are and for that reason decline to participate in feasting and dancing."

Except for those who did participate and thought it a splendid reception, most of the country agreed with Senator Wade. Mrs. Lincoln was called a "Delilah" and castigated for serving the finest wines, champagnes, and "French dishes for dainty stomachs," at the same time that the men on the battlefield were given coffee and hardtack.

Mary Lincoln simply could not win. Still, she was not entirely blameless for her disastrous public image. Short-tempered and insecure, the first lady was not one to take criticism, even if offered constructively, as it was in early October 1861. Attending the funeral of Lincoln's close friend Gen. Edward Baker, killed at the battle of Ball's Bluff, Mrs. Lincoln showed up all decked out in a "lilac silk dress, with bonnet and gloves to match." Many thought her attire inappropriate, and when it was brought to her attention, she acidly remarked, "I wonder if the women of Washington expect me to muffle myself up in mourning for every soldier killed in this great war?" And she added for good measure, "I intend to wear what I please."

Her extravagance was yet another problem. Whether it be a shopping spree for items in the White House (Congress had appropriated

$20,000 for refurbishing and redecorating the mansion) or for her own personal use, it all seemed out of place in view of the war. But Mary, self-centered as ever, went about spending vast sums, each shopping trip and her purchases reported in detail by the press. At a time when American families were trying to make ends meet as their menfolk were away at war, the president's wife was buying a set of china for the White House for $3,195, French wallpaper for $6,800, and a carpet for the East Room costing $2,500. These price tags were bad enough, but had the public known that Mrs. Lincoln had exhausted the congressional allocation in less than a year, actually exceeding it by $6,700, the fallout would have been a lot worse. In any event, when Lincoln got word of it, he was furious at his wife for overrunning "an appropriation of $20,000 for *flub dubs* for this damned old house, when the soldiers cannot have blankets." Eventually, a sympathetic congressman bailed out the first lady by slipping the extra expenditure in the next year's White House budget.

A compulsive shopper, Mary learned nothing from the experience. She continued to run up thousands of dollars of personal debt, purchasing such items as black point lace shawls for $650 each, "a real camel hair cashmere" one at $1,000, along with "bonnets, gowns, slippers . . . diamond ear knobs, tiny gilt clocks, sets of china, silver, and crystal." In later years a journalist recalled the indignation felt toward Mrs. Lincoln: "While her sister-women scraped lint, sewed bandages, and put on nurses' caps, and gave their all to country and to death, the wife of its President spent her time in rolling to and fro between Washington and New York, intent on extravagant purchases for herself and the White House."

The "stabs given Mary," to use Lincoln's phrase, would never cease, and would pursue her well beyond her years as first lady. Unable to concede that perhaps some of the criticism was justified, Mary dismissed it all as vicious and slanderous. In the spring of 1864, when a supporter suggested that she take a public stand against her detractors, she responded that it was unnecessary. "Since I have known real sorrow—since little Willie died," she explained, "all these shafts have no power to wound me." Given the grief caused by her son's death, for the moment, Mary might have convinced herself that her critics could no longer do her harm. But no matter how much personal tragedy she endured, the gossip and press attacks would always remain a source of great pain to her.

FIRST LADY

Although it is a common title today, the wife of the president of the United States has not always been called the first lady. Prior to the Civil War, the chief executive's wife went by a variety of titles. Martha Washington, for example, was called Lady Washington, while other presidential wives were referred to as Mrs. President or Presidentress, or sometimes as the Republican or Democratic Queen (the terms being used in a philosophical rather than in a partisan sense).

Some modern authors have alleged that it was Julia Grant who was the first to be called first lady. Others have said it was Lucy Hayes. Neither is correct. The first presidential wife to be referred to as first lady was Mary Todd Lincoln. Writing for a Washington, D.C., paper in November 1861, a social columnist spoke of Mrs. Lincoln as "the first Lady in the Land." Other journalists then began using the expression, especially Noah Brooks, a frequent visitor to the White House and Washington correspondent for the *Sacramento Daily Union.* The term soon found its way abroad, thanks to the English Civil War reporter William Howard Russell, who noted it in his book, *My Diary North and South,* published in 1863 and widely read on both sides of the Atlantic.

Since Noah Brooks was a close friend of the Lincoln family, it's possible that Mrs. Lincoln was aware of the title, although there is no mention of it in those of her letters still existing, but if so, it was no doubt a source of pleasure to her. She so desperately wanted to be at the center of Washington society, to be admired and respected as "the first Lady in the Land." In the end, however, plagued by emotional problems, personal tragedy, and a bad public image, Mary Lincoln never fully achieved what her new title implied.

THE PRESIDENT'S THEATERGOING

Abraham Lincoln and Mary Todd, as ill matched as they might have appeared, had more in common than one would have imagined. A burning desire to get ahead, to prosper, to play an influential role in the political process—these were but a few of the shared aspirations that bound the couple closer together. Even in matters of recreation, the president and first lady had similar interests, both having developed early in life a love for the theater.

As a young prairie lawyer traveling the circuit, Lincoln, according to one of his colleagues, "was fond of going all by himself to any little show or concert." Mary, too, enjoyed seeing plays "but had a special predilection for the opera." In her adolescence, she had confided to a friend that the foremost requirement she sought in a husband was a willingness to let her go to the theater as often as she wished. In this regard, Mary was not to be disappointed. Once settled in Washington, the Lincolns were the first presidential couple to attend the theater on a more or less regular basis.

Whenever time permitted, the president and first lady—sometimes just the two of them, but occasionally accompanied by a small group of friends—went to see plays or hear concerts at Grover's Theatre on E Street between Thirteenth and Fourteenth, at Ford's Theatre on Tenth Street between E and F, or at one of the smaller theatrical halls in the city. If Mary was indisposed or out of town, Lincoln might go by himself, take his son Tad, or invite one or both of his private secretaries, John Hay and John Nicolay.

The president enjoyed all forms of entertainment, ranging from plays, opera, and concerts to dancing girls and blackface minstrel singers. Shakespearean productions appealed to him the most. Back in Springfield, Lincoln had been an avid reader of the bard, but he had never seen any of the plays performed. Often invited by Washington theater owners who provided him with a complimentary private box, Lincoln rarely turned down an opportunity to see Shakespeare on stage. The productions were usually performed by some of the finest actors of the day, including Edwin Booth, whom the president saw in *Richard III, Julius Caesar, The Merchant of Venice,* and *Hamlet.* In early November 1863 the president also attended a dramatic presentation starring Edwin's younger brother, John Wilkes Booth. The performers, however, were not important to Lincoln; it was the profound truths of the plays that attracted him. "It matters little to me," he said, "whether Shakespeare be ill or well played. The *thoughts* are enough."

Whatever meanings he derived from Shakespeare, Lincoln's theatergoing was less a learning experience and more a means of lifting his flagging spirits. Even when it came to Shakespearean plays, he preferred reading the tragedies at home but seeing the comedies on stage with their bawdy scenes, hilarious absurdities, and double-entendre-filled dialogue. To those who felt that it was inappropriate for him to seek amusement during such troubled times, the president refused to be apologetic. "Some people find me wrong to attend the theater," Lincoln commented, "but it serves me well to have a good laugh with a crowd of people."

The theater also served as a respite, a momentary escape from the awful burdens of office. On one occasion, while attending a play with Mary and several others, the president seemed uninterested, appearing "worn and weary." When a member of his party asked if he was enjoying the performance, Lincoln replied: "I have not come for the play, but for the rest. . . . It is simply to get two or three hours' relief that I am here."

As the war drew to a close, the president's theatergoing caused concern among those responsible for his safety. Lincoln's hate mail had increased, assassination rumors were rampant, and the capital itself was becoming more and more infested with spies and malcontents. Ward Hill Lamon, the president's old Illinois friend and self-appointed bodyguard, was more alarmed than ever. Lincoln's presence at a crowded theater, without security, was an invitation to disaster. In December 1864, after the president, unprotected, returned from a performance, Lamon could contain himself no longer. "Tonight, as you have done on several previous occasions," Lamon berated the president, "you went unattended to the theatre. When I say unattended I mean you went alone with [Sen.] Charles Sumner [of Massachusetts] and a foreign minister, neither of whom could defend himself against an assault from any able-bodied woman in this city. And you know or ought to know that your life is sought after and will be taken unless you and your friends are cautious, for you have many enemies within our lines."

Prophetic though Lamon's words were, Lincoln paid them little heed. The president and first lady continued to attend the theater without adequate security right up to that fateful evening of April 14, 1865.

CHAPTER 13

Honoring the Living and the Dead

I n the early 1800s, when Napoleon instituted the Legion of Honor, providing titles, annuities, and medals to France's "notables" in military or civil life, he remarked somewhat cynically that "it is with baubles that men are led." Not everyone agreed. The Revolution's faithful took issue with the general, objecting vehemently to this new system of honors. Without firm republican traditions in France, however, the opposition was no match for Napoleon, who went on to make himself emperor in 1804.

Americans, on the other hand, with their strong democratic antecedents, nurtured a longstanding hostility toward titles, decorations, or anything that smacked of aristocracy. Only occasionally did they make exceptions. During the American Revolution, the Continental Congress authorized that a medal be struck for George Washington in gratitude for his role in driving the British from Boston in 1776. Other commanders, notably Gen. Horatio Gates and Capt. John Paul Jones, were similarly honored. But these were isolated instances; no formal award system was adopted until Washington himself took the initiative. On August 7, 1782, the general signed an order declaring that if a soldier engaged in a "singularly meritorious action," he would be "permitted to wear on his facings, over his left breast, the figure of a heart in purple cloth, or silk, edged with narrow lace or binding." Above all, Washington hoped that the "Purple Heart," as it became known, would show that "the road to glory in a citizen's army is thus open to all."

Yet Washington's gesture did not set a precedent. As far as can be determined, only three Purple Hearts were ever awarded during the

Revolution, and then the very concept of the decoration was forgotten. When it was revived a century and a half later in 1932, the emphasis was on honoring those killed or wounded in action.

Neither the War of 1812 nor the Mexican War (1846–48) was productive of combat medals. Congress continued to resist such aristocratic affectations, though during the conflict with Mexico, lawmakers in Washington were willing to authorize "certificates of merit" for soldiers who demonstrated gallantry on the battlefield. Eventually 539 men received these certificates, signed by the president and entitling each of them to an increase in pay of $2 per month. A signal (and profitable) honor to be sure, but without a medal pinned on a uniform for all to see, most certificate holders received minimal recognition from either their comrades or the public at large.

It was not until the Civil War that Congress finally relented and authorized a combat medal for actions on both land and sea. With the very destiny of the nation at stake, the Union was willing to exercise whatever means necessary to inspire its fighting men.

THE MEDAL OF HONOR

The Medal of Honor, America's highest military decoration, was born during one of the nation's darkest times. In July 1861 Northern forces had taken a beating at the hands of the Confederates at Bull Run. Strategically, the Southern victory was of little significance, but psychologically, it was a shattering blow to the morale of the Union army—an army in desperate need of having its confidence rebuilt.

While many hoped that its new commander, Gen. George B. McClellan, could revive the flagging spirit of the North's main military force, Lt. Col. Edward D. Townsend, an assistant adjutant general of the army, had came up with an idea of his own. Why not provide battlefield decorations for enlisted men? After all, officers who engaged in noteworthy actions were given brevet ranks (honorary promotions with no increase in pay), a system that was corrupt at times, yet it served its purpose, imperfect as it was. But there was no such mechanism to reward common soldiers, and perhaps a combat medal for these men would serve a similar purpose.

Townsend's proposal got nowhere. Winfield Scott, general in chief of the Union army, insisted that decorations were too elitist for American democratic sensibilities. But as the old general ruminated on European-style privilege and aristocratic taste, Secretary of the Navy Gideon Welles took a different tack. Increasingly frustrated with the lack of spirit in the navy, and convinced that it could use a morale boost, Welles seized upon Townsend's idea and enlisted the support of Sen. James Grimes of Iowa, chairman of the committee on naval affairs. In December 1861 Congress approved a measure creating the naval Medal of Honor—the first time ever that the U.S. Congress authorized a combat decoration.

James Pollock, director of the U.S. mint in Philadelphia, was selected to design the medal. Pollock came up with an inverted five-pointed star, two inches in length, suspended from an anchor, which in turn is attached to a red, white, and blue ribbon. At the center of the star were two humanlike figures, one, the Roman goddess Minerva representing the Union, who with shield in one hand and fasces in the other was defending herself against the second figure, a male symbolizing the Confederacy, who in a crouching position was holding in his hands serpents with forked tongues ready to attack. The engraving would become known as "Minerva Repulsing Discord."

The naval Medal of Honor was intended only for enlisted men; naval officers did not become eligible until 1915. At first the army followed the same policy. In fact, the Congressional resolution creating an army Medal of Honor (signed into law on July 12, 1862) contained language almost identical to the naval measure. Even the design of the medal was very similar; the only difference was that in lieu of an anchor suspended from the ribbon, there was the figure of a spread-winged eagle standing on a crossed cannon and cannonballs. In one respect, however, there was a significant difference; within less than a year (March 1863), army officers were made eligible for the decoration.

Intended originally "to improve the efficiency" of Union forces only in the Civil War, the medal's overall value to the military was quickly realized. In 1863 the Medal of Honor—for both branches of the service—was made a permanent fixture.

The Confederacy also planned to issue medals, but for reasons not entirely clear, the effort proved stillborn. In the fall of 1862 the Southern Congress passed a measure approving medals of valor for the army. A year later, however, the inspector general's office of the Confederacy announced without explanation that it had encountered "difficulties in procuring the medals and badges of distinction." Instead, names were placed on a "Roll of Honor," which (like the Mexican War certificates) had little impact, emotional or otherwise.

Few, if any, accolades in American history parallel the Medal of Honor. High-ranking generals, and even those who have held the highest office in the land, have coveted the award. Gen. George S. Patton once remarked that he would give his "immortal soul" for the decoration. Theodore Roosevelt, for another, made no secret of his desire for the award. And Harry S. Truman was heard on more than one occasion telling the men to whom he presented the medal, "I would rather have that medal than be president of the United States."

"ABOVE AND BEYOND THE CALL OF DUTY"

Although the army Medal of Honor bill was signed into law in the summer of 1862, some eight months passed before the decoration was actually awarded. On March 25, 1863, six survivors of the "Andrews Raiders"—a group of men who had stolen a Confederate locomotive and led Southerners on a wild and freewheeling chase in northern Georgia—received the medal, the first soldiers in American history to be so honored. Eventually eight other survivors of the mission were granted the decoration, while posthumous awards went to the families of four of the raiders hanged by the Confederates. Two others who were executed, including James J. Andrews, leader of the group, were denied the honor because of their civilian status.

By the latter part of the war, the medal became far more popular, and awards quickly accelerated. In 1864 nearly 100 medals were granted, and in 1865 more than 300 were issued. Most candidates, however, received their medals after the conflict was over, in some cases many years after they had performed their heroic deeds. All told, 2,438 Medals of Honor were issued to those who served in the Civil War— more awards than in any other subsequent American conflict.

Since so many were awarded the Medal of Honor years after they had earned it, a distinction has to be made between the first time the decoration was earned and the first time it was received. As noted above, the first recipients of the honor were the Andrews Raiders, but the first U.S. soldier to earn the accolade was Assistant Surgeon Bernard J. D. Irwin. The events that made him a candidate for the award took place two months before the outbreak of the war itself. Like most soldiers of the antebellum regular army, Dr. Irwin was stationed in the West primarily to protect settlers and lines of communication from hostile Indians. In February 1861 Irwin was posted in southern Arizona, where the sheer stupidity of a Lt. George Bascom precipitated a war with the Chiricahua Apaches led by Cochise. Bascom brought Cochise in for a parley concerning some stolen cattle and a kidnapped boy, but the Apache leader denied all knowledge of the matter. Unconvinced, the rash lieutenant ordered Cochise's arrest, and a general melee erupted in the council tent. Cochise used his knife to rip a vent in the canvas and escape, but several of his party were captured, including a brother and a nephew. Bascom's ill-advised act had started an Indian war that would last over a decade.

Later, Bascom found himself besieged by Cochise at a fortified mail station at the ironically named Apache Pass. When word of the lieutenant's predicament reached Fort Breckenridge, a small rescue party was organized, with Surgeon Irwin, the only officer to volunteer for the mission, placed in charge. Leading his detachment on a grueling, two-day, hundred-mile trek in a blinding snowstorm, Irwin and his rescue party came on a band of Apaches leading stolen cattle; after a brief fight, the cattle were retaken and three Indians captured. Knowing Bascom would need supplies, Irwin proceeded to Apache Pass with cattle and prisoners in tow. The surgeon reached the mail post and helped relieve the surrounded soldiers, actions for which he would receive in 1894—thirty-three years later—the Medal of Honor.

Dr. Irwin went on to serve in the Union army during the Civil War. At the battle of Shiloh, he earned still another distinction, organizing, for the first time in medical history, a field hospital entirely under canvas.

The first man to earn the Medal of Honor during the Civil War itself was Cpl. Francis Brownell of the New York Zouaves, a regiment recruited from the city's fire department. They sported baggy red trousers and short vests, topped off by tasseled hats, similar to the uniforms worn by Algerian troops who fought in the French Army. As colorful and dashing as the Zouaves were, so was their commander, Col. Elmer Ellsworth, who happened to be a former student in Lincoln's law office and whom the president regarded almost as a son.

In late May 1861 Ellsworth took his men to Alexandria, Virginia, just across the Potomac from Washington. Confederate troops had evacuated the town, but its citizens were still Southern sympathizers. When Ellsworth saw a Confederate flag flying on top of an Alexandria hotel, he rushed in to tear it down. The young colonel went upstairs, tore the banner down, and was descending with it in hand when he met the hotel owner armed with a double-barreled shotgun. The hotel owner discharged one barrel into Ellsworth's chest, killing him instantly.

Corporal Brownell, who had accompanied Ellsworth on the flag-tearing mission, was the owner's next target. As the Southerner lowered the weapon, Brownell managed to knock it aside before the trigger was pulled. Acting instinctively in self-defense, the corporal shot the hotel owner in the face, then bayoneted him in the chest for good measure. Brownell received the Medal of Honor for his actions, though it could be argued that his deeds were hardly above and beyond the call of duty. In any case, the basis for Brownell's award would prove to be the exception, not the norm. Beginning in 1862, the majority of medals were distributed for battlefield bravery.

The entire process, for that matter, was far more egalitarian than its early critics (who were concerned with the trappings of Old World privilege) could have imagined. In actuality, the Medal of Honor was well within the precepts of American democracy. The common denominator was courage, the common currency, valorous deeds. All else was equal. As long as one performed in a truly heroic manner, any serviceman was eligible, from the highest general to the lowliest private. Even drummer boys could win the prize.

Gen. Oliver O. Howard won his Medal of Honor by personally leading his men in a charge at the Battle of Fair Oaks on the Peninsula in the spring of 1862. During the advance, Howard was wounded twice in the right arm, injuries that later required the limb to be amputated. Around the same time, but on the other end of the scale, fourteen-year-old drummer boy William H. Horsfall of the 1st Kentucky Infantry earned a medal by rescuing a wounded officer at Corinth, Mississippi. Under heavy fire, Horsfall reached the stricken man and managed to drag him safely back to Union lines.

There were many who received the decoration for either capturing an enemy flag or preventing it from falling into enemy hands—the so-called "flag awards." On both sides, regimental colors were literally the symbolic heart of any unit, talismans that evoked its cohesion and fighting spirit. They were potent symbols that went beyond any functional value. To defend a flag was a point of honor, to lose a flag in enemy action the ultimate disgrace.

Seizing an enemy flag was no easy task, because the color bearer was usually protected by a guard of well-armed comrades. Still, hundreds of Union soldiers risked their lives to capture Rebel banners. Possibly the most famous—at least to Civil War buffs—was Lt. Thomas W. Custer, younger brother of the celebrated cavalryman George Armstrong Custer. Tom Custer (who, like his brother, would die in 1876 at the battle of the Little Big Horn) distinguished himself by seizing not one but two flags in two separate incidents during the last year of the war, earning a Medal of Honor for each flag.

Although many serving in the navy saw their share of action, on the whole, Union sailors were not afforded the numerous opportunities that their land-bound brothers in arms had to prove themselves under fire. Much of the naval war was blockading the Southern ports, where the greatest enemy was boredom, not Confederates. Nevertheless, the men of the U.S. Navy or, as Lincoln liked to call them, "Uncle Sam's Web-feet," did not lack courage when given the opportunity to display their valor.

The first sailor to earn the Medal of Honor (keeping in mind the distinction between earning and receiving it) was John Williams of the USS *Pawnee* during an attack on Mathias Point, Virginia, on June 26, 1861. As for the first U.S. seamen to receive the decoration, there were some twenty in number, all of them having participated in the capture of New Orleans. On April 24, 1862, the sailors demonstrated conspicuous bravery when Forts Jackson and St. Philip unleashed a merciless barrage of fire on their vessels as they sailed toward the city. Seaman Thomas Lyon aboard the USS *Pensacola,* for example, lashed himself off the port bow to take depth soundings, despite Rebel snipers. Another sailor, Quartermaster James Buck, was at the wheel of Admiral David Farragut's flagship *Brooklyn* when the vessel came under punishing fire from Confederate batteries. Remaining at his post for seven hours, even when wounded severely by a flying splinter, Buck refused to abandon his station and go below. And then there was Gunner's Mate J. B. Frisbee on the USS *Pinola,* who noticed that the fire on board his vessel was creeping dangerously close to the ship's powder magazine. Without giving it a second thought, he ran into the magazine, shut the door behind him, and stood ready to extinguish any sparks that might penetrate the chamber.

Within its ranks, the U.S. Navy also included seagoing soldiers, namely marines, who, though few in number, were still able to compile a distinguished record of bravery. The first of seventeen U.S. marines to win the Medal of Honor during the Civil War was Sgt. John Mackie. On May 15, 1862, during the attack on Fort Darling at Drewry's Bluff on the James River in Virginia, he was cited for "gallant conduct." Serving on board the USS *Galena,* Mackie "fearlessly maintained his musket fire against the rifle pits along the shore" and filled "vacancies at guns caused by men wounded and killed in action."

All Medal of Honor winners belonged to a fraternity of courage, regardless of their racial, ethnic, or religious background. The first African-American to earn a Medal of Honor was Sgt. William H. Carney, Company C, 54th Massachusetts Colored Infantry. A twenty-three-year-old runaway slave, Carney won his medal on July 18, 1863, during the attack on Fort Wagner. Described as "a carnival of death and a hell of terror," the assault on the South Carolina fortress was a particularly bloody one. When the original color bearer of the 54th went down, Carney seized the standard, then moved forward at the head of the advancing troops. Wounded twice, he managed to bring back the flag when the assault failed. Bloody, his uniform speckled with sand and dirt, Carney was triumphant. The enemy had not captured his precious burden, and, as he revealed proudly to his fellow soldiers, "The flag never touched the ground, boys." Carney was one of seventeen African-Americans who received the accolade. Black sailors, too, were honored; four of them won the medal during the course of the war.

Other minorities also had ample opportunities to display their courage. Sgt. Leopold Karpeles of the 57th Massachusetts Infantry was a color bearer during the sanguinary Wilderness campaign. On May 6, 1864, he rallied his comrades and induced them to stem an enemy advance at no small personal risk to himself. Karpeles was the first of four Jewish servicemen to earn the Medal of Honor.

For the most part, medal recipients richly deserved it. Sometimes, though, political concerns, or the expediency of the moment, dictated the decision. Just before the battle of Gettysburg, for instance, there was concern that Washington might not be adequately protected while the bulk of the Union army was in the field against Lee's invasion. The 25th and 27th Maine regiments could have easily provided defense for the capital, but their time of service had expired and they were about to disband. Not a single man in the 25th agreed to remain during the emergency, but some 309 soldiers in the 27th stepped forward, while the remaining 555 in the regiment chose to go home. Pleased by those willing to stay, Secretary of War Edwin M. Stanton ordered a Medal of Honor for each of the volunteers. Through some bureaucratic mixup, however, all 864 of the men in the 27th regiment were granted the medal.

Other noncombat awards were given to the twenty-nine soldiers who served as Lincoln's funeral guard and seven others to miscellaneous recipients. There were also five scouts and guides (among them William "Buffalo Bill" Cody) who earned the medal in action but were technically ineligible in view of their civilian status.

In 1916 Congress passed a measure creating a "Medal of Honor Roll." Those who had won the award and had reached the age of sixty-five would be entitled to a special lifetime pension of $10 a month. But the real intent of the act was its second provision, calling for a board of army examiners to review all winners since 1863. Only those involved in "actual conflict with the enemy, distinguished by conspicuous gallantry . . . at the risk of life above and beyond the call of duty" would be allowed to retain their medal.

Between October 1916 and January 1917, the board reviewed all the data concerning the 2,625 Medals of Honor that had been awarded up to that time. The combat service under review was not just the Civil War, but the Spanish-American conflict, the so-called "Philippine Insurrection," the Boxer Rebellion in China, and the Mexican Expedition in pursuit of Pancho Villa. Altogether, 911 medals, all involving Civil War recipients—the 864 given to the 27th Maine, the 29 granted to Lincoln's funeral guard, the 5 awarded to the civilian scouts, and 13 others, *not* including Corporal Brownell's (the soldier who shot the hotel keeper)—were rescinded by the board.

MILITARY PENSIONS

It is common knowledge that the Civil War caused more military deaths and disabilities than any other American conflict, but what is far less known is the fate of those who survived—the wounded, the widowed, the orphaned. To its credit, Congress acted swiftly to ease the burden of the war's living victims. In the summer of 1861 it approved a bill providing for "invalid pensions" for the wounded or disabled and payments to widows or heirs. But it was not until the following year, on July 14, 1862, that President Lincoln signed into law a measure that became the basis for all subsequent pension legislation until 1890.

The 1862 act provided monthly payments to a soldier or sailor "disabled by reason of any wound received or disease contracted while in the service of the United States, and in the line of duty." The amount to be paid would be determined by the extent of the limitations suffered from the wound or illness. If deemed "totally disabled," a private, for example, would get $8 a month, while officers would receive more, depending on their rank, reaching a ceiling of $30 a month for a lieutenant colonel or above. By the end of the war Congress amended the legislation, providing higher payments to veterans with specific injuries of a serious nature. A soldier or sailor who suffered the loss of both hands or the sight of both eyes would be granted $25 a month; the loss of both feet or the loss of one hand and one foot, $20 a month. Subsequent legislation included other specific disabilities eligible for higher than standard pension payments.

The 1862 revenue measure also made provision for the widow or dependent children. In order to qualify for a pension, the deceased soldier's wife (if there was no wife, his child or children) would have to prove that the death was from a service-related disease or wound. Once established, his widow or minor dependents would "receive the same pension as the husband or father would have been entitled to had he been totally disabled," again anywhere between $8 and $30 a month. In 1868 minor children were included in the pension plan even if their mother was alive; a widow receiving a private's pay was now entitled to $2 for each dependent child under the age of sixteen. If the woman remarried, the pension payments ceased, though if widowed again, the pension would resume. In 1886 Congress decided to raise the stipend from $8 to $12 for widows and dependent relatives of deceased privates.

These sums seem low, almost minuscule, today, but they must be set against the wages and purchasing power of the times. The pensions were particularly favorable to women. Twelve dollars a month meant $144 a year, not a bad supplemental income when average annual salaries in 1890 were $438. In other words, widows would receive about one-third of the average male worker's salary, but in actuality, it was even more, since at this time a woman could expect to earn only about three-fifths of the wages of an adult man.

In 1890 further pension legislation was enacted that proved highly favorable to veterans, a direct result of their enormous political clout. It's no mere coincidence that in 1890 the Union veterans' organization, the Grand Army of the Republic, reached its peak in membership— 428,000—a number that few Washington politicians could afford to ignore. The new pension law provided that anyone who had been enrolled for ninety days or more in the Union military, had been honorably discharged, and was disabled (whatever the cause, war related or not) was entitled to a pension. Equally generous terms were also extended to a widow, who would be granted $8 a month regardless of the cause of her husband's death, as long as he had met the above criteria and they were married before June 27, 1890.

Given these new and less demanding regulations, it is not surprising that veterans and their dependents applied for pensions in increasing numbers, escalating costs to unprecedented heights. To obtain some idea of how unprecedented these costs really were, one only has to compare the total amounts spent on military pensions before and after the Civil War. From the founding of the Constitutional government in 1789 to the outbreak at Fort Sumter in 1861, Federal military pension expenditures amounted to $90 million. In 1915, on the fiftieth anniversary of the surrender at Appomattox, the government paid out almost sixty times that amount—$5 billion. By 1932 the United States became the first country in history to pay its veterans and their dependents pensions totaling more than twice the cost of the war itself. In fact, as late as

1987, sixty-six widows and children of Civil War veterans could still be found on the Federal pension rolls.

The American people had clearly responded in the affirmative to President Lincoln, who, in his second inaugural address on March 4, 1865, had called upon his fellow citizens "to care for him who shall have borne the battle, and for his widow, and his orphan."

MIAs

Civil War Americans had to endure much suffering, but perhaps nothing was more heart-wrenching for them than not knowing what happened to their loved ones on the battlefield. The war that raged between North and South was actually the first conflict in American history in which substantial numbers of servicemen, both Union and Confederate, were MIAs—men missing in action.

In retrospect it's not difficult to see why there were so many MIAs. Civil War battlefields were far flung, armies advanced and retreated rapidly, and the destructive power of weapons produced a bitter and massive harvest of death. Disease proved even more deadly, ravaging Union and Confederate troops with a lethal impartiality. Unfortunately, record keeping was poor, especially when hasty interments were made after battles by details of troops lacking proper supervision.

As for the casualties themselves, they were easy enough to be misidentified, if they were identified at all. Dead bodies would decompose rapidly, particularly in warm weather. The corpses, a soldier on burial detail remembered, would be "swollen to twice their natural size, black as Negroes in most cases." Under such horrible circumstances, without any recognizable personal effects on the body, identification was next to impossible.

The metal dog tags of today would have helped remedy such a problem. As a matter of fact, some Union soldiers did pin pieces of paper or cloth on their uniforms with their names, units, home addresses, and next of kin on them. That way, if they were numbered among the fallen, at least their families would know their fate. Yet the affixing of identification tags on uniforms was a grim reflection of reality, not a general practice. For the most part, soldiers only pinned papers on when they thought they were going to almost certain death, as in the Union assault on Cold Harbor in early June 1864.

Battle fatalities were only one part of the story when it came to MIAs; prison deaths were quite another. Large numbers of men who were reported missing were former inmates of prison camps, where hardship and disease took a heavy toll. As malnutrition, typhoid, and other illnesses swept through the camps, prison authorities buried thousands of victims without properly recording their identities. Of the few records that were kept, most of them undoubtedly were destroyed by the chaos of war.

Clara Barton, best known for her nursing efforts during the war, was one of the first to address the problem of MIAs. As the conflict drew to a close, Barton started receiving letters from women all over the North asking her for help in locating missing husbands and sons whom they had reason to fear had languished or died in Southern prisons. Convinced that this was now "the most pressing necessity" of the hour, Barton committed herself wholeheartedly to the task at hand. Even Lincoln aided her with a letter of support. "To the friends of missing persons," the president wrote, "Miss Clara Barton has kindly offered to search for missing prisoners of War. Please address her at Annapolis, Maryland giving name, regiment, and company of any missing prisoner."

One of Barton's main concerns was the identification of the many thousands of Union prisoners who had perished at Andersonville, in southwestern Georgia, the Confederacy's most notorious prisoner of war camp. After finding a former Andersonville POW named Dorence Atwater, who had secretly kept a roster of those who died at the prison, Barton's mission was made easier, but not any less grimmer.

She took Atwater, forty coffin makers, and a crew of grave diggers and went to the Andersonville site. The work was depressing, even stomach-turning, but Barton would not be swayed. Bodies were exhumed for identification and reburial; if some trace of identity was established, the name was checked off against the Atwater list. After five months (June through October 1865), and in spite of the ovenlike heat of the Georgia summer, Barton and her team exhumed 12,912 Union bodies, of which 451 remained unidentified. Once exhumation and identification were completed, the dead were reburied in graves four feet deep, each with an inscribed headboard.

After leaving that "sad and terrible" place, Barton, for the next three years, continued her work on behalf of the MIAs. Summing up her labors in a detailed statement to Congress in 1868, she reported that her office had received 63,182 inquiries, written 41,885 letters, and mailed 58,693 printed circulars. Above all, however, Barton and her staff had identified 22,000 men, including those who had died at Andersonville.

It was truly an impressive achievement, but despite Barton's herculean efforts, the numbers of unidentified Union soldiers and sailors who made the ultimate sacrifice were staggering. Of the 360,000 Union servicemen who lost their lives, more than 40 percent (148,000) lie buried in graves marked "unknown," and some 7 percent (25,000) lie in unknown graves.

Not surprisingly, the percentage of Confederate MIAs is larger. In view of the South's rapid decline in the last two years of the war, its total collapse after Appomattox, and its failure to preserve necessary records, scholars have concluded that of the 260,000 Confederates who perished, at least half, probably more, are in resting places that are either unmarked or unknown.

As for Clara Barton, she went on to even greater fame as the founder of the American Red Cross. Yet none of her accomplishments were as poignant as her efforts to identify those who had made the ultimate sacrifice in defense of their country.

NATIONAL MILITARY CEMETERIES

The United States was the first nation in the world to establish national military cemeteries. In Europe, where wars and revolution were endemic, there was no systematized approach to the burial of military dead until the First World War. Soldiers might be buried in churchyards if the battlefield was near a church, or interred in mass graves where they fell, but nothing was set aside specifically for the purpose. During the Franco-Prussian War (1870–71), a German military cemetery was established "almost by accident," more an isolated event rather than a precedent.

The first American military cemeteries appeared during the Civil War. On July 17, 1862, Congress passed a law authorizing the president "to purchase cemetery grounds, and cause them to be securely enclosed, to be used as a national cemetery for the soldiers who shall die in the service of the country."

Although the Federal government ultimately would be responsible for the creation of scores of military burial sites, state officials and private citizens actually founded the very first one—at Gettysburg. Those three days of combat (July 1–3, 1863) in southern Pennsylvania were the bloodiest of the war, producing combined casualties for Union and Confederate forces of more than 50,000 dead, wounded, or missing. The Union's Army of the Potomac suffered 23,049 of those casualties: 3,155 killed, 14,529 wounded (some 2,000 of them mortally), and 5,365 missing.

Soon after the fighting, Gettysburg attorney David Wills, with the support of officials from Pennsylvania and other Northern states whose troops fought in that engagement, procured seventeen acres of the battlefield (at Cemetery Hill west of the Baltimore Pike) to be set aside as the "Soldiers' National Cemetery." Dedicated on November 19, 1863, the burial grounds were immortalized—and in later years somewhat overshadowed—by Lincoln's famous Gettysburg Address.

Following the ceremonies at Gettysburg, with the war still raging and some of the worst fighting yet to come, the Union had neither the energy nor the resources to create a national network of military cemeteries. Instead, the efforts undertaken were basically piecemeal to meet local emergencies. Thus, by war's end, there were only ten areas designated as military resting grounds. But in the half decade after the conflict, with the Union at peace and eager to honor those who had perished in its defense, sixty-three new national cemeteries were created. Several additional ones were set up after 1870, bringing the total number to seventy-nine. Every state involved in the Civil War has at least one of these national burial grounds, the largest single site at Vicksburg, Mississippi, where 16,000 servicemen are at rest.

In 1908 a government survey established that the Civil War national cemeteries hold the bodies of 315,830 Union soldiers and sailors, leaving about 44,000 men interred in private plots or unknown graves.

DECORATION DAY

Decoration Day, now called Memorial Day, was a direct outgrowth of the Civil War. In the immediate postwar period the Grand Army of the Republic, representing Union veterans, lobbied strenuously for the holiday, and their efforts paid off. On May 30, 1868, for the first time, Americans commemorated what would become an annual day of observance in honor of those who, as Lincoln expressed it at Gettysburg, "gave the last full measure of devotion."

Initially intended as an occasion to decorate the graves of fallen Civil War heroes, as time went on Memorial Day honored all American military personnel who died in wartime. Although it has taken on the trappings of a joyful national holiday, a rival of the Fourth of July, with parades, picnics, retail sales, sports events, and the like, Memorial Day has not entirely lost its original purpose. That the holiday has survived to this day and has retained more than a semblance of solemnity can be explained, according to Amy E. Holmes in her study of Civil War widowhood, in terms of "the great need of a society to recover from and continually justify a huge sacrifice."

CHAPTER 14

Assassination

The first half of April 1865 was one of the most eventful two-week periods in American history. On Sunday, April 2, the Rebels began the evacuation of their capital, Richmond. The following morning Union troops entered the city. Less than a week later, on April 9, at a tiny Virginia village called Appomattox Courthouse, Robert E. Lee surrendered his Army of Northern Virginia to Ulysses S. Grant, ending the Civil War (though there were still other Southern armies in the field). Then, on Good Friday, April 14, the inconceivable occurred: the nation's chief executive was cut down by an assassin. Northern victory celebrations turned into funeral dirges of mourning, red, white, and blue bunting replaced by black crepe. "This past week has presented a sequence of personal and national events, happy and horrible, fuller of interest than any other in my life," young Lester Ward (later to become a distinguished sociologist) noted in his diary on April 16. Rarely had so many Americans experienced such a range of contrasting emotions—from fevered exultation to deep sorrow—in a matter of days.

The exultation, which was first inspired by the fall of the Rebel capital, reached its highest level in the Union when news of Lee's surrender became known. Northerners, observed Secretary of the Navy Gideon Welles, were "delirious with joy," both on and off the battlefield.

It was about 3:30 in the afternoon of April 9 when official word reached the Army of the Potomac, delivered by no less a personage than their commander, Gen. George Meade. "It's all over, boys!" Meade shouted, hat in hand, hair ruffled by the wind as he galloped along. The troops had been waiting for just such an announcement, and the news opened the floodgates of emotions that had been bottled up for weeks. The men responded with a deep, full-throated roar of approval, then the whole scene dissolved into noisy, joyous chaos. Maj. Henry Lee recalled that he saw men falling "on each others' necks and laugh and cry by turns. Huge, lumbering, bearded men embrace and kiss like schoolgirls, then dance and sing and shout." Erupting fountains of hats, shirts, knapsacks, and boots filled the air, while bands joined the merriment by playing patriotic tunes. At the same time, batteries of cannons boomed in salute, adding to the exuberant cacophony.

As word spread, other Union armies responded in similar fashion. Gen. William Tecumseh Sherman's troops were near Raleigh, North Carolina, when the men heard the news. Even senior officers demonstrated their elation. Gen. Charles Woods took a big brass drum and began pounding it, while other officers grabbed horns and blew them as loud as they could. They then paraded about the camp with the "jolly old general" in the lead.

Returning from a visit to Richmond, President Lincoln had been aboard the steamer *River Queen* when the surrender occurred. Upon arriving in the capital early in the evening on April 9, Secretary of War Edwin M. Stanton greeted him with the good tidings. The two men embraced, and Stanton permitted his emotions, usually under tight leash, to break through his no-nonsense facade.

By the following morning word of Appomattox had spread across the land, and the joy was infectious, passing from person to person with almost bewildering speed. In the bigger cities like New York, Philadelphia, and Chicago, thousands thronged the streets, hugging each other, parading, singing songs, exploding fireworks, and setting alight huge bonfires.

But nowhere was the celebration more joyful than in the nation's capital, where the residents were aroused from sleep on the morning of April 10 by a cannon salute of hundreds of guns, their thunderous booms breaking out windows in Lafayette Square. Government offices were closed in honor of the occasion, and, as journalist Noah Brooks reported, the streets "were all alive with people, cheering and singing, carrying flags and saluting everybody, hungering and thirsting for speeches."

Many of the revelers gravitated to the White House, hoping to catch a glimpse of the president and perhaps hear a few words, but with no success. Later in the day most of them returned to the grounds of the executive mansion, along with thousands of others, and called for the president to deliver a speech. Lincoln's son Tad made a mischievous appearance at a huge open window, delighting the crowd by waving a captured Confederate flag, until "he was lugged back by the slack of his trousers by some discreet domestic."

Then Lincoln appeared at the window, "and for a moment the scene was of the wildest confusion; men fairly yelled with delight, tossed up their hats, and screamed like mad." Once quiet was restored, the president promised his audience that he would deliver a speech the following evening. For now, however, he called upon one of the bands in the crowd to strike up "Dixie." It was a lively tune, and one of his favorites. "Our adversaries over the way attempted to appropriate it," Lincoln playfully told his listeners. With Northern victory now in hand, the president went on, amid laughter and applause, the song "is our lawful prize." The band played "Dixie" as Lincoln requested, then followed up with "Yankee Doodle" as a patriotic encore.

The next day, Tuesday, April 11, Lincoln kept his promise and delivered an address to another large group that assembled at the White House. The theme was reconstruction, a matter much on the president's mind and a task he would have to tackle in the next four years. How the South was going to be restored to the Union was a problem "fraught with great difficulty," Lincoln frankly admitted, especially so since there was much dispute "as to the mode, manner, and means of reconstruction." To avoid further contention and possible deadlock, the president informed his listeners, Congress must be willing to work with those Southern Unionists who wanted to restore their states to "proper practical relations" with the Union.

Much of what Lincoln said, in one form or another, had been said on previous occasions. But the chief executive added something new to the mix. For the first time publicly, Lincoln expressed his support for granting the vote to some African-Americans, namely, "the very intelligent" (i.e., literate) and those who served as soldiers. To most whites, North or South, convinced of the black man's inherent inferiority, such a proposal was disconcerting and far too radical in its implications. Yet Lincoln hoped that under the right circumstances perhaps some would be willing to acquiesce to his suggestion. Not so in the case of at least one in the crowd, who listened to the president's speech with rising contempt and anger. John Wilkes Booth, actor and Confederate sympathizer, passionately believed in the moribund Southern cause. The idea of black equality with whites, real or implied, was anathema to him. Lincoln's proposal, Booth remarked to a companion, meant "nigger citizenship. Now, by God, I'll put him through. That is the last speech he will ever make."

"SIC SEMPER TYRANNIS!"

From the moment John Wilkes Booth fired a bullet into the head of Abraham Lincoln on the evening of April 14, 1865—committing the first presidential assassination in American history—the killer's motivation has been a source of endless debate.

Born on May 10, 1838, Booth was raised on a farm near Bel Air, Maryland, not far from Baltimore. His father was Junius Brutus Booth, an English-born immigrant, who, despite suffering from alcoholism and bouts of mental instability, was considered the finest American actor of his generation. Three of the four Booth sons (there were six surviving children in all) became actors, even though Junius did not want them to follow in his footsteps.

John Wilkes, or "Johnnie" as he was called in his youth, had a happy childhood by most accounts; attempts to connect his future action with his early upbringing have come to naught. As he entered his teenage years, however, he developed a dark side to his personality, slumping into periods of sadness, provoked in part, according to his biographers, by the taunting of schoolmates once it became known that Booth's parents had never married (they finally did so on Johnnie's thirteenth birthday). In any case, Booth's occasional melancholia did not stifle his ambition. The young man was something of a dreamer, his imagination fired by his father's success. He, too, wanted to make his mark in the world, and acting seemed a sure passport to fame and fortune.

After a shaky start—he was once hooted off the stage—he soon became an accomplished thespian. By 1861, at twenty-three, he was what one would call today a "Hollywood star," blessed with dashing good looks, accentuated by his "sweeping black hair" and the "most wonderful black eyes in the world"; a personable, almost seductive, manner; and a natural flair for the theatrical. He even dressed the part, wearing flowing capes and fur-lined collars. Although he had many women friends and fans, more than a few of whom were involved with him romantically, he also had enough charisma to charm men, a quality that would come in handy when he hatched his pro-Confederate plots.

A Southerner by birth, Booth was also one by instinct and inclination. "This country," he always believed, "was for the *white* not for the black man. And looking upon *African slavery* from the same standpoint . . .," he continued, "I for one, have ever considered *it,* one of the greatest blessings (both for themselves and us) that God ever bestowed upon a favored nation."

When the war came, it would have been logical for Booth to go South and join the Confederate army. But as he confided to his brother Edwin, he had promised their mother that he "would keep out of the quarrel," ruefully adding that he was sorry that he had said so. Yet Booth, ever the chameleon, gave his sister Asia another explanation that might be closer to the truth: He would be more valuable to the South as a spy. "I have only an arm to give," he explained, but "my brains are worth twenty men, my money worth an hundred. I have free pass everywhere, my profession, my name, is my passport."

At first Booth's involvement with the Southern cause was modest, smuggling desperately needed medical supplies such as quinine. But soon he became a full-fledged spy, passing all kinds of intelligence to Confederate agents. Touring extensively, even in Southern areas under Union occupation, the actor bragged to his sister that the pass he had received from Ulysses S. Grant had given him "freedom of range"— without the Union general realizing what a good deed he had done for the South.

By 1864 the Confederacy was in dire straits. Gone was the euphoria of the first two years of the war, when Southern independence seemed only a matter of time. Now, with Rebel armies in retreat on most major fronts, hopes for victory were fading rapidly. Like most Southerners, Booth was filled with despair, made worse by the possibility that Lincoln might win a second term in office. To Booth, the incumbent was determined to trample the Constitution and establish himself as "king of America." "You'll see—you'll see," the actor told his sister, "that *reelection* means *succession.*"

No matter how preposterous his prediction, Booth was convinced that it would come to pass. Something bold, something audacious would have to be undertaken to thwart Lincoln's monarchical ambitions and at the same time turn the tide in favor of the South.

In the summer of 1864 Booth was offered an opportunity to accomplish both objectives in one sweeping action. It involved a plan to kidnap the president, a plan that was formulated, according to the most recent scholarship, not by Booth, as previously thought, but by Confederate leaders in Richmond. Meeting with Southern intelligence agents in July 1864 in Boston and later in October in Montreal, the hotheaded actor learned of the abduction scheme and apparently offered his services to carry it out.

The plan might have been far-fetched, though its premise was not. The South's manpower was finite, the North's seemingly infinite. Tens of thousands of Confederate soldiers languished in Northern prisons, and their presence on the battlefield was sorely missed. There had been a prisoner exchange program earlier in the war, but it had been stopped because of the South's stubborn refusal to treat African-American Union soldiers as legitimate prisoners of war. At any rate, the idea was to kidnap Lincoln, smuggle him to Richmond, and hold him for ransom in return for the release of all Confederate POWs, who in turn would fill the depleted ranks of the Southern armies.

Beginning in September 1864, Booth recruited followers for the kidnap plot. Samuel B. Arnold and Michael O'Laughlen, both of whom had served brief stints in the Confederate army and were boyhood friends of the actor, seem to have fallen under his spell and signed on. Another conspirator was John H. Surratt, a secret Confederate courier, whose widowed mother, Mary, ran a boardinghouse in the capital where Booth and his band of malcontents sometimes gathered. Soon others joined, including George Atzerodt, a middle-aged German-born wagon painter from Maryland; David E. Herold, a nineteen-year-old unemployed drugstore clerk, who was described by some contemporaries as "feeble-minded"; and Lewis Powell (alias "Paine," or "Payne"), a big, brawny twenty-year-old Confederate veteran, who also might have been slightly retarded.

By January 1865 all the groundwork was laid for the presidential kidnapping. Now all that was needed was a clear opportunity to do the deed. But Lincoln's movements were unpredictable, making it difficult to pin him down. Time and again, the plot was plagued by bad luck, bad timing, and misinformation. Booth began to chafe at the delay; the Confederacy was on its last legs, and something needed to happen soon. Finally, the newspapers announced that on March 17 the president was scheduled to attend a play at a soldiers' hospital near Washington. Booth and his men swung into action, planning to abduct Lincoln after the performance, as he made the return trip to the White House. At the last moment, however, the president decided to remain in the capital and review a returning regiment of troops instead of attending the performance.

For Arnold, O'Laughlen, and Surratt this was the last straw. All three left Washington and wanted no further involvement in the scheme. Booth was crushed by the failure of the mission, made worse only by the news in early April that Richmond had fallen, followed less than a week later by Lee's surrender of the Army of Northern Virginia. Utterly devastated, the actor began to drink heavily, on some evenings polishing off a quart of brandy in the space of two hours. "For six months we had worked to capture [Lincoln]," Booth scribbled in his pocket daybook. "But our cause being almost lost, something decisive & great must be done."

Even before the kidnap plot had fallen apart, Booth had given thought to murdering the president. Attending Lincoln's inauguration on March 4, 1865, Booth, so consumed by his own hatreds and so certain that the president was another "Bonaparte," heard nothing on that day to convince him otherwise. Lincoln's call for reconciliation with the South—"With malice toward none; with charity for all"—when it came to Booth, fell on deaf ears. As far as the fanatical young actor was concerned, the inauguration ceremony was a missed opportunity. "[What] an excellent chance to kill the President if I had wished," he confided to a friend. Not long afterward, on the evening of April 11, after hearing Lincoln speak of his desire for limited African-American suffrage, Booth once again thought of doing the president in. Around this time, moreover, it is now known, thanks to the investigative research of several modern scholars, that Booth had traveled to Boston and New York, where he had contact with Confederate agents who apparently were planning to blow up the White House and kill Lincoln and members of his cabinet. Once that plan failed to be implemented, Booth might very well have been under the impression that his homicidal scheme now had the blessings of the Confederate hierarchy.

Not that he needed them. By the time Booth had finally decided to commit the assassination, there was no doubt in his mind that Lincoln was "a false president yearning for kingly succession" and therefore had to be eliminated. The actor would follow in the footsteps of his hero, Brutus, and save the country by ridding it of its "Julius Caesar." Lincoln's abolitionist policies might well die with him, and—who knew—the South might be able to rise again and establish independence in the wake of the chaos that "Caesar's" death would inevitably bring.

Delusional perhaps, but Booth was not clinically insane as some writers have alleged. His motives were strictly political, as can be seen by the fact that the plot also included the assassination of Vice President Andrew Johnson and Secretary of State William H. Seward. The intention was nothing less than the decapitation of the U.S. government by the elimination of its top executive officers. George Atzerodt was assigned to kill the vice president, and Lewis Powell, with David Herold serving as his guide through the streets of Washington, was to dispatch the secretary of state.

The story of Lincoln's assassination is familiar to most Americans. When Booth found out that Lincoln was going to attend Ford's Theatre on the evening of April 14, he realized that he had a perfect opportunity for killing the president. Booth was well-acquainted with the theater, and as a famous actor, he had free access to the building. He was also familiar with the play that was running, *Our American Cousin,* and knew that act 3, scene 2 had a line that usually brought gales of laughter from the audience. The laughter would mask the sound of a gunshot, and even better, there was only one actor onstage at that moment.

As planned, the assassin managed to sneak into the president's box and fired a .44-caliber slug into the back of Lincoln's head. Maj. Henry Rathbone, a guest in the presidential party, tried to grapple with the assailant, but Booth took a concealed knife and slashed the officer's arm to the bone. Jumping from the box to the stage, Booth apparently caught his spur on some of the bunting, and it caused him to partly lose his balance. The assassin landed heavily, and by some accounts, it was at this time that he broke a shinbone, though others claim he hurt his leg later in a horse fall while in flight from the authorities. In any case, Booth rose and shouted "Sic Semper Tyrannis!" ("Thus always to tyrants") to the startled and puzzled crowd. Always the actor, it's probable that he gave his exit line much thought. The dual meaning of the phrase no doubt appealed to his sense of the dramatic. On the one hand, "Sic Semper Tyrannis" was the motto of Virginia, the most prestigious state of the former Confederacy, and on the other, Booth was providing a fitting epitaph for Lincoln, whom he considered a tyrant.

The other conspirators failed miserably in their assignments. Atzerodt lost his nerve; even "Dutch courage" in the form of heavy drinking could not induce him to kill Vice President Johnson. Lewis Powell did manage to badly wound Secretary of State Seward with a knife. Fortunately, the secretary's previous injuries suffered in a carriage accident probably saved him, since the neck brace that he was wearing protected him from Powell's attempt to slash his throat.

President Lincoln was not as fortunate; he died the next day at 7:22 A.M. As for his murderer, he had no remorse. "I do not repent the blow I struck," Booth jotted in his diary while on the run. In fact, the fugitive could not understand why so many had turned against him for doing no more than "what Brutus was honored for." It was a mission that had to be fulfilled, Booth truly believed, for the "country groaned beneath this tyranny and prayed for this end."

Booth might have thought that he had killed a tyrant and that the country would be grateful to him, but the unprecedented outpouring of grief at home (at least in the North) as well as abroad following the news of the president's death suggested otherwise. The assassin, obsessed by his belief that Lincoln had tyrannical ambitions, was simply incapable of anticipating the public's sorrow and outrage over the murder. Nor could he have understood, even remotely, the senselessness of his crime. From across the Atlantic, *The Times* of London probably expressed it best:

> Abraham Lincoln was as little of a tyrant as any man who ever lived. He could have been a tyrant had he pleased, but he never uttered so much as an ill-natured speech. . . . In all America there was, perhaps, not one man who less deserved to be the victim of this revolution than he who has just fallen.

"THE BIGGEST MANHUNT IN AMERICAN HISTORY"

There was no question in anyone's mind who had assassinated Abraham Lincoln. Despite the pandemonium that reigned in the horrifying minutes after the shot was fired, John Wilkes Booth was recognized almost immediately as he jumped from the presidential box to the stage on his way to the back-door exit. He made no attempt to disguise himself, as if he wanted the world to know that he was responsible for the deed. Booth and his brothers had often performed mock killings in Shakespearean plays; now life was imitating art. As Booth viewed it, this was the greatest role of his career, and every actor needs an audience.

But this was not a one-man show. When news came of the violent attack on Secretary of State William H. Seward, it was clear that more people were involved. Determined to bring all the conspirators to justice, Secretary of War Edwin M. Stanton took charge of the investigation, dispatching soldiers, War Department agents, and civilian investigators throughout the Washington–Maryland area. Whether the secretary of war realized it or not, he was coordinating the first major manhunt ever undertaken by the U.S. government.

Within a week of the murder, most of those allegedly involved were picked up and jailed by the authorities. On April 17 Edman Spangler was arrested. A scene shifter at Ford's Theatre, Spangler had asked a fellow employee to hold Booth's horse at the rear of the theater, though it's likely he had no idea what the actor had been up to. On the same day Spangler was apprehended, Booth's boyhood friends and participants in the abortive kidnapping plot, Samuel B. Arnold and Michael O'Laughlen, were captured. Another member of the abduction team, John H. Surratt, was also identified, leading pursuers to a boardinghouse on H Street run by his mother, Mary. John was nowhere to be found, but government agents decided to take Mary Surratt into custody, since it was learned that her boardinghouse was a known hangout for Booth and his gang. Just as they were about to escort Mary out of the residence, Lewis Powell arrived at the doorstep. Identifying himself as a laborer hired by Mrs. Surratt to dig a gutter, he was arrested on suspicion and later positively identified as the assailant of Secretary of State Seward. Three days later, on April 20, an inebriated George Atzerodt, who had been assigned to murder Vice President Johnson but had been unable to muster the courage to do so, was arrested in western Maryland. This left three major suspects at large: Booth; David E. Herold, who had joined up with the actor in Maryland and was his companion in flight; and John Surratt, who reportedly had fled the country.

The government manhunt was now in high gear. Stanton was determined to bring the fugitives to justice no matter what it took. Swarms of government agents, provost marshals, and whole regiments of troops fanned out to apprehend the remaining conspirators. Journalist George A. Townsend, arriving in Washington the day after Lincoln's death to cover the story, was astonished by the large number of "Detective Police" he encountered in the city. In addition to the thousands of soldiers and hundreds of investigators assigned to the case, Stanton was willing to employ every means possible to track the fugitives down, including the distribution of the first man-wanted posters ever published with photographs. The secretary also appealed directly to the public, announcing that "all good citizens are exhorted to aid public justice on this occasion." And if patriotism could not produce the desired information, perhaps money could. As an added inducement, Stanton authorized a $50,000 reward for the capture of Booth and $25,000 each for Herold and Surratt.

Cavalry patrols scoured the countryside, and it was during one of these sweeps, on April 26, that Booth and his accomplice, Herold, were cornered in a tobacco barn near Port Royal, Virginia. Twelve days had passed since the assassination. For the fleeing actor, it had been a time of cold, hunger, despair, and severe physical pain, a consequence of the leg injury he had sustained after committing the murder.

Troopers surrounded the barn and demanded surrender. Herold complied, hands held high. Booth refused to come out. He had been an eyewitness to the hanging of John Brown in 1859 and was probably resolved not to die such an ignominious death. The barn was set on fire in an effort to smoke the fugitive out. Soldiers caught fleeting glimpses of Booth through barn slats, a hobbling figure silhouetted against rising flames. Orders had been given to take the assassin alive, but Sgt. Boston Corbett, a religious fanatic who believed that he answered to a higher authority, shot Booth in the neck, rendering him paralyzed.

The stricken actor was dragged out of the burning barn. Rambling a bit, at one point Booth asked his captors to "tell Mother I die for my country." Two or three pain-wracked hours later, he was pronounced dead.

Of all those allegedly involved in the assassination, only John Surratt escaped what has been called "the biggest manhunt in American history."

MARY E. SURRATT

The trial of the Booth conspirators was one of the most controversial in American history. Denied the right to be heard by a jury of their peers, the suspects, all civilians, were tried by a military commission. Their actions, it was argued, were military-related since Lincoln was killed in his capacity as commander in chief of U.S. armed forces actively engaged in war (all Confederate troops had not yet surrendered). Of course, this was the official rationale to deny the accused any right to a trial in a civil court. The real reason, as Secretary of War Edwin M. Stanton conceded in private, was that the rules of evidence in a military proceeding were less likely to be bogged down in legal technicalities, and the punishment was more likely to be severe and swift.

A nine-member military tribunal was assembled to hear the case against the conspirators. Composed of six generals and three colonels (including Gen. Lew Wallace, who later would procure a measure of immortality by writing the novel *Ben Hur*), the board was presided over by Maj. Gen. David Hunter, well known for his radical antislavery views and his wartime efforts to organize black military regiments. None of the members of the commission, however, had any legal training to speak of.

The chief prosecutor was Judge Advocate General Joseph Holt. Born and raised in Kentucky, Holt was nonetheless a firm Unionist, who, early in the war, had gone on record insisting that "rebels and traitors" should be subjected to harsh punishment. Along with the other members of his legal team, Holt exploited every possible advantage afforded the prosecution in a military trial. And there were many.

The military commission convened on May 8, 1865, but the actual trial did not begin until May 10 (ironically, what would have been Booth's twenty-seventh birthday). The proceedings were held on the third floor of the Old Penitentiary, located on the grounds of the Washington Arsenal (where Fort Lesley J. McNair is now located). The eight suspects on trial were Lewis Powell, George Atzerodt, and David E. Herold, each involved in both the kidnapping and assassination conspiracies; Samuel B. Arnold and Michael O'Laughlen, known to have played roles in the abduction scheme and suspected of having knowledge of what was to transpire at Ford's Theatre; Edman Spangler, who had arranged to have Booth's getaway horse held in the rear of the theater; Mary E. Surratt, charged with complicity in the kidnapping and assassination plots; and Dr. Samuel A. Mudd, the physician who set Booth's fractured leg while he was in flight from the authorities. All of the accused were tried under a blanket indictment, charging them with treason for their participation in either the kidnapping scheme or the assassination, or both, in order to deprive the nation of its military leadership in time of war.

Although members of the military tribunal were not vengeance-obsessed "hanging judges," as some have claimed, there's no denying that their decisions regarding the rules of procedure clearly favored the prosecution. First of all, the accused were not told of the charges against them until they were read on the first day of the trial. How could an adequate defense be mounted in their behalf if there was no prior knowledge of the charges until the opening day of court? Second, the prosecutors were not required to present an advance list of witnesses, while defense attorneys were. This meant that witnesses against the defendants could be called at any time without prior notice to their lawyers, who were prepared neither to counter the testimony nor to procure witnesses who might do so. Third, the attorneys for the accused were not permitted to confer with their clients privately, but instead had to consult with them in the courtroom and within earshot of the guards. Finally, and perhaps most disconcerting in view of the fact that conviction could result in a death sentence, the military tribunal did not have to render a unanimous verdict; a vote of six of the nine members was all that was needed to declare a defendant guilty.

Of the various cases, the one against forty-eight-year-old Mary Surratt was the shakiest. As a known Confederate sympathizer who ran a boardinghouse in Washington frequented by Booth and his men, she may have been guilty of poor judgment, but there was no concrete evidence linking her to the abduction plan or to the assassination conspiracy. All things considered, the case against her was largely circumstantial, hinging on the testimony of two witnesses. The first, John M. Lloyd, who rented a tavern from Mrs. Surratt, testified that about a month and a half before Lincoln's murder, Herold, Atzerodt, and John H. Surratt (Mary's son) had hidden two carbines, ammunition, a rope, and a monkey wrench at the tavern. Then, just before the assassination, on two separate occasions, Lloyd informed the court, Mrs. Surratt had told him to have the "shooting irons" ready to be picked up, which the fleeing Booth and Herold actually did pick up around midnight on April 14. A second witness, Louis Weichmann, a boarder at the Surratt house, testified that he had seen Mary and John Wilkes Booth holding several private conversations, one on the day of the assassination. Added to this was the appearance of Lewis Powell on Surratt's doorstep forty-eight hours after he had attacked Secretary of State Seward, and Mary's refusal at first to admit that she knew him. And then there was the matter of her son John, the only member of the conspiracy still at large. In sum, it seemed as if there was enough evidence, if it went unchallenged, to send Mary to the gallows.

Mrs. Surratt's only hope rested with Sen. Reverdy Johnson of Maryland, who had volunteered to defend her without compensation. If anyone could expose the weakness in the prosecution's case it was Johnson, a former U.S. attorney general and one of the most prominent trial lawyers of the day. But during his very first appearance, the senator ran afoul of the military commission when two of its members questioned his loyalty to the Union. Personally offended, and convinced that his standing before the court was compromised, Johnson refused to continue as Mary's defense counsel and left matters to two junior attorneys.

Johnson's departure has been viewed by some scholars as a bold act of defiance against a biased court. That may be, but there are also hints that the senator personally cared little about Mary Surratt's fate. It's possible that he may have initially accepted the case to take a stand against military tribunals, which he abhorred. Once that statement was made, Johnson seemingly abandoned his client.

On June 30, after deliberating less than a day, the commission handed down the verdicts. Arnold, O'Laughlen, and Mudd received life sentences at hard labor; Spangler, six years at hard labor. The remaining four—Powell, Herold, Atzerodt, and Surratt—were sentenced to be hanged.

The only surprise in the outcome was a clemency recommendation for Mrs. Surratt. Signed by five members of the military tribunal, it requested that in light of Mary's "sex and age," her death sentence be commuted to life in prison. The plea for mercy was supposed to end up on President Andrew Johnson's desk, though he denied ever seeing the petition. Clouded by controversy, the issue has been unraveled by modern historians, who are of the opinion that the president was telling the truth. Determined to see all the major conspirators die, Judge Advocate General Holt was the one responsible for intentionally suppressing the clemency plea.

On July 7, 1865, the four condemned prisoners were hanged, including Mary E. Surratt, the first woman ever executed by the U.S. government. Was she guilty? No one can say with absolute certainty, especially after the passage of 135 years, but all indicators suggest that she was unaware of the Lincoln murder plot and that she may have known little or nothing of the earlier scheme to kidnap the president. Mrs. Surratt was clearly a victim of the times as much as she was a victim of circumstance.

As for the conspirators who escaped the hangman's noose, they were shipped to a penal island in the Dry Tortugas, off the Florida coast, sometimes called "America's Devil's Island." None of them, however, would serve out their sentences. In 1869, during the last weeks of his presidency, Andrew Johnson pardoned Mudd, Arnold, and Spangler; O'Laughlen had died in prison. The president also ordered the bodies of Booth and the four who were executed exhumed from their interment underneath a stone floor of a warehouse on the Washington Arsenal grounds and returned to their families.

JOHN H. SURRATT

John H. Surratt is best known as the only member of the Lincoln conspiracy to evade Secretary of War Stanton's massive dragnet. Possessing neither ability nor intellect, Surratt's escape from justice was more a result of sheer luck and governmental indecision rather than any clever or brilliant maneuvering on his part.

If there was one distinguishing characteristic of John Surratt, it was—similar to that of his hero Booth—a blind, almost fanatical loyalty to the Confederate cause. Shortly after Rebel batteries opened fire on Fort Sumter in April 1861, seventeen-year-old Surratt, who was attending a Catholic divinity school not far from Baltimore, dropped out in order to help his beloved South. As he explained years later in a self-serving public lecture, by the time he reached his eighteenth birthday, he was "sending information regarding the movements of the United States Army stationed in Washington and elsewhere, and carrying dispatches to the Confederate boats on the Potomac."

In 1864 Surratt left Maryland with his widowed mother, Mary, and his sister, Anna (his older brother, Isaac, was a Confederate soldier), and relocated to Washington, where Mary ran the now famous boarding-house on H Street. It was about this time that Surratt met John Wilkes Booth, and he soon became his right-hand man in the scheme to kidnap the president. But once the plan proved abortive, Surratt washed his hands of the actor and the rest of the gang, and picked up where he had left off as a spy and message bearer for the Confederate secret service.

After word of the assassination spread, Surratt probably realized that one way or another he would be implicated in the plot. He fled first to Montreal, where a Confederate agent provided him with some money and a disguise, enabling him to keep a low profile. Then, in September 1865, he boarded a steamer for Liverpool. During the voyage, Surratt got a little too talkative and confessed to the ship's doctor that he was the famous American fugitive. Once the vessel got into port, the doctor, anxious to collect the $25,000 reward on Surratt's head, reported the matter to the American consul, who in turn conveyed the information to Washington. To the enormous surprise of everyone involved, Secretary of War Stanton and Judge Advocate General Joseph Holt advised that "no action be taken in regard to the supposed John Surratt at present." Not long afterward, Stanton also announced that the reward money for the arrest of Surratt had been rescinded. Obviously, those who had been connected with the prosecution of the eight Booth accomplices were not interested in bringing Surratt to justice, fearful perhaps that his trial (which inevitably would take place in a civil court) might bring to light the legal improprieties as well as the weaknesses in the cases of several if not all of the original conspirators.

Whether they were aware of Washington's concerns or not, diplomatic officials in the field decided to take matters into their own hands. In the spring of 1866 Rufus King, head of the U.S. delegation to the Papal States, was tipped off that John Surratt had left England and enrolled in the papal guard at the Vatican. Seeking authority from the State Department to place Surratt under arrest, King was subjected to a runaround that lasted for months, until he finally seized the initiative in early November and requested that the Vatican turn Surratt over to him, which it agreed to do. But somehow Surratt escaped from the papal soldiers guarding him, fled to Naples, and from there boarded a steamer bound for Egypt. Upon his arrival in Alexandria, the fugitive was detained until the American consul general, Charles Hale, conferred with the Egyptian government. Four days later, on November 27, 1866, John H. Surratt was taken into custody to be returned to the United States for trial—the first American citizen ever extradited by the U.S. government.

The case of the last Booth conspirator began on June 10, 1867. Fortunately for Surratt, the hysteria and trauma of Lincoln's murder had died down, resulting in a far more dispassionate judicial climate than the one his mother and the other seven defendants had experienced two years earlier. During the two-month trial held in the Criminal Court of the District of Columbia, Surratt's attorneys presented evidence convincing most jurors that their client had been in Elmira, New York, at the time of the assassination, and therefore could not have been involved in the crime. By a vote of eight to four in the defendant's favor, the jury deadlocked, which meant a retrial. At the second trial, Surratt's defense counsel pointed out that the time limit on the indictment against his client had expired, which led the judge to dismiss all charges.

John Surratt was a free man. He settled in Baltimore, worked as an auditor, and in 1870 attempted to explain his wartime activities (and salvage his reputation) by delivering a lecture in Rockville, Maryland. Admitting his role as a Confederate spy and acknowledging his complicity in the scheme to abduct Lincoln, but not to murder him, he insisted that his actions were carried out "by a sincere desire to assist the South in gaining her independence." No one seemed to care. Even Southerners found it hard to consider John Surratt a hero. Somehow he could never erase the fact that he remained in hiding while his mother was tried and executed. He died in 1916.

LINCOLN'S WIDOW

The bullet fired by John Wilkes Booth on that Good Friday in April 1865 destroyed two Lincolns, not one. Mary Todd Lincoln never recovered from that shattering blow. As she prepared to leave the White House after more than a month of seclusion, she wrote in confidence: "I go hence, broken hearted, with every hope almost in life—crushed." Without her husband, Mary believed, she "had nothing, *was* nothing." Such thoughts, to be sure, reflected grief instead of reason, but they were not entirely untrue. Departing Washington on May 23, "there was scarcely a friend to tell her good-by. . . . The silence was almost painful."

The Lincolns—Mary and her sons, Robert (who would begin studying law) and twelve-year-old Tad—settled in Chicago, taking residence at various hotels, none ever meeting the exacting standards of the former first lady. "Living in a boarding house, is most revolting to my sons & myself," she complained to Simon Cameron, a former secretary of war in Lincoln's cabinet and currently a senator from Pennsylvania. What Mrs. Lincoln wanted was her own home, not the one in Springfield, haunted by memories, but a new one befitting her position as the widow of the "sainted" president. She had hoped that Cameron could help raise through private donations $20,000, perhaps as much as $30,000, to enable her to procure and furnish the house she had in mind. The senator agreed to solicit contributions in her behalf.

Not that Mary was penniless. Lincoln's estate was valued at some $110,000, but since the president did not leave a will, the money was divided equally among his wife and sons and placed in a trust. Mrs. Lincoln's share generated somewhere between $1,500 to $1,800 a year, equivalent to about four times the annual income of an average wage earner. Unimpressed by the amount, she dismissed it as "a war clerk's salary." It was hardly adequate to meet her needs, especially since she had run up $10,000 in personal debts during her residency in the White House, debts that had yet to be paid. For years she had lived well beyond her means and was able to get away with it, having been given special consideration as the president's wife. Now she was treated like everyone else, with creditors threatening her if she did not pay.

Just before Christmas 1865, Mary got an early and unexpected holiday gift. Congress voted her the equivalent of one year of her late husband's salary—$25,000. It was enough to buy a home, but there would be little left to furnish and maintain it. Convincing herself that Senator Cameron would raise the additional funds, Mary, impulsive as ever, went ahead and purchased a stone-fronted row house on West Washington Street in Chicago. Soon after assuming possession, however, she got word from Cameron that he could not come up with the money. Within a year, unable to meet her expenses, she rented out the house and moved back into a hotel.

Despite Cameron's lack of success, Mary had not given up on the possibility of being rescued from her financial difficulties by what was called "subscription funds." At a time when pensions and life insurance were in their infancy, it was not uncommon for wealthy admirers to contribute money and gifts to public heroes or their widows. But thus far, no one stepped forth to assist the president's widow. Particularly galling, in Mary's eyes, was the overwhelming generosity contributors had shown toward Gen. Ulysses S. Grant. Not only had wealthy supporters raised the $30,000 necessary to pay off the mortgage on Grant's Washington home, but the general was given two other houses, one in his hometown of Galena, Illinois, and the other in Philadelphia. To Mary, this made no sense. "Roving generals," she protested to a friend, "have elegant mansions showered upon them, and the American people leave the family of the Martyred President, to struggle as best they may! Strange justice."

Rather than wait for what may never materialize, Mary decided to raise some money on her own. In the fall of 1867, with the help of Elizabeth (Lizzie) Keckley, an ex-slave who had served as the former first lady's seamstress, Mary arranged to sell most of her jewelry and clothes through a brokerage house in New York City. Promised by the promoters that she could easily earn $100,000 within a few weeks, she was ecstatic. But the project, poorly planned and managed, proved a fiasco. People came to the sale largely out of curiosity, rather than to buy. The press referred to it as the "Old Clothes Scandal" and savagely attacked Mary as "that dreadful woman . . . in the open market with her useless finery . . . [who] persists in forcing her repugnant individuality before the world." Shocked and saddened by this new "round of newspaper abuse," Mary believed that she had done nothing wrong, that her motives were of the "purest" kind. "What a world of anguish this is— and how I have been made to suffer!" she confided to Lizzie Keckley. "If I had committed murder in every city in this blessed Union, I could not be more traduced."

Failing to gain support, financial or otherwise, and humiliated by the "vampyre press," Mary decided to take Tad and live abroad for a while. In the fall of 1868 they took passage on a steamer for Bremen, Germany. Upon arrival, mother and son traveled to Frankfurt-am-Main, where Tad was enrolled in school and Mary rented a room in a nearby hotel. At first things seemed to go well. In this "land of strangers," Mary wrote to a friend, she experienced a sense of solace, which she "was not allowed" back home. But as in the past, whatever inner peace the former first lady felt was usually cut short by a resurgence of her fears and anxieties. What troubled Mary most, once again, was her financial situation. It was "quite as expensive," she soon realized, to live in Europe as in the States. Hotel bills, tuition for Tad's schooling, and physician fees (for her "ill health caused by great mental distress") ate up much of her income. If only she could find a way to supplement it.

Toward the end of 1868, it appeared that Congress might provide Mary with the additional funds she so desperately wanted. Sen. Charles Sumner of Massachusetts, a longtime family friend of the Lincolns', was planning to introduce a bill providing a yearly pension for the president's widow. Supporters of the impending legislation paved the way by arguing that Lincoln had been killed while serving as commander in chief, and thus his wife was as much entitled to an annual allotment as were the wives of other officers and men who perished in the war.

As soon as Mary heard of the effort to secure her a pension, she swung into action. Writing to several congressmen, she discussed in detail her straitened financial circumstances and her ill health, at the same time never letting them forget that her husband's life "was sacrificed to his country's service."

The pension resolution, finally introduced in the Senate in early 1869, called for Mrs. Lincoln to receive an annual payment of $5,000. It was referred to the committee on pensions, which after ten days issued a report recommending rejection of the proposed allotment. A bitter and heated debate ensued in the Senate. Those who objected to the pension argued that Mary was far from destitute. Why should she demand public funds? Other widows, equally—perhaps even more— worthy, had to live on much less. The widow of Gen. Edward Baker, for example, was getting only $600 a year. Was Mrs. Lincoln deserving of more than eight times that amount?

The bill languished for more than a year and a half. Unwilling to concede defeat, its supporters periodically brought the issue before the full chamber. At last their tenacity paid off when, on July 14, 1870, a consensus was reached. The Senate agreed to grant Mary Lincoln $3,000 (later increased to $5,000) a year—the first time a president's widow ever received an annual pension.

Less than a year later, Mary and Tad returned to the States. Although the former first lady had hoped for a larger yearly allotment, she was still grateful for what had transpired. Not only had she received a permanent supplement to her income, but she was also given long overdue recognition from the government her husband had so faithfully served.

Things were looking up for Mary, and even her friends noticed a positive change in her personality. But like so many other times in her life, whatever happiness and satisfaction she felt did not last for long. Mary was one of those unfortunate people who somehow was destined to have more—much more—than her share of human tragedy. In July 1871, Tad, only eighteen years of age, died, probably of tuberculosis.

Inconsolable over the loss of her son, Mary's mental state, fragile as it was, further deteriorated. Within four years, her erratic behavior— obsessions with imagined poverty, wild spending sprees, delusions that some one was stalking her—persuaded her only surviving son, Robert, to have her committed to a sanitarium on the grounds of insanity. In September 1875, after several months of confinement, Mary was released, whereupon she took passage to Europe, settling in France. For the next half decade she lived abroad, until she suffered a bad fall that injured her back. Forced to return home, Mary was invited to live with her sister in Springfield, Illinois. Half blind, partially paralyzed, and plagued by severe emotional problems, she confined herself to an upstairs bedroom, with a money belt strapped to her waist and surrounded by all her worldly possessions. On July 16, 1882, Mary Todd Lincoln suffered a stroke and died at the age of sixty-four. Her oft-repeated wish "to rejoin my Husband, who loved me so devotedly & whom I idolized" finally had been fulfilled.

Notes

PREFACE (Pages xi–xiii)

(xi)   **Catton**: Bruce Catton, *Reflections on the Civil War,* ed. by John Leekley (Garden City, N.Y.: Doubleday & Company, 1981), 14.

(xi)   **William Tecumseh Sherman**: William T. Sherman, *Memoirs of General William T. Sherman* (New York: D. Appleton and Company, 1875), 2: 227.

(xi)   **Emma Mordecai**: John Rader Marcus, *Memoirs of American Jews: 1775–1865* (Philadelphia: The Jewish Publication Society of America, 1955), 3: 344.

(xi)   **Young Southern Lieutenant**: John Sergeant Wise, *The End of an Era,* ed. by Curtis Carroll Davis (New York: Thomas Yoseloff, 1965), 454.

(xi)   *Montgomery Daily Advertiser*: July 1, 1864.

(xi)   **Louisiana Planter**: James M. McPherson, *Abraham Lincoln and the Second American Revolution* (New York: Oxford University Press, 1990), vii.

(xi–xii)   **Black Army Chaplain**: Leon F. Litwack, *Been in the Storm So Long: The Aftermath of Slavery* (New York: Alfred A. Knopf, 1979), 96.

(xii)   **Lucy Buck**: Elizabeth R. Baer, ed., *Shadows on My Heart: The Civil War Diary of Lucy Rebecca Buck of Virginia* (Athens: University of Georgia Press, 1997), 5.

(xii)   **Thomas Long**: James M. McPherson, *The Negro's Civil War: How American Negroes Felt and Acted During the War for the Union* (New York: Pantheon Books, 1965), 213.

(xii)   **Robert Purvis**: Ibid., 12, 309.

(xii)   **Wendell Phillips**: Eric Foner and Olivia Mahoney, *A House Divided: America in the Age of Lincoln* (New York: W. W. Norton & Company, 1990), 133.

(xii)   *New York Times*: October 9, 1867.

(xii)   **George Ticknor**: George Ticknor, *Life, Letters, and Journals of George Ticknor* (Boston: Houghton Mifflin Company, 1909), 2: 485.

(xii)   **Karl Marx**: Morton Keller, *Affairs of State: Public Life in Late Nine-
         teenth Century America* (Cambridge, Mass.: Harvard University Press,
         1977), 6.

(xii)   **Benjamin Disraeli**: Belle Becker Sideman and Lillian Friedman, eds.,
         Europe Looks at the Civil War (New York: The Orion Press, 1960), 233.

(xii)   **Charles Dickens**: Edgar Johnson, *Charles Dickens: His Tragedy and
         Triumph* (New York: Simon and Schuster, 1952), 2: 1093.

(xiii)   **Keller**: Keller, *Affairs of State,* 1–2; see also Marcus Cunliffe, *Soldiers
         and Civilians: The Martial Spirit in America, 1775–1865* (Boston: Lit-
         tle, Brown and Company, 1968), 434; J. Matthew Gallman, *The North
         Fights the Civil War: The Home Front* (Chicago: Ivan R. Dee, 1994),
         194, 196; Anne C. Rose, *Victorian America and the Civil War* (New
         York: Cambridge University Press, 1992), 13; David T. Gilchrist and W.
         David Lewis, eds., *Economic Change in the Civil War* (Greenville,
         Del.: Eleutherian Mills-Hagley Foundation, 1965), 107–108, 172–174.

(xiii)   **Vandiver**: Frank E. Vandiver, *Blood Brothers: A Short History of the
         Civil War* (College Station: Texas A&M University Press, 1992), 178.

(xiii)   **McPherson**: See the following works by James M. McPherson: *Battle
         Cry of Freedom: The Civil War Era* (New York: Oxford University
         Press, 1988), 452, 861–862; *Drawn with the Sword: Reflections on the
         American Civil War* (New York: Oxford University Press, 1996), vii;
         and *Abraham Lincoln and the Second American Revolution,* vii–viii;
         see also W. R. Brock, *An American Crisis: Congress and Reconstruc-
         tion, 1865–1867* (New York: Harper & Row, 1963), 1; Mark Grimsley,
         The American Civil War: The Emergence of Total Warfare (Lexington,
         Mass.: D. C. Heath and Company, 1996), 33; Peter Batty and Peter
         Parish, *The Divided Union: The Story of the Great American War*
         (Topsfield, Mass.: Salem House Publishers, 1987), 199.

(xiii)   **50,000 books**: McPherson, *Drawn with the Sword,* 56.

(xiii)   **Hesseltine**: William B. Hesseltine, ed., *The Tragic Conflict: The Civil
         War and Reconstruction* (New York: George Braziller, 1962), 5.

CHAPTER 1: ON THE EVE OF CIVIL WAR (Pages 1–35)

(1–2)   **Introduction**: Stephen B. Oates, *To Purge This Land with Blood: A
        Biography of John Brown* (New York: Harper and Row, 1970), 353–
        356; Allan Nevins and Milton Halsey Thomas, eds., *The Diary of
        George Templeton Strong: The Turbulent Fifties, 1850–1859* (New
        York: The Macmillan Company, 1952), 2: 480; Allan Nevins, *The
        Emergence of Lincoln: Prologue to Civil War, 1859–1861* (New York:
        Charles Scribner's Sons, 1950), 2: 129–130.

(2–3)   **William Pennington**: Prior to Pennington, the only other freshman
        congressman elevated to the speakership (besides the very first speaker
        of the house, Frederick A. C. Muhlenberg of Pennsylvania) was Henry

Clay of Kentucky, on November 4, 1811. Emerson D. Fite, *The Presidential Carnpaign of 1860* (1911; reprint, Port Washington, N.Y.: Kennikat Press, 1967), 33, 43–44; Nevins, *The Emergence of Lincoln,* 2: 116–124, 405; Ollinger Crenshaw, "The Speakership Contest of 1859–1860: John Sherman's Election a Cause of Disruption?" *Mississippi Valley Historical Review* 29 (December 1942), 323–338; Roy F. Nichols, *The Disruption of American Democracy* (1948; reprint, New York: The Free Press, 1967), 271–276.

(3–4) **Rabbi Morris J. Raphall**: Morris U. Schappes, ed., *A Documentary History of the Jews in the United States: 1654–1875* (New York: Schocken Books, 1971), 406, 684; Bertram W. Korn, *American Jewry and the Civil War* (1951; reprint, New York: Atheneum, 1970), 16–20.

(4–5) **"Buchaneers"**: The title of this section comes from a chapter heading in Mark Summers, *The Plundering Generation: Corruption and the Crisis of the Union, 1849–1861* (New York: Oxford University Press, 1987), 239; see also 242–260; Michael Holt, *The Political Crisis of the 1850s* (New York: John Wiley & Sons, 1978), 214; Nevins, *The Emergence of Lincoln*, 2: 196–200; David E. Meerse, "Buchanan, Corruption and the Election of 1860," *Civil War History* 12 (June 1966), 116–131.

(5–7) **Democratic National Convention**: Nevins, *The Emergence of Lincoln*, 2: 203–228; Joseph Nathan Kane, *Facts about the Presidents: A Compilation of Biographical and Historical Information* (New York: The H. W. Wilson Company, 1989), 92; Charles P. Roland, *An American Iliad: The Story of the Civil War* (Lexington: University Press of Kentucky, 1991), 19–20; David M. Potter, *The Impending Crisis, 1848–1861* (New York: Harper & Row, 1976), 407–413; Robert W. Johannsen, *Stephen A. Douglas* (New York: Oxford University Press, 1973), 758–759, 771.

(7–8) **Chicago**: Nevins, *The Emergence of Lincoln*, 2: 247–248; Robert H. Jones, *Disrupted Decades: The Civil War and Reconstruction Years* (New York: Charles Scribner's Sons, 1973), 52; Reinhard Luthin, *The First Lincoln Campaign* (1944; reprint, Gloucester, Mass.: Peter Smith, 1964), 20–21; Stephen B. Oates, *With Malice Toward None: The Life of Abraham Lincoln* (New York: New American Library, 1977), 184.

(8–9) **The "Wigwam"**: Murat Halstead, "The Republicans Nominate Lincoln," in Hesseltine, ed., *The Tragic Conflict*, 100; William B. Hesseltine, ed., *Three Against Lincoln: Murat Halstead Reports the Caucuses of 1860* (Baton Rouge: Louisiana State University Press, 1960), 143; Nevins, *The Emergence of Lincoln*, 2: 248; Bruce Catton, *The Centennial History of the Civil War: The Coming Fury* (Garden City, N.Y.: Doubleday & Company, 1961), 1: 49, 62.

(9–10) **Republican National Convention**: David Herbert Donald, *Lincoln* (New York: Simon and Schuster, 1995), 247–250; Hesseltine, ed., *Three Against Lincoln*, 165, 171; Paul F. Boller, Jr., *Presidential Cam-*

paigns (New York: Oxford University Press, 1984), 104–105; Nevins, *The Emergence of Lincoln*, 2: 229, 249, 251; Roy F. Nichols, *The Stakes of Power: 1845–1877* (New York: Hill and Wang, 1961), 81; Oates, *With Malice Toward None*, 191–194.

(10– **Japanese Diplomatic Mission**: Lewis Bush, *77 Samurai: Japan's First*
12)   *Embassy to America* (Tokyo: Kodansha International Ltd., 1968), 163–
       179; W. G. Beasley, *Japan Encounters the Barbarian: Japanese Travellers in America and Europe* (New Haven, Conn.: Yale University Press, 1995), 56–66; *Kodansha Encyclopedia of Japan* (Tokyo: Kodansha International Ltd., 1983), 8: 174; Philip Shriver Klein, *President James Buchanan: A Biography* (University Park: The Pennsylvania State University Press, 1962), 348; Nevins, *Emergence of Lincoln*, 2: 174; Peter Duus, ed., *The Japanese Discovery of America* (Boston: Bedford Books, 1997), 23–25; Masao Miyoshi, *As We Saw Them: The First Japanese Embassy to the United States (1860)* (Berkeley: University of California Press, 1979), 43, 74–84.

(13– **The Prince of Wales**: Klein, *President James Buchanan*, 350; George
14)   Dangerfield, *Victoria's Heir: The Education of a Prince* (New York: Harcourt, Brace and Company, 1941), 111–113; Giles St. Aubyn, *Edward VII: Prince and King* (New York: Atheneum, 1979), 47–48; Robin W. Winks, *Canada and the United States: The Civil War Years* (Baltimore: The Johns Hopkins University Press, 1960), 5–7.

(14– **Campaign Biographies of Lincoln**: Ernest James Wessen, "Campaign
16)   Lives of Abraham Lincoln, 1860: An Annotated Bibliography of the Biographies of Abraham Lincoln Issued during the Campaign Year," *Papers in Illinois History and Transactions* 44 (1937), 192, 195, 199; Douglas L. Wilson, *Honor's Voice: The Transformation of Abraham Lincoln* (New York: Alfred A. Knopf, 1998), 3–4; Reinhard Luthin, *The Real Abraham Lincoln* (Englewood Cliffs, N.J.: Prentice-Hall, 1960), 223, 225; Grace Locke Scripps Dyche, "John Locke Scripps: Lincoln Campaign Biographer," *Journal of the Illinois State Historical Society* 17 (October 1924), 335–338; Donald, *Lincoln*, 19; Oates, *With Malice Toward None*, 196–197; Jones, *Disrupted Decades*, 150–151.

(16– **"Little Giant"**: Johannsen, *Douglas*, 778, 797–799, 802–803, 871–872;
17)   Gerald M. Capers, *Stephen A. Douglas: Defender of the Union* (Boston: Little, Brown and Company, 1959), 207–208; Boller, *Presidential Campaigns*, 109–110; David R. Barbee and Milledge L. Bonham, Jr., eds., "The Montgomery Address of Stephen A. Douglas," *Journal of Southern History* 5 (November 1939), 527, 551; Potter, *The Impending Crisis*, 440–441.

(18– **The Campaign of 1860**: The only other presidential election in which
19)   eligible voters cast more ballots (82.6 percent) was in 1876. From 1904 to the present, no presidential election has attracted more than 65.7 percent of the electorate. A. James Reichley, ed., *Elections American Style*

(Washington, D.C.: The Brookings Institution, 1987), 113–114; Harold W. Stanley and Richard G. Niemi, *Vital Statistics on American Politics* (Washington, D.C.: Congressional Quarterly, 1994), 85; Glyndon G. Van Deusen, "Why the Republican Party Came to Power," in Harmon Knoles, ed., *Crisis of the Union: 1860–1861* (Baton Rouge: Louisiana State University Press, 1965), 11; Boller, *Presidential Campaigns*, 111–112; *Harper's Weekly*, October 13, 1860; Nevins, *The Emergence of Lincoln*, 2: 305; Fite, *Presidential Campaign of 1860*, 225–231; New York *Daily Tribune*, November 8, 1860.

(19–20) **Abraham Lincoln**: Boller, *Presidential Campaigns*, 102; Luthin, *The First Lincoln Campaign*, 224–225; McPherson, Battle Cry of Freedom, 232–233; Don E. Fehrenbacher, *Prelude to Greatness: Lincoln in the 1850s* (Stanford, Calif.: Stanford University Press, 1962), 159–160; Potter, *The Impending Crisis*, 446–447; Richard Nelson Current, "'Right Makes Might': Lincoln and the Race for President, 1859–1860," in Mario M. Cuomo and Harold Holzer, eds., *Lincoln on Democracy* (New York: HarperCollins Publishers, 1990), 146–147; Robert W. Johannsen, *Lincoln, the South, and Slavery: The Political Dimension* (Baton Rouge: Louisiana State University Press, 1991), 108.

(21–22) **Henry Villard**: John L. Moore, *Speaking of Washington: Facts, Firsts, and Folklore* (Washington, D.C.: Congressional Quarterly, 1993), 260; J. Cutler Andrews, *The North Reports the Civil War* (Pittsburgh: University of Pittsburgh Press, 1955), 77–79; *Dictionary of American Biography* (1936; reprint, New York: Charles Scribner's Sons, 1964), 10: 273–275; Henry Villard, *Memoirs of Henry Villard: Journalist and Financier, 1835–1900* (Boston: Houghton Mifflin and Company, 1904), 1: 1–8, 89–96, 136–138, 140–152; Louis M. Starr, *Reporting the Civil War: The Bohemian Brigade in Action, 1861–1865* (1954; reprint, New York: Collier Books, 1962), 24–25; Harold G. and Oswald Garrison Villard, eds., *Lincoln on the Eve of '61: A Journalist's Story by Henry Villard* (New York: Alfred A. Knopf, 1941), 96–98.

(22–23) **Grace Bedell's Letter**: Douglas L. Wilson and Rodney O. Davis, eds., *Herndon's Informants: Letters, Interviews, and Statements about Abraham Lincoln* (Urbana: University of Illinois Press, 1998), 517; Kane, *Facts about the Presidents*, 97–98; Benjamin P. Thomas, *Abraham Lincoln: A Biography* (New York: Alfred A. Knopf, 1952), 221; Robert S. Harper, *Lincoln and the Press* (New York: McGraw–Hill, 1951), 84–85.

(23–26) **Kate Warne**: James Mackay, *Allan Pinkerton: The First Private Eye* (New York: John Wiley & Sons, 1997), 74–75, 100, 102–103; James D. Horan, *The Pinkertons: The Detective Dynasty That Made History* (New York: Bonanza Books, 1967), 29, 52–59; Norma B. Cuthbert, ed., *Lincoln and the Baltimore Plot: 1861* (San Marino, Calif.: The Huntington Library, 1949), 21, 40–45, 70, 76–82; Alan Axelrod, *The War Between the Spies: A History of Espionage During the American Civil*

War (New York: The Atlantic Monthly Press, 1992), 11–22; Donald, *Lincoln*, 277–278; Oates, *With Malice Toward None*, 229–230; Theodore Roscoe, *The Web of Conspiracy: The Complete Story of the Men Who Murdered Abraham Lincoln* (Englewood Cliffs, N.J.: Prentice-Hall, 1959), 6–10; Richard Wilmer Rowan, *The Pinkertons: A Detective Dynasty* (Boston: Little, Brown and Company, 1931), 109– 115; Allan Pinkerton, *The Spy of the Rebellion* (New York: G. W. Carleton and Co., 1883), 91–99.

(26–27) **The Confederate States of America**: William C. Davis, *"A Government of Our Own": The Making of the Confederacy* (New York: The Free Press, 1994), 76, 227–228, 246, 251, 256–261, 294–295; Emory M. Thomas, *Robert E. Lee: A Biography* (New York: W. W. Norton, 1995), 72, 173, 184; Kenneth M. Stampp, *The Peculiar Institution: Slavery in the Ante-Bellum South* (New York: Alfred A. Knopf, 1956), 27–33; Frank E. Vandiver, *Their Tattered Flags* (New York: Harper & Row, 1970), 24–25; Thomas E. Schott, *Alexander H. Stephens of Georgia: A Biography* (Baton Rouge: Louisiana State University Press, 1988), 3–4, 20–21, 306–313, 321–322; Edward McPherson, *The Political History of the United States of America during the Great Rebellion* (Washington, D.C.: Philip & Solomons, 1865), 103.

(27–29) **An Armed Camp**: John S. D. Eisenhower, *Agent of Destiny: The Life and Times of Winfield Scott* (New York: The Free Press, 1997), 353–355; Potter, *The Impending Crisis*, 566; Axelrod, *The War Between the Spies*, 22–23; Roy Meredith, *Mr. Lincoln's Camera Man: Mathew B. Brady* (New York: Charles Scribner's Sons, 1946), 68; Elbert B. Smith, *The Presidency of James Buchanan* (Lawrence: The University Press of Kansas, 1975), 191; Charles W. Elliot, *Winfield Scott: The Soldier and the Man* (New York: The Macmillan Company, 1937), 694–695; Kenneth M. Stampp, *And the War Came: The North and the Secession Crisis, 1860–1861* (Baton Rouge: Louisiana State University Press, 1950), 197.

(29–30) **Born in Kentucky**: Wilson and Davis, eds., *Herndon's Informants*, 27–28, 67, 257; Donald, *Lincoln*, 22–24, 36; Oates, *With Malice Toward None*, 5, 7–8, 16–17.

(30–31) **Lincoln's Working-Class Roots**: Wilson, *Honor's Voice*, 86–89, 91–93, 96–100; Wilson and Davis, eds., *Herndon's Informants*, 120–121, 124–125; Walter B. Stevens, *A Reporter's Lincoln*, edited by Michael Burlingame (Lincoln: University of Nebraska Press, 1998), 168; Thomas, *Abraham Lincoln*, 23–43; Roy P. Basler, ed., *The Collected Works of Abraham Lincoln* (New Brunswick, N.J.: Rutgers University Press, 1953), 3: 462; Carl Sandburg, *Abraham Lincoln: The War Years—II* (1939; reprint, New York: Charles Scribner's Sons, 1948), 4: 590– 591.

(31–32) **Five Former Presidents**: At the time of President Bill Clinton's inauguration on January 20, 1993, the five ex–presidents still alive were

Richard Nixon, Gerald Ford, Jimmy Carter, Ronald Reagan, and George Bush. Moore, *Speaking of Washington*, 119; Donald Cole, *Martin Van Buren and the American Political System* (Princeton, N.J.: Princeton University Press, 1984), 425–426; John Niven, *Martin Van Buren: The Romantic Age of American Politics* (New York: Oxford University Press, 1983), 610–612; Boller, *Presidential Campaigns*, 100; Robert J. Rayback, *Millard Fillmore: Biography of a President* (Buffalo, N.Y.: Buffalo Historical Society, 1959), 423, 430.

(32– **Maj. Robert Anderson**: Maury Klein, *Days of Defiance: Sumter,*
35) *Secession, and the Coming of the Civil War* (New York: Alfred A. Knopf, 1997), 168, 215, 296: W. A. Swanberg, *First Blood: The Story of Fort Sumter* (New York: Charles Scribner's Sons, 1957), 135–136, 141, 323, 333–335; McPherson, *Battle Cry of Freedom*, 264–274; Starr, *Reporting the Civil War*, 7–8; John T. Hubbell and James W. Geary, eds., *Biographical Dictionary of the Union: Northern Leaders of the Civil War* (Westport, Conn.: Greenwood Press, 1995), 146–147; *New York Times*, January 4, 1861; D. Mark Katz, *Witness to an Era: The Life and Photographs of Alexander Gardner* (New York: Viking, 1991), 19–20; Klein, *President James Buchanan*, 402; Richard N. Current, *Lincoln and the First Shot* (Philadelphia: J. B. Lippincott Company, 1963), 24, 44–45, 96–102.

(35) **New York *Herald***: Starr, *Reporting the Civil War*, 24; Allan Nevins, *The War for the Union: The Improvised War, 1861–1862* (New York: Charles Scribner's Sons, 1959), 1: 262; Douglas Fermer, *James Gordon Bennett and the New York Herald: A Study of Editorial Opinion in the Civil War Era, 1854–1867* (New York: St. Martin's Press, 1986), 324.

CHAPTER 2: RAISING AND ADMINISTERING AN ARMY
(Pages 37–66)

(37– **Introduction**: Jeffrey Rogers Hummel, *Emancipating Slaves, Enslav-*
39) *ing Free Men: A History of the American Civil War* (Chicago: Open Court, 1996), 156, 159; Herman M. Hattaway, "The Civil War Armies: Creation, Mobilization, and Development," in Stig Förster and Jörg Nagler, eds., *On the Road to Total War: The American Civil War and the German Wars of Unification, 1861–1871* (New York: Cambridge University Press, 1997), 181–183; George T. Ness, *The Regular Army on the Eve of the Civil War* (Baltimore: Toomey Press, 1990), 1, 3, 250–251; Peter J. Parish, *The American Civil War* (New York: Holmes & Meier Publishers, 1975), 132–133; Russell F. Weigley, *Quartermaster General of the Union Army: A Biography of M. C. Meigs* (New York: Columbia University Press, 1959), 319; Basler, ed., *The Collected Works of Abraham Lincoln*, 4: 437; Philip Shaw Paludan, *"A People's Contest:" The Union and Civil War, 1861–1865* (New York: Harper &

Row Publishers, 1988), 18; T. Harry Williams, *The Selected Essays of T. Harry Williams* (Baton Rouge: Louisiana State University Press, 1983), 150; James M. McPherson, *For Cause and Comrades: Why Men Fought in the Civil War* (New York: Oxford University Press, 1997), 46; Fred Albert Shannon, *The Organization and Administration of the Union Army, 1861–1865* (1928; reprint, Gloucester, Mass.: Peter Smith, 1965), 1: 152–153; Bell Irvin Wiley, *The Life of Billy Yank: The Common Soldier of the Union* (Indianapolis: The Bobbs-Merrill Company, 1951), 25–27.

(39–
45)   **Conscription**: Hummell, *Emancipating Slaves, Enslaving Free Men*, 158–159; James I. Robertson, Jr., *Soldiers Blue and Gray* (Columbia: University of South Carolina Press, 1988), 8–9, 12–13, 36–40; Paludan, "A People's Contest," 15–18; Eugene C. Murdock, *One Million Men: The Civil War Draft in the North* (Madison: The State Historical Society of Wisconsin, 1971), 4–8, 24–25, 81, 201–203, 218–220, 334–335, 340–342; James W. Geary, *We Need Men: The Union Draft in the Civil War* (Dekalb: Northern Illinois University Press, 1991), 3–5, 66–67, 138, 167–169, 173–174; Richard N. Current, ed., *Encyclopedia of the Confederacy* (New York: Simon & Schuster, 1993), 1: 396–399, 2: 467; James M. McPherson, *Ordeal by Fire: The Civil War and Reconstruction* (New York: McGraw-Hill, 1992), 353–355; Richard H. Sewell, *A House Divided: Sectionalism and Civil War, 1848–1865* (Baltimore: The Johns Hopkins University Press, 1988), 88–89, 102; James G. Randall and David Donald, *The Civil War and Reconstruction* (Lexington, Mass.: D. C. Heath and Company, 1969), 251–252, 264–265, 268–269, 315–318, 328–329; Randall C. Jimerson, *The Private Civil War: Popular Thought during the Sectional Conflict* (Baton Rouge: Louisiana State University Press, 1988), 192–193, 196–197; Bell Irvin Wiley, *The Plain People of the Confederacy* (1944; reprint, Chicago: Quadrangle Books, 1963), 65; Gallman, *The North Fights the Civil War*, 62–63, 65–66; Geoffrey C. Ward, *The Civil War: An Illustrated History* (New York: Alfred A. Knopf, 1990), 242–244; Nevins and Thomas, eds., *The Diary of George Templeton Strong*, 3: 479; Iver Bernstein, *The New York City Draft Riots: Their Significance for American Society and Politics in the Age of the Civil War* (New York: Oxford University Press, 1990), 123–124; Adrian Cook, *The Armies of the Street: The New York City Draft Riots of 1863* (Lexington: The University Press of Kentucky, 1974), 194–203; Bruce Catton, *America Goes to War* (Middletown, Conn.: Wesleyan University Press, 1958), 44–46.

(45–
52)   **African-American Soldiers**: Dudley Taylor Cornish, *The Sable Arm: Negro Troops in the Union Army, 1861–1865* (New York: W. W. Norton, 1966), 3; James M. McPherson, *The Struggle for Equality: Abolitionists and the Negro in the Civil War and Reconstruction* (Princeton, N.J.: Princeton University Press, 1964), 192, 197; McPherson, *The*

Negro's Civil War, 20, 163–165; Wiley, *The Life of Billy Yank*, 120; Litwack, *Been in the Storm So Long*, 66, 70; Philip S. Foner, *History of Black Americans: From the Compromise of 1850 to the End of the Civil War* (Westport, Conn.: Greenwood Press, 1983), 3: 368; Elizabeth Ware Pearson, *Letters from Port Royal: Written at the Time of the Civil War* (Boston: W. B. Clarke, 1906), 43; Worthington Chauncey Ford, ed., *A Cycle of Adams Letters, 1861–1865* (Boston: Houghton Mifflin Company, 1920), 1: 171; Basler, ed., *The Collected Works of Abraham Lincoln*, 5: 423; *Douglass' Monthly* 4 (September 1861), 516, and 5 (August 1863), 852; William Cullen Bryant II, ed., "A Yankee Soldier Looks at the Negro: Extracts from the Civil War Letters of Henry M. Cross, 1863–1865," *Civil War History* 7 (June 1961), 144; V. Jacque Voegeli, *Free but Not Equal: The Midwest and the Negro During the Civil War* (Chicago: The University of Chicago Press, 1967), 102; McPherson, *For Cause and Comrades*, 126–127, 152–153; Joseph T. Glatthaar, *Forged in Battle: The Civil War Alliance of Black Soldiers and White Officers* (New York: The Free Press, 1990), 31–32, 134, 155–159, 167, 178–180, 250–251; Herman Hattaway, *Shades of Blue and Gray: An Introductory Military History of the Civil War* (Columbia: University of Missouri Press, 1997), 159–160; Benjamin Quarles, *The Negro in the Civil War* (Boston: Little, Brown and Company, 1953), 31, 118–119, 205–207; *The War of the Rebellion: A Compilation of the Official Records of the Union and Confederate Armies* (Washington, D.C.: Government Printing Office, 1889), Series 1, Vol. 24, Pt. 1, 106, Series 2, Vol. 6, 163, Series 3, Vol. 3, 696; Noah Andre Trudeau, *Like Men of War: Black Troops in the Civil War, 1862–1865* (Boston: Little, Brown and Company, 1998), 44–45, 166–169, 466–467; McPherson, *Ordeal by Fire*, 349, 351–353; Sewell, *A House Divided*, 177–179; Harold Holzer, ed., *The Lincoln Mailbag: America Writes to the President, 1861–1865* (Carbondale: Southern Illinois University Press, 1998), 163–164, 166–167; Joseph T. Glatthaar, "Black Glory: The African-American Role in Union Victory," in Gabor S. Boritt, ed., *Why the Confederacy Lost* (New York: Oxford University Press, 1992), 152; W. E. Burghardt Du Bois, *Black Reconstruction in America* (1935; reprint, Cleveland: The World Publishing Company, 1964), 104.

(52–56) **Free Military School for Applicants for Commands of Colored Troops**: Soon after the school closed, it reopened under a new name—the U. S. Military School for Officers—but it was no longer free. Candidates were required to pay tuition. The school remained in operation through the rest of the war, continuing to turn out officers for black units. Ira Berlin, Joseph P. Reidy, and Leslie S. Rowland, eds., *Freedom: A Documentary History of Emancipation, 1861–1867*. Series II. *The Black Military Experience* (Cambridge, England: Cambridge University Press, 1982), 303–329, 406–411; Glatthaar, *Forged in Battle*,

8–9, 35–59, 176, 182; James G. Hollandsworth, Jr., *The Louisiana Native Guards: The Black Military Experience during the Civil War* (Baton Rouge: Louisiana State University Press, 1995), 270–283; Hondon B. Hargrove, *Black Union Soldiers in the Civil War* (Jefferson, N.C.: McFarland & Company, 1988), 109–110; Jimerson, *The Private Civil War*, 101; Cornish, *The Sable Arm*, 217–228.

(56–
59)   **"The Sergeant Turns Out to Be a Woman"**: Mary Elizabeth Massey, *Bonnet Brigades* (New York: Alfred A . Knopf, 1966), 78–80, 84–85; Earl Schenck Miers, ed., *When the World Ended: The Diary of Emma LeConte* (New York: Oxford University Press, 1957), 90; Kate Mason Rowland and Mrs. Morris L. Croxall, eds., *The Journal of Julia LeGrand: New Orleans, 1862–1863* (Richmond: Everett Waddey Co., 1911), 52–53; Drew Gilpin Faust, *Mothers of Invention: Women of the Slaveholding South in the American Civil War* (Chapel Hill: The University of North Carolina Press, 1996), 202; Elizabeth Leonard, *All the Daring of the Soldier: Women of the Civil War Armies* (New York: W. W. Norton, 1999), 165, 310–311; DeAnne Blanton, "Women Soldiers of the Civil War," *Prologue* 25 (Spring 1993), 27, 29–33; Lauren Cook Burgess, ed., *An Uncommon Soldier: The Civil War Letters of Sarah Rosetta Wakeman, alias Private Lyons Wakeman, 153rd Regiment, New York State Volunteers* (New York: Oxford University Press, 1994), xi, 1–7; Ann Douglas Wood, "The War Within a War: Women Nurses in the Union Army," *Civil War History* 18 (September 1972), 202; Catherine Clinton, *Tara Revisited: Women, War, and the Plantation Legend* (New York: Abbeville Press, 1995), 99; Richard Goldhurst, *Many Are the Hearts: The Agony and the Triumphs of Ulysses S. Grant* (New York: Reader's Digest Press, 1975), 34; Richard Hall, *Patriots in Disguise: Women Warriors of the Civil War* (New York: Paragon House, 1993), xiii, 20–26, 98–106, 156–160; M. H. Mahoney, *Women in Espionage: A Biographical Dictionary* (Santa Barbara, Calif.: ABC–CLIO, 1993), 76–77; Catherine Clinton, "'Noble Women as Well,'" in Robert Brent Toplin, *Ken Burns's The Civil War: Historians Respond* (New York: Oxford University Press, 1996), 71–73.

(59–
63)   **"Holy Joes"**: Parker C. Thompson, *From Its European Antecedents to 1791: The United States Army Chaplaincy* (Washington, D.C.: Office of the Chief of Chaplains, Department of the Army, 1978), 1: xiv–xx; Herman A. Norton, *Struggling for Recognition: The United States Army Chaplaincy, 1791–1865* (Washington, D.C.: Office of the Chief of Chaplains, Department of the Army, 1977), 2: 1–19, 64–68, 82–109; John Tracy Ellis, *American Catholicism* (Chicago: The University of Chicago Press, 1969), 98; Benjamin J. Blied, *Catholics and the Civil War* (Milwaukee: privately printed, 1945), 36, 108–111; Edward J. Longacre, *Army of Amateurs: General Benjamin F. Butler and the Army of the James, 1863–1865* (Mechanicsburg, Penn.: Stackpole Books, 1997), 56;

Gerald Sorin, *Tradition Transformed: The Jewish Experience in America* (Baltimore: Johns Hopkins University Press, 1997), 27; Stanley Feldstein, *The Land That I Show You: Three Centuries of Jewish Life in America* (Garden City, N.Y.: Anchor Press, 1978), 89–90; Korn, *American Jewry and the Civil War*, 56–97; Rollin W. Quimby, "Congress and the Civil War Chaplaincy," *Civil War History* 10 (September 1964), 250–251, 254; *U.S. Statutes at Large*, 12: 595; Edwin S. Redkey, "Black Chaplains in the Union Army," *Civil War History* 33 (December 1987), 331–333, 337–349; Berlin, Reidy, and Rowland, eds., *Freedom: The Black Military Experience*, 348–349; Rollin W. Quimby, "The Chaplain's Predicament," *Civil War History* 8 (March 1962), 27–31; Bell Irvin Wiley, "'Holy Joes' of the Sixties: A Study of Civil War Chaplains," *The Huntington Library Quarterly* 16 (May 1953), 287– 290.

(63–
65) **Montgomery C. Meigs, Quartermaster General, U.S.A.**: Parish, *The American Civil War*, 150–151; Weigley, *Quartermaster General of the Union Army*, 3–5, 13–77, 255–257; Allan Nevins, *The War for the Union: The Organized War, 1863–1864* (New York: Charles Scribner's Sons, 1971), 3: 291–295; Paul P. Van Riper and Keith A Sutherland, "The Northern Civil Service: 1861–1865," *Civil War History* 11 (December 1965), 369.

(65–
66) **Taps**: Hubbell & Geary, eds., *Biographical Dictionary of the Union*, 76–77; Oliver W. Norton, *Army Letters, 1861–1865* (Chicago: O. L. Deming, 1903), 327–329; Robertson, *Soldiers Blue and Gray*, 87–88.

CHAPTER 3: THE LAND WAR (Pages 67–104)

(67–
68) **Introduction**: Thomas A. Palmer, "Military Technology," in Melvin Kranzberg and Carroll W. Pursell, Jr., eds., *Technology in Western Civilization: The Emergence of Modern Industrial Society, Earliest Times to 1900* (New York: Oxford University Press, 1967), 1: 497; Earl J. Hess, "Tactics, Trenches, and Men in the Civil War," in Förster and Nagler, eds., *On the Road to Total War*, 482–483; Grimsley, *The American Civil War*, 159; Parish, *The American Civil War*, 128–130; Edward Hagerman, *The American Civil War and the Origins of Modern Warfare: Ideas, Organization, and Field Command* (Bloomington: Indiana University Press, 1988), xi–xii; Sewell, *A House Divided*, 126–127; Albert A. Nofi, *The Civil War Notebook: A Collection of Little-Known Facts and Other Odds-and-Ends about the Civil War* (Conshohocken, Penn.: Combined Books, Inc., 1993), 74; Ward, *The Civil War*, 267.

(68–
70) **The Minié Ball**: Robert V. Bruce, *Lincoln and the Tools of War* (Indianapolis: Bobbs-Merrill Company, 1956), 37–38; Joseph T. Glatthaar, "Battlefield Tactics," in James M. McPherson and William J. Cooper, eds., *Writing the Civil War: The Quest to Understand* (Columbia: University of South Carolina Press, 1998), 63–64, 67–71; Robertson, *Sol-

diers Blue and Gray, 55; Hattaway, *Shades of Blue and Gray*, 2–3; Gerald F. Linderman, *Embattled Courage: The Experience of Combat in the American Civil War* (New York: The Free Press, 1987), 135–139; Hummel, *Emancipating Slaves, Enslaving Free Men*, 186– 188; Grady McWhiney, "Who Whipped Whom? Confederate Defeat Reexamined," *Civil War History* 11 (March 1965), 7–8; Charles C. Fennell, Jr., "The Civil War: The First Modern War," in John M. Carroll and Colin F. Baxter, eds., *The American Military Tradition: From Colonial Times to the Present* (Wilmington, Del.: Scholarly Resources, 1993), 66–67; Catton, *America Goes to War*, 17–19; Grady McWhiney and Perry D. Jamieson, *Attack and Die: Civil War Military Tactics and the Southern Heritage* (University, Ala.: The University of Alabama Press, 1982), 48–49, 60, 139, 146.

(70– **Breechloaders and Repeating Rifles**: Bruce, *Lincoln and the Tools of*
76)   *War*, 99–111, 154–156, 204–206, 285–287; Robertson, *Soldiers Blue and Gray*, 55–56, 221; Emory M. Thomas, *The American War and Peace: 1860–1877* (Englewood Cliffs, N.J.: Prentice-Hall, 1973), 71–72; James A. Huston, *The Sinews of War: Army Logistics, 1775–1953* (Washington, D.C.: U.S. Government Printing Office, 1966), 157–158; Carl L. Davis, *Arming the Union: Small Arms in the Civil War* (Port Washington, N.Y.: Kennikat Press, 1973), 126–131, 135–138, 157–159; Charles A. Stevens, *Berdan's United States Sharpshooters in the Army of the Potomac, 1861–1865* (St. Paul: The Price-Mcgill Company, 1892), 309–311; W. Eugene Sloan, "The Spencer: Revolution in Weaponry—Goodbye to the Single-Shot Musket," *Civil War Times Illustrated* 23 (May 1984), 31, 33; Glatthaar, "Battlefield Tactics," 64–65; Nevins, *The War for the Union*, 3: 306–308; John W. Rowell, *Yankee Artillerymen: Through the Civil War with Eli Lilly's Indiana Battery* (Knoxville: University of Tennessee Press, 1975), 53–55, 60–61, 65–67; John D. McAulay, *Civil War Breech Loading Rifles: A Survey of the Innovative Arms of the American Civil War* (Lincoln, R.I.: Andrew Mowbray, 1987), 73–86; Frank Moore, ed., *The Rebellion Record: A Diary of American Events, with Documents, Narratives, Illustrative Incidents, Poetry, Etc.* (New York: D. Van Nostrand, Publisher, 1864), 7: 58 ("Poetry and Incidents"); Oscar Osburn Winther, ed., *With Sherman to the Sea: The Civil War Letters, Diaries & Reminiscences of Theodore F. Upson* (Baton Rouge: Louisiana State University Press, 1943), 157–158; Nevins, *The War for the Union*, 1: 369.

(76– **Machine Guns**: Paul Wahl and Donald R. Toppel, *The Gatling Gun*
80)   (New York: Arco Publishing Company, 1965), 1–5, 9–10, 12, 26; Garry James, "The Search for the Ultimate Weapon," *Civil War Times Illustrated* 31 (January/February 1993), 49–56; Ian V. Hogg, *Weapons of the Civil War* (New York: Military Press, 1987), 50–55; Jack Coggins, *Arms and Equipment of the Civil War* (Garden City, N.Y.: Doubleday &

Company, 1962), 43–55; Bruce, *Lincoln and the Tools of War*, 118–123, 194–200, 282–283, 290; New York *Evening Post*, April 25, 1862; Holzer, ed., *The Lincoln Mailbag*, 142–143; Lester L. Swift, ed., "The Recollections of a Signal Officer," *Civil War History* 9 (March 1963), 50; Shannon, *The Organization and Administration of the Union Army*, 1: 146–147; Huston, *The Sinews of War*, 193–194.

(80– **Musket Shells**: Wayne Austerman, "Abhorrent to Civilization: The
82) Explosive Bullet in the Civil War," *Civil War Times Illustrated* 24 (September 1985), 37–40; Washington *Evening Star*, June 6, 1862; Bruce, *Lincoln and the Tools of War*, 190–192, 257; Coggins, *Arms and Equipment of the Civil War*, 27.

(82– **Gas Warfare**: Bruce, *Lincoln and the Tools of War*, 247–248; F. Stans-
84) bury Haydon, "A Proposed Gas Shell, 1862," *The Journal of the American Military History Foundation* 2 (Spring 1938), 52–54; Peter Young and J. P. Lawford, eds., *History of the British Army* (New York: G. P. Putnam's Sons, 1970), 219.

(84– **Land Mines**: W. Davis Waters, "'Deception Is the Art of War': Gabriel
87) J. Rains, Torpedo Specialist of the Confederacy," *The North Carolina Historical Review* 66 (January 1989), 30–38, 45–46, 49–50, 53–60; Mark E. Neely, Jr., "Was the Civil War a Total War?" *Civil War History* 37 (March 1991), 12–13; Milton F. Perry, *Infernal Machines: The Story of Confederate Submarine and Mine Warfare* (Baton Rouge: Louisiana State University Press, 1965), 58–60, 165, 179–180; Hattaway, *Shades of Blue and Gray*, 159.

(87– **Brass Pounders**: Bern Dibner, "The Beginning of Electricity," in
90) Kranzberg and Pursell, eds., *Technology in Western Civilization* 1: 454–455; Palmer, "Military Technology," 496; George Raynor Thompson, "Civil War Signals," *Military Affairs* 18 (Winter 1954), 190–191, 199– 200; Coggins, *Arms and Equipment of the Civil War*, 108; Peter Maslowski, "Military Intelligence Sources during the American Civil War," in James E. Dillard and Walter T. Hitchcock, eds., *The Intelligence Revolution and Modern Warfare* (Chicago: Imprint Publications, 1996), 46–49; Alvin F. Harlow, *Brass-Pounders: Young Telegraphers of the Civil War* (Denver, Colo.: Sage Books, 1962), 26–28; Francis Trevelyan Miller, ed., *The Photographic History of the Civil War* (1911; reprint, New York: Thomas Yoseloff, 1957), 8: 342–343, 348, 350, 363; Paul J. Scheips, "Union Signal Communications: Innovation and Conflict," *Civil War History* 9 (December 1963), 403, 419; James A. Rawley, *Abraham Lincoln and a Nation Worth Fighting For* (Wheeling, Ill.: Harlan Davidson, 1996), 74; Edwin C. Fishel, *The Secret War for the Union: The Untold Story of Military Intelligence in the Civil War* (Boston: Houghton Mifflin Company, 1996), 146; Hagerman, *The American Civil War and the Origins of Modern Warfare*, 36–37, 41, 87.

(90–   **Col. Albert J. Myer, U.S. Army Signal Corps**: Nevins, *The War for*
95)   *the Union*, 1: 267; Editors of the Army Times, *A History of the U.S. Sig-*
        nal Corps (New York: G. P. Putnam's Sons, 1961), 7–8, 11–13, 18,
        38–40, 52–57, 64; Scheips, "Union Signal Communications," 399–406,
        412–415, 420–421; Thompson, "Civil War Signals," 188–192, 194–
        198; Fishel, *The Secret War for the Union*, 10, 37–38, 146; Maslowski,
        "Military Intelligence Sources during the American Civil War," 45–48;
        Hagerman, *The American Civil War and the Origins of Modern War-*
        fare, 43–44, 52, 86–87, 103–104; Miller, ed., *The Photographic History*
        of the Civil War, 8: 312–313, 318, 322, 340; Swift, "The Recollections
        of a Signal Officer," 41, 44; Longacre, *Army of Amateurs*, 26–27.

(95–   **The Railroads**: George Rogers Taylor, *The Transportation Revolution:*
100)   *1815–1860* (New York: Holt, Rinehart and Winston, 1962), 84–86, 144;
        Hogg, *Weapons of the Civil War*, 134–138; McPherson, *Battle Cry of*
        Freedom, 12, 671–681; George Edgar Turner, *Victory Rode the Rails:*
        The Strategic Place of the Railroads in the Civil War (Indianapolis: The
        Bobbs-Merrill Company, 1953), 17–18, 87, 246–247, 288–294; Thomas
        Weber, *The Northern Railroads in the Civil War: 1861–1865* (1952;
        reprint, Westport, Conn.: Greenwood Press Publishers, 1970), 30, 105,
        134–136, 199–200, 219–221; Thomas, *Abraham Lincoln*, 262–263;
        Francis A. Lord, *Lincoln's Railroad Man: Herman Haupt* (Rutherford,
        N.J.: Fairleigh Dickinson University Press, 1969), 261; Allan Nevins,
        The War for the Union: The Organized War to Victory, 1864–1865 (New
        York: Charles Scribner's Sons, 1971), 4: 151–152; James A. Rawley, *The*
        Politics of Union: Northern Politics during the Civil War (Hinsdale, Ill.:
        The Dryden Press, 1974), 59; Huston, *The Sinews of War*, 207, 209–210;
        Parish, *The American Civil War*, 352; Sherman, *Memoirs*, 2: 398.

(100–   **Gen. Ulysses S. Grant**: Gen. Winfield Scott also held three-star rank,
104)   but that was by brevet, which meant that it was honorary, with no
        increase in pay. Geoffrey Perret, *Ulysses S. Grant: Soldier and Presi-*
        dent (New York: Random House, 1997), 86–88, 107–113, 202–208,
        287–288, 290, 294–298, 368, 478; Ulysses S. Grant, *Personal Memoirs*
        of U. S. Grant (New York: Charles L. Webster & Company, 1885), 1:
        24, 38, 53; William S. McFeeley, *Grant: A Biography* (New York:
        W. W. Norton, 1981), 29–30, 99–151; Richard Goldhurst, *Many Are the*
        Hearts, 33–34; Earl J. Hess, *The Union Soldier in Battle: Enduring the*
        Ordeal of Combat (Lawrence: University Press of Kansas, 1997), 64–
        72; Russell F. Weigley, *The American Way of War: A History of United*
        States Military Strategy and Policy (New York: Macmillan Publishing
        Co., 1973), 142–152; Linderman, *Embattled Courage*, 147; Sewell, *A*
        House Divided, 155–159; Charles Royster, *The Destructive War: Wil-*
        liam Tecumseh Sherman, Stonewall Jackson, and the Americans (New
        York: Alfred A. Knopf, 1991), 286, 332–339.

CHAPTER 4: THE NAVAL WAR (Pages 105–132)

(105) **Introduction**: Ivan Musicant, *Divided Waters: The Naval History of the Civil War* (New York: HarperCollins Publishers, 1995), 1–2; Parish, *The American Civil War,* 417; Joseph Durkin, *Stephen R. Mallory: Confederate Navy Chief* (Chapel Hill: The University of North Carolina Press, 1954), 150; Randall and Donald, *The Civil War and Reconstruction,* 440.

(105– **Secretary of the Navy Gideon Welles**: Nevins, *The War for the Union,*
107) 3: 27, 285–286; Hubbell and Geary, eds., *Biographical Dictionary of the Union,* 578–579; Musicant, *Divided Waters,* 3–5; Richard S. West, Jr., *Gideon Welles: Lincoln's Navy Department* (Indianapolis: The Bobbs-Merrill Company, 1943), 120–121, 147; Richard S. West, Jr., *Mr. Lincoln's Navy* (New York: Longmans, Green and Company, 1957), 52; Bern Anderson, *By Sea and by River: The Naval History of the Civil War* (New York: Alfred A. Knopf, 1962), 17–20.

(107– **The Blockade**: McPherson, *Battle Cry of Freedom,* 369, 380–382;
108) Nevins, *The War for the Union,* 3: 339–341; Coggins, *Arms and Equipment of the Civil War,* 126–127, 151, 153–154; Robert E. May, ed., *The Union, the Confederacy, and the Atlantic Rim* (West Lafayette, Ind.: Purdue University Press, 1995), 4; James M. Merrill, *The Rebel Shore: The Story of Union Seapower in the Civil War* (Boston: Little, Brown and Company, 1957), 69; Dean B. Mahin, *One War at a Time: The International Dimensions of the American Civil War* (Washington, D.C.: Brassey's, 1999), 161–173; Anderson, *By Sea and by River,* 230; Rawley, *The Politics of Union,* 168.

(108– **The CSS *Virginia***: Durkin, *Stephen R. Mallory,* 43–44; Musicant,
111) *Divided Waters,* 134–154; McPherson, *Battle Cry of Freedom,* 373–375; Ward, *The Civil War,* 100; Virgil Carrington Jones, *The Civil War at Sea* (New York: Holt, Rinehart and Winston, 1960–1962), 3: 403; William N. Still, Jr., *Iron Afloat: The Story of the Confederate Armorclads* (Nashville, Tenn.: Vanderbilt University Press, 1971), 25; Anderson, *By Sea and by River,* 73.

(111– **The USS *Monitor***: John Niven, *Gideon Welles: Lincoln's Secretary of*
113) *the Navy* (New York: Oxford University Press, 1973), 404–406; James Tertius deKay, *Monitor: The Story of the Legendary Civil War Ironclad and the Man Whose Invention Changed the Course of History* (New York: Walker and Company, 1997), 86–137; Still, *Iron Afloat,* 32; William M. Fowler, Jr., *Under Two Flags: The American Navy in the Civil War* (New York: W. W. Norton & Company, 1990), 81–84; Musicant, *Divided Waters,* 155–169; H. Allen Gosnell, *Guns on the Western Waters: The Story of the River Gunboats in the Civil War* (Baton Rouge: Louisiana State University Press, 1949), 3; *Dictionary of American Biography* (1930; reprint, New York: Charles Scribner's Sons, 1958), 3: 171–176; Nofi, *The Civil War Notebook,* 49; Howard P. Nash, Jr., *A*

Naval History of the Civil War (New York: A. S. Barnes and Company, 1972), 83–87; Bert Hubinger, "Can We Ever Raise the Monitor?," *Civil War Times Illustrated* 36 (June 1997), 42–43; Arthur Farr, "The Real Genius behind the Monitor," *Civil War Times Illustrated* 36 (June 1997), 34–36.

(113– **Encounter at Hampton Roads**: deKay, *Monitor*, 150–221; Ward, *The*
115) *Civil War*, 101; West, *Gideon Welles*, 153–154; Albert A. Nofi, *A Civil War Treasury: Being a Miscellany of Arms and Artillery, Facts and Figures, Legends and Lore, Muses and Minstrels, Personalities and People* (1992; reprint, New York: Da Capo Press, 1995), 188; Musicant, *Divided Waters*, 169–178; Jones, *The Civil War at Sea*, 1: 429–437; Still, *Iron Afloat*, 33–34; Fowler, *Under Two Flags*, 83; McPherson, *Battle Cry of Freedom*, 377; Hubinger, "Can We Ever Raise the Monitor?," 38–48.

(115– **By Sea to the Peninsula**: McPherson, *Battle Cry of Freedom*, 336, 424;
116) Weigley, *Quartermaster General of the Union Army*, 2–3, 243–245; Joseph P. Cullen, *The Peninsula Campaign, 1862: McClellan & Lee Struggle for Richmond* (Harrisburg, Penn.: Stackpole Books, 1973), 15–16, 30–31, 178–179; Stephen Sears, "Lincoln and McClellan," in Gabor S. Boritt, ed., *Lincoln's Generals* (New York: Oxford University Press, 1994), 33–39.

(116– **Torpedoes**: Perry, *Infernal Machines*, 4–6, 188, 199–201; Current, ed.,
118) *Encyclopedia of the Confederacy*, 4: 1603–1604; Francis Leigh Williams, *Matthew Fontaine Maury: Scientist of the Sea* (New Brunswick, N.J.: Rutgers University Press, 1963), 367–368, 378–379, 608; Francis A. Lord, *Civil War Collector's Encyclopedia* (1963; reprint, Edison, N.J.: Blue & Grey Press, 1995), 2: 200, 202.

(118– **Minesweepers**: John C. Wideman, *The Sinking of the USS* Cairo (Jack-
119) son: University Press of Mississippi, 1993), 25–27; Nash, *A Naval History of the Civil War*, 151; Fowler, *Under Two Flags*, 199–200; Jones, *The Civil War at Sea*, 2: 292–294.

(119– **USS *Cairo***: The USS *Cairo* was raised in the mid-1960s and is now on
120) exhibit at the Vicksburg National Military Park. Wideman, *The Sinking of the USS* Cairo, ix–x, 27–39, 81; Raimondo Luraghi, *A History of the Confederate Navy*, trans. by Paolo E. Coletta (Annapolis, Md.: Naval Institute Press, 1996), 246–247; Jones, *The Civil War at Sea*, 2: 294–297; Fowler, *Under Two Flags*, 201; Perry, *Infernal Machines*, 33–36.

(120– **CSS *David***: Perry, *Infernal Machines*, 81–85; Luraghi, *A History of the*
121) *Confederate Navy*, 260–262; Lord, *Civil War Collector's Encyclopedia*, 1: 178; Jones, *The Civil War at Sea*, 3: 52–60; Lydel Sims, "The Submarine That Wouldn't Come Up," *American Heritage* 9 (April 1958), 51, 107; Nofi, *A Civil War Treasury*, 259.

(122) **The University of Virginia**: Williams, *Matthew Fontaine Maury*, 376–377; Robert V. Bruce, *The Launching of Modern American Science: 1846–1876* (New York: Alfred A. Knopf, 1987), 310.

(122– **A Torpedo Gone Awry**: Bruce, *Lincoln and the Tools of War*, 177–178;
123) Lord, *Civil War Collector's Encyclopedia*, 1: 178; Washington *Evening Star*, December 11, 1862.

(123– **Adm. David Glasgow Farragut**: James P. Duffy, *Lincoln's Admiral:*
126) *The Civil War Campaigns of David Farragut* (New York: John Wiley & Sons, 1997), 44–45, 83, 193–194, 219–220, 238–248, 253, 257–259; Charles Lee Lewis, *David Glasgow Farragut: Admiral in the Making* (Annapolis, Md.: United States Naval Institute, 1941), 292–293; Niven, *Gideon Welles*, 382–384; McPherson, *Battle Cry of Freedom*, 418–420; Edward L. Beach, *The United States Navy: 200 Years* (New York: Henry Holt and Company, 1986), 310–316; Anderson, *By Sea and by River*, 240–247.

(126– **Adm. David Dixon Porter**: West, *Gideon Welles*, 199–201; Tamara
128) Moser Melia, "David Dixon Porter: Fighting Sailor," in James C. Bradford, ed., *Captains of the Old Steam Navy: Makers of the American Naval Tradition, 1840–1880* (Annapolis, Md.: Naval Institute Press, 1986), 231–232; Fowler, *Under Two Flags*, 203–207; Chester G. Hearn, *Admiral David Dixon Porter* (Annapolis, Md.: Naval Institute Press, 1996), 33–35, 91–104, 141–143; Hubbell and Geary, eds., *Biographical Dictionary of the Union*, 411–412; Nevins, *The War for the Union*, 3: 72–73; Richard S. West, Jr., *The Second Admiral: A Life of David Dixon Porter: 1813–1891* (New York: Coward-McCann, 1937), 179, 232; Jones, *The Civil War at Sea*, 2: 424–426.

(128– **Submarine School**: Perry, *Infernal Machines*, 94–103; Sims, "The
130) Submarine That Wouldn't Come Up," 48–51, 107–108; Luraghi, *A History of the Confederate Navy*, 256–257; Current, ed., *Encyclopedia of the Confederacy*, 4: 1556–1558; Nofi, *Civil War Treasury*, 257–259.

(130– **Remaining Underwater**: Sims, "The Submarine That Wouldn't Come
131) Up," 109–110; Perry, *Infernal Machines*, 103–105; Luraghi, *A History of the Confederate Navy*, 257; Jones, *The Civil War at Sea*, 3: 125.

(131– **CSS *H. L. Hunley***: Current, ed., *Encyclopedia of the Confederacy*, 4:
132) 1558; Sims, "The Submarine That Wouldn't Come Up," 48, 110–111; Perry, *Infernal Machines*, 105–108; Luraghi, *A History of the Confederate Navy*, 257–259; Coggins, *Arms and Equipment of the Civil War*, 149–150; Daniel Lenihan, "Time Capsule: Objects in History," *American History* 32 (August 1997), 74; *New York Times*, August 9, 2000.

CHAPTER 5: FIGHTING THE WAR FROM THE AIR
(Pages 133–153)

(133– **Introduction**: F. Stansbury Haydon, *Aeronautics in the Union and Con-*
135) *federate Armies: With a Survey of Military Aeronautics Prior to 1861* (Baltimore: Johns Hopkins University Press, 1941), 1, 24–26, 28, 32; Douglas Botting, *The Great Airships* (Alexandria, Va.: Time-Life

Books, 1981), 20; Donald Dale Jackson, *The Aeronauts* (Alexandria, Va.: Time-Life Books, 1980), 14, 82; R. S. Waters, "Ballooning in the French Army During the Revolutionary Wars," *The Army Quarterly* 23 (January 1932), 330–332; J. Duane Squires, "Aeronautics in the Civil War," *American Historical Review* 42 (July 1937), 654.

(135– **John Wise**: Haydon, *Aeronautics in the Union and Confederate Ar-*
137)   *mies*, 57–81; *Dictionary of American Biography*, 10: 428–429.

(137– **Thaddeus S. C. Lowe**: Haydon, *Aeronautics in the Union and Confed-*
140)   *erate Armies*, 155–165, 167–175; Eugene B. Block, *Above the Civil War: The Story of Thaddeus Lowe, Balloonist, Inventor, Railway Builder* (Berkeley, Calif.: Howell-North Books, 1966), 11–56; *Dictionary of American Biography*, 10: 428; Bruce, *Lincoln and the Tools of War*, 85; *The War of the Rebellion: Official Records*, Series 3, Vol. 3, 254; Christopher Andrew, *Secret Intelligence and the American Presidency from Washington to Bush* (New York: HarperCollins Publishers, 1995), 20; Moore, ed., *The Rebellion Record*, 1: 108.

(140– **Aerial Reconnaissance**: Haydon, *Aeronautics in the Union and Con-*
141)   *federate Armies*, 181–185; Dino A. Brugioni, "Arlington and Fairfax Counties: Land of Many Reconnaissance Firsts," *Northern Virginia Heritage* (February 1985), 3.

(141) **Mapmaking in the Air**: Haydon, *Aeronautics in the Union and Con-
       federate Armies*, 186; Brugioni, "Arlington and Fairfax Counties," 6.

(142– **Flying over Enemy Territory**: Samuel S. Cox, *Three Decades of Fed-*
144)   *eral Legislation: 1855 to 1885* (San Francisco: Occidental Publishing Co., 1885), 158; Block, *Above the Civil War*, 68–70; Horace Sawyer Mazet, "Lincoln—Patron of Military Aviation," *The American Legion Monthly* 18 (February 1935), 32; *The War of the Rebellion: Official Records*, Series 3, Vol. 3, 258; Brugioni, "Arlington and Fairfax Counties," 4; Haydon, *Aeronautics in the Union and Confederate Armies*, 192–193.

(144– **An American Air Corps**: Squires, "Aeronautics in the Civil War," 658,
146)   661–663; Haydon, *Aeronautics in the Union and Confederate Armies*, 194–195, 233, 238–240, 264–270, 278; Nofi, *A Civil War Treasury*, 177; Brugioni, "Arlington and Fairfax Counties," 5; Jackson, *The Aeronauts*, 89; *The War of the Rebellion: Official Records*, Series 3, Vol. 3, 280–281, 294, 314; Mazet, "Lincoln—Patron of Military Aviation," 44; Jeremiah Milbank, Jr., *The First Century of Flight in America: An Introductory Survey* (Princeton, N.J.: Princeton University Press, 1943), 126.

(147– **John La Mountain and the USS *Fanny***: Haydon, *Aeronautics in the*
148)   *Union and Confederate Armies*, 35, 85–86, 96, 147–149, 152–153; Milbank, *The First Century of Flight in America*, 64; Brugioni, "Arlington and Fairfax Counties," 8; Jackson, *The Aeronauts*, 87.

(148– **Aerial Spotting of Artillery Fire**: Haydon, *Aeronautics in the Union*
149) *and Confederate Armies*, 212–213; *The War of the Rebellion: Official Records*, Series 3, Vol. 3, 262–263.

(149– **Bombardment of Island No. 10**: Haydon, *Aeronautics in the Union*
151) *and Confederate Armies*, 388, 393–397; *The War of the Rebellion: Official Records*, Series 3, Vol. 3, 269, 302–304, 316–318; Jackson, *The Aeronauts*, 90; Bruce, *Lincoln and the Tools of War*, 88; Squires, "Aeronautics in the Civil War," 668; Maslowski, "Military Intelligence Sources during the American Civil War," 45.

(151– **The "Silk Dress Balloon"**: Squires, "Aeronautics in the Civil War,"
152) 663–664; Jon L. Wakelyn, *Biographical Dictionary of the Confederacy* (Westport, Conn.: Greenwood Press, 1977), 130; Nofi, *A Civil War Treasury*, 177–178; Clinton, *Tara Revisited*, 142–143; Coggins, *Arms and Equipment of the Civil War*, 109.

(152– **Propaganda Leaflets from the Air**: Hans L. Trefousse, *Ben Butler:*
153) *The South Called Him Beast!* (New York: Twayne Publishers, 1957), 110–112, 147–150; T. Harry Williams, *Time-Life History of the United States: The Union Restored* (New York: Time-Life, 1963), 6: 117; Herman Belz, *Reconstructing the Union: Theory and Policy during the Civil War* (Ithaca, N.Y.: Cornell University Press, 1969), 156–157; Nevins, *The War for the Union: The Organized War to Victory, 1864– 1865* (New York: Charles Scribner's Sons, 1971), 4: 47; Bruce, *Lincoln and the Tools of War*, 73.

CHAPTER 6: INTELLIGENCE GATHERING AND SECURITY MEASURES (Pages 155–174)

(155– **Introduction**: Edwin C. Fishel, *The Secret War for the Union*, 8–9;
156) Stephen F. Knott, *Secret and Sanctioned: Covert Operations and the American Presidency* (New York: Oxford University Press, 1996), 13– 15, 136; Andrew, *For the President's Eyes Only*, 7–14.

(156– **Allan Pinkerton**: Mackay, *Allan Pinkerton*, 15–105, 137–170; Fishel,
159) *The Secret War for the Union*, 3, 21–22, 53–55, 75, 160–163, 237–239; Edwin C. Fishel, "Pinkerton and McClellan: Who Deceived Whom?" *Civil War History* 34 (June 1988), 115–142; Horan, *The Pinkertons*, 1– 36, 62–68, 115–136.

(159– **Bureau of Military Information**: Fishel, *The Secret War for the*
161) *Union*, 3–4, 24–28, 287–299, 318–322, 410–411; Andrew, *For the President's Eyes Only*, 18–22; Edwin C. Fishel, "The Mythology of Civil War Intelligence," in John T. Hubbel, ed., *Battles Lost and Won: Essays from Civil War History* (Westport, Conn.: Greenwood Press, 1975), 95– 97; Axelrod, *The War Between the Spies*, 188–189; Maslowski, "Military Intelligence Services during the American Civil War," 33–34.

(161– **Women Spies**: Lyde Cullen Sizer, "Acting Her Part: Narratives of
165) Union Women Spies," in Catherine Clinton and Nina Silber, eds.,
Divided Houses: Gender and the Civil War (New York: Oxford University Press, 1992), 115; Maslowski, "Military Intelligence Services during The American Civil War," 37, 54; Clinton, *Tara Revisited,* 69–70, 89–98; Mary Elizabeth Massey, *Bonnet Brigades* (New York: Alfred A. Knopf, 1966), 96–104, 269; Fishel, *The Secret War for the Union,* 57–62, 66–68, 551–553; M. H. Mahoney, *Women in Espionage: A Biographical Dictionary* (Santa Barbara, Calif.: ABC-CLIO, 1993), 24–27, 101–104, 215–218; Drew Gilpin Faust, *Mothers of Invention: Women of the Slaveholding South in the American Civil War* (Chapel Hill: University of North Carolina Press, 1996), 214–219; Hubbell & Geary, eds., *Biographical Dictionary of the Union,* 540–541; Earl Conrad, *Harriet Tubman* (1943; reprint, New York: Paul S. Eriksson, 1969), 164–175; Harnett T. Kane, *Spies for the Blue and Gray* (Garden City, N.Y.: Hanover House, 1954), 12–13, 17–67, 129–155, 231–249; Nofi, *A Civil War Treasury,* 291–293.

(165– **Lincoln's Suspension of Habeas Corpus**: Mark E. Neely, Jr., *The Fate
167) of Liberty: Abraham Lincoln and Civil Liberties* (New York: Oxford University Press, 1991), 123, 130–131, 137–138, 232–234; Basler, ed., *The Collected Works of Abraham Lincoln,* 5: 436–437, 6: 267; Stephen B. Oates, *Abraham Lincoln: The Man behind the Myths* (New York: Harper & Row Publishers, 1984), 121–122; Donald, *Lincoln,* 303–304 Gallman, *The North Fights the Civil War,* 145.

(167– **Passports**: United States. Passport Office. Department of State, *The
168) United States Passport: Past, Present, Future* (Washington, D.C.: Department of State Publication, 1976), 4–5, 181–186, 195–198; Gaillard Hunt, *The American Passport: Its History and a Digest of Laws, Rulings and Regulations Governing Its Issuance by the Department of State* (Washington, D.C.: Government Printing Office, 1898), 50–53.

(168– **Federal Troops as Strikebreakers**: *New York Times,* July 2, 1863;
170) Philip S. Foner, *History of the Labor Movement in the United States: From Colonial Times to the Founding of the American Federation of Labor* (New York: International Publishers, 1947), 1: 328–329; Sewell, *A House Divided,* 102–103; David Montgomery, *Beyond Equality: Labor and the Radical Republicans, 1862–1872* (New York: Alfred A. Knopf, 1967), 96–100; Grace Palladino, *Another Civil War: Labor, Capital, and the State in the Anthracite Regions of Pennsylvania, 1840–68* (Urbana: University of Illinois Press, 1990), 141–146, 169; John L. Blackman, Jr., "The Seizure of the Reading Railroad in 1864," *The Pennsylvania Magazine of History and Biography* 111 (January 1987), 49–58.

(170– **White House Security**: Thomas, *Abraham Lincoln,* 454–455, 458;
172) Robert V. Remini, *Andrew Jackson and the Course of American*

Democracy, 1833–1845 (New York: Harper & Row Publishers, 1984),
3: 60–61, 228–229; John William Ward, *Andrew Jackson: Symbol for
an Age* (New York: Oxford University Press, 1955), 114; Noah Brooks,
Washington in Lincoln's Time, ed. by Herbert Mitgang (Chicago: Quadrangle Books, 1971), 44; Oates, *With Malice Toward None,* 267–268,
452–453; Roscoe, *The Web of Conspiracy,* 12–13; Margaret Leech,
Reveille in Washington: 1860–1865 (New York: Harper & Brothers,
1941), 357–358.

(172– **United States Secret Service**: Andrew, *For the President's Eyes Only,*
174) 24; David R. Johnson, *Illegal Tender: Counterfeiting and the Secret
Service in Nineteenth Century America* (Washington, D.C.: Smithson-
ian Institution Press, 1995), xiv–xvii, 37, 43–45 66–72; Walter S.
Bowen and Harry Edward Neal, *The United States Secret Service*
(Philadelphia: Chilton Company Publishers, 1960), 12–17.

CHAPTER 7: HEALTH AND MEDICAL CARE (Pages 175–218)

(175– **Introduction**: Lloyd Lewis, *Sherman: Fighting Prophet* (New York:
176) Harcourt, Brace and Company, 1932), 635–636; McPherson, *Ordeal by
Fire,* 386, 487; Nevins, *The War for the Union,* 3: 312; George A. Bender, *Great Moments in Medicine* (Detroit: Northwood Institute Press,
1966), 261–262, 272–273; Robertson, *Soldiers Blue and Gray,* 146–
151; George Worthington Adams, *Doctors in Blue: The Medical History of the Union Army in the Civil War* (New York: Henry Schuman,
1952), 4; William Quentin Maxwell, *Lincoln's Fifth Wheel: The Political History of the United States Sanitary Commission* (New York:
Longmans, Green & Co., 1956), 245.

(177– **Standards for Physicians**: Howard D. Kramer, "Effect of the Civil
178) War on the Public Health Movement," *Mississippi Valley Historical
Review* 35 (December 1948), 452, 458; Adams, *Doctors in Blue,* 49–55;
Frank R. Freemon, *Gangrene and Glory: Medical Care During the
American Civil War* (Madison, N.J.: Fairleigh Dickinson University
Press, 1998), 24–26; Bonnie Ellen Blustein, "'To Increase the Effi-
ciency of the Medical Department': A New Approach to U.S. Civil War
Medicine," *Civil War History* 33 (March 1987), 28–31, 36–37; Robert-
son, *Soldiers Blue and Gray,* 155–156; Stewart Brooks, *Civil War Med-
icine* (Springfield, Ill.: Charles C. Thomas Publisher, 1966), 27; Bell
Irvin Wiley, *The Life of Johnny Reb: The Common Soldier of the Con-
federacy* (Indianapolis: Bobbs-Merrill Company, 1943), 267–268; H. H.
Cunningham, *Doctors in Gray: The Confederate Medical Service*
(Baton Rouge: Louisiana State University Press, 1960), 264–266.

(178– **The "Letterman System"**: Maxwell, *Lincoln's Fifth Wheel,* 75, 337;
181) Edwin S. Barrett, *What I Saw at Bull Run* (Boston: Beacon Press,
1886), 26; Louisa May Alcott, *Hospital Sketches,* ed. by Bessie Z.

Jones (Cambridge: Harvard University Press, 1960), xxii; P. M. Ashburn, *A History of the Medical Department of the United States Army* (Boston: Houghton Mifflin Company, 1929), 69–71, 79; Jonathan Letterman, *Medical Recollections of the Army of the Potomac* (New York: Appleton and Company, 1866), 23–30, 52–53, 57–63, 157; Adams, *Doctors in Blue,* 67, 88–89, 91–92; Freemon, *Gangrene and Glory,* 44–48, 67–76; Fred B. Ryons, "The United States Army Medical Department, 1861–1865," *The Military Surgeon* 79 (November 1936), 354–356; John D. Billings, *Hardtack and Coffee: The Unwritten Story of Army Life,* ed. by Richard Harwell (Chicago: R. R. Donnelley & Sons, 1960), 336–339, 348–349; Brooks, *Civil War Medicine,* 36; Nofi, *A Civil War Treasury,* 263; Frank R. Freemon, *Microbes and Minie Balls: An Annotated Bibliography of Civil War Medicine* (Rutherford, N.J.: Fairleigh Dickinson University Press, 1993), 10; McPherson, *Ordeal by Fire,* 387.

(182– **The U.S. Sanitary Commission**: Young and Lawford, *History of the*
185) *British Army,* 159–160; McPherson, *Battle Cry of Freedom,* 480–483; Maxwell, *Lincoln's Fifth Wheel,* 1–30, 299, 308–310; Adams, *Doctors in Blue,* 5–9, 73; Robert H. Bremner, *The Public Good: Philanthropy and Welfare in the Civil War Era* (New York: Alfred A. Knopf, 1980), 38–39, 42–44, 54–55, 62–65, 70, 78; Marilyn Mayer Culpepper, *Trials and Triumphs: Women of the American Civil War* (East Lansing: Michigan State University Press, 1991), 249, 254–261, 333–334; Freemon, *Microbes and Minie Balls,* 130; Emerson David Fite, *Social and Industrial Conditions in the North during the Civil War* (New York: Macmillan Company, 1910), 278, 280–283; Daniel A. Sutherland, *The Expansion of Everyday Life, 1860–1876* (New York: Harper & Row Publishers, 1989), 89–90.

(185– **America's "Florence Nightingales"**: Agatha Young, *The Women and*
189) *the Crisis: Women of the North in the Civil War* (New York: McDowell, Oblensky, 1959), 18–19, 98, 154–155; Young and Lawford, *History of the British Army,* 160; Adams *Doctors in Blue,* 176–179, 181–184; David Gollaher, *Voice for the Mad: The Life of Dorothea Dix* (New York: The Free Press, 1995), 7–41, 404–422; Michael Burlingame and John R. Turner Ettlinger, eds., *Inside Lincoln's White House: The Complete Civil War Diary of John Hay* (Carbondale, Ill.: Southern Illinois University Press, 1997), 3; McPherson, *Ordeal by Fire,* 391; Culpepper, *Trials and Triumphs,* 317–318, 323–330, 345–346, 353; Elizabeth D. Leonard, "Civil War Nurse, Civil War Nursing: Rebecca Usher of Maine," *Civil War History* 41(September 1995), 199–200, 206–207; M. A. Newcomb, *Four Years of Personal Reminiscences of the War* (Chicago: H. S. Mills & Co., Publishers, 1893), 43; Stephen B. Oates, *A Woman of Valor: Clara Barton and the Civil War* (New York: The Free Press, 1994), 23, 376–377, 508; Hubbell & Geary, eds., *Biographical*

Dictionary of the Union, 30; Jane E. Schultz, "Race, Gender, and Bureaucracy: Civil War Army Nurses and the Pension Bureau," *Journal of Women's History* 6 (Summer 1994), 45, 53–59, 63; Sister Mary Denis Maher, *To Bind Up the Wounds: Catholic Sister Nurses in the U.S. Civil War* (Westport, Conn.: Greenwood Press, 1989), 1, 38–40, 51, 69–71, 152; Massey, *Bonnet Brigades*, 63; Phyllis Read and Bernard L. Witlieb, *The Book of Women's Firsts* (New York: Random House, 1992), 447; Clinton, *Tara*, 82–89; Bonnie Bullough and Vern Bullough, "The Origins of Modern American Nursing: The Civil War Era," *Nursing Forum* 2 (1963), 25–26.

(189–192) **Pavilion Hospitals**: The 8 percent mortality rate was for white Union soldiers. African-American soldiers suffered approximately a 20 percent death rate from wounds and disease, reflecting a clear inequality in medical treatment. Glatthaar, *Forged in Battle*, 187–188, 227, 250–251; Allan Nevins, "A Major Result of the Civil War," *Civil War History* 5 (September 1959), 241; Huston, *The Sinews of War*, 248–249; F. William Blaisdell, "Medical Advances during the Civil War," *Archives of Surgery* 123 (September 1988), 1048, 1050; Adams, *Doctors in Blue*, 26–27, 150–156, 172–173; Frank R. Freemon, "Lincoln Finds a Surgeon General: William A. Hammond and the Transformation of the Union Army Medical Bureau," *Civil War History* 33 (March 1987), 7–10, 19–20; Maxwell, *Lincoln's Fifth Wheel*, 151–152, 241; Cunningham, *Doctors in Gray*, 51–53; Robertson, *Soldiers in Blue and Gray*, 166–167; Brooks, *Civil War Medicine*, 43, 47.

(192–193) **Annie Wittenmyer**: Elizabeth D. Leonard, *Yankee Women: Gender Battles in the Civil War* (New York: W. W. Norton & Company, 1994), 51–103, 162–165; Annie T. Wittenmyer, *Under the Guns: A Woman's Reminiscences of the Civil War* (Boston: E. B. Stillings & Co. Publisher, 1895), 72–73; Francis E. Willard, *Woman and Temperance: Or, The Work and Workers of the Woman's Christian Temperance Union* (Hartford, Conn.: Park Publishing Co., 1884), 160–163; James O. Henry, "The United States Christian Commission in the Civil War," *Civil War History* 6 (December 1960), 374–375, 382, 385.

(193–196) **Hospital Ships**: Huston, *The Sinews of War*, 244–245; Estelle Broadman and Elizabeth B. Carrick, "American Military Medicine in the Mid-Nineteenth Century: The Experience of Alexander H. Hoff, M.D.," *Bulletin of the History of Medicine* 64 (Spring 1990), 71–72; Adams, *Doctors in Blue*, 82; John Van R. Hoff, "Memoir of Alexander Henry Hoff," *The Military Surgeon* 31 (1912), 50–51; Kristie Ross, "Arranging a Doll's House: Refined Women as Union Nurses," in Clinton and Silber, *Divided Houses*, 99–101; Edward C. Kenney, "From the Log of the *Red Rover*, 1862–1865: A History of the First U.S. Navy Hospital Ship," *Missouri Historical Review* 60 (1965), 31–49; Louis H. Roddis, *A Short History of Nautical Medicine* (New York: Harper and Brothers,

1941), 288–291, Steven Louis Roca, "Presence and Precedents: The USS *Red Rover* during the American Civil War, 1861–1865," *Civil War History* 44 (June 1998), 91–110.

(196– **Hospital Trains**: McPherson, *Battle Cry of Freedom*, 12; Turner, *Vic-*
197) *tory Rode the Rails*, 297–307; Thomas Weber, *The Northern Railroads in the Civil War: 1861–1865* (1952; reprint, Westport, Conn.: Greenwood Press, 1970), 227; I. Bernard Cohen, "Science and the Civil War," *Technology Review* 48 (1946), 168–169; Robertson, *Soldiers Blue and Gray*, 164; Francis A. Lord, *Lincoln's Railroad Man: Herman Haupt* (Rutherford, N.J.: Fairleigh Dickinson University Press, 1969), 272–274.

(197– **Disabled Veterans**: Brooks, *Civil War Medicine*, 97–98; McPherson,
199) *Ordeal by Fire*, 386; Dixon Wecter, *When Johnny Comes Marching Home* (1944; reprint, Westport, Conn.: Greenwood Press, 1970), 209–214; Harold Elk Straubing, *In Hospital and Camp: The Civil War through the Eyes of Its Doctors and Nurses* (Harrisburg, Penn.: Stackpole Books, 1993), 7–8.

(199– **Foot Problems**: Edgar Erskine Hume, *Victories of Army Medicine: Sci-*
201) *entific Accomplishments of the Medical Department of the United States Army* (Philadelphia: J. B. Lippincott, 1943), 176–178; Robertson, *Soldiers Blue and Gray*, 63–64; Allan Nevins, *The War for the Union: War Becomes Revolution, 1862–1863* (New York: Charles Scribner's Sons, 1960), 2: 493–494; Wiley, *The Life of Johnny Reb*, 119–121; William C. Davis, *Lincoln's Men: How President Lincoln Became Father to an Army and a Nation* (New York: Free Press, 1999), 113–114; Martin Windrow and Gerry Embleton, *Military Dress of North America: 1665–1970* (New York: Charles Scribner's Sons, 1973), 100; Ira M. Rutkow, *The History of Surgery in the United States: 1775–1900* (San Francisco, Norman Publishing, 1988), 1: 250–251.

(201– **Dental Care**: Cunningham, *Doctors in Gray,* 19, 243–246, 273; Brooks,
202) *Civil War Medicine*, 26–27, 47, 123; George Winston Smith, *Medicines for the Union Army: The United States Army Laboratories during the Civil War* (Madison, Wis.: American Institute of the History of Pharmacy, 1962), 78–79.

(202– **Medical Storekeepers**: Smith, *Medicines for the Union Army,* 5–6;
203) Henry N. Rittenhouse, "U.S. Army Medical Storekeepers," *American Journal of Pharmacy* 37 (1865), 87–90; Nevins, *The War for the Union,* 3: 314, 316.

(204) **Veterinary Surgeons**: Everett B. Miller, "A Veterinarian's Notes on the Civil War," *Veterinary Heritage: Bulletin of the American Veterinary History Society* 8 (1985), 10–25.

(205– **Dr. Mary Walker**: Young, *The Women and the Crisis,* 9; Charles
208) McCool Snyder, *Dr. Mary Walker: The Little Lady in Pants* (New York: Vantage Press, 1962), 12–16, 41–47, 53–54, 61, 78–79, 88, 123, 145,

150–151; Leonard, *Yankee Women,* 105–157, 263–264; Lois Decker O'Neill, ed., *The Women's Book of World Records and Achievements* (Garden City, N.Y.: Anchor Press, 1979), 534.

(208– **Alexander T. Augusta, M.D.**: Quarles, *The Negro in the Civil War,*
209) 203–204; Berlin, Reidy, and Rowland, eds., *Freedom: The Black Military Experience,* 354–355; Holzer, ed., *The Lincoln Mailbag,* 83–84; Glatthaar, *Forged in Battle,* 187–188, 280; Charles M. Christian, *Black Saga: The African American Experience* (Boston: Houghton Mifflin Company, 1995), 204–205.

(210– **Battling Venereal Disease**: Thomas P. Lowry, *The Story the Soldiers*
212) *Wouldn't Tell: Sex in the Civil War* (Mechanicsburg, Penn.: Stackpole Books, 1994), 78–87; James Boyd Jones, Jr., "A Tale of Two Cities: The Hidden Battle against Venereal Disease in Civil War Nashville and Memphis," *Civil War History* 31 (September 1985), 270–276; Robertson, *Soldiers Blue and Gray,* 117–120; John D'Emilio and Estelle B. Freedman, *Intimate Matters: A History of Sexuality in America* (New York: Harper & Row Publishers, 1988), 134, 148; Sewell, *A House Divided,* 107; Wiley, *The Life of Billy Yank,* 257–261; Sutherland, *The Expansion of Everyday Life: 1860–1876,* 17; Culpepper, *Trials and Triumphs,* 114–116; Massey, *Bonnet Brigades,* 262–264.

(212– **Post-Traumatic Stress Disorder**: The foremost authority on this sub-
214) ject as it relates to the Civil War is Eric T. Dean, Jr. See his *Shook over Hell: Post-Traumatic Stress, Vietnam, and the Civil War* (Cambridge, Mass.: Harvard University Press, 1997), especially chapters 3–8; Grant, *Memoirs,* 1: 356; Leander Stillwell, *The Story of a Common Soldier of Army Life in the Civil War* (Erie, Kan.: The Erie Record, 1917), 35; Ernest Linden Waitt, *History of the Nineteenth Regiment, Massachusetts Volunteer Infantry, 1861–1865* (Salem, Mass.: The Salem Press Co., 1906), 242; Norton, *Army Letters,* 93, 107; Wecter, *When Johnny Comes Marching Home,* 154–155.

(215– **Racism Confirmed**: John S. Haller, "Civil War Anthropometry: The
216) Making of a Racial Ideology," *Civil War History* 16 (December 1970), 309–324; Glatthaar, *Forged in Battle,* 253–255.

(216– **Army Medical Museum**: Robert S. Henry, *The Armed Forces Institute*
218) *of Pathology: Its First Century, 1862–1962* (Washington, D.C.: Office of the Surgeon General, 1964), 1–3, 11–18, 29–31, 51, 62, 82–84, 395–396, 401; John H. Brinton, "Address at the Closing Exercises of the Session 1895–96, Army Medical School," *The Journal of the American Medical Association* 26 (March 1896), 601–602; W. A. Swanberg, *Sickles the Incredible* (New York: Charles Scribner's Sons, 1956), 49–55, 63–66, 216–225; Hume, *Victories of Army Medicine,* 51–53.

CHAPTER 8: REPORTING THE WAR (Pages 219–242)

(219– **Introduction**: L. Edward Carter, "The Revolution in Journalism during
220) the Civil War," *Lincoln Herald* 73 (1971), 232; Nevins, *The War for the Union*, 1: 261–262; Frank Luther Mott, *American Journalism: A History, 1690–1960* (New York: The Macmillan Company, 1962), 303–304; Brayton Harris, *Blue & Gray in Black & White: Newspapers in the Civil War* (Washington, D.C.: Brassey's, 1999), 3–14; Royster, *The Destructive War*, 238; Edwin Emery, *The Press and America: An Interpretive History of the Mass Media* (Englewood Cliffs, N.J.: Prentice-Hall, 1972), 237.

(220– **The "Specials"**: Havilah Babcock, "The Press and the Civil War," *The
222) Journalism Quarterly* 6 (March 1929), 1; Rupert Furneaux, *News of War: Stories and Adventures of the Great War Correspondents* (London: Max Parrish & Co. Ltd., 1964), 33; Joseph J. Mathews, *Reporting the Wars* (Minneapolis: University of Minnesota Press, 1957), 80–84; Fermer, *James Gordon Bennett and the New York* Herald, 200–201; Royster, *The Destructive War*, 237; Starr, *Reporting the Civil War*, 4, 46, 49–50, 289; Harris, *Blue & Gray in Black & White*, 14, 119–135; J. Cutler Andrews, *The North Reports the Civil War* (Pittsburgh: University of Pittsburgh Press, 1955), 20–21, 60–61, 643–644, 650–653; Carter, "The Revolution in Journalism during the Civil War," 230, 235–236, 240; J. Cutler Andrews, *The South Reports the Civil War* (Princeton, N.J.: Princeton University Press, 1970), 536–539, 542; Elmer Davis, *History of the New York Times: 1851–1921* (New York: New York Times, 1921), 53; James Parton, "The *New York Herald* from 1835–1866," *North American Review* 102 (April 1866), 375–378, 403, 418.

(222– **Aerial News Coverage**: *Boston Daily Journal*, November 22, 1861;
223) Haydon, *Aeronautics in the Union and Confederate Armies*, 129–130.

(223– **Journalistic Artists**: W. Fletcher Thompson, Jr., *The Image of War:
226) The Pictorial Reporting of the American Civil War* (New York: Thomas Yoseloff, 1959), 30, 42, 50–53, 74–76, 81–85, 128; Starr, *Reporting the Civil War*, 207–210; *New York Times*, October 21, 1890, September 28, 1912.

(226– **Thomas Morris Chester**: R. J. M. Blackett, *Thomas Morris Chester,
228) Black Civil War Correspondent: His Dispatches from the Front* (Baton Rouge, Louisiana State University Press, 1989), 3–42, 46–91; McPherson, *The Negro's Civil War*, 59–60; Andrews, *The North Reports the Civil War*, 635; Noah Andre Trudeau, *Out of the Storm: The End of the Civil War, April–June 1865* (Boston: Little, Brown and Company, 1994), 78, 82.

(228– **Captured Journalists**: Starr, *Reporting the Civil War*, 150–159; An-
231) drews, *The South Reports the Civil War*, 85, 165–166, 256, 278, 508;

Bernard A. Weisberger, *Reporters for the Union* (Boston: Little, Brown and Company, 1953), 178, 286; Emmet Crozier, *Yankee Reporters: 1861–65* (New York: Oxford University Press, 1956), 318–405; Andrews, *The North Reports the Civil War*, 613–614.

(231– **A Leak in the White House**: Gerry Van der Heuvel, *Crowns of Thorns*
232)   *and Glory: Mary Todd Lincoln and Varina Howell Davis: The Two First Ladies of the Civil War* (New York: E. P. Dutton, 1988), 123–125; Richard B. Kielbowicz, "The Telegraph, Censorship, and Politics at the Outset of the Civil War," *Civil War History* 40 (June 1994), 116–117; Donald, *Lincoln*, 324–325; Michael Burlingame, *The Inner World of Abraham Lincoln* (Urbana: The University of Illinois Press, 1994), 304–306.

(232– **News Transmission**: Carter, "The Revolution in Journalism during the
233)   Civil War," 231–232; Andrews, *The North Reports the Civil War*, viii, 6–7, 31; James L. Crouthamel, *Bennett's New York Herald and the Rise of the Popular Press* (Syracuse: Syracuse University Press, 1989), 121–122; Starr, *Reporting the Civil War*, 277, 288.

(233– **Official News Bulletins**: Mathews, *Reporting the Wars*, 88, 91–92; F.
235)   B. Marbut, *News from the Capital: The Story of Washington Reporting* (Carbondale: Southern Illinois University Press, 1971), 126–131; Starr, *Reporting the Civil War*, 244–253.

(235– **Government Censorship**: Kielbowicz, "The Telegraph, Censorship,
237)   and Politics at the Outset of the Civil War," 96, 100–105, 118; Emery, *The Press and America*, 239–243; Phillip Knightley, *The First Casualty: From the Crimea to Vietnam: The War Correspondent as Hero, Propagandist, and Myth Maker* (New York: Harcourt Brace Jovanovich, 1975), 27; Starr, *Reporting the Civil War*, 146–150; Andrews, *The North Reports the Civil War*, 378–383; Weisberger, *Reporters for the Union*, 108–114; Crozier, *Yankee Reporters*, 291–305; John F. Marszalek, *Sherman's Other War: The General and the Civil War Press* (Memphis: Memphis State University Press, 1981), 146–149; Stanley P. Hirshson, *The White Tecumseh: A Biography of General William T. Sherman* (New York: John Wiley & Sons, 1997), 146–149.

(237– **Bylines**: Starr, *Reporting the Civil War*, 160–161; Carter, "The Revolu-
238)   tion in Journalism during the Civil War," 235; Sidney Kobre, *Development of American Journalism* (Dubuque, Iowa: Wm. C. Brown Company Publishers, 1969), 335.

(238– **Front-Line Newsboys**: McPherson, *For Cause and Comrades*, 92–93;
239)   Fermer, *James Gordon Bennett and the New York Herald*, 200, 206; Cullen "Doc" Aubrey, *Recollections of a Newsboy in the Army of the Potomac: 1861–1865* (Milwaukee: n.p., 1904), 9–18, 138–139; Starr, *Reporting the Civil War*, 176–177.

(239– **New Orleans *Tribune***: Actually, the *Tribune* was published only six
242)   days a week; it did not appear on Monday. But it was still considered,

for all intents and purposes, a daily. Current, ed., *Encyclopedia of the Confederacy*, 3: 1137; John W. Blassingame, *Black New Orleans: 1860–1880* (Chicago: University of Chicago Press, 1973), 9–15; McPherson, *The Negro's Civil War*, 276; Edward Larocque Tinker, *Creole City: Its Past and Its People* (New York: Longmans, Green & Co., 1953), 107–110, 169–170; Gerald M. Capers, *Occupied City: New Orleans under the Federals, 1862–1865* (Lexington: University of Kentucky Press, 1965), 1–5, 10, 180; David C. Rankin, ed., *My Passage at the New Orleans Tribune: A Memoir of the Civil War Era [by] Jean-Charles Houzeau* (Baton Rouge: Louisiana State University Press, 1984), 2–18, 22–29, 33–37, 47–48, 55–56; New Orleans *Daily Picayune*, April 27, 1868.

CHAPTER 9: PHOTOGRAPHING THE WAR (Pages 243–255)

(243– **Introduction**: Dorothy Meserve Kunhardt and Philip B. Kunhardt, Jr.,
244) *Mathew Brady and His World* (Alexandria, Va.: Time-Life Books, 1977), 38–39; Brian Coe, *The Birth of Photography: The Story of the Formative Years, 1800–1900* (London: Ash & Grant, 1976), 26–29; Meredith, *Mr. Lincoln's Camera Man*, 16–18; Robert Taft, *Photography and the American Scene: A Social History, 1839–1889* (New York: Dover Publications, 1938), 6–14; Naomi Rosenblum, *World History of Photography* (New York: Abbeville Press, 1997), 15, 24–27, 32–37.

(245– **Wartime Photography**: Thompson, *The Image of War*, 18; Jorge Lew-
247) inski, *The Camera at War: A History of Photography From 1840 to the Present Day* (New York: Simon & Schuster, 1978), 37; Taft, *Photography and the American Scene*, 223–225, 484–485; Rosenblum, *A World History of Photography*, 180–184; Current, ed., *Encyclopedia of the Confederacy*, 3: 1205–1207; William F. Stapp, "Introduction," in Constance Sullivan, ed., *Landscapes of the Civil War* (New York: Alfred A. Knopf, 1995), 18; Ward, *The Civil War*, 404.

(247– **Mathew B. Brady**: Katz, *Witness to an Era*, 11–12; Meredith, *Mr. Lin-
250) coln's Camera Man*, vii, 16, 18; Kunhardt and Kundhardt, *Mathew Brady and His World*, 56, 63–66, 90; Cheryl Sloan Wray, "Photographer Mathew Brady fulfilled his stated objective 'to preserve the faces of historic men'—living and dead," *America's Civil War* 10 (September 1997), 20, 22; Roy Meredith, *The World of Mathew Brady: Portraits of the Civil War Period* (Los Angeles: Brooke House Publishers, 1976), 7; Alan Trachtenberg, *Reading American Photographs: Image as History, Mathew Brady to Walker Evans* (New York: Hill and Wang, 1989), 41–42, 81; Rosenblum, *A World History of Photography*, 190–191; Thompson, *The Image of War*, 32, 41–42.

(250– **The Camera as a Tool of War**: Katz, *Witness to an Era*, 3–7, 31; Jo-
252) sephine Cobb, "Alexander Gardner," *Image: Journal of Photography*, 7

(June 1958), 127–132; Meredith, *Mr. Lincoln's Camera Man,* 144– 145; Thompson, *The Image of War,* 76–77; Kunhardt and Kunhardt, *Mathew Brady and His World,* 57; Miller, ed., *The Photographic History of the Civil War,* 1: 25, 31, 42, 44; Current, ed., *Encyclopedia of the Confederacy* 3: 1206.

(252– **Capt. Andrew J. Russell, U.S. Army**: William Gladstone, "Captain
253) Andrew J. Russell: First Army Photographer," *Photographica* 10 (February 1978), 7–9; Josephine Cobb, "Photographers of the Civil War," *Military Affairs* 26 (Fall 1962), 127; Thomas Westin Fels, *Destruction and Destiny: The Photographs of A. J. Russell: Directing American Energy in War and Peace, 1862–1869* (Pittsfield, Mass.: The Berkshire Museum, 1987), 11–12; Miller, ed., *The Photographic History of the Civil War,* 1: 42; Trachtenberg, *Reading American Photographs*, 107–110.

(253– **"The Dead of Antietam"**: Jan Zita Grover, "The First Living-Room
255) War: The Civil War in the Illustrated Press," *Afterimage* 11 (February 1984), 9–10; *New York Times*, October 20, 1862; O. W. Holmes, "Doings of the Sunbeam," *The Atlantic Monthly* 12 (July 1863), 11–12; William A. Frassanito, *Gettysburg: A Journey in Time* (New York: Charles Scribner's Sons, 1975), 27–28; Liva Baker, *The Justice from Beacon Hill: The Life and Times of Oliver Wendell Holmes* (New York: HarperCollins Publishers, 1991), 125–136: Katz, *Witness to an Era,* 47, 61, 63; Trachtenberg, *Reading American Photographs,* 89; Rosenblum. *A World History of Photography,* 34–35; Stanley B. Burns, *Early Medical Photography in America: 1839–1883* (New York: Burns Archive, 1983), 794–796, 945–946.

CHAPTER 10: THE WARTIME PRESIDENCY (Pages 257–277)

(257– **Introduction**: Michael P. Riccards, *The Ferocious Engine of Democ-
258) racy: A History of the American Presidency, from the Origins through William McKinley* (Lanham, Md.: Madison Books, 1995), 1: 281; Edward Campbell Mason, *The Veto Power: Its Origin, Development and Function in the Government of the United States (1789–1889)* (1890; reprint, New York: Russell & Russell, 1967), 214; Donald, *Lincoln,* 303; McPherson, *Abraham Lincoln and the Second American Revolution,* 37.

(258– **An "Unlimited Despot"**: Basler, ed., *The Collected Works of Abraham
260) Lincoln,* 4: 191, 429, 440, 7: 281; Arthur M. Schlesinger, Jr., *The Imperial Presidency* (Boston: Houghton Mifflin Company, 1973), 58–63; Rawley, *The Politics of Union,* 27; Horace Greeley, *The American Conflict: A History* (Washington, D.C.: National Tribune, 1899), 497–498; Frank Freidel, ed., *Union Pamphlets of the Civil War, 1861–1865* (Cambridge, Mass.: Harvard University Press, 1967), 1: 537; Donald, *Lin-*

coln, 301–303; Marcus Cunliffe, *American Presidents and the Presidency* (New York: McGraw-Hill Book Company, 1976), 100–101; Wilfred E. Binkley, *President and Congress* (1937; reprint, New York: Vintage Press, 1962), 154–155; Herman Belz, *Abraham Lincoln, Constitutionalism, and Equal Rights in the Civil War Era* (New York: Fordham University Press, 1998), 41–43, 97–99.

(260–   **Presidential Accessibility to the Press**: James E. Pollard, *The Presi-*
262)   *dents and the Press* (1947; reprint, New York: Octagon Books, 1973), 312, 348, 371, 389–390; Harper, *Lincoln and the Press*, 186–187; Howard K. Beale, ed., *Diary of Gideon Welles: Secretary of the Navy under Lincoln and Johnson* (New York: W. W. Norton, 1960), 2: 131; Sandburg, *Abraham Lincoln*, 4: 114; Menahem Blondheim, *News over the Wires: The Telegraph and the Flow of Public Information in America, 1844–1897* (Cambridge, Mass.: Harvard University Press, 1994), 134; Starr, *Reporting the Civil War*, 125–134; Paul F. Boller, *Presidential Anecdotes* (New York: Oxford University Press, 1981), 126–127.

(262–   **"Public Opinion Baths"**: Cunliffe, *American Presidents and the Pres-*
264)   *idency*, 98; Oates, *With Malice Toward None*, 264–266; Donald, *Lincoln*, 311; *Sacramento Daily Union*, December 4, 1863; C. Van Santvoord, "A Reception by President Lincoln," *The Century Magazine* 25 (February 1883), 613;. Wilson and Davis, eds., *Herndon's Informants*, 561–562.

(264–   **Lincoln among the Troops**: Luthin, *The Real Abraham Lincoln*, 408–
266)   409; Ira Seymour Dodd, *The Song of the Rappahannock* (New York: Dodd, Mead and Company, 1898), 141–142; Davis, *Lincoln's Men*, 130–145; Princess Felix Salm-Salm, *Ten Years of My Life* (New York: R. Worthington, 1877), 44; Julia Lorrilard Butterfield, *A Biographical Memoir of General Daniel Butterfield, Including Many Addresses and Military Writings* (New York: Grafton Press, 1904), 159; Ruth L. Silliker, ed., *The Rebel Yell & the Yankee Hurrah: The Civil War Journal of a Maine Volunteer* (Camden, Me.: Down East Books, 1985), 75; Robert L. Willett, Jr., *One Day of the Civil War: America in Conflict, April 10, 1863* (Washington, D.C.: Brassey's, 1997), 17–24; Donald, *Lincoln*, 515–516; Royster, *The Destructive War*, 243; Michael Burlingame, ed., *Lincoln Observed: Civil War Dispatches of Noah Brooks* (Baltimore: Johns Hopkins University Press, 1998), 39–45.

(266–   **Haiti and Liberia**: Calvin D. Linton, ed., *American Headlines: Year by*
269)   *Year* (Nashville: Thomas Nelson Publishers, 1984), 170; Clyde N. Wilson and W. Edwin Hemphill, eds., *The Papers of John C. Calhoun* (Columbia: University of South Carolina Press, 1977), 10: 39; Basler, ed., *The Collected Works of Abraham Lincoln*, 5: 39, 192; McPherson, *The Political History of the United States of America during the Great Rebellion*, 374–375; *Douglass' Monthly* (September 1862), 5: 707; Henry Mayer, *All On Fire: William Lloyd Garrison and the Abolition of*

Slavery (New York: St. Martin's Press, 1998), 538–539; Oates, *With Malice Toward None*, 338–339; Rawley, *The Politics of Union*, 77.

(269– **Lincoln's Bid for Reelection**: David E. Long, *The Jewel of Liberty:*
273) *Abraham Lincoln's Re-Election and the End of Slavery* (Mechanicsburg, Penn.: Stackpole Books, 1994), 153–166, 179, 193, 216–234, 255–259, 270–271; David E. Long, "I Shall Never Recall a Word," in Frank J. Williams, William D. Pederson, and Vincent J. Marsala, eds., *Abraham Lincoln: Sources and Style of Leadership* (Westport, Conn.: Greenwood Press, 1994), 93–96; Davis, *Lincoln's Men*, 192–227; Phillip Shaw Paludan, "A People's Contest," 245–257; John C. Waugh, *Reelecting Lincoln: The Battle for the 1864 Presidency* (New York: Crown Publishers, 1997), 282–294, 317–321, 328–330, 340–343, 354; Oates, *With Malice Toward None*, 431–433; Mark E. Neeley, Jr., "The Civil War and the Two–Party System," in James M. McPherson, ed., *"We Cannot Escape History": Lincoln and the Last Best Hope of Earth* (Urbana: University of Illinois Press, 1995), 94; William Frank Zornow, *Lincoln & the Party Divided* (Norman: University of Oklahoma Press, 1954), 179–183, 215–216; Donald, *Lincoln*, 537, 544; Holzer, ed., *The Lincoln Mailbag*, 176–178; McPherson, *Battle Cry of Freedom*, 803–804; Royster, *The Destructive War*, 243; Joseph Allan Frank, *With Ballot and Bayonet: The Political Socialization of American Civil War Soldiers* (Athens: University of Georgia Press, 1998), 93–97; Basler, ed., *The Collected Works of Abraham Lincoln*, 8: 100n.; Allan Nevins, ed., *George Templeton Strong: Diary of the Civil War, 1860–1865* (New York: The Macmillan Company, 1962), 511; McPherson, *The Political History of the United States of America, during the Great Rebellion*, 607.

(273– **"The Black Man's President"**: Basler, ed., *The Collected Works of*
275) *Abraham Lincoln*, 3: 145–146, 7: 542–543; Leslie H. Fishel and Benjamin Quarles, eds., *The Black American: A Brief Documentary History* (Glenview, Ill.: Scott, Foresman and Company, 1970), 150–151; Quarles, *The Negro in the Civil War*, 139–140, 252–255; Donald, *Lincoln*, 475, 541; McPherson, *The Negro's Civil War*, 253–255, 273, 275, 305; George Sinkler, *The Racial Attitudes of American Presidents, from Abraham Lincoln to Theodore Roosevelt* (Garden City, N.Y.: Doubleday, 1971), 42–43; Luthin, *The Real Abraham Lincoln*, 585; Allen Thorndike Rice, ed., *Reminiscences of Abraham Lincoln by Distinguished Men of His Time* (New York: North American Review, 1888), 191–193; Merrill D. Peterson, *Lincoln in American Memory* (New York: Oxford University Press, 1994), 30, 59.

(276– **Lincoln and Organized Labor**: Philip S. Foner, *History of the Labor*
277) *Movement in the United States: From Colonial Times to the Founding of the American Federation of Labor* (New York: International Publishers, Co., 1947), 1: 331–333, 353–354; Basler, ed., *The Collected Works*

of Abraham Lincoln, 3: 468, 5: 52; David Montgomery, *Beyond Equality: Labor and the Radical Republicans, 1862–1872* (New York: Alfred A. Knopf, 1967), 97; Massey, *Bonnet Brigades*, 144–146.

CHAPTER 11: THE WARTIME CONGRESSES (Pages 279–309)

(279– **Introduction**: McPherson, *Battle Cry of Freedom*, 450–452; Heather
280)   Cox Richardson, *The Greatest Nation of the Earth: Republican Economic Policies during the Civil War Era* (Cambridge, Mass.: Harvard University Press, 1997), 2–7; Phillip Shaw Paludan, *"A People's Contest,"* 88.

(280– **Wartime Taxation**: Hummel, *Emancipating Slaves, Enslaving Free
282)   Men*, 221–223; Ward, *The Civil War*, 127; Richardson, *The Greatest Nation of the Earth*, 115–116, 129–133; Robert Stanley, *Dimensions of Law in the Service of Order: Origins of the Federal Income Tax, 1861–1913* (New York: Oxford University Press, 1993), 40–42, 53–55; James G. Blaine, *Twenty Years of Congress: From Lincoln to Garfield* (Norwich, Conn.: The Henry Bill Publishing Company, 1884), 1: 433; Leonard P. Curry, *Blueprint for Modern America: Nonmilitary Legislation of the First Civil War Congress* (Nashville: Vanderbilt University Press, 1968), 149, 169, 179–180, 247–248; *U.S. Statutes at Large*, 12: 432–489; George S. Boutwell, *Reminiscences of Sixty Years in Public Affairs* (New York: McClure, Phillips & Co., 1902), 1: 303–315; Van Riper and Sutherland, "The Northern Civil Service: 1861–1865," 358; Paludan, *"A People's Contest,"* 118–119.

(282– **"Financier of the War"**: Nevins, *The War for the Union*, 3: 228; Rich-
284)   ardson, *The Greatest Nation of the Earth*, 37–38, 41–57, 62–64; Henrietta M. Larson, *Jay Cooke: Private Banker* (1936; reprint, New York: Greenwood Press Publishers, 1968), 109, 119–151, 164–175; Paludan, *"A People's Contest,"* 115–117; McPherson, *Battle Cry of Freedom*, 443; John Niven, *Salmon P. Chase: A Biography* (New York: Oxford University Press, 1995), 261–268; Roland, *An American Iliad*, 96; David Donald, ed., *Inside Lincoln's Cabinet: The Civil War Diaries of Salmon P. Chase* (New York: Longmans, Green and Co., 1954), 40; Fite, *Social and Industrial Conditions in the North during the Civil War*, 133.

(284– **"Greenbacks"**: Herman E. Krooss, ed., *Documentary History of Bank-
287)   ing and Currency in the United States* (New York: Chelsea House Publishers, 1969), 2: 1261–1263; Paludan, *"A People's Contest,"* 108–112; McPherson, *Battle Cry of Freedom*, 445–447; Gallman, *The North Fights the Civil War*, 47, 96; Rawley, *The Politics of Union*, 50–51; Richardson, *The Greatest Nation of the Earth*, 70–75, 82–84; Charles A. Jellison, *Fessenden of Maine: Civil War Senator* (Syracuse, N.Y.: Syracuse University Press, 1962), 147–149; Parish, *The American Civil War*, 356–357.

(287– **A National Bank System**: Paludan, *"A People's Contest,"* 108; Hum-
289) mel, *Emancipating Slaves, Enslaving Free Men*, 224; Fite, *Social and Industrial Conditions in the North during the Civil War*, 113–115; Parish, *The American Civil War*, 360–361; Curry, *Blueprint for Modern America*, 197–205; Richardson, *The Greatest Nation of the Earth*, 67–68, 86, 91–94; McPherson, *Ordeal by Fire*, 206–207; Krooss, *Documentary History of Banking and Currency in the United States*, 2: 1264–1266; Robert P. Sharkey, "Commercial Banking," in Gilchrist and Lewis, eds., *Economic Change in the Civil War Era*, 23–24;

(289) **"In God We Trust"**: John J. Pullen, *A Shower of Stars: The Medal of Honor and the 27th Maine* (Philadelphia: B. Lippincott Company, 1966), 54–55; Joseph J. Kane, *Famous First Facts: A Record of First Happenings, Discoveries, and Inventions in American History* (New York: H. W. Wilson Company, 1981), 394; Daryl Lyman, *Civil War Wordbook: Including Sayings, Phrases and Slang* (Conshohocken, Penn.: Combined Books, 1994), 90, 172.

(289– **Department of Agriculture**: Richardson, *The Greatest Nation of the*
292) *Earth*, 149–157; G. S. Boritt, *Lincoln and the Economics of the American Dream* (Memphis: Memphis State University Press, 1978), 215–216; Basler, ed., *The Collected Works of Abraham Lincoln*, 3: 480; Paul W. Gates, *Agriculture and the Civil War* (New York: Alfred A. Knopf, 1965), 306–308, 319–323; A. Hunter Dupree, *Science in the Federal Government: A History of Policies and Activities to 1940* (Cambridge, Mass.: Harvard University Press, 1957), 150–152, 172; Van Riper and Sutherland, "The Northern Civil Service," 367; Nevins, *The War for the Union*, 3: 263; Paludan, *"A People's Contest,"* 166.

(292– **The Homestead Act**: Richardson, *The Greatest Nation of the Earth*,
293) 140–149; Basler, ed., *The Collected Works of Abraham Lincoln*, 4: 202; Paludan, *"A People's Contest,"* 134–135; Curry, *Blueprint for Modern America*, 101–108, 248–249; Gates, *Agriculture and the Civil War*, 290–294; McPherson, *Battle Cry of Freedom*, 450–451; Robert Cruden, *The War That Never Ended: The American Civil War* (Englewood Cliffs, N.J.: Prentice-Hall, 1973), 179.

(293– **Higher Education**: Richard Hofstadter, *Anti-Intellectualism in Ameri-*
296) *can Life* (New York: Alfred A. Knopf, 1964), especially 272–279; Gates, *Agriculture and the Civil War*, 251–252, 268–271; Edward Danforth Eddy, Jr., *Colleges for Our Land and Time: The Land Grant Idea in American Education* (New York: Harper & Brothers, 1956), 23–51; Fite, *Social and Industrial Conditions in the North during the Civil War*, 235–236; Richardson, *The Greatest Nation of the Earth*, 154–160; Paludan, *"A People's Contest,"* 130–132; Rawley, *The Politics of Union*, 67.

(296– **The Transcontinental Railroad**: Richard B. Rice, William A. Bul-
298) lough, and Richard J. Orsi, *The Elusive Eden: A New History of California* (New York: McGraw-Hill, 1996), 192–194, 260–262; Richard-

son, *The Greatest Nation of the Earth,* 170–187; Curry, *Blueprint for Modern America,* 116–136, 246–247; Weber, *The Northern Railroads in the Civil War,* 22–23; Cruden, *The War That Never Ended,* 180–181; Randall and Donald, *The Civil War and Reconstruction,* 288.

(298–   **Encouraging Immigration**: Richardson, *The Greatest Nation of the*
299)   *Earth,* 19–20, 162, 167–168; Boritt, *Lincoln and the Economics of the American Dream,* 221–223; Basler, ed., *The Collected Works of Abraham Lincoln,* 7: 40; Richard Nelson Current, *Speaking of Abraham Lincoln: The Man and His Meaning for Our Times* (Urbana: University of Illinois Press, 1983), 119; Murdock, *One Million Men,* 323–324, 328; Parish, *The American Civil War,* 367–368.

(299–   **Postal Service Reform**: McPherson, *For Cause and Comrades,* 11;
302)   Dodd, *The Song of the Rappahannock,* 129; Robertson, *Soldiers Blue and Gray,* 105; Mary A. Livermore, *My Story of the War: A Woman's Narrative of Four Years Personal Experience* (Hartford: A. D. Worthington and Company, 1891), 660–661; Wayne E. Fuller, *The American Mail: The Enlarger of the Common Life* (Chicago: University of Chicago Press, 1972), 70–71, 166–168, 246–247; Gerald Cullinan, *The United States Postal Service* (New York: Praeger Publishers, 1973), 80–85, 195–196; Fite, *Social and Industrial Conditions in the North during the Civil War,* 138–139; Sutherland, *The Expansion of Everyday Life,* 202–203.

(302–   **Antiobscenity Legislation**: D'Emilio and Freedmen, *Intimate Matters,*
304)   131–132; Lowry, *The Story the Soldiers Wouldn't Tell,* 54–56, 59–61; James C. N. Paul and Murray L. Schwartz, *Federal Censorship: Obscenity in the Mail* (New York: Free Press of Glencoe, 1961), 17–18, 254–260; *U.S. Statutes at Large,* 13: 507.

(304–   **Yosemite**: Joseph H. Engbeck, Jr., *State Parks of California: From*
306)   *1864 to the Present* (Portland, Oreg.: Graphic Arts Center Publishing Co., 1980), 17–19; Hans Huth, "Yosemite: The Story of an Idea," *Sierra Club Bulletin* 33 (March 1948), 47–48, 62–70, 74; Hans Huth, *Nature and the American: Three Centuries of Changing Attitudes* (Berkeley: University of California Press, 1957), 146–151; Rice, et. al., *The Elusive Eden,* 290–291.

(306–   **The Freedmen's Bureau**: Basler, ed., *The Collected Works of Abraham*
309)   *Lincoln,* 4: 506; Trefousse, *Ben Butler,* 78–79; Eric Foner, *Reconstruction: America's Unfinished Revolution, 1863–1877* (New York: Harper & Row, Publishers, 1988), 68–70, 142–144, 150–153, 169–170; James Marten, *The Children's Civil War* (Chapel Hill: University of North Carolina Press, 1998), 128–136, 196–197; Bremner, *The Public Good,* 83, 118–120, 125; Donald G. Nieman, *To Set the Law in Motion: The Freedmen's Bureau and the Legal Rights of Blacks* (Millwood, N.Y.: KTO Press, 1979), xiii–xv, 221–222; Herman Belz, *Emancipation and Equal Rights: Politics and Constitutionalism in the Civil War Era* (New

York: W. W. Norton, & Company, 1978), 72–73; John Hope Franklin, *Reconstruction: After the Civil War* (Chicago: University of Chicago Press, 1961), 36–39; Kenneth M. Stampp, *The Era of Reconstruction: 1865–1877* (New York: Alfred A. Knopf), 1966), 134–135.

CHAPTER 12: THE FIRST FAMILY (Pages 311–324)

(311– **Introduction**: Oates, *With Malice Toward None*, 103–105, 108, 312–
314) 313; Wilson and Davis, eds., *Herndon's Informants*, 453, 465; Luthin, *The Real Abraham Lincoln*, 131–141, 410; Douglas L. Wilson, *Lincoln before Washington: New Perspectives on the Illinois Years* (Urbana: University of Illinois Press, 1997), 99–125; Jean H. Baker, *Mary Todd Lincoln: A Biography* (New York: W. W. Norton & Company, 1987), 102, 125–129, 131–132; Donald, *Lincoln*, 108–109, 159; Geoffrey Ward, "The House at Eighth and Jackson," *American Heritage* 40 (April 1989), 76–78; Katherine Helm, *The True Story of Mary, Wife of Lincoln* (New York: Harper and Brothers, 1928), 140; Charles B. Strozier, *Lincoln's Quest for Union: Public and Private Meanings* (New York: Basic Books, 1982), 71–91.

(314– **"Happy and Unrestrained by Parental Tyranny"**: William Hanchett,
316) *Out of the Wilderness: The Life of Abraham Lincoln* (Urbana: University of Illinois Press, 1994), 72; Baker, *Mary Todd Lincoln*, 120–125; Wilson and Davis, eds., *Herndon's Informants*, 181, 357; Justin G. Turner and Linda Levitt Turner, *Mary Todd Lincoln: Her Life and Letters* (New York: Alfred A. Knopf, 1972), 41–42, 120; Donald, *Lincoln*, 159–160; Ruth Painter Randall, *Lincoln's Sons* (Boston: Little, Brown and Company, 1955), 92–127, 140–141.

(316– **"The Hope and Stay of Her Old Age"**: Oates, *With Malice Toward*
318) *None*, 312–315; Baker, *Mary Todd Lincoln*, 202–222; Helen Nicolay, *Lincoln's Secretary: A Biography of John G. Nicolay* (New York: Longmans, Green & Co., 1949), 132–133; Elizabeth Keckley, *Behind the Scenes; Or, Thirty Years as a Slave, and Four Years in the White House* (New York: G. W. Carleton & Co., Publishers, 1868), 103; Strozier, *Lincoln's Quest for Union*, 136–138; Donald, *Lincoln*, 336–337; Randall, *Lincoln's Sons*, 128–142; Turner and Turner, *Mary Todd Lincoln*, 121–124; Van der Heuvel, *Crowns of Thorns and Glory*, 169–171.

(318– **"Stabs Given Mary"**: Paul F. Boller, Jr., *Presidential Wives* (New
321) York: Oxford University Press, 1988), 110–113; Keckley, *Behind the Scenes*, 101, 136; Turner and Turner, *Mary Todd Lincoln*, 78–79, 88–89, 100–101, 110–111, 162–163, 187–190; Oates, *Abraham Lincoln: The Man behind the Myths*, 178; Baker, *Mary Todd Lincoln*, 110–111, 222–223; Oates, *With Malice Toward None*, 297, 409; E. H. Gwynne-Thomas, *The Presidential Families* (New York: Hippocrene Books, 1989), 169–170; Thomas, *Abraham Lincoln*, 297–298; Burlingame, *The*

Inner World of Abraham Lincoln, 298–300; Leech, *Reveille in Washington,* 295; Van der Heuvel, *Crowns of Thorns and Glory,* 120–123; Mary Clemmer Ames, *Ten Years in Washington: Life and Scenes in the National Capital, As a Woman Sees Them* (Hartford: A. D. Worthington & Co., Publishers, 1880), 237.

(322) **"First Lady"**: Hanchett, *Out of the Wilderness,* 77; Moore, *Speaking of Washington,* 108; Kane, *Facts about the Presidents,* 310; Burlingame, ed., *Lincoln Observed,* 88; William Howard Russell, *My Diary North and South* (Boston: T. O. H. P. Burnham, 1863), 566–567.

(322– **The President's Theatergoing**: Wilson and Davis, eds., *Herndon's In-*
324)   *formants,* 648; Turner and Turner, *Mary Todd Lincoln,* 218; Gene Smith, "The Booth Obsession," *American Heritage* 43 (September 1992), 109; Burlingame and Ettlinger, eds., *Inside Lincoln's White House,* 104, 128; Holzer, ed., *The Lincoln Mailbag,* 143; Donald, *Lincoln,* 568–570; Auguste Laugel, *The United States during the Civil War,* ed. by Allan Nevins (Bloomington: Indiana University Press, 1961), 261–262, 315–316; Timothy S. Good, ed., *We Saw Lincoln Shot: One Hundred Eyewitness Accounts* (Jackson: University Press of Mississippi, 1995), 3; Don E. Fehrenbacher and Virginia Fehrenbacher, eds., *Recollected Words of Abraham Lincoln* (Stanford, Calif.: Stanford University Press, 1996), 188; Clint Clay Tilton, "Lincoln and Lamon: Partners and Friends," *Transactions of the Illinois State Historical Society* (1932), 215.

CHAPTER 13: HONORING THE LIVING AND THE DEAD
(Pages 325–338)

(325– **Introduction**: Bernard Chevalier, *Napoleon,* trans. Thomas Michael
326)   Gunther (Memphis: Lithograph Publishing Company, 1993), 32; Georges Lefebvre, *Napoleon: From 18 Brumaire to Tilsit, 1799–1807* (New York: Columbia University Press, 1969), 144, 150, 159; Editors of Boston Publishing Company, *Above and Beyond: A History of the Medal of Honor from the Civil War to Vietnam* (Boston: Boston Publishing Company, 1985), 3.

(326– **The Medal of Honor**: Editors of Boston Publishing Company, *Above*
328)   *and Beyond,* 2–5, 15, 53; Pullen, *Shower of Stars,* 54–66.

(328– **"Above and Beyond the Call of Duty"**: Bruce Jacobs, *Heroes of the*
333)   *Army: The Medal of Honor and Its Winners* (New York: W. W. Norton & Company, 1956), 17–40, 169–172; Editors of Boston Publishing Company, *Above and Beyond,* 18–21, 43–44, 49–55; Burlingame, ed., *Lincoln Observed,* 30–33; Frank Donovan, *The Story of the Medal of Honor* (New York: Dodd, Mead & Company, 1962), 11–20; B. J. D. Irwin, "The Days Gone By: The Apache Pass Fight," *The Military Sur-*

geon 73 (October 1933), 197–203; Stewart Brooks, *Civil War Medicine* (Springfield, Ill.: Charles C. Thomas, Publisher, 1966), 38; Thomas, *Abraham Lincoln,* 269–270; Pullen, *A Shower of Stars,* 67–81, 134–137; Joseph Nathan Kane, *Famous First Facts: A Record of First Happenings, Discoveries, and Inventions in American History* (New York: H. W. Wilson Company, 1981), 371; Joseph B. Mitchell, *The Badge of Gallantry: Recollections of Civil War Congressional Medal of Honor Winners* (New York: Macmillan Company, 1968), 12, 132–134, 145–147; Schappes, ed., *A Documentary History of the Jews in the United States,* 700; Irvin H. Lee, *Negro Medal of Honor Men* (New York: Dodd, Mead & Company, 1967), 4–5, 24–50, 129–130; Glatthaar, *Forged in Battle,* 275–278; Brian C. Pohanka, "Carnival of Death," *America's Civil War* 4 (September 1991), 36.

(333– **Military Pensions**: Amy E. Holmes, "'Such Is the Price We Pay':
335)   American Widows and the Civil War Pension System," in Maris A Vinovskis, ed., *Toward a Social History of the American Civil War: Exploratory Essays* (New York: Cambridge University Press, 1990), 171–174; 194–195; Bremner, *The Public Good,* 144–145; Maris A. Vinovskis, "Have Social Historians Lost the Civil War? Some Preliminary Demographic Speculations," in Vinovskis, *Toward a Social History of the American Civil War,* 21–23; *U.S. Statutes at Large,* 12: 566–569; Stuart McConnell, *Glorious Contentment: The Grand Army of the Republic, 1865–1900* (Chapel Hill: The University of North Carolina Press, 1992), 15; Linderman, *Embattled Courage,* 270–271, 275; Mary R. Dearing, *Veterans in Politics: The Story of the G.A.R.* (Baton Rouge: Louisiana State University Press, 1952), 399–401; Basler, ed., *The Collected Works of Abraham Lincoln,* 8: 333.

(335– **MIAs**: McPherson, *Battle Cry of Freedom,* 574; Edward Steere, "Evo-
337)   lution of the National Cemetery System, 1865–1880," *The Quartermaster Review* 32 (1953), 22–24; Catton, *Reflections on the Civil War,* 236; Gallman, *The North Fights the Civil War,* 160; Oates, *A Woman of Valor,* 295–297, 304, 309, 313–336, 367–368; Robert E. Denney, *Civil War Medicine: Care & Comfort of the Wounded* (New York: Sterling Publishing Co., 1994), 381–383.

(337– **National Military Cemeteries**: George L. Mosse, *Fallen Soldiers: Re-
338)   shaping the Memory of the World Wars* (New York: Oxford University Press, 1990), 45–46; *U.S. Statutes at Large,* 12: 596; Steere, "Evolution of the National Cemetery System, 1865–1880," 22–24, 123–124; Harry W. Pfanz, *Gettysburg—Culps Hill and Cemetery Hill* (Chapel Hill: University of North Carolina Press, 1993), 374–375; Webb Garrison, *Civil War Curiosities: Strange Stories, Oddities, Events, and Coincidences* (Nashville: Rutledge Hill Press, 1994), 208; William H. Price, *The Civil War Centennial Handbook* (Arlington, Va.: Prince Lithograph Co., 1961), 14.

(338) **Decoration Day**: Sutherland, *The Expansion of Everyday Life*, 260;
      Holmes, "'Such Is the Price We Pay': American Widows and the Civil
      War Pension System," 193–194; Basler, ed., *The Collected Works of
      Abraham Lincoln*, 7: 23.

CHAPTER 14: ASSASSINATION (Pages 339–358)

(339– **Introduction**: Bernhard J. Stern, ed., *Young Ward's Diary* (New York:
 341) G. P. Putnam's Sons, 1935), 168; Beale, ed., *Diary of Gideon Welles*, 2:
      278; Nevins, *The War for the Union* 4: 313–314; James I. Robertson, Jr.,
      ed., *The Civil War Letters of General Robert McAllister* (New Bruns-
      wick, N.J.: Rutgers University Press, 1965), 607–608; Emmy E. Werner,
      Reluctant Witnesses: Children's Voices from the Civil War (Boulder,
      Colo.: Westview Press, 1998), 140–141; Oates, *With Malice Toward
      None*, 458–461; Paludan, *"A People's Contest,"* 392; *Sacramento Daily
      Union*, May 8, 1865; Basler, ed., *The Collected Works of Abraham Lin-
      coln*, 8: 393, 400–401, 403; William Hanchett, *The Lincoln Murder Con-
      spiracies* (Urbana: University of Illinois Press, 1983), 37.

(342– **"Sic Semper Tyrannis!"**: John Rhodehamel and Louise Taper, eds.,
 347) *"Right or Wrong, God Judge Me": The Writings of John Wilkes Booth*
      (Urbana: University of Illinois Press, 1997), 1–2, 4–8, 10–16, 125, 154–
      155; W. Emerson Reck, *A. Lincoln: His Last 24 Hours* (1987; reprint,
      Columbia: University of South Carolina Press, 1994), 63–66; Asia
      Booth Clarke, *The Unlocked Book: A Memoir of John Wilkes Booth by
      his Sister Asia Booth Clarke* (New York: G. P. Putnam's Sons, 1938),
      115–116, 124–125; Edwina Booth Grossmann, *Edwin Booth: Reflec-
      tions by his Daughter* (New York: Century Co., 1894), 227; Clara E.
      Laughlin, *The Death of Lincoln: The Story of Booth's Plot, His Deed
      and the Penalty* (New York: Doubleday, Page & Company, 1909), 59–
      60; Hanchett, *The Lincoln Murder Conspiracies*, 35–58; William A.
      Tidwell, James O. Hall, and David Winfield Gaddy, *Come Retribution:
      The Confederate Secret Service and the Assassination of Lincoln* (Jack-
      son: University Press of Mississippi, 1988), 5, 28, 262–295, 416–424;
      William A. Tidwell, *April '65: Confederate Covert Action in the Amer-
      ican Civil War* (Kent, Ohio: Kent State University Press, 1995), 7, 137,
      144–148, 156–157, 162–164, 175; William Hanchett, "Shooting the
      President as a Military Necessity," in Charles M. Hubbard, ed., *Lincoln
      and His Contemporaries* (Macon, Ga.: Mercer University Press, 1999),
      145, 147–148; Luthin, *The Real Abraham Lincoln*, 612–618; Good, ed.,
      We Saw Lincoln Shot, 10–26; *The Times* of London, April 29, 1865.

(347– **The Biggest Manhunt in American History**: Hanchett, *The Lincoln
 349) Murder Conspiracies*, 61, 65, 176; Rhodehamel and Taper, eds., *"Right
      or Wrong, God Judge Me": The Writings of John Wilkes Booth*, 16–18;
      Benjamin P. Thomas and Harold M. Hyman, *Stanton: The Life and*

Times of Lincoln's Secretary of War (New York: Alfred A. Knopf, 1962), 400, 419–421; Oates, *Abraham Lincoln: The Man behind the Myths,* 164–165; Luthin, *The Real Abraham Lincoln,* 665–666; Hanchett, *Out of the Wilderness,* 117.

(349– **Mary E. Surratt**: Thomas Reed Turner, *Beware the People Weeping:*
352) *Public Opinion and the Assassination of Abraham Lincoln* (Baton Rouge: Louisiana State University Press, 1982), 145, 152, 155–156, 169–171, 174–179, 181, 251–252; Thomas and Hyman, *Stanton,* 423, 426–430, 434; Edward A. Miller, Jr., *Lincoln's Abolitionist General: The Biography of David Hunter* (Columbia: University of South Carolina Press, 1997), 250–251, 255; Roscoe, *The Web of Conspiracy,* 431, 441–442, 446–447, 475–476, 481–482, 487–488; Trudeau, *Out of the Storm,* 360–362, 374–375; Gene Smith, "The Booth Obsession," *American Heritage* 43 (September 1992), 108, 110; Guy W. Moore, *The Case of Mrs. Surratt: Her Controversial Trial and Execution for Conspiracy in the Lincoln Assassination* (Norman: University of Oklahoma Press, 1954), 100–102, 105–113, 115–117.

(352– **John H. Surratt**: Roscoe, *The Web of Conspiracy,* 50–55, 507, 510;
354) Osborn H. Oldroyd, *The Assassination of Abraham Lincoln* (Washington, D.C.: O. H. Oldroyd, 1901), 229, 231, 238–239; Hanchett, *The Lincoln Murder Conspiracies,* 47–48, 86–88; Turner, *Beware the People Weeping,* 227, 250, 252; John Bassett Moore, *A Treatise on Extradition and Interstate Rendition* (Boston: The Boston Book Company, 1891), 1: 104–105; Oates, *Abraham Lincoln: The Man behind the Myths,* 168–169.

(354– **Lincoln's Widow**: Turner and Turner, *Mary Todd Lincoln,* 228, 231,
358) 236, 264–265, 349–356, 429–433, 440–441, 489–500; Baker, *Mary Todd Lincoln,* 254–267, 298–302, 367–368; Oates, *Abraham Lincoln: The Man behind the Myths,* 180–187; Van der Heuvel, *Crowns of Thorns and Glory,* 184–188, 199–203, 207–221; Paul F. Boller, Jr., *Presidential Wives* (New York: Oxford University Press, 1988), 116–117.

Bibliography

PUBLISHED PRIMARY SOURCES

Alcott, Louisa May. *Hospital Sketches.* Edited by Bessie Z. Jones. Cambridge: Harvard University Press, 1960.

Ames, Mary Clemmer. *Ten Years in Washington: Life and Scenes in the National Capital, as a Woman Sees Them.* Hartford: A. D. Worthington & Co., Publishers, 1880.

Aubrey, Cullen "Doc." *Recollections of a Newsboy in the Army of the Potomac: 1861–1865.* Milwaukee, n.p., 1904.

Barbee, David R., and Milledge L. Bonham, Jr., eds. "The Montgomery Address of Stephen A. Douglas." *Journal of Southern History* 5 (November 1939): 527–552.

Bare, Elizabeth R., ed. *Shadows on My Heart: The Civil War Diary of Lucy Rebecca Buck of Virginia.* Athens: University of Georgia Press, 1997.

Barrett, Edwin S. *What I Saw at Bull Run.* Boston: Beacon Press, 1886.

Basler, Roy P., ed. *The Collected Works of Abraham Lincoln.* 9 vols. New Brunswick, N.J.: Rutgers University Press, 1953.

Beale, Howard K., ed. *Diary of Gideon Welles: Secretary of the Navy under Lincoln and Johnson.* 3 vols. New York: W. W. Norton, 1960.

Berlin, Ira, Joseph P. Reidy, and Leslie Rowland, eds. *Freedom: A Documentary History of Emancipation, 1861–1867.* Series II. *The Black Military Experience.* Cambridge, England: Cambridge University Press, 1982.

Billings, John D. *Hardtack and Coffee: The Unwritten Story of Army Life.* Edited by Richard Harwell. Chicago: R. R. Donnelley & Sons, 1960.

Blaine, James G. *Twenty Years of Congress: From Lincoln to Garfield.* 2 vols. Norwich, Conn.: Henry Bill Publishing Company, 1884–1886.

Boutwell, George S. *Reminiscences of Sixty Years in Public Affairs.* 2 vols. New York: McClure, Phillips & Co., 1902.

Brinton, John H. "Address at the Closing Exercises of the Session 1895–96, Army Medical School." *The Journal of the American Medical Association* 26 (March 1896): 599–605.

Brooks, Noah. *Washington in Lincoln's Time.* Edited by Herbert Mitgang. Chicago: Quadrangle Books, 1971.

Bryant II, William Cullen, ed. "A Yankee Soldier Looks at the Negro: Extracts from the Civil War Letters of Henry M. Cross, 1863–1865." *Civil War History* 7 (June 1961): 133–148.

Burgess, Lauren Cook, ed. *An Uncommon Soldier: The Civil War Letters of Sarah Rosetta Wakeman, alias Private Lyons Wakeman, 153rd Regiment, New York State Volunteers.* New York: Oxford University Press, 1994.

Burlingame, Michael, ed. *Lincoln Observed: Civil War Dispatches of Noah Brooks.* Baltimore: Johns Hopkins University Press, 1998.

Burlingame, Michael, and John R. Turner Ettlinger, eds. *Inside Lincoln's White House: The Complete Civil War Diary of John Hay.* Carbondale: Southern Illinois University Press, 1997.

Butterfield, Julia Lorrilard. *A Biographical Memoir of General Daniel Butterfield, Including Many Addresses and Military Writings.* New York: The Grafton Press, 1904.

Clarke, Asia Booth. *The Unlocked Book: A Memoir of John Wilkes Booth by his Sister Asia Booth Clarke.* New York: G. P. Putnam's Sons, 1938.

Cuthbert, Norma B., ed. *Lincoln and the Baltimore Plot: 1861.* San Marino, Calif.: Huntington Library, 1949.

Dodd, Ira Seymour. *The Song of the Rappahannock.* New York: Dodd, Mead and Company, 1898.

Donald, David, ed. *Inside Lincoln's Cabinet: The Civil War Diaries of Salmon P. Chase.* New York: Longmans, Green and Co., 1954.

Fishel, Leslie H., and Benjamin Quarles, eds. *The Black American: A Brief Documentary History.* Glenview, Ill.: Scott, Foresman and Company, 1970.

Ford, Worthington Chauncey, ed. *A Cycle of Adams Letters, 1861–1865.* 2 vols. Boston: Houghton Mifflin Company, 1920.

Freidel, Frank, ed. *Union Pamphlets of the Civil War, 1861–1865.* 2 vols. Cambridge, Mass.: Harvard University Press, 1967.

Good, Timothy S., ed. *We Saw Lincoln Shot: One Hundred Eyewitness Accounts.* Jackson: University Press of Mississippi, 1995.

Grant, Ulysses S. *Personal Memoirs of U. S. Grant.* 2 vols. New York: Charles L. Webster & Company, 1885–1886.

Grossmann, Edwina Booth. *Edwin Booth; Reflections by his Daughter.* New York: Century Co., 1894.

Halstead, Murat. "The Republicans Nominate Lincoln." In *The Tragic Conflict: The Civil War and Reconstruction,* edited by William B. Hesseltine, 98–117. New York: George Braziller, 1962.

Hesseltine, William B., ed. *Three Against Lincoln: Murat Halstead Reports the Caucuses of 1860.* Baton Rouge: Louisiana State University Press, 1960.

Holmes, O. W. "Doings of the Sunbeam." *The Atlantic Monthly* 12 (July 1863): 1–15.

Holzer, Harold, ed. *The Lincoln Mailbag: America Writes to the President, 1861–1865*. Carbondale: Southern Illinois University Press, 1998.

Irwin, B. J. D. "The Days Gone By: The Apache Pass Fight." *The Military Surgeon* 73 (October 1933): 197–203.

Keckley, Elizabeth. *Behind the Scenes; Or, Thirty Years as a Slave, and Four Years in the White House*. New York: G. W. Carleton & Co., Publishers, 1868.

Laugel, Auguste. *The United States during the Civil War*. Edited by Allan Nevins. Bloomington: Indiana University Press, 1961.

Laughlin, Clara E. *The Death of Lincoln. The Story of Booth's Plot, His Deed and Penalty*. New York: Doubleday, Page & Company, 1909.

Letterman, Jonathan. *Medical Recollections of the Army of the Potomac*. New York: Appleton and Company, 1866.

Livermore, Mary A. *My Story of the War: A Woman's Narrative of Four Years Personal Experience*. Hartford: A. D. Worthington and Company, 1891.

Marcus, Jacob Rader. *Memoirs of American Jews: 1775–1865*. Vol. 3. Philadelphia: Jewish Publication Society of America, 1955.

McPherson, Edward. T*he Political History of the United States of America during the Great Rebellion*. Washington, D.C.: Philip & Solomons, 1865.

Miers, Earl Schenck, ed. *When the World Ended: The Diary of Emma LeConte*. New York: Oxford University Press, 1957.

Moore, Frank, ed. *The Rebellion Record: A Diary of American Events, with Documents, Narratives, Illustrative Incidents, Poetry, Etc.* 8 vols. New York: G. P. Putnam, 1861–1863. D. Van Nostrand, Publisher, 1864–1868.

Nevins, Allan, ed. *George Templeton Strong: Diary of the Civil War, 1860–1865*. New York: Macmillan Company, 1962.

Nevins, Allan, and Milton Halsey Thomas, eds. *The Diary of George Templeton Strong*. 4 vols. New York: Macmillan Company, 1952.

Newcomb, M. A. *Four Years of Personal Reminiscences of the War*. Chicago: H. S. Mills & Co., Publishers, 1893.

Norton, Oliver W. *Army Letters, 1861–1865*. Chicago: O. L. Deming, 1903.

Parton, James. "The *New York Herald* from 1835–1866." *North American Review* 102 (April 1866): 373–419.

Pearson, Elizabeth Ware. *Letters from Port Royal: Written at the Time of the Civil War*. Boston: W. B. Clarke, 1906.

Pinkerton, Allan. *The Spy of the Rebellion*. New York: G. W. Carleton and Co., 1883.

Rankin, David C., ed. *My Passage at the New Orleans Tribune: A Memoir of the Civil War Era [by] Jean-Charles Houzeau*. Baton Rouge: Louisiana State University Press, 1984.

Rhodehamel, John, and Louise Taper, eds. *"Right or Wrong, God Judge Me": The Writings of John Wilkes Booth*. Urbana: University of Illinois Press, 1997.

Rice, Allen Thorndike, ed. *Reminiscences of Abraham Lincoln by Distinguished Men of His Time.* New York: North American Review, 1888.

Rittenhouse, Henry N. "U.S. Army Medical Storekeepers." *American Journal of Pharmacy* 37 (1865): 87–90.

Robertson, Jr., James I., ed. *The Civil War Letters of General Robert McAllister.* New Brunswick, N.J.: Rutgers University Press, 1965.

Rowland, Kate Mason, and Mrs. Morris L. Croxall, eds. *The Journal of Julia LeGrand: New Orleans, 1862–1863.* Richmond: Everett Waddey Co., 1911.

Russell, William Howard. *My Diary North and South.* Boston: T. O. H. P. Burnham, 1863.

Salm-Salm, Princess Felix. *Ten Years of My Life.* New York: R. Worthington, 1877.

Schappes, Morris U., ed. *A Documentary History of the Jews in the United States: 1654–1875.* New York: Schocken Books, 1971.

Sherman, William T. *Memoirs of General William T. Sherman.* 2 vols. New York: D. Appleton and Company, 1875.

Sideman, Belle Becker, and Lillian Friedman, eds. *Europe Looks at the Civil War.* New York: Orion Press, 1960.

Silliker, Ruth L., ed. *The Rebel Yell & the Yankee Hurrah: The Civil War Journal of a Maine Volunteer.* Camden, Me.: Down East Books, 1985.

Stern, Bernhard J., ed. *Young Ward's Diary.* New York: G. P. Putnam's Sons, 1935.

Stevens, Walter B. *A Reporter's Lincoln.* Edited by Michael Burlingame. Lincoln: University of Nebraska Press, 1998.

Stillwell, Leander. *The Story of a Common Soldier of Army Life in the Civil War.* Erie, Kan.: Erie Record, 1917.

Straubing, Harold Elk. *In Hospital and Camp: The Civil War through the Eyes of Its Doctors and Nurses.* Harrisburg, Penn.: Stackpole Books, 1993.

Swift, Lester L., ed. "The Recollections of a Signal Officer." *Civil War History* 9 (March 1963): 36–54.

Ticknor, George. *Life, Letters, and Journals of George Ticknor.* 2 vols. Boston: Houghton Mifflin Company, 1909.

United States Statutes at Large. 12 (December 1859–March 1863), 13 (December 1863–December 1865).

Van Santvoord, C. "A Reception by President Lincoln." *The Century Magazine* 25 (February 1883), 612–614.

Villard, Henry. *Memoirs of Henry Villard: Journalist and Financier, 1835–1900.* 2 vols. Boston: Houghton Mifflin and Company, 1904.

Villard, Harold G., and Oswald Garrison Villard, eds. *Lincoln on the Eve of '61: A Journalist's Story by Henry Villard.* New York: Alfred A. Knopf, 1941.

The War of the Rebellion: A Compilation of the Official Records of the Union and Confederate Armies. 128 vols. Washington, D.C.: Government Printing Office, 1880–1901.

Wilson, Clyde N., and W. Edwin Hemphill, eds. *The Papers of John C. Cal-houn.* Vol. 10. Columbia: University of South Carolina Press, 1977.

Winther, Oscar Osburn, ed. *With Sherman to the Sea: The Civil War Letters, Diaries & Reminiscences of Theodore F. Upson.* Baton Rouge: Louisiana State University Press, 1943.

Wise, John Sergeant. *The End of an Era.* Edited by Curtis Carroll Davis. New York: Thomas Yoseloff, 1965.

Wittenmyer, Annie T. *Under the Guns: A Woman's Reminiscences of the Civil War.* Boston: E. B. Stillings & Co., Publisher, 1895.

NEWSPAPERS

Boston Daily Journal
Douglass' Monthly
Montgomery Daily Advertiser
New Orleans *Daily Picayune*
New York *Daily Tribune*
New York *Evening Post*
New York Times
Sacramento Daily Union
The Times of London
Washington *Evening Star*

BOOKS

Adams, George Worthington. *Doctors in Blue: The Medical History of the Union Army in the Civil War.* New York: Henry Schuman, 1952.

Anderson, Bern. *By Sea and by River: The Naval History of the Civil War.* New York: Alfred A. Knopf, 1962.

Andrew, Christopher. *Secret Intelligence and the American Presidency from Washington to Bush.* New York: HarperCollins Publishers, 1995.

Andrews, J. Cutler. *The North Reports the Civil War.* Pittsburgh: University of Pittsburgh Press, 1955.

———. *The South Reports the Civil War.* Princeton, N.J.: Princeton University Press, 1970.

Ashburn, P. M. *A History of the Medical Department of the United States Army.* Boston: Houghton Mifflin Company, 1929.

Axelrod, Alan. *The War Between the Spies: A History of Espionage during the American Civil War.* New York: Atlantic Monthly Press, 1992.

Baker, Jean H. *Mary Todd Lincoln: A Biography.* New York: W. W. Norton & Company, 1987.

Baker, Liva. *The Justice from Beacon Hill: The Life and Times of Oliver Wen-dell Holmes.* New York: Harper-Collins Publishers, 1991.

Batty, Peter, and Peter Parish. *The Divided Union: The Story of the Great American War.* Topsfield, Mass.: Salem House Publishers, 1987.

Beach, Edward L. *The United States Navy: 200 Years.* New York: Henry Holt and Company, 1986.

Beasley, W. G. *Japan Encounters the Barbarian: Japanese Travellers in America and Europe.* New Haven, Conn.: Yale University Press, 1995.

Belz, Herman. *Abraham Lincoln, Constitutionalism, and Equal Rights in the Civil War Era.* New York: Fordham University Press, 1998.

———. *Emancipation and Equal Rights: Politics and Constitutionalism in the Civil War Era.* New York: W. W. Norton & Company, 1978.

———. *Reconstructing the Union: Theory and Policy during the Civil War.* Ithaca, N.Y.: Cornell University Press, 1969.

Bender, George A. *Great Moments in Medicine.* Detroit: Northwood Institute Press, 1966.

Bernstein, Iver. *The New York City Draft Riots: Their Significance for American Society and Politics in the Age of the Civil War.* New York: Oxford University Press, 1990.

Binkley, Wilfred E. *President and Congress.* 1937. Reprint, New York: Vintage Press, 1962.

Blackett, R. J. M. *Thomas Morris Chester, Black Civil War Correspondent: His Dispatches from the Front.* Baton Rouge: Louisiana State University Press, 1989.

Blassingame, John W. *Black New Orleans: 1860–1880.* Chicago: University of Chicago Press, 1973.

Blied, Benjamin J. *Catholics and the Civil War.* Milwaukee: privately printed, 1945.

Block, Eugene B. *Above the Civil War: The Story of Thaddeus Lowe, Balloonist, Inventor, Railway Builder.* Berkeley, Calif.: Howell-North Books, 1966.

Blondheim, Menahem. *News over the Wires: The Telegraph and the Flow of Public Information in America, 1844–1897.* Cambridge, Mass.: Harvard University Press, 1994.

Boller, Jr., Paul F. *Presidential Anecdotes.* New York: Oxford University Press, 1981.

———. *Presidential Campaigns.* New York: Oxford University Press, 1984.

———. *Presidential Wives.* New York: Oxford University Press, 1988.

Bolting, Douglas. *The Great Airships.* Alexandria, Va.: Time-Life Books, 1981.

Boritt, G. S. *Lincoln and the Economics of the American Dream.* Memphis: Memphis State University Press, 1978.

Bowen, Walter S., and Harry Edward Neal. *The United States Secret Service.* Philadelphia: Chilton Company Publishers, 1960.

Bremner, Robert H. *The Public Good: Philanthropy and Welfare in the Civil War Era.* New York: Alfred A Knopf, 1980.

Brock, W. R. *An American Crisis: Congress and Reconstruction, 1865–1867.* New York: Harper & Row, 1963.

Brooks, Stewart. *Civil War Medicine.* Springfield, Ill.: Charles C. Thomas Publisher, 1966.

Bruce, Robert V. *Lincoln and the Tools of War.* Indianapolis: Bobbs-Merrill Company, 1956.

———. *The Launching of Modern American Science: 1846–1876.* New York: Alfred A. Knopf, 1987.

Burlingame, Michael. *The Inner World of Abraham Lincoln.* Urbana: University of Illinois Press, 1994.

Burns, Stanley B. *Early Medical Photography in America: 1839–1883.* New York: Burns Archive, 1983.

Bush, Lewis. *77 Samurai: Japan's First Embassy to America.* Tokyo: Kodansha International Ltd., 1968.

Capers, Gerald M. *Occupied City: New Orleans under the Federals, 1862–1865.* Lexington: University of Kentucky Press, 1965.

———. *Stephen A. Douglas: Defender of the Union.* Boston: Little, Brown and Company, 1959.

Catton, Bruce. *America Goes to War.* Middletown, Conn.: Wesleyan University Press, 1958.

———. *Reflections on the Civil War.* Edited by John Leekley. Garden City, N.Y.: Doubleday & Company, 1981.

———. *The Centennial History of the Civil War: The Coming Fury.* Vol. 1. Garden City, N.Y.: Doubleday & Company, 1961.

Chevalier, Bernard. *Napoleon.* Translated by Thomas Michael Gunther. Memphis: Lithograph Publishing Company, 1993.

Christian, Charles M. *Black Saga: The African American Experience.* Boston: Houghton Mifflin Company, 1995.

Clinton, Catherine. *Tara Revisited: Women, War, and the Plantation Legend.* New York: Abbeville Press, 1995.

Coe, Brian. *The Birth of Photography: The Story of the Formative Years, 1800–1900.* London: Ash & Grant, 1976.

Coggins, Jack. *Arms and Equipment of the Civil War.* Garden City, N.Y.: Doubleday & Company, 1962.

Cole, Donald. *Martin Van Buren and the American Political System.* Princeton, N.J.: Princeton University Press, 1984.

Conrad, Earl. *Harriet Tubman.* 1943. Reprint, New York: Paul S. Eriksson, 1969.

Cook, Adrian. *The Armies of the Street: The New York City Draft Riots of 1863.* Lexington: University Press of Kentucky, 1974.

Cornish, Dudley Taylor. *The Sable Arm: Negro Troops in the Union Army, 1861–1865.* New York: W. W. Norton, 1966.

Crouthamel, James L. *Bennett's New York Herald and the Rise of the Popular Press.* Syracuse, N.Y.: Syracuse University Press, 1989.

Crozier, Emmet. *Yankee Reporters: 1861–1865.* New York: Oxford University Press, 1956.

Cruden, Robert. *The War That Never Ended: The American Civil War.* Englewood Cliffs, N.J.: Prentice-Hall, 1973.

Cullen, Joseph P. *The Peninsula Campaign, 1862: McClellan & Lee Struggle for Richmond.* Harrisburg, Penn.: Stackpole Books, 1973.

Cullinan, Gerald. *The United States Postal Service.* New York: Praeger Publishers, 1973.

Culpepper, Marilyn Mayer. *Trials and Triumphs: Women of the American Civil War.* East Lansing: Michigan State University Press, 1991.

Cunliffe, Marcus. *American Presidents and the Presidency.* New York: McGraw-Hill Book Company, 1976.

———. *Soldiers and Civilians: The Martial Spirit in America, 1775–1865.* Boston: Little, Brown and Company, 1968.

Cunningham, H. H. *Doctors in Gray: The Confederate Medical Service.* Baton Rouge: Louisiana State University Press, 1960.

Current, Richard N. *Lincoln and the First Shot.* Philadelphia: J. B. Lippincott Company, 1963.

———. *Speaking of Abraham Lincoln: The Man and His Meaning for Our Times.* Urbana: University of Illinois Press, 1983.

Current, Richard N., ed. *Encyclopedia of the Confederacy.* 4 vols. New York: Simon and Schuster, 1993.

Curry, Leonard P. *Blueprint for Modern America: Nonmilitary Legislation of the First Civil War Congress.* Nashville: Vanderbilt University Press, 1968.

Dangerfield, George. *Victoria's Heir: The Education of a Prince.* New York: Harcourt , Brace and Company, 1941.

Davis, Carl L. *Arming the Union: Small Arms in the Civil War.* Port Washington, N.Y.: Kennikat Press, 1973.

Davis, Elmer. *History of the New York Times.* New York: New York Times, 1921.

Davis, William C. *"A Government of Our Own": The Making of the Confederacy.* New York: Free Press, 1994.

———. *Lincoln's Men: How President Lincoln Became Father to an Army and a Nation.* New York: Free Press, 1999.

Dean, Jr., Eric T. *Shook over Hell: Post-Traumatic Stress, Vietnam, and the Civil War.* Cambridge, Mass.: Harvard University Press, 1997.

Dearing, Mary R. *Veterans in Politics: The Story of the G.A.R.* Baton Rouge: Louisiana State University Press, 1952.

deKay, James Tertius. *Monitor: The Story of the Legendary Civil War Ironclad and the Man Whose Invention Changed the Course of History.* New York: Walker and Company, 1997.

D'Emilio, John, and Estelle B. Freedman. *Intimate Matters: A History of Sexuality in America.* New York: Harper & Row Publishers, 1988.

Denney, Robert E. *Civil War Medicine: Care & Comfort of the Wounded.* New York: Sterling Publishing Co., 1994.

Dictionary of American Biography. 20 vols. 1929–1936. Reprint (20 vols. in

10), New York: Charles Scribner's Sons, 1957–1964.

Donald, David Herbert. *Lincoln.* New York: Simon and Schuster, 1995.

Donovan, Frank. *The Story of the Medal of Honor.* New York: Dodd, Mead & Company, 1962.

Du Bois, W. E. Burghardt. *Black Reconstruction in America.* 1935. Reprint, Cleveland: World Publishing Company, 1964.

Duffy, James P. *Lincoln's Admiral: The Civil War Campaigns of David Farragut.* New York: John Wiley & Sons, 1997.

Dupree, A. Hunter. *Science in the Federal Government: A History of Politics and Activities to 1940.* Cambridge, Mass.: Harvard University Press, 1957.

Durkin, Joseph. *Stephen R. Mallory: Confederate Navy Chief.* Chapel Hill: University of North Carolina Press, 1954.

Duus, Peter, ed. *The Japanese Discovery of America.* Boston: Bedford Books, 1997.

Eddy, Jr., Edward Danforth. *Colleges for Our Time: The Land Grant Idea in American Education.* New York: Harper & Brothers, 1956.

Editors of the Army Times. *A History of the U.S. Signal Corps.* New York: G. P. Putnam's Sons, 1961.

Editors of Boston Publishing Company. *Above and Beyond: A History of the Medal of Honor from the Civil War to Vietnam.* Boston: Boston Publishing Company, 1985.

Eisenhower, John S. D. *Agent of Destiny: The Life and Times of Winfield Scott.* New York: Free Press, 1997.

Elliot, Charles M. *Winfield Scott: The Soldier and the Man.* New York: Macmillan Company, 1937.

Ellis, John Tracy. *American Catholicism.* Chicago: University of Chicago Press, 1969.

Emery, Edward. *The Press and America: An Interpretive History of the Mass Media.* Englewood Cliffs, N.J.: Prentice-Hall, 1972.

Engbeck, Jr., Joseph H. *State Parks of California: From 1864 to the Present.* Portland, Oreg.: Graphic Arts Center Publishing Co., 1980.

Faust, Drew Gilpin. *Mothers of Invention: Women of the Slaveholding South in the American Civil War.* Chapel Hill: University of North Carolina Press, 1996.

Fehrenbacher, Don E. *Prelude to Greatness: Lincoln in the 1850s.* Stanford, Calif.: Stanford University Press, 1962.

Fehrenbacher, Don E., and Virginia Fehrenbacher, eds. *Recollected Words of Abraham Lincoln.* Stanford, Calif.: Stanford University Press, 1996.

Feldstein, Stanley. *The Land That I Show You: Three Centuries of Jewish Life in America.* Garden City, N.Y.: Anchor Press, 1978.

Fels, Thomas Westin. *Destruction and Destiny: The Photographs of A. J. Russell: Directing American Energy in War and Peace, 1862–1869.* Pittsfield, Mass.: Berkshire Museum, 1987.

Fermer, Douglas. *James Gordon Bennett and the New York Herald: A Study of*

Editorial Opinion in the Civil War Era, 1854–1867. New York: St. Martin's Press, 1968.

Fishel, Edwin C. *The Secret War for the Union: The Untold Story of Military Intelligence in the Civil War.* Boston: Houghton Mifflin Company, 1996.

Fite, Emerson D. *Social and Industrial Conditions in the North during the Civil War.* New York: Macmillan Company, 1910.

———. *The Presidential Campaign of 1860.* 1911. Reprint, Port Washington, N.Y.: Kennikat Press, 1967.

Foner, Eric. *Reconstruction: America's Unfinished Revolution, 1863–1877.* New York: Harper & Row, Publishers, 1988.

Foner, Eric, and Olivia Mahoney. *A House Divided: America in the Age of Lincoln.* New York: W. W. Norton & Company, 1990.

Foner, Philip S. *History of Black Americans: From the Compromise of 1850 to the End of the Civil War.* Vol. 3. Westport, Conn.: Greenwood Press, 1983.

———. *History of the Labor Movement in the United States: From Colonial Times to the Founding of the American Federation of Labor.* Vol. 1. New York: International Publishers, 1947.

Fowler, Jr., William M. *Under Two Flags: The American Navy in the Civil War.* New York: W. W. Norton & Company, 1990.

Frank, Joseph Allan. *With Ballot and Bayonet: The Political Socialization of American Civil War Soldiers.* Athens: University of Georgia Press, 1998.

Franklin, John Hope. *Reconstruction: After the Civil War.* Chicago: University of Chicago Press, 1961.

Frassanito, William A. *Gettysburg: A Journey in Time.* New York: Charles Scribner's Sons, 1975.

Freemon, Frank R. *Gangrene and Glory: Medical Care during the American Civil War.* Madison, N.J.: Fairleigh Dickinson University Press, 1998.

———. *Microbes and Minie Balls: An Annotated Bibliography of Civil War Medicine.* Rutherford, N.J.: Fairleigh Dickinson University Press, 1993.

Fuller, Wayne E. *The American Mail: The Enlarger of the Common Life.* Chicago: University of Chicago Press, 1972.

Furneaux, Rupert. *News of War: Stories and Adventures of the Great War Correspondents.* London: Max Parrish & Co. Ltd., 1964.

Gallman, Matthew J. *The North Fights the Civil War: The Home Front.* Chicago: Ivan R. Dee, 1994.

Garrison, Webb. *Civil War Curiosities: Strange Stories, Oddities, Events, and Coincidences.* Nashville: Rutledge Hill Press, 1994.

Gates, Paul W. *Agriculture and the Civil War.* New York: Alfred A. Knopf, 1965.

Geary, James W. *We Need Men: The Union Draft in the Civil War.* Dekalb: Northern Illinois University Press, 1991.

Gilchrist, David T., and W. David Lewis, eds. *Economic Change in the Civil War.* Greenville, Del.: Eleutherian Mills-Hagley Foundation, 1965.

Glatthaar, Joseph T. *Forged in Battle: The Civil War Alliance of Black Soldiers and White Officers.* New York: Free Press, 1990.

Goldhurst, Richard. *Many Are the Hearts: The Agony and Triumphs of Ulysses S. Grant.* New York: Reader's Digest Press, 1975.

Gollaher, David. *Voice for the Mad: The Life of Dorothea Dix.* New York: Free Press, 1995.

Gosnell, H. Allen. *Guns on the Western Waters: The Story of the River Gunboats in the Civil War.* Baton Rouge: Louisiana State University Press, 1949.

Greeley, Horace. *The American Conflict: A History.* Washington, D.C.: National Tribune, 1899.

Grimsley, Mark. *The American Civil War: The Emergence of Total Warfare.* Lexington, Mass.: D. C. Heath and Company, 1996.

Gwynne-Thomas, E. H. *The Presidential Families.* New York: Hippocrene Books, 1989.

Hagerman, Edward. *The American Civil War and the Origins of Modern Warfare: Ideas, Organization, and Field Command.* Bloomington: Indiana University Press, 1988.

Hall, Richard. *Patriots in Disguise: Women Warriors of the Civil War.* New York: Paragon House, 1993.

Hanchett, William. *The Lincoln Murder Conspiracies.* Urbana: University of Illinois Press, 1983.

———. *Out of the Wilderness: The Life of Abraham Lincoln.* Urbana: University of Illinois Press, 1994.

Hargrove, Hondon B. *Black Union Soldiers in the Civil War.* Jefferson, N.C.: McFarland & Company, 1988.

Harlow, Alvin F. *Brass-Pounders: Young Telegraphers of the Civil War.* Denver, Colo.: Sage Books, 1962.

Harper, Robert S. *Lincoln and the Press.* New York: McGraw-Hill, 1951.

Harris, Brayton. *Blue & Gray in Black & White: Newspapers in the Civil War.* Washington, D.C.: Brassey's, 1999.

Hattaway, Herman. *Shades of Blue and Gray. An Introductory Military History of the Civil War.* Columbia: University of Missouri Press, 1997.

Haydon, F. Stansbury. *Aeronautics in the Union and Confederate Armies: With a Survey of Military Aeronautics Prior to 1861.* Baltimore: Johns Hopkins Press, 1941.

Hearn, Chester G. *Admiral David Dixon Porter.* Annapolis, Md.: Naval Institute Press, 1996.

Helm, Katherine. *The True Story of Mary, Wife of Lincoln.* New York: Harper and Brothers, 1928.

Henry, Robert S. *The Armed Forces Institute of Pathology: Its First Century, 1862–1962.* Washington, D.C.: Office of the Surgeon General, 1964.

Hess, Earl J. *The Union Soldier in Battle: Enduring the Ordeal of Combat.* Lawrence: University of Kansas Press, 1997.

Hesseltine, William B., ed. *The Tragic Conflict: The Civil War and Reconstruction.* New York: George Braziller, 1962.

Hirshson, Stanley P. *The White Tecumseh: A Biography of General William T. Sherman.* New York: John Wiley & Sons, 1997.

Hofstadter, Richard. *Anti-Intellectualism in American Life.* New York: Alfred A. Knopf, 1964.

Hogg, Ian V. *Weapons of the Civil War.* New York: Military Press, 1987.

Hollandsworth, Jr., James G. *The Louisiana Native Guards: The Black Military Experience during the Civil War.* Baton Rouge: Louisiana State University Press, 1995.

Holt, Michael. *The Political Crisis of the 1850s.* New York: John Wiley & Sons, 1987.

Horan, James D. *The Pinkertons: The Detective Dynasty That Made History.* New York: Bonanza Books, 1967.

Hubbell, John T., and James W. Geary, eds. *Biographical Dictionary of the Union: Northern Leaders of the Civil War.* Westport, Conn.: Greenwood Press, 1995.

Hume, Edgar Erskine. *Victories of Army Medicine. Scientific Accomplishments of the Medical Departments of the United States Army.* Philadelphia: J. B. Lippincott, 1943.

Hummel, Jeffrey Rogers. *Emancipating Slaves, Enslaving Free Men: A History of the American Civil War.* Chicago: Open Court, 1996.

Hunt, Gaillard. *The American Passport: Its History and a Digest of Laws, Rulings and Regulations Governing Its Issuance by the Department of State.* Washington, D.C.: Government Printing Office, 1898.

Huston, James A. *The Sinews of War: Army Logistics, 1775–1953.* Washington, D.C.: Office of the Chief of Military History, 1966.

Huth, Hans. *Nature and the American: Three Centuries of Changing Attitudes.* Berkeley: University of California Press, 1957.

Jackson, Donald Dale. *The Aeronauts.* Alexandria, Va.: Time-Life Books, 1980.

Jacobs, Bruce. *Heroes of the Army. The Medal of Honor and Its Winners.* New York: W. W. Norton & Company, 1956.

Jellison, Charles A. *Fessenden of Maine: Civil War Senator.* Syracuse, N.Y.: Syracuse University Press, 1962.

Jimerson, Randall C. *The Private Civil War: Popular Thought during the Sectional Conflict.* Baton Rouge: Louisiana State University Press, 1988.

Johannsen, Robert W. *Lincoln, the South, and Slavery: The Political Dimension.* Baton Rouge: Louisiana State University Press, 1991.

———. *Stephen A. Douglas.* New York: Oxford University Press, 1973.

Johnson, David R. *Illegal Tender: Counterfeiting and the Secret Service in Nineteenth Century America.* Washington, D.C.: Smithsonian Institution Press, 1995.

Johnson, Edgar. *Charles Dickens: His Tragedy and Triumph.* 2 vols. New York: Simon and Schuster, 1952.

Jones, Robert H. *Disrupted Decades: The Civil War and Reconstruction Years.* New York: Charles Scribner's Sons, 1973.

Jones, Virgil Carrington. *The Civil War at Sea.* 3 vols. New York: Holt, Rinehart and Winston, 1960–1962.

Kane, Harnett T. *Spies for the Blue and Gray.* Garden City, N.Y.: Hanover House, 1954.

Kane, Joseph Nathan. *Facts about the Presidents: A Compilation of Biographical and Historical Information.* New York: H. W. Wilson Company, 1989.

———. *Famous First Facts: A Record of First Happenings, Discoveries, and Inventions in American History.* New York: H. W. Wilson Company, 1981.

Katz, D. Mark. *Witness to an Era: The Life and Photographs of Alexander Gardner.* New York: Viking, 1991.

Keller, Morton. *Affairs of State: Public Life in Late Nineteenth Century America.* Cambridge, Mass.: Harvard University Press, 1977.

Klein, Maury. *Days of Defiance: Sumter, Secession, and the Coming of the Civil War.* New York: Alfred A. Knopf, 1997.

Klein, Philip Shriver. *President James Buchanan: A Biography.* University Park: Pennsylvania State University Press, 1962.

Knightley, Phillip. *The First Casualty: From the Crimea to Vietnam: The War Correspondent as Hero, Propagandist, and Myth Maker.* New York: Harcourt Brace Jovanovich, 1975.

Knott, Stephen F. *Secret and Sanctioned: Covert Operations and the American Presidency.* New York: Oxford University Press, 1996.

Kobre, Sidney. *Development of American Journalism.* Dubuque, Iowa: Wm. C. Brown Company Publishers, 1969.

Kodansha Encyclopedia of Japan. Tokyo: Kodansha International Ltd., 1983.

Korn, Bertram W. *American Jewry and the Civil War.* 1951. Reprint, New York: Atheneum, 1970.

Krooss, Herman E., ed. *Documentary History of Banking and Currency in the United States.* Vol. 2. New York: Chelsea House Publishers, 1969.

Kunhardt, Dorothy Meserve, and Philip B. Kunhardt, Jr., *Mathew Brady and His World.* Alexandria, Va.: Time-Life Books, 1977.

Larson, Henrietta M. *Jay Cooke: Private Banker.* 1936. Reprint, New York: Greenwood Press Publishers, 1968.

Leech, Margaret. *Reveille in Washington: 1860–1865.* New York: Harper & Brothers, 1941.

Lefebvre, Georges. *Napoleon: From 18 Brumaire to Tilsit, 1799–1807.* New York: Columbia University Press, 1969.

Leonard, Elizabeth. *All the Daring of the Soldier: Women of the Civil War Armies.* New York: W. W. Norton, 1999.

———. *Yankee Women: Gender Battles in the Civil War.* New York: W. W. Norton, 1994.

Lewinski, Jorge. *The Camera at War: A History of Photography From 1840 to the Present Day.* New York: Simon & Schuster, 1978.

Lewis, Charles Lee. *David Glasgow Farragut: Admiral in the Making.* Annapolis, Md.: United States Naval Institute, 1941.

Lewis, Lloyd. *Sherman: Fighting Prophet.* New York: Harcourt, Brace and Company, 1932.

Linderman, Gerald F. *Embattled Courage: The Experience of Combat in the American Civil War.* New York: Free Press, 1987.

Linton, Calvin D., ed. *American Headlines: Year by Year.* Nashville: Thomas Nelson Publishers, 1984.

Litwack, Leon F. *Been in the Storm so Long: The Aftermath of Slavery.* New York: Alfred A. Knopf, 1979.

Long, David E. *The Jewel of Liberty: Abraham Lincoln's Re-Election and the End of Slavery.* Mechanicsburg, Penn.: Stackpole Books, 1994.

Longacre, Edward J. *Army of Amateurs: General Benjamin F. Butler and the Army of the James, 1863–1865.* Mechanicsburg, Penn.: Stackpole Books, 1997.

Lord, Francis A. *Civil War Collector's Encyclopedia.* 1963. Reprint (5 vols. in 2), Edison, N.J.: Blue & Grey Press, 1995.

———. *Lincoln's Railroad Man: Herman Haupt.* Rutherford, N.J.: Fairleigh Dickinson University Press, 1969.

Lowry, Thomas P. *The Story the Soldiers Wouldn't Tell: Sex in the Civil War.* Mechanicsburg, Penn.: Stackpole Books, 1994.

Luraghi, Raimondo. *A History of the Confederate Navy.* Translated by Paolo E. Coletta. Annapolis, Md.: Naval Institute Press, 1996.

Luthin, Reinhard. *The First Lincoln Campaign.* 1944. Reprint, Gloucester, Mass.: Peter Smith, 1964.

———. *The Real Abraham Lincoln.* Englewood Cliffs, N.J.: Prentice-Hall, 1960.

Lyman, Daryl. *Civil War Wordbook: Including Sayings, Phrases and Slang.* Conshohocken, Penn.: Combined Books, 1994.

Mackay, James. *Allan Pinkerton: The First Private Eye.* New York: John Wiley & Sons, 1997.

Maher, Sister Mary Denis. *To Bind Up the Wounds: Catholic Sister Nurses in the U.S. Civil War.* Westport, Conn.: Greenwood Press, 1989.

Mahin, Dean B. *One War at a Time: The International Dimensions of the American Civil War.* Washington, D.C.: Brassey's, 1999.

Mahoney, M. H. *Women in Espionage: A Biographical Dictionary.* Santa Barbara, Calif.: ABC-CLIO, 1993.

Marbut, F. B. *News from the Capital: The Story of Washington Reporting.* Carbondale: Southern Illinois University Press, 1971.

Marszalek, John F. *Sherman's Other War: The General and the Civil War Press.* Memphis: Memphis State University Press, 1981.

Marten, James. *The Children's Civil War.* Chapel Hill: University of North Carolina Press, 1998.

Mason, Edward Campbell. *The Veto Power: Its Origin, Development and Function in the Government of the United States (1789–1889)*. 1890. Reprint, New York: Russell & Russell, 1967.

Massey, Mary Elizabeth. *Bonnet Brigades*. New York: Alfred A. Knopf, 1966.

Mathews, Joseph J. *Reporting the Wars*. Minneapolis: University of Minnesota Press, 1957.

Maxwell, William Quentin. *Lincoln's Fifth Wheel: The Political History of the United States Sanitary Commission*. New York: Longmans, Green & Co., 1956.

May, Robert E., ed. *The Union, the Confederacy, and the Atlantic Rim*. West Lafayette, Ind.: Purdue University Press, 1995.

Mayer, Henry. *All On Fire: William Lloyd Garrison and the Abolition of Slavery*. New York: St. Martin's Press, 1998.

McAulay, John D. *Civil War Breech Loading Rifles: A Survey of the Innovative Arms of the American Civil War*. Lincoln, R.I.: Andrew Mowbray, 1987.

McConnell, Stuart. *Glorious Contentment: The Grand Army of the Republic, 1865–1900*. Chapel Hill: University of North Carolina Press, 1992.

McFeeley, William S. *Grant: A Biography*. New York: W. W. Norton, 1981.

McPherson, James M. *Abraham Lincoln and the Second American Revolution*. New York: Oxford University Press, 1990.

———. *Battle Cry of Freedom: The Civil War Era*. New York: Oxford University Press, 1988.

———. *Drawn with the Sword: Reflections on the American Civil War*. New York: Oxford University Press, 1996.

———. *For Cause and Comrades: Why Men Fought in the Civil War*. New York: Oxford University Press, 1997.

———. *The Negro's Civil War: How American Negroes Felt and Acted during the War for the Union*. New York: Pantheon Books, 1965.

———. *Ordeal by Fire: The Civil War and Reconstruction*. New York: McGraw-Hill, 1992.

———. *The Struggle for Equality: Abolitionists and the Negro in the Civil War and Reconstruction*. Princeton, N.J.: Princeton University Press, 1964.

McWhiney, Grady, and Perry D. Jamieson. *Attack and Die: Civil War Military Tactics and the Southern Heritage*. University, Ala.: University of Alabama Press, 1982.

Meredith, Roy. Mr. *Lincoln's Camera Man: Mathew B. Brady*. New York: Charles Scribner's Sons, 1946.

———. *The World of Mathew Brady: Portraits of the Civil War Period*. Los Angeles: Brooke House Publishers, 1976.

Merrill, James M. *The Rebel Shore: The Story of Union Seapower in the Civil War*. Boston: Little, Brown and Company, 1957.

Milbank, Jr., Jeremiah. *The First Century of Flight in America: An Introductory Survey*. Princeton, N.J.: Princeton University Press, 1943.

Miller, Jr., Edward A. *Lincoln's Abolitionist General: The Biography of David Hunter.* Columbia: University of South Carolina Press, 1997.

Miller, Francis Trevelyan, ed. *The Photographic History of the Civil War.* 1911. 10 vols. Reprint, New York: Thomas Yoseloff, 1957.

Mitchell, Joseph B. *The Badge of Gallantry: Recollections of Civil War Congressional Medal of Honor Winners.* New York: Macmillan Company, 1968.

Miyoshi, Masao. *As We Saw Them: The First Japanese Embassy to the United States (1860).* Berkeley: University of California Press, 1979.

Montgomery, David. *Beyond Equality: Labor and the Radical Republicans, 1862–1872.* New York: Alfred A. Knopf, 1967.

Moore, Guy W. *The Case of Mrs. Surratt: Her Controversial Trial and Execution for Conspiracy in the Lincoln Assassination.* Norman: University of Oklahoma Press, 1954.

Moore, John Bassett. *A Treatise on Extradition and Interstate Rendition.* Boston: Boston Book Company, 1891.

Moore, John L. *Speaking of Washington: Facts, Firsts, and Folklore.* Washington, D.C.: Congressional Quarterly, 1993.

Mosse, George L. *Fallen Soldiers: Reshaping the Memory of the World Wars.* New York: Oxford University Press, 1990.

Mott, Frank Luther. *American Journalism: A History, 1690–1960.* New York: Macmillan Company, 1962.

Murdock, Eugene C. *One Million Men: The Civil War Draft in the North.* Madison: State Historical Society of Wisconsin, 1971.

Musicant, Ivan. *Divided Waters: The Naval History of the Civil War.* New York: HarperCollins Publishers, 1995.

Nash, Jr., Howard P. *A Naval History of the Civil War.* New York: A. S. Barnes and Company, 1972.

Neely, Jr., Mark E. *The Fate of Liberty: Abraham Lincoln and Civil Liberties.* New York: Oxford University Press, 1991.

Ness, George T. *The Regular Army on the Eve of the Civil War.* Baltimore: Toomey Press, 1990.

Nevins, Allan. *The Emergence of Lincoln: Prologue to Civil War, 1859–1861.* Vol. 2. New York: Charles Scribner's Sons, 1950.

———. *The War for the Union.* 4 vols. New York: Charles Scribner's Sons, 1959–1971.

Nichols, Roy F. *The Disruption of American Democracy.* 1948. Reprint, New York: Free Press, 1967.

———. *The Stakes of Power: 1845–1877.* New York: Hill and Wang, 1961.

Nicolay, Helen. *Lincoln's Secretary: A Biography of John G. Nicolay.* New York: Longmans, Green & Co., 1949.

Nieman, Donald G. *To Set the Law in Motion: The Freedmen's Bureau and the Legal Rights of Blacks.* Millwood, N.Y.: KTO Press, 1979.

Niven, John. *Gideon Welles: Lincoln's Secretary of the Navy.* New York: Oxford University Press, 1973.

————. *Martin Van Buren: The Romantic Age of American Politics.* New York: Oxford University Press, 1983.

————. *Salmon P. Chase: A Biography.* New York: Oxford University Press, 1995.

Nofi, Albert A. *The Civil War Notebook: A Collection of Little-Known Facts and Other Odds-and-Ends about the Civil War.* Conshohocken, Penn.: Combined Books, 1993.

————. *A Civil War Treasury: Being a Miscellany of Arms and Artillery, Facts and Figures, Legends and Lore, Muses and Minstrels, Personalities and People.* 1992. Reprint, New York: Da Capo Press, 1995.

Norton, Herman A. *Struggling for Recognition: The United States Army Chaplaincy, 1791–1865.* Washington, D.C.: Office of the Chief of Chaplains, Department of the Army, 1977.

Oates, Stephen B. *Abraham Lincoln: The Man behind the Myths.* New York: Harper & Row Publishers, 1984.

————. *To Purge This Land with Blood: A Biography of John Brown.* New York: Harper & Row, 1970.

————. *With Malice Toward None: The Life of Abraham Lincoln.* New York: New American Library, 1977.

————. *A Woman of Valor: Clara Barton and the Civil War.* New York: Free Press, 1994.

Oldroyd, Osborn H. *The Assassination of Abraham Lincoln.* Washington, D.C.: O. H. Oldroyd, 1901.

O'Neill, Lois Decker, ed. *The Women's Book of World Records and Achievements.* Garden City, N.Y.: Anchor Press, 1979.

Palladino, Grace. *Another Civil War: Labor, Capital, and the State in the Anthracite Regions of Pennsylvania, 1840–1868.* Urbana: University of Illinois Press, 1990.

Paludan, Philip Shaw. *"A People's Contest:" The Union and Civil War, 1861–1865.* New York: Harper & Row Publishers, 1988.

Parish, Peter J. *The American Civil War.* New York: Holmes & Meier Publishers, 1975.

Paul, James C. N., and Murray L. Schwartz. *Federal Censorship: Obscenity in the Mail.* New York: Free Press of Glencoe, 1961.

Perret, Geoffrey. *Ulysses S. Grant: Soldier and President.* New York: Random House, 1997.

Perry, Milton F. *Infernal Machines: The Story of Confederate Submarine and Mine Warfare.* Baton Rouge: Louisiana State University Press, 1965.

Peterson, Merrill D. *Lincoln in American Memory.* New York: Oxford University Press, 1994.

Pfanz, Harry W. *Gettysburg—Culp's Hill and Cemetery Hill.* Chapel Hill: University of North Carolina Press, 1993.

Pollard, James E. *The Presidents and the Press.* 1947. Reprint, New York: Octagon Books, 1973.

Potter, David M. *The Impending Crisis, 1848–1861.* New York: Harper & Row, 1976.

Price, William H. *The Civil War Centennial Handbook.* Arlington, Va.: Prince Lithograph Co., 1961.

Pullen, John J. *A Shower of Stars: The Medal of Honor and the 27th Maine.* Philadelphia: J. B. Lippincott Company, 1966.

Quarles, Benjamin. *The Negro in the Civil War.* Boston: Little, Brown and Company, 1953.

Randall, James G., and David Donald. *The Civil War and Reconstruction.* Lexington, Mass.: D. C. Heath and Company, 1969.

Randall, Ruth Painter. *Lincoln's Sons.* Boston: Little, Brown and Company, 1955.

Rawley, James A. *Abraham Lincoln and a Nation Worth Fighting For.* Wheeling, Ill.: Harlan Davidson, 1996.

———. *The Politics of Union: Northern Politics during the Civil War.* Hinsdale, Ill.: Dryden Press, 1974.

Rayback, Robert J. *Millard Fillmore: Biography of a President.* Buffalo, N.Y.: Buffalo Historical Society, 1959.

Read, Phyllis, and Bernard L. Witlieb. *The Book of Women's Firsts.* New York: Random House, 1992.

Reck, Emerson W. *A. Lincoln: His Last 24 Hours.* 1987. Reprint, Columbia: University of South Carolina Press, 1994.

Reichley, A. James, ed. *Elections American Style.* Washington, D.C.: Brookings Institution, 1987.

Remini, Robert V. *Andrew Jackson and the Course of American Democracy, 1833–1845.* Vol. 3. New York: Harper & Row Publishers, 1984.

Riccards, Michael P. *The Ferocious Engine of Democracy: A History of the American Presidency, from the Origins through William McKinley.* Vol. 1. Lanham, Md.: Madison Books, 1995.

Rice, Richard B., William A. Bullough, and Richard J. Orsi. *The Elusive Eden: A New History of California.* New York: McGraw-Hill, 1996.

Richardson, Heather Cox. *The Greatest Nation of the Earth: Republican Economic Policies during the Civil War Era.* Cambridge, Mass.: Harvard University Press, 1997.

Robertson, Jr., James I. *Soldiers Blue and Gray.* Columbia: University of South Carolina Press, 1988.

Roddis, Louis H. *A Short History of Nautical Medicine.* New York: Harper and Brothers, 1941.

Roland, Charles P. *An American Iliad: The Story of the Civil War.* Lexington: University Press of Kentucky, 1991.

Roscoe, Theodore. *The Web of Conspiracy: The Complete Story of the Men Who Murdered Abraham Lincoln.* Englewood Cliffs, N.J.: Prentice-Hall, 1959.

Rose, Anne C. *Victorian America and the Civil War.* New York: Cambridge University Press, 1992.

Rosenblum, Naomi. *World History of Photography.* New York: Abbeville Press, 1997.

Rowan, Richard Wilmer. *The Pinkertons: A Detective Dynasty.* Boston: Little, Brown and Company, 1931.

Rowell, John W. *Yankee Artillerymen: Through the Civil War with Eli Lilly's Indiana Battery.* Knoxville: University of Tennessee Press, 1975.

Royster, Charles. *The Destructive War: William Tecumseh Sherman, Stonewall Jackson, and the Americans.* New York: Alfred A. Knopf, 1991.

Rutkow, Ira M. *The History of Surgery in the United States: 1775–1900.* Vol. 1. San Francisco: Norman Publishing, 1988.

Sandburg, Carl. *Abraham Lincoln: The War Years—II.* Vol. 4. 1939. Reprint, New York: Charles Scribner's Sons, 1948.

Schlesinger, Jr., Arthur M. *The Imperial Presidency.* Boston: Houghton Mifflin Company, 1973.

Schott, Thomas E. *Alexander H. Stephens of Georgia: A Biography.* Baton Rouge: Louisiana State University Press, 1988.

Sewell, Richard H. *A House Divided: Sectionalism and Civil War, 1848–1865.* Baltimore: Johns Hopkins University Press, 1988.

Shannon, Fred Albert. *The Organization and Administration of the Union Army, 1861–1865.* 1928. 2 vols. Reprint, Gloucester, Mass.: Peter Smith, 1965.

Sinkler, George. *The Racial Attitudes of American Presidents, from Abraham Lincoln to Theodore Roosevelt.* Garden City, N.Y.: Doubleday, 1971.

Smith, Elbert B. *The Presidency of James Buchanan.* Lawrence: University Press of Kansas, 1975.

Smith, George Winston. *Medicines for the Union Army: The United States Army Laboratories during the Civil War.* Madison, Wis.: American Institute of Pharmacy, 1962.

Snyder, Charles McCool. *Dr. Mary Walker: The Little Lady in Pants.* New York: Vantage Press, 1962.

Sorin, Gerald. *Tradition Transformed: The Jewish Experience in America.* Baltimore: Johns Hopkins University Press, 1997.

Stampp, Kenneth M. *And the War Came: The North and the Secession Crisis, 1860–1861.* Baton Rouge: Louisiana State University Press, 1950.

———. *The Era of Reconstruction: 1865–1877.* New York: Alfred A. Knopf, 1966.

———. *The Peculiar Institution: Slavery in the Ante-Bellum South.* New York: Alfred A. Knopf, 1956.

Stanley, Harold W., and Richard G. Niemi. *Vital Statistics on American Politics.* Washington, D.C.: Congressional Quarterly, 1994.

Stanley, Robert. *Dimensions of Law in the Service of Order: Origins of the Federal Income Tax, 1861–1913.* New York: Oxford University Press, 1993.

Starr, Louis M. *Reporting the Civil War: The Bohemian Brigade in Action, 1861–1865.* 1954. Reprint, New York: Collier Books, 1962.

St. Aubyn, Giles. *Edward VII: Prince and King.* New York: Atheneum, 1979.

Stevens, Charles A. *Berdan's United States Sharpshooters in the Army of the Potomac, 1861–1865.* St. Paul: Prince-Mcgill Company, 1892.

Still, Jr., William N. *Iron Afloat: The Story of the Confederate Armorclads.* Nashville: Vanderbilt University Press, 1971.

Strozier, Charles B. *Lincoln's Quest for Union: Public and Private Meanings.* New York: Basic Books, 1982.

Sullivan, Constance, ed. *Landscapes of the Civil War.* New York: Alfred A. Knopf, 1995.

Summers, Mark. *The Plundering Generation: Corruption and the Crisis of the Union, 1849–1861.* New York: Oxford University Press, 1987.

Sutherland, Daniel A. *The Expansion of Everyday Life, 1860–1876.* New York: Harper & Row Publishers, 1989.

Swanberg, W. A. *First Blood: The Story of Fort Sumter.* New York: Charles Scribner's Sons, 1957.

———. *Sickles the Incredible.* New York: Charles Scribner's Sons, 1956.

Taft, Robert. *Photography and the American Scene: A Social History, 1839–1889.* New York: Dover Publications, 1938.

Taylor, George Rogers. *The Transportation Revolution: 1815–1860.* New York: Holt, Rinehart and Winston, 1962.

Thomas, Benjamin P. *Abraham Lincoln: A Biography.* New York: Alfred A. Knopf, 1952.

Thomas, Benjamin P., and Harold M. Hyman. *Stanton: The Life and Times of Lincoln's Secretary of War.* New York: Alfred A. Knopf, 1962.

Thomas, Emory M. *Robert E. Lee: A Biography.* New York: W. W. Norton, 1995.

———. *The American War and Peace: 1860–1877.* Englewood Cliffs, N.J.: Prentice-Hall, 1973.

Thompson, Parker C. *From Its European Antecedents to 1791: The United States Army Chaplaincy.* Washington, D.C.: Office of the Chief of Chaplains, Department of the Army, 1978.

Thompson, Jr., W. Fletcher. *The Image of War: The Pictorial Reporting of the American Civil War.* New York: Thomas Yoseloff, 1959.

Tidwell, William A. *April '65: Confederate Covert Action in the American Civil War.* Kent, Ohio: Kent State University Press, 1995.

Tidwell, William A., James O. Hall, and David Winfield Gaddy. *Come Retribution: The Confederate Secret Service and the Assassination of Lincoln.* Jackson: University Press of Mississippi, 1988.

Tinker, Edward Larocque. *Creole City: Its Past and Its People.* New York: Longmans, Green & Co., 1953.

Trachtenberg, Alan. *Reading American Photographs: Image as History, Mathew Brady to Walker Evans.* New York: Hill and Wang, 1989.

Trefousse, Hans L. *Ben Butler: The South Called Him Beast!* New York: Twayne Publishers, 1957.

Trudeau, Noah Andre. *Like Men of War: Black Troops in the Civil War, 1862–1865.* Boston: Little, Brown and Company, 1998.

———. *Out of the Storm: The End of the Civil War, April–June 1865.* Boston: Little, Brown and Company, 1994.

Turner, George Edgar. *Victory Rode the Rails: The Strategic Place of the Railroads in the Civil War.* Indianapolis: Bobbs-Merrill Company, 1953.

Turner, Justin G., and Linda Levitt Turner. *Mary Todd Lincoln: Her Life and Letters.* New York: Alfred A. Knopf, 1972.

Turner, Thomas Reed. *Beware the People Weeping: Public Opinion and the Assassination of Abraham Lincoln.* Baton Rouge: Louisiana State University Press, 1982.

United States. Passport Office. Department of State. *The United States Passport: Past, Present, Future.* Washington, D.C.: Department of State Publication, 1976.

Van der Heuvel, Gerry. *Crowns of Thorns and Glory: Mary Todd Lincoln and Varina Howell Davis: The Two First Ladies of the Civil War.* New York: E. P. Dutton, 1988.

Vandiver, Frank E. *Blood Brothers: A Short History of the Civil War.* College Station: Texas A & M University Press, 1992.

———. *Their Tattered Flags.* New York: Harper & Row, 1970.

Voegeli, Jacque. *Free but Not Equal: The Midwest and the Negro during the Civil War.* Chicago: University of Chicago Press, 1967.

Wahl, Paul, and Donald R. Toppel. *The Gatling Gun.* New York: Arco Publishing Company, 1965.

Waitt, Ernest Linden. *History of the Nineteenth Regiment, Massachusetts Volunteer Infantry, 1861–1865.* Salem, Mass.: Salem Press Co., 1906.

Wakelyn, Jon L. *Biographical Dictionary of the Confederacy.* Westport, Conn.: Greenwood Press, 1977.

Ward, Geoffrey C. *The Civil War: An Illustrated History.* New York: Alfred A. Knopf, 1990.

Ward, John William. *Andrew Jackson: Symbol for an Age.* New York: Oxford University Press, 1955.

Waugh, John C. *Reelecting Lincoln: The Battle for the 1864 Presidency.* New York: Crown Publishers, 1997.

Weber, Thomas. *The Northern Railroads in the Civil War: 1861–1865.* 1952. Reprint, Westport, Conn.: Greenwood Press Publishers, 1970.

Wecter, Dixon. *When Johnny Comes Marching Home.* 1944. Reprint, Westport, Conn.: Greenwood Press Publishers, 1970.

Weigley, Russell F. *The American Way of War: A History of United States Mil-*

itary Strategy and Policy. New York: Macmillan Publishing Co., 1973.

————. *Quartermaster General of the Union Army: A Biography of M. C. Meigs.* New York: Columbia University Press, 1959.

Weisberger, Bernard A. *Reporters for the Union.* Boston: Little, Brown and Company, 1953.

Werner, Emmy E. *Reluctant Witnesses: Children's Voices from the Civil War.* Boulder, Colo.: Westview Press, 1998.

West, Jr., Richard S. *Gideon Welles: Lincoln's Navy Department.* Indianapolis: Bobbs-Merrill Company, 1943.

————. *Mr. Lincoln's Navy.* New York: Longmans, Green and Company, 1957.

————. *The Second Admiral: A Life of David Dixon Porter: 1813–1891.* New York: Coward-McCann, 1937.

Wideman, John C. *The Sinking of the USS Cairo.* Jackson: University Press of Mississippi, 1993.

Wiley, Bell Irvin. *The Life of Billy Yank: The Common Soldier in the Union.* Indianapolis: Bobbs-Merrill Company, 1951.

————. *The Life of Johnny Reb: The Common Soldier of the Confederacy.* Indianapolis: Bobbs-Merrill Company, 1943.

————. *The Plain People of the Confederacy.* 1944. Reprint, Chicago: Quadrangle Books, 1963.

Willard, Francis E. *Woman and Temperance; Or, the Work and Workers of the Woman's Christian Temperance Union.* Hartford, Conn.: Park Publishing Co., 1884.

Willett, Jr., Robert L. *One Day of the Civil War: America in the Conflict, April 10, 1863.* Washington, D.C.: Brassey's, 1997.

Williams, Francis Leigh. *Matthew Fontaine Maury: Scientist of the Sea.* New Brunswick, N.J.: Rutgers University Press, 1963.

Williams, T. Harry. *The Selected Essays of T. Harry Williams.* Baton Rouge: Louisiana State University Press, 1983.

————. *Time-Life History of the United States: The Union Restored.* New York: Time-Life, 1963.

Wilson, Douglas L. *Honor's Voice: The Transformation of Abraham Lincoln.* New York: Alfred A. Knopf, 1998.

————. *Lincoln before Washington: New Perspectives on the Illinois Years.* Urbana: University of Illinois Press, 1997.

Wilson, Douglas L., and Rodney O. Davis, eds. *Herndon's Informants: Letters, Interviews, and Statements about Abraham Lincoln.* Urbana: University of Illinois Press, 1998.

Windrow, Martin, and Gerry Embleton. *Military Dress of North America: 1665–1970.* New York: Charles Scribner's Sons, 1973.

Winks, Robin W. *Canada and the United States: The Civil War Years.* Baltimore: Johns Hopkins Press, 1960.

Young, Agatha. *The Women and the Crisis: Women of the North in the Civil War.* New York: McDowell, Oblensky, 1959.

Young, Peter, and J. P. Lawford, eds. *History of the British Army.* New York: G. P. Putnam's Sons, 1970.

Zornow, William Frank. *Lincoln & the Party Divided.* Norman: University of Oklahoma Press, 1954.

CHAPTERS AND ARTICLES

Austerman, Wayne. "Abhorrent to Civilization: The Explosive Bullet in the Civil War." *Civil War Times Illustrated* 24 (September 1985): 36–40.

Babcock, Havilah. "The Press and the Civil War." *The Journalism Quarterly* 6 (March 1929): 1–5.

Blackman, Jr., John L. "The Seizure of the Reading Railroad in 1864." *The Pennsylvania Magazine of History and Biography* 111 (January 1987): 49–60.

Blaisdell, F. William. "Medical Advances during the Civil War." *Archives of Surgery* 123 (September 1988): 1045–1050.

Blanton, DeAnne. "Women Soldiers of the Civil War." *Prologue* 25 (Spring 1993): 27–33.

Blustein, Bonnie Ellen. "'To Increase the Efficiency of the Medical Department:' A New Approach to U.S. Civil War Medicine." *Civil War History* 33 (March 1987): 22–41.

Broadman, Estelle, and Elizabeth B. Carrick. "American Military Medicine in the Mid-Nineteenth Century: The Experience of Alexander H. Hoff, M.D." *Bulletin of the History of Medicine* 64 (Spring 1990): 63–78.

Brugioni, Dino A. "Arlington and Fairfax Counties: Land of Many Reconnaissance Firsts." *Northern Virginia Heritage* (February 1985): 3–8.

Bullough, Bonnie, and Vern Bullough. "The Origins of Modern American Nursing: The Civil War Era." *Nursing Forum* 2 (1963): 13–27.

Carter, L. Edward. "The Revolution in Journalism during the Civil War." *Lincoln Herald* 73 (1971): 229–241.

Clinton, Catherine. "Noble Women As Well." In *Ken Burns's The Civil War: Historians Respond,* edited by Robert Brent Toplin, 61–80. New York: Oxford University Press, 1996.

Cobb, Josephine. "Alexander Gardner." *Image: Journal of Photography* 7 (June 1958): 124–136.

———. "Photographers of the Civil War." *Military Affairs* 26 (Fall 1962): 127–135.

Cohen, I. Bernard. "Science and the Civil War." *Technology Review* 48 (1946): 167–170, 192–193.

Crenshaw, Ollinger. "The Speakership Contest of 1859–1860: John Sherman's Election a Cause of Disruption?" *Mississippi Valley Historical Review* 29 (December 1942): 323–338.

Current, Richard Nelson. "'Right Makes Might': Lincoln and the Race for President, 1859–1860." In *Lincoln on Democracy,* edited by Mario M. Cuomo and Harold Holzer, 141–147. New York: HarperCollins Publishers, 1990.

Dibner, Bern. "The Beginning of Electricity." In *Technology in Western Civilization: The Emergence of Modern Industrial Society, Earliest Times to 1900,* edited by Melvin Kranzberg and Carroll W. Pursell, Jr., 1: 452–467. New York: Oxford University Press, 1967.

Dyche, Grace Locke Scripps. "John Locke Scripps: Lincoln's Campaign Biographer." *Journal of the Illinois State Historical Society* 17 (October 1924): 333–351.

Farr, Arthur. "The Real Genius behind the Monitor." *Civil War Times Illustrated* 36 (June 1997): 34–36.

Fennell, Jr., Charles C. "The Civil War: The First Modern War." In *The American Military Tradition: From Colonial Times to the Present,* edited by John M. Carroll and Colin F. Baxter, 61–94. Wilmington, Del.: Scholarly Resources, 1993.

Fishel, Edwin C. "The Mythology of Civil War Intelligence." In *Battles Lost and Won: Essays from Civil War History,* edited by John T. Hubbell, 83–106. Westport, Conn.: Greenwood Press, 1975.

———. "Pinkerton and McClellan: Who Deceived Whom?" *Civil War History* 34 (June 1988): 115–142.

Freemon, Frank R. "Lincoln Finds a Surgeon General: William A. Hammond and the Transformation of the Union Army Medical Bureau." *Civil War History* 33 (March 1987): 5–21.

Gladstone, William. "Captain Andrew J. Russell: First Army Photographer." *Photographica* 10 (February 1978): 7–9.

Glatthaar, Joseph T. "Battlefield Tactics." In *Writing the Civil War: The Quest to Understand,* edited by James M. McPherson and William J. Cooper, 60–80. Columbia: University of South Carolina Press, 1998.

——— "Black Glory: The African-American Role in Union Victory." In *Why the Confederacy Lost,* edited by Gabor S. Boritt, 133–162. New York: Oxford University Press, 1992.

Grover, Jan Zita. "The First Living-Room War: The Civil War in the Illustrated Press." *Afterimage* 11 (February 1984): 8–11.

Haller, John S. "Civil War Anthropometry: The Making of a Racial Ideology." *Civil War History* 16 (December 1970): 309–324.

Hanchett, William. "Shooting the President as a Military Necessity." In *Lincoln and His Contemporaries,* edited by Charles M. Hubbard, 139–148. Macon, Ga.: Mercer University Press, 1999.

Hattaway, Herman M. "The Civil War Armies: Creation, Mobilization, and Development." In *On the Road to Total War: The American Civil War and the German Wars of Unification, 1861–1871,* edited by Stig Förster and Jörg Nagler, 173–198. New York: Cambridge University Press, 1997.

Haydon, F. Stansbury. "A Proposed Gas Shell, 1862." *The Journal of the American Military History Foundation* 2 (Spring 1938): 52–54.

Henry, James O. "The United States Christian Commission in the Civil War." *Civil War History* 6 (December 1960): 374–388.

Hess, Earl J. "Tactics, Trenches, and Men in the Civil War." In *On the Road to Total War: The American Civil War and the German Wars of Unification, 1861–1871,* edited by Stig Förster and Jörg Nagler, 481–496. New York: Cambridge University Press, 1997.

Hoff, John Van R. "Memoir of Alexander Henry Hoff." *The Military Surgeon* 31 (1912): 47–51

Holmes, Amy E. "'Such Is the Price We Pay': American Widows and the Civil War Pension System." In *Toward a Social History of the American Civil War: Exploratory Essays,* edited by Maris A. Vinovskis, 171–196. New York: Cambridge University Press, 1990.

Hubinger, Bert. "Can We Ever Raise the Monitor?" *Civil War Times Illustrated* 36 (June 1997): 38–48.

Huth, Hans. "Yosemite: The Story of an Idea." *Sierra Club Bulletin* 33 (March 1948): 47–78.

James, Garry. "The Search for the Ultimate Weapon." *Civil War Times Illustrated* 31 (January–February 1993): 48–55.

Jones, Jr., James Boyd. "A Tale of Two Cities: The Hidden Battle against Venereal Disease in Civil War Nashville and Memphis." *Civil War History* 31 (September 1985): 270–276.

Kenney, Edward C. "From the Log of the *Red Rover*, 1862–1865: A History of the First U.S. Navy Hospital Ship." *Missouri Historical Review* 60 (1965): 31–49.

Kielbowicz, Richard B. "The Telegraph, Censorship, and Politics at the Outset of the Civil War." *Civil War History* 40 (June 1994): 95–118.

Kramer, Howard D. "Effect of the Civil War on the Public Health Movement." *Mississippi Valley Historical Review* 35 (December 1948): 449–462.

Lenihan, Daniel. "Time Capsule: Objects in History." *American History* 32 (August 1997): 74.

Leonard, Elizabeth D. "Civil War Nurse: Rebecca Usher of Maine." *Civil War History* 41 (September 1995): 190–207.

Long, David E. "I Shall Never Recall a Word." In *Abraham Lincoln: Sources and Style of Leadership,* edited by Frank J. Williams, William D. Pederson, and Vincent J. Marsala, 89–108. Westport, Conn.: Greenwood Press, 1994.

Maslowski, Peter. "Military Intelligence Sources during the American Civil War." In *Intelligence Revolution and Modern Warfare,* edited by James E. Dillard and Walter T. Hitchcock, 33–60. Chicago: Imprint Publications, 1996.

Mazet, Horace Sawyer. "Lincoln—Patron of Military Aviation." *The American Legion Monthly* 18 (February 1935): 30–33.

McWhiney, Grady. "Who Whipped Whom? Confederate Defeat Reexamined." *Civil War History* 11 (March 1965): 5–26.

Meerse, David E. "Buchanan, Corruption and the Election of 1860." *Civil War History* 12 (June 1966): 116–131.

Melia, Tamara Moser. "David Dixon Porter: Fighting Sailor." In *Captains of the Old Steam Navy: Makers of the American Naval Tradition, 1840–1880,* edited by James C. Bradford, 227–252. Annapolis, Md.: Naval Institute Press, 1986.

Miller, Everett B. "A Veterinarian's Notes on the Civil War." *Veterinary Heritage: Bulletin of the American Veterinary History Society* 8 (1985): 10–25.

Neely, Jr., Mark E. "The Civil War and the Two-Party System." In *"We Cannot Escape History:" Lincoln and the Last Best Hope of Earth,* edited by James M. McPherson, 86–104. Urbana: University of Illinois Press, 1995.

———. "Was the Civil War a Total War?" *Civil War History* 37 (March 1991): 5–28.

Nevins, Allan. "A Major Result of the Civil War." *Civil War History* 5 (September 1959): 237–250.

Palmer, Thomas A. "Military Technology." In *Technology in Western Civilization: The Emergence of Modern Industrial Society, Earliest Times to 1900,* edited by Melvin Kranzberg and Carroll W. Pursell, Jr., 1: 489–502. New York: Oxford University Press, 1967.

Pohanka, Brian C. "Carnival of Death." *America's Civil War* 4 (September 1991): 30–36.

Quimby, Rollin W. "The Chaplain's Predicament." *Civil War History* 8 (March 1962): 25–37.

———. "Congress and the Civil War Chaplaincy." *Civil War History* 10 (September 1964): 246–259.

Redkey, Edwin S. "Black Chaplains in the Union Army." *Civil War History* 33 (December 1987): 331–350.

Roca, Steven Louis. "Presence and Precedents: The USS *Red Rover* during the American Civil War, 1861–1865." *Civil War History* 44 (June 1998): 91–110.

Ross, Kristie. "Arranging a Doll's House: Refined Women as Union Nurses." In *Divided Houses: Gender and the Civil War,* edited by Catherine Clinton and Nina Silber, 97–113. New York: Oxford University Press, 1992.

Ryons, Fred B. "The United States Army Medical Department, 1861–1865." *The Military Surgeon* 79 (November 1936): 341–356.

Scheips, Paul J. "Union Signal Communications: Innovation and Conflict." *Civil War History* 9 (December 1963): 399–421.

Schultz, Jane E. "Race, Gender, and Bureaucracy: Civil War Army Nurses and the Pension Bureau." *Journal of Women's History* 6 (Summer 1994): 45–69.

Sears, Stephen. "Lincoln and McClellan." In *Lincoln's Generals,* edited by Gabor S. Boritt, 1–50. New York: Oxford University Press, 1994.

Sharkey, Robert P. "Commercial Banking." In *Economic Change in the Civil War Era,* edited by David T. Gilchrist and W. David Lewis, 23–31. Greenville, Del.: Eleutherian Mills-Hagley Foundation, 1965.

Sims, Lydel. "The Submarine That Wouldn't Come Up." *American Heritage* 9 (April 1958): 48–51, 107–111.

Sizer, Lyde Cullen. "Acting Her Part: Narratives of Union Women Spies." In *Divided Houses: Gender and the Civil War,* edited by Catherine Clinton and Nina Silber, 114–133. New York: Oxford University Press, 1992.

Sloan, W. Eugene. "The Spencer: Revolution in Weaponry—Goodbye to the Single-Shot Musket." *Civil War Times Illustrated* 23 (May 1984): 31–33.

Smith, Gene. "The Booth Obsession." *American Heritage* 43 (September 1992): 104–119.

Squires, J. Duane. "Aeronautics in the Civil War." *American Historical Review* 42 (July 1937): 652–669.

Stapp, William F. "Introduction." In *Landscapes of the Civil War,* edited by Constance Sullivan, 17–21. New York: Alfred A. Knopf, 1995.

Steere, Edward. "Evolution of the National Cemetery System, 1865–1880." *The Quartermaster Review* 32 (1953): 22–24, 120–125.

Thompson, George Raynor. "Civil War Signals." *Military Affairs* 18 (Winter 1954): 188–201.

Tilton, Clint Clay. "Lincoln and Lamon: Partners and Friends." *Transactions of the Illinois State Historical Society* (1932): 175–228.

Van Deusen, Glyndon G. "Why the Republican Party Came to Power." In *Crisis of the Union: 1860–1861,* edited by Harmon Knoles, 3–20. Baton Rouge: Louisiana State University Press, 1965.

Van Riper, Paul P., and Keith A. Sutherland. "The Northern Civil Service: 1861–1865." *Civil War History* 11 (December 1965): 351–369.

Vinovskis, Maris A. "Have Social Historians Lost the Civil War? Preliminary Demographic Speculations." In *Toward a Social History of the American Civil War: Exploratory Essays,* edited by Maris A. Vinovskis, 1–30. New York: Cambridge University Press, 1990.

Ward, Geoffrey. "The House at Eighth and Jackson." *American Heritage* 40 (April 1989): 68–79

Waters, R. S. "Ballooning in the French Army during the Revolutionary Wars." *The Army Quarterly* 23 (January 1932): 327–340.

Waters, W. Davis. "'Deception Is the Art of War': Gabriel J. Rains, Torpedo Specialist of the Confederacy." *The North Carolina Historical Review* 66 (January 1989): 29–60.

Wessen, Ernest James. "Campaign Lives of Abraham Lincoln, 1860: An Annotated Bibliography of the Biographies of Abraham Lincoln Issued during the Campaign Year." *Papers in Illinois History and Transactions* 44 (1937): 188–220.

Wiley, Bell Irvin. "'Holy Joes' of the Sixties: A Study of Civil War Chaplains." *The Huntington Library Quarterly* 16 (May 1953): 287–304.

Wood, Ann Douglas. "The War within a War: Women Nurses in the Union Army." *Civil War History* 18 (September 1972): 197–212.

Wray, Cheryl Sloan. "Photographer Mathew Brady Fulfilled His Stated Objective 'To Preserve the Faces of Historic Men'—Living and Dead." *America's Civil War* 10 (September 1997): 20–22.

Index